Acclaim for James D. Hornfischer
and

SHIP OF GHOSTS

"Hornfischer exhaustively details the full story: the visceral terror of a naval battle, savage treatment by Japanese captors, and post-traumatic stress disorder." —*Entertainment Weekly* (An EW Pick—Grade: A)

"Hornfischer (who wrote the equally powerful *The Last Stand of the Tin Can Sailors*) follows these survivors without ever missing a beat, proving himself to be one of our greatest WWII historians."
—*Book-of-the-Month Club News*

"The author of *The Last Stand of the Tin Can Sailors* gives us another excellent volume of World War II naval history. . . . Drawing on the survivors' accounts and extensive published resources, Hornfischer has painted a compelling picture of one of the most gallant ships and one of the grimmest campaigns in American naval history. He has a positive genius for depicting the surface-warfare sailor in a tight spot. May he write long and give them more memorials."
—*Booklist* (starred review)

"Chronicles a nearly forgotten chapter of U.S. naval history with a gripping intensity that should satisfy salty dogs and landlub-bers. . . . Hornfischer has emerged as a major World War II mar-itime historian by weaving together the human and strategic threads of a fascinating tale. What kind of yarn is *Ship of Ghosts*? Put Stephen Ambrose aboard the cruiser. . . . Next bring along Patrick O'Brien for nautical detail and high-seas drama. Then factor in Joseph Conrad for tales of men under stress in exotic climes."
—*Metro West Daily News*

"For Hornfischer . . . the tale of the *Houston* and the Death Railway is all the more poignant because it is relatively unsung, at least com-pared to such well-documented horrors as the Bataan Death March. . . . The scenes he paints are riveting."
—*Pittsburgh Post-Gazette*

"A gripping narrative . . . Harrowing and frank, this story of a gritty band of men—starved, isolated and working under excruciating conditions—reflects the triumph of will over adversity . . . [a] long-overdue saga of the famous ship." —*Kirkus Reviews*

"Engrossing . . . a superb evocation of naval combat . . . a gripping, well-told memorial to Greatest Generation martyrdom."
—*Publishers Weekly*

"*Ship of Ghosts* would be an unforgettable book if only for its brilliantly wrought account of the massive, chaotic sea battle that destroyed the USS *Houston*. But that is only the beginning of a story that grows more harrowing with every chapter, and that finally leaves the reader amazed at what human beings are capable of achieving and enduring." —Stephen Harrigan, author of *Challenger Park* and *The Gates of the Alamo*

"On sea and on land, these intrepid sailors endured enough for a thousand lifetimes. In this riveting account, Hornfischer carefully reconstructs a story none of us should be allowed to forget."
—Hampton Sides, author of *Blood and Thunder* and *Ghost Soldiers*

"Hornfischer has produced another meticulously researched naval history page-turner in *Ship of Ghosts*. He manages to fuse powerful human stories into the great flow of historical events with a singular storytelling talent." —John F. Lehman, former Secretary of the Navy, author of *On Seas of Glory*

"Hornfischer has done it again. His narrative is fine-tuned and always compelling but where he truly excels is in his evocative, often lyrical descriptions of combat at sea. Those who enjoyed his previous bestseller will love *Ship of Ghosts*—military history at its finest."
—Alex Kershaw, author of *The Few*

"Masterly . . . [the] descriptions of the huge and terrifying naval engagements are as overwhelming a stretch of historical writing as I have ever come across. . . . Beautifully written and heart-gripping."
—Adam Nicolson, author of *God's Secretaries*

"Recounts perhaps the most devastating untold saga of World War II in piercing detail." —Donovan Webster, author of *The Burma Road*

"Hornfischer has hit another home run." —Paul Stillwell, former director, History Division, U.S. Naval Institute; author of *Battleship Arizona*

"Excellent . . . Hornfischer details amazing stories of survival and horrifying stories of death. He tells of the trials that brought punishment to the perpetrators and of the difficulties survivors had in adapting to freedom." —*San Antonio Express-News*

"Finally . . . a new book about the *Houston,* her crew, and their 'lost years' has reached stores. James D. Hornfischer's *Ship of Ghosts* accomplishes what its predecessors never quite did." —*America in WWII*

"Hornfischer rivets the reader's attention. . . . The crew relate, through Hornfischer's superb narrative style, their individual accounts in a seamless tale of bravery and uncommon personal fortitude. . . . Jim Hornfischer has crafted a terrific read and every U.S. Navy sailor and every WWII history buff will want to read *Ship of Ghosts*." —*Tin Can Sailor*

"James D. Hornfischer is . . . a first-rate World War II naval historian. . . . [His] book is ultimately an evocative testament to the human spirit." —*Austin Monthly*

"The author . . . brings to life another little-known chapter of World War II in the Pacific. . . . I highly recommend *Ship of Ghosts*. While it is historical, its fast and exciting pace reminds me of *The Sand Pebbles,* one of my favorite novels." —Col. Gordon W. Keiser, USMC (ret.), U.S. Naval Institute *Proceedings*

"Certain to appeal to many types of readers—scholars, navy buffs, armchair sailors and military historians among them." —Associated Press

SHIP of GHOSTS

The Story of the USS Houston,
*FDR's Legendary Lost Cruiser, and
the Epic Saga of Her Survivors*

★

James D. Hornfischer

BANTAM BOOKS

SHIP OF GHOSTS
A Bantam Book

PUBLISHING HISTORY
Bantam hardcover edition published November 2006
Bantam trade paperback edition / September 2007

Published by Bantam Dell
A Division of Random House, Inc.
New York, New York

The author is grateful for the permission of the copyright holders to quote
selections from the following works:

The Ghost That Died in Sunda Strait by Walter G. Winslow, excerpted with
the permission of the author's daughter, Delsa W. Amundson.

Last Man Out by H. Robert Charles, excerpted with permission of the
author.

Out of the Smoke and *Into the Smother* by Ray Parkin, excerpted with the
permission of The Sir Edward Dunlop Medical Research Foundation,
Brunswick, Australia.

Book design by Susan Hood
Maps by Robert Bull

Library of Congress Catalog Card Number: 2006047530

ISBN 978-0-553-38450-5

Printed in the United States of America
Published simultaneously in Canada

www.bantamdell.com

BVG   10   9   8   7   6   5   4   3   2

The day will come when even this ordeal will be a sweet thing to remember.

—Virgil, THE AENEID

CONTENTS

SHIP OF GHOSTS

This is the ancient history of a forgotten ship, forgotten because history is story, because memory is fragile, and because the human mind—and thus the storytellers who write the history—generally accepts only so much sorrow before the impulse prevails to put the story on a brighter path. The Pacific war's desperate days were dark enough to obscure one of the great naval epics of this or any century. The story of the USS *Houston* (CA-30) was largely unknown even in its own time. Since then, what may have been the most trying ordeal to beset a ship's company has lain in puzzling obscurity.

Even readers who have explored the Navy's war against Japan in some depth are unlikely to have read much about the *Houston*'s battles and the forty-two-month ordeal that her survivors endured. The men who gave life to the legend of Franklin D. Roosevelt's favorite warship fought their war in isolation, hidden, it seems, behind the pall of smoke standing over the armored carcasses of Pearl Harbor. Eight thousand miles from home, trapped on the wrong side of the tear that Imperial Japan rent in the fabric of the Pacific Ocean's realm, they ran a gauntlet through the war's first eighty-four days that would have been an epic unto itself in any other time. And yet the history books scarcely report it. Any number of good histories of the Pacific war pass over the story of the U.S. Asiatic Fleet and her redoubtable flagship as if they had never existed. The classic serial documentary *Victory at Sea* does not mention it. Nor does the epic television series *World at War*. Accordingly, we know little of the exploits of the Galloping Ghost of the Java Coast, of her crew's gallantry against the guns and torpedo batteries of a superior Japanese fleet, and of the darker trial that awaited them after Java fell.

Newspapers carried sketchy reports of the *Houston*'s final action. But as the calamity of a two-ocean war engulfed America in 1942, no one could say what became of her survivors, how many there were, where they were taken, what trials they suffered, when if ever they might return home. The *Houston*'s survivors, barely a third of her complement, would come to envy her dead. Captured and made slaves on one of history's most notorious engineering projects, they were lost for the duration of World War II, enfolded in a mystery that would not be solved until America's fleets and armies had subdued one of the most potent military machines ever set loose on the world, and freed its prisoners and slaves. Even today we know little of the staggering trials of her survivors, a seagoing band of brothers whose resilience was tested on the project that encompassed the drama depicted in David Lean's classic film *The Bridge on the River Kwai*. Few people understand that there were Americans there. And fewer still appreciate how their spirit of resistance, defiance, and sabotage enabled them to keep their dignity, and how their conspiracies to espionage eventually conjoined with those of the OSS in Thailand during the most fraught hours of the Asian war.

The *Houston* carried 1,168 men into the imperiled waters of the Dutch East Indies at the start of the war. Just 291 of them returned home. In the end, when the puzzle of their fate was at last solved, the euphoric rush of victory swept their tale into the dustbin of dim remembrance. The story of the *Houston* got lost in a blizzard of ticker tape.

The surviving men of the USS *Houston* have lived and aged gracefully, seldom if ever asking for attention or demanding their due. Now they are old, and they are leaving us. They numbered sixty-five when this project began in 2003. As I write in February 2006, that number is down to forty-two. Only the ship's hardiest representatives are left. The time is fast coming when the eyewitnesses to

World War II will be gone, and historians left with their documents and nothing more. So it is time now to remember the *Houston* and what may well be the most trying ordeal ever suffered by a single ship's company in World War II. At the very least, we owe them some overdue thanks before it is time for them to go.

Part One

ON ASIA STATION

★

"I knew that ship and loved her. Her officers and men were my friends."

—Franklin D. Roosevelt, letter to Houston mayor Neal Pickett, Memorial Day, 1942

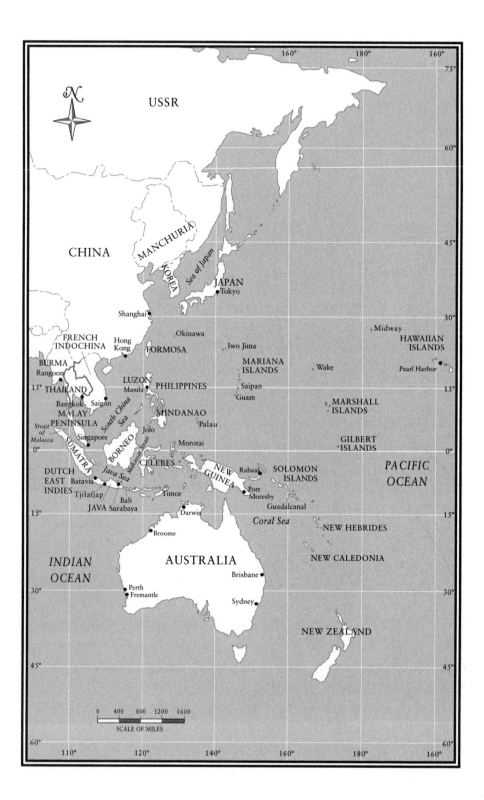

CHAPTER 1

Off the island of Bali, in the silhouette of mountains made sacred by the favor of local gods, a warship plied the black waters of an equatorial sea. The night of February 4, 1942, found her moving swiftly toward a port on the southern coast of the adjoining island of Java. She had sustained a deep wound that day, an aerial bomb striking her after turret, charring and melting the gun house and its entire stalk. The great blast killed forty-six men. Her captain now sought port to patch his ship and bury his dead with honors. For the flagship of the U.S. Asiatic Fleet, this was the first blow of a war not yet sixty days old.

The USS *Houston,* a heavy cruiser, was the largest combat vessel the U.S. Navy had committed to the Dutch East Indies. She was bound for the port of Tjilatjap. Its colliding consonants compelled American sailors to give the town the more symphonious nickname "Slapjack" or, chewing their words more bitterly, "that lousy dump." As the thunder of Japan's opening offensive washed over Indonesia in early 1942, Tjilatjap was one of three havens that Allied warships still maintained in these dangerous waters. With the enemy's invasion fleets pressing down from the north and his planes attacking from land bases ever closer to Java, those harbors were fast becoming untenable. The previous day, February 3,

Japanese bombers struck Surabaya, the city in the island's east that was home to Adm. Thomas C. Hart's threadbare squadron of surface combatants. To the west, the port at Batavia (now Jakarta) was a marked target too. As Hart's commanders well knew, Japan's aviators had needed just forty-eight hours after the start of war on December 8 to smash American airpower in the Philippines, sink the two largest Allied warships in the region—the British battleship *Prince of Wales* and the battlecruiser *Repulse*—and land an invasion force on Luzon. The Imperial red tide knew no pause. Flowing southward, operating at high tempo by day and by night, the Japanese executed a leapfrogging series of amphibious invasions down the coasts of Borneo and Celebes, each gain consolidated and used to stage the next assault. The shadow of the Japanese offensive loomed over Java, where the Allies would make a last stand in defense of the old Dutch colonial outpost and aim to blunt Japan's onrushing advance toward Australia.

At midnight of February 3, alerted by Allied aircraft to the presence of a Japanese invasion fleet in Makassar Strait, north of Java, the *Houston* had departed Surabaya with a flotilla of U.S. and Dutch warships—the aged light cruiser USS *Marblehead,* the Dutch light cruisers *De Ruyter* and *Tromp,* and an escort of eight destroyers. Under Dutch Rear Adm. Karel W. F. M. Doorman, the striking force steamed by night to avoid Japanese aircraft. But the distance to their target was such that the Allied ships had no choice but to cross the Flores Sea by daylight on February 4. No friendly fighter planes were on hand to cover them. It was about ten o'clock on that bright morning when Japanese bombers began appearing overhead, ending Doorman's mission before it ever really began.

That day had started as so many of them did, with the *Houston*'s Marine bugler putting his brass bell to the public address microphone and blowing the call to air defense. As men sprinted to their general quarters stations, they could look up and see the Japanese bombers droning by, one wave after the next, nine at a time, fifty-four in all, locked in tight V formations, silvery fuselages glinting in the sun. Nosing over into shallow power glides from seventeen thousand feet, the twin-engine G3M Nells began their bombing runs.

Capt. Albert Harold Rooks steered his ship through the maelstrom of splashes, some of the bombs landing close enough aboard to fracture rivets belowdecks, some falling in patterns dense enough to conceal the six-hundred-foot-long ship behind a temporary mountain range of foamy white seawater. Watching the *Houston* under bombardment, a sailor on another ship said, "All this water just sort of hung in the air. Then it started to fall back, and out from underneath all this stuff comes the *Houston* going thirty knots." A master ship handler, the fifty-year-old skipper had an intuitive sense of his cruiser's gait. He was expert in dodging the bombs that fluttered earthward in the midmorning sun, never hesitating to stretch the limits of the engineering plant or test the skill and endurance of the throttlemen and water tenders and machinists, who gamely kept pace with the sudden engine orders and speed changes, risking the destruction of their delicate machinery by the slightest misstep. Relying on the smart reactions of his snipes as an extension of his own hand, Rooks maneuvered his cruiser like none the crew had ever seen, accelerating and slowing, ordering "crashbacks" that wrenched his engines from full ahead straight into full astern, thus steering not only by rudder but by counterturning the propeller screws, the starboard pair surging ahead while the port pulled astern. "He handled that ship like you or I would handle a motorboat," said Howard R. Charles, a private in the *Houston*'s seventy-eight-man Marine detachment.

By acclamation Rooks was one of the brightest lights to wear four gold bars in the prewar U.S. Navy. He had been Admiral Hart's aide when the Asiatic Fleet boss was superintendent of the Naval Academy. On the teaching staff at the Naval War College in Newport, Rhode Island, in 1940, Rooks showed a keen analytical mind, and it was with no evident sarcasm that colleagues called him the second coming of the great naval strategist Alfred Thayer Mahan. In the few months since taking over the *Houston* in Manila, the quietly authoritative skipper had moved out of the shadow of a beloved predecessor and won, it seems, a reputation as a sort of minor deity.

An SOC Seagull floatplane was on the *Houston*'s catapult, propeller whipping the air at full throttle, its pilot ready for an explosive-charged launch. Under normal conditions in the days before radar, the SOCs were used for reconnaissance and gunnery spotting. Flung aloft from catapults mounted on the quarterdeck amidships, the biplanes would fly out ahead of the ship, climb to around two thousand feet, and spend two or three hours weaving back and forth on either side of the cruiser's base course heading. In combat, they could loiter over an enemy fleet, signaling corrections to the gunnery department. The Seagulls were light enough to grip the air at a speed as low as sixty miles per hour, permitting a leisurely reconnaissance pattern. But now the idea was to get the vulnerable, combustible planes off the ship before the Japanese got lucky with one of their bombs.

As another formation of bombers crossed overhead, the antiaircraft officer couldn't stand waiting for the SOC to get airborne. His five-inch guns, elevated high, roared. At once the muzzle blast, just ten feet from the plane, tore the canvas skin right off the plane. As Lt. Harold S. Hamlin recalled, "the pilot found himself sitting on a picked chicken—the blast had removed every stitch of fabric from the plane. Pilot and crewman scrambled out, and the forlorn-looking plane, naked as a jay-bird, was jettisoned."

The *Houston* belched so much smoke from her after stack that the antiaircraft crews lost use of the aft rangefinder, bathed in black soot. So they aimed by eye. Good as the crews on her eight open-mount five-inch guns were, they were shocked to find that their ammunition was of little use. Their first salvo arced skyward right into the midst of the bombers. But only one of the four rounds was seen to explode. That sorry proportion held up through the day. Of the four hundred odd antiaircraft shells the *Houston*'s crews fired, nearly three hundred were duds. In the prewar years, the Navy Department, mindful of costs, had refused to let its ships fire live rounds in antiaircraft gunnery drills. The *Houston*'s gunnery officer had appealed time and again for permission to use live ammunition but was turned down. The projectiles thus saved had been left to sit and age in the magazines. Now, as the realization dawned on them that most of their stored projectiles were little more than outsize paperweights, the antiaircraft crews became "mad as scalded dogs" and fired all the faster, if to little result.

During the bombardment that rained down on them that morning, the light cruiser *Marblehead* was straddled perfectly by a stick of seven bombs, engulfing the old ship in giant splashes. Two struck home, and a near miss, detonating underwater close aboard to port, did as much damage as the direct hits. Fifteen men were killed as fires raged fore and aft. With part of her hull dished in, scooping in seawater at high pressure, seams and rivets leaking, the *Marblehead* listed to starboard, settling by the head, her rudder jammed into a hard port turn. Seeing her distress, Captain Rooks turned the

Houston toward her to bring his gunners to bear on the attackers. As he did so, another V of bombers passed overhead at fifteen thousand feet. A second flock of bombs wobbled earthward. They missed—all of them except for the stray.

Some say that the lone five-hundred-pounder must have gotten hung up in the Japanese plane's bomb bay on release. With its carefully calculated trajectory interrupted, it wandered from the path of its explosive peers, arcing down outside the field of view from the pilothouse, where Rooks, head tilted skyward, binoculars in hands, was watching the flight of ordnance and conning his ship to avoid it. Unseen until it was far too late, the wayward bomb found the ship. It punched through the searchlight platform mounted midway up the *Houston*'s sixty-foot-high mainmast, rattled down through its great steel tripod, and struck just forward of the aft eight-inch gun mount, whose triple barrels were trained to port, locked and loaded to fend off low-flying planes.

The bomb's blast reverberated all along the *Houston*'s length, and up and down its seven levels of decks. The sickened crew felt the cruiser lift, rock, and reel. When fires ignited the silk-encased powder bags stored in the number-three hoist, a vicious flash fire engulfed the gun chamber and reached down into the powder circle. Yellow-white smoke washed over the fantail.

Intense heat inside the heavily perforated gun house, or perhaps a firing circuit shorted out in the deluge from the fire hoses, caused the center eight-inch rifle to discharge. The untimely blast startled the crew, and they collided with one another diving for cover. The powder-fed storm of flames took nearly four dozen of Captain Rooks's best men. They never stood a chance, not the doomed crew inside Turret Three, nor the men in the powder circle and handling room below them, nor the after repair party, cut down nearly to a man at their general quarters station, right under the hole in the main deck. In nearby crew's quarters, men were found blown straight through the springs of their bunks. Scraps of clothing stuck in the springs were all that remained of them, identification made possible only by the stenciling on their shirts. They could not have known what hit them. But far worse was in store for everyone aft should the flames reach the eight-inch powder bags piled in the magazine.

Fearing a catastrophic explosion, Cdr. Arthur L. Maher, the *Houston*'s gunnery officer, rallied the firefighting crews and sent two petty officers into the scorched ruin of the gun mount searching for survivors. One of them, aviation machinist's mate second class John W. Ranger, played a hose on the other, Charles Fowler, to keep him cool. Then Ranger joined Fowler inside, armed with a carbon dioxide canister to fight the flames, the heat from which was already bubbling grease smeared on the eight-inch projectiles kept in ready storage.

By the light of a battle lantern in the turret's lower chambers, gunner's mate second class Czeslaus Kunke and seaman second class Jack D. Smith dogged down the metal flaps that separated the magazine from the burning handling room and flooded the magazine and powder hoist. "I told John [Ranger] if we had not stopped the fire before it arrived at the magazine he would have been the first Navy astronaut," Smith wrote. Their quick thinking and a measure of good fortune saved the ship from a final calamity.

With the *Houston*'s main battery hobbled and the *Marblehead* damaged, Admiral Doorman aborted the mission, ordering the wounded cruisers to Tjilatjap for repair. As evening fell, Captain Rooks steered his bruised ship toward safety, out of the Flores Sea through Alas Strait, then west into the easternmost littorals of the Indian Ocean. Steaming in the shadows of the holy peaks of Lombok and Bali, the *Houston*'s crew gathered their dead shipmates on the fantail. The *Houston*'s two medical officers, Cdr. William A. Epstein and Lt. Clement D. Burroughs, exhausted themselves patching up the wounded and easing the worst of them into death. "I'm convinced they were never the same again," wrote Marine 2nd Lt. Miles Barrett. "For weeks their nerves were completely shattered." An ensign named John B. Nelson had the chore of identifying the charred corpses as they lay in makeshift state. Nelson's eyes filled with tears as he studied the remains, identifying some and guessing at others. Then they were covered with a canvas tarpaulin to await burial. A carpenter's mate oversaw the crew detailed to assemble caskets from scrap lumber. Their hammers tapped and tapped, marking time through the night. "War came to us in a real way. It knocked all the cockiness out of us," said Sgt. Charley L. Pryor Jr. of the ship's Marine detachment. "We saw what war could be in its real fury, just in those brief few moments."

A ceremonial watch was set in honor of the dead. Seaman first class John Bartz, a stout Minnesotan from the Second Division, held his rifle at attention on the midwatch, fidgeting in the starlit darkness. What unsettled him was not so much the corpses but their un-expected movements at sudden intervals: arms and legs twitching, rising and reaching in death's stiffening grip.

"I'm telling you, it was spooky," Bartz said. "It was really scary when you're standing there, a young kid about eighteen years old. I was glad to see my relief at four."

CHAPTER 2

The horrors of the bomb blast challenged the mettle of a crew that had developed its esprit from altogether different experiences. By 1942, only a few of them had been on board long enough to remember the ship's heyday in the thirties, when a president was proud to call himself their shipmate. Most of those who had sailed on those unforgettable voyages had left the ship. Yet the high spirits lived in the older sailors' memories. It was a sort of living dream, a skein of folk history that wove itself into the banter in the mess halls and set the *Houston*'s men apart from the other seadogs in the fleet. The five-year reign the ship enjoyed as Franklin D. Roosevelt's favorite ride would survive the worst onslaughts of the Japanese.

Four times in the 1930s FDR had joined the *Houston* on long interoceanic trips. Whether it was because she had been launched in September 1929, right before the stock-market crash that brought on the Depression, and thus stood as a sort of shining symbol of the nation in its heyday, or whether it was an accident of circumstance, no one quite knew. Most of them seemed willing to accept it as the natural by-product of their shipshape tradition of discipline. "The spit and polish of the U.S. Navy was ingrained in us," one sailor wrote, "and up to the moment he arrived on board we worked every minute to have the ship in readiness. Not a speck of dust, or corrosion on bright work, paint work, and our white teakwood decks shone with a snowy whiteness that came from many hours of scrubbing and holystoning. The ship was in perfect order." The wheelchair-bound commander in chief appreciated the custom-engineered conveniences the shipfitters and metalsmiths installed whenever he came aboard. Ladders were replaced with electric lifts, handrails bolted along bulkheads, and ramps laid here and there to enable him to explore her decks and compartments.

"Bring the boat around," Roosevelt would tell the brass at the Navy Department whenever the urge or the opportunity beckoned. In 1934, he rode on board the *Houston* from Annapolis to Portland, Oregon, by way of the Panama Canal and Honolulu. In October 1935, he went from San Diego to Charleston following much the same southern route.

On the morning of July 14, 1938, as the ship was approaching San Francisco, the rumor circulated that the president was readying himself to join them once again. As the *Houston* eased into the harbor, some sharp-eyed sailors on deck could see the dockworkers breaking out the telltale fittings that heralded the arrival of a special visitor. FDR drew a rousing crowd at the new San Francisco–Oakland Bay Bridge. Shortly after the *Houston* tied up to a pier, another crowd began to form. At 2:30 P.M., the ship's loudspeaker announced, "All hands shift into the uniform of the day: officers, full dress blue; crew, dress blue. Affirm." Less than an hour later the crew was manning the rail, the honor guard and band assembled on the quarterdeck, the quartermaster standing ready to break the presidential flag at the mainmast.

When the crowd began cheering, a sailor named Red Reynolds spotted the presidential limousine. He was surprised to see that FDR's wheelchair was already on board the ship. It sat empty on the quarterdeck, at the end of a forty-foot-long ramp, a steep "brow," reaching down to the dock. The limousine pulled up on the pier and stopped at the brow's base.

"I was wondering, *What now?*" Reynolds wrote. "The President is paralyzed. His legs were shriveled. No larger than my arms. How will he come aboard? Then, to my amazement, I watched him lean from the back seat, reach out, grab the brow rails with both hands, and, hurtling through the air, draw himself to an upright position. Then hand over hand, he slowly progressed up the brow, his feet dangling inches above the deck of the brow. Stopping occasionally, smiling and nodding to the crowd. Saying a few words to the crowd and leading off with his old familiar words, 'My friends.' As he reached the top of the brow, he reached out, grasping the arms of his wheel chair, swinging his body into the air. Raising his right hand to a smart sailors' salute to 'Old Glory,' as she waved back from her station on the main deck aft. As he dropped the salute all honors were rendered and his first words were, 'It's good to be back home again, Captain.' The feelings of the crew were perhaps best expressed by all shouting, 'What a shipmate!' "

Further out in the harbor, the battleships and heavy cruisers of the United States Fleet awaited their commander in chief's review. They were lined up in four rows, "so evenly spaced that a giant ruler might have been laid among them, touching each," observed Reynolds. It was said to be the largest concentration of U.S. naval power assembled to date. At 3:45, the *Houston* backed away from Oakland Pier. Roosevelt parked himself on the communications deck to take in the spectacle.

Steaming beneath the San Francisco–Oakland Bay Bridge and turning west, the *Houston* stood out of San Francisco Harbor, making ten knots. As she came abreast of the fleet flagship, the *Pennsylvania,* the battleship let loose a full broadside in salute. The roar had scarcely faded when the *Houston* passed by the *Idaho.* She issued a salute with a blast from her own battery. The fleet review progressed in a stately, thunderous rhythm, the baton of the ceremonial cannonade passing from one battleship to the next as the *Houston* slid past, the band on her quarterdeck playing "The Star-Spangled Banner," crews on all ships lining the rails, officers resplendent in full parade dress, epaulets, braid, and buttons shining gold against deep blue in the afternoon sun. When the last battleship had discharged its honors, the heavy cruisers of the Scouting Force picked up the powder-charged tribute. When the majestic show ended, the *Houston* set course for San Diego.

On arrival there, the president left the ship on some matter of business, then returned to make yet another grand entrance, thrilling the crowds on Kettner Boulevard. This time Eleanor Roosevelt was on hand, sitting dockside on one of the bollards around which the mooring lines were slung. Bantering with sailors through open portholes on the cruiser's second deck, she told the crew to take good care of Franklin. She said, "Don't let him get too tired, don't let him catch cold, don't let him smoke too much." At

5:15 P.M., the *Houston* backed from the pier in San Diego and got under way again. Surrounded by pleasure craft, she stood out of the harbor, passing Fort Rosecrans, and set course for the far side of the continent, Pensacola by way of Panama.

In the twenty-four days that ensued, the president would for the third time win his stripes as a friend of the *Houston* and a fisherman worthy of the tallest tales. When he fished, he shunned the sleek, custom-built forty-foot cabin boat, perched on deck with its black hull trimmed with gold plating and a gold presidential seal affixed on each side of the bow. He preferred the cruiser's regular motor launch. And instead of venturing out accompanied by the chief boatswain's mate, the motor machinists, and a select cadre of officers, FDR asked—insisted, in fact—that a twenty-year-old coxswain named Russell be his personal guide. He liked the kid. Hailing from coastal Maine, Russell had fishing in his blood. That was good enough for Roosevelt. As soon as the carpenter's mates had removed the special chair from the presidential cabin boat and bolted it to the deck of the launch, the aviation crane hoisted out the small craft and Coxswain Russell and his crew of enlisted kids went fishing with the leader of the free world.

Yellowtails and sea bass, groupers, big jacks and small sharks— they hit ravenously and often. The president, flush with jokes and stories, had the boat party rolling with laughter. Returning to the ship one evening, he told Russell to take the boat out again and angle alone for a change. Spotting his coxswain pulling away in the launch without orders, Capt. George Nathan Barker ordered him sharply to come back alongside. Whereupon, Red Reynolds recalled, "the President turned and told the Captain to simmer down, that he had told Russell to fish some if he liked. That was one of a number of times the Captain had to tuck his tail and back-water. Barker was captain of the ship, but Roosevelt was the Supreme Commander."

FDR had a knack for remembering names and faces from previous times on board. When the baker, Donahue, offered him a doughnut, the president said, "Get Kielty to give us some coffee." He went up to another sailor he recognized, a gunner's mate named Wicker, and said, "I thought you told me in '34 you were getting out of the Navy. What did you do, ship over?" Wicker replied, "Well, sir, I was going out, but I figured you'd make another cruise on *Houston,* so I shipped over for another four years so I could be with you again."

Roosevelt smacked him on the hip and said, "Don't give me any of that blarney. You're a career man."

Barker ran a tight ship, but the buoyant presence of the president encouraged him to let up. One day the boatswain's pipe shrilled and routine inspections were called. There followed a pause and then another rising whistle. "Belay that last word," came the announcement. "Repeat, belay that last word. There will be no field day; there will be no inspection. . . . By the word of the President all of us are on a three-week vacation."

Whatever virtue lay in the idea of recreation lasted roughly until the *Houston* had crossed the equator, on its ninth day out of San Diego, July 25. The enlisted men at that point discovered their commander in chief's well-developed fondness for membership in exclusive clubs. It was on boisterous display during the traditional crossing-the-line ceremony, the gaudily theatrical hazing ritual inflicted upon sailors who have not sailed across the equator before by those who have. The pollywogs learned to their dismay that FDR had crossed the line eighteen times already. As "senior shellback," the president reveled in the festivities. Though his entourage of aides and Secret Service agents declined to participate in the silliness, their demurral did not withstand the power of high-pressure saltwater hoses and some time to reflect while bound to stanchions, baking dry in the sun.

Roosevelt gave up a day of fishing to wheel around topside, relaying orders from King Neptune and taunting pollywogs with tales of the ocean deity's vengeance. The details of what happened next are privileged, as proceedings of the ceremony tend to be. The following noon, as lunch was being served to as many new shellbacks as could rouse themselves from their bunks, the ship entered the volcano-flanked anchorage at Tagus Cove in the Galápagos Islands and the boats were hoisted out for another presidential fishing charter. Roosevelt seemed to think an important rite of passage had been completed. That evening, returning to the ship with catches in hand, he was overheard telling his mates, "Today you became men."

That the president loved the ship was not altogether surprising, for warships have a way of seizing the hearts of those who come to know them. The *Houston* was like that. Her captains tended to be bighearted and popular disciplinarians whose personalities helped animate her sleek, powerful lines. That she was neither stout enough to stand and slug with her foreign peers nor modern enough to track them with radar and destroy them from afar was immaterial to the mythology that grew up around her. After Roosevelt's 1938 tour, the *Houston* was designated as the flagship of the United States Fleet. She had that distinction fleetingly, from September to December. But she would ever after be known as FDR's cruiser, and that legacy would stay with the *Houston* through the ordeal ahead, when the ship and the president who loved her were oceans apart and fighting their own wars.

As the damaged cruiser raced for port on the night of February 4, 1942, the Pacific war in full vicious swing, memories of antebellum pomp and circumstance lay in shrouds. The story of its crew's struggle would unfold far beyond the reach of the president, far from the Pacific Fleet, battered and smoldering in Pearl Harbor. They were forgotten, if not by their loved ones then certainly by a public outraged by losses much closer to home, and discarded by war planners who had no choice but to leave them to fight a holding action of indefinite length while their nation retrenched for a struggle whose theater of first priority was on the other side of the world. There were, for now, no more planes to send them, no more ships to reinforce them. Franklin D. Roosevelt was busy with a war plan that would leave his favorite warship fending for herself against increasingly doubtful odds.

CHAPTER 3

The *Houston* had been christened in line with the ambitions of its namesake city's elite. In January 1927, wishing to paint Houston's name on the gray hull of a newly forged symbol of America's might, the city's leaders rallied behind former mayor Oscar Holcombe in petitioning the Navy Department to name a cruiser for the second-largest city in the American South. In short order, a blitz of entreaties from Houston's citizenry was hitting the desk of Navy Secretary Curtis D. Wilbur—nearly two hundred resolutions from civic organizations, five hundred Western Union telegrams from individuals, and five thousand "classically composed appeals" from "home-loving boys and girls who comprise our scholastic population," wrote William A. Bernrieder, executive secretary of the Cruiser Houston Committee. Within nine months of the campaign's start, the Navy announced that its newest cruiser would be named the *Houston*. She would be a flag cruiser fitted to accommodate an admiral's staff and designated to replace the USS *Pittsburgh* (CA-4) as flagship of the U.S. Asiatic Fleet.

Electric-welded, lightweight, and fast, the USS *Houston* (originally designated CL-30) was drawn up to pack 130,000 shaft horsepower, more than the entire U.S. fleet did in 1898. The shipbuilders at Newport News Shipbuilding and Drydock in Newport News,

Virginia, birth state of Sam Houston, launched her on September 7, 1929, at a cost of $17 million. On that grand day, the citizens of Houston showed up in Virginia in numbers that powerfully impressed Newport News president Homer L. Ferguson, who attested, "Out of 319 launchings at the yards none was more colorful, nor bore more unmistakable signs of careful preparation."

"No detail, however small, was overlooked by naval architects, engineers and scientists in making this cruiser the supreme combination of all that is superb and efficient in fighting ships," William Bernrieder would tell Houston's KPRC radio audience. The crew slept not on hammocks but on actual berths with springs and mattresses. There were mailboxes throughout the ship, a large recreation hall with modern writing desks and reading lamps, footlockers instead of musty old seabags for personal storage, and hot and cold running water—not just for officers but for the crew as well.

Commissioned in the summer of 1930 and reclassified from light cruiser to heavy cruiser a year later, the *Houston* acquired her lifelong identification with the fabled U.S. Asiatic Fleet from the beginning. The ship was the Asiatic Fleet's flagship until 1933. By the time she returned in that capacity in November 1940 under Capt. Jesse B. Oldendorf, relieving the *Augusta,* tensions with Japan were escalating dangerously.

The Asiatic Fleet was, in effect, the frontier detachment of the turn-of-the-century Navy. In the tradition of Theodore Roosevelt's Great White Fleet, its ships toured Asia's imperial wilderness, showing the U.S. flag. Though it was always led by a single heavy cruiser or battleship that served as its flagship, the fleet's signature vessel was the gunboat, 450-tonners that ranged inland—as far as thirteen hundred miles up the Yangtze River—to safeguard U.S. interests in China. One officer who commanded a Yangtze gunboat called them "seagoing fire departments." By virtue of its exotic station, basing its ships wherever the seasons or the tremors of faltering European empires required—Shanghai, Tsingtao, Manila—the fleet enjoyed a cachet among sailors that always outweighed its meager physical assets. Free from stateside hierarchies and rigmarole, Asiatic Fleet sailors acquired a signal swagger and style. Admiral Hart held a high opinion of them. "Like their officers, the men were regulars and were of longer average service and experience than the rest of the Navy. . . . No man ever commanded a better lot." In 1905, a midshipman named Chester Nimitz had served his first sea duty with the fleet, on board the twelve-thousand-ton battleship *Ohio*. Thirty years later he was back, commanding the fleet's flagship, the cruiser *Augusta*.

Few American military men have served their nation as isolated and far removed from support as the men on "Asia Station." On the world maps that schoolchildren studied—Mercator projections that invariably centered on the North American continent and whose edges cleaved the world vertically at 110 degrees east longitude— they patrolled the extreme edges of the planet. It was not possible to be farther from home. In such an exotic setting, even the most worldly American boy would have been an innocent, but the *Houston*'s crew were provincials by most any measure. Decades before, as the Navy was pushing to build a modern battle fleet—an ambition that got a boost with the victory over Spain in 1898—the commandant of the Newport Naval Training Station declared, "We want the brawn of Montana, the fire of the South and the daring of the Pacific slope." As a Navy Department official wrote in 1919, "The boy from the farm is considered by the naval recruiting service to be the most desirable material." At a time when judges were still sentencing criminals to rehabilitation by service in the fleet, the Navy would take whatever able-bodied, hardy-souled young men it could find. The arrangement was useful for all concerned. In the Depression and immediately afterward, new recruits joined not to redeem the free world but to save their hardscrabble selves. In a ship such as the *Houston,* the children of the "hungry thirties" entered a self-contained meritocracy in which they might find a way to thrive.

Smart discipline could mold the hardest cases into sailors. Pfc. John H. Wisecup from New Orleans, tall, lean, profane, and shockingly effective in a fight, no longer got into fisticuffs in the disciplined confines of the *Houston*'s Marine detachment. Such behavior had nearly brought a premature end to his Navy career. Driven by an aggressive machismo that seemed to have no greater expression than a drunken brawl, he had a checkered service record but enjoyed the saving good fortune to have had at least one commanding officer along the way who, when Wisecup crossed the line, saw enough virtue in him to spare him from a general court-martial.

Prominent among those virtues was his fastball. A dominating right-hander, Wisecup had taken his New Orleans Jesuit Blue Jays to an American Legion regional title and had played in the minor leagues before enlisting in the Corps and finding himself hotly recruited to play for the Marines' Mare Island squad. The commander there was a colonel named Thompson. A devout baseball fan, he took a liking to Wisecup—or at least to his right arm. He had seen what it could do to the Army and semipro teams that challenged the Marines for supremacy on the base. That fondness paid dividends for Wisecup when he got into a boozy fistfight with another Marine who happened to work as a guard at the base prison, famously known as "84" after its building number. Wisecup took the guy apart.

The next day Colonel Thompson hauled in the private, heard his story, and passed along some dire news: "You know, they want your blood at '84,' John." Wisecup said that he suspected as much. "If I give you a general court-martial," the colonel said, "you're going to do your time right over there. You know what's going to happen?" Again Wisecup said he knew. The colonel offered him a way out. The USS *Chaumont* was in port. The 8,300-ton Hog Island Type B transport had won fame as the ship that had first landed Marines in Shanghai in 1927. It was a coveted billet for anyone looking to join the fabled Fourth Marines on Asia Station. The colonel told Wisecup the *Chaumont* was at the pier and that if he was smart he'd go along with a new assignment. "Go pack your gear and get aboard," Thompson said. In pulling that string for his ace, the colonel gave him a free ticket not only out of the doghouse but to glory road.

Wisecup boarded the *Chaumont*—and blew the opportunity on his very first liberty. Overstaying his leave, he returned to the ship and was given an immediate deck court-martial. Tried and found guilty, he got ten days of bread and water and a stiff boot out of the China Marines. Halfway through his sentence, another ship moored alongside, and Wisecup was ordered to transfer to her and finish serving his sentence there. The other ship was the USS *Houston*.

Wisecup was not meant to be a China Marine. But he was clearly meant to stand out on the *Houston*. When the troublemaker hauled his seabag up the gangway, he saluted the officer of the deck and announced, "Sir, Private Wisecup, reporting for duty. Where's the brig?" Wisecup did his time and managed to stay out of the lockup thereafter. He adapted to a world of regimentation and polished pride. Captain Rooks's Marines were not allowed topside except in full dress, shoes polished and shirts triple-creased. Forced to vent his insuppressible rages privately, Wisecup maintained a serviceable reputation, though in time his steel locker door was permanently bowed in.

The tradition of the seagoing Marine dated to the Revolutionary War, when Marines shot muskets from a man-of-war's fighting tops. It spoke to the depth of the leadership tradition that grew from the *Houston*'s heady early days, and of the talents of 1st Lt. Frank E. Gallagher, Gunnery Sgt. Walter Standish, and 1st Sgt. Harley H. Dupler of the *Houston*'s detachment in particular, that a man such as John Wisecup was put in a position to make something of himself. It was true of all the crew to one degree or another, such was the contrast between life on board ship and the deprivation of the times. A sailor named James W. Huffman left his faltering family farm in the San Joaquin Valley, California, in 1933 and hustled his skinny frame to the San Diego Naval Training Center mostly in order to eat. And because the Depression destroyed families as well as livelihoods, more than a few *Houston* sailors had enlisted to escape broken homes. Howard R. Charles, a *Houston* Marine private, put himself in the path of a world war by escaping the wildfires of another: an escalating violent struggle with his stepfather back home in Hutchinson, Kansas. Melfred L. "Gus" Forsman, a seaman first class, didn't need a push. He left Iowa in April 1939 to become a *Houston* sailor, dreaming of seeing faraway lands. But as he soon learned, anyone aspiring to a life of adventurous globetrotting found he had been sold a bill of goods. Fuel was expensive, and ships were kept in port as often as possible. Most enlisted men found their ambitions checked by a system of class that generally reserved the prestige of an officer's commission for the white, the Episcopal, and the wealthy. The accoutrements of the good life found in officers' country—silver service worthy of Hyde Park, a Steinway baby grand in the wardroom, all gifts of the citizens of Houston—were as much the ornaments of expectation as of accomplishment.

Several members of the *Houston*'s Marine detachment were veterans of the illustrious Fourth Marine Regiment, the unit that helped defend Shanghai's International Settlement from the brushfires of combat between Japanese and Chinese forces. According to a veteran of Asia Station, Rear Adm. Kemp Tolley, the Fourth Marines were "the seaward anchor of the Yangtze Patrol during the period which might be called the Patrol's heyday: 1927 to its flaming end on Corregidor." One of its battalion commanders, the colorful Maj. Lewis B. "Chesty" Puller, had served in the *Augusta*'s Marine detachment under Captain Nimitz. The *Houston*'s Sgt. Charley L. Pryor Jr. had gotten his first stripe from Puller himself during his tour on the *Augusta*. In 1940, liberty in Tsingtao was an adventure unto itself. "Marines were never slow in tangling with men of the various other foreign detachments," Tolley would write. "A very satisfactory state of belligerency could be established by a leading question or a facetious remark concerning a Seaforth Highlander's kilt."

Brawling frolics with soldiers of friendly nations were one thing. The Japanese were another. Charley Pryor had seen them training for war, witnessed their exercises, saw squads and company-sized units drilling in the hills and on the beaches in and around Shanghai. He wrote his parents in Littlefield, Texas, of brawls between Marines and militant Japanese nationals. "Everyone hates the Japs and though we are all told to take anything they say or do to us, it just won't be done. I will try to kill the Japanese who so much as lays a hand on me. I am just like everyone else so I know the rest will do the same thing."

As Hitler's armies tore through Europe and Russia, the International Settlement became electric with energy, swelling with Jewish refugees from Austria. They brought some of Vienna with them, erecting bistros and wienerschnitzel stands alongside the tea and silk shops. String combos played on the streets. But by December 1940, as many people were fleeing the Settlement as arriving there. Distress was in the air. A *Time* correspondent wrote:

> The first sting of winter hung over a dying city. Its tide of fleeing foreigners has reached flood last month with the evacuation of U.S. citizens; its foreign colony has shrunk to a scattering of bitter enders. . . . The roulette tables at Joe Farren's, the Park Hotel's Sky Terrace, Sir Ellis Victor Sassoon's Tower Night Club has none of their old sparkle. Industrial Shanghai is sinking fast.

The Marines' experience in China was excellent preparation for what the *Houston*'s officers had in store for them. For thirteen months leading to the outbreak of war, Cdr. Arthur L. Maher, the gunnery officer, had run a training program rooted in the idea that competition through intersquad rivalry was the key to high performance. The 1,168-man wartime complement was full of senior petty officers who had a talent for promoting competition between divisions. In the deck force, it was up to men such as boatswain's mate first class Shelton "Red" Clymer—"a real tough old bird," said one sailor—to get green recruits ready for war. In the engineering department belowdecks, any number of experienced hands kept the screws turning. Lt. Cdr. Richard H. Gingras and his hard-driving machinists ran the ship's two steam power plants. "The caliber of the senior petty officers was way above anything that I'd seen in these other ships," said Lt. Robert B. Fulton, the ship's assistant engineering officer. "Other ships were struggling to get basic things together. None of them could compare to the caliber of personnel on the *Houston*."

In dealing with the Japanese leading up to war, the U.S. Congress had been considerably less surly than the leathernecks of the Fourth Marines. Certainly, Japan had not always been America's enemy. During World War I the two nations had enjoyed a de facto alliance, Japan fondly remembering Teddy Roosevelt's anti-Russian posture during the Russo-Japanese War and eager for the chance to relieve Germany of its colonial island holdings in the Central Pacific: the Mariana, Caroline, and Marshall Islands. Worried about provoking Japan, the U.S. Congress voted in February 1939 against appropriating $5 million to upgrade the Navy's forward base in Guam. Though in April 1940 Adm. Harold R. Stark, the chief of naval operations, had relocated the United States Fleet from the West Coast to Pearl Harbor in Hawaii, overseas the Navy would make do with the bases it already possessed.

The imperial Japanese notion of peace was as consistent in application as it was different from the rest of the world's understanding of the term. Serene dominion over continental and oceanic Asia was the Tokyo militarists' idea of peace, clearly articulated by Japan but widely misunderstood in the West. "Japan was the only important nation in the world in the twentieth century which combined modern industrial power and a first-class military establishment with religious and social ideas inherited from the primitive ages of mankind, which exalted the military profession and regarded war and conquest as the highest good," wrote the historian Samuel Eliot Morison. The Japanese Imperial Army, which by 1931 had become the dominant voice in Japanese government, adopted the ancient ambition of Japan's mythical founder, Emperor Jimmu: the principle of *hakku ichiu*, "bringing the eight corners of the earth under one roof."

With Formosa and Korea in hand, spoils of previous wars, Japan cast its ambitious eye on China and its iron- and coal-rich northern provinces. Imperial troops had been there in sizable force since the "Manchuria Incident" in 1931. In a malevolent gambit that seemed to preview the Reichstag fire in 1933 Weimar Germany, the Japanese garrison conspired to bomb the South Manchuria Railway, which it controlled, in order to justify more aggressive moves against its enemy. An escalating cycle of provocation and skirmish ensued. In July of 1937, a year in which Emperor Hirohito's Japan allocated sixty-nine percent of its budget to the military, the intensifying fighting provoked Japan to launch a full offensive in northern China. Aiming to avoid embargoes mandated by the U.S. Neutrality Acts, Japan called its savage campaign against civilians and city-dwelling foreigners a benevolent occupation. But the strain of China operations soon compelled Japan to look farther afield for oil, timber, rubber, tin, and other materials to wage the war. Playing on the tensions between the Soviet Union and Germany to maximize its freedom of action in Asia, Tokyo turned its covetous eyes southward, to the Dutch East Indies.

Sumatra, Java, Borneo, Celebes, Bali, Timor, and the 17,500 other islands in the scimitar-shaped archipelago held a world of natural wealth. Ten thousand species of birds, fish, flora and fauna were its surface manifestations: exotic deerlike pigs, dwarf buffalo, tree kangaroos, Komodo dragons, one-horned rhinos, and freshwater dolphins. Land's boundary line with the sea was smudged every year by the onset of monsoons, typhoons, and windblown wave crests during the rainy season. But it was the treasures below the ground—oil, tin, manganese, roots that gave life to rice plants, and trees bearing rubber—that interested Japan.

In the years preceding war, American diplomats had driven a hard bargain with the Japanese, constraining them with naval arms treaties and holding out the threat of boycott and embargo to compel them to walk the line. Americans watched but did not seem to appreciate the fervor with which Japan was seizing control of the Asian mainland. Weary of war, some believed that messy foreign entanglements could be avoided, saving their suspicions for their own military or for Wall Street financiers and arms traders who they thought had profiteered during the Great War. In June 1940 the U.S. Army's total enlistment stood at 268,000 men. It was inconvenient to contemplate that during the first six weeks of the Rape of

Nanking, nearly half that number of Chinese civilians and prisoners of war, as well as some American civilians, had been slaughtered by the Japanese Army.

The naivete of the isolationists concerning Imperial Japan's ambitions was matched only by the ignorance of the average enlistee concerning its capabilities. Most American servicemen saw the Japanese as too many newspaper cartoonists sketched them: bucktoothed simpletons who would wilt when faced with U.S. Marines and tough sailors in their impregnable ships. But the perking belligerence of the Japanese dispelled any such misguided popular stereotypes among U.S. military planners. They saw the threat. As 1940 wound down, with the Japanese drawing up plans to seize the Dutch East Indies, American military dependents were sent home from the Philippines. Admiral Hart relocated the Asiatic Fleet from Shanghai to Manila in November 1941, allowing Rear Adm. William A. Glassford to stay on as long as he could in Shanghai as head of the Naval Purchasing Office and nominal boss of the Fourth Marines. The American position on the mainland was, according to Kemp Tolley, "about as hopeful as lighting a candle in a typhoon."

★

In August 1941, Edith Rooks traveled from Seattle to Honolulu to say farewell to her husband as he prepared to take command of the USS *Houston* in Manila. Understanding the temperature of the times, Captain Rooks could not restrain himself from a moment of candor. He took stock of the developing crisis over China and told Edith that he would be unlikely to come home from this assignment alive. As his son would explain, "He said the power of the Japanese was far greater than what we could muster, and he did not expect to return."

The 1914 Naval Academy graduate, having made captain in February, was a star performer and seemed bound for flag rank. His assignment to the Asiatic Fleet flagship was for two years—the minimum length of sea duty to make him eligible for promotion to rear admiral. On August 28, Rooks found the *Houston* at Cavite Navy Yard in Manila and two days later relieved Capt. Jesse B. Oldendorf as her commander. The next day he wrote Edith and reiterated his mixed feelings. "It's a shame to wish away time at our age, but two years is a long time, and I don't look forward to it with pleasure." In 1941 even a keen observer such as Rooks, long a student of geopolitics and now able to observe the Pacific theater firsthand, had trouble teasing out the flow of events. "My opinion of the Jap situation keeps changing. If I understand the press reports coming out of Tokyo, they are making some very grave decisions right now. I think they will finally decide against war with us, but I certainly might be wrong."

In other writings, Rooks's pessimism prevailed. His analytical mind told him that whatever her industrial advantages over the long term, America would not long stand up against a determined Japanese offensive in the western Pacific. He appreciated the Japanese Navy's capabilities. Samuel Eliot Morison would write, "Few Allied naval officers other than Captain Rooks of the USS *Houston* believed the Japanese capable of more than one offensive operation, but they exceeded even his expectation."

If he did not wish away time entirely, Rooks marked its passing with the precision of a chronometer. "Well, September is almost gone," he wrote Edith after a month in command of his ship, abandoning longhand and breaking in his new Underwood typewriter, acquired in Manila for forty-five dollars. "Day after tomorrow it will be one month since I took over the *Houston,* and two months since I left you in Honolulu. That makes two twenty-sixths of the time, or 1/13 gone. When you say it that way, it doesn't sound so interminable, does it?"

In time he seemed to realize the cumulative effect on Edith of reiterating his pessimism. In his correspondence to her during the ensuing months leading up to war, one can sense him doing penance for his earlier candor. "The longer they keep from striking, the less chance that they will start anything. For one thing, America is growing stronger every day," he wrote on October 5.

He told Edith he thought the Japanese would attack Siberia if they attacked at all. "They are really in what must be for them a very unsatisfactory position. An attack on Siberia will not solve their pressing need to obtain oil and other supplies. In a movement to the South, where such supplies are, they will inevitably be opposed by the combined power of the United States, the British Empire, and the Netherlands East Indies. If they make no move at all, our embargo will slowly but surely sap their economic and industrial strength and will probably ultimately defeat their effort in China." Two weeks later he noted that "the Jap situation is sizzling this week end, with the fall of the cabinet, and with the torpedoing of our destroyer *Kearny* on the east coast. I suppose it means real trouble. . . . Well, come what may, I am ready for it."

For a short time still, the Philippine capital would be a sanctuary from the kind of chaos that was overtaking Shanghai. A few months into his tenure as captain, with the *Houston* moored at Cavite, Rooks returned to his stateroom after an evening on the town and wrote Edith, "It is an interesting fact to me that there seems to be no particular fear or nervous tension here at all. Everyone seems calm, cool, and cheerful. They have of course been facing such crises for months, not to say years, and are inured to them. . . . As for me, I face the future with the utmost confidence. My job is turning into one of the biggest in the Navy at this time, and I am fortunate to have it. The ship is in excellent condition as far as material and training is concerned. Whatever weaknesses she has are those of design. Service in these hot southern waters is of course very uncomfortable when the ships are sealed up for war operations, but we will have to take that."

He seemed eager to revoke his farewell prophecy in Honolulu. "I have a feeling that fate is going to be kind to me," Rooks wrote to Edith, "and that on some happier tomorrow we will be walking the streets of Seattle in company, as we now do in spirit."

CHAPTER 4

In November 1941, the tension that gripped the naval base at Cavite was palpable. A war warning was circulating. Aware of the Asiatic Fleet's vulnerability in Manila, Admiral Hart scattered the vessels.* The *Houston* was stripped down for action. The admiral's flag quarters were cleared of all unnecessary accoutrements. The nicer furniture was stored ashore in Manila, including the silver service and the baby grand piano. One afternoon, when the *Houston's* softball team went out to meet a challenge from sailors at Canacao Naval Hospital, the familiar peacetime routine prevailed. Three hours later, the ballplayers returned to find the well-ordered chaos of a warship preparing to get under way.

A shore patrol went to round up stragglers still on liberty. Yard workers hustled to reinstall the ship's four carbon arc searchlights, which had been detached and set aside for replacement by newer models. They doubled their efforts to install two additional four-barreled 1.1-inch antiaircraft mounts. Welders dropped over the sides to burn portholes shut. The ship's degaussing cable, wrapped

---

*The U.S. Asiatic Fleet consisted of the *Houston,* the *Marblehead,* thirteen old destroyers (Destroyer Squadron Twenty-nine), twenty-six submarines, six gunboats, and assorted support vessels.

around the ship's hull to produce a magnetic field to defeat magnetic-triggered mines, was hurriedly tested and calibrated. The *Houston* was going to sea. FDR would fish with it now from afar, pursuing more formidable quarry.

At nine A.M. on December 1, the *Houston* set course for Iloilo, 238 miles south of Manila, while the light cruiser *Marblehead* and the destroyers headed for bases in Borneo. Navy war plans had long provided for such a withdrawal. The prewar consensus had been that the Asiatic Fleet would leave the area entirely, biding time in the Indian Ocean until the main Pacific Fleet had advanced far enough west to join in a counteroffensive. Hart was initially reluctant to abandon the Philippines without a fight. As late as October 1941 he suggested keeping his small fleet in Manila and fighting alongside General MacArthur. But Secretary Frank Knox's Navy Department deemed it too risky. A compromise was reached under which the *Houston* would move further south but stay nominally in the region, leading the fleet from Surabaya, Java.

Stopping at Iloilo, Rooks rendezvoused with Admiral Glassford, recently evacuated from China. When Glassford's Catalina flying boat splashed down in the bay just before dark on December 7, a motor launch from the *Houston* retrieved him and brought him to the ship. "Let's get the hell out of here," Glassford reportedly said upon stepping aboard. The *Houston* was soon en route to Surabaya.

The *Houston*'s escape was a close one. The Japanese swung their blade east and south on December 8 (December 7 in the United States). The *Houston* radioman who received Admiral Hart's Morse code transmission perfunctorily copied the block of characters, dated the sheet three A.M. local time, tossed it into the basket, then asked himself, "What did that thing say?" It said: "JAPAN STARTED HOSTILITIES. GOVERN YOURSELVES ACCORDINGLY." "We had hardly cleared Iloilo entrance when we heard gunfire astern of us and saw a ship aflame," Cdr. Arthur Maher recalled. Hidden in the dark backdrop of Panay's mountain ranges, the *Houston* avoided notice of the Japanese pilots. She joined a pair of Asiatic Fleet destroyers, the *Stewart* and the *John D. Edwards,* in escorting two fleet oilers and the old seaplane tender *Langley* out of the war zone.

Anyone overconfident about America's prospects against Japan might have asked why the invincible U.S. fleet was on the run. En route to Surabaya, Captain Rooks called his officers and department

heads to the executive officer's cabin and informed them that war
had started. On December 10 more than fifty twin-engine Japanese
bombers struck Cavite unopposed, burning out most of its key installations, destroying the harbor facilities, and sinking a transport
ship. When Tokyo Rose came on the radio that night, she purred an
optimistic report that President Roosevelt's favorite heavy cruiser
had been sunk. The men of the *Houston* were at once flattered and
unnerved by the attention. Embracing their status as a priority target not only of the Japanese military but of its propagandists too,
they would coin a defiant nickname for the ship: the Galloping
Ghost of the Java Coast.

Their cocky optimism took a blow when the toll of the Pearl
Harbor raid and the destruction of General MacArthur's air force on
Luzon were reported in dispatches. A Navy Department communiqué that arrived on December 15, typed up and posted in the mess
hall, detailed the losses: the *Arizona* sunk, the *Oklahoma* capsized.
The damage to the Pacific Fleet left the United States with, in
Samuel Eliot Morison's words, "a two-ocean war to wage with a less
than one-ocean Navy. It was the most appalling situation America
had faced since the preservation of the Union had been assured." The
crew was stunned, if unsure what it all meant for them beyond an
end to fifty-cent eight-course dinners and nickel shots of whiskey in
Manila's cabarets.

By Christmas, Wake Island had fallen. Manila, under daily air attack from Formosa, had been abandoned and declared an open city
by MacArthur, whose soldiers, with the men of the Fourth Marines,
would soon be bottled up on the Bataan peninsula. Singapore faced a
siege. Where might the Allies finally hold the line? On New Year's
Day 1942, with Japanese amphibious forces closing in on Borneo
and Celebes to the north, an American submarine entered Surabaya's
harbor in Java flying the flag of a four-star admiral. Admiral Hart
disembarked weary, having made the thousand-mile journey from
Cavite mostly submerged, breathing stale air. Ashore, he gathered
his energies and took a train west to Batavia, headquarters of the
Dutch Naval Command. It was clear to all the Allied commanders
in the theater that their last stand in the southwest Pacific would be
made in Java.

The British and the Americans had formalized their joint command relationship at the end of December, at the Arcadia Conference

in Washington, where President Roosevelt and Prime Minister Churchill endorsed a Europe-first strategy and established the Combined Chiefs of Staff to centralize American and British strategic decision making. To defend the Dutch East Indies, and ultimately Australia, a four-nation joint command, ABDACOM, was organized on January 15, combining American, British, Dutch, and Australian forces under the overall command of British Field Marshal Sir Archibald Wavell. Ground forces on Java included principally Dutch and Australian garrisons, about 40,000 strong, under Dutch Lt. Gen. Hein ter Poorten. ABDA's meager and ill-supported air forces were placed under Royal Air Force Air Marshal Sir Richard Peirse. As senior naval commander in the area, Admiral Hart was named head of the naval component, formally colloquialized as "ABDAfloat."

Low-level confusion, or at least a lack of focus and unity of purpose, surrounded most every aspect of the ABDA naval command. The confusing unit nomenclature reflected this. The *Houston* and the other combatants of the U.S. Asiatic Fleet were known as "Task Force Five" when they were on convoy duty, but were part of the "Combined Striking Force" during joint offensive operations. When Admiral Hart was named commander of ABDAfloat, he put Admiral Glassford in command of Task Force Five and installed his capable chief of staff, Rear Adm. William R. Purnell, an old hand at working with the British and Dutch, as acting Asiatic Fleet commander, based at Hart's former Surabaya waterfront headquarters. Hart himself relocated to Field Marshal Wavell's ABDA flag headquarters in the mountain resort town of Lembang, seventy-five miles southeast of Batavia and several hundred miles from Surabaya. The interlocking responsibilities and haphazard lines of international communication were a recipe for frustration.

Hart readily saw that conflicting national priorities would hamper everyone's ability to fight. In the prewar conferences attended by Admiral Purnell, it became clear that the Royal Navy was worrying less about defending Java than about saving its imperial crown jewel, Singapore, at the tip of the Malay peninsula. Long before war began, the Americans and the British had debated the merits of holding Singapore. The Americans considered it hopeless once Japanese land-based airpower came to bear on it. But Wavell insisted that the British garrison there could endure a Japanese assault indefinitely. "Our whole fighting reputation is at stake, and the

honour of the British Empire," he wrote after the island came under
Japanese assault, in a February 10 letter that largely paraphrased a
cable he had received from Prime Minister Churchill that same day.
"The Americans have held out on the Bataan Peninsula against
heavier odds; the Russians are turning back the picked strength of
the Germans; the Chinese with almost complete lack of modern
equipment have held the Japanese for four and a half years. It will be
disgraceful if we yield our boasted fortress of Singapore to inferior
forces."

Hart preferred to orient the Allied effort toward the defense of
Australia. Already the Americans were setting up a major base for
its service force—supply ships, tenders, and other auxiliaries—at
Darwin in northwestern Australia, the receiving point for convoys of
troops, equipment, and supplies arriving from points north and east.
The U.S. Asiatic Fleet surface battle group, Task Force Five, consisting of the *Houston,* the *Marblehead,* and the thirteen old destroyers of
Destroyer Squadron Twenty-nine, joined by the modern light
cruiser *Boise,* was well positioned at Surabaya to guard the lifeline to
Australia.* The British made their home port at Batavia, four hundred miles to the west, a better position for running convoys to
Singapore. The heavy cruiser HMS *Exeter,* which had won fame in
1939 hunting the *Graf Spee* in a legendary pursuit that ended with
the German pocket battleship's scuttling at Montevideo, was the
largest Royal Navy ship in the theater.

Painfully aware of Germany's occupation of their continental
homeland, the Dutch were naturally displeased that an American,
Hart, was to head the naval defense of their homeland in exile. His
appointment to lead ABDAfloat put him in natural conflict with the
head of Dutch naval forces in the area, Vice Adm. Conrad E. L.
Helfrich, a jut-jawed bulldog of a commander who preferred attack
to retreating defense. Born on Java, he knew the region's straits,
coves, and shallows. At the Surabaya conference he reportedly
pounded the table and demanded a squadron of heavy cruisers to resist the Japanese onslaught. Though he discovered there were limits
to the resources America and Britain could assign to his cause, he

---

*The *Boise* (CL-47) was not originally part of the Asiatic Fleet. Assigned to the Pacific
Fleet's Cruiser Division Nine, she was pressed into Asiatic Fleet service after escorting
a convoy to Manila that arrived on December 4, 1941, just in time to get trapped there
by the outbreak of the war.

still thought Allied surface forces could stymie the enemy convoys, even without air cover.

In a secret prewar analysis that he completed on November 18, 1941, labeled "Estimate of the Situation," Rooks showed his almost prescient strategic acuity, detailing in 107 typed and hand-annotated legal pages the soon-to-be-exploited weaknesses of the scattered Allied forces in the Pacific. From Singapore's vulnerability to blockade and land assault to Manila's exposure to air raids, Rooks catalogued the full range of the Allies' shortcomings.

The remedy, he argued, was boldness, commitment, and unity. As Captain Rooks sized things up, the best way to contain the enemy's swelling tide was to base a combined Allied superfleet at Singapore. For a time in 1941, the British discussed reinforcing the Far Eastern Fleet with as many as seven additional battleships. Rooks argued that such a force, augmented by Allied cruisers and destroyers, might contest Japanese control of the South China Sea and block Japanese aggression against the Philippines, Borneo, and Indochina. "When this fleet becomes strong enough to prevent Japanese control of the South China Sea the war will be well on its way to being won," Rooks wrote. But he ultimately recognized the futility in it. Such a dramatic effort would require an unlikely concentration of resources and will. He saw that without stronger air forces to cover them, with long lines of supply and replenishment, and led by commanders un-acquainted with local waters, even a fleet of dreams would have had a hard time of it. Alas, the means had to carry the end. When Rooks took the *Houston* out of Darwin and headed for the combat zone in the Dutch East Indies, he left behind a copy of his "Estimate" with a colleague. He left behind his optimism too. Historians would be the arbiters of Albert H. Rooks's ability to divine the shape of things to come.

It would fall to the scattered navies of four nations to save the Dutch East Indies. It would fall to Franklin Roosevelt's favorite ship; to the *Exeter* and three smaller cruisers of a Dutch flotilla de-fending its own imperial shores; to an Australian light cruiser, the *Perth,* whose pugnacious skipper had made his name in the Mediterranean; to several squadrons of old destroyers still capable of running with bone in teeth but whose better days were behind them; to Capt. John Wilkes's submarine force, operating on the run without spare parts or a good supply of torpedoes. It would fall to ships and submarines because there were not enough planes. The ineffectiveness of the aerial campaign over Java would make the ships' work all the tougher. At the dawn of the age of naval air power, ushered in by its leading and most audacious practitioners, the Japanese, Thomas C. Hart's ABDA naval force would fight largely without wings. But it would most certainly fight.

CHAPTER 5

In the two months leading up to the *Houston*'s catastrophic bomb hit in the Flores Sea on February 4, ABDA ships had seen action only sporadically. To the chagrin of her crew, the *Houston*'s primary task during that period was convoy escort. Per orders of the Navy Department, Rooks's cruiser joined the seagoing wagon train of transports ferrying American and Australian troops from Australia to Java. As often as not, the easternmost leg was Darwin, but sometimes the *Houston* steamed east as far as Torres Strait to pick up convoys coming up from Sydney and around Cape York Peninsula.

For infuriating stretches of time, the *Houston* stood at anchor off Darwin, swinging to the tides. The crew chafed to grapple with the Japanese fleet. "It got to be so bad," wrote Walter Winslow, a *Houston* floatplane pilot, "that when I was in the company of Australian naval officers, I began to feel almost ashamed to be a part of the vaunted United States Navy." A heavy cruiser with presidential pedigree deserved better than shepherding the sows of the service force.

Failing that, her crew certainly deserved a liberty call more interesting than what Darwin had to offer. The outpost of fifteen hundred souls was the capital of the Northern Territory, but that title was out of proportion to the dimensions of the town's grid, three blocks by two, its single-story buildings roofed in corrugated iron, horses and carts providing the only public transportation. The flinty terrain and the red clay streets that swirled up with dust when they weren't boggy with rain evoked memories of the nineteenth-century frontier. Sailors from America's rural precincts may have enjoyed the fleeting illusion that they had come home again. For most of the *Houston*'s crew, though, the town was a disappointment. Hopes of meeting Australian girls faded in light of the reality that mostly only men were there. The first major Allied combat unit in the area was the 147th Field Artillery, a federalized South Dakota National Guard unit that was trucked up from Brisbane on January 18 to help defend Australia's northern frontier. Drinking warm beer with Australians and South Dakotans was a pleasing diversion as far as it went. But it grew sour when the town's beer supply vanished. Such shortages had struck Darwin before—its buildings had the broken windows to prove it. No sooner had the town restocked from the last run on its beer supply than a bunch of thirsty Yanks descended upon them again. The town's supplies of canned food disappeared too, snapped up by *Houston* men eager to have snacks handy in the gun tub.

When the mayor of Darwin complained to Captain Rooks about the market-crashing effects of his crew's appetite, the fleet's service force replenished the town with fresh fruits and vegetables, canned peaches, hams, fruit cocktail, and olives, all originally meant for the U.S. troops in now-abandoned Manila. One of the *Houston*'s senior floatplane pilots became a small-town celebrity by procuring some American beer from a supply vessel in the harbor and bringing it ashore. "That's the closest I've ever been to becoming the president of Australia," Lt. Tommy Payne said.

Offensive operations fell to other ships of the ABDA fleet. On the night of January 22–23, a U.S. submarine patrolling Makassar Strait, the *Sturgeon,* intercepted a Japanese invasion force bound for the key oil center of Balikpapan, Borneo, closed with the convoy, and fired a spread of torpedoes. Seeing several bright explosions, Cdr. William L. Wright radioed his higher-ups, "Sturgeon *no longer virgin.*" When PBY-4 Catalina flying boats spotted more enemy shipping heading for Balikpapan, there was no doubt as to the enemy's intentions.

Word was relayed to the other ships of Task Force Five, awaiting orders in Kupang Bay in eastern Timor. With the *Houston* busy far to the east, escorting a convoy from Torres Strait back to Surabaya, Admiral Glassford had at his disposal the *Boise* and the *Marblehead* and the destroyers *John D. Ford, Pope, Parrott,* and *Paul Jones.* He was excited about the approach of a Japanese surface force in a place where his ships might finally be able to do something about it. What followed was the U.S. Navy's first offensive operation of World War II and its first major surface action since the Spanish-American War. And the Asiatic Fleet's largest ships would miss out on it.

On the morning of January 23, Glassford's flotilla set out to strike at the Japanese landings at Balikpapan. The *Boise,* Glassford's flagship, hit an uncharted pinnacle rock, tearing a long gash near her keel and forcing her to Tjilatjap for repairs. No sooner had Glassford transferred his flag to the *Marblehead* than trouble struck that ship too. Mechanical problems with a turbine limited her to a speed of fifteen knots. The *John D. Ford, Pope, Parrott,* and *Paul Jones* sortied alone to ambush the Japanese landing force off Balikpapan that night.

Approaching the big Dutch oil center near midnight, Commodore Paul Talbot, in the *John D. Ford,* discerned a dozen transports anchored in rows outside the harbor, neatly silhouetted against the fires consuming Balikpapan's refining and storage facilities, set ablaze by the Dutch in retreat. The destroyers accelerated to twenty-seven knots.

The Japanese *marus* never saw them coming. On the first run, the *Parrott* sent three torpedoes bubbling toward a row of transports anchored about five miles outside the harbor entrance. The other American ships followed suit, and as Talbot reversed course back to the south, explosions began to rend the night. The 3,500-ton transport *Sumanoura Maru* threw a tower of flame five hundred feet high. Rear Adm. Shoji Nishimura, in the light cruiser *Naka,* took his ships away from the action in search of his presumed assailant, a U.S. submarine. But his impulsiveness left Talbot's squadron alone with its quarry. Another transport, the *Tatsukami Maru,* erupted and sank, as did an old destroyer. The *Kuretake Maru* actually got up steam, not unlike the *Nevada* at Pearl Harbor. But the *Paul Jones* got her, putting a torpedo into the five-thousand-tonner's starboard bow and leaving her sinking, stern high out of the water. A last torpedo, from the *John D. Ford*, damaged still another transport. Their lethal work done, Talbot's ships joined up and headed for Surabaya as Nishimura's destroyers chased phantoms.

Given the totality of the surprise, their success in the Battle of Balikpapan was only middling: four of twelve transports sunk and one torpedo boat. The Japanese seized the valuable oil port anyway. But in the context of disastrous circumstances, the attack was a lift to the spirits.

*

Admiral Hart never got word from Washington about when, if ever, more combat ships would arrive to help him against the on-rushing enemy. Nor was he told when the main Pacific Fleet would finally go on the attack and relieve the pressure he was facing from the Japanese. Though Vice Adm. William F. Halsey's aircraft carriers struck the Marshall and Gilbert Islands on February 1, the Japanese were making bolder strides to seize control of the western Pacific.

Life would have been easier for Hart if the Japanese military were his only foe. Internecine squabbles hampered him—but more threatening still were the daggers being sharpened in private. Field Marshal Wavell was of mixed mind regarding Hart's suitability for command. He complained to Winston Churchill via telegram that the fall of Manila had given the American "exaggerated ideas of Japanese efficiency." Wavell described Hart as "a quiet attractive character and seems shrewd. But he is old and openly says so and gives me the impression of looking over his shoulder rather too much." Hart was conscious that "almost no one had ever been retained in a sea-going command beyond the age of 64." There was, he wrote, "a movement toward youth in all sea commands." Tall, thin, and white-haired, the sixty-four-year-old habitually joked about being an "old man." This might have been a gambit to build collegiality through self-effacement, but it only eroded the Allies' confidence in him. Tommy Hart was, in his own words, "a worrier who never could sit back and coast until whatever was in hand was tied down and double-rivetted." He would compose a diary of three thousand pages, the handwriting decaying into a shaky, arthritic scrawl by the end.

Hart was caught in a political crossfire from both east and west.

At home, as the U.S. Army and Navy maneuvered to assign blame for the Pearl Harbor debacle, General MacArthur was trying to saddle him with the loss of the Philippines. Hart had to contend, too, with the Dutch admiralty's bitterness over their exclusion from ABDA leadership. Admiral Helfrich was not only commander in chief of the Royal Dutch East Indies Navy but minister of marine in the Dutch government. His civilian authority underscored the awkward fact that Hart superseded him in the military hierarchy. Helfrich's counterpart, General ter Poorten of the Dutch Army, was a co-equal of Hart's. For Helfrich to stand beneath his peer seemed hard for him to take. He ribbed Hart about the inefficacy of U.S. submarines in the theater. The American suspected Helfrich might have withheld information from him, and even lied about the readiness of Dutch warships for counterattacks against the Japanese.

Hart sympathized with the Dutch and took pains to suggest to Helfrich that he had accepted the ABDAfloat post only reluctantly and had not lobbied for it. "I did not like to be commanding Admiral Helfrich on his own home ground," he later wrote. As a sop to Dutch national pride he delegated to Helfrich the task of dealing directly with Rear Adm. Doorman, the commander of the Dutch surface combatants in ABDA, whom Hart would later put in command of a reconstituted Combined Striking Force.

Restrained and decorous in public, Hart never criticized the Allies in the press. In private, though, he was candid, even blunt, incapable of endorsing sunny pretenses about the military situation as he saw it. He could be intimidating to underlings. An Asiatic Fleet destroyer captain remarked, "I was scared of the old devil. It was a well known fact that he could shrivel an individual to a cinder with but a single glance of those gimlet like eyes." When it came to jousting with foreign contemporaries, however, he appears to have been something of a pushover. Hart's candor would be his own worst enemy. As disarming as he must have hoped his references to his age might be, it only gave Helfrich leverage in his back-channel effort to undermine him. If Hart's combat instincts and the readiness of his ships would determine his fortunes in theater, his political survival would hinge on battles fought in Washington, a continent away.

Word of the "strategic withdrawal" of British troops down the

Malay Peninsula arrived on January 31. The erosion of their position defied the royal imagination. Yet there the Japanese were, somehow vaulting the length of the jungle-sotted peninsula, on the verge of seizing "the Gibraltar of the East," Singapore, Britannia's most important naval base east of Ceylon. The quick collapse highlighted the futility of the British preference for convoying troops, and the grand waste of using all available Royal Navy and Dutch surface ships to escort convoy after convoy of troops bound for precipitous surrender.

Admiral Hart's position within ABDA was nearly as tenuous as that of the British stronghold. On February 5 he received a telegram from Adm. Ernest J. King, the commander in chief of the United States Fleet, informing him that an "awkward situation" had arisen in Washington. Wavell, thinking that Hart's pessimism was sapping the vigor of the naval campaign, urged Churchill to find a "younger more energetic man" for the job. Churchill in turn cultivated Franklin Roosevelt's doubts, already seeded by General MacArthur. As a result, when King contacted Hart it was to suggest that Hart request detachment for health reasons and yield his command to Admiral Helfrich. Anguished that he might depart under a pall, Hart complied, and the Dutchman was promptly named his successor. Hart confided to his diary on February 5, "It's all on the laps of the gods." Two days later, the U.S. Asiatic Fleet was officially dissolved and renamed U.S. Naval Forces, Southwest Pacific, nominally under Admiral Glassford. The American flotilla took its place as a component of the Combined Striking Force, under the overall command of Helfrich, who in turn delegated its tactical control to Rear Admiral Doorman.

Doorman was aggressive, but even the boldest deployment of cruisers faced dim prospects under enemy-controlled skies. The Combined Striking Force's February 3 sortie, abandoned after the *Houston* took that terrible bomb hit on Turret Three, revealed the difficulties that even the most powerful surface squadron would have in a theater dominated by enemy planes. As his damaged ship docked at Tjilatjap in the first week of February, Captain Rooks might well have seen the evolving Allied predicament as similar to Spain's doomed attempt in 1898 to hold Cuba and Puerto Rico during the Spanish-American War as an American invasion loomed. He had studied it at the War College. The commander of Spain's

CHAPTER 6

Romantic ideals dissolved quickly in the Pacific war's early days. As the last Allied base in the Sunda chain beyond the reach of Japanese bombers, located in the center part of the island's south coast, away from the pincers of Japanese airpower encroaching from east and west, Tjilatjap had drawn a multinational crowd of ships, naval and merchant alike, seeking to elude the onslaught. It was clear that nothing could be done for the grievous wound to the *Houston*'s after turret. Although support ships were on hand to service destroyers and submarines short on ordnance, stores, and parts, the *Houston*'s after turret was a permanent ruin, its internal circuitry burned out, breechblocks and firing locks frozen into place. The crew used a dockside crane to hoist the turret assembly back onto its roller bearings. Shipfitters patched the roof of the gun house with a big steel plate, draped a canvas shield over the turret's side, and trained it aft, creating the appearance of combat readiness. Two fractured longitudinal support beams under the main deck were replaced with rails from the train yard near the docks. The *Houston*'s forward antiaircraft director was jury-rigged back into service, and stocks of antiquated five-inch projectiles were replaced with five hundred live rounds taken from the *Boise*. The most modern ship in the theater, the *Boise* had been forced to Ceylon after running aground off Timor. Her last contribution was leaving her valuable ordnance behind.

The most important service was rendered to the *Houston*'s deceased. The crew stood at attention in their dress whites as the dead followed the wounded ashore. As they were loaded onto Dutch Army flatbed trucks, the ship's band performed Chopin's funeral dirge. The solemn procession marked the turning of a page. Among the men killed in the inferno in Turret Three was warrant officer Joseph A. Bienert, a boatswain, whose last act before the bomb struck was to order one of his electricians forward to check the circuitry on a malfunctioning five-inch projectile hoist. The order spared Howard Brooks his life. The electrician's mate returned aft to find Bienert sitting there with his insides blown out. "Oh, don't bother with me," Bienert said. "Go help someone that you can help. Don't bother with me." Bienert was the only man among the *Houston*'s fifty-four officers and warrants who had been on board for President Roosevelt's memorable cruise in 1938, when the band was playing a very different tune.

As the funeral procession motored off along Tjilatjap's dusty streets to the beachside cemetery, an uneasy feeling became palpable among the newly war-wise sailors. Crossing-the-line initiations, tropical fishing expeditions, and the ceremonial frivolities of peacetime life seemed a world away. "Suddenly," Lt. (jg) Walter Winslow wrote, "I had the weird impression that we were all standing on the brink of a yawning grave."

The ship's twenty wounded, along with about fifty more from the *Marblehead,* were put on a Dutch train for transport to Petronella Hospital in the town of Jogjakarta. Meanwhile, work parties, having used up the supply of lumber in the holds, gathered more of it ashore and returned to the ship to continue making coffins, forty-six for their own dead and thirteen more for the *Marblehead*'s. All available hands kept busy hewing the rough native mahogany until they could no longer stay awake. For the second time in as many days, exhausted crewmen collapsed to the lullaby of saw on wood and hammer on nail, which didn't trail off until about two A.M. "A weird silence enveloped the ship, broken only by the slow tread of sentries making their rounds," recalled Walter Winslow.

★

On February 8, three days into his tenure as a lame duck, Admiral Hart flew from Lembang to Tjilatjap and surveyed the damage done to his ships. The *Marblehead,* arthritic even in the best of repair, was finished. A Dutch naval architect managed to hoist her bow onto the little floating dry dock so her breached hull could be patched. But nothing could be done for her damaged rudder. In a few days the *Marblehead* would be westbound to the Brooklyn Navy Yard by way of Ceylon, steering with her engines and staying afloat via submersible pump and bucket brigade.

What to do with the *Houston* was a more complicated question. Hart knew that his star skipper deserved a voice in the matter.

For his part, Captain Rooks wondered about his family. He had received no mail of any kind since November, had had no word about Edith or his two sons, Albert junior, just twelve, and Hal, breezing through Navy ROTC at Harvard and destined for a Pacific tour in a heavy cruiser of his own. He was eager to share news of the battle with them within the censor's necessary limits.

From Tjilatjap he cabled Seattle to assure Edith he was okay before she saw any publicity about the hit the ship had taken in the Flores Sea. "Well, the big news is that we have been in action. We were in the so-called Battle of the Flores Sea," he wrote her. "I cannot give you any details inasmuch as I do not know whether our Navy Department has made any announcement of it or not. . . . I was not hurt, and came out of it with a good reputation. The crew delegated the ship's chief master at arms to congratulate me on the way the ship was handled. . . . Throughout I remained cool and composed, and suffered no nervous or other shocks as a result of the experience."

In the middle of the combat theater Admiral Hart was able finally to take the full measure of the *Houston*'s fifty-year-old captain. "When it comes to judging the ability of men as cruiser captains, one usually cannot tell how they will turn out until they are tried," Hart would later tell Edith. At Tjilatjap, Hart observed the demeanor of his onetime aide and wrote, "Rooks still had perfect poise. His nerves were absolutely unshaken, his attitude and outlook as to the future were perfect and, in fact, I could see nothing whatever upon which I could base the slightest criticism (and, as you know, I am exacting and critical). After I left the *Houston* I told myself, 'Well, now I know that I have in Rooks just the kind of cruiser captain that the situation out here calls for.' "

Under normal circumstances, a damaged main battery was cause for a mandatory appointment with the yardbirds. But nothing about ABDAfloat's circumstances was normal. The striking force could not afford to do without one of its two heavy cruisers. Conferring with Rooks on the day of the funeral, Hart could see that sending the *Houston* home for repairs was an unaffordable luxury, at least until the promised new light cruiser *Phoenix* arrived in early March to take her place. Even with its cauterized after turret, the *Houston* still packed a stiff punch in its forward eight-inch battery.

But Hart feared that ordering the damaged ship to remain in theater and contend with the coming storm would amount to a death sentence for one of the best-trained, highest-morale crews in the fleet. He reportedly told Rooks that he "didn't want our folks to accuse him of manslaughter, and there was a battle coming that was already lost before it was fought."

Hart's worries about "manslaughter" were probably overstated in view of the crew's eagerness to assume the risk. It was exactly what most of them wanted. Some of the men got together and wrote a letter to their captain pledging that wherever he and the ship went, that's where they would go too. Though it was a truism to a degree—deserters don't get far at sea—the sentiment was emotionally genuine. "I think they looked at him as just another god," said Gus Forsman. "Admiration for the Captain bordered on worship," some officers would later write. "Everybody believed that the Good Lord had His hand on his shoulder for the things that he brought us through," said Paul Papish, a storekeeper third class. That knack for inspiring confidence seemed to come naturally to Rooks. But it would never get too deeply into his head. According to Frank E. (Ned) Gallagher, a second lieutenant with the Marine detachment, "He always knew who he was and never wanted to be anybody else."

For Albert H. Rooks, whose ship had been bloodied without the opportunity to respond in kind, there was no other decision but to stay and fight. He would not see the *Houston* pulled out at the very moment she was needed most. Though he longed for home, was in fact counting the days, his own concerns came secondary to his role as commander of the most powerful U.S. warship in the Asiatic theater.

Although Tommy Hart would live to regret putting the ship's fate in the hands of her proud skipper, there was no denying that the ship still had some wallop left in her. "After telling me that he would take his ship out again in a few hours," Hart wrote, "Rooks pointed to the wreck of his after turret and said, 'A Jap cruiser will have one strike on us, but with the two remaining we will try to break up his game.' Such was the spirit."

CHAPTER 7

Valentine's Day 1942 was one of emotional reckonings and commitments to faith. Rooks wrote Edith in longhand, his penmanship more hurried than it had been before. "I am going out into the troubled zone this evening," he wrote, "and I don't know where we will end up. Two nights ago a dispatch came indicating we were to return to the United States. You can imagine the thrill we got—I dreamed about it all the rest of the night. But the next morning a dispatch came correcting the other. Our name had got there by mistake."

The present was as heavily shrouded by doubt as the future. The *Houston*'s captain took refuge in the notion that a man's destiny was out of his hands. "I trust that everything is going well with you and the boys and your father," he wrote. "Keep your spirits up. In these times one must cultivate a faith in his fate. May God protect and strengthen you."

That night Tommy Hart joined sixteen soon-to-be-former Asiatic Fleet colleagues at the Savoy Hotel in Bandung, Java, for a farewell dinner. He was feeling more than a little fraught about it. Haunted first by the fear he was leaving behind good men to die under foreign command, he worried too that his reputation had been sullied by his abrupt and awkward dismissal, that the perception might arise in

Washington that he was guilty of some failing of character or competence. No doubt at the end of the twenty-five-day, eight-thousand-mile journey back to the nation's capital, his political foes would await his return with some relish.

The Asiatic Fleet's officers toasted their veteran leader's retirement. Then Hart stood to speak but could not summon words. As a brash young officer, he had once declared his wish to end his naval career on the bridge of his flagship, blown to eternity by a large-caliber salvo. He settled for a less dramatic exit. Faltering with grief, he at last managed only to say: "Well, boys, we all have a busy day tomorrow, so we'd better break this up." In the receiving line afterward, his fleet intelligence officer, Lt. Cdr. Redfield Mason, grabbed Hart's hand with both of his and said, "Goodbye, sir, you are the finest man I've ever known." Hart couldn't recognize anyone through the brine that welled in his eyes. That night he wrote in his diary, "Oh it was hard." Wartime farewells were always wrenching, but "leaving them out here in the face of a dangerous enemy and commanded by God knows whom or how" was more than the old admiral could stand.

The next day he was driven to Batavia in a battered sedan for transit west. He was last seen in Java standing alone on the pier in Tanjung Priok, Batavia, wearing civilian clothes, awaiting the arrival of a bomb-damaged British light cruiser to ferry him home.

*

If a fighting spirit prevailed, the men of the *Houston* would have to suffer through one more turn as a convoy escort before exercising it. The cruiser was ordered to Darwin once again on February 10.

She began the return journey on February 15 leading a convoy of troop ships to Timor, the easternmost of the Lesser Sunda Islands. All hope of keeping supplies flowing between Australia and Java required that Timor stay in Allied hands. The outpost held the only airfield, at Kupang, that enabled Allied fighter planes to cover the sea-lanes to and from Darwin.

The four transports, escorted by the *Houston,* the destroyer USS *Peary,* and the Australian escort sloops *Warrego* and *Swan,* carried a few thousand Australian Pioneers, infantry specially trained in construction and engineering, as well as a battalion of the U.S. 148th Field Artillery Regiment, a federalized Idaho National Guard unit once earmarked to reinforce General MacArthur in the

Philippines before his lines collapsed. They found themselves in Australia by accident. Their convoy had been one week out of Pearl Harbor when the war started. Now, as Admiral Hart was donning his civilian clothes to depart Java, the troops set sail for Timor, the Australians filling the 11,300-ton U.S. Army transport *Meigs* and the 5,400-ton Matson Line freighter SS *Mauna Loa* and the Americans boarding the British cargo ship SS *Tulagi* and the transport SS *Port Mar*.

Around noon on the first day at sea, the *Houston*'s bugler sounded the call to air defense. As the men ran to battle stations, a Japanese H6K Mavis flying boat appeared overhead, circling out of gun range. The plump four-engine plane lumbered in and made a pair of bombing runs on the cruiser from ten thousand feet, but the *Houston*'s concentrated flak drove her away. The Mavis was chased by a lone P-40 Warhawk fighter scrambled from Darwin and guided toward the Mavis by the *Houston*'s gunners, who sent a volley of five-inch shells bursting in the aircraft's direction. The two planes disappeared over the horizon, leaving the sailors to guess which one's demise caused the subsequent flash of fire and the pillar of black smoke.

The fact that enemy air power could reach them just one day out of Darwin was more troubling to the crew than the attack's negligible results. "We believed that by being south of the Malay barrier we had nothing to fear from the Japanese bombers and would have time to rest our jangled nerves," Walter Winslow wrote. The Japanese knew full well they were coming. As Tokyo Rose announced that afternoon, "*I see the USS* Houston *is escorting four transports to Timor, and they're going to be in for a big surprise.*"

Around eleven A.M., the promised surprise came: a formation of nine Mavises and thirty-six twin-engine Mitsubishi Type 97 bombers, flying from the newly secured airfield at Kendari on Celebes. As they formed up into the dreaded nine-plane Vs and began their runs, the *Houston* drew most of their attention.

Lt. Jack Lamade climbed into his aircraft on the port catapult and its gunpowder charge detonated, propelling him to sixty miles per hour in a fifty-foot run. As his biplane clawed skyward the lieutenant set course for Broome, a coastal town five hundred nautical miles to the southwest. Lieutenant Winslow was unable to get airborne at all. The concussion of the five-inch guns shredded the fabric of his wings and fuselage.

Most of the troops embarked in the transports had never witnessed the U.S. Navy in action. The *Houston* made an impressive spectacle as Captain Rooks circled his charges, trying to draw the attention of the planes. "She was a wonderful sight, a fighting cruiser racing away at the uttermost limits of her energy," wrote a sailor on the *Warrego*. "Above the smoke of her guns poured a smoke screen, as her bow like a hissing knife slashed through the 'drink' at speed that churned a stern wave boiling almost up to her after rails. We stared dumbfounded."

Since the Japanese planes always seemed to drop their bombs from the same altitude and release point relative to the *Houston*'s course and speed, the cruiser's senior aviator, Lt. Tommy Payne, had devised a "maneuvering table" that helped Captain Rooks calculate when to order the helm turned to avoid bombs, as he had done with such success in earlier actions. Rooks lay on the deck on the bridge, watching the planes with his binoculars and shouting helm orders as the bombs fell.

"They dropped them so close to us that the shrapnel just pecked along our splinter shields all around us," said Charley Pryor, who manned gun number eight, the portside five-inch mount closest to the fantail. Like even the oldest salts on the ship, Sergeant Pryor was stunned by Rooks's audacity at the helm. The skipper turned the cruiser so sharply that seawater washed up over the quarterdeck. There were moments, Pryor recalled, when "in the foretops, all they could see under them was green sea, no ship." For harrowing moments, the swirling flood reached to the knees of men standing on deck.

"I'd often wondered and worried . . . whether I'd be capable of doing my job or not," said pharmacist's mate Griff L. Douglas, an eighteen-year-old who had earned a decade's worth of wisdom on February 4 while patching together maimed survivors. "I knew I'd been trained well, but it worried me all the time. I thought, 'Well, I know I'm scared,' and I'd think, 'Well, maybe I can't do my job.' But after that, I never worried about it anymore."

The ship spat skyward so much flak that she appeared to burn. Her gallery of eight five-inch guns put up a total of 930 rounds, two and a half rounds a minute for each gun for forty-five minutes straight. The projectiles taken from the *Boise* made a startling difference in the conduct of the enemy planes. "You could just see them rocking up there," said Marine Pvt. Lloyd V. Willey. With the concentrated smoky black bursts whistling shrapnel past their windscreens, the bombers retreated to a higher altitude. Seven fell victim to the *Houston*'s gunners. Already worn down from day after day of steady vigilance, the crews were relieved by men from other stations as the heat exhaustion got to them.

The soldiers on the transports had little else to do but gape as the cruiser shaped a weaving course around and through them. A yellow-orange curtain of fire seemed to envelop the *Houston,* while overhead another curtain—the black shroud of the heavy cruiser's shell bursts—sheltered the transports from the planes. Bombs landed all around her—"All the sea boiled up and *Houston* was gone," wrote E. L. Cullis. Another *Warrego* sailor said, "Good God! They've got her!" But then, Cullis wrote, "from walls of water surely two hundred feet high, from clouds of flame-shot smoke, *Houston* emerged, racing ahead. A miracle. We sighted her mast. Then her upper deck—it was a rippling sheet of flame. She was surging and bouncing and skidding like a toy ship spinning upon whirlpools." By the time the bombers vanished, the only friendly casualty was a U.S. soldier on the *Mauna Loa,* hit by shrapnel from a near miss. He was taken aboard the *Houston,* but her pharmacist's mates were helpless to save him.

As the convoy slugged north by night, the startling news came that Timor was already in enemy hands. The convoy promptly turned around and set course again for Darwin. The frustration aboard the *Houston* was palpable, leavened only briefly by the consoling wild cheers the troops in the four transports sent up—the Australians the loudest—as their sleek protector took station at the head of their column on the return journey. Ham sandwiches and cups of coffee in hand, faces and dungarees black with gun grease, the crewmen of the *Houston* came topside to bask in the celebratory roar. "It was a proud moment," recalled Bill Weissinger, a gunner on the number-one five-inch mount on the starboard side. "The men were crying and may not even have realized it. The tears were streaming down their face and making clean channels down their cheeks."

CHAPTER 8

The astonishing progress of the Japanese in oceanic Asia was putting the entire issue of defending Java into doubt. They were advancing in a pincer movement. The Imperial Navy's Western Attack Group, with seven cruisers, twenty-five destroyers, and fifty-six transports and cargo ships, was under way from Camranh Bay, Indochina, on course for Batavia and western Java. The Japanese Eastern Attack Group, with one cruiser, six destroyers, and forty-one transports, accompanied by three cruisers and seven destroyers of the Eastern Covering Group, threatened Surabaya and eastern Java. Fighting blind, without air cover or reconnaissance, the ABDA nations would be hard-pressed to muster enough strength to stop either arm.

On February 15, Singapore capitulated, less than a week after Field Marshal Wavell declared its unbreachable strength. That same day, with the *Houston* at sea between Timor and Darwin, Admiral Doorman led his striking force up the Karimata Strait to challenge the enemy's advance toward the Sumatran oil center of Palembang. The Japanese found him first, hitting him with a naval air raid that damaged the Australian light cruiser *Hobart* and two U.S. destroyers. Doorman returned to Batavia with nothing to show for his dash. In the east, prospects were no brighter. The capture of Timor meant that Surabaya, Java's capital, would come under regular land-based air attack. Allied ships would operate in the Java Sea at their deep peril, exposed to attack from three directions.

The *Houston* returned to Darwin with her Timor convoy on the afternoon of February 18, refueled from a barge, and set sail again around 5:30 P.M., under orders to rejoin Doorman. It was just as well for the *Houston* to be clear of Darwin's waters. The next night, the crew heard Tokyo Rose announce that the Japanese First Carrier Fleet, under Vice Adm. Chuichi Nagumo, leader of the Pearl Harbor striking force, had launched a devastating surprise attack on the port.

A strike of 188 fighters and dive-bombers from the *Akagi, Kaga, Hiryu,* and *Soryu,* fresh from the Pearl Harbor raid, overwhelmed the ten American P-40 Warhawks sent to intercept them and, bolstered by fifty-four bombers flying from Kendari and Ambon, left the airdrome a shambles, its storage facilities ravaged, and thirteen ships sunk, including the *Meigs,* the *Mauna Loa,* and the destroyer *Peary* with most of her crew. Tokyo Rose added the *Houston* to the list, a fictional flourish so familiar by now that it no longer much amused anyone. That day too Japanese fighters swept over Surabaya and elements of the Japanese Sixteenth Army, ferried across the Java Sea from Makassar Town, went ashore on Bali.

With his ships dispersed near and far, from Sumatra to Tjilatjap and from Surabaya to Darwin, Doorman could not mount a concentrated naval assault on the forces creeping toward him. Field Marshal Wavell was losing heart altogether: "I am afraid that the defense of the ABDA area has broken down," he observed on the twenty-first. Two days later he received orders from London to abandon Java altogether. On February 25 he secretly boarded a plane and departed with his staff for Ceylon, leaving Java's defense to the Dutch. There was no longer an ABDA naval force for Admiral Helfrich to lead. With Wavell's departure, the multinational command ceased formally to exist and Helfrich became his nation's own last hope.

As for the Americans, consigned to defeat by the U.S. Navy and poised to make a last stand under a foreign flag, their final lot was now cast. At dusk on February 21, the *Houston* arrived again at Tjilatjap. The crew was angered to find that the Dutch crews who manned the fueling station were nowhere to be found. Refueling would be a matter of self-service. A working party from the ship's engineering department went ashore and took whatever the lines would give them—just three hundred tons—before the glow of dawn forced Captain Rooks to leave port for the comparative safety of sea.

As the *Houston* threaded the protective minefield outside the harbor and turned west toward Sunda Strait, accompanied by the destroyers *Paul Jones* and *Alden,* Walter Winslow asked the navigator, Cdr. John A. Hollowell Jr., where they might be headed. "In a fatherly way, he draped his arm around my shoulder and, as though talking to himself, said, 'Son, we're going to hell, we're going to hell.'" As the ship navigated the strait, rudder and engines straining against the strong currents, Ens. Charles D. Smith looked back at that perilous stretch of water and remarked, apropos of nothing, "Say, didn't I just hear a gate clang shut behind us?" This struck Paul Papish as a premonition. The storekeeper would never shake the memory.

*

Making a successful transit north through Sunda Strait, the *Houston* rejoined Rear Adm. Karel Doorman's striking force in Surabaya on the afternoon of February 24. The harbor of the capital city in east Java was marked by a towering column of smoke, the product of repeated Japanese air raids whose latest victim was a freighter, her hull laid open and sprawled on her side with a full cargo of rubber aflame. By day the smoke was a handy navigation aid for inbound Japanese aircraft. By night, its flames would be a beacon for any warships or submarines stalking the port. Captain Rooks anchored the *Houston* in midstream, a few hundred yards from the docks, where several warehouses were on fire. The crew watched sailors and soldiers ashore scrambling around with hoses.

That night, with their ship still tied up, the crew topped off the *Houston*'s capacious fuel oil bunkers, then watched in fascination as a Dutch minelayer opened fire on the grounded merchantman with her deck gun, trying to quench her blazing cargo of rubber by shattering the hull and letting in the sea. Instead of sinking, the vessel just burned more fiercely. A Dutch torpedo boat motored in and launched a torpedo at her, to no better effect. For sailors on the *Houston,* these attempts to scuttle the floundering inferno made quite a spectacle. "With all the confusion going on around us," Walter Winslow wrote, "we slept very little that night."

Even with the return of the *Houston*, Admiral Doorman's ability to blunt the Japanese drive against Java was limited at best. Before leaving the theater, Field Marshal Wavell had written Winston Churchill, describing the intractable problem of defending a six-hundred-mile-long island with a handful of cruisers and destroyers. "If this [naval force] is divided between the two threatened ends of the island it is too weak for either. If kept concentrated it is difficult, owing to distance involved, to reach a vital point in time. Wherever it is, it is liable to heavy air attack." Without fighter cover, the number of ships the Allies had to oppose the Japanese was almost academic. The *Houston*'s sailors marked time by the regular appearances of Japanese bombers overhead, three and four times a day.

The members of the threadbare U.S. fighter squadron charged with providing land-based fighter cover in the Dutch East Indies were mostly veterans of the Philippines campaign, evacuated and taken to Brisbane, Australia, where they set up a makeshift training program for the green second lieutenants arriving from the States and cobbled together several squadrons from available parts and personnel. It wasn't the way the Army Air Forces preferred to organize itself, but there were enough planes and people on hand to patch together five squadrons. Assigned to Java, the Seventeenth Pursuit Squadron (Provisional) came into being on January 10. Maj. Charles A. Sprague's pilots had flown their P-40E Warhawks from Brisbane to Darwin and then on a thirteen-hundred-mile, six-leg flight up to Java.

Under the overall command of Col. Eugene L. Eubanks in Malang, Sprague's pilots found a home at the Ngoro (or Blimbing) airdrome, located about forty miles southwest of Surabaya. Flying from the sodden rice fields of their hidden hive, they took to the skies daily in flights of eight, twelve, and sixteen P-40Es to intercept Japanese air strikes and escort the AAF's own bombing strikes against Japanese targets in the area. The Dutch air warning service relayed ground observers' aircraft sightings and all-clear signals to Surabaya via wire or native drumbeats. Sprague's aviators typically got no more than twenty-five minutes of advance notice to get into the air. By the time they reached interception altitude of 21,000 feet or more, as often as not the bombs had already fallen. Gamecock-tough but ill-equipped, they could do little to prevent the daily pasting Surabaya was taking from Japanese bombers. Their own airdrome was substantially safer, owing to their proficiency at hiding their planes under tangles of tapioca brush.

After the fall of Kendari on January 26, the attacks had been coming incessantly. All during February, the squadron's pilots waged a determined campaign to intercept the inbound bombers, flying occasional reconnaissance and strike missions over Bali, Lombok, and the surrounding Java Sea as well. They suffered every handicap possible for a gang of aviators, from shortages of spare parts, fuel, and Prestone to muddy airstrips, perpetual bad weather, and a lack of early warning about enemy strikes. That the Japanese opposing them were fiercely well trained, with skills sharpened through years of war on the Asian mainland, was the final imbalance. Nearly every day this pickup squad took to the skies in their P-40s to tangle with the Japanese. Even when the Dutch coast watchers gave them sufficient warning, sometimes the old planes couldn't get the job done. The oily life was being flown out of them. Their weary engines often had trouble reaching the bombers' cruising altitude—around 27,000 feet—which was close enough to the P-40E's service ceiling to make interception difficult even on the best of days.

Refusing to wear insignia, not only out of egalitarian esprit but also from fear of Japanese snipers, Sprague got up every day and fought, driven by pure, haunted anger. The Japanese had captured his wife and children in the Philippines. His anguish over their fate was well-known to his men. Soon enough they would be anguishing over him.

On the morning of February 20, the squadron escorted a motley dive-bomber strike against Japanese shipping off Bali following that island's fall. While a handful of Douglas A-24 Banshees zoomed down to attack the ships, Sprague turned his sixteen Warhawks against a swarm of Japanese Zeros closing to intercept.* In the ensuing melee, the American fliers claimed four Zeros. Four P-40s were lost. Returning to Blimbing, the pilots were saddened to find that Major Sprague was among the missing. Eventually word reached the squadron through the native rumor mill that their commander had been taken captive by the Japanese. With their commander missing, Sprague's squadron, seldom noted or written about, acquitted

---

*The Banshee was the Army version of the Navy's SBD Dauntless dive-bomber.

themselves proudly as the dark clouds of war scudded south, flying and fighting in conditions as bad as anything outside the Flying Tigers' better-publicized aerial domain. Over time, though, they bled out through attrition.

*

As February drew to an end, the threat from the air seemed to herald worse tidings from the sea. The snooping eyes of submariners aboard the USS *Seal* reported a convoy of Japanese troop transports off Bawean Island, just a hundred miles north of Surabaya. On the morning of February 24 Admiral Helfrich ordered five ships of his Western Striking Force, led by the HMS *Exeter,* the HMAS *Perth,* and three British destroyers, to leave Batavia and join Doorman at Surabaya. He projected that Japanese troops would reach Java's shores by the morning of the twenty-seventh. On February 25, belated word arrived from General MacArthur that a hundred Japanese ships had been seen gathering at Jolo. That same day a reconnaissance plane reported that some eighty enemy vessels were en route south in Makassar Strait. The aircraft was destroyed before further details could be sent. On the twenty-sixth, the crew of a Catalina patrol plane spotted fifty to sixty transports and destroyers farther west, in Karimata Strait between Borneo and Sumatra. Japan's serpentine arms were reaching out to seize Java. The sightings put urgency to the growing certainty that the Allies needed a decisive victory, and soon.

On the morning of February 26, the *Houston* returned from a fruitless nighttime sweep of the waters between Surabaya and Bawean Island with the Dutch cruisers *De Ruyter* and *Java,* dropped anchor in the channel between Java and Madura Island, and endured yet another assault by Japanese aircraft. With the harbor defenses by and large abandoned, the *Houston* was the port's principal antiaircraft installation and its most inviting target. "It was the first time we'd ever fired at anchorage," remembered Charley Pryor, "and we fired right up to the maximum limits . . . about eighty-eight degrees. And so we fired that way, and then the opposite battery would pick them up when they crossed over." With their five-inch guns elevated to fire nearly straight up, the crews had to reckon with their own ordnance coming right back down on them. The larger chunks weighed as much as three pounds, "jagged things a half-inch thick, maybe three or four inches wide at one place," said Pryor. At one point the Dutch authorities in Surabaya asked that the ship refrain from directing its antiaircraft fire over the city for fear of harm to its residents.

For the crew, awake all night at general quarters and unable to sleep by day as bombers attacked overhead, there were no breaks for meals. The best they could hope for was ham sandwiches and coffee served at their battle stations. "At the end of three or four days of this, we were really at the end of our physical and psychological endurance," seaman first class Otto Schwarz recalled. But high spirits endured. At the sounding of the all-clear siren, the *Houston's* band would gather on the quarterdeck and bounce out swing tunes, bucking up crewmen exhausted by the full-time alerts.

If the *Houston's* luck in ducking the bombardment was cause for celebration, the arrival of reinforcements for the Combined Striking Force should have inspired a ticker-tape parade. At 2:30 on February 26, three British destroyers stood in, followed thirty minutes later by the HMS *Exeter* and light cruiser HMAS *Perth*. "I cannot ever remember a more heartening sight than those five grey ships steaming into the harbor," wrote Lieutenant Hamlin. The arrival of Capt. Oliver Gordon's *Exeter* in particular lifted everyone's spirits. Though she was armed lightly for a heavy cruiser, with just six twin-mounted eight-inch guns, and displaced less than nine thousand tons, typical given the requirements of the naval treaties, she was highly regarded for her part in hunting, with two other Royal Navy cruisers, the German pocket battleship *Graf Spee* halfway across the Atlantic in 1940. It was among the legendary chapters in the Royal Navy's history. Such gallantry the Allies would need again now.

As the British ships were arriving, Admiral Helfrich, in Bandung, sent an urgent message to Doorman reporting a force of thirty Japanese transports on the move 180 miles northeast of Surabaya. "STRIKING FORCE IS TO PROCEED TO SEA IN ORDER TO ATTACK ENEMY AFTER DARK. AFTER ATTACK, STRIKING FORCE IS TO PROCEED TOWARDS TANJUNG PRIOK. ACKNOWLEDGE." Helfrich's instructions suggested both optimism and desperation. He was clearly hoping that the Combined Striking Force could repel the Japanese invasion force in the east and then, continuing to Tanjung Priok— Batavia—stage an encore against the western group.

Late in the afternoon of the twenty-sixth, Doorman summoned his commanders to his new headquarters in an electric company office in a residential neighborhood of Surabaya. Speaking fluent

English, he said that British radio intercepts of Japanese naval communications indicated that Japanese convoys were steaming east and west of Borneo. He even knew which destroyer squadrons were escorting them. Doorman reviewed the plan for Java's defense, discussed the formations the Combined Striking Force would use by day and by night, and described each vessel's role in them. He reviewed the status of his ships, reminding his skippers of the grave wound the *Houston* had taken. The bomb blast on February 4 had cost him three of his fifteen eight-inch guns. Without her aft turret, the *Houston* was unfit to bring up the rear of a column.

With the fall of Borneo, Celebes, and Bali, the enemy's land-based planes were even closer now. Carriers were nearby and possibly battleships too. A *Kongo*-class battleship had been reported near Singapore, and another in Makassar Strait. Doorman said the probable landing site for Japanese troops would be either the north shore of Madura Island or the oil fields at Rembang in the west. Accordingly, he warned them, a new minefield had been laid off Tuban, west of Surabaya. Then Doorman said something that perked the ears of every captain in the room—and provoked more than one cynical laugh: "There is a possibility in this action we may have some fighter protection."

The prospect of air cover had been tantalizing. Great promises had been heard about shiploads of planes and pilots en route from the United States via Australia to bolster the defense of the Dutch East Indies. Doorman was expecting the imminent arrival at Tjilatjap of the seaplane tender USS *Langley,* bound from Fremantle with a load of thirty-two ready-to-fly P-40Es and thirty-three pilots, and the cargo ship *Sea Witch,* loaded with twenty-seven more Warhawks, disassembled and packed in crates. Helfrich had ordered them to head for Tjilatjap in a daylight run—a bold decision that carried considerable risk.

Those risks would materialize for the worst. The two ships parted company en route—the *Sea Witch* could not keep up—and the *Langley* crossed paths with land-based bombers of the Japanese Eleventh Air Fleet, patrolling south of Java to extinguish just such an effort. Nearing Tjilatjap on the morning of February 27, the old carrier was set upon by Japanese fliers, struck by five bombs, and left to be scuttled seventy-five miles south of Tjilatjap. The *Sea Witch* later made port undetected, unloaded her crates, and withdrew to Australia. But there would be no time to assemble, much less deploy, the Warhawks. They never got out of their crates. As the officers gathered in Admiral Doorman's headquarters seemed already to know, the gallant fliers of the threadbare Seventeenth Pursuit Squadron had all the aircraft they were going to get.

At 8:55 P.M. that night, barely an hour before Admiral Doorman was to get under way, Admiral Helfrich amplified the spirit of urgency with one further exhortation to his *Eskader Commandant*: "YOU MUST CONTINUE ATTACKS TILL ENEMY IS DESTROYED." This much can be said for the outclassed Dutch admirals: In defense of their second homeland, they did not shy from a fight. For the first time their best ships were gathered in one force. If their enemy's exact whereabouts still lay shrouded in some mystery, there was no doubt they planned to announce themselves soon. Karel Doorman's force would enter that fight one-eyed if not blind, and with only the dimmest sense of the forces marshaled against it. But the showdown for Java was coming. Captain Rooks's *Houston* and the rest of the Combined Striking Force would be ready.

Part Two

A BLOODSTAINED SEA

★

Life brings its own education, and the life of the sea permits no truancy. It says to a man, learn to be a seaman, or die. It takes no slurring answer, it gives no immunity. . . . The ocean cannot be cheated. . . . It may not be crossed except by those who know the stars.

—Lincoln Colcord

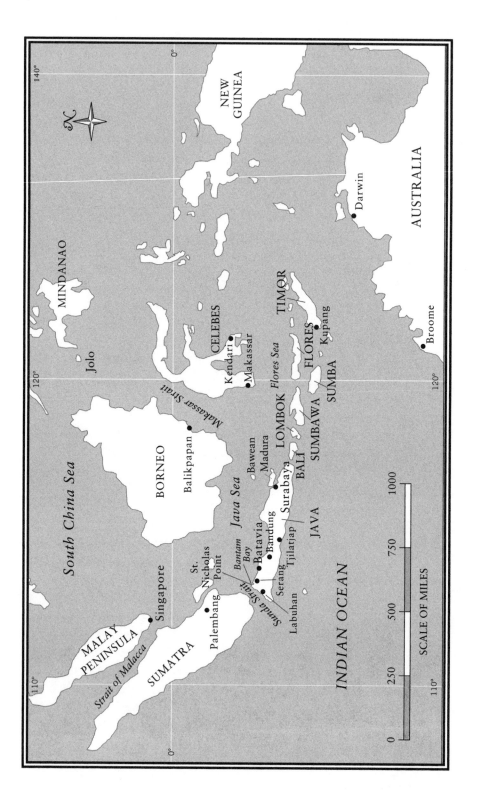

CHAPTER 9

The invasion convoy was twenty miles long, arrayed around two parallel columns of troop transports steaming a mile apart, 650 yards between ships, their extended line humped upward gently by the curve of the earth. Heavy with arms and vehicles and khaki-shirted soldiers enflamed with pride of empire, with backpacks, leather boots, and bundles of battle flags that leached red dye in the squalls and deck wash, the transports of the Japanese Eastern Attack Group pushed through the seas, zigzagging at ten knots.

The majestic sight of it transfixed the captain of the destroyer *Amatsukaze,* escorting the formation to port. But Cdr. Tameichi Hara's awe contended with his better judgment. Befitting a responsible commander, he fretted about the uncertainties and risks of the audacious operation. As the rhetoric of conquest was reduced to actual soldiers and ships and planes moving by complex schedules, human imperfection and weakness were becoming all too evident. Hara worried that Allied submarines would be drawn by the transport captains' carelessness—the black smoke churning from their stacks, their loose attitude toward radio discipline and nighttime blackout doctrine. The flare of a cigarette, seen through the wrong submarine's periscope, could bring ruin to the entire group.

The two heavy cruisers assigned to guard them, the *Haguro* and the *Nachi,* the latter the flagship of Rear Adm. Takeo Takagi's Eastern Covering Group, trailed the vulnerable convoy by some two hundred miles, exhibiting the supercilious leisure of a triumphant fleet. Those ships would be essential in a face-off with Allied cruisers. Each cruiser carried a main battery of ten eight-inch guns mounted in five double turrets, plus sixteen torpedo tubes loaded with the new Type 93 heavy torpedo, nicknamed the "Long Lance." Oxygen-fueled and wakeless at a racing-boat speed of as much as forty-nine knots, they delivered a hull-busting thousand-pound warhead up to 43,600 yards—over four times the range of American torpedoes.

Conceit seemed to flow from the highest levels of the Japanese command. The Combined Fleet commander in chief, Adm. Isoroku Yamamoto, flying his flag in the battleship *Nagato,* moored near Kure in the Japanese home islands, was little bothered by the small force of Allied warships reported to be gathering against him. When he ordered Admiral Nagumo's carrier force to strike Darwin on February 19, he urged the destruction of dockside storehouses and shore facilities and instructed Nagumo to let the few Allied warships in the area slip away if necessary. "We must secure oil and other resources of the Dutch East Indies," Yamamoto announced. "That is of higher priority than pursuing any small American force." The USS *Houston* had been declared sunk more than once; why trouble with her now? He ordered his invasion forces to sail against Java even before Nagumo and his carriers could join them in support. "The landing operation does not require the support of a major task force," he declared. He deemed the Allied fleet "completely demoralized" and "no longer in shape to attempt any major action."

Under the overall command of Rear Adm. Shoji Nishimura in the light cruiser *Naka,* the Eastern Attack Group had sailed from Jolo on February 19, embarking the Imperial Japanese Army's 48th Division, veterans of the Philippines conquest. General MacArthur had duly reported them to ABDA. Stopping at Balikpapan, the convoy absorbed most of the 56th Regiment. As Nishimura's group approached Java from the east, farther to the west Vice Adm. Jisaburo Ozawa's Western Attack Force, originating from Camranh Bay in Indochina, was southbound with fifty-six transports. The two invasion forces reached slowly south toward their prize.

★

Rear Adm. Karel Doorman, flying his flag in the light cruiser *De Ruyter,* left Surabaya harbor near sunset on February 26 sure that invasion was imminent, though less certain what course he should take to head it off. As his ships departed, the wrecked docks were dotted with old men, women, and children—relatives of Dutch sailors, perhaps—waving farewell. Spirits were high, but his squadron's departure went less than smoothly. As the striking force was getting under way, the *De Ruyter* struck a tugboat hauling a water barge, sinking both of the smaller ships.

Doorman's flotilla—*De Ruyter* in the lead, followed by the *Houston,* the *Exeter,* the light cruisers *Java* and *Perth,* and nine destroyers from three nations—cleared the narrows between the west coast of Madura Island and Java and reached open water. The time for hedging bets had passed. After months of indecision and scattershot planning, the Allies had a powerful surface force under one command. Doorman would take it to sea and risk everything in defense of his homeland's exotic outpost.

As the *Houston* made way, the *Exeter* turned out and passed her. From her mainmast the British heavy cruiser was flying a bright white battle ensign, twelve feet on a side, illuminated by a ray of the setting sun. Paul Papish on the *Houston,* seeing the British ship, couldn't help but think that as impressive a spectacle as it made, the ensign tended to defeat the elaborate camouflage painted on her hull. As the *Exeter* went by, sailors on the *Houston* could hear a tune playing over the British ship's loudspeakers: "A-Hunting We Will Go . . ." The buglers on the Dutch destroyers blew what sounded like a hunting song too. "Even when we found that it was merely a bugle call to close water-tight doors it still had a fine challenging lilt to it," remembered Lieutenant Hamlin.

Admiral Doorman took his column east along Madura Island until about 1:00 A.M., turned north, then reversed course west for the rest of the night. He led his ships as far as Rembang, then doubled back east. The Japanese fleet continued to elude him. Probing the night by eye, his lookouts found nothing. Then dawn came, dependably bringing with it the drone of Japanese aircraft. The air-search radar on the *Perth* detected them above the cloud layer. At nine o'clock a plane broke through and dropped a stick of bombs that splashed harmlessly in the vicinity of the destroyer HMS *Jupiter*. The attack was a mere gesture. It was the fact that the Japanese had spotted them that carried the greatest threat. Appearing sporadically over Doorman's Combined Striking Force through the morning of February 27, the Japanese fliers shadowed it and kept Nishimura apprised. Duly alerted, the commanders of the heavy cruisers *Nachi* and *Haguro* doubtless knew they would have plenty of time to catch up with the transports and form up for battle.

By noon, with his destroyers' oil bunkers getting light, Admiral Doorman chose to return to Surabaya. The consecutive nights' failure to find and engage the enemy did not sit well with Admiral Helfrich. On hearing of Doorman's return to port, he signaled his striking force commander, "NOTWITHSTANDING AIR ATTACK YOU ARE TO PROCEED TO SEARCH FOR AND ATTACK ENEMY." But the air attack was not the reason for Doorman's withdrawal. He responded to Helfrich, "WAS PROCEEDING EASTWARD AFTER SEARCH FROM SAPOEDI TO RAMBANG. SUCCESS OF ACTION TONIGHT DEPENDS ABSOLUTELY ON GETTING GOOD RECONNAISSANCE INFORMATION IN TIME, WHICH LAST NIGHT FAILED ME." To underscore the condition of his ships and men, Doorman signaled Helfrich at 12:40 P.M., "THIS DAY THE PERSONNEL REACHED THE LIMIT OF ENDURANCE. TOMORROW THE LIMIT WILL BE EXCEEDED."

About that there was little doubt. The only question was how well and for how long the Striking Force's sailors could function beyond human limits. Some of the gunners on the *Houston* had been on alert for twenty-one consecutive hours—an unheard-of marathon of tension, concentration, and strain. On the other ships, things were no better. "Throughout *Perth* there was general frustration and weariness, accentuated by the enemy's power to sit over them with aircraft and make fools of them on the surface," a quartermaster on that ship observed.

At 2:27 P.M. the Allied ships were entering the channel through the protective minefield that lay outside Surabaya's harbor when at last it happened. From Admiral Doorman came word that a Dutch PBY had sighted southbound Japanese transports twenty miles west of Bawean Island. Doorman had wanted good reconnaissance. Now, it seemed, he had gotten it. "The word spread like wildfire throughout the *Houston*," wrote Walter Winslow. "Suddenly, men were no longer tired. This time we were hunting no specter force." The enemy, long sought and seldom encountered, was less than a hundred miles away. Doorman passed the order to turn around in midchannel and led his squadron back out to sea.

CHAPTER 10

No perfect account can be written of the major naval battle that ensued north of Java on the afternoon and night of February 27, 1942. The documentary record of the Battle of the Java Sea suffers from the deaths of so many key participants and from the loss of so many sunken ships' logbooks that any narrative is bound to disappoint those who expect naval actions to be carefully tracked and cataloged. But if the details don't always collate, the truth of the battle is not difficult to tease out.

At 2:45 P.M., as Karel Doorman led his squadron to sea, he sent this message to his captains: "AM PROCEEDING TO INTERCEPT ENEMY UNITS. FOLLOW ME. DETAILS LATER." Absent more specific orders, they would be left to ponder those details for themselves. In the *Houston,* Captain Rooks called "a hurried but deadly serious" conference in his wardroom, where his gunnery officer, Cdr. Arthur Maher, outlined the obvious and daunting objective: to destroy the enemy invasion convoy, after first disposing of any combatant vessels that might be escorting it. While there was no telling how many Japanese warships might be lurking nearby to protect the valuable flotilla, reportedly it was an inviting target, consisting of thirty-five to forty troop transports.

If only Doorman's aviators could get a look at it for themselves.

The *Houston*'s aviation contingent had been sidelined. Rooks had just one of his original four Seagull floatplanes left. Enlisted pilot Lanson Harris, Lt. Thomas B. Payne, Ens. John B. Stivers, and Lt. (jg) Walter G. Winslow had practically as little to do as Lt. Jack Lamade, who was still cooling his heels on the Australian west coast. With the onset of the air attacks on the Striking Force in Surabaya, Captain Rooks realized the futility and risk of maintaining his own aircraft. He ordered Lt. Payne, the ship's senior pilot, to fly the last operable SOC off the ship and find a safe place to hide it while the fleet was at sea. As the crew raced to battle stations, Lanson Harris joined the other idlers from the aviation division seeking a good place to watch the coming battle. Walter Winslow climbed to the signal bridge, scanning the northwestern horizon for Japanese ships and looking on with no small amount of anticipation.

Three British destroyers, the *Jupiter,* the *Electra,* and the *Encounter,* were arrayed left to right in line abreast, forming a van scouting line perpendicular to and about five miles ahead of the cruiser column. Doorman's *De Ruyter* led the main body of the Striking Force, followed at nine-hundred-yard intervals by the *Exeter,* the *Houston,* the *Perth,* and the *Java.* Though the formation looked impressive, its deployment suggested its shortcomings. The Striking Force's destroyers had been run so hard during the previous few weeks that Doorman could not deploy them as he would have wished. Hamstrung by cranky engineering plants, the *John D. Edwards, Alden, Paul Jones,* and *John D. Ford* weren't fast enough to pass to the head of the formation and take up position on Doorman's port bow. They settled instead for following in column astern the cruisers. Doorman's two Dutch tin cans, the *Kortenaer* and the *Witte de With,* steamed on his port beam in part because the *Kortenaer* had boiler trouble that limited her speed to twenty-four knots. Destroyers were called many things—dogs, wolves, cans, thoroughbreds—but never albatrosses.

The Striking Force's other deficiencies were less apparent to the eye, if equally likely to hamper its lethality. Foremost among these were communications. Despite the development of radio and years spent by different navies creating signal flag systems, Doorman's ships had a hard time talking to each other. Each nation had its own signals and communications in good order. A naval authority called the system used by the U.S. Navy "a tactical instrument of collective genius, as reliable and thoroughly tested as the laws of physics. It was a treasure of efficiency, cohesiveness and clarity." But within this multinational force, those virtues were notably overboard. The squadron's communications were hastily jury-rigged in a futile attempt to accommodate differences in language and protocol.

On the *De Ruyter,* Doorman broadcast his orders to the Striking Force via a shortwave transmitter in his native Dutch. This was fine for the *Java,* the *Kortenaer,* and the *Witte de With.* But the English-speaking vessels confronted unneeded complexity. A U.S. Navy liaison officer stationed on the *De Ruyter,* Lt. Otto F. Kolb Jr., and a signalman first class, Marvin E. Sholar, translated the orders concurrently and relayed them via signal light or tactical radio to the *Houston,* which in turn passed the orders to the *Exeter,* the *Perth,* and the destroyers. As a consequence of the translation and rebroadcast, confusion could easily arise as to the sequence of orders. Commanders often could not reconcile them. Even a common language did not guarantee effective communications. If signal flags had to be used, the British and the Americans might as well have been speaking alien tongues, because the British used signal flags that no one else could read.

"Everyone knows that you cannot assemble eleven football players who have never seen each other before, and go out and beat Notre Dame," Lieutenant Hamlin wrote. "Even if they are good, they need to have some workouts to learn the signals and get to know each other. This team never got any workouts. Two hours after it assembled it was out on patrol."

"FOLLOW ME," Doorman had ordered. Traditionally, such a command enabled an admiral to lead his column without need of signals. Understated simplicity could work well enough if the squadron shared a foundational understanding of how the commander preferred to maneuver and fight. In this case, noting the murky situation faced by the newly gathered ships of the abortive ABDA organization, critics have said that more should have been required of its commander. The unasked follow-up to Doorman's order might have been "AND THEN WHAT?"

*

The battle proper begins at 4:02 P.M., when lookouts on a British destroyer spot three Japanese floatplanes in the north. Visibility is clear, northeasterly winds at Force 1 or 2, the seas rolling with ten-foot swells. On the horizon a blur of gray smoke appears. It grows into a thicker streak of smoke, revealing the presence of distant ships. The minutes pass and soon, by 4:14, steel masts and the tops of foreign superstructures are rising on the northern horizon. Spotting the sprouting thicket of steel, a British destroyer in the van, the *Electra,* signals to Admiral Doorman: "ONE CRUISER, LARGE DESTROYERS, NUMBER UNKNOWN, BEARING 330, SPEED 18, COURSE 220 DEGREES." Three minutes later, the *Electra* sends a signal that brings chills: "TWO BATTLESHIPS, ONE CRUISER, SIX DESTROYERS." Before the report of battleships has a chance to register, another British ship returns a correction: "TWO HEAVY CRUISERS."

Anyone privy to the signals exhales in relief, for the difference between battleships and heavy cruisers is as between life and death. Battleships were known to be about. Admiral Nagumo's carrier group sailed with two of them, the swift *Kongo* and *Haruna,* tracking these waters without enemy peer. But these are not battleships—if they had been, their presence would have been forcefully announced at a range of twenty miles. Much to the relief of Commander Hara and the rest of the Japanese destroyer captains, the cruisers *Nachi* and *Haguro* are with them now. Admiral Takagi has ordered Nishimura's troop carriers to withdraw while the cruisers and destroyers settle the question of their access to Java's beaches.

Within minutes, Lt. Bruce D. Skidmore, stationed high in the *Houston*'s foremast, reports enemy cruisers bearing thirty degrees relative to starboard, steaming southwest on a nearly perpendicular course to the northwesterly oriented Allied line. The enemy fleet reveals itself slowly, like a winter forest growing out of the equatorial sea. The steel branches proliferate. There is no telling how large it is. On the *Houston,* a sinking feeling sets in that they are outnumbered. Yet somehow it manages to coexist with a prickle of excitement that the ship is finally going to get to do what it was built for. "We realized help would come, but not today," said Marine Pfc. Marvin Robinson. "The feeling was—and I think the skipper had a large part to do with this feeling—'Looky fellows, let's give them hell. Let's give them all we've got. They'll be here.'" There is not a man on the *Houston* who doubts the crew's morale, even in these most adverse conditions.

A halo of copper-orange flame envelops the silhouettes of two heavy cruisers, the *Nachi* and the *Haguro,* before clouds of cordite smoke conceal them and a light reverberation of thunder rolls in behind. Excitement has gotten the better of the Japanese. Admiral Takagi's flagship and its sister ship in Cruiser Division Five have opened fire at nearly thirty thousand yards. The range is too long by some two thousand yards. The projectiles take more than a minute to travel that far. Well ahead of Doorman's column, white towers of seawater rise, stand briefly, then collapse from their base, the spray-whipped peaks drifting as mist.

Doorman evaluates his predicament, gauges time and motion, worries that the Japanese ships might beat him to the intersection of their converging courses. If that happens, the enemy will cross his formation's T, thereby exposing his lead ships to full broadsides from the entire opposing line. Doorman changes course twenty degrees to the left, paralleling the course of the enemy cruisers. The maneuver momentarily hangs the three leading British destroyers out on the cruisers' starboard bow, closest to the Japanese. The HMS *Electra,* the right-hand ship in the scouting line, attracts vicious fire. From fifteen thousand yards, the light cruisers and even a few destroyers can reach her. A spectrum of dye-colored foam rises around her. The *Electra*'s commanding officer, Cdr. C. W. May, has the ship "twisting like a hare" chasing shell splashes. Whether by reason of signaling problems or Admiral Doorman's tactical preference, the lead British destroyers are kept on a leash. They do not form up to attack with torpedoes. Doorman orders His Majesty's tin cans to scurry to the safety of the Allied column's disengaged port side and form up into a column, awaiting their moment.

From overhead comes the buzzing of aircraft, as yet out of sight. Admiral Doorman has requested air support, but the call has gone unheeded. These planes are probably not friendly. On this day Surabaya's air defense command will concentrate its meager resources on bombing Nishimura's convoy, not protecting Doorman's fleet. In the late afternoon, three A-24s escorted by eleven P-40s attack some Japanese troop transports heading for Java, claiming one sunk. Meanwhile, direct support comes from surprising quarters: A PBY Catalina, the type that has first spotted the Japanese fleet this morning, unloads a bomb at a Japanese destroyer. The big patrol bomber would have been more profitably used keeping station over the enemy force, reconnoitering it for Doorman's benefit. A few U.S. Army B-17s of the Nineteenth Bomb Group, operating from Malang, make bombing runs over the Japanese escorts as well, but to no result.

Watching from the starboard side of the *Houston*'s signal bridge, Walter Winslow is awestruck by the sight of the fabled *Exeter* in action, her forward eight-inch twin turrets engaging a light cruiser just coming within range nearly dead ahead. His reverie ends a moment later when he is seized as if by a great hand and thrown against the signal bridge's gray steel bulkhead, his battle helmet skittering across the deck. The *Houston*'s own main battery has let loose. Lieutenant Skidmore in Spot One watches the salvo's flight all the way to its laddering impact, red-dyed splashes rising amid the Japanese cruisers. Via sound-powered phones he sends word from the foretop: "No change to opening range." Winslow dares to rejoice: Though the first salvo has drawn no blood, it is right on target.

★

The *Houston* had a reputation as one of the best gunnery ships of her type. However, as in the gunnery departments of the other members of the *Northampton* class, things were done the old-fashioned way. She carried no radar to automate the gunlayer's craft, no remote-control servo motors to take muscle and sweat out of the business of training and elevating guns. Ranges were triangulated by eye, as the fire-control officer optically centered his twin scopes on the target, their angle of convergence registering on a mechanical indicator dial that showed the range in yards. That datum was shouted down a voice tube to the plotting room, or Central Station, deep belowdecks, where the plotting room officer, Lt. Cdr. Sidney L. Smith, operated the ship's mechanical analog computer. Smith cranked other vital data into the machine—the target's bearing from the gun director, estimates of its course and speed, and the *Houston*'s own course from the gyrocompass repeater and her speed from the pitometer—and as the guns lashed out and shells landed, observers spied the shell splashes and called down to Commander Smith gun angle corrections, or "spots." "Our first shots were fired almost ahead, only about twenty degrees on the starboard bow," wrote Lieutenant Hamlin, "and with the ship charging ahead at twenty-eight knots the backward kick of those two forward turrets shook the old *Houston* like a leaf."

The spotters on the *Houston* had a clear enough view of the forces arrayed against them: two heavy cruisers just ahead of their starboard beam, and two light cruisers, each leading a pack of destroyers, closer in but farther to the west, bearing about thirty degrees relative.

As the pointer in Turret Two, James W. Huffman sat on a brass bicycle seat in a tight corner of the gun house, sweating in the dim red glow of the battle lanterns. Gripping a two-handled wheel that elevated the three guns, "Red" Huffman kept his eyes fixed on a large synchro-driven indicator dial within which a pair of small illuminated lightbulbs, or "bugs," revolved in concentric tracks indicating the guns' actual and on-target elevations. When the turret officer— Ens. Charles D. Smith commanded Turret Two—ordered him to "match bugs," he would crank his hand wheels to align the bug showing the battery's actual elevation with the outer bug showing the elevation needed to bring it on target. At the sound of a buzzer activated by the turret captain (a chief petty officer) Huffman would jerk the trigger built into the grip of his left-hand elevation wheel and the big guns would fire. The roar and recoil of the triple eight-inch rifles arrayed beneath him could unhinge the five senses. "Jesus Christ, you just can't imagine," Huffman said. "You lose track of every damn thing." To reload, Huffman lowered the guns to a five-degree elevation so the loaders and rammers below him could stuff the breeches with projectiles and enough powder bags to suit the range. Then he matched bugs again, jerked the handle trigger, cringed at the deep rocking report, and repeated the cycle again.

Turret One developed mechanical difficulties from the fifth salvo, when a fuse box jarred loose from the turret's bulkhead, disabling the electro-hydraulic ramming mechanism.

From that point on, according to Lieutenant Hamlin, the crew in the *Houston*'s forwardmost turret loaded and rammed the breech by hand, keeping pace with Turret Two on all but a few salvos. "This is a thing that you couldn't do in peacetime," Hamlin wrote, "no gun crew could do it, but they did."

Some seventy men worked in each of the *Houston*'s two functioning main battery mounts. Below, loading the two hydraulic hoists that fed the handling room from the *Houston*'s magazines was exhausting work. Seaman second class William M. Ingram said they were at general quarters so often that he scarcely ever slept in the First Division's crew compartment. He barely even knew where his bunk was. He kept a pillow and a blanket in the starboard-side powder box. Spartan accommodations and relentless working hours notwithstanding, the gun crews sent five, sometimes six projectiles a minute rushing out at Japanese cruisers that were doing the same thing right back to them.

Scoring a hit with a naval rifle at the extreme range of more than eighteen statute miles was a bit like rolling snake eyes twice in a row. Arcing down after seventy seconds of flight, the projectiles fell at angles nearly vertical to the sea, both minimizing the chance of a hit and rendering a crippling waterline blow virtually impossible. Further reducing the odds was the erratic path of the targets, each ship turning in irregular zigs and zags. This kind of fight had been long rehearsed in exercises wherein victory emerged through seamanship: forming columns quickly to take the initiative, keeping the column closed and free of gaps to concentrate firepower and simplify command, and orienting it to greatest advantage relative to the enemy and the elements, a challenge complicated by wind, heavy seas, and smoke.

For some fifteen minutes as the opening salvos flashed and roared over the Java Sea, the Japanese concentrated their gunfire on the *Exeter,* leaving the *Houston* undisturbed. Captain Rooks's target was the rear Japanese heavy cruiser, the *Haguro,* trailing Takagi's flagship *Nachi* by about half a mile. The *Houston*'s guns roared, landing 260-pound projectiles all around the enemy ship. Japanese spotter planes launched by catapult from the *Nachi* and other of Takagi's ships ranged up and down the length of the Allied column on its disengaged side, safely out of reach of the *Houston*'s expert gunners. Takagi's cruisers made good use of the floatplanes' spotting reports: Their salvos straddled the *De Ruyter, Houston,* and *Perth* as well as the *Exeter.* From the third salvo on, the *Nachi*'s and *Haguro*'s "overs" were missing the *Exeter* by as little as three yards to the disengaged side, indicating the steepness of the projectiles' fall. Captain Gordon reported a "near-miss underwater well aft" that flooded some compartments and "had the apparent effect of lifting the whole ship in a most remarkable manner."

But Admiral Takagi wanted a torpedo fight. It was the Japanese Navy's way of war. Even if he could outshoot his enemy—his cruisers' eight-inch guns numbered twenty to Doorman's twelve—his navy's tactical doctrine favored the undersea missiles as the weapon of decision. His destroyer squadrons were well practiced in the deadly craft. And already Rear Adm. Shoji Nishimura's destroyers were racing in to demonstrate it. The enemy ships were as yet beyond the range of *Houston*'s secondary battery of five-inch guns, but the six-inchers of Doorman's light cruisers would soon take them up. Capt. Hector M. L. Waller of the *Perth* grew frustrated at his uselessness in a long-range duel. "What possible bloody good can we do here? We should be in there having a whack at them—not sitting here waiting to be sunk."

At 4:30 the *Naka* and the seven destroyers with her had closed to within sixteen thousand yards of Doorman's force. They swung out to port and the torpedoes began hitting the sea. The *Haguro* joined this volley too, sending eight Long Lances bubbling toward the *Exeter*. The Japanese ships fired forty-three in all. Admiral Doorman also favored closing the range. His destroyers had torpedoes, but more urgent was the need to bring into the fight his light cruisers' six-inch guns, the one category of arms in which the Combined Striking Force had superiority.

While the *Exeter* threw salvos at a light cruiser, broad on the starboard beam, the *Houston*'s forward main batteries slammed away at a heavy cruiser. After the sixth salvo Lieutenant Skidmore announced, "Straddle." Four salvos later, flames and enemy blood flowed. Supervising his crew as they rammed the breeches by hand, Lieutenant Hamlin in Turret One couldn't see much from within his shuddering armored gun house. But through the turret periscope he did see "a dull red glow of the exploding shells" on an enemy cruiser. "I saw us hit this enemy cruiser one very good wallop indeed. I saw flames shoot up from her after high turret and smoke and flames come up in the waist in the neighborhood of the ack-ack battery." Hamlin recalled:

> I whooped lustily and dashed for the voice tube to the gun chamber. The gun crews there do a job requiring closer timing and teamwork than any other game in the world. They have no time to watch the show. I shouted, "We've just kicked hell out of a ten-gun Jap cruiser." The boys came back with a short cheer and I turned to find the talker happily occupying the periscope.

Commander Maher, the gunnery officer, whose vantage point was considerably better than Hamlin's, observed that the *Houston*'s target was "put on fire early in the engagement" and mentioned "a fire in the vicinity of the forward turrets." According to Maher, at 4:55 P.M., a little over half an hour into the battle, "the target was aflame both forward and amidships. The target ceased firing and fell out of column under the cover of the smoke from the fires and from her own funnel." Ray Parkin, the *Perth* quartermaster, wrote, "Clouds of black smoke poured out of her top up to three-hundred feet high, but she kept firing." Captain Gordon of the *Exeter,* his gunnery officer, and members of his fire-control team saw hits around the "lower bridge structure." An aerial photo taken by an American P-40 pilot around this time shows a fast-moving Japanese ship trailing an outsize column of black smoke. When men on the *Houston* heard that a Japanese ship had ceased fire, turned, and withdrawn, spontaneous cheers rose.

With the apparent momentary withdrawal of one of the enemy heavies, the *Houston* turned her guns on the second. But she would score no further hits on the Japanese cruisers. A frayed electrical lead in the forward main gun director, coupled with the whipping back and forth of the towering foremast housing, led to problems with the *Houston*'s gunnery deflection adjustments. "The range was perfect," the turret officer in Turret Two, Ens. Charles Smith, recalled, "but as we continued to fire on this second ship, we could not tell just exactly where the salvo was going to land. Sometimes it would be five mills to the left, sometimes on and sometimes ten mills to the right." To a ship that prided itself on gunnery, the failure was intolerable.

The Japanese machinery of war was far from perfect too. As more than forty torpedoes were racing toward the Allied cruisers, several were seen to explode prematurely, rending the sea just a few minutes out of their tubes. Captain Hara on the *Amatsukaze* lamented the defective mechanisms. And he marveled at the apparent professionalism of the Allied captains. They seemed to know just when to throw the helm, combing the wakes of the Japanese torpedoes and presenting the smallest possible profile to the deadly fish.

For the Allies, the seeming ritual nature of the engagement ended less than an hour after it began. A medium-caliber projectile struck the *Java,* while an eight-incher arced down and slammed into the *Houston.* The latter passed through main deck aft of the anchor windlass, penetrated the second deck, and tore through the starboard side above the waterline without exploding. Another hit ruptured an oil tank on the *Houston*'s port side aft, but it too failed to explode. Either the warheads were duds or the ship's treaty-mandated limitations on weight, which dictated lighter armor protection than would become typical for a heavy cruiser, paid the dividend of failing to detonate a projectile engineered to sink ships with heavier hides.

CHAPTER 11

Salvo after salvo exploded into the sea around us," wrote Walter Winslow, the grounded aviator. "I was mesmerized by the savage flashes of enemy guns, and the sight of their deadly shells flying toward us like giant blackbirds." Torpedoes approached more stealthily. Their initial release, seldom seen, had to be inferred from the movements of ships. Shortly after five P.M., the *Jintsu* and six of the eight destroyers with her in Destroyer Squadron Two snaked in toward Doorman's force, approached nearly head-on until they were about seventeen thousand yards away, and then withdrew behind a smoke screen. The telltale sequence meant that a second wave of torpedoes was on the way, this time sixty-eight in all, forty-eight from the six destroyers and a total of twenty more from the *Jintsu* and the two heavy cruisers. Trailing the Allied column, the captains of the U.S. destroyers couldn't see much, but one commander wrote, "Throughout this madness, everyone was painfully aware that torpedoes were knifing their way through the sea toward us, yet Admiral Doorman took no evasive action."

Then, all at once, all of Doorman's ships seemed to be swerving out of line. The *Exeter,* in line ahead of the *Houston,* had taken a hit. An eight-inch projectile punched through a gun shield on her starboard secondary battery, killing six, then penetrated downward and exploded inside a boiler in the B fireroom, killing ten more men. Power to her main battery failed, quieting her guns. As burst steam pipes screamed, Captain Gordon's ship slowed to eleven knots, hauling sharply out to port. "We were appalled," Walter Winslow wrote, "to see a billowing white cloud of steam spewing from the *Exeter* amidships."

The British cruiser's portside sheer threw Doorman's column into confusion. The concussive quakes of the *Houston*'s gunfire had shaken her Talk Between Ships radio into malfunction. The delicate arcs in the ship's signal spotlights were shattered too, and smoke obscured the alphabet flags and Aldis lamps used for communications in their stead. Captain Rooks, unable to communicate, saw the *Exeter* turn and suspected he had missed a signal from Admiral Doorman. The flagship *De Ruyter* lay ahead somewhere, shrouded in the smoke. So Rooks turned too, coming abreast of and then passing the wounded *Exeter*. Maher ordered the *Houston*'s main batteries to check fire as the turrets rotated in unison, rumbling about to stay on target through the turn. The *De Ruyter* continued on course for a moment before Doorman, realizing what was happening behind him, threw a hard port rudder to avoid losing his squadron.

As the cruiser column frayed amid the mounting confusion, Captain Waller of the *Perth* noticed the sorry state of the *Exeter*, billowing steam from the depths of her engineering plant. Aiming to cover the British heavy with a smoke screen, he swung the *Perth* in a counterclockwise loop to the north, racing astern of the south-turning *Houston* eight hundred yards to the engaged side and firing floating smoke pots into the sea that churned out white clouds. The thirty-foot-high wall of smoke gave the *Exeter* a reprieve.

The sight of Waller's ship in action stirred Lieutenant Hamlin's pride: "I'll never forget the *Perth* as she came by there. She was a magnificent sight. Absolutely at top speed, streaming smoke and with battle flags flying at both yardarms and a great big white ensign aft, all guns firing and she looked like a warship really should. One of the finest sights I have ever seen." In the chaos brought about by the *Exeter*'s sudden trauma, however, no one seemed to realize the risk in turning south while enemy torpedoes were coming in from the west.

"The sea seemed alive with torpedoes running from all quarters," recalled Walter Winslow. Some surfaced and porpoised as they ran out of fuel. Others erupted in blasts of spray and debris, self-destructing at the end of their long-range runs. One of them, drifting along at the end of its run, actually hit the *Houston,* gently glancing off the cruiser's hull. "It was not going at sufficient speed to detonate," wrote Ensign Smith, "and it bounced off and fell away." Not knowing the astonishing range of the Japanese Type 93, many officers thought they had come from submarines. The Dutch destroyer *Kortenaer,* trailing the cruisers on the disengaged side and now, with the southward turn, screening them to the west, found herself broadside to a spread of Long Lances. One struck her on the starboard side.

A tremendous explosion produced a tower of seawater that swallowed her nearly from forecastle to fantail. When the splash crashed back down upon itself, the ship was revealed again, lying broken in two, jackknifed and foundering, each ruined half of her gray-green camouflaged hull pointing helplessly to the sky like a partly submerged V. According to Ensign Smith on the *Houston,* "There was only fifteen or twenty feet separating her bow from her stern."

"Passing close aboard," wrote Winslow, "we saw a few men desperately scrambling to cling to her barnacled bottom while her twin propellers, in their last propulsive effort, turned slowly over in the air." A few sailors flashed a thumbs-up sign at the passing American heavy before the remains of their ship disappeared beneath the swells. "No ship stopped to take on survivors," Winslow wrote, "for any that did could easily have shared the same fate." The *Kortenaer* was gone within a minute, her crew left alone to contend with the sea.

Admiral Doorman had ordered his ships to leave survivors alone. In torpedo-riven waters, the risks of stopping were too great. The captains of the leading British destroyers did what they could under the circumstances, scrambling to lay smoke around the *Exeter* and give Doorman time to reassemble his cruiser line. Though they built a solid smoke wall, it had no roof. Japanese spotting aircraft droned overhead, radioing back details of the chaos.

At around six P.M., as daylight was beginning to fade, the *De Ruyter* appeared through the smoke and haze, blinkering the signal "FOLLOW ME," a repeat of Doorman's earlier cryptic command. Captain Rooks, watching the sea for torpedoes and ordering his guns to engage any Japanese ships closing with the wounded *Exeter,* took the *Houston* in a clockwise circle and steadied the helm on an easterly course behind the flagship. Captain Waller, having finished laying smoke around the *Exeter*, saw Doorman's signal and fell back into line with his retiring peers. The *Java* followed.

The *Exeter*'s engineering crew, struggling to coax electrical power from their shattered machinery, seemed to be making progress. Before long, her main battery came back to life, throwing salvos through the smoke at targets somewhere to the north.

*

Admiral Helfrich was helpless to aid his fleet in its hour of need. At 5:25 P.M., from Bandung, ABDA's naval commander ordered Admiral Glassford, commander of U.S. naval forces in the theater, to send his submarines to intercept the Japanese convoy, as yet hovering out of sight to the northwest. For Admiral Doorman, there was no telling what the silent service was up to, but his destroyers had torpedoes and now the tin cans were finally able to respond in kind, if not in unison. Doorman signaled, "BRITISH DESTROYERS COUNTERATTACK." Too widely dispersed to form up in column, they made individual sorties.

The *Electra*, first into the breech, met ferocious gunfire from the Japanese. In quick succession, three shells struck her. The first, below the bridge, severed internal communications and the gun director's signals to the mounts. Another hit the forward switchboard, shutting down power in the forward part of the ship. The third destroyed the after boiler room, and with that the *Electra* shuddered to a stop. When a fusillade of projectiles tore away the ship's forward gun mount, the searchlight platform, and then one of the rear guns, the captain, Commander May, ordered the ship abandoned. The two other British destroyers in Doorman's force, the *Encounter* and the *Jupiter*, arrived in time to see the *Electra* burning and dead in the water. The *Encounter* fired her torpedoes through an opening in the smoke. Attacking separately, the *Jupiter* was unable to get a torpedo solution on the enemy, and so she stood close by the *Exeter*, driving off with her gunfire two Japanese destroyers probing the smoke for the wounded cruiser.

The *Perth* was doing her own probing, firing her six-inch main battery at mastheads visible above the smoke. Once Doorman's cruisers dialed in the range, the Japanese ships withdrew, and the *Exeter*, now making fifteen knots, was finally spared. Five miles to his east, through dusk's failing light, Captain Gordon spied a shaded signal lamp on the *Witte de With* instructing him to follow the Dutch destroyer back to Surabaya immediately. The two ships would peel away and head south. Leaving the battle scene, they reached port without further drama.

*

All throughout the engagement, the American destroyers had little clue what was expected of them. The commander of the *John D. Edwards,* Lt. Cdr. Henry E. Eccles, would remark acidly, "The crystal ball was our only method of anticipating the intention of Commander, Combined Striking Force." When orders finally did come, they did little to dispel the need for wizardry. As his cruisers retired south, Doorman signaled the destroyers to turn north and make a torpedo attack. Then he canceled the order. Shortly he issued a new one: "COVER MY RETIREMENT." At that point, low on fuel, the destroyers had little else to contribute to the battle. Their swimming torpedoes didn't contribute much either. From long range, as could be expected, they all missed.

The fog of war was billowing out thicker than any smoke screen. One question loomed large: At 6:30 Admiral Doorman radioed Helfrich at Bandung, *"Enemy retreating west. Where is convoy?"* In the *De Ruyter,* Doorman curled sharply back toward the northwest, leading the *Perth, Houston, Java,* and four U.S. destroyers, perhaps in search of an opening through which to locate and attack the Japanese troopships. Clearing some smoke around 7:30, they again ran into the ubiquitous *Nachi* and *Haguro.*

As Captain Hara related it, the two heavy cruisers were unprepared for the encounter, having stopped to retrieve floatplanes they had launched at the battle's outset. As the Allies approached, the *Nachi*'s boatswains were busy with the amidships crane. When they finished hooking up and bringing the last plane on board, the *Nachi*'s engines roared to life. The Japanese ships laid smoke to cover their withdrawal and within a few minutes were at eighteen knots. Though Admiral Takagi refrained from using his searchlights because he knew he was vulnerable, his ships opened fire with their main batteries at thirteen thousand yards. The cruisers traded salvos for about ten minutes until the *Perth*'s Captain Waller, spotting flashes along the length of the silhouetted enemy ships and suspecting a torpedo launch, turned sharply away. Evidently wishing to spare his cruiser's faltering ammunition stocks, and perhaps despairing of his chances of blazing a path to the invasion convoy through the gunfire of its most powerful escorts, Doorman broke off the engagement. He swung his squadron away to the south.

The *Nachi* and *Haguro,* both of which would go on to post gaudy combat records through the Pacific war, had escaped a most dangerous trap. In Doorman's failure to see the plight of the momentarily exposed Japanese cruisers, he forfeited his best chance yet of reaching the transports concealed behind them over the northern horizon. The record reflects no sign that the Allies ever appreciated the tactical opportunity that had just washed over their bows and drained out the gunwales. Like so many opportunities, it had arrived unannounced and vanished without ceremony. They would get only one more like it.

CHAPTER 12

Night fell. The wind went away with the sun, and the torn seas were permitted to slumber, smooth and glassy and glinting with the light of a rising full moon. The Japanese ships were gone. What wounds they might be tending were, and might ever remain, unknown. The wounds suffered by the Combined Striking Force were many and manifest. And for all their sacrifices, the danger to the Dutch East Indies loomed as great as ever. Thousands of Japanese troops were out there still, no doubt growing restless as soldiers out of their element will. They would bide their time at sea.

As Admiral Doorman led his ships southward toward Java's northern coast, he received from the Dutch commander of the Surabaya naval district a three-hour-old report from a U.S. bomber that forty-five enemy transports, three cruisers, and twelve destroyers were just twenty miles from Bawean Island. Given the unfortunate vintage of the sighting report and the swift setting of the sun, his chances of intercepting them seemed about as good as the prospects for his home island in general.

The persistence of daylight had been his last hope to find and destroy an enemy who was all too lethally well trained to fight after dark. Ahead a lighthouse stood near Toeban, warning Doorman of his proximity to land. Nearly as dangerous as the newly planted minefields off that coastal town were the shoal waters that threatened the keels of his deepest-draft ships.

During the lull on the *Houston*, hastily prepared sandwiches and coffee were distributed. Crews in the engineering compartments, gun mounts, and magazines, worn from the nonstop action, paused to eat and rest. Their hardware had withstood similar strain. Turret One had fired 261 salvos since installation, 97 just that afternoon. Turret Two had fired 264, 100 that afternoon. The life of an eight-inch gun was about 300 salvos. From the long barrels of the rifles, the liners were creeping out as much as an inch or more from the muzzle. The gun casings were so hot they could not be touched for hours. The ventilation systems in the shell decks, handling rooms, and magazines were utterly inadequate. Fighting 140-degree heat, men who didn't lose consciousness altogether during the battle stood in three inches of melted gun grease, sweat, and urine. The violent sheering of the ship sloshed that fetid brew everywhere, into the breech trays and onto the powder cases. The mixture of human and industrial stenches crept into every compartment without a watertight seal.

Doorman changed course to the west, paralleling the north coast of Java. Shortly after nine P.M., the four U.S. destroyers that had so doggedly brought up the Striking Force's rear had become too low on fuel to continue. The destroyers weren't the only Allied ships low on critical consumables. The *Houston* had passed word to the *Perth*'s Captain Waller via voice circuit that her two forward mounts were nearly out of eight-inch ammunition. The shortage was the unavoidable result of an unprecedented four-hour gunnery marathon. At one point Otto Schwarz of the *Houston,* stationed on the shell deck below Turret One, had been assured by a chief that naval battles were always over in a hurry. He told Schwarz there had never been a naval battle that lasted longer than twenty or twenty-five minutes. The limited stock of ready ammunition in the turret would be all the gunners would need. Some eight hours later, the men in Schwarz's compartment were still hauling greasy shells out of the storage racks. When they were gone, the crew began the backbreaking job of hand-carrying 260-pound projectiles, swaddled in slings made from cloth sheets, from the aft magazine up through the labyrinthine passageways leading forward, across the deck, and down into the two forward handling rooms.

Twice between eight and nine P.M., lookouts called out sightings of enemy destroyers to the east. But they were phantoms, alive only in the imaginations of the watch personnel skittish from four hours of combat. What other threats lurked in the night could only be guessed. Mysterious yellow lights appeared in the water, seeming to rise from the deep in the wake of Doorman's ships as they steamed. Some observers thought the lights marking their path were the by-product of their disturbance of a shallow sea. "As fast as we popped one group of lights astern, another popped up about a hundred yards to port," Walter Winslow wrote.

In fact, the lights were not surfacing from below. They were float-ing down from the sky, parachute-harnessed calcium flares dropped by Japanese spotter plane pilots every time Doorman changed course. The flares traced their track so relentlessly that Jim Gee thought the Japanese had tied them together on strands to be caught by the *Houston*'s prow and dragged along behind her "like a long string of Christmas lights." What little chance Doorman had to break through and attack the transports vanished. Takeo Takagi knew his every move.

★

Karel Doorman was about twenty minutes into his westward coastal run when a great blast swallowed the last ship in his line. The flash of the explosion settled into a moonlit flood of steam, and against that hellish backdrop sailors on the Dutch light cruiser *Java* looking astern could make out a lamp signaling, "*JUPITER* TORPE-DOED."

At least it seemed like a torpedo. The explosion tore the British destroyer's hull on the starboard side, abreast of the number-two boiler room's forward bulkhead. Though more Long Lances lay in store for this Allied fleet, this was not one of them. It was a mine, part of a Dutch field planted off the coast that very day in anticipa-tion of the coming invasion. Admiral Takagi had declined to pursue Doorman south out of this very fear. Her back broken, the *Jupiter* floundered and settled and took her time sinking, joining the *Kortenaer* and the *Electra* in death. Just seventy-eight of her crew reached the beach, and another handful were later retrieved from the sea by the Japanese.

Perhaps thinking he might seize a last opportunity to reach the convoy, Doorman steered north again, knowing that with every thumping turn of his ships' steam-driven screws, Japanese aircraft watched him from overhead. At about 9:50 P.M., Captain Waller spied one, glinting by the moon's light. Shortly thereafter the Allies' new northerly course was etched in blazing calcium, another string of floating flares tracing their track.

Nerves rattled as the ships passed back through waters that had been their battlefield in the afternoon. The swells here and there were dotted with men adrift—survivors of the *Kortenaer*. The orders to ignore them stood. The area was still too hot for a rescue attempt. Clinging to or standing in their life rafts, the Dutch sailors blew whistles and hollered, looking for help. As the *Houston* passed within sight of the survivors, her deck force threw a raft overboard and illuminated the area with a flare. The HMS *Encounter* stopped—on whose authority it remains unclear—and took aboard 113 in all.

There was yet an enemy to hunt, and the quarry reappeared around 10:30 P.M. The *Nachi* and the *Haguro,* last seen some four hours earlier, now materialized to port, bearing down from the north on an opposite parallel course before looping around and tracing a parallel northerly course at a range of thirteen thousand to sixteen thousand yards. Concerned with dwindling ammunition stocks— the two cruisers had fired more than twelve hundred rounds that afternoon, and 348 more after dark—their commanders fired at a deliberate pace. It was futile to engage at that range by night. Star shells couldn't reach that far. The phosphorous-filled projectiles needed to burst beyond their target in order to silhouette it properly. The *Houston* fired several illumination rounds, but they fell short, as did those fired by the Japanese. But the night afforded its own illumination. Lieutenant Hamlin wrote, "We stopped shooting star shells and settled down to just shooting at each other by the starlight."

A few projectiles landed close enough aboard to thrash the sides of the *Houston*'s hull underwater like chains flailing at a tin roof. Japanese guns scored on the *De Ruyter,* hitting the flagship on the quarterdeck. For good measure, the *Nachi* and the *Haguro* put a dozen more torpedoes into the water, sixty degrees to starboard, at targets eleven thousand yards away. The ships entered a rainsquall as their commanders counted down the torpedo runs.

Captain Waller was conning the *Perth* behind his squadron flagship. Seeing the *De Ruyter* turn and surmising that Doorman had spotted inbound torpedoes, he changed course on cue. The *Houston* and the *Java* followed the *Perth,* pregnant minutes passing before the night was again lit by a blast. It was the *Java,* taking a torpedo aft. Charley Pryor, scanning the *Houston*'s port quarter with binoculars, saw her blow. He saw bodies flying through the air, silhouetted by flames, the water burning. Red and pink streamers flew everywhere from the column's rear. The blast was powerful enough to be felt by crewmen topside on the *Perth.* Flames leaped above *Java*'s bridge. She sank so quickly—in about eight minutes—that her steel had no time to melt.

Another torpedo struck the *De Ruyter* so soon after the first one hit the *Java* that some witnesses took it as a simultaneous cataclysm or confused their sequence. The flagship "blew up with an appalling explosion and settled aft, heavily afire," Captain Waller observed. "It happened with the suddenness and completeness that one sees in the functioning of a good cigarette-lighter—a snap and a burst of flame," wrote Lieutenant Hamlin. The inferno's heat was so intense that sailors on the *Perth,* following several hundred yards behind the flagship, could feel it on their faces. "I thought it would fry us," one Australian recalled. "It was so close you could smell burning paint and a horrible stink like burning bodies."

Reprising what happened that afternoon with the *Exeter,* the sudden crippling of the *De Ruyter* derailed the column like a jackknifing freight train. "Captain Rooks frantically maneuvered his cruiser to avoid torpedoes," Walter Winslow wrote, "and then ordered the *Houston* into a hard right turn, unaware that the *Perth,* whose captain was now the senior officer, was overtaking us to starboard in an effort to assume the lead." Captain Waller had to stop his port engine and turn the helm all the way over to port, and the *Perth* "just scraped by the port side" of the burning flagship. The *Houston* sheered out to starboard, nearly colliding with the *Perth.* Rooks ordered emergency full astern while Ens. Herbert A. Levitt grabbed the wheel from the helmsman and brought the ship back to port, avoiding the Australian cruiser by a mere twenty-five yards.

As the *De Ruyter*'s crew gathered forward to escape the flames eating the back half of the ship, the fires reached the forty-millimeter antiaircraft ammunition stowage, and small explosions began popping amid the sailors. Glowing metal fragments shot into the night as the ordnance went off en masse. As the fires worsened, Admiral Doorman had no choice but to order abandon ship. One of his last earthly acts was to instruct the last two serviceable vessels under his command, the *Houston* and *Perth,* to head for Batavia rather than stand by to recover his survivors. The standing order that disabled friendlies should be "left to the enemy's mercy" came with no exemption for an admiral. Left behind, the *De Ruyter* fought the clutches of the sea for nearly an hour and a half before she finally sank. Ensign Smith in the *Houston* "counted nine separate and distinct explosions before we cleared the horizon."

Karel Doorman was never seen again. Admiral Helfrich had ordered him to fight to the end, and that is precisely what he did. "The *Houston* and *Perth* raced on into the night," wrote Walter Winslow. "Behind us blazed the funeral pyres of our comrades-in-arms, whom we deeply mourned."

CHAPTER 13

As the growl of naval gunfire washed ashore on Java, only the most naive of the battle's proximate witnesses could fail to appreciate its sinister meaning. An American B-17 pilot stationed there recalled, "Walking to the telephone building I could hear a dull rumble in the hot midnight air coming from far over the water. The few people in the blacked-out streets assumed it was distant thunder. I knew it was the little Dutch Navy in its final agony out there in the dark." The men of the U.S. Nineteenth Bomb Group at Malang were closely acquainted with the mounting disaster. The sound of the naval battle out to sea seemed to herald the end. A pilot recalled, "Java died that night in the gunfire which came rolling in over the water."

But two ships yet lived. By night the *Houston* and the *Perth* raced westward, bound for refuge and replenishment. For a time, the Japanese pursued them. Admiral Takagi, whose cruisers had ranged miles to the northwest by the time their torpedoes hit the two Dutch cruisers, had wanted to finish them off. As crewmen on the decks of the *Nachi* and *Haguro* leaped and danced and shouted "*Banzai!*" as fires raged on the waters to their southeast, Takagi approached the *Java* and the *De Ruyter* in their death throes and instructed his gunners not to waste precious ammunition on them. "They are done for," he said coolly.

At midnight the *Nachi* and *Haguro* spotted silhouettes to the south-southeast. As Takagi's destroyers sought in vain to locate and engage them, his cruisers opened fire on "four cruisers." But whatever they were shooting at slipped away. Puzzled by the disappearance of the surviving Allied ships, Takagi called off his search around three A.M. Commander Hara would call the admiral's inability to finish off the survivors "the last Japanese mistake of the battle," though it would become clear soon enough that mistakes had been predominantly the domain of the Allies.

The *Houston* and the *Perth* formed a short column and chased rainsqualls to elude their pursuers. Standing orders were for all ships to sail to Batavia if the squadron got scattered. They were to make the three-hundred-mile run to refuel, then pass through Sunda Strait, head down to Tjilatjap to evacuate Allied soldiers and airmen gathering on Java's south coast, then continue on to Australia. At 8:40 P.M. on the night of February 27, the *Houston* sent a dispatch labeled "Urgent" to Admiral Glassford: "HOUSTON AND PERTH RETIRING TO BATAVIA ARRIVE ABOUT 1000 TOMORROW X REQUEST PILOTS AND AIR PROTECTION IF AVAILABLE." Whoever could manage it found a place to sack out on deck. The heat and smell in the lower decks were simply too much. Hatches were thrown open, letting the hot ferment of battle vent into the night.

Though the ship's stocks of ammunition and fuel were low, the crew's morale, as ever, was improbably high. It had been high when they were spending day after day at general quarters at Surabaya, helpless against the droning assault of Japanese bombers. It had been high when they finally entered battle against the Japanese Navy, and high still as their enemy routed them. Now, more understandably, morale was high because at last, against all odds, they were about to see sunrise on February 28. When one Allied ship after another was bursting into flames all around them, no one would have put much money on it.

The terror they had experienced was a frightening preview of the trials the U.S. Navy would face after dark against their well-practiced enemy. Before the war, plenty of reasons were found—compelling enough in peacetime—to neglect difficult and dangerous night exercises. Adm. James O. Richardson, commander in chief of the United

States Fleet, wrote, "In the era before radar, close-in night exercises brought great risk of collision, loss of life, and expensive ship repairs." In other words, they were very much like actual night battles. He might have endorsed them by the same measure. As a result of this hesitancy, Navy commanders would not see nighttime torpedo attacks launched by hard-charging cruiser and destroyer captains until they confronted the real thing under the least forgiving of circumstances.

Captain Rooks was well aware of the rigorous emphasis his enemy had given to night fighting. In his analysis of the Japanese threat titled "Estimate of the Situation," written just three weeks before Pearl Harbor and turned over to a colleague for safekeeping when the *Houston* was in Darwin in January, Rooks referred to the Japanese claim to being "the world's most capable users of the torpedo" and described their aggressively realistic doctrine for their use in night actions. There was no denying their lethality. The Allies' bloody discipleship at the feet of the Imperial Japanese Navy's torpedo virtuosos began with the Battle of the Java Sea. That Rooks, his ship, and gallant crew had survived it was sheerest happenstance.

*

Once daylight came, revealing no enemy ships nearby, it seemed reasonable for the first time to hope that the *Houston* might escape the flash flood of Japanese power and regroup in Australia for the long war ahead. "I don't think there was ever a minute that we didn't feel that we were going to make it, that we were going to come out on top of this," said Jim Gee of the *Houston*'s Marine detachment.

Arriving at Batavia in the early afternoon of February 28, the two ships were stalked briefly by a flight of Japanese torpedo bombers before Dutch Hurricane fighters scattered them in a rare and probably accidental moment of interservice cooperation. At three o'clock Admiral Glassford reached Captain Rooks via secure telephone. "He was so very cheery," Glassford would write to Edith, "and the more so because [he] had gallantly engaged the enemy." As the admiral gave Rooks his instructions, a harbor boat met them outside the breakwater and its pilot guided them through its protective minefield.

There wasn't much to protect. As the *Houston* and *Perth* entered port, several merchant ships could be seen resting at odd angles on the harbor floor. What the Japanese planes had not yet smashed lay abandoned in place. Once bustling with industry, Batavia's port district, Tanjung Priok, looked like a ghost town. As the cruisers moored to the pier to refuel, keeping up steam for an early-morning departure, it was clear that most of the harbor workers were gone. The Javanese and Malayan natives had learned to resent four centuries of European rule. But the Japanese were an as yet unknown quantity. The natives heard promising talk of a Greater East Asian Co-Prosperity Sphere. They would find a safe place to await the arrival of the "liberators."

Rooks and Waller went ashore and took the Australian officer's staff car to the British Naval Liaison Office. There they received an encouraging report. According to Dutch air reconnaissance, Sunda Strait was wide open. The closest imperial warships were seventy miles to their northeast, heading east. The enemy had nothing within a ten-hour sail of the passage. Rooks and Waller were warned not to fire on any friendly patrol craft that would likely be watching Sunda Strait.

Escape seemed to be on everyone's mind. Ashore, the Dutch were more interested in rendering the port useless to the Japanese than servicing the Allied ships that now needed them. With evacuation plans in motion, sappers were readying to blow up the dockside warehouses and other facilities. Workers at the soon-to-be-demolished canteen store were generous with their inventory, allowing the sailors to make off with whiskey, cigarettes, and other goods previously earmarked for the "Victualling Officer, Singapore." Captains Rooks and Waller divvied up a dozen large life rafts that were stacked up on the dock. But more precious cargo eluded them.

The supply of fuel oil available to ABDA naval forces was desperately short. With the sea route from the massive refineries at Palembang, Sumatra, imperiled by Japanese forces, tankers could no longer make the run to Java. The island was down to its native capacity, just 22,000 tons per month. Java's storage facilities, though large, were located inland and now effectively inaccessible given the abandonment by many native workers. Admiral Helfrich accordingly notified his naval commanders, "OIL POSITION IS SERIOUS. EVERY EFFORT MUST BE MADE TO REDUCE EXPENDITURE PROVIDED OPERATIONS AGAINST THE ENEMY ARE NOT PREJUDICED . . . IT IS ESSENTIAL THAT OIL BE MOVED FROM SURABAYA TO TJILATJAP AND TANJUNG PRIOK AS SOON AS POSSIBLE."

When it was sprayed into the furnaces that heated a ship's boilers,

the Dutch oil, lighter and less viscous than standard American
Bunker B, didn't produce enough volume for a ship to generate full
power. With the warm Java Sea waters already impairing the efficiency of her condensers, the best the *Houston* could do was twenty-
seven or twenty-eight knots, well short of her rated thirty-two. At
Tanjung Priok on February 28, only 760 long tons of furnace fuel
were on hand, and the Dutch were inclined to be miserly with it.
Admiral Helfrich had instructed the port authority at Tjilatjap to
keep the available fuel for their own nation's fleet. "NO FURTHER
FUEL WILL BE ISSUED TO U.S. NAVAL VESSELS," Glassford informed his commanders. "UNLESS OTHERWISE INSTRUCTED WE
WILL FUEL OUR [SHIPS] FROM [THE OILER] *PECOS*."

The harbor authorities rebuffed the *Houston*'s and *Perth*'s requests
for fuel, informing Lt. Robert Fulton, in charge of fueling, that it
was on reserve for Dutch warships.

When the Americans and Australians informed them of the disaster off Surabaya and the loss of most of the Dutch Navy, the harbor
masters yielded a bit. Some cajoling and arm-twisting got three
hundred tons of oil pumped into the *Perth,* bringing her bunkers to
half capacity. The *Houston* got somewhat less. One of the dud projectiles that struck her during the Java Sea action had penetrated her oil
tanks, making it impossible to fill them above a certain level without leaking an oil trail. But some thought her 350,000 gallons on
hand was adequate to reach Australia.

It was clear the *Houston* would not make the trip in her accustomed high style. Like the *Perth,* she was about as battered and salt-
worn as her crew. "Concussion from the main batteries had played
havoc with the ship's interior," Walter Winslow wrote. "Every un-
locked dresser and desk drawer had been torn out and the contents
spewed all over. In lockers, clothes were wrenched from hangers and
dumped in muddled heaps. Pictures, radios, books and anything else
not bolted down had been jolted from normal places and dashed to
the deck." The well-appointed admiral's cabin, which marked the
Houston as a flagship, standing ready for use by any flag officers or adventurous U.S. presidents who might happen to come aboard, was a
mess of ruined luxuries: overturned furniture, shattered glass and
china, and drifts of soundproof insulation torn and jarred from the
bulkheads. Scarcely a piece of glass was intact. Portholes, lightbulbs,
mirrors, searchlight lenses, crystal tumblers, picture frames—all
had been shattered by the impact of battle. The concussion of Turret

Two, which often fired while rotated to an extreme after bearing, had popped rivets and metal fittings and battered the weather shields girding the bridge, as well as damaged the signal searchlights on the navigation bridge. The guns themselves needed replacement.

The *Perth* was equally bad off. After the battle, an exhausted Hector Waller went to his cabin to rest for a spell. The forty-one-year-old captain sorely needed it. "He had been off-color for days," remembered a *Perth* sailor. Jaundice had cast his skin in a pale yellow. Arriving in his cabin, he had to sweep his bunk clean of glass shards before lying down to rest.

On both ships, the buzz now centered on two things: what might have been in the disastrous battle they had just survived, and what might yet come to pass in the urgent days ahead. As to the first question, the American sailors speculated how it might have gone differently had the *Boise* or *Marblehead* or *Phoenix* been with them. For the men of the *Perth,* the absent savior was their old Mediterranean squadronmate, the heavy cruiser HMAS *Australia,* whose gunnery, they said, was as good as it got. The Aussies felt that if a proven fighter such as "ol' Hec" had been in command rather than Admiral Doorman, the Combined Striking Force would have been handled more aggressively and decisively.

Captain Waller's reputation had swelled with his successes in the Mediterranean. Commanding the destroyer HMAS *Stuart,* he had won two Distinguished Service Orders, one for his gallant turn during the Battle of Matapan, where the *Stuart* contributed more than a destroyer's share to the Royal Navy's greatest victory since Trafalgar and helped end Italy's challenge to the naval balance of power. Waller had a reputation as a fighter and a hands-on commander. He liked to read and send his own signals. He proved his marksmanship by blasting floating mines with his own rifle. Visiting the governor's palace in Malta, he had had both the temerity to tell the island's First Lady that her famous rose garden was poorly pruned and the skill to wield the clippers himself and improve it. "Leaning against his bridge rail or walking the quarterdeck or even in civilian clothes he seemed to broadcast strength—the inner controlled strength of a man who knew where he was going, and knew why," Ronald McKie wrote. Heavy-shouldered and balding, with rounded facial features, he was stern and serious-minded but given to seasonable playfulness. His odd mix of traits enabled his dour aspect to become its own brand of charm. Though his full given name, Hector Macdonald

Laws Waller, might have suggested he had been bred to dine with fine silver, he lacked pretense utterly. A naval career had in fact been his sole professional purpose since the age of nine.

The consensus among the Monday-morning quartermasters was that the three light cruisers should have operated independently of the heavies and charged with the destroyers straight at the Japanese, while the *Houston* and the *Exeter* blasted away from afar. The Americans could only guess at the destruction they would have wrought had their after eight-inch battery been working. Its untapped potential was plain to see—and haul. For the better part of that afternoon in Tanjung Priok, the crew continued loading projectiles from the after magazine on bedsheets and carrying them six hundred feet to the depleted forward magazines and handling rooms. The treacherous hike was considerably easier to do while the ship was moored rather than pitching and rolling at sea in the midst of battle.

Beyond the second-guessing, most of the sailors were elated to have survived at all. Having paid their way, they felt they had earned some respite now in safer harbors. "Everyone was lighthearted, and thinking that we had done our share, and done our best," Lloyd Willey said. "We thought it would be great to see the United States again." Others looked forward to more immediate good times in Australia.

While the crew was trying to get refueled, the *Houston* floatplane pilot who had stayed behind with his aircraft in Surabaya, Lt. Tom Payne, radioed word that he would fly to Tanjung Priok that afternoon to rejoin the ship. When he arrived, approaching the harbor from the sea, the raw-nerved crew of a Dutch shore battery opened fire on his Seagull at long range. As explosions of flak burst all around him, Payne touched down beyond the breakwater, cursing vigorously. As he began to taxi in, a Dutch torpedo boat motored out to inspect him. The *Houston*'s crew watched with some trepidation, unable to inform the boat that it was their shipmate. To their relief, it circled Payne's aircraft and escorted him back into the harbor. "Tom was hoisted on board," Walter Winslow wrote, "perplexed, to say the least, by his less than cordial welcome."

CHAPTER 14

Naval service is a highly technologized trade. In it, life is simplified to the degree possible around the practical application of repetition-driven training. In the age of practical mechanics, efficiency was the route to advancement—and, in war, to survival. Training was designed in part to reduce war's emotional calamities to the mastery of innumerable arcana, mechanics, and procedures. And yet somewhere along the way this rational world seemed to turn back on itself and touch a spiritual plane. As sailors' worlds contracted around their narrow specialties, it was easy for them to feel as much like initiates in a mysterious brotherhood as cogs in a machine. Vestiges of the mystical remained. And despite their determined optimism, dark superstitions lurked everywhere.

While she was preparing to leave Fremantle for the East Indies, the *Perth* had been recalled three times before finally receiving orders to depart at 11:30 on February 13. Confronted with the unlucky date, Captain Waller intentionally delayed standing out till after midnight on the fourteenth. One did not idly tempt the fates. Unease was already rife on that ship. The *Perth* sailors realized at one point that two chaplains were on the roster, and contemplated the apocalyptic implications. "One was bad enough," Ronald McKie wrote, "but two—that was lethal." Another omen: While the *Perth* was firing on Japanese planes, a portrait of Marina, Duchess of Kent—it was she who had rechristened the ship as the *Perth* in 1939 after she was acquired from the Royal Navy as the HMS *Amphion*— fell from the wardroom bulkhead and crashed to the floor. Clearly dark ghosts were at work.

But perhaps the most striking portent involved the feline mascots of the *Houston* and the *Perth*. "I don't know if Captain Rooks had anything to do with this or not, but it seemed very strange," remembered Seldon Reese, a seaman first class on the *Houston*. As Rooks walked down the gangplank for a meeting of commanders, the ship's cat "took off down that pier into Java like some big hound dog. You never saw a cat move so fast in your life." Apparently the animal had had enough of life on the ship, be it a favorite of the president or not. Crewmen who witnessed the incident were nearly as spooked as their feline ex-shipmate. It gave substance to a fear expressed by Lieutenant Winslow—"that, like a cat, the *Houston* had expended eight of its nine lives and that this one last request of fate would be too much."

The *Perth*'s black cat, Red Lead, had been given to a sailor at a New Year's Eve party in Sydney in 1941. The feline had lived life as seagoing contraband until one day his owner devised to sneak topside and release the cat when Captain Waller was on duty on the bridge. The affection-starved animal snaked around Waller's legs. To the delight of the sailor, the captain adopted the cat, removing the risk of its expulsion by officers junior in rank but superior in adherence to the book. In port now, Red Lead tried three times to desert the ship. The master-at-arms finally had to put him in "irons," sticking his paws in a kerosene can with holes cut in it. The animal seemed to know something.

*

At dusk on February 28 the two ships got under way from Batavia. The Dutch destroyer *Evertsen,* also in port, ought to have joined them, but her commander had no orders and her boilers had no steam, and either deficiency was enough to keep her in port no matter how much the cruiser captains may have wanted her as an escort. Without a harbor pilot to guide them, trusting their own charts and the coming full moon—it would be bright enough to allow the antiaircraft rangefinders to take navigational fixes on shore—Rooks and Waller led their ships through the minefield channel without incident, and increased their speed to twenty-two knots. Their bid to reach Australia was all that remained.

Walter Winslow wandered out on the quarterdeck by the port-side catapult tower. Looking astern, he watched Java's darkening junglescape shrink in the flow of the ship's trailing white wake. "Many times before I had found solace in its beauty, but this night it seemed only a mass of coconut and banana palms that had lost all meaning. I was too tired and too preoccupied with pondering the question that raced through the mind of every man aboard. 'Would we get through Sunda Strait?'"

On the *Perth,* officers in whites assembled on their own quarter-deck to salute the striking of the ensign at sunset. Captain Waller held Red Lead, scratching him absently as the bugle pealed. An officer on the *Houston* had asked, as his ship was passing north through Sunda Strait on February 24, whether anyone had heard what he had: the sound of a gate clanging shut. The *Perth*'s engineering officer, Lt. Frank Gillan, felt a similar breath on his neck as he saluted the falling flag. According to Ronald McKie, "He felt that this moment at sundown was a dividing line between the past and the future and that somewhere a decision had been made affecting his life and the lives of them all."

Another night fell, quieter than the last. The two ships sailed west toward what they hoped would be a more promising tomorrow.

CHAPTER 15

The sea was calm. The moon would soon rise, bright and full. Those who managed to sleep did so fitfully. Those who could not sweltered in the nighttime heat. On the bridge, Captain Rooks and the rest of the officers of the watch clung to the reassuring Dutch reconnaissance report that the strait to the west was clear. Though the Japanese fleet seemed to be everywhere, at the moment the two ships seemed to be catching a break. The Japanese controlled all of the waterways leading out of the Java Sea except one. Sunda Strait, the narrow outlet into the Indian Ocean, lay open.

They had nothing to guide them but their eyesight. The *Houston,* with no radar, relied on the limited capabilities of the *Perth*'s air-search set, but it was generally confounded by the mess of islands cluttering these waters. So all eyes watched the dark. Off duty and hungry for sleep, Walter Winslow went to his cabin, navigating by the dim blue glow of battle lights set close to the deck at his feet. He switched on a flashlight briefly to find his cabin door, stepped in, and moved to his desk. Sitting on top of it was a carved wooden figurine, a Balinese head that he had bought on his first visit to Surabaya and had seen fit to name Gus. Standing in the dark, Winslow said, "We'll get through this O.K., won't we, Gus?" He felt sure his little friend on the totem had responded with a nod.

Eleven o'clock came and went. Soon the lighthouse on Babi Island was visible about a mile and a half off the starboard bow. Ahead and to port, Java's coastline dropped away where Bantam Bay opened up, then returned in the form of St. Nicholas Point, marking the northern opening of Sunda Strait. About seventy miles separate St. Nicholas Point, located at the strait's fifteen-mile-wide north-eastern bottleneck, and the Java Head lighthouse that marks its southwestern opening into the Indian Ocean. In the center of the strait lies a rocky cluster of islands whose very name evokes cata-clysm. The explosive self-destruction of the island of Krakatoa in 1883 reverberated from Bangkok to western Australia, shook the hulls of ships eighty-five miles east in Tanjung Priok, sent aloft the ashen remains of six square miles of rock, and killed some 36,000 people. It had reformed the contours of this rocky passage between the Sumatran and Javanese headlands. Because the entire Dutch East Indies lie along the fault line between the Eurasian and Australian tectonic plates, Java and the seas surrounding it are ever alive with volcanic activity.

Sunda Strait's powerful currents run always to the south, counter-parts to the northerly flows that prevail in the straits east of Java, in a sense making the entire island a vortex in a whirlpool more than six hundred miles across. Krakatoa's remnants are eddies in Sunda's flow, creating currents and rips strong enough to sink ships, the wreckage of which swiftly washes into the wide Indian Ocean. The deep paroxysms of geology that opened the celebrated passage had catered to the needs of traders and adventurers ever after. Merchants and travelers alike would use Sunda Strait for east-west transit. For those getting rich selling pepper and nutmeg, or exploring Oriental and Polynesian frontiers, it was the gateway to opportunity and dis-covery. And it had known war as well. For Kublai Khan, transiting the strait in the year 1293 with a thousand ships and twenty thou-sand men, it was an avenue to pacifying an upstart Javanese king who had snubbed the Mongol leader by sending his ambassador home less his nose. For Captain Rooks, who had brought his ship north through this strait seeking a fight with the enemy, it offered a route to survival.

"Ever since the night of the 23rd," wrote Lieutenant Hamlin, "when I last looked at this body of water, I had been getting on fine with a thoroughly fatalistic attitude. Not pessimism, just a fatalistic attitude. Now I began to see rosy visions of the *Houston* steaming into an Australian port. Then the long trip home for a new turret, and a visit with my wife."

On the *Perth,* yeoman of signals Eric Piper was "pacing the flag deck exhorting everyone to be alert." It was no idle pep talk; many of the sailors were faltering from exhaustion. When Lt. Lloyd Burgess finished his four-to-eight-P.M. navigator's watch that evening, he was so tired he couldn't remember a single order he had given or the name of a single crewman he had spoken to.

The strait ahead demanded the strictest vigilance. On either side, land formed a backdrop that rendered ship silhouettes invisible after dark. Commanding the machine-gun platform high in the *Houston's* foremast, Marine gunnery sergeant Walter Standish remarked to Sgt. Joseph M. Lusk and Pfc. Howard R. Charles, "They could hide a battleship out there, and we'd never see it until it attacked." The shoreline's shadows were a hazard of sorts, but after long stretches of combat duty on the open sea, Charles welcomed the sight of the Java mainland. "If we sink, at least there's land nearby," he thought, making a mental note of a constellation, the Southern Cross, that would mark the way to shore if the worst came to pass.

Around 11:15, Captain Waller spotted something, a dim silhouette low and dark on the water lying in the embrace of the shadows. He took it for a Dutch patrol craft and ordered his chief yeoman to flash a challenge on the Aldis signal lamp. After several prickling seconds the response came, a greenish light blinking a stream of nonsense. A stickler for good signal work—it was one of the few subjects where the captain's sense of humor left him—Waller ordered the challenge repeated, and as his yeoman did so, the unidentified vessel turned, revealing the telltale silhouette of a Japanese destroyer even as it started making smoke.

Captain Rooks spotted the ship just a beat after Waller did. Keeping station on the *Perth* nine hundred yards astern, he too considered it a Dutch picket until it became clear it was moving much faster than a patrol boat would. He ordered general quarters as a precaution and relieved his officer of the deck, Lieutenant Hamlin, who scrambled down to take station in the officer's booth of Turret One.

On the flag deck of the *Perth,* whose magazines were even lighter than the *Houston's,* with just twenty rounds per six-inch gun, Bill Bee sensed activity on the bridge above him. Manning the starboard eighteen-inch carbon arc spotlight, he noticed the cruiser's A and B turrets, the twin-mounted six-inch batteries just forward of him, swinging out to starboard. "I looked in the same direction as the guns were pointing and without the aid of night binoculars I could make out four objects which appeared to be destroyers coming towards us bearing about 020 degrees." The *Perth* turned slightly to port. The *Houston* followed. The first hint most of the American cruiser's crew got that anything was amiss was the sudden, startling flash and shock of the *Perth*'s main guns ripping into the night up ahead.

As the general quarters alarm began its dissonant electronic barking (its energizing effect never diminished: even a veteran like Lieutenant Winslow leapt from his bunk and "found myself in my shoes before I was fully awake"), Lieutenant Hamlin could see a red Very flare arc skyward from the vicinity of the unidentified ships. Captain Rooks, spying the dim shapes dead ahead and to starboard, ordered the after five-inch guns to illuminate them. They barked, lofting star shells to seven thousand yards, but the rounds burst short, producing a bright white glare and no silhouettes for the *Houston*'s gunners to range on. Another salvo extended the range, but still the phosphorous rounds failed to reach beyond and silhouette the target. When the *Houston*'s own main battery let loose, the range was just five thousand yards.

From his cinematic vantage point on the *Perth*'s flag bridge, Bill Bee was optimistic about the gunfire's results. "Our first salvos appeared to strike home on the leading DD's and I was expecting another burst from the forward turrets when flashes of gunfire from a number of directions diverted my attention. *Houston* too had now joined in the fray." The blast of the *Houston*'s first salvos nearly knocked Ens. Charles D. Smith clean overboard as he raced from his stateroom to his battle station in the officer's booth of Turret Two. In short order Smith's guns joined the fight. Exactly how many ships they faced, and of what type, was as yet unclear. The *Houston* had just fifty rounds left per eight-inch gun after the marathon engagement in the Java Sea. "We were desperately short of those eight-inch bricks," wrote Lieutenant Winslow, "and I knew the boys weren't wasting them on mirages."

Run for the strait or attack into the bay? For Captains Rooks and Waller, there was no real choice at all. With a full moon rising, the night offered only a thin cloak to movement. The long silhouettes slipping through the narrow waters around Sunda Strait could not fail to find them. Of course, cruiser commanders only ever go to sea with one purpose in mind: the destruction by gun salvo of every enemy ship they can bring within reach.

When the *Houston* was preparing to depart Tanjung Priok, seaman first class William J. Stewart had overheard an officer in the communications department tell Captain Rooks that the ship's stash of confidential publications was gathered and ready in case it became necessary to dispose of them by throwing them overboard. Stewart knew enough about security procedures to appreciate the implication that danger lay ahead. "I figured we were in for trouble that night."

Around 11:30 P.M., the *Houston*'s communications department transmitted the message that would be the last clue to the ship's fate the world would have for more than three years. For the ship whose death had already been announced gleefully and repeatedly by Japanese propagandists, that had avoided one trap after another, that was now steaming at flank speed toward the engagement the best minds of the Allied navies had sought, entering battle again was no cause to wax dramatic.

The last that anyone would ever hear from the USS *Houston,* the HMAS *Perth,* their remarkable commanders, or so many of their superb crews was a final radio transmission that Captain Rooks sent before the approaching cataclysm swallowed him forever. To Admiral Glassford, to the commander of the Sixteenth Naval District, to Radio Corregidor, and to the chief of naval operations, he reported: "ENEMY FORCES ENGAGED."

CHAPTER 16

Howard Brooks dared to hope they might make it through Sunda Strait. But when the star shells started bursting, illuminating the ship so terrifically as to render academic the setting of the sun, he despaired of it entirely. He could hear the drone of a single-engine plane. The damn thing was dropping flares all around them from up on high, tracking them just as the bobbing phosphorous pots had marked their night run after the Java Sea battle. The planes seemed to have lights for every occasion. The Japanese were professional sea warriors, no question about that. The *Houston* had all she could handle.

The first Japanese ship to respond to the surprising intrusion by the *Houston* and *Perth* into Bantam Bay was the destroyer *Fubuki*. Her commander was as startled by the encounter as his two counterparts were. Cdr. Yasuo Yamashita, spotting them about eleven thousand yards east of Babi Island, was unsure of their identity but confident his ship had not yet been seen. He rounded in behind them, keeping a safe distance of about five miles. He shadowed them until he saw the leading Allied ship flash a challenge on her signal lamp. At that point he ordered his torpedomen to fire nine Type 90 torpedoes while the destroyers *Harukaze* and *Hatakaze*, patrolling closer to the beach, laid a defensive smoke screen. As the two Allied cruisers accelerated, guns roaring, the *Fubuki* signaled the commander of other Japanese forces out there in the dark: "TWO MYSTERIOUS SHIPS ENTERING THE BAY."

The *Houston* and the *Perth,* had they been alerted to the presence of an enemy fleet, might have sought a way around it, even despite their weeks-long effort to grapple with it. Sufficiently forewarned, the Japanese invasion force might well have chosen to let the two cruisers slip by. There was great risk in exposing the important operation they were undertaking that night in a gun battle with two cruisers, even if their destruction would have eliminated Allied naval strength in the area.

The *Fubuki*'s early warning brought a prompt reaction from Rear Adm. Kenzaburo Hara, commander of the screening force accompanying the Western Attack Group. Immediately he ordered the light cruiser *Natori* and the six destroyers of the 5th and 11th Destroyer Divisions into action, and requested the help of two heavier hitters, the *Mikuma* and *Mogami* of Cruiser Division Seven, providing cover about fourteen nautical miles to the north. The two heavy cruisers hustled south, accompanied by the destroyer *Shikinami.* The Japanese warships fired illumination rounds. They rose in swift arcs and dropped white contrails that glowed in the blaze of drifting chemical suns.

In the officer's booth in Turret One, Lieutenant Hamlin got one last chance to peek through his periscope before the careening rush of strobe-lit events absorbed him completely in the management of his rocking main battery. He saw the *Perth* turning north and felt his own ship turning in behind her. The long shadows of enemy ships lurked at almost every compass point, flashes of gunfire blinking out all around. In the *Perth*'s plotting room, through the voice tube, Schoolmaster N. E. Lyons heard someone on the bridge say, "There are four to starboard." Then, "There are five on our port side." Then, "By God, they're all round us."

Marine private Jim Gee ran below to his general quarters station in the five-inch magazine. "You could see the ships just all over because we immediately turned on searchlights. And the Japanese turned on searchlights. . . . The place was like Fifth Avenue, you know. And I guess for the first time, I myself felt some apprehension but I went down in the magazine and things were moving so fast that you really didn't have time to think about the situation."

The *Perth* led the *Houston* in a tight circle, engaging targets as they revealed themselves with their searchlights, silhouettes, or flash of guns. While the Japanese searchlights reached them easily, those of the Allied ships lacked the reach to be effective in turn. "We were firing at any target that [we] saw, point blank—pick your target, fire at will," said Gee, part of the eight-man team of sailors and Marines in his magazine. The volume of fire coming back on them was heavy. Gee said, "We knew they were having hell upstairs."

Set up as a medical triage at general quarters, the *Houston*'s wardroom was full of corpsmen and stretcher-bearers waiting for something to do. Walter Winslow asked them what they knew about the enemy they were fighting. No one seemed to have much information. He started climbing a steel ladder toward the bridge, holding tight to the rail as the main battery's concussion jarred his grip. He ran across the communications deck, passing one of the ship's four quad-mounted 1.1-inch machine guns along the way. "Momentarily," Winslow recalled, "I caught a glimpse of tracers hustling out into the night. They were beautiful." By the time he reached the bridge, it seemed every mount on the *Houston* was firing.

> How reassuring it was to hear, at measured intervals, the blinding crash of the main battery, the sharp rapid crack of the five-inch guns, the steady, methodic *pom, pom, pom, pom* of the one-point-one's; and above all that, from their platforms high in the foremast and in the mainmast, came the continuous sweeping volleys of fifty-caliber machine guns which had been put there as anti-aircraft weapons, but which now suddenly found themselves engaging enemy surface targets.

Throughout the Battle of Sunda Strait, the fire controlmen, spotters, and gunners on the *Houston* and the *Perth* had no burden of identification to put pause in their work. Because there were only the two of them, as long as the ships stayed in line ahead with guns on broadside bearings, one ship never feared hitting the other. Keeping a simple column was not an entirely simple task—amid the maelstrom the cruisers could not always clearly see each other. But targets were plentiful. They appeared at ranges as close as fifteen hundred yards.

The Allied sailors had no firm idea of how many ships they faced. Under the circumstances they were impossible to count. The *Perth*'s first report was one destroyer and five unknowns. In the space of several awakening minutes, that became one cruiser and five destroyers. As the number climbed, the sense emerged that still larger things loomed out there in the dark. Five cruisers and ten destroyers. Twenty destroyers. Closer to shore, something else could be made out: the shadows of merchantmen and transports. There were dozens of them. As the spotters on the *Houston* and *Perth* came closer, they realized something astonishing: The enemy fleet they were fighting was the covering force for a landing operation.

Ahead and to port, clustered all around St. Nicholas Point, transports and auxiliaries were at anchor or on the beach, unloading their cargos of men, vehicles, weapons, and supplies as fast as the sergeants of Japan's Sixteenth Army could manage. Now, ostensibly looking to escape, two Allied cruisers had stumbled into the opportunity that the sharpest minds of their naval command had for difficult weeks tried to create for them. They had surprised a Japanese invasion force at the moment of its greatest vulnerability. Samuel Eliot Morison called it "the largest landing yet attempted in the Southwest Pacific."

The Japanese Western Attack Group's covering force included the heavy cruisers *Mogami* and the *Mikuma* as well as three divisions of destroyers and the light cruiser *Natori*. The landing force itself consisted of fifty-six transports and auxiliaries carrying Lt. Gen. Hitoshi Imamura's Sixteenth Army and its supply train, anchored all around the head of St. Nicholas Point, clear around to Merak on Sunda Strait.

General Imamura's sea route to western Java had finally opened when Admiral Helfrich sent the *Exeter* and her consorts east to join Admiral Doorman at Surabaya. Like the Allies, the Japanese too had thought their path would be free now of enemy ships. But in losing track of the *Houston* and the *Perth* after the Java Sea action, Japanese aerial reconnaissance had failed its fighting forces as surely as the Allied spotters had failed theirs.

The Allied ships should in fact have known that a Japanese force was headed their way. As would be revealed later, while they were docked in Tanjung Priok, the HMAS *Hobart* had spotted the Western Attack Group idling to the north near Banka Island. But the Australian light cruiser's report never got past the authorities in Bandung. According to Walter Winslow, Captain Rooks was innocent too of another vital piece of intelligence. As he and Captain

Waller were meeting with the Dutch at Batavia, a piece of paper sat on the desk of Maj. Gen. Wijbrandus Schilling, commander of the Dutch East Indian First Army in western Java, who was headquartered in the same building as the British Naval Liaison Office. It was an aircraft sighting report registering the approach of the southbound convoy the *Hobart* had seen. The enemy force was too large to miss. It had been spotted 150 miles north of Sunda Strait, steaming south at fifteen knots. But according to Walter Winslow, General Schilling did not know the *Houston* and the *Perth* were in port. As a consequence, the ships learned nothing of this important piece of reconnaissance work until its subjects were under their guns. On the way to Java with his convoy, General Imamura had fretted that he might land unopposed. Part of him seemed to crave a showdown with the enemy's samurai. He was getting his wish.

Given the close quarters of the bay, the Japanese had a hard time avoiding hitting their own ships. The two enemy cruisers were running a course straight through their midst, exposing the Japanese ships to either side—transports and patrol boats to the west, combatants to the east—to friendly fire with almost every salvo. While the Americans could see innumerable gun flashes on nearly every bearing, there were moments when very few shell splashes were landing near the *Houston*. Were the Japanese firing at their own?

As the *Perth* and *Houston* looped to port, changing course from the north back toward Bantam Bay, the main batteries and the starshell-firing after five-inch guns engaged targets to starboard. The forward five-inch guns trained to port. "The fight evolved into a melee with the *Houston* engaging targets on all sides at various ranges," Commander Maher wrote.

Deep in the bowels of the ship, plotting room officer Lt. Cdr. Sidney L. Smith had a rather less complicated view of the battle. There the sound of the gunners' labors arrived not as the cracking cacophony that rang eardrums topside but as a deep concussion whose reverberations were more readily felt in the sternum. He listened to the reports from the spotters, gunners, and rangefinders on his sound-powered phones and dialed that information into the Ford Instrument Company Range Keeper Mark 8. Its shafts, cams, rotors, and dials spun and turned and produced corrections that Commander Smith relayed to the gun mount crews.

Japanese destroyers bore in out of the darkness in groups of three and four, angling for a torpedo attack. The ships of Destroyer Division Twelve, which had been idling on the other side of St. Nicholas Point, roared out of Sunda Strait and curved around into Bantam Bay. They were dashingly commanded, rushing in to just a few hundred yards and firing furiously at a ship more than four times their size. At 11:40 the *Shirayuki* and the *Hatsuyuki,* following the *Natori,* loosed nine torpedoes each. The *Asakaze* unloaded six more, the light cruiser *Natori* four. Captain Rooks swerved the ship as he had done during the aerial bombardments in the Flores Sea, seeking now to avoid not aerial bombs but the even more forbidding threat of torpedoes streaking unseen under the waves. None of these first twenty-eight fish found the mark.

The enemy tin cans stabbed the Allied ships with their search-lights. The illumination benefited the gunners on the *Mogami* and *Mikuma,* lying off in the darkness. Having hustled south to engage the unexpected raiders, the two cruisers stood off some twelve thousand yards away, protected from return fire by the blinding glare of the destroyers' spots. The *Houston's* machine gunners locked in fresh belts and raced to quench the lights with lead. In the lethal game of hide-and-seek, the Japanese alternated their searchlight beams, shuttering one and opening another to avoid drawing fire. According to Ray Parkin in the HMAS *Perth,* "The tactics were to expose the beam of one light for a few seconds to bathe *Perth* stark against the night; then that beam would be folded back within the iris shutters and another, elsewhere, would take its place. Heavy shell-fire criss-crossing them tore the sea to shreds and raised white monuments caught in the beams of light."

At 11:26 the *Perth* took a projectile through the forward funnel. Another hit the flag deck a few minutes later. About ten minutes before midnight, under sustained fire from the *Mogami* and *Mikuma,* she took a waterline hit on the starboard side, starting severe flooding in the seamen's mess.

Commander Maher and the men in the *Houston's* forward main battery directors were confronting their own challenges. Owing to the extreme height of their placement in *Northampton*-class cruisers, the blending of the enemy with the coastline, and the obscuring effects of enemy searchlights and smoke, the crew in Director One had trouble training their big batteries on the speedy targets. But every officer on the *Houston's* bridge saw three Japanese destroyers cross their wake at about three thousand yards. Minutes later, a pair of torpedoes were seen bubbling in from astern, one to each side of the ship. Some forty-five minutes had passed since the *Houston*'s general quarters alarm started screaming.

Commander Maher had the conn now. He steered straight ahead, cutting a narrow path between the torpedoes chasing from astern and allowing them to pass, one ten feet to port and the other about ten yards to starboard. His guns were madly engaged in all directions. Whenever Japanese destroyers approached, every gun that could bear zeroed in on the close-range threat. Crews assigned to illuminate with star shells had all they could handle trying to silhouette targets for the main battery amid the heavy smoke and Captain Rooks's frequent course changes.

The cataclysmic crash of the cruiser's salvos were echoed by the flash and roar of Japanese guns, as if returning from the far wall of a canyon. The *Houston* took her first hit when a projectile struck the forecastle, starting fires in the paint locker that danced brightly for about a quarter of an hour. The night air was rancid with cordite. Though the winds were still, the wisps of gray-white muzzle smoke flying from the *Houston*'s guns fell quickly away, left behind like an airborne wake covering her trail of foam.

★

Warships are divided into two worlds. One—encompassing the bridge, conning tower, and signal platforms—is devoted to observation, judgment, and command. The other—down in the engine rooms and firerooms, in the gun mounts and turrets, handling rooms and magazines, aid and repair stations—functions by procedure, repetition, and rote. Vital though the work belowdecks is, little of it depends on what the men there see around them, for indeed they see very little. They experience the battle through the skin: the deep, vibrating hum of the power plant, the rumblings and crashing of the gun batteries.

Deep in the *Houston,* in the forward powder magazine, seaman second class Otto Schwarz only knew what he could hear on the intercom and on the headsets. Layers of armor and steel decking insulated him from the sounds of battle. Near misses announced themselves with a staccato cascade of shrapnel against the steel hull. "It sounded like somebody throwing pebbles at the ship."

Ray Parkin, as the *Perth*'s chief quartermaster, was better positioned to take in the spectacle of the pyrotechnics directed the two cruisers' way.

> The whole ship was alive with orders streaming out and information streaming in, like the blood pounding through the heart of a human body. The glare of searchlights; the flash, blast and roar of her own guns; tracer ammunition stitching light across the sky; phosphorescent wakes entangling; ships on fire; star-shells festooned in short strings in the sky—all these confused the evidence of one's eyes. Brilliance and blackness struggled for supremacy. Smoke trails hung jumbled like curtains in the flies and wings of some immense stage.

Time rushed by in freeze-frame sequence, an adrenaline-enabled illusion that permits even the most confused crazy quilt of events to unfold in clear slow motion. It was collective survival in action. There was an overwhelming imperative to perform one's duty perfectly, mechanically, in the stop-time of life-and-death concentration. They had to have faith that their unseen shipmates manning other stations were locked into the cycle with that same stone-cold focus. As a sailor from another war put it, "This kind of fighting demands the purest form of courage. . . . We must not let our imaginations run riot. . . . A man has to exercise perfect mastery over his emotions, carrying out his duties in a mechanical manner."

Stationed on a hoist in one of the five-inch magazines, seaman second class Donald Brain saw the power to his compartment die and the hydraulics fail, making it necessary to work the hoist by hand. Brain grabbed some hand cranks out of the ready locker, set them up, and was so busy cranking five-inch projectiles up to the gun deck that he had no time to fret when an enemy shell came plowing through the side of the ship just forward of his station, rumbling like a freight train. "That is just what it sounded like . . . just a rumble and a bang and a crash, and on it went." He would crank that hoist until the magazine was empty.

The furious but uncoordinated nature of the *Houston*'s gunnery—directors abandoned and manned again, rangefinders disabled, turrets switched to manual control and from director to director—meant that though a large number of Japanese ships were engaged in the battle, seldom was the *Houston*'s fire concentrated sufficiently to sink any given ship.

Her five-inch gunners did the best they could. Most of them had been together since the ship left the States in October 1940. Commander Maher had worked them hard and it bore fruit now. Even on local control, the captains of the five-inch mounts performed superbly. Their fire struck the destroyer *Harukaze* on the bridge and in the engine room, damaging her rudder, killing three, injuring fifteen, and forcing her to abort a torpedo launch. Their volleys also ravaged the destroyer *Shirayuki*. Though the *Houston* had just one working thirty-six-inch searchlight on each side, her gunners managed to range on the *Mikuma,* hitting her with a projectile that disabled her main electrical switchboard and silenced her batteries and searchlights for several minutes. But Capt. Shakao Sakiyama's electricians wired around the trouble, enabling her to resume the bombardment with even greater effectiveness as she closed to within ten thousand yards.

Having gone through the Java Sea battle, Howard Brooks recognized the tenor of the enemy cruisers' eight-inch main battery fire. The big guns sounded much closer now than they had the previous afternoon. The destroyers were far easier to see. "We could see the whole outline of these Japanese destroyers that were firing at us," Brooks said. "We could see the guys on the guns, Japanese sailors, their forms, moving around the guns. They were pouring fire right into our ship."

"Oh Lord, sometimes you felt like you could reach out and shake their hands," said John Bartz. He took shelter behind the back of his gun's seat as bullets pinged all around the makeshift metal shield. The Marine second lieutenant in charge of his mount, Edward M. Barrett, ordered him to keep shooting, and Bartz did so, keeping to his unorthodox shielded firing position, reaching around the seat back to elevate and depress the guns, and grabbing the foot-pedal trigger with his other hand to fire.

"The tin cans got so close to us . . . that when they got under two hundred yards, you couldn't train on them. . . . You'd hit the top of their stacks," said John Wisecup, on gun number seven, aftermost on the boat deck's starboard side. With some satisfaction Wisecup could tell that the 1.1-inch pom-poms were getting to the enemy. "They'd rake that topside, and you could hear them yelling over there. You could see their faces. You could hear the guys on the bridge hollering because they were that close when they hit them."

High in the *Houston's* foremast, standing on a twenty-by-twenty-foot corrugated steel platform where four .50-caliber machine guns were mounted, Howard Charles had a commanding view of the battle. There he had a measurable advantage over gunners stationed closer to the sea. It was easier to fire down on a target than to hit it firing straight out over the water. With orders to quench enemy searchlights wherever they might shine, he steered his tracers into the glare of the unshuttered enemy lenses. All things considered, he preferred this lofty view to the cloistered depths of the magazines or handling rooms. Ever since the ship departed Tanjung Priok, he had been stirring restlessly in his bid for a little sleep before his mid-watch shift began at midnight. But a kapok life jacket made a lousy mattress and a steel helmet an even worse pillow. So he had lain there watching the stars slide through the heavens until more compelling lights and clouds seized his attention.

Charles lost track of how many belts he and his loader had ripped through the gun chamber of his .50. Each time a new one was in place, the loader would tap him on the shoulder and he would pull the cocking lever twice and seize down on the handle bar trigger, showering red tracers at any Japanese ship that dared to brandish her beams. It might have seemed like a county fair target gallery, except that the Japanese ships sliding into view out of the night returned fire all too vigorously. The day before, during the Battle of the Java Sea, the ship's machine gunners had stood by uselessly as the main batteries traded salvos at a range of a dozen miles or more. Now even the smallest guns played a part in the main event.

*

The men of the *Houston's* engineering department had all the work they could handle keeping their complex machinery from yielding to the violent shakedown the cruiser's helmsman and gunners were giving it. Changes in speed, sudden course adjustments, the impact of hits delivered and received—all conspired against the orderly operation of a steam-driven power plant. Heavy and powerful though the 107,000-horsepower geared-turbine power plant was, its operation was a delicate business that required experience up and down the chain of command, and an intuitive understanding between men at different stations. A radical maneuver such as a crashback, designed to pull a sharp emergency turn by putting the shafts on the inside of the turn suddenly into reverse, requires the entire black gang to work together flawlessly. The throttleman watching the engine order telegraph responds to the bridge's order by spinning the large handwheels to cut the flow of steam through the "ahead" throttle and simultaneously cracks the "astern" throttle to slow down and stop the turbine wheels. As he opens wide the astern throttle, he risks much: Too much steam can strip the turbine blades; too little risks a slow response to a vital order—equally sinful in the snap-to-it world of a shipboard engineering department, and more so under fire.

Only an experienced fireroom watch can contend with the sudden reduction to zero of the system's demand for their steam. Trained intensively to observe the spray of vaporized bunker oil from the burners and monitor the efficiency of the nozzles and their combustion cones, they cut in or shut off burners to keep steady pressure in the main and auxiliary steam lines. Water tenders watch the boiler water level—too high a level sends water into the turbines with the steam, wrecking the turbines; too low and the boilers can burn out. Machinist's mates stay busy working thirty-odd pumps to meet the plant's rapidly fluctuating water demands. Meanwhile, the system's efficiency is subject to any number of external variables, from the temperature of the water outside the hull, which influences the effectiveness of the condenser that returns boiler water to the system, to the viscosity of the bunker oil sprayed through the burners.

"We were making full power," Lt. Robert Fulton recalled. "The throttle was wide open. We were rolling along and the machinery in this one engine room was working just fine." Around 12:15 A.M., the ship took a grievous hit aft on the starboard side. Fulton felt a slight tremor, and no more. Others felt it more heavily, though no one could ever quite tell whether it was a torpedo hit or a salvo of heavy projectiles. Whatever it was shattered the after engine room.

A shower of giant sparks cascaded through the bulkhead separating the number-four fireroom from the after engine room. Paint chips flew off the bulkhead and tore into exposed flesh like little blades. With the destruction of the main feedwater pumps in the after engine room, the four boilers in firerooms three and four were suddenly starved for water. The glasses indicating the water level inside the boilers went dry. A water tender started the emergency feed pumps, but they delivered too little too late. Before fireman first class George Detre's horrified eyes, the brickwork of two of the boilers driving the ship's inboard pair of screws were turned into molten slurry.

In the forward engine room, Lieutenant Fulton wondered what had happened in the after engine room. The only evidence he had of the compartment's fate was a sudden loss of communication with his chief engineer, Lt. Cdr. Richard Gingras. It could not have been pretty, the great blast ripping open the hull, tossing the crew about like puppets, melting the steel floor gratings in a flash, opening the way for the sea to flow in and quench the roasting steel, summoning a hissing wash of seawater and steam.

Fulton's glimpse of that hell was a narrow and quick one, and it came via an unlikely window: the engine order telegraph. "When the ship was underway my job was to see to it that the two shafts of the forward engine room operated exactly the same as those in the after engine room," Fulton said. When the captain signaled an engine order, it was relayed via the bridge's engine order telegraph to Commander Gingras in the after control engine room, which drove the ship's two inboard shafts. Gingras matched the setting on his own telegraph, thus confirming to the bridge his compliance with the order and passing the order to Fulton in the forward engine room, who mimicked his superior's actions.

Looking at the dial of the engine order telegraph, Fulton saw something curious happen. All of a sudden the indicator's pointer, which usually moved so deliberately in response to specific orders, was waving back and forth quickly. "It made no sense at all," Fulton said. "We couldn't understand it." He thought the telegraph had malfunctioned somehow. But synchros didn't go haywire like that. Nor, to say the least, did the engine orders, so faithfully mimicked downstream from the bridge. Fulton tried both of the available JV phone circuits but got no answer on either one. It would dawn on him later that the wagging indicator pointer was in all likelihood the act of a human hand, an improvised emergency signal from someone attempting in his scalding final moments to communicate disaster to the captain on the bridge. "It is exactly the kind of quick thinking that was typical of Mr. Gingras," Fulton wrote.

Up on deck, above the after engine room, gusts of steam from shattered high-pressure pipes kept repair parties from doing their job. On the boat deck, the venting steam forced men on the five-inch guns and after antiaircraft gun director to abandon their stations. The after guns were manned mostly by the ship's Marine detachment. There was not a moment of panic among them. Before abandoning their steam-swamped battle stations, they actually requested permission to do so—and promptly returned to the boat deck as soon as the heat subsided.

CHAPTER 17

Reaching the signal bridge, Walter Winslow found that Captain Rooks had decamped from the bridge and gone one deck below to the armored conning tower, a protected command station with narrow slits affording a limited view right out over Turret Two. It was a much safer place from which to command a warship in battle, and Rooks needed every advantage he could get. Efficient communication was nearly impossible owing to the racket of the ship's own gunfire. Every available phone circuit was abuzz with urgent reports and orders and acknowledgments. "I wanted desperately to know what we were up against, but to ask would have been absurd," Winslow recalled. "From the captain to the men talking on the overburdened battle-phones, everyone in conn was grimly absorbed in fighting the ship."

Rooks was doubtlessly having a hard time following the *Perth* up ahead. The only sign of the Australian ship was the yellow-orange strobes of her guns biting into the smoky night. Unlike the *Houston,* she still carried torpedoes, 21-inchers. The U.S. Navy had decided in 1933 that it was risky to field the volatile weapons on its heavy cruisers. So the *Houston's* torpedo mounts were taken off and the open hull spaces plated over. Hec Waller managed to fire four of the

Perth's eight torpedoes at the outlines of targets looming to starboard.

Waller stood on the bridge with nine other officers and chiefs. As the forward batteries sustained their measured cadence, flashing hell at the enemy and jarring to pieces furniture and other loosely anchored fixtures, Waller maintained an outward calm, his voice steady as he issued helm orders. He periodically vented pressure, as when a spotlight stabbed him—"For God's sake shoot that bloody light out!" But by and large he kept so quiet that silence became contagious. Lloyd Burgess "felt his heart hammering and all sound was within himself, so that he could almost hear the blood pumping through his body." Waller's composure defied the increasing tempo of the apocalypse swirling outside his pilothouse. He kept calm even when the worst happened and the first Japanese torpedo bore down and struck the *Perth,* marking the beginning of its end.

She was barreling along at twenty-eight knots when the fish struck near the forward engine room. The crash and the roar shook her and departed, leaving behind a strange silence in her guts. "Some vital pulse had stopped," Ray Parkin remembered. The intercom crackled with the report, "Forward engine room out. Speed reduced," to which Captain Waller's response was, "Very good."

Gunfire battered the *Perth,* knocking away the seaplane catapult back aft. Word followed that B turret forward and X and Y turrets aft were out of projectiles, and that the loaders were ramming practice rounds boosted by an extra bag of powder for better hitting effect. Then A turret checked in, reporting just five projectiles left. Waller acknowledged each piece of bad news by saying, "Very good."

The *Perth* started slowing with the first torpedo hit, her gyro smashed and the fire-control system gone with it, guns switched over to local control. The crews on her two forward four-inch mounts were all killed by blasts. The men on the other secondary guns, also out of ammunition, were left to fire star shells and practice rounds at the enemy. When a sailor wondered aloud in the dark, "What do we use after these?" an older man suggested they raid the potato locker for ordnance.

The *Perth's* deck lurched again as a second torpedo struck. This one seemed to lift the ship from a point right under the bridge. The rising deck threw Captain Waller and his nine officers and chiefs upward, and they fell down again, knocked to their knees.

"Christ, that's torn it," Waller said. "Abandon ship."

The gunnery officer, Peter Hancox, asked, "*Prepare* to abandon ship, sir?"

"No," the captain said. "Abandon ship." Waller's instincts about ships were not prone to be wrong.

The usual procedure was to secure the engines so that the ship would drift to a stop, thus allowing crewmen to leave the ship in the vicinity of lifeboats as they were lowered from the halyards. Waller instead ordered the chief quartermaster to leave the engines at half speed ahead. "I don't want the Old Girl to take anyone with her," he said. The suction of a sinking ship could draw survivors under. Perhaps Waller considered it a matter of choosing one's poison. The crews of the *Perth*'s A and B turrets left their gun houses and rushed out on deck to release the life rafts, but their timing was unfortunate. They reached the open air just in time to be cut down by heavy shellfire.

John Harper, the navigator, ran through passageways spreading the captain's order to abandon ship. Reaching the sick bay, he found carnage. The scattered mess of bloodied sailors in their white uniforms reminded him of strings of red and white ceremonial flags, stricken and piled in a red and white heap. Survivors sat there "stupefied with shock" and required sharp reminders to get moving. Collapsed bulkheads and piles of debris nearly blocked their exit through interior passageways, and outside, they found the whole port side amidships buried by the haphazardly cantilevered ruins of the catapult and crane. The glare of Japanese searchlights helped Harper pick his way to the rail and illuminated a clear expanse of water into which to leap.

He swam to a small balsa raft and hung on as he watched the *Perth* draw away from him, still making headway. The quarterdeck was crowded with sailors hesitant to go overboard for fear of landing in the cutting swirl of the ship's outboard propellers. Then, Ray Parkin wrote, "across the sea and under the sky came a great roar."

> From under X turret a huge ragged geyser of shattered water spouted skywards, ringed with debris and oil-fuel. The right and left six-inch guns of X turret jumped their trunnions, and each gun was left pointing outwards from the other. The ship gave a violent nervous twitch. Against the ice-

white light the mass of milling figures shot into the air, turning over and over like acrobats or tossed rag-dolls.

Leading seaman H. Keith Gosden, escaping Y turret's lobby, was thrown skyward by one of the torpedo blasts. "Light, almost gay, in that mad moment," he felt the urge to sing and dance in the air. When he hit the deck again a wave of water produced by the explosion washed him overboard, and as he fell into the sea he envisioned the telegram his mother would receive announcing his loss, and the tears that would fall from her eyes upon learning the news.

John Harper "was suddenly appalled at the amount of shellfire falling amongst the survivors." It was worse still on the ship. She had taken on a hard list to port. "Pieces could be seen flying off as salvoes exploded with wicked flashes all over her," he wrote. The *Perth*'s navigator lay in the water and watched as his ship died. In his heart, sadness warred with pride.

When a ship turns onto its side, the world goes ninety degrees off kilter. Without the sky to orient them, sailors trying to escape from belowdecks find the familiar interior of the ship has become a house of mirrors. Decks become bulkheads and bulkheads decks, ladders become rails running surrealistically sideways, and athwartship passageways become deep wells yawning at one's feet.

Lt. Frank Gillan, one of the *Perth*'s engineers, was struggling to get free of the turtling ship. Stationed with three other men in the fireroom, or stokehold as the Aussies called it, they were losing their bearings as their steel-enclosed world made a disorienting ninety-degree rotation. Leaving the fireroom, they realized their best route to the main deck was a hatch some distance down the passageway they were standing in. The hatch opened to the level above them, the enclosed torpedo space below the four-inch-gun deck. It was a path they had trodden many times when the world was on its feet. Now, with the ship nearly on her side, a significant obstacle lay in their path: the athwartship passage opened below them like a five-foot-wide trapdoor into an abyss. One of the stokers that Lieutenant Gillan had helped escape from the fireroom tried to jump across, but his boots slipped on takeoff and he fell short, vanishing into the depths of the upended passageway that swallowed his scream.

The other two men with Gillan successfully leaped the pit and kept running. Wearing a Royal Australian Navy ball cap with a coal miner's lamp strapped to it, Gillan followed, but the seconds that separated them were meaningful. Ahead, he could see ocean water cascading through the hatch leading upward to his freedom. He froze for a moment, feeling the natural impulse to prefer a delayed but sure drowning to a more immediate but only slightly less certain one. Then he gathered his courage, took a deep breath, and plunged upward into the water, fighting his way up through the hatch. He succeeded, but even in his success he had to confront a sickening question. If the ship finally capsized, where would "up" finally take him? In moving toward the main deck, he might in fact be seeking her bottom as the ship turned turtle and came down on top of him.

She hadn't gone fully over yet. Gillan could still feel that the ship was making forward headway while sinking by the bow. He realized this meant the water must be entering the ship from the forward compartments and flowing toward the rear. And he knew the inflow would carry with it assorted flotsam—entangling lines and nets, as well as heavier objects—that could prove dangerous if he fought against the natural progression of things.

In a moment of clarity, Gillan realized that his only hope was to surrender to the sea. If he relaxed and let it take him, it might just carry him free of the ship as it sought its own escape from the labyrinth. He tucked his knees up under his chin and began rolling aft as the water embraced him. Like a small boulder at the bottom of a rushing stream, he tumbled backward through a wreckage-filled passageway, gulping enough air to survive and thinking all along, *Thank God my Mae {West} isn't fully inflated. I'd be up against the roof if it was and would never get out.*

Lungs burning, Gillan felt himself bump up against the ship's rail. He was finally free of the enclosed torpedo space. The cord to his miner's lamp snagged momentarily on the rail, but then he was floating again, being washed up and down, unsure of which direction the surface was. He felt currents whirlpooling around him. The sensation evoked an amusement park ride before the flashing of red, green, and purple lights marked the possibility that his brain was starving for oxygen as he drowned.

Then the sea seemed to yield. There were no more currents, no more detritus of a battered ship grasping at him. All was still. He basked for a moment in a dying repose before it occurred to him, *If I don't struggle now I'll drown.* He clawed at the water around him, sensing the surface above and reaching furiously for it. At last there came an explosion of water and tarry black bunker oil as Lieutenant Gillan broke the surface and sucked air again.

Any frail hope for the *Perth* was lost when a fourth torpedo struck the ship forward on the port side, throwing high another foaming column of seawater. This broke her. As survivors scrambled overboard and swam clear, they looked back and saw her not so much sink as drive herself under water. "Her four propellers came clear of the sea," Ray Parkin wrote. "Three of the shafts were now broken, but the fourth was still turning. She went down for all the world as if she were steaming over the horizon from them. 'She did not sink,' they said, 'she *steamed* out.'"

Frank Gillan caught the very last sight of the ship. Surfacing, he grabbed a biscuit tin floating nearby and fastened his arms around it, then turned and looked back in the direction of the ship. About a hundred feet away from him, a large curved blade—one of the *Perth*'s propeller screws—flicked the air one last time and disappeared beneath the ocean's surface, carrying Captain Waller, dead on the bridge, and hundreds of others to their final resting place at twenty fathoms.

"I'm the last man out of that ship alive," Gillan announced to the stars overhead. "God, I thank you."

CHAPTER 18

At about ten minutes after midnight, the *Perth* could be seen from the *Houston*'s bridge and forward deck spaces, apparently dead in the water and sinking. "When Captain Rooks realized she was finished and escape was impossible," Walter Winslow wrote, "he turned the *Houston* back toward the transports, determined to sell his ship dearly. From that moment on, every ship in the area was an enemy, and we began a savage fight to the death."

The *Houston* was alone, facing attacks not only from the *Mikuma* and *Mogami* looming some twelve thousand yards to the north but also from two full destroyer squadrons and assorted armed auxiliaries. In their concentrated assault, direct hits from Japanese gunfire were following fast and furious, smashing the *Houston* up forward, producing a killing storm of shrapnel and flames. In the warren of passageways and compartments below, the noise came as a nearly continuous roaring, droning hum.

"We couldn't see," Jim Gee said. "We knew that we'd been hit a few times. We knew we had a good list on the ship. We knew that we were getting real close to the bottom of that ammunition deck, and all we had to send up were star shells. And, of course, we could hear a loud-speaker; every now and then, the captain would come on the loud-speaker and say something." So long as that voice was there, strong and fatherly, all would be well. The intangible qualities of leadership emerged from small, prosaic things such as being there and speaking for yourself when the moment required it. Any number of minutiae connected to personality and judgment coalesced into something larger and could pay good dividends in terms of performance when the time came. The *Houston*'s time was now.

Spotlights reached for Captain Rooks's cruiser and missed, summoning the shapes of Japanese transports nearer to shore. The *Houston*'s forward Mark 19 antiaircraft director got their range and fed an accurate setup to the main and secondary batteries, which banged away to port in roaring acknowledgment of the gift. Whenever a wayward searchlight beam settled on a transport or a support vessel, they would work her over furiously.

Then, amid the chaotic melee out to sea, a series of sharp detonations could be heard closer to the beach. Within sixty minutes of their first encounter with the Allied cruisers, the Japanese ships cutting the shell-torn seas outside Sunda Strait had put eighty-seven torpedoes into the water. More than a few hit appropriately hostile targets. But most of them churned harmlessly on toward the Japanese transports and auxiliaries clustered near shore. No fewer than four Japanese transports took torpedoes in their bellies, most all of them fired by Japanese destroyers. By widespread eyewitness accounts, at least four transports and a minesweeper were sunk or heavily damaged in the fratricidal undersea crossfire.

Among these was the *Shinshu Maru*, the headquarters vessel of Lt. Gen. Hitoshi Imamura himself.* As that shattered transport rolled over, tons of heavy equipment, including badly needed radio equipment belonging to the Sixteenth Army, slid from its decks into the sea. Joining hundreds of his troops in the water, Imamura rode driftwood for several hours before a boat finally retrieved him. When he was at last delivered to shore, the drenched general parked himself on a pile of bamboo and was finally forced to confront the humor in the debacle as an aide congratulated him on a successful landing on Java.

Imamura thought that torpedoes from the *Houston* had hit his ship. Given her proximity, it was natural to make this assumption, though it was of course patently impossible, as the *Houston* no longer carried torpedo tubes. Still, the general's own chief of staff allowed

---

*Imamura's flagship is called the *Ryujo Maru* in some accounts.

the notion to stand. Later, receiving a Japanese commodore sent to apologize to him for the navy's error, he discouraged the apology, preferring the honor of taking a blow from enemy samurai to the embarrassment of fratricide. "Let the *Houston* have the credit," he said.

Over on the *Houston,* just as the flow of steam was stanched from the destroyed after engine room, permitting the after director crew to return to their stations, the ship lost use of her brain. A torpedo struck the ship to starboard below the communications deck, plunging Central Station and the plotting room into darkness. They could hear the thunder of the *Houston*'s own gunfire, the rumble and snort of the enemy shells striking. At least once came a horrible, high-pitched metallic grinding sound that might have been the sound of a dud torpedo nosing along the side and bottom of the ship's hull. The crew from Plot, on the starboard side of the ship, withdrew into Central Station, away from the vulnerable sides of the hull.

By the red glow of emergency battle lanterns, they weighed their options. With his rangekeeper out of action, Lt. Cdr. Sidney Smith decided there was little point in staying put. He got on the phone to the bridge and asked permission to abandon Central Station. He and his plotting department team were ordered topside to assist as needed.

Escaping from Central Station was among the most harrowing gauntlets to run. With the watertight doors sealed for battle, the only way out was straight up through the hollow trunk of the foremast, which reached down through all the *Houston*'s decks like a taproot into Sidney Smith's netherworld. Studded inside with steel rungs, it provided a direct route to the main deck and superstructure. Traversing that vertical chute for the first time, in pitch blackness and in the midst of combat, was an ordeal that radioman second class David Flynn would not soon forget. "You didn't know where the hell you were," he said. "I had never used this escape route in my life before." He began climbing, estimating his progress by triangulating to the frightening cacophony of battle outside.

Clarence "Skip" Schilperoort, an electrician's mate assigned to the main battery battle telephone switchboard in Plot, was the second man up the trunk. He found the hatch to the officers' stateroom, exited and walked aft toward the quarterdeck, came to another hatch, and unscrewed the peephole that enabled a cautionary glance through. All he could see were flames. On the intercom he had heard

the hue and cry as spotters called out sightings for the fire controlmen and gun crews. Now, moving forward through a passageway
and looking for the hatch to the main deck between Turrets One and
Two, Schilperoort reached open air and saw enemy destroyers driving in close and peeling away. "I thought I was looking at a moving
picture," he said. Deciding that standing there and gawking was a
sure way to get himself killed, he retreated behind Turret One, lee-
ward of the gunfire.

David Flynn kept climbing up the foremast's trunk. He must
have missed the hatch, because he emerged three levels above the
main deck, behind the conning tower in the flag plotting station. A
hatch to the outside was open, and he exited just in time to see the
flash of an explosion that blew shrapnel into his left leg. Shortly
thereafter he got the word that Captain Rooks had been hit too.

CHAPTER 19

In the choking confines of Turret Two, the ripe air heavy with heat, Red Huffman was head down on the indicator dial, listening for the gun captain's signal to fire. The enemy ships were so close now that the guns were elevated downward, below zero degrees. Having rammed and fired twenty-seven salvos, the turret crew was hoisting and loading the twenty-eighth when there came a sharp metallic shock and an intense spray of sparks. The gun house had taken a direct hit square on the faceplate by a shell from a Japanese cruiser lying off somewhere in the dark.

The projectile failed to explode, but because the turret's powder flaps had been opened to enable the men in the powder circle to pass powder bags into the gun chamber, the sparks alone were deadly. They splashed into the gun house and flowed all around the bags, igniting them. A flash fire engulfed the entire gun mount and roared down into the powder circle and shell deck.

The only men inside who were fully shielded from the inferno were Ens. Charles D. Smith, his talker, and two rangefinder operators stationed in the flameproof turret officer's booth. Smith pulled the lever that activated the turret's sprinkler system and peered through the booth's glass port to assess the damage. All he could see was "a red haze as if on a foggy night." The smoke from the fires was tinted scarlet by all the burning particles of powder flying around as if seeking an exit from the blazing enclosure.

"Everything lit up," Huffman said. "Oh God, it was all flames." Seated above and forward of the triple mount's gun breeches, he was lashed by a long tongue of flame that came reaching up around the turret's split-level deck. Because the pointer's station was severely cramped for headroom, he wasn't able to don his battle helmet. The fire burned away the hair on the back of his head and roasted his back.

"I'm telling you what I did when I had my senses about me," Huffman said. "After that, you operated automatically. You knew what to do and you did it, and you didn't know *when* you did it or *how* you did or *what* you did, but you did it. You were trained to do it. For years I trained on that damn thing. All of us did. Everybody knew exactly what to do. We were trained to fight to the death, and that was what we did. It's a hell of a thing to say, but it's true."

Stunned by shock, badly burned, hands moving with sharp purpose but unguided by active thought, Huffman opened the gun house's port-side hatch and climbed through it. "I was getting out of there. It was a raging inferno. I didn't know what I was doing." With the turret trained out to starboard, the hatch led not to the communications deck but out into a void of space with a ten-foot drop straight down to the main deck. "There was nothing under me but air," Huffman said. "But I never had that all in my mind. I really wasn't thinking at all. I was just getting away from all that fire." He landed hard on the teak. Memory failed him for a time from that point on. According to Ensign Smith, only seven of the fifty-eight men in Turret Two's assembly—the turret, the magazine, the powder circle, the gun deck, and so on—escaped alive. Aside from Smith, Huffman, gunner's mate third class James L. Cash, seaman first class Ray Goodson, and some lucky souls inside the officer's booth, everyone else succumbed to the inferno of powder bags.

When the fires inside the turret grew hot enough to begin cracking the thick glass of his viewing port, Smith and the others abandoned the officer's booth and scrambled clear of the turret as it burned up from within. Looking back, they were astonished to see the booth hatch open again and seaman first class Henry S. Grodzky stumble out onto the communications deck. Burned worse than Red Huffman was, he collapsed. Smith ran to him and carried him to the lee of the radio shack, where a medical triage had been set up.

On Turret Two's shell deck, seaman first class William J. Stewart felt a slight jarring impact and saw a bright spark fly through an opening in the top of the barbette. Knowing that the tightly sealed gun housing was not readily permeable to flames, Stewart saw the spark as a sign of a terrible conflagration above. "We knew the turret was on fire and that if we were to survive, why, we had better start getting out," he said. When he and the six other men on the shell deck wrestled open the four-foot-high watertight hatch, they were met by a pressurized blast of flame. "It was just like coming out of a blow torch and was bouncing off the bulkhead about eight feet in front of us," Stewart said. He might have made it unscathed, but his dungarees got snared on the hatch and fire washed all around him. Bare from the waist up, he suffered horrible black burns on his exposed torso, face, and ears. His hair, thoroughly drenched with sweat, "burned down to a charcoal mat and apparently protected the top of my head," Stewart wrote. He worked his dungarees free and, numb but soon to be in need of morphine, escaped with the six others. He headed to the aid station, high on his own adrenaline.

Red Huffman and another sailor were struggling with a fire hose, trying to train it on Turret Two, but it pulled no water. Back near the number-one radio room, Ensign Smith and some others found another hose and played it into the burning enclosure. To Smith's surprise, the lights were still on inside, but they did not long survive the torrent from the fire hose. The electrical circuit and the lights died with the flames. The firefighters had no inclination to explore the dark turret's blowtorched innards any further. Terrible fumes from inside drove them back.

The flames churning out of Turret Two had briefly cast the *Houston* in sharp relief for enemy gunners. In the *Mikuma,* sailors boisterously celebrated the tall lance of flame that leaped from what appeared to them to be the *Houston's* bridge. Although those fires were swiftly quenched, projectiles flew to the ship like flies to a porch lamp, striking in rapid succession and filling the air with shrapnel, dust, and debris.

The random nature of the carnage made it futile to anticipate or avoid. "It's coming from all sides," Paul Papish said. "You don't know where to go on the ship for protection. . . . Up the ladder you go, and you figure, 'Well, bull! This isn't the place to be!' So you head back down." The sick bay, the brig, the life jacket locker, the wardroom, and the foremast machine gun platform all took direct hits. A series of burning belowdecks compartments were ordered flooded. When a fire broke out in magazine number two, timely flooding by Commander Maher prevented a catastrophic explosion. Word followed that the small-arms magazine between magazines one and two was afire, and it was flooded too. Then Lieutenant Hamlin in Turret One was surprised to hear a report of fire in his own magazine.

He had had no suggestion of it from the men best situated to know, those stationed in the magazine itself. Presumably a high temperature reading sent up a red flag to magazine flood control, so Commander Maher had ordered magazine number one flooded as well. As a precaution, Hamlin ordered the sprinklers activated in the lower powder hoists. But the wrong switch was thrown and the upper hoist and powder circle got wet too. As a consequence, he lost several salvos that were ready in the upper hoist. One last salvo remained in Turret One's breeches. It was duly fired, and from that point onward the *Houston* was without the services of its largest guns.

With a ten-degree starboard list, the *Houston* was fighting with her lightest weapons. Two motor torpedo boats sped in, attracting the attention of the .50-caliber gunners in the tops and the 1.1-inch gunners below them. One boat was seen to disintegrate in the storm. The other was sawed clean in half yet managed in the seconds available to it to fire a torpedo, which ran on the surface and struck the *Houston* on the starboard side forward of the catapult tower.

"The ship seemed to be thrown sideways, and the deck jumped so bad I was knocked to my knees," remembered seaman second class Bill Weissinger. "That explosion must have shot a couple of tons of water into the air, because when I started to get up, it came pouring down, and Bam! Down I went again. Man, it was heavy." The explosion jarred the catapult track loose from its mounting, and it collapsed across the quarterdeck.

With Japanese ships pressing so close that *Houston* sailors could hear the roar of their firerooms, the battle harked back to an earlier day when naval battles were fought within man-to-man reach, without industrial tools to enable long-distance killing cleansed of a personal aspect. "It was point-blank. It wasn't any of this arcing over yonder," said Frank King, "it was just right broadside." Seaman first class Gus Forsman, on a port-side five-inch gun, said, "It was invigorating to be in a battle like that to where you didn't wait for orders to fire or anything. You just picked a target and fired at it."

The light guns kept up a busy chatter, but the five-inch mounts were running short of ammunition. Resigning himself to the inevitable, seaman second class Earl C. Humphrey, the rammer on Forsman's gun, backed up against a ready box full of star shells, cradling one of his mount's last projectiles in his arms. He told Forsman, "I thought I was going to get it, and when I got it well, I wanted to go all the way." But when the gun captains ran out of common five-inch ammunition and started raiding that ready box for ordnance, Humphrey's express ticket to a painless death started to look a little less certain.

Star shells were deadly at close range. The captain's talker, aviation machinist's mate second class John Ranger, a hero of the February 4 fire in Turret Three, stood just outside the conning tower, still tethered to his phones even though Captain Rooks had left to escape the flames from Turret Two. Standing there, Ranger could hear the hollering of the Japanese sailors as their ships were struck with the sizzling phosphorous rounds. The shells made a lot of noise too. "You could hear them cooking," he said.

Bright lights warred with darkness for possession of the night. "My God, those magnesium flares just light a place up," said Paul Papish, stationed in the after battle dressing station. "It's a ghostly effect. You just can't actually imagine in your mind what it looks like. . . . But it's indescribable. A Japanese destroyer had illuminated us, and I remember hearing somebody holler, 'Put out that goddamned light!' And they fired point blank, that star shell, into that searchlight, which couldn't have been more than the length of [a] building away from us. You could hear screams coming from the Japanese ship."

CHAPTER 20

Surrounded by enemy ships on all offshore bearings, the *Houston* was about five miles northwest of Panjang Island and about the same distance east-northeast from St. Nicholas Point, on an eastward course at twenty knots. It was a little after midnight. The ship was taking on water and listing hard, restricting both her speed and her maneuverability. Her main guns were silent, Turrets Two and Three shattered and burned out, Turret One starved for ammunition with flooded magazines and hoists. "Because of the overwhelming volume of fire and the sheer rapidity with which hits were being scored on the *Houston*, it was impossible to determine in many instances whether a shell, torpedo, or bomb hit had occurred," Commander Maher wrote.

Lost in the numbing stop-time of battle, few of the *Houston*'s sailors could step back and evaluate the ship's overall prospects. That was the job of the officers and the captain. Walter Winslow was standing next to Captain Rooks on the signal bridge. Having been forced to leave the conn by the intensity of Turret Two's flames, Rooks summoned the ship's Marine bugler, Jack Lee. "In a strong, resolute voice," Winslow recalled, "[Rooks] spoke the fateful words: 'Bugler, sound abandon ship.'" Pvt. Lloyd Willey marveled at the clarity of the horn player's tone. "He never missed one beat on that bugle. It would have been absolutely beautiful if it had been any-where else but at that time." Lee blew his clean tones into the ship's PA system. The abandon ship order went out over the battle tele-phones and the general announcing system.

Their commanding officer had foreseen this. His prescient "Estimate of the Situation" had described the swift, multipronged nature of the coming Japanese offensive. He had predicted Luzon's vulnerability to air attack, had warned of Singapore's exposure, and knew Japan would exploit it with its hard-hitting aviation corps. The devastating Darwin raid was no surprise to him either. He ap-preciated the skill of the Japanese officer corps and the dedication of their enlisted force. The Allies' chances had never looked very good to Albert Harold Rooks. "If widely dispersed over the Far East, from Manila to Surabaya to Singapore," he had written, "[the Allied ships] will be capable of only the most limited employment, and many of them will come to an untimely end."

The captain was descending the ladder from the signal bridge when a salvo hit the number-one 1.1-inch mount on the ship's star-board side, killing or wounding everyone in its vicinity. The blast threw a torrent of shrapnel into an athwartship passageway aft of the number-one radio room just as Rooks was coming off the ladder. It caught him in the head and upper torso. Ens. Charles D. Smith, the Turret Two officer, saw him stagger and collapse about ten feet from where Smith was standing. Rooks lay there, soaked with blood on the left side of his head and shoulders. Smith ran to him, but "he was too far gone to talk to us," the young officer wrote.

Smith opened his first aid kit and stuck his commanding officer with two syrettes of morphine. "He died within a minute," Smith would write. Then he laid a blanket over him and sought out the ex-ecutive officer, Cdr. David W. Roberts, and the navigator, Cdr. John A. Hollowell Jr., and reported their captain's death.

One of Captain Rooks's mess attendants, a heavyset Chinaman named Ah Fong but nicknamed "Buda" by the crew, came across the skipper in his last moments. According to Walter Winslow, "Rocking slowly back and forth, he held Captain Rooks as though he were a little boy asleep and, in a voice overburdened with sorrow, repeated over and over, 'Captain dead, *Houston* dead, Buda die too.' " The Chinese were generally terrified of the water. Though several others would be successfully urged overboard at gunpoint, Buda wouldn't budge.

★

The order to abandon ship took Robert Fulton by surprise when it came in over a phone circuit. "We were really roaring along," the assistant engineering officer recalled. His forward engine room was turning the outboard screws at some 330 revolutions per minute. With all four screws going at that speed, the ship would normally make thirty-two knots. But the inboard screws were dead, just dragging through the sea. The best the *Houston* could do now was about twenty-one knots. Except for the dead phone circuits and the peculiar wagging of the after engine room's telegraph pointer, Fulton had had no indication anything was really wrong with the *Houston*. The abandon ship order seemed precipitous.

Thinking some kind of mistake had been made, he called the bridge and requested verification of the abandon ship order. Several minutes passed during which Fulton and his crew had no idea what they should be doing. Finally, after several minutes of chafing silence, a second order to abandon ship was received. Fulton passed the order to the rest of the dozen-odd men with him in the forward engine room and commenced the shutdown of the cruiser's last working propulsion plant.

The fireroom crews shut down the burners under the boilers, leaving valves open to bleed off the high-pressure steam in the system. Though this was a standard procedure that removed the risk of injuries from the release of high-pressure steam in the propulsion system, it could not stop the ship with its ten thousand tons' worth of inertia. As a consequence, the *Houston* continued to make headway as the first life rafts were lowered over the side. They were lost as the ship sailed on before crews could climb down into them.

With Captain Rooks's passing, the ship's senior surviving officer and exec, Commander Roberts, took charge. At 12:29 A.M., having noticed the loss of several rafts as the ship made way, he countermanded the abandon ship order. The cancellation went out over an intercom system that was too shattered to carry the message everywhere. Some heard it, turned away from the rail, and took shelter in less exposed areas of the ship. But many others never did, and they continued helping themselves and their shipmates overboard.

Quite a few sailors who returned to their battle stations were only too glad to get back into the fight. The prospect of leaving the ship was rife with uncertainty. During a lull in shooting, Gus Forsman was having a cigarette on the boat deck with gunner's mate second class Elmer L. McFadden when he heard Commander Roberts on the intercom ordering all hands back to their battle stations. Forsman thought: *Well, that's more like it.*

No matter how bad off a ship may be, there must always be a plan going forward, an objective to reach for, an opening to gain, a reprieve to win. How else should a sailor invest his hopes? The ship itself looms so large in his life that her end can be quite inconceivable.* But the near certainty of the ship's end dawned on even the most unshakably optimistic of the ship's crew. As he was returning gladly to his gun mount, even the gung-ho Forsman found himself thinking, *I wonder how the water is.*

*

---

*Several *Houston* survivors have claimed that Captain Rooks wanted to steer the *Houston* toward Panjang Island in an effort to beach her, presumably to save his men and turn his ship into an unsinkable artillery emplacement. According to Quentin C. Madson, the captain's last words were, "Head for the nearest land. We've got to give the men a chance." William J. Weissinger Jr. recalled the PA announcement: "All hands stand-by for a ram. The Captain is going to try to beach. All hands stand-by! Belay abandon ship!" Seaman first class Seldon D. Reese told an interviewer, "Captain Rooks passed the word, 'Don't abandon ship! I'm going to beach it!'" Others, however, dispute the willingness of a top captain such as A. H. Rooks to risk turning his cruiser into a Japanese war prize. The longtime president of the USS *Houston* Survivors Association, Otto Schwarz, called the claim "a short-lived rumor" and "comic book propaganda." Rear Adm. Robert B. Fulton observed that the *Houston* had no steering control once the after engine room was disabled, and regarded the idea that Captain Rooks was aiming to ground his ship as not only impracticable, but an insult to his reputation. "No capable and responsible commanding officer would ever beach his ship where it could pass into the hands of the enemy," Fulton wrote to the author. "That would constitute a violation of the most basic rules in our Navy. . . . In the wardroom we had several discussions as to how we could best sink the ship if forced to that action to avoid capture. . . . The talk of beaching the ship is just nonsense. The originators of those stories, I think, were just trying to say something complimentary about their Captain, whom we all revered. . . . But those stories show a total lack of understanding of all that our Captain had to face." In an August 28, 1945, letter to Edith Rooks, Ens. Herbert A. Levitt, the *Houston*'s signal officer, stated that the captain said to him, "We'll beach her, man, and fight her from there" before he, "reluctant and with tremulous voice," ordered Levitt to sound the abandon ship. In context, the remark, if it was actually made, seems more a fleeting and emotional exclamation than an order.

Though they could tell "we were really getting the devil knocked out of us," Jim Gee and the other sailors and Marines belowdecks in the five-inch magazine had frozen in disbelief when the first abandon ship order was passed around. The hatch above them was dogged down from above. Unlike the hatches in the main battery's magazines, there were no dogs on the underside. They had no way out. For a time, they did not move from their stations. Yet their confidence was still whole. "No one in the magazine ever said 'I guess we won't make it!' or something of this nature," Gee said. "I have never seen eight men face the absolute end so calmly," said Pfc. Marvin E. Robinson. When the second abandon ship order came, at 12:33, minutes after the first one, with reports of flooding circulating on the battle phones, they decided it was time to go. Marine corporal Hugh Faulk appeared overhead, wrestling open the hatch and hollering down to Gee and his crew, "Y'all come on out, and hurry!" Faulk was awash to his ankles in water, its level almost overspilling the top of the hatch. According to Robinson, "I told the boys, 'We've had it.' There was no panic, nothing." Someone said, "Well, we might as well go topside."

Jim Gee climbed up the ladder out of the magazine, took a long drink of surprisingly cold, fresh water from a scuttlebutt that had no business working, and started wading forward through water that got deeper with every step. "We were going to go up and see if there was something that we could do to help someone because a lot of people were in trouble."

"It looked like high noon on the boat deck," Bill Weissinger said. He recalled watching a Japanese destroyer off the ship's starboard beam. "I went through the steam that was pouring out of an engine room vent to the port side of the boat deck. With the bright beams of the searchlight filtering through the cloud of steam, which was drifting aft on a light breeze, the scene that met my eyes had an eerie quality about it. I had a fleeting impression that I was on a strange ship. What I was looking at was unrecognizable to me. Everything was in disarray." Weissinger removed his shoes, laid them side by side on the deck, and jumped overboard.

Leaving the forward powder magazine and heading topside toward his abandon ship station, Otto Schwarz was knocked unconscious by a great blast. He awoke in a grayed-out landscape of smoke, unsure of where he was. Feeling his way around the bulkhead, unshirted and wearing khaki pants, he found a rifle rack and realized he was in the Marine compartment. He finally reached the quarterdeck, then ran forward to the forecastle. "When I got there it was just like the Fourth of July," he said. "The Japanese ships were out there in a semicircle. You could see their searchlights and muzzle flashes and all." Tracers whipping all around him, he ran to the life jacket locker but found it was on fire. He went farther forward, where other sailors were milling, unsure what to do with an abandon ship order in effect but with the ship still making way at about ten knots, to Schwarz's eye. He was running back aft when a series of explosions buffeted him, knocking him to the deck. Looking up, he could see the night air filled with debris, metal chunks, and flotsam, burning and falling toward him, a red-hot rain of steel. Out of nowhere a sailor wearing a life jacket jumped on top of Schwarz.

People pass through our lives fleetingly, touch us once, and go. The sailor, a seaman first class named Raleigh Barrett, touched Schwarz's life meaningfully at that moment. "All of a sudden this guy jumped on top of me, and he had a life jacket on. So he absorbed the shrapnel that was falling down that would have hit me, and I had no clothing on at all, just a pair of marine khaki pants," Schwarz said. "So he jumps on top of me, then rolls off. I never saw him after that. He didn't survive."

By one o'clock in the morning, few if any of the crew remained on deck. Even the men in the forward engine room had managed to get off the ship. But the machine-gunners in the tops lived in a separate world. On the foremast machine-gun platform, Howard Charles had been so intent in guiding the snaking curve of his .50-caliber tracers into the bright searchlight beams snapping on and off around him that he was surprised to find himself contemplating an unexpected silence and a vague, ringing memory of a bugle call below. As he knelt to pull another ammo belt from the metal locker at his feet, he took stock of his surroundings. He was alone on the foremast gun platform with Gunnery Sgt. Walter Standish, the two Marines outnumbered by the three other gun mounts standing abandoned around them.

Charles shielded his eyes as a new Japanese searchlight stabbed the ship. He snapped another belt into place and hammered at it for a bit, then felt a strong hand on his shoulder. "Better go, Charlie. It's all over. Finished."

"What about you?" he asked Standish. "You going with me?"

As Charles remembered it, the portly gunny grinned. "I'd never make it," he said. "Go, now. Swim away before you're pulled under."

Charles could see an orange life raft hanging over the nearly awash starboard rail, half in the water. To port, men were leaping straight down into the sea and paddling hard away from the ship and its expected undertow. In the aviation hangars aft of the quarterdeck, fires were everywhere. Acrid smoke wafted upward from Turret Two. Flames were grabbing at the base of the foremast.

When Charles looked up, Commander Maher was there, having come down from the gunnery officer's booth in the foretop. Maher urged Sergeant Standish down, nodding to the ladder. Charles joined the plea. "Come on, Sarge," he said. "You and me, we'll make it." He saw land beneath the twinkling heavenly fixture of the Southern Cross, which he had taken note of earlier—in another life, it seemed. "It isn't very far to that island."

But Standish couldn't swim. He shook his head and said calmly, "Goodbye, Charlie."

The ship shuddered again, and with that Howard Charles grabbed the rungs of the ladder and started down the foremast. He wrote:

> Down I went past the bridge and the conning tower, decks strewn with bodies and crooked steel lit up like day in the searchlights. Past a groaning man with one leg torn off, the stump forming a black-red pool. Over the lifeless shapes, an arm, a hand, my shoes slipping on slime and defecation. Through smells of fried flesh and hair, like odors of animal hides scorched by branding irons.

Choking on his own vomit, he continued, "feeling direction, sensing purpose, body moving as if propelled by someone else." The hangar fires backlit a slaughterhouse on the quarterdeck. Japanese destroyers and patrol boats were close by on all sides. "Muzzle bursts were blinking under searchlights, and out of the darkness came the red streaks arcing in across the starboard side, ripping into bodies caught on the lifelines," Charles would write.

He had it in his mind to look for a friend, Howard Corsberg, who he knew couldn't swim. As he was crossing the quarterdeck aft, a torpedo hit on the starboard side, sending a wave of seawater over the deck and washing Charles against the seaplane catapult tower.

Hanging on to it, the hard taste of oil filling in his mouth, he thought, *Is this the way it is? Is this the way you go?*

The wave drained away and Charles saw an enemy ship nearby, its gun crew stitching tracers into the *Houston*. He felt anger rising in his belly. Then he settled into a place beyond raw emotions, a place of detachment, the self at arm's length, as if he were floating through the ordeal. He would wonder later if it was a form of trauma, and would feel the urge to study it. He dropped to his hands and knees and crawled to the port side, where things seemed a little less dangerous. As the seaplane hangar behind him exploded and flames licked at the back of his shirt, he found another buddy in the Marine detachment, Sgt. Joe Lusk, standing there.

Lusk was leaning his tall frame against a line, smoking a cigarette. He tossed the butt overboard and asked, "You ready?" The younger Marine said he was, though the voice he heard coming out of his mouth sounded like a stranger's. "You gotta get off here, Charlie," Lusk said, then flung himself over the port rail, landing in the black water with a large splash. Charles followed him.

"I could feel the heat of the roaring inferno on my back as I tightened the straps of my lifejacket searching the sky for the Southern Cross," Charles said. "I reached out and grabbed a lifeline. No matter what happened, I would swim toward those six bright stars hanging over the tiny black strip of land that had to be Java."

Lieutenant Hamlin got off the ship by sliding down the port side of the bow as the ship rolled over to starboard. "I nearly fell through a hole back into the anchor windlass room, which would have discouraged me tremendously," he wrote. Taking note of "a great many unauthorized holes" up forward, Hamlin reached the waterline and found he could stand on the hull. He walked aft, over the bulge amidships. "I hit the water on the other side of that bulge and gave the best imitation of a torpedo that I could, trying to get away from suction."

"There were dead fish floating all around," one sailor noted. "It was a very badly shark-infested area, but there was no danger from sharks that night. They were dead, too."

They drifted on the swells, watching Japanese destroyers have their way with their ship. "I thought of her as she was when I joined her— just back from a Presidential cruise," Lieutenant Hamlin recalled. "She shone from end to end with new paint and shining brass and polished steel. Well, there wasn't much spit and polish to her now."

Hamlin put a few hundred feet of water between him and his ship, then turned back to take a look at her. "She was full of holes all through the side, these close-range destroyer shells had gone right through one side and out the other, a good many of them. . . . Her guns were askew, one turret pointing one way, and another the other, and five-inch guns pointing in all directions."

★

Listing hard to starboard, settling by the bow, the *Houston* was bathed from stem to stern in hostile white light, wooden decks splintering under gales of machine-gun fire. She seemed on the verge of capsizing, yardarms nearly touching the sea, when, according to John Wisecup, "she righted herself like a dog shaking water off its back," perhaps momentarily counterflooded by an unnoted and gratuitous torpedo hit. When that happened, the colors, brought to life by the beams of hot carbon arcs, just seemed to snap to and wave over the watery battlefield. "Perhaps I only imagined it," Walter Winslow wrote, "but it seemed as though a sudden breeze picked up the Stars and Stripes still firmly two-blocked on the mainmast, and waved them in one last defiant gesture."

As the *Houston* sank, going down by the broken bow, red tracers were seen, right to the end, still whipping down from the foremast's machine gun platform. Gunnery Sergeant Standish, Wisecup wrote, "living up to Marine Corps legend, was a warrior to the end.

"Many years have gone by," wrote Wisecup, "but I can still vividly recall the scene. The stars and stripes still fast on the mainmast streaming aft in the breeze. The 'Gunny's' fifty-caliber machine gun still sending out a line of tracers toward the Japs as the tired old *Huey Maru* slowly sank beneath the waters of the straits.

"Not a word was uttered by anyone on the raft as they gazed at the spot where our ship had gone down."

Once upon a day, William Bernrieder, the booster who had led the USS *Houston* campaign, called her "the Nation's safest insurance against foreign aggression—the expression of might upholding the right. . . . May we always regard her as the emissary of peace, but if fight she must—may the Cruiser *Houston*—the pride of our Navy— never strike her colors to an enemy." That was the one thing her survivors would remember, as clearly as a first child's birthday, long after they were left alone in the nighttime sea. She never struck her colors.

Part Three

THE EMPEROR'S GUESTS

★

War is hell, but that's not the half of it, because war is also mystery and terror and adventure and courage and discovery and holiness and pity and despair and longing and love. War is nasty; war is fun. War is thrilling; war is drudgery. War makes you a man; war makes you dead.

—Tim O'Brien
The Things They Carried

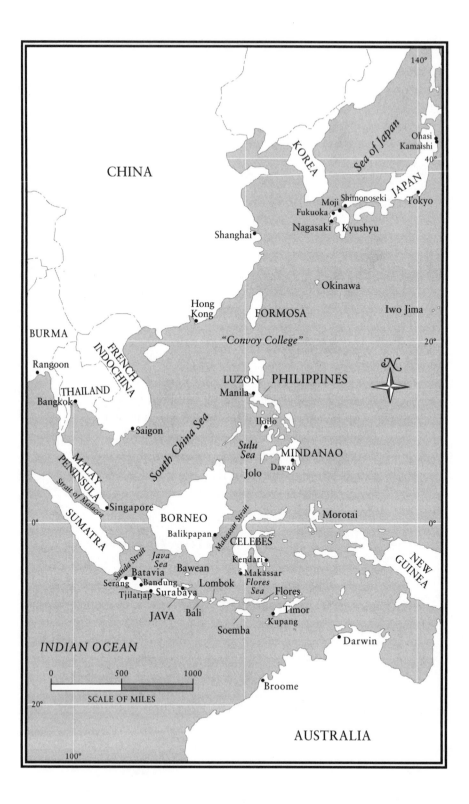

CHINA

KOREA

Sea of Japan

JAPAN

Ohasi
Kamaishi

140°

40°

Moji • Shimonoseki
Fukuoka •
Nagasaki • Kyushyu

Tokyo

Shanghai •

Okinawa

Hong
Kong •

FORMOSA

Iwo Jima

BURMA

FRENCH
INDOCHINA

"Convoy College"

20°

Rangoon •

THAILAND

LUZON   PHILIPPINES

Bangkok •

Manila •

Saigon •

Iloilo •

MALAY
PENINSULA

Sulu
Sea

MINDANAO

Strait of Malacca

Davao •

Jolo

SINGAPORE

Singapore •

BORNEO

Morotai •

0°

0°

SUMATRA

Balikpapan •

CELEBES

NEW
GUINEA

South China Sea

Makassar Strait

Java
Sea

Kendari •

Bawean •

Makassar •

Sunda Strait

Batavia •

Flores
Sea

Serang • Bandung •   Lombok
Tjilatjap • Surabaya

Flores

JAVA   Bali

Timor •
Kupang

Soemba

INDIAN OCEAN

Darwin •

0   500   1000

Broome •

SCALE OF MILES

20°

AUSTRALIA

100°

CHAPTER 21

The *Houston*'s survivors were never far from shore. Their ship came to rest a few miles west of Panjang Island, and about the same distance east of St. Nicholas Point. The *Perth* settled several miles north of the *Houston*.

Despite the proximity to the coast, the obstacles to reaching land were formidable. Although 368 *Houston* survivors would finally be rounded up ashore—less than a third of the ship's wartime complement—by all accounts many more than that survived the ship's immediate trauma and loss. The final tally would take years to sort out. According to the ship's action report, 150 men who made it into the water alive were never seen again. Lt. Harold Hamlin would write, "I saw hundreds of unwounded men go over the side there, whom I haven't seen since." So many men never reached the beach. With most of the lifeboats shattered by gunfire and torpedo blasts, and with any number of life rafts dropped prematurely on the first call to abandon ship, out of reach as the dying ship drifted to a halt, survivors clung to the handiest wreckage. The powerful surge draining out of the Java Sea through Sunda Strait took hold of them and whatever flotsam they were holding to—rafts, furniture, mattresses, spent shell cases—and pulled it toward a fathomless oblivion in the Indian Ocean.

From the moment the USS *Houston* and the HMAS *Perth* sank, hundreds of separate dramas set out on diverging paths. The currents feeding Sunda Strait saw to that. They spread the survivors far and wide. They dangled them within a hard swim of land all around St. Nicholas Point and near islands in the strait's northern channel, and pulled them away on a natural whim. Survivors contended with predators under the sea and on land. They were set upon by native hillmen eager to settle scores with the white man and embrace the arriving Japanese. They were hauled aboard Imperial Army transports. They were shot in the water where they swam, never given a chance.

Sailors have earned places in legend for exploits less than what these men did up to the time of their sinking. Surely few naval personnel have ever performed more resolutely while running such a demanding gauntlet through enemy-controlled seaways. But when March 1, 1942, dawned, the eighty-fourth day of the Pacific war, their ordeal was in fact only beginning. No one could quite have guessed at the dimensions it would finally acquire.

The destruction of the Allied fleet in the Dutch East Indies was proof of Capt. Albert H. Rooks's foresight. His "Estimate of the Situation" foretold the entire fiasco. "There is an adage at war colleges that he who wills the end must will the means," he had written. "For this task the means are lacking."

Just as he had predicted, the other ships of the ABDA naval force, used in scattered piecemeal defense, came to sad ends. Once the *Houston* and the *Perth* were gone, there was little hope left for the stragglers. The Dutch destroyer *Evertsen* got under way a few hours after the two cruisers departed on their final voyages, clearing Tanjung Priok's minefield by 9:15 P.M. on February 28. Shortly thereafter her captain reported flashes of gunfire ahead. A surprised Admiral Helfrich relayed to Rooks and Waller a message from Admiral Glassford reporting the start of the battle: "EVERTSEN REPORTS SEA BATTLE IN PROGRESS OFF ST. NICHOLAS PT. . . . IF ANY OF ADDRESSEES ARE ENGAGED WITH ENEMY OTHERS RENDER ASSISTANCE AS POSSIBLE." This was not news to anyone in the *Houston* or the *Perth*. But since the *Evertsen* herself was soon thereafter attacked and sunk by two Japanese destroyers, Helfrich's message created the misunderstanding in the Navy Department that the *Houston* had been lost while going to the *Evertsen*'s aid.

On the morning of March 1, Helfrich received notice from his chief of staff, British Rear Adm. A. F. E. Palliser, that all Royal Navy ships would withdraw from the theater. Helfrich argued for a time but eventually relented, perhaps recognizing the intractable conflict of national interests within his own headquarters. He then instructed Admiral Glassford to send the remaining U.S. ships to Australia. The old destroyers *Parrott* and *Whipple,* three gunboats, and two minesweepers were the only ones to reach Fremantle. The new *Brooklyn*-class light cruiser USS *Phoenix,* released from convoy duty and speeding to reinforce Java, was ordered back to Exmouth Gulf, Australia. It is said that when sailors from the old Asiatic Fleet encountered *Phoenix* crewmen later in the war, they ascribed that necessary decision to a lack of nerve. Sharp words occasionally followed, and a fisticuff or two.

The HMS *Exeter,* hastily repaired at Surabaya after the Java Sea debacle, tried to escape the waters of the conquered archipelago. On the morning of March 1, she was hunted down south of Borneo by four Japanese cruisers and sunk with the destroyers USS *Pope* and HMS *Encounter.* That same day, the USS *Edsall* was caught south of Java by the battleships *Hiei* and *Kirishima.* With their fourteen-inch salvos the battleships blew the old destroyer's keel literally out of the water. The saddest story may belong to the *Edsall*'s sister ship, the USS *Stewart.* She had capsized in dry dock at Tjilatjap and was scuttled by her crew as the Allies abandoned the port. The Japanese repaired, refitted, and commissioned her as their own Patrol Boat No. 102, making that destroyer the only U.S. surface warship in World War II to be salvaged and made operational by her enemy. Through the rest of the war American pilots, recognizing her lines despite the modified uptakes and mast, would be mystified by the idea of an American ship operating so deep in enemy territory.

In his "Estimate of the Situation," Captain Rooks leveled no criticism at his superiors, though it was plain enough that he would have done things differently had the campaign been his to direct. Politics had trumped operational strategy at every turn. As Rooks suggested, a failure of foresight and a shortage of matériel sealed their doom. Adm. Ernest King was said to have called the campaign to defend the southwestern Pacific "a magnificent display of very bad strategy." Samuel Eliot Morison saw little strategic use in ABDA's ultimate martyrdom. Still, in the loss of the *Houston* and the other

CHAPTER 22

For Otto Schwarz, after abandoning ship there had been no longing looks back at Old Glory whipping from the mainmast truck, just a deltoid-burning crawl stroke away from the gunfire and the explosions. Stopping to rest, he donned the life vest he had been dragging with him, then noticed the moonlit mountaintops in the indeterminate distance. Alone, he set out for them, arms chopping the sea all through the night.

Over the water Schwarz could hear shouts, the *pop-pop* of machine guns, faint screams, and silence. Then, startlingly closer, he heard the rumbling gurgle and swish of diesel engines, and sensed a small craft nearing him. He went motionless just as a searchlight beam grabbed at him. The boat came closer. He heard Japanese voices and tensed, waiting for bullets to come. A Japanese sailor prodded Schwarz with something long and sharp, a boathook perhaps. There was more jabbering discussion, then the searchlight switched off, the engines roared to life, and the boat was gone.

Word passed swiftly over the waters that the Japanese were shooting survivors where they swam. Jim Gee heard the reports—from stunned word of mouth and from the gun barrels themselves. The Marine could hear urgent advice passing between his shipmates: *Swim that way. No, that way. Oil over here. Land's that way.* He settled for treading water. With no life vest or doughnut ring, he calmly kept his place afloat for about an hour as Japanese boats played yellow-white searchlights in all directions, looking for his like.

But in time Gee grew exhausted, deeply so. The consequence of rescue by the enemy was plain to the ear as gunshots ricocheted over the water. He thought of his shipmates killed in action. *Well, a lot of them have already gone. There's no need for me to do otherwise.* What made him special? The existential vertigo became so unbearable that he despaired and finally just gave up. He quit the air and let himself slide under the water.

Gee stayed down long enough for a desperate reflex to kick in. "I took a deep drink of that sea water and I knew that wasn't really where I wanted to be." He kicked himself back to the surface and to his good leatherneck senses. A thought finally reached him that re-oriented his thinking and told him that all was far from lost: "I had a round-trip ticket home. . . . I was going back home. From that point, I never wavered any one minute in believing that I wouldn't make it."

For some, the decision to survive was abrupt, coming in a flash. For others it was a function of staying on autopilot and letting the will regather its might. According to Charley Pryor, "You're just completely beyond exhaustion but still you go. At a time like that you've got some reservoir of strength you never knew you had until you have to use it. Within ten minutes you feel, 'Well, I can't swim another stroke,' but then eleven hours later you're still going."

Seaman second class Eugene Parham was on a lifeboat led by Lt. Cdr. Sidney Smith, the plotting room officer, when it drifted into a herd of Japanese troop transports anchored offshore. Soldiers and sailors lined the rails, jeering unintelligibly. When Commander Smith gave them permission to surrender if they so chose, Parham and some others climbed aboard a transport and submitted to their captors. Shortly afterward, a motorboat towing an empty *Houston* life raft puttered by and the next thing Parham and six other Americans on the transport knew, the Japanese were forcing them into the raft. A Japanese officer flashed his sword, the towline was severed, and they were cast loose again.

They drifted for the better part of the day, picking up a few more survivors before catching a current and losing sight of land. As the raft drifted along, Parham and two others decided their best chance at survival lay in jumping overboard and swimming toward the mountaintops visible on the horizon. Four hours of hard swimming paid an unexpected dividend: A mile from the Java beach, an outrigger canoe found them. Two natives were at the oars, but the hands that hauled them aboard were American. Ens. John B. Nelson was in charge of the craft, having leased it from natives for rescue work for the price of his U.S. Naval Academy ring. It bought Parham's life, but no one on the lifeboat he had originally abandoned—not Commander Smith nor anyone else—was ever seen again.

At least one other native caught the entrepreneurial spirit, but this one overplayed his hand. A Javanese at the helm of a fishing boat motored up to a group of struggling *Houston* survivors, meaning to do some brisk business. "This jerk was picking up guys if they could pay him something of value," seaman second class William M. Ingram Jr. said. "He kept picking up exhausted guys, more and more of them, and taking their wedding bands, money, and watches. All I had was a jackknife on a lanyard tied to my belt, and a cheap ring I'd picked up in Honolulu," Ingram said. "The native wanted both of them. I gave him what he wanted because, hell, I had to get on that boat, and there wasn't any time to bargain." Eventually, outraged by the price gouging, a bunch of the Americans rose and, said Ingram, "threw his ass overboard."

In their new boat, Ingram and his shipmates headed for land, fighting stiff currents all the way. As they passed close by a small island, several sailors got anxious and jumped for it, only to get swept away by the fast-moving water. Sometimes staying with a raft saved you. Other times it was a sure route to oblivion; by inference, more than a few rafts had to have been swept into the Indian Ocean. Ingram's remaining group made it to the beach, but their lucky judgment did them no good. "We weren't ashore five minutes when along came a bunch of Jap soldiers, who took us prisoner," he recalled.

*

Exhausted from treading water, Jim Gee paddled in search of something buoyant to cling to, finally catching sight of a Seagull floatplane pontoon drifting loose. As he approached, he found a bunch of *Houston* survivors holding on to it, perhaps twenty of them, some badly burned. The ship's chaplain, Cdr. George S. Rentz, was among them, doing what he had been put on the earth to do: minister to those in need.

Gee had little need of his chaplain's services. The Marine private was not injured, merely tired. He clutched the side of the float, gathering strength and wind for another run toward shore. When he finally set out again, he discovered that no one, not even a strong-swimming Marine, could contend with the currents off Java. "I could feel myself being carried out to sea. There are certain things you can just tell. I could tell that I wasn't going in a straight path." He found just enough strength to return to the pontoon.

Gee got back in time to witness the making of a Navy legend. Chaplain Rentz, at fifty-nine, had been the oldest man on the ship, nine years senior to Captain Rooks and only about a year away from retirement when the *Houston* went down. The native of Lebanon, Pennsylvania, had been a pastor at churches in Pennsylvania and New Jersey before joining the Navy during World War I. That war was nearly over when Rentz, as a junior-grade lieutenant, was named acting chaplain to the Eleventh Marine Regiment, deployed to France in October 1918, just a month before the armistice. After the war, Rentz fulfilled a series of sea-duty assignments in the peacetime Navy, making commander in 1924. He needed nearly two decades more to find his ultimate calling as shepherd to the survivors of a U.S. Navy cruiser in extremis.

The surplus pontoon, taking on water through a hole in its top, was slowly losing its buoyancy. Several times during the night Rentz tried to swim away to keep it from sinking. "You men are young, with your lives ahead of you," he said. "I am old and have had my fun." Each time, a different sailor from the group ignored Rentz's entreaty and retrieved him.

At one point Lloyd Willey saw Rentz huddled with a sailor on the float. The kid, seaman first class Walter L. Beeson, was hanging on, head down, apparently wounded, though it was hard to see where or how badly. He didn't have a life jacket. According to Beeson, Rentz, unhurt himself, "told me his heart was failing him; told me he couldn't last much longer." Gasping for breath, the chaplain said a brief prayer for the men in the group, removed his life jacket, and offered it to the young sailor. Perhaps ashamed to take it, Beeson accepted it but declined to put it on, at least not until Rentz had kicked away from the float and submitted to the sea. According to Jim Gee, "No one realized what had happened. It's just one of those things that one minute he's there, and the next minute you look around and you take a head count, and sure enough, he wasn't there." Only when the finality of Rentz's sacrifice had sunk in did Walter Beeson pull on the life jacket. The group stayed together and drifted the rest of that night, humbled by the spirit of their chaplain right to the end.

*

As dawn broke over Bantam Bay on March 1, the *Houston*'s survivors could at last see the full extent of the Japanese landing operation and their own incidental place in its midst. "The bay was as slick as glass, not a ripple anywhere except in the wake of the landing barges plying between the transports and the shore with their loads of supplies and troops," wrote Bill Weissinger, floating with a group of *Houston* survivors led by Lt. Joseph F. Dalton. "The surface was dotted with all sorts of objects: boxes, crates, lumber, all types of containers, and life jackets—some empty . . . some occupied." According to John Wisecup, on another raft, "Transports lined the beach as far as the eye could see, busily discharging troops and equipment with little visible resistance." Too tired to swim for shore, the Americans drifted, watching the barges going back and forth, wondering if one might come for them. In time, a barge hauled out in their direction.

As the thirty-footer pulled alongside, Dalton urged his shipmates to remove any insignia that might identify their ship. The Japanese engineer in charge of the craft motioned them aboard, seated them on deck, then began making "strange guttural-snarling sounds which we found out later was the Japanese language," Weissinger wrote. With the life raft towed behind it, the barge got under way and headed for one of the large transports. The Japanese engineer and his coxswain passed around cigarettes. Then the coxswain approached Lieutenant Dalton.

"*Ingeris, ka?*"

English? Dalton didn't hesitate to correct him. "No. American," he said.

The enemy sailor dismissed this out of hand. "*No America. All America finis. Ingeris.*" The two men disputed the question of nationality in pidgin for a few minutes until the barge reached the transport, then the Japanese sailor gave up.

The coxswain threw over a line, went up the gangway, and conferred with the troop carrier's officer of the deck. Then without comment he came back down and released the line. The engineer throttled up again and steered the barge toward another vessel. They had no more luck with that one. In all, four different transports refused custody of the Dalton gang. "Nobody wanted us," wrote Bill Weissinger. The engineer was finally left with no alternative but to cast them loose again. The coxswain cut the line towing the raft listlessly behind, and indicated that the survivors were to swim for it. As they went overboard again, three rifle-armed soldiers on the large transport walked along the rail. The troopship was moving just fast enough to keep the survivors on its beam. The Americans braced for gunfire. Reaching the raft and ducking behind its lee side, they cowered and drifted until they were out of range and their only enemy, once again, was the sea.

★

Some sailors drifted for days. Others were lucky enough to reach shore right away. Survivors who struggled ashore at the first opportunity were almost always rewarded with a quick capture. This was the fate of Frank Gillan, the lucky *Perth* lieutenant who appears to have been the last man off his ship.

Gillan rode a series of floating vehicles to survival, each one more seaworthy than the one before: a wooden plank, a Carley float, and finally a lifeboat, where he joined about seventy of his shipmates. An able sailor, Gillan got the mast and sails up, fashioned a tiller out of driftwood, and turned toward Sumatra before adverse headwinds forced him to shape a course back toward Java. Going slowly blind from the bunker oil clotting in his eyes, Gillan turned over the tiller to a sailor named McDonough. When the wind died at nightfall, they had to row. They were soon desperate with exhaustion. One sailor who started vomiting up oil was relieved of rowing but sat there for a time still pulling an invisible oar until someone eased him to the bottom boards, slick with the blood of the injured, to sleep. With a combination of "bullying and blarney and child psychology," McDonough kept them bending to the oars. Two bodies were slid overboard as a chaplain named "Bish" Mathieson intoned the last rites. Finally, in the early hours of Monday, March 2, scarcely twenty-four hours since the *Perth* went down, they reached Java's shore. They spread out the lifeboat's sail on the beach like a tarp and arranged five wounded men on it. Then they slept.

At dawn Gillan awoke and the decision was made to split up their party, leaving the wounded on the beach while the healthy hiked north and south looking for help. Gillan paired up with Bill Hogman, a stoker, who, unasked, took his hand and served as his eyes, leading him after the others all that day and far into the night, guiding his steps, explaining what the country looked like. At the village of Labuhan, miles south of their original landfall, they met a *Houston* officer—this might have been Lt. Joseph Dalton or Lt. (jg) Leon Rogers, who both reached Labuhan and met *Perth* survivors. The American told them to wait while he went to another village where other Yanks were said to be. The Dutch, he said, would provide them with transportation. About an hour later a native policeman showed up and handed them a handwritten note from the same U.S. officer saying there were no vehicles after all and advising the Australians to head for the hills and attempt a rendezvous with Dutch ground forces.

Crossing the coastal paddies toward higher ground, the two Australians encountered Chinese shopkeepers who gave them food. The offerings of the natives were harsher: spitting and unintelligible threats. At a hillside village that night, they slept in a small hospital, where they met a Dutch officer. "Can you get us arms and medical supplies?" Gillan wanted to know. An encouraging promise was made, but it did not survive the night. In the morning the Dutchman was gone.

"We can fight in the hills," Gillan said, still unable to see. He and his mates walked all day up-country through plantations and jungle, hoping to find Dutch soldiers. What they found instead were sarong-clad hillmen armed with gleaming parangs and knives. Though Gillan was enjoying the return of his eyesight—he could see if he pulled his lids open with his fingers—he could do little to resist. When the natives became preoccupied with arguing among themselves, he and Hogman scrabbled together some good rocks to throw. Gillan carried a heavy stick too, which he waved threateningly at an armed hillman who approached him. Though they were outnumbered and overmatched, the standoff held. It lasted, at least, until a truck motor shredded the jungle's peace. A small Japanese flag flew from its hood. The natives scattered.

As the vehicle sped into view, the Australians saw the vehicle's occupants and resigned themselves to capture. There were three of them, all Indonesians. All wore white armbands emblazoned with a red rising sun. One of them leaped out and, pointing imperatively at the truck, said, "You prisoner. You be well treated." Gillan, exhausted and numb, complied. He and Hogman joined other prisoners in the truck as the driver got in, hit the gas, and began navigating the winding hillside roads. When they arrived at the town of Pandeglang, about twenty miles northeast of Labuhan, and parked near the town jail, crowds of natives filled the streets. They jeered, "*English finish, English finish!*", spat at them, and smacked them with sticks.

Gillan, an engineer, was a machine-minded westerner. His dreams were of a familiar world he had learned to love: engine rooms, roaring burner fires, hissing boilers, screaming turbines, the smell of oil mixing with sweat. Now, like the rest of the sailors in captivity, he began adjusting to a different reality, an alien and primitive one. Somewhere along the way Gillan saw fit to speak a quick, quiet prayer: "Please, God, help us and deliver us all and look after our families at home."

*

The men on John Wisecup's life raft, whose senior man was a gravely wounded young lieutenant junior grade named Francis B. Weiler, fought Sunda Strait's currents by using pieces of flotsam as oars and making fast a bowline that was towed by several of the stronger swimmers. Weiler had a gouge near his spine and a wound in his arm deep enough to show bone in the moonlight. After a day or two soaking in bunker oil, his arm festered and began to turn gangrenous. It swelled to twice its size. Drifting with the current, Weiler used his good arm to splash water on the parched, exhausted men who were doing the paddling. They worked doggedly, but thirst and fatigue pushed them toward madness. There were some outlandish conversations on that raft. Each time dawn came, Wisecup noticed, a few faces had gone missing.

Though morning on the third day revealed no land within sight, they knew enough to keep rowing, and somehow that afternoon the tide gave them a break, steering the currents back toward shore. With Weiler still lurching around the raft with one good arm, splashing water on folks and taking no notice of his wounds, John Wisecup looked toward the bowline and saw that the swimmers towing it had somehow changed their stroke. From the way their shoulders were moving above water, in fact, Wisecup was delighted to realize that they must be standing on the bottom. They hauled the raft toward the welcoming nearby beach. Two sailors carried

Weiler ashore and sat him against a coconut tree. Then several eld-
erly Javanese men appeared with machetes. They cut the tops off
some green coconuts and let the sailors drink their fill.

Few of the *Houston's* survivors had seen the need to keep their
shoes when they left the ship. Faithful to regulations to the end,
most had placed them neatly by the gunwales before going overboard. "The deck looked like a used shoe store display," Wisecup recalled. As the survivors pulled themselves over coral and rocks and
onto land, they realized their mistake. Much later some of them
would dream of the abandoned footwear as they wrapped their
bleeding feet in rags, leaves, and carvings from rubber tires. Sailors
from the deck force got by the best going barefoot. Months of trudg-
ing the *Houston's* hot decks with holystones and hoses in hand had
toughened their soles as the yeomen and radio operators could only
have wished.

Survivors washed ashore at any number of scattered points. They
organized themselves and tried to round up their friends, to heal
them or get them healed. Pursuing varied routes of evasion and escape, they acquired stories divergent and dramatic enough to keep a
Hollywood producer busy making wartime epics for the rest of his
career. In search of help, they hiked mountains and dirt roads, forded
streams and hailed rickshaws. But as often as not, the help turned
out to be in league with the newly arriving Japanese.

Several centuries of weighty colonial administration had not disposed Java's nationalists to like the Americans any better than they
did the Dutch. Some say the Japanese, perhaps not quite appreciat-
ing their new subjects' readiness to collaborate with them, put a
fifty-guilder reward on white men captured dead or alive. The cash
might not have been necessary. Rhetoric of a "Greater East Asian
Co-Prosperity Sphere" fueled nascent Javanese nationalism and paid
dividends of loyalty in the early going, netting the Imperial Army
scores of prisoners. Survivors who caught wind of the natives' hostility hid out in the hills, subsisting on water, coconuts, and scraps
from friendly Sundanese villagers. These acts of kindness and generosity—providing nourishment, concealment, shelter, and likely
routes toward Allied army positions—were frequent enough to prevent the question of trusting the locals from ever becoming completely decided.

Ens. Charles D. Smith and coxswain Red Huffman, old hands
from Turret Two, washed ashore on a small island about three

hundred yards off St. Nicholas Point. Worn beyond hope, they slept until daylight on March 2 and woke to find that five others had joined them, Marine sergeant Joe Lusk and four sailors. The presence of Japanese ships and aircraft complicated the job of reaching the Java mainland, but in the morning a rainsquall passed through, providing sufficient medium-range concealment for them to swim ashore safely by daylight. They gathered themselves on the beach, slipped across the Japanese-patrolled coast road, then climbed to high ground and looked over the other side of the hill to the sea.

About five miles down the beach, they could see six or eight transports anchored off St. Nicholas Point. Beyond them, prowling the edge of Bantam Bay, was a light cruiser, three destroyers, and some patrol boats. No doubt the Japanese were still reeling from the sudden, spectral appearance of Allied cruisers in their midst. The price the two ships had extracted from the landing operation was plain to see. Swimming ashore, more than a few *Houston* survivors saw the hulks of three large Japanese merchant ships, sunken and lying on their sides, as well as a seaplane tender or some other kind of major auxiliary vessel with its flight deck mostly awash.

The problem with the survivors' proto-heroic efforts at evasion and escape was that ultimately there was no way out. All Allied personnel who could manage it had fled to Tjilatjap and evacuated Java a week before. Now there were no ships or planes left to catch. Though there remained some ground battles yet to be fought for control of the island, the surviving sailors were stuck well behind Japanese lines, in a terrible position to link up with friendly troops. What the location and number of the few remaining Allied units might be, no one quite seemed to know.

CHAPTER 23

Before their ships were sunk together, the sailors of the *Houston* and the *Perth* had been no more than friendly strangers. With a wide ocean stretching between them, they waved from distant rails but seldom saw each other for the man beneath the uniform. The collective ordeal propelled them into a deeper alliance; many would end it as lifelong friends. "Those Aussies," said Otto Schwarz. "If you ever have to get captured, get captured with Aussies."

One of the traits the Americans seemed to have in common with the Australians was a boundless sense of the possible. Unlike the British, who struck many of the Americans as repressed by traditions and hierarchies, or the Dutch colonials, orderly and risk-averse like landed gentry, the Australians tended to be maverick optimists. While the Dutch were preparing themselves for surrender, the American and Australian sailors had fight left in them and showed it.

In fact, for some survivors of the *Perth,* it wasn't enough merely to reach shore on Java or some barren island in Sunda Strait. There were a couple of well-led groups that hatched plans to travel like castaways all the way home to Australia. They built boats and jury-rigged them for sea. They set sail and felt their way home, navigating by starlight, convinced that their war had only begun. Going home was an option unavailable to all but the most fantasy-prone Americans. But if the Aussies had their way, they might yet fulfill Admiral Glassford's February 28 order sending them to Tjilatjap in preparation for a run down under.

Leading seaman Keith Gosden—who had flown suddenly and exuberantly off the *Perth* when the torpedo hit near Y turret's lobby—refused to be rescued when he had his chance. Alongside his raft came an Imperial Navy destroyer. Already holding *Perth* survivors in custody, its crew threw down lines. One of them called, "Come aboard," but Gosden and his shipmates saw rescue as a synonym for surrender and pushed off from the warship. A *Perth* man shouted, "You know where to stick it, mug—we'd rather drown!" The Japanese replied, "So, you say Nippon no bloody good. You wait till tomorrow." The ship vanished.

Soon afterward the tables were turned. Gosden felt someone pulling at his legs. Startled, he looked down and saw his assailant: a swimming Japanese soldier with a rifle and in full battle gear trying to get aboard his raft. The survivors of the *Houston* and the *Perth* were not the only victims of the Battle of Sunda Strait to contend with the violent sea. All around Gosden and his fellow survivors imperial troops floundered, some facedown, dead and drowned, others struggling toward the raft, holding their rifles "like periscopes." When the soldier grabbing at Gosden tried to say something, the sailor replied with a sharp kick to the face. The soldier reached again for the Australian sailor's boots—he had kept them in anticipation of getting ashore, but they made fair weapons too. Gosden kicked at the face again and again until it was no longer there to be kicked. His resistance spurred his shipmates to a rather frenzied defense of the raft. Soon the only Japanese visible nearby were facedown and inert. They were Gosden's enemy, and he would neither accept rescue by them nor do them that favor. He was going home. As he would remind himself on the difficult journey ahead: *There's a plan for every man, and when that plan is completed that is the end. This is not my time. My death is not determined yet. I will get home.*

By first light on March 1, the southerly flow through Sunda Strait was carrying Keith Gosden and his float full of survivors into the wedge of sea separating Toppers and Sangiang Islands. Gosden's shipmate, Lieutenant Gillan, and his boys, like the Americans Hamlin and Huffman and Harris and Schwarz and so many others, were able to scramble ashore. Gosden and his mates went for a ride.

Toppers Island, near the up-current northeastern end of Sunda

Strait, was a small lump of rock that sported an important light-house. Survivors of both the *Houston* and the *Perth* found refuge on its compact shore. Sangiang Island, larger and more verdant, was visible as a low line of rocks, fringed by bushes and taller palm trees that enclosed a narrow inner plain full of broad-leafed swordgrass and younger banana palms. Watching the islands as they appeared to slide north along the distant mainland coast, Gosden could see that he might be missing his only chance to reach land before the current expelled him remorselessly into the Indian Ocean. He told his shipmates he was going to swim for Sangiang. They scoffed. He persisted. The argument was not settled until Gosden slid off the raft and began swimming, along with a persuadable Royal Australian Air Force corporal, Ronald Bradshaw. The waters near Sangiang's shore whorled and ripped, sometimes bubbling like rapids. Fifty yards from the beach Gosden and Bradshaw got caught in this watery revolving door and were spun out farther from the is-land.

Many others had fought these currents and lost. From Lt. Joseph Dalton's group, two American sailors, seaman first class Isaac A. Black and signalman first class Edward T. Carlyle, set out for the Java shore. They dived off the raft and rode a shore-bound current for a time, but Lieutenant Dalton could soon see that they were moving faster down-current than toward shore. Black, about a half mile south of Dalton and his men, seemed to be in trouble. He be-gan waving and shouting, but the wind and waves erased his words. Carlyle was farther away but apparently having better luck. Some-how he had gotten on board a banca boat, which he began rowing in Dalton's direction. But when another boat, a native fishing craft, was spotted heading in their direction, the men in Dalton's raft took their attention away from their two distant shipmates. Pursuing their own survival, they piled from the raft into the small craft, nearly swamping it, giddily showering their rescuers with the cash they had in the pockets of their khakis. When they finally settled in, they realized they had lost sight of Black and Carlyle. "They had both disappeared," wrote Bill Weissinger. "It is a mystery we could never find an answer for."

Keith Gosden had better outcomes in mind for himself. Moving again toward Sangiang, he treaded water for a while to catch his breath, and as he did the current brought a body his way. The body was on its back, arms outstretched. As it drew nearer, the Australian recognized it as a *Perth* telegraphist, Peter Nelson. As Nelson drifted nearer still, Gosden was startled to realize that he was alive—asleep in fact, and snoring robustly. When Gosden yelled and splashed water on him, the telegraphist awoke and, sleepily incensed, asked, "What's biting you?" But the risks were apparent: they were drifting so fast that they stood to miss the island altogether. Gosden waved at Nelson and Bradshaw, indicating he was going to swim for Sangiang's beach. Again the currents seized him, but this time he was pulled toward the island's sheltered lee side, where the waters relaxed and purposeful swimming became possible. The Adelaide native chose a wave with the shape and strength to take him in. Hitting the shallows in an avalanche of foam, he felt the redemptive stinging scrape of live coral against his belly.

Twenty-two Australians gathered at Sangiang, eventually congregating under the leadership of Lt. Cdr. P. O. L. "Polo" Owen, the *Perth*'s paymaster. Owen took charge and split them into groups and they went right to work. Ducking the odd Japanese aircraft, they gathered corn, green papaws, tomatoes, native tobacco, and coconuts. They found some tins of kerosene and used it to dissolve the corrosive coat of bunker oil that clung to them. They scoured the beach for useful treasures, prominent among them a wooden lifeboat well stocked with provisions, oars, sails, and flares. They found three sheep shut up in a hut, slaughtered them, and made a fine pink stew. And they slept. Hard.

They rose the next day to find four of their number missing, along with the lifeboat. Someone said, "If that's the sort they are, we're better without them." What was there to do but accept the frail criminality of human nature? All agreed it would be a death sentence to stay where they were.

Seeing Japanese air activity in the east, Commander Owen guessed that Batavia was an enemy hive. There was no point trying to reach it. But he felt if the men could get from Sangiang to the Java mainland, they might find transportation there to Tjilatjap and rejoin Allied forces. On Wednesday, March 4, having gorged on as much stew as they could manage with bare hands, shells, or palm leaves as spoons, they overloaded a twenty-five-man boat with food and forty-one souls and shoved off for the last battlefield in the Dutch East Indies.

Once on Java, Owen wanted to go to Labuhan by land. Keith Gosden and some others preferred to travel by sea. The seafarers, who found a leader in Lt. John A. Thode, felt they could get all the way to Australia on their own. Owen and Thode agreed to disagree as to means, but they settled on an interim rendezvous at Labuhan. Owen and one group would walk there. Thode and his group would go by sea, hugging the coast.

Owen's journey turned quickly into a deadly misadventure. Four of his fellow travelers, unable to keep his aggressive pace after a few miles, decided to head for Batavia instead of Labuhan. Their reward for breaking ranks was an ambush by Javanese hillmen that left three dead and the survivor badly slashed but able to tell the story. Owen and the others continued south and their line straggled out before they reached a small village. Coming to a rise in the road, they glimpsed the sea. Owen saw a lifeboat out there, oars dipping and pulling, up and down, and the sight of Thode's crew reenergized his steps through the paddies and coconut plantations. He headed a line that stretched out now for miles.

Just before sundown, Owen came to another village and met a young man, well dressed in a linen coat and a black and orange sarong, who pointed the way to Labuhan. The man said he had worked as a schoolmaster in Batavia before the Japanese came. He warned them of armed bands of Javanese who had looted and burned Labuhan's Chinese-owned shops. They could be relied upon to do worse to white men, he said, adding that there had not been any Dutchmen in Labuhan for some time, and that transportation to Tjilatjap was unavailable.

Marching into a sparsely developed fishing outpost, Commander Owen's party saw out in its bay a modest fleet of small gondolas painted green and scarlet and yellow. One boat among them looked decidedly out of place. It was the lifeboat carrying Lieutenant Thode's party. Owen called out and waved to them. As he led his men toward the beach, a score of parang-armed natives picked up their stride and started trailing them. The Australians began running. They passed through a coconut grove and reached the water. They sloshed quickly through the coral-bottomed shallows until the water was deep enough to swim. Reaching Thode's lifeboat, they were pulled aboard and were reunited with their shipmates from Sangiang.

Discouraging though Owen's experience ashore might have been, he held on to his wish to go over land to Tjilatjap. He pressed the issue again with Thode, and the lieutenant finally had no choice but to stand firm. The disagreement endured. Thode returned his superior to land with some two dozen others. As Owen's men vanished among the huts of Labuhan, Thode and his nine castaways, including Gosden, rowed their lifeboat back to sea. It was then that their mini-epic adventure truly began.

*

They ran south with the currents, rowing mostly and taking whatever help the light winds could blow into the split canvas bag they used for a sail. Always within view of Krakatoa's cone, looming in the northwest, they made the thirty-five-mile run from Labuhan to Princes Island in the southwestern end of Sunda Strait in one day. On that rocky beach they found five dozen crates that had been shoved around and scattered by the tides. Dreaming of canned asparagus, steak, beans, and beer, they tore into them but found only two types of loot, and lots of it: ammonia and bundle upon bundle of paper currency. Since the latter proved to be Japanese occupation money, and since the sailors aimed to avoid that jurisdiction altogether, they cursed the treasure and tossed the bundles into the surf. But one last box of the trove had not been opened yet. One of the sailors found it wedged in some rocks where the beach ended. He smashed it open with a pair of rocks and was dumbfounded to find what they needed even more than food: sails, a full set of them—mainsail, foresail, and jib. "Boys," said Lieutenant Thode as the group surrounded the find, "this definitely means we'll get home."

Before departing they used a piece of iron binding from one of the boxes to saw down a coconut tree and feasted on its eight fruits, garnished with some periwinkles pulled from the rocks. The next morning, Friday, March 6, they set course for Tjilatjap. They would need twelve days to cover the three hundred miles to the friendly port. From there, the optimists calculated, reaching Australia would mean five more weeks at sea.

They rowed all day in shifts. The absence of wind caused their muscles to burn as surely as the sun did their oil-stained skin. When the heat became oppressive, the castaways could dip themselves in the sea, but only briefly and only so long as a shipmate could stand by, oar at the ready, to fend off the trailing sharks. The nights were clear, the moon bright between dusk and nine o'clock. On some nights the stars stayed visible longer than that, providing a fix to navigate by. But usually it rained, forcing them to sail blind. More than once they discovered that they had wasted the night rowing in a big circle.

When morning broke on the twelfth day past Princes Island, Thode said, "If we're lucky we'll see a monolith at the entrance to Tjilatjap some time today." The announcement was met skeptically—out of food, the men were growing suspicious of cheap gambits to boost morale. But early that afternoon land appeared, and as they drew closer they could see, in a gap between hills, the monolith.

The inlet to Tjilatjap harbor was a narrow passage between the mainland and the coastal island of Kanbangan. Entering it, the Aussies could see on one side of the harbor, on a faraway shore, hundreds of soldiers dressed in khaki. Were they Japanese? Weak from exhaustion and perhaps reluctant to consider the worst, Thode steered on, heading the opposite way. He tied up on a wharf next to a patrol boat flying the Dutch flag. Two Dutch officers in green uniforms met them. One carried a pistol, the other a light machine gun. "Who are you?" the latter demanded, speaking first in Dutch, then in English. Thode approached the Dutchmen, identified himself, then described their ordeal and their ambition going forward. He requested food for the journey ahead. The officer with the pistol shook his head. "Nippon is your friend. You must give up your plan to reach Australia and go to him for protection."

Thode returned to consult with his men. "You heard what he said. What's it to be? Surrender, or shall we have a crack at them?" The strength left in their bodies did not match the anger in their veins. Certainly they were powerless against a submachine gun and a pistol. One of them muttered, "You bastards. You yellow, fifth-column bastards." And so at friendly gunpoint the heroes of the HMAS *Perth* surrendered the fight. Stunned as they were by the turn of events, they were more shocked still to find that their actual mortal enemy—the Japanese—was more inclined to show them kindness than their putative friends. The Dutch officers marched the captives to a makeshift Japanese headquarters in town. As imperial troops beat looters with rifle butts outside, the Dutchmen, speaking in Japanese, called out to the headquarters' occupants. A Japanese colonel appeared. When Thode identified his band as survivors of the *Perth,* the Imperial Army officer said in clean English, "You sank our ships in Sunda Strait. Look at me. I'm still covered in oil. I can't get the stuff off."

The Australians were taken to a place where they could wash. When the oil residue did not come off, Japanese soldiers helped them scrub down, and at this point it struck Gosden that the unexpected generosity had to have a catch. The Japanese were known to be brutes. Yet who could deny this charity: The Aussies were fed, given tea with milk, cigarettes, and matches. They slept for a bit, then were awakened and given clothes and more cigarettes. In light of the dark rumors circulating about the Japanese, they could scarcely believe their luck.

The colonel interrogated Thode that afternoon, took down the names of his party, then made the lieutenant a surprising offer. He would be allowed to choose his prison camp. That day Thode, escorted by the colonel's sergeant major, inspected several of them and settled on a camp outside of Tjilatjap. At the time, there was no way anyone might guess that this would be the last act of enemy-sanctioned free will that most of them would exercise for more than three years.

CHAPTER 24

For a time, the Australians who reached Tjilatjap were permitted to think that their gallantry would win them some type of preferred treatment. The rest of the survivors, and certainly most of the Americans, had less encouraging introductions to prisoner life.

The morning after his ship was destroyed, after two weeks at battle stations and thirteen hours fighting Sunda's currents, Otto Schwarz was retrieved by a Japanese landing boat and deposited on the beach. So tired he could scarcely stand, the eighteen-year-old from Newark, New Jersey, joined a group of about nineteen other *Houston* sailors. He cast off his life vest, leaving himself wearing only his khaki pants, and tried to seat himself on a crate. Almost immediately a Japanese guard ran up to him and bashed him to the ground. An officer took him behind some palm trees, leveled a pistol at his head, and asked, "Do you want to see your family again?" He demanded to know how many airplanes the Americans had, and how many battleships. A seaman second class never knew much, but any Allied sailor in the theater would have laughed at the idea that battleships or aircraft had a prominent place in early-1942 Allied orders of battle. Schwarz said as much. The officer grew belligerent but shoved Schwarz back to his group, where they all became stevedores for Gen. Hitoshi Imamura's beachmasters.

Prodded at bayonet point and bashed by rifle butts, the group of twenty Americans, including Schwarz, Lt. Cdr. William Galbraith, Ens. John Nelson, and Marines Charley Pryor and Howard Charles, spent three days and four nights hauling pony carts full of food, supplies, and ammunition from barges to depots ashore. A Japanese officer who could manage a little English said, "You are prisoners of war. Your lives will be spared." But reassurance wasn't what Pryor, for one, needed. "I had no fear of these people. It didn't worry me from one minute to another whether or not they wanted to line me up and shoot me."

As it happened, the beasts that had been earmarked to pull those carts had gone down with one of the merchantmen sunk the night before. So the Americans worked in their stead late into the night. The asphalt road ground their bare feet raw. Schwarz developed a huge single blister running from toe to heel. Taken to a local schoolhouse, he was allowed to rest a bit, then a Japanese soldier approached him with a pair of tweezers and tore off the blister and doused the wound with iodine. "All my life I was the kind of person who just went from one event to another. I never worried about the door closing behind me," he would say. "I always took everything day by day. I realized life was not going to be pleasant after that. I found out in quick order what it was going to be like to be a prisoner of war."

Capture was an anticlimactic end to grandiose plans to evade and escape. When Ens. Charles D. Smith, Red Huffman, and Sergeant Lusk came ashore, they had tried to avoid the well-patrolled coast road, cross the mountains, and reach Dutch lines. But at midday on March 3, after two and a half days of subsisting on rainwater and growing weak from the deprivation, they encountered a native whose wary hospitality got them a meal of fish heads and rice but not much more. As they were eating, he evidently hailed a Japanese army patrol nearby. They scarcely had time to duck into the bushes before they were rounded up without a fight. Shackled as a chain gang and marched through a village, they realized they might be better off with the Japanese than with the natives. In the village, the locals were waving small flags emblazoned with imperial rising suns. The Japanese officer in charge of the prisoners assigned a guard to protect them.

Thoughts of escape gave way to the reality of their physical limitations, to exhaustion and the absence of routes to Allied lines. All roads led to prison. Taken to the nearest villages, they were packed into local jails emptied for use as POW pens. Into Pandeglang came Lt. (jg) Leon Rogers and Lt. Joseph Dalton, similarly betrayed by natives, Otto Schwarz and the beachside work party, and John Wisecup and the rest of the men from Lieutenant Weiler's raft. Most of the prisoners were finally force-marched or packed in trucks and driven to Serang, the largest town west of Batavia. Except for the preponderance of olive-green Japanese army vehicles shuttling soldiers and equipment hither and yon, the trading center's bustling streets reminded some Americans of good old Manila. General Imamura had established his temporary Sixteenth Army headquarters in the municipal building there until sturdier facilities were found in a southern suburb of Batavia. Imamura liked what he heard of local cooperation with his invasion forces. His army was received as the Asian liberator foretold in Indonesian prophecy since the 1700s. The general told a village elder, "You and the Japanese are brothers. We are fighting the Dutch so that you can recover your freedom."

*

Pandeglang, Rangkasbitung, Serang. To Western ears, the names were alien. But for three weeks in March these places were home to most of the U.S. and Australian survivors who straggled in from the surrounding jungles and beaches of Java. It was strange territory to them, but even to those familiar with it, the contours of this corner of the universe were in flux. The Japanese troops were on the move, consolidating a foothold in western Java and jousting with Allied forces in the east.

Amid the confusion, reunions with other shipmates had an aspect of excitement. Lieutenant Thode's men rejoined Commander Owen and his group. The senior officer had worked his way from village to village, pleading with the village *wadanas* (or chieftains) to help his men until the inevitable betrayal. The *Houston* survivors compared notes on their last sea battle ("How many do you think we lost?") and on who got off the ship, where, and when ("Did so-and-so make it? Have you seen him?"). One sailor reported having seen Sergeant Standish, the grizzled Marine who was thought to have fired those last bursts from the *Houston*'s toppling foremast, cleaning his .45 pistol on the beach and then vanishing into the bush. Few of the others thought that could be possible.

The municipal jail was cleared of its local felons and jammed on March 8 with as many Allied prisoners as would fit. Most of the *Houston*'s officers were imprisoned there. They compiled a muster roll of all of the known survivors from the ship. By authoritative tallies, 368 men from the *Houston*'s complement of 1,168, and 324 of the *Perth*'s 681, survived to become prisoners of war. At Serang, there was a total of about 1,500 prisoners, an odd rabble of captives that included sailors of four nations, Royal Air Force personnel, British troops evacuated from Singapore, and local Dutch, including women and children. Dressed in whatever they happened to wash ashore with—oil-stained khaki shorts or perhaps just a loincloth—they slept on hard floors in square fourteen-foot cells. The officers had a tub for a latrine, which was emptied once a day into an open drain running through the cell and outside into a small creek. The rest of the men were crammed into an abandoned movie theater, where the seats had been stripped out, leaving a sloping concrete floor as a POW campground.

Frightened as they were, the prisoners in the Serang theater had to laugh at their captors' futile attempts to count them. During the roll calls, which the Japanese would teach them to call *tenkos*, the men were forced to sit erect and cross-legged while the guards took a count. "On the first nine occasions their counts varied between 1,620 and 1,483," wrote Rohan Rivett, an Australian radio journalist who had escaped Singapore only to be captured on Java. "They've now decided after several more counts on some intermediate figure, but their system of counting is so weird and wonderful that I doubt if they really know to the nearest fifty just how many of us they've got jammed into this [bloody] hellhole." But the prisoners' laughter welled in the shadow of death. In the balcony above them, a tripod-mounted machine gun pointed out over the stage like a lethal spotlight.

Bearding and filthy, their injuries untreated, the sailors were "packed together," Rivett wrote, "like penguins or seals on one of those rocky beaches which the publishers of natural history books love to photograph." Under strict orders to neither speak nor move, the men pressed bones to concrete for hours on end. Only a few had serious wounds. The swift ocean currents, by killing the weak, had largely prescreened survivors for a minimum level of health. Any number of the severely injured who got off the ship never made it ashore. William Stewart, burned while escaping the shell deck beneath the inferno of Turret Two, didn't appear to have very good prospects. Lieutenant Burroughs, the *Houston*'s junior medical officer, figured Stewart wouldn't last two days. The ragged burns on his back and chest prevented him from lying down, so he had to sit. A *Houston* pharmacist's mate wrapped the sailor's charred body in a large swatch of canvas theater curtain, keeping it moist with water cajoled from the Japanese guards and changing and remoistening the dressing with religious regularity each morning after peeling away the dead skin. An Australian doctor saved his left arm by deft application of cod liver oil.

Those with high fevers were sent outside to lie on the bamboo platform that covered the latrine. At night they reclined and slept as sardines in a can, arranged tightly with chests against spines across the full length of the theater. One man's attempt to roll over required a whole row of his fellows to do the same. Food was available only in starvation rations: bare spoonfuls of nearly raw rice. Native cooks mixed it in a concrete bin with a shovel. The result stuck fast to a plate turned upside down. Sufficient water rations went only to those willing to risk execution by slipping outside near the pit latrine during a rain and drinking what fell through the downspouts from the gutters.

The *Houston*'s officers were taken aside in turns for interrogation by the Japanese secret military police, or Kempeitai, in a private residence in Serang that bustled with the comings and goings of Imperial Army jeeps and motorcycles. The small but resounding professional kindnesses the *Perth*'s men experienced in Tjilatjap were not to be found here. Rank brought no privileges. The interrogators worked them over severely. The Americans could hear the tortured screams of a kid from the Royal Australian Air Force. "We thought we were dead pigeons more than once," Lieutenant Barrett wrote.

The Japanese had declared the *Houston* sunk so many times that the flesh-and-blood presence of her survivors fresh from battle might well have struck them as a mass apparition. "They just didn't want to believe we were off the *Houston*," said Charley Pryor. Lieutenant Hamlin, captured and taken to a Japanese merchant ship, was questioned extensively about American attitudes toward the war and whether or not he thought America could win. The information the Americans received or inferred from the interrogators might have given them confidence that victory could be had. Lt. Tommy Payne was told that seven Japanese warships had been sunk on the night of

February 28, including heavy and light cruisers, destroyers, and a seaplane tender. Like Otto Schwarz, he was pressed to reveal how many battleships had been in the Allied force that night. Ens. Herbert Levitt was told that three Japanese cruisers were sunk, along with nine destroyers, a seaplane tender, two transports, and a hospital ship. The extravagant falsity of these claims was matched by odd reports at Serang, supposedly originating with senior Dutch officials, that the American Pacific Fleet was off Java, bombarding Japanese forces near its principal cities, that Allied troops had landed on Timor, Bali, and Java itself, and that, farther afield, four million American, British, and Canadian soldiers had invaded the Bordeaux region of France. Flirtations with fantasy kept morale up, but the news would get worse before it would get better. On the evening of March 24, the stragglers in the contingent of *Houston* survivors, including ship's doctor William Epstein, arrived at Serang and were locked up in the town jail. Two days later, word reached them that the first of their captured shipmates had passed away. On March 26, Lieutenant Weiler, who had tried so gallantly to rally the men of his raft despite his own severe wounds, died at the small Dutch hospital in Pandeglang. A Japanese army officer pocketed his Naval Academy ring as a souvenir.

★

At first, they put great hopes in the idea that friendlies were just around the next coconut palm. "For the first four or five days at Serang," Lanson Harris said, "we were very up. We thought any minute now the Marines were going to come crashing through the door and rescue us. I didn't know where the Marines were going to come from. All I knew is that Marines were pretty good at this kind of stuff." Others were less sure, although the confidence certainly was contagious.

Months before, the Marines had turned in a performance in defense of Wake Island that was as inspirational to home morale as the *Houston*'s exploits might have been had full details reached the mainland. But those Marines were Japanese prisoners now. Their brothers in the Corps were still several months away from settling on Guadalcanal as their first major objective. It took only a few weeks for the mood to darken. "We began to mellow out and to think, *Boy, we're a thousand miles from home and nobody's going to come get us out,*" Harris said.

Their world contracted around the here and now. Food was the top priority in that world, and the Japanese did little to satisfy it. "We were hungry to the point of it being actual torture," said Charley Pryor, held at the Serang jail. They learned that the feeling of extreme hunger was both mental and physical, a transition phase from relative abundance to a crisis of want. They would grow accustomed to far worse. The sign of trouble would be when their hunger pangs disappeared altogether.

"After about two weeks, things began to get very uptight," Lanson Harris said. "We began to hear a lot of stupid arguments. There were a lot of fights. I remember a fellow named Blackie Strickland who was arguing with another fellow over how many pancakes he could eat. *I can eat twenty-six pancakes. You're a damn liar! You can't eat twenty-six pancakes.* Next thing you know they're down on the deck punching holes in each other."

Six weeks in Serang were a short education in the utility of discipline, leadership, and unit integrity. The Japanese, apparently seeing the risks inherent in those same things, undertook to erode them. The first week of April, they ordered most of the *Houston*'s officers to board trucks. Eight of them—Al Maher, William Galbraith, Joseph Dalton, Bob Fulton, Frank Gallagher, Harlan Kirkpatrick, Tommy Payne, and Walter Winslow—were taken from the camp to the docks of Tanjung Priok and put on a prison ship destined for Japan. Three line officers stayed behind, Lt. Russell R. Ross, buckled with dysentery, Lieutenant Hamlin, and Ensign Smith, as well as the two ship's doctors, Cdr. William Epstein and Lt. Clement Burroughs. The departing officers would arrive at Shimonoseki, Japan, on May 4, beginning a journey entirely distinct from the one that would engulf the men left behind on Java.

The scattering of the *Houston*'s men to the far corners of Asia achieved something that the Japanese never quite could with guns and torpedoes. Tokyo Rose wouldn't be crowing about it, but the dispersal of the survivors ensured that one of the fleet's best-drilled fighting crews, the officers and bluejackets who had given life to a presidential flagship, ceased finally to exist. They would forge their identities afresh in the crucible of captivity.

CHAPTER 25

On February 28, 1942, the Navy Department had issued to the press Communiqué No. 48, making vague reference to a "major action" fought by an Allied fleet against a much larger Japanese force trying to land troops on Java. "From fragmentary reports received in the Navy Department," it read, "American naval forces participating in this action consisted of one heavy cruiser and five destroyers." Two weeks later, on March 14, the Navy put out Communiqué No. 54, recounting in more detail the great battle the *Houston* had fought on February 27. The report stated she had survived this encounter and, having refueled, continued west on February 28 in the company of an Australian cruiser. That night the Allied ships met the enemy again, entering battle at about 11:30 P.M. "Nothing, however, has been heard from the HMAS *Perth* or the USS *Houston* since that time," the communiqué read. "The next of kin of the USS *Houston* are being informed accordingly."

Communiqué No. 54 became the basis for an Associated Press report that led the front page of the March 15, 1942, *Los Angeles Examiner*. Jane Harris, who lived in Los Angeles, saw it. The eighty-point sans-serif headline declared, "12 Allied Warships Lost in Java Battle—U.S. Cruiser *Houston*, Destroyer *Pope* Among Japanese Victims—13th Vessel Beached; 8 Nipponese Craft Sunk in Fight."

But since the piece didn't mention her husband, as far as Jane Harris cared, it might as well not have run.

The ambiguity grew worse five days later. On March 20, the Navy delivered a telegram to 1601½ North Broadway Street in Santa Ana, regretting to inform Lanson Harris's parents of their son's MIA status. "Santa Ana Flyer Listed as Missing," announced the home-town paper. Newspapers around the country reported the various lo-cal reverberations of the Navy's communiqués and casualty lists. "Kin of Missing Sad but Proud, Some Hopeful," reported the *New York Herald Tribune*. In April, a wire report detailed the exploits of *Houston* crewmen who fought an inferno ignited by an aerial bomb that hit the cruiser's after gun turret. That was the last certain knowledge to be had of their worldly acts. "Heroes of Cruiser Fire Now Missing," the *Los Angeles Times* reported on April 15.

A United Press dispatch published in some U.S. papers on April 24 opened the possibility of hope. It reported a Japanese propaganda announcement that gloatingly claimed that the *Houston*'s gunnery officer, Cdr. Arthur Maher, was in captivity in "the southern re-gions." According to the Domei News Agency, which broadcast the dispatch, Maher had told his interrogators that only a few of the *Houston*'s complement had been rescued after "the Battle of Java."

The potential enormousness of the ship's loss was itemized on May 14, when the Navy published "Casualty List No. 3," naming the 2,495 officers and enlisted men missing in action from the Pearl Harbor attack through the middle of April, as well as 2,995 more killed in action during that period. The entire crew of the *Houston* appeared on the MIA list. What fate had befallen any one of them was unknown.

People received news in approximate proportion to their mental and emotional wherewithal to collate scattered and fragmentary dis-patches. They had to read the right newspaper at the right time, or have friends or family in other cities to keep track of out-of-town sources. For some people, the uncertain grief of a missing loved one eroded the concentration needed to scan and absorb relevant infor-mation from the stream of world developments, just as it intensified the need to do so. With four theaters of war in full furious swing—a struggle that Franklin D. Roosevelt had described in a fireside chat as "a new kind of war . . . different from all other wars of the past. Not only in its methods and weapons but also in its geography"—it was easy to miss the smallest report that could unlock a mystery.

★

The telegram from the Postal Telegraph Co. reached 705 McGilvra Boulevard in Seattle on March 4, about ten days before she would learn that anything had happened to her husband's ship. The local receiving station had date-stamped it 12:44 P.M. Though it was printed with any number of alphanumeric codes, the space reserved for the point of origin simply said, "Sans Origine." But its message seemed to establish an essential fact that Edith Rooks would cling to in the difficult months ahead. It was simply this: "EVERYBODY WELL. LOVE, HAROLD ROOKS."

If that was so as of the date it was stamped, it did not matter to the captain's wife where the telegram had originated. She told a reporter, "That means he and the ship are okay. When he meant himself in cablegrams to me, he said, 'All well.' If he meant himself and the ship, he said, 'Everybody well.'" From the signature line itself, the telegram might well have come from her son Harold R. Rooks, then a junior at Harvard University. Ten days later, however, she heard from him too. He sent a Western Union dispatch from Cambridge, saying, "JUST HEARD THAT HOUSTON WAS SUNK. HAVE YOU HEARD ANYTHING? WILL STAY IN IF YOU WANT TO PHONE ELIOT 1546. LOVE, HAROLD."

Edith had indeed heard something. But as word of the sinking of the *Houston* began to make headlines, the March 4 message from her husband was her talisman against the dark reality pressing down around her. It was a miracle of miracles. He was alive. When the Navy Department's "We regret to inform you" notice arrived on March 14, the day of her son's inquiry, informing her that her husband was missing following action against the enemy, she could dismiss it as a mistake, a bureaucrat being overzealous with the boilerplate.

The *Houston* was lost but her husband was fine, and she was so very proud of her older son. Nineteen-year-old Harold was busy with a naval reserve officer curriculum that would propel him in his father's path. Edith applauded his ambition. Her March 18 letter to Admiral Hart was, as Hart told her in reply, "characteristic of you in having no hesitation about your son carrying on in his father's footsteps." The Rooks family was fully vested in this war. And Hart was not giving up on the skipper of the *Houston*. He wrote Edith on March 25, "I, myself, am by no means without hope of seeing Rooks in the flesh again. It is quite true that we may not hear from him for a long time, since he may be a prisoner of war. But the experiences of ships sinking in action in that warm water is that there are many survivors in most of the cases. You see, water is warm, not rough, and men can endure until they are picked up."

A few weeks later, the Secretary of the Navy put a sharp dent in Edith's hopes, elaborating on the Western Union telegram.

> It is with deep regret that I confirm the Navy Department's dispatch informing you that your husband, Captain Albert Harold Rooks, United States Navy, is missing following action in the service of his country.
>
> The meager report received shows that the vessel to which he was attached has been reported missing and must be presumed to be lost. As you know, battle conditions delay communications, and it may be months before we have definite information. However, as soon as further details as to his status are received, you will be notified. . . .
>
> As a recent law has been passed providing for continuing payment of salary and certain allotments for missing officers, it is suggested that you communicate with the Navy Department concerning allotments that may lapse.
>
> I desire to express to you my deepest sympathy in your anxiety.

For a few months her only source of news, and the only theater for her despair, was private correspondence. In late April, Edith received a letter from a Navy captain named J. W. Woodruff saying that the mother of *Houston* aviator Lt. John B. Stivers "had word from a most responsible source" that Captain Rooks was a prisoner of war in Formosa. No vague blandishment from the Secretary of the Navy could wash away the hope that grew from these heartening nuggets.

In a May 21 encomium to her husband, Admiral Glassford described him as "a tower of strength in getting our scattered forces together, providing safe conduct for hundreds of merchant ships escaping to the southward out of the fighting area to the north, and in planning not only our operations . . . but for our operations against the enemy. . . . It would be difficult for me to tell you how I relied on your husband's advice to me during those days. So much so that I had determined quite definitely after I relieved Admiral Hart to get Captain Rooks out of his ship at the first opportunity and attach him to my staff as the Deputy Chief of Staff. He never knew of this. . . . I needed just such a man."

*

Years of activism by William A. Bernrieder and other Houston civic leaders to name CA-30 after their city reflected a level of pride that wartime only strengthened. If the launching of the *Houston* had been cause for front-page headlines and champagne celebrations, her loss was, for Bernrieder, akin to the loss of a loved one.

He was visiting the Navy Department on that sad day in early March when he heard that the *Houston* had been sunk. "There was a bell in the naval office which tolled every time a ship was lost," Bernrieder said. "I'm not a crying man; I've probably cried twelve times in my life. But when I saw that dispatch and heard the toll, I went down the hall into a bathroom and cried." The emotional resonance of the name *Houston* was no longer exclusive to Texas. In short order following the news of the cruiser's loss, Navy secretary Frank Knox announced that a sleek new *Cleveland*-class light cruiser under construction at Newport News and slated to be christened the *Vicksburg* would be renamed *Houston*. The new *Houston* (CL-81) was scheduled for a June 1943 launching. And the people of the city of Houston were preparing an even more resounding salute to the lost ship.

"There's never been anything like it, before or since," a city magazine would write four decades later of Memorial Day 1942 in Houston. More than ten thousand Houstonians jammed Main Street between McKinney and Lamar to ensure that the memory of their late namesake cruiser would never be lost. They had read with the rest of America the Navy dispatches and scant news reports sketching the events of her demise. They hungered for news that at least some of the crew might have survived. If it would fall to the Navy to build a new *Houston,* the city itself would take the job of finding the men to replace the human toll.

The old heavy cruiser embarked 1,168 men. The goal of the "Houston Volunteers" recruitment drive was to find a thousand more to replace them. The throng in downtown Houston that day had come to witness the swearing in of a group chosen from the more than three thousand who answered the call. Few of the eager volunteers were likely aware that according to Navy superstition, it was powerfully bad luck for a ship to have its name changed after the keel was laid. There was a war to be won and a campaign of boosterism to sustain. The volunteers included ranch hands and cowboys, college kids and middle-aged men. "I'm ready to fight," one of them told a recruiter after the word went out just two weeks before Memorial Day. "I want to join the Houston Volunteers and get a chance to avenge the boys of the cruiser *Houston*." The volunteers would indeed later become known as the "Houston Avengers."

Though a Navy edict would block family members from serving on the same ship, there was no shortage of familial pledges. Brothers volunteered with brothers; fathers showed up with their sons. A fifty-three-year-old logger named William Harrison Watson tried to sign up but was turned away because of his age and poor eyesight. His four boys took the oath instead. The Junior Chamber of Commerce commissioned a sixty-foot model of the old *Houston* and displayed it outside the naval recruiting office. The keynote speaker that day was the last admiral to fly his flag from *Houston*'s truck, Admiral Glassford, extracted from the doomed Asiatic theater.

Like Glassford, William Bernrieder must have marveled at how times had changed. When the executive secretary of the Cruiser Houston Committee was a naval reservist in the twenties, he had walked down this very same thoroughfare in uniform and been jeered at by pacifists. Now it seemed people couldn't jam themselves tightly enough into the downtown intersection to join this street festival of patriotism. After Glassford finished the swearing-in ceremony, Houston's mayor, Neal Pickett, read a letter from President Roosevelt over the loudspeakers:

> On this Memorial Day, all America joins with you who are gathered in proud tribute to a great ship and a gallant company of American officers and men. That fighting ship and those fighting Americans shall live forever in our hearts.
>
> I knew that ship and loved her. Her officers and men were my friends.
>
> When ship and men went down, still fighting, they did not go down to defeat. They had helped remove at least two cruisers and probably other vessels from the active list of the enemy's rank. . . .
>
> The officers and men of the USS *Houston* drove a hard bargain. They sold their liberty and their lives most dearly.

The spirit of these officers and men is still alive. That is being proved today in all Houston, in all Texas, in all America.

Not one of us doubts that the thousand recruits sworn in
today will carry on with the same determined spirit shown by
the gallant men who have gone before them. . . .

Our enemies have given us the chance to prove that there
will be another USS *Houston,* and yet another USS *Houston* if
that becomes necessary, and still another USS *Houston* as long
as American ideals are in jeopardy. . . .

The officers and men of the USS *Houston* have placed us all
in their debt by winning a part of the victory which is our
common goal. Reverently, and with all humility, we acknowledge this debt.

To those officers and men, wherever they may be, we give
our solemn pledge that the debt will be repaid in full.

At the close of the ceremony, the new boots marched down to the
railway station, where five trains would take them to west coast
training centers. Ultimately, only one of the Avengers would actually come out of the personnel pool assigned to the new *Houston*: a reservist named William A. Kirkland, who worked as a banker in
town. The rest were given to the Navy's general personnel pool,
which Secretary Knox called "an unparalled gift of manpower."

The fate of those they were replacing remained a vexing open
question when an AP wire dispatch published on July 2 cited a
Japanese announcement that a thousand survivors of the USS
Houston and HMAS *Perth* were being held at Batavia. No doubt
mindful that the Japanese had been announcing the sinking of the
Houston just about every other week since the start of the war, the AP
discounted the news, referring to the essential untrustworthiness of
enemy pronouncements.

The avenging impulse carried on. Later that year the city would
organize a fund-raising campaign to pay for the new ship. By the
time it closed on December 21, 1942, Houston residents rich and
poor would pledge $85 million to cover the construction costs of the
new *Houston*, delivered by check from FDR's secretary of commerce,
Jesse H. Jones, to Secretary Knox. And there was enough money to
fund not only a new *Houston* but an aircraft carrier as well. In January
1943, a light carrier already under construction at New York
Shipbuilding in Camden, New Jersey, was christened the *San Jacinto*

(CVL-30) after Texas's signature victory in its war for independence. That ship would slingshot a sometime Houstonian and future American president into desperate air battles in the far western Pacific. George H. W. Bush's aircraft carrier would join a fleet that the survivors languishing on Java could only have fantasized about.

CHAPTER 26

Serang would be a way station to larger prisons. Consolidating the unexpected mob of prisoners—what imperial officer worth his sake could ever have imagined so many men surrendering?—the Japanese determined that more spacious accommodations were needed. On April 13 Imperial Army trucks arrived and the prisoners were mustered and told to prepare to move out. A Japanese officer ordered the Americans to line up against the jail's wall. "Officer? Any officer?" he demanded to know. An American stepped forward. "Yes, I'm a naval officer." It was Lieutenant Hamlin.

The Japanese, in broken English, elicited some basic biographical information from Hamlin. He was none too pleased to learn his prisoner was from the *Houston*. The Japanese officer alluded to a hospital ship sunk in Bantam Bay—"No good. No good," he said—then he turned to weightier questions of honor. He asked Hamlin, "Who is the better man, Tojo or Roosevelt?"

"Roosevelt," answered the lieutenant.

The Japanese officer turned and hollered at his troops, who jumped away from the American as machine gunners swiveled their weapons and trained them on the prisoners.

There was a weighty silence, then the officer stepped forward again. "Who is the better man, Tojo or Roosevelt?" Again Hamlin responded in favor of his commander in chief.

The machine gun barrels converged on Hamlin now. The Japanese officer repeated the question, "Who's the better man? Tojo or Roosevelt?"

Though he might have had special reason to know, given FDR's famous affection for his old ship, Hamlin simply said this time, "Roosevelt is my leader." This seemed to satisfy the Japanese officer. He barked at his troops and they began breaking down their machine guns. When they were finished, they began herding the Americans into trucks for a journey to God knew where.

It wasn't a long trip. The trucks drove them some sixty miles to Java's capital city, Batavia. A Dutch installation there, known as "Bicycle Camp," had been the headquarters of the colonial army's Tenth Battalion, a unit of bicycle troops, before General Imamura's troops seized it and turned it into a prison. The trucks passed through the gate and unloaded the prisoners along the long macadam road running straight through the camp. On either side of the entrance road, long barracks stretched a hundred yards or more, separate ones for the Dutch, Australian, British, and Americans. Constructed from concrete blocks, the barracks had smart red tile roofs and porches running the length of them on both sides. The sleeping quarters inside had no bunks as such. Prisoners slept on bamboo platforms that lined either wall. The barracks were subdivided into cubicles, each holding five or six men. Though the compound was ringed with concertina wire, it was full of relative luxuries such as running water and sewers. After the squalor of Serang, Lloyd Willey thought Bicycle Camp "looked like the Hilton." About five thousand Allied prisoners of war would call it home in the summer of 1942.

For the *Houston*'s seasoned crew, it was boot camp all over again. Whenever a guard walked into the camp area, which they did day and night, the first man to see him shouted "*Kiotsuke*"—attention! "The whole camp froze," said Jim Gee. "You stood like statues. Rank didn't make a bit of difference. As long as you were a prisoner, you froze. And if the Japs saw you move, if you were a hundred yards away and you moved, you kicked something, or you picked up something, boy he'd walk directly to you and knock you right down with the butt of his rifle or do whatever he wanted to."

Several times a day, whenever a Japanese officer saw fit, muster was called. Whenever *tenkos* were ordered, the prisoners counted off—"*Ichi, ni, san, shi, go* . . ." If a guard came within forty feet, a crisp, forty-five-degree bow was required, arms straight at the sides. The slightest failure—of posture, of appearance, of obedience to the babel of commands—brought a swift blow to the head by open hand, fist, stick, or rifle butt. The prisoners adopted the British term for this abuse, "bashings."

It was no special form of torture. It was standard treatment in the Imperial Army, which routinely enforced discipline through physical abuse, humiliation, and corporal punishment. Though the Japanese had little regard for an enemy who surrendered—the Japanese army's interpretation of the code of Bushido gave no such option to the emperor's troops—the bashings were little different from what they gave their own troops. In the Imperial Army pecking order, the beatings flowed downhill from the sergeants to corporals to the several levels of privates, to the Korean conscripts, and finally to the prisoners. "When a guy got out of line, they didn't bawl him out. He had to stand at attention, and they belted the piss out of him," said John Wisecup. "Officers did it to one another, so they did it to us, only more so."

Many of the Japanese noncoms initially at Bicycle Camp were first-team combat veterans with years of experience in Manchuria and China. Though their odd split-toed *tabi* sneakers and oversized uniforms struck the Americans as comical, their prowess was evident enough. "They were hard cases," said Wisecup. The front-line troops, who temporarily administered the camps until combat operations ended, were tough, disciplined, occasionally brutal, and every so often surprisingly humane. "They were looking for a soft billet," said *Houston* sailor George Detre. "They just wouldn't bother you unless they had to." Later, when rear-echelon support troops arrived and Korean conscripts were given charge over the prisoners, the treatment would grow much worse.

The only reliable way to avoid a bashing was to will yourself into the woodwork. Taller guys had a hard time being inconspicuous, and because the Japanese and later Korean guards seemed sensitive to the racial height disparity, taller prisoners were often made to stand in pits or sink to their knees so the guards could knock them around. The Marines, chosen for Asiatic Fleet service in part for their stature, paid a price for their genetic blessings. John Wisecup was an imposing specimen, long and lean, with a squint of New Orleans character in his looks. Jim Gee stood six foot three, one of the better boxers in the fleet, nicknamed "Caribou" for the size of his frame. According to Gee, "Some of them were so short that when they'd start to hit you with their fists you could sort of straighten up and miss it. And that would make them mad! Oh, they'd get mad when you'd do that! And so once, being a tall person, one of them was so little that I could miss his slap every time he'd try it. So he marched me over to a building, and he stood upon the porch, and I stood down on the ground, and he literally slapped me back and forth until I decided, 'I really shouldn't do that anymore. I'll just let him hit me once or twice next time and miss the rest of it.'"

The worst thing a prisoner could do while under assault, short of retaliating, was to fall down. "You did your damnedest to hold your feet, and you did your damnedest to hold in any kind of a groan or anything like that," said Seldon Reese. They learned to stand and take it. "After a while, hell, a bashing didn't mean nothing to you," said Wisecup. "Christ, it was a way of life."

Amid the daily grind at Bicycle Camp, local Dutch women appeared outside the barbed wire from time to time, riding by on bikes, flashing the prisoners a V for victory, cheering them on, sometimes offering them food, soap, sugar, or news. This incensed the Japanese, who more than once knocked the women off their bikes and beat them on the ground. The prisoners learned to dread the women's friendly gestures, knowing the likely reaction from the guards. But their courage was inspiring. "I must say that if they were fighting the war, it might have turned out differently," said Jim Gee. "The women and the kids had more intestinal fortitude than any group of people that I have ever seen or know of."

The guards' conduct confirmed the basest Western stereotypes of the Japanese even as it shocked them with its brutality. "The Japanese soldier placed great emphasis on his masculinity, lowering his voice several notches by force to make it sound deeper, meaner, and harsher," Howard Charles would write. "He strutted, pulling the corners of his mouth down like an actor in a Kabuki play. He appeared to engineer his anger, starting at one level and building his rage to the point of explosion. If you never hated before, you did now. But you could not let it show, if you wanted to live."

Other guards showed kindness and generosity to their captives. A three-star private nicknamed Smiley professed to be a Christian and said that he had a brother who lived in the Sacramento Valley in

California. "I'll always thank some good Christian missionary, I guess, for his work with this individual," said Charley Pryor. "This old boy had a mouthful of gold teeth. He opened his mouth, and it looked like the sun coming up." His time in the States seemed to dispose him kindly to his prisoners. "At nighttime you'd hear some noise around your cell door, and there'd be a little tin of water he slid under the door or maybe a tin of rice that he had taken from the natives' kitchen," Pryor said. But such behavior was exceptional. Once in a while, a prisoner would start to feel his oats a little too fully, bringing a reprisal that reasserted powerfully who was in charge.

One day at Bicycle Camp a guard was hollering at a big Australian kid, who couldn't understand what was being demanded of him. The guard slapped him. The Australian reared back and struck the guard right in the jaw, knocking him back several steps. "All these other Jap guards rushed out immediately, and they started beating on this Australian," Lloyd Willey said. "They beat him all afternoon. They made him stand at attention, and anytime that he dropped down, they'd go out and beat him some more. That lasted almost three days, until he just laid on the ground. He was practically dead, and then they started kicking him until he was dead. Then they tied a rope around his ankles, and they pulled him up and down every street in Bicycle Camp." They called the Allied officers over. " 'This man died an easy death compared to what the next man will get who hits a Japanese guard.' "

CHAPTER 27

In the deprived conditions at Bicycle Camp, hygiene was difficult to practice. An outbreak of dysentery at Serang had left hundreds of men unable to crawl to the latrine. A few days after the officers' departure to Japan on April 8, Marine Pvt. Donald W. Hill, removed to the courtyard outside the Serang theater, died of the disease. He couldn't stomach the food the Japanese were serving. According to Marvin Robinson, Hill "willed himself to die" by repeating these words as his dysentery drained him: *"This is not the way my mother made bread. . . ."*

The *Houston* sailors had long ago adjusted their constitutions to resist the contagions of Asiatic Fleet service. Sudden sicknesses were liable to wash over the crew at any moment. Once, before war broke out, the ship's sick bay became so overcrowded that the Marines had to be evicted from their berthing area to make room for the ill. They got savvy to the ways sickness spread, controlling contagions by careful hygiene, requiring coffee be drunk from disposable paper cups.

Though an enterprising Marine sergeant had procured a shower-head down at the Batavia docks and converted the rudimentary plumbing in the Navy barracks into showers, dysentery and malaria were rife. To combat them, the Japanese gave prisoners access to the camp hospital, where medical officers and pharmacist's mates worked as staff. The *Houston*'s entire medical department, including its two doctors, Commander Epstein and Lieutenant Burroughs, and pharmacist's mates Al Kopp, Eugene Orth, Raymond Day, Griff Douglas, and Lowell W. Swartz, worked there. Proper medicine was unavailable. They had lab dyes, slides, and cover glasses but no microscope. One day, Burroughs cajoled a Japanese optometrist into finding them a new microscope. In the morning he smuggled in a 1920 vintage Himmler model.

But when disease came, their defenses were unprepared. John Wisecup fell ill with bacillary dysentery and then its amoebic cousin. He came close to death. Passing blood and growing anemic, he dropped thirty pounds from his normal weight of 175. "This stuff is just like a knife in your guts," he said. "The smell of any kind of chow made me sick." Not treatment by charcoal solution nor rice soup or salts cured him. "I was a walking wreck. People wouldn't even come near me. . . . I could see them looking at me: 'Jesus! This son-of-a-bitch is going to die!' You know, I looked that bad."

The worst case belonged to the senior surviving line officer from the *Houston*, Lt. Russell R. Ross. They called him "Rosie." He had contracted a case of bacillary dysentery that defied the best work of the men at Bicycle Camp's hospital. Hamlin repeatedly asked the camp commander, a lieutenant named Suzuki, to allow him to go to Batavia to buy medicine, where there was known to be an ample supply. The Japanese refused. According to Hamlin, "Finally a British colonel interceded and told the Japs it would be plain murder if they did not permit the purchase of medicine for Lt. Ross and an Australian soldier who was also critically ill." The medicine was delivered, but it arrived too late. Ross died on May 5, the Australian a day or two later.

According to John Wisecup, Ross could not seem to summon the will to live in captivity. "He gave up a long time ago," Wisecup said. "This guy was an overaged lieutenant. He was in his thirties and was a very moody type of guy." Senior officers, who usually had the best access to information and were well suited to evaluate it, could be the most despondent prisoners in the camp. Commander Epstein succumbed to the despair that education and knowledge sometimes brought. According to Al Kopp, where others with more hopeful outlooks managed to work their way through the most difficult days on naive faith, Epstein, though well loved by the sailors, who could be his sons, became mired in pessimism. Thus, when Lieutenant Ross died, it was another lieutenant, a Naval Academy man and a line officer, who ascended to lead the *Houston* contingent. Having shown his mettle trying to save Ross from contagion, the man who helped bury him, Lt. Harold S. Hamlin, took over as commander of the Navy company.

With the *Houston*'s other senior officers pulled away and shipped to Japan, and with the officers left in camp housed in separate quarters, Hamlin feared the enlisted men would dissociate without the officers there to lead them. He thought they might conclude that they were "all in this together on an equal footing." Such egalitarianism was unacceptable to Hamlin. He worried that small acts of rebellion unconscionable on a Navy ship were becoming everyday occurrences. Enlisted men stole from the waterfront. Some dispensed with saluting and used first names or nicknames with officers. John Wisecup, a gifted cartoonist who was as ruthless with the sketch pad as he was with mouth and fists, lampooned one and all with his illustrated satires of camp life. He resisted the temptation to spoof the camp guards only at the behest of shipmates with a surer sense of self-preservation. As useful as this leveling idea might have been from a survivalist's perspective—and as useful as it would occasionally prove later, when life got worse—there was value in hierarchy and internal accountability. Prison morale grew from the sense of order and structure that the captives built independent of that which the Japanese imposed upon them. It helped them keep their dignity and thus built a foundation for survival.

Lieutenant Hamlin called several meetings of his men and, quoting Navy regulations from memory, reminded them that the authority of officers extended beyond the hull of the ship. "Generally speaking," he wrote, "petty officers behaved splendidly in this respect and after I had held 'Captain's Mast' and assigned extra duties as punishment, discipline returned to normal."

According to Hamlin, "Organization was kept in every way as similar to normal Naval organization as the circumstances would permit." The group was subdivided into divisions commanded by an officer assisted by a chief petty officer. Lt. (jg) Leon W. Rogers was appointed executive officer. The supply officer, Ens. Preston R. Clark, assisted in the preparation and distribution of food. The third senior officer, Ens. J. M. Hamill, was appointed first lieutenant and, assisted by the carpenter, was in charge of the upkeep and cleanliness of the barracks. The medical department was under Commander Epstein. Hamlin arranged for a rotating schedule of daily watches and installed two yeomen, John C. Reas and John A. Harrell, in a Japanese-equipped office to compile personal records. They kept one copy for their captors and another, secretly, for themselves.

The officers and NCOs cobbled together battle reports for the actions in the Java Sea and Sunda Strait. Lt. Leon Rogers interviewed survivors and began to keep a log of their movements, disciplinary offenses, and so on. "We were professional sailors," said George Detre, "and this was the only way we went." Throughout the ordeal, the enlisted men would benefit from the strength and station of their officers. "If you got your brass, you got a chance. If you don't, you're strictly on your own," said John Wisecup.

*

The hyperactive machismo of a guy such as Wisecup, reined in over time by the likes of senior sergeants including Walter Standish and Harley Dupler, bred the Marines' reputation for aggressive efficiency that led so many prisoners to vest their hopes in rescue. When would it finally come? Despite a mounting impression that no one was riding to their aid, the prisoners kept an eager ear on the news.

News was a gold-standard commodity, as valuable to the mind as food was to the body. It was power. It was strength, the key to withstanding the psychic assaults of the guards at *tenko*. Somewhere along the line at Bicycle Camp, Charley Pryor found a Malay-English dictionary. He studied it like a Bible in catechism. Three weeks of cramming enabled him to talk with natives and get the scoop on the outside world. "They would tell us about great naval battles and what the Allied forces had destroyed and that they were on Ambon, or they'd landed to the north in the Celebes or on Borneo, and they were on Sumatra. Oh, it was just a matter of a few days, you know, and they'd be on Java."

There were plenty of reasons to question the sunny outlook. On a work party out at the Dunlop tire factory one afternoon, Paul Papish was stacking tires, cussing a blue streak. "What's the matter, sailor?" a voice behind him asked. Papish replied, "These damned Japs don't know where they want this stuff." Reaching for another tire, he saw out of the corner of his eye a split-toed *tabi* belonging to a Japanese sergeant.

Turning, Papish stood and looked around for the speaker. "I don't know where this voice is coming from, speaking just as good English as I am," Papish said. As he realized it must have been the Japanese, shock spread across the American's face, and the sergeant grinned and said, "That's all right." Papish could not have guessed how all right it was. As it happened, this soldier had more in common with a New York cabbie than with one of Tojo's finest. He told Papish that before the war started he had in fact been a taxi driver in Manhattan. On December 8, the date of the Pearl Harbor attack in Japan, he was home visiting his aging parents. Stuck thereafter in Nippon, he was conscripted into the army and there was no looking back.

"Listen, I want to tell you something," the sergeant said. "There's a lot of Japanese who speak good English. They won't be like me. Remember that." The sergeant gave Papish a cigarette later that day, as well as some canned beef to mix with his rice. Papish asked him, "Look, tell me something. What do you think of this war?"

"Well, sailor, I'll tell you this. You and I both know who's going to win, but it's going to be a long one. Yes, it's going to be a long one."

Paul Papish had persuaded himself that liberation was just around the corner. If denial morphed into fantasy, and the result bucked up the spirits, why not cling to it? The Japanese might have the upper hand at the moment, but it wouldn't be for long, he consoled himself. Yet the English-speaking sergeant's candor eroded his confidence that the war would go well. "That just kind of took the wind out of my sails," Papish said. A Catholic, he sought out a Dutch priest and asked if he had anything he could pray with. The priest gave him a rosary.

The frightful possibilities had a few weeks to gain a foothold in the sailors' minds before, as expected, United States troops finally appeared, marching on the gates of Bicycle Camp. But it was not the U.S. Marines who came for the *Houston* men. The Army did the honors instead.

CHAPTER 28

The four-hundred-odd soldiers who appeared at Bicycle Camp on May 14, 1942, belonged to the Second Battalion of the 131st Field Artillery Regiment of the Thirty-sixth Infantry Division, Texas National Guard. Reaching Bicycle Camp under the command of Col. Blucher S. Tharp, the soldiers, in full dress, marched in hauling duffles and all manner of diverse equipment. The sudden commotion was a pleasant surprise to the Navy prisoners. "They sure looked good," said Donald Brain. "They looked awfully good coming in there." Otto Schwarz and Gus Forsman felt their hearts swell at the sharp appearance of their countrymen.

The Texans, a world away from their headquarters at Camp Mabry in Austin, had become orphans on the Army's organizational chart shortly after their unit was placed under federal control on November 25, 1940. After conducting maneuvers in the Louisiana swamps and pine forests in the summer of 1941, the Texans were "surplused"—detached from the Thirty-sixth Division and sent to the Pacific, earmarked for a secret location named "PLUM." They left San Francisco on board the SS *Republic* just two weeks before the Pearl Harbor raid. PLUM turned out to be the Philippines. Their mission was to support Allied forces under General MacArthur.

For the *Houston* survivors, the arrival of this sharply uniformed, well-supplied battalion of ostensible liberators was the long-awaited moment of deliverance, the restoration of the natural order of an America-centered universe. At least it was all of these things for a few minutes. Like their dream fantasies about roast beef and fresh bread and sweet pork and beans vanishing at the end of hungry slumbers, the idea that the Army had come to free them shimmered briefly and gave way to scraping reality. It dawned quickly on the *Houston* men that the Texans were not rescuers. Herded into Bicycle Camp, they were coming to kneel alongside the Navy company in submission to Imperial Japan. Back home, their fate unknown, the unit would acquire a nickname that had the ring of legend: "The Lost Battalion."

As the fleet-wide assignment of the Houston Volunteers showed, the Navy Department forbade its ships from having the kind of provincial identity that characterized the Lost Battalion. Each of its batteries was drawn from a single Texas town—D Battery from Wichita Falls, E Battery from Abilene, F Battery from Jacksboro, Headquarters Battery from Decatur, and so on. Though the *Houston's* crew hailed from all across America, it had a number of Lone Star Staters, including Marvin Robinson, Charley Pryor, Jim Gee, Frank "Pinky" King, and Bert Page. A few of them actually had friends in common with the Guardsmen. It highlighted the clannish nature of the Texans—and also their greatest strength. By virtue of their selection as Asiatic Fleet flagship and the president's private fishing yacht, the *Houston* men had developed a special sense of identity that became the basis for everything they did. But the Texans of the 131st were born with it. The Alamo spirit grew out of small-town friendships, rooted in local pride. As it happened, more than a few of the *Houston* sailors could relate to them on that level. Pinky King's older sisters had gone to school with 2nd Lt. Clyde Fillmore's wife back in Wheeler County. They had to meet halfway around the world in an enemy prison camp to discover it.

The first asset the artillerymen brought to camp was their number. With the arrival of the 534 Texans, there were a total of 902 Americans at Bicycle Camp. "We felt very good because we felt that in numbers there was strength. We needed that," said Jim Gee. If some of the *Houston* Marines wondered what kind of soldiers these Guardsmen were, others had seen some of their handiwork earlier, on the long march to Serang. Charley Pryor had seen Japanese trucks burning by the roadside, trees denuded of foliage, and the odd corpse of an Imperial Army soldier in khaki and split-toed boots. Who was doing the fighting they could hardly have known. Swift though the Japanese conquest had been, it was not a complete walkover.

The Texans, appalled by the ragged condition of the Navy "gobs," responded with generosity that brought the sailors a step back toward humanity. Their extra clothing and gear was distributed among the bedraggled *Houston* men until everyone had gotten something. They passed around blankets, pants, shirts, smokes, cans of Spam, spoons, plates, cups, razors, and tools. "Whatever you needed, they seemed to come up with it," said Gus Forsman. Rumors floated that the battalion's officers had brought a considerable sum of cash into the camp. With the arrival of the 131st came, somehow, money that was used to buy supplies. The men were paid by their rank and took all opportunities to buy food from locals. The 131st brought a full field kitchen with them. Once it was set up, the Americans had the best in the camp.

Like the *Houston* survivors, the Lost Battalion had tangled with the Japanese and come away monstrously frustrated. Sailing westward during the countdown to war, embarked on the SS *Republic* and escorted by the heavy cruiser *Pensacola*, even the experienced troops among them had wondered, "How could there be so much water in the world?" Under way for the Philippines, they were redirected to Brisbane, arriving three days before Christmas 1941. There they ran into some locals who greeted them boisterously, "Hey, Yanks!" The artillerymen responded, "Hey, ANZACs!"* When the protest came, "We're not ANZACs, we're Australians," the Guardsmen replied, "Well, we're not Yanks, we're Texans."

On January 11, 1942, they landed at Surabaya, Java, eventually to deploy around Camp Singosari, an airstrip amid the muddy tapioca fields outside nearby Malang. The artillerymen worked as the Nineteenth Bombardment Group's ground support unit, as their mess, their equipment maintenance, communications, and air defense staff. They rigged their World War I–vintage seventy-five-millimeter field guns for antiaircraft duty, planting them in pits to improve their firing angles. They sprang into action whenever they heard the drum signals of native spotters along the coast warning them of inbound Japanese planes.

---

*ANZAC is an acronym for Australia and New Zealand Army Corps, dating to 1915.

Like their naval counterparts within ABDA, they had been poorly employed under multinational command. Perhaps no one invested any great hope in them. On January 18, Field Marshal Wavell himself inspected them and did not seem impressed. There was little they could do to protect the home of the overmatched, overworked B-17 Flying Fortress crews at Singosari. On February 27, what was left of the Nineteenth Bombardment Group, ravaged by Japanese air attacks, withdrew from Java. The Second Battalion was released, too. "We were still in an *Alice in Wonderland* world," said Jess Stanbrough, a technical sergeant and radio specialist with the unit. "It was just another Louisiana maneuver. Nobody was frightened of the situation. We certainly didn't realize how bad it was. We thought there were a lot of other people around to help." Like the sailors on the *Houston,* they idled and wondered when the Japanese amphibious assault would finally come.

The commander of ABDA's ground forces needed artillery. Dutch Lt. Gen. Hein ter Poorten had two Australian infantry battalions, the 2/3 Machine Gun and 2/2 Pioneers (combat engineers) under Brigadier Arthur S. Blackburn; twenty-five British light tanks of the Third Hussars; and 25,000 Dutch troops, the majority of them ethnic Indonesians with a low level of readiness and training. What he lacked was artillery. The Americans filled the bill. When the fight for Java was joined on the ground, the 131st's E Battery was assigned to clean up the battalion's equipment and then withdraw to Surabaya. The rest of the battalion went west to fight alongside the Australians.

As they departed, the Americans drove their trucks in circles to convince Japanese observers there were more of them than the four hundred or so there actually were. "We would pass through a village, make a wide sweep, rearrange our vehicles and enter that village from another direction," remembered Kyle Thompson, a sergeant with Headquarters Battery. "It all seemed useless to me, but then the idea was to make the people think they had tons of support from the United States Army."

The 131st dug in new positions in a rubber plantation outside the Dutch governor's grounds at Buitenzorg (now Bogor). Soon they withdrew to Bandung. The plan was for Brigadier Blackburn's Australians, combat-hardened veterans of fighting in North Africa, Greece, and Crete, to hold the Japanese from prepared positions in western Java while the Dutch troops counterattacked on the flanks.

If the worst happened, the artillerymen knew they could count on the Navy to retrieve them from the beach and carry them to safety. The British had done it at Dunkirk.

Japanese troops came ashore on March 1 and before long they seemed to be everywhere. They were too many and too swift. With Japanese aircraft controlling the skies—soldiers from the 131st were dismayed to find American fighter planes at Bandung still in crates stacked on flatcars—the Aussies and the Dutch were left fighting a piecemeal defense that never congealed into a force capable of a counteroffensive.

On March 4, near Buitenzorg, the 131st, two and a half miles behind the Australian front lines, went into action supporting friendly infantry, firing till dark. During the next couple of days the artillerymen played hide-and-seek as Japanese patrols sought to locate them. Maj. Winthrop H. ("Windy") Rogers, the battery's commander, told Sergeant Thompson, "There's only a few hundred of them over there. We'll have them wiped out by tomorrow noon, and within a week there won't be a Jap left on Java."

On March 5, scouts from D Battery came across a large, modern hotel, the Savoy, and parked their command car by the entry. Dozens of Dutch officers in dress uniform milled about, escorting women in fine formal wear. A good orchestra was playing, a seven-course dinner in progress. "We entered right off the road, dressed in our fatigues, dirty and bearded, and carrying our .45 pistols. We were utterly amazed to see this big party going on with bright lights blazing with a full-scale war going on just down the road," said Jess Stanbrough. The Americans sat down and gorged themselves.

Two days later a courier arrived from the front with a message for Colonel Tharp: "The Australian Brigadier says it's getting pretty hot up there. He advises an immediate withdrawal. The first line of Japs already have crossed the river. We can't possibly stop them—we're outnumbered at least 100 to 1."

Tharp ordered his batteries to retreat and join him in Buitenzorg as Dutch engineers blew up bridges over Java's western rivers. "The impact of this hit us like a ton of bricks," wrote Kyle Thompson. "At last we fully realized that the war had caught up with us." One moonless night, the Texans began pulling out. Because Thompson's command car had radio equipment that needed to stay hooked up to the command post, he was the last one out. With Japanese forces advancing directly behind him, he raced through the night, headlights blazing in violation of blackout orders.

At his command post, Colonel Tharp gathered his men on the morning of March 8 and said, "Well, men, it's quite obvious that we aren't running the Japs off the island and we aren't likely to. It looks like this whole thing will fall through. We are under the direct command of the Dutch, and what they say, we have to do. I think they will surrender by the tenth at the latest. We have one chance left. There may be a ship down on the south coast. We'll try to make it through to it."

With Japanese bombers controlling the skies, the Imperial Second Army took Batavia and Tjilatjap, overcame light resistance outside Surabaya, and was converging on the old ABDA headquarters at Bandung from two sides. At nine A.M. on March 8, as Tharp's men were still aiming to escape, General ter Poorten announced that the Dutch fight for Java was at an end. Two hours later, a Dutch messenger reached the 131st's headquarters on a motorcycle. He was carrying a message: "We are forced to surrender. It is useless to try to hold out any longer. You are ordered to surrender immediately with your men and equipment, unconditionally, to the Imperial Japanese Army. You are to wait with your men and equipment at Goerett."

"On whose orders?" Colonel Tharp asked.

"The Governor General's office, Batavia, sir. I am also instructed to tell you that it's useless to attempt an escape. There is no way out."

Allied leadership would be as fractious in surrender as it had been in battle. "We were stunned, speechless," wrote Kyle Thompson. "Some of us were crying out of fear of an uncertain future." A few slipped out of camp against orders and headed for the coast in hopes of escape. But there was none. Instructed by the Dutch to surrender their equipment in good order, the battalion rebelled. The Texans depressurized the recoil mechanisms on their artillery pieces, buried their small arms, rolled hundred-dollar bills into cigars and smoked them. They drained the oil pans of their trucks and held a morbid competition to see which make lasted longest without engine lubrication. The Ford died first, then the Dodge, then the Chevy.

Word came that some Americans had been able to evacuate at Tjilatjap. The soldiers had heard rumors that the *Houston* and perhaps other ships were standing by to take them off the island. "We still had this eternal hope, prayer for the *Houston*," Sgt. Wade H. Webb of the 131st said. "We lived on that, and actually we lived on that right up until they capitulated. Even a few days after, there was talk of breaking to the coast on the south . . . We clung to that possibility that we would get on the *Houston* and get off Java." They knew nothing of the Battle of Sunda Strait, the heroism of Captain Rooks, or the stoutness of Sergeant Standish's heart. They could go south and take their chances there, or surrender and roll the dice with the enemy.

Though some newspaper reports back home would describe the capture of the Lost Battalion as if it had been a repeat of the Alamo, the reality was far less dramatic. For the duration of the war it would burn the Texans that they had been cashed out by the Dutch and forced to submit with scarcely a fight. Rounded up at Goerett, they were taken to a train station and presented to a Japanese officer who made a welcoming speech. "I guess that was the first time I'd seen a Jap or heard them speaking," said Staff Sgt. Roy M. Offerle. "He would scream and holler and yell, and then the interpreter would say, 'The commander says he is very happy to see you.' Then he would scream and holler like he was threatening to kill us, and then they would say, 'You will soon go to a camp.' " On April 1, they were imprisoned at Batavia's port district, Tanjung Priok.

Six weeks later, the artillerymen were marched to Bicycle Camp, where they came face-to-face with the sailors who were supposed to have been their rescuers. The sailors stared back, reciprocal expectations evident in many eyes. Through no fault of their own, each had let down the other. All were disappointed, if not altogether surprised, to find that they were not the only Americans who had failed to turn back an ambitious emperor's bid for control of the Asian world.

CHAPTER 29

Capture was a crucible that turned the dynamics of success upside down. Strengths became weaknesses, weaknesses strength. Where at the Naval Academy a well-developed aura of entitlement and patrician self-esteem could propel one to success, now those traits were potential paths to ruin. A disdainful look in the eye or a failure to submit, so carefully inculcated in children of privilege, got you beaten. A harder upbringing, on the other hand—a lifestyle of rural labor, of daily brinksmanship with an abusive stepfather—could produce a psychological carapace that enabled survival amid horrible adversity. Such improbable strength was not uncommon among the hardscrabble kids who enlisted in the military in the late 1930s and early 1940s. The trick to living in Japanese captivity was to navigate the divide separating subservience and defiance. Independent-minded boots who once thought the world revolved around their own tough selves might have wondered at the calculated brutality of their drill instructors. They would learn soon enough the higher purpose behind it all.

Otto Schwarz had left Newark at sixteen in the summer of 1940, joined the Civilian Conservation Corps, and worked on road construction crews in the Sierra Nevadas. After a Navy recruiter visited his work site one day, Schwarz asked his mother to sign his enlistment papers. She seemed to know that the military offered him a chance for a better life. Howard R. Charles grew up in Kansas fantasizing about killing his abusively tyrannical stepfather. Ultimately his method of coping was to run away. By the time he reached Bicycle Camp, he knew how to take a punch. "That's the way I handled myself with my stepfather. 'Howard,' he would say, 'I'm gonna fix you, you little sonuvabitch.' And then he would beat me, always in private, sometime with fists, sometimes with that blacksnake whip, promising to kill me if I ever so much as breathed a word about it to my mother particularly, or anyone else. . . . I reacted to the guards who beat the prisoners as I did to my stepfather. I would never deliberately antagonize them. I would let them get their kicks from beating me, and I would wait, and one day . . ."

There were times when the Japanese seemed vulnerable to a surprisingly effective group countermeasure devised by the prisoners. It worked like this: when one of their number was taking a bashing, rather than cower, they gathered as an audience. They would call each other's attention to the victim and point and laugh at him. "Hey, old Joe's really getting a pounding . . . !" In effect it turned the offending guard into a performer on the prisoners' stage. This psychological aikido could have striking results. "That really embarrassed the Japanese," said Seldon Reese. "It had a hell of a psychological effect on them. . . . They got to where they didn't really hound the Americans and Australians and Scots nearly as much as the English and the Dutch. . . . They got far worse bashings than us guys that laughed." It was a bit like slowing the progress of a forest fire by burning down the woods in its path. But it paid dividends, at least initially, at Bicycle Camp.

*

Every morning at daybreak, after *tenko,* the Japanese sent the prisoners down to the dockyards at Tanjung Priok and to other military and industrial sites to salvage useful things from the rubble of war. At the Dunlop tire factory, they stacked tires and loaded them onto ships. Out at an airfield, they moved gasoline and oil drums. At the partially scuttled Shell Oil Company refinery, they used hand pumps to move gasoline from the few storage tanks that the Dutch hadn't ruined with sugar into fifty-five-gallon drums, then rolled them onto trucks for transport to a makeshift storage area out on a golf course. There were plenty of smaller drums of grease and oil to queue up on the docks. Autos were cannibalized for their carburetors and spark plugs and sheet metal. Industrial machinery—large gears, small nuts and bolts, generators, refrigerators—was crated up and shipped to the home islands. What furniture and other treasures could be looted from Java's Dutch mansions and villas were likewise jammed onto cargo ships and taken to Japan.

A barge sunk in the harbor was found to be full of gin, whiskey, and spirits. Japanese divers retrieved much of it, selling bottles in camp for two guilders. Prisoners could usually flip such delicacies for a profit, though if a guy got caught doing arbitrage the penalty was severe. "In Bicycle Camp, you tried to get out on a working party rather than get out of work," Paul Papish said. "It was survival. You had a chance to get something to eat." Prisoners assigned to stack sacks of sugar learned to tear open a sack and leak some into their boot. A ship's cook used the contraband to make candy with coconut and peanuts.

The Batavia waterfront was a scavenger's paradise, and the prisoners benefited from it as surely as their masters did. They snatched anything at hand that offered some potential use in captivity: nails, paint, medicine, Vaseline, kerosene, gasoline, gin. Service in a warship's closed universe made Navy men resourceful. John Wisecup fashioned a prison mess kit out of some old peach cans. Bamboo stalks became spoons or chopsticks. He could take a beer bottle, tie string around the middle, and set the string on fire. When it burned through, he would tap the bottle on concrete and break it around the middle, then sand down the edges to make a serviceable drinking glass. Two sailors, Blackie Strickland and Manuel Castro, found some timbers and built a four-sided vat. Mixing sugar, available from locals for a price, and a sweet fruit that looked like a long peanut, they brewed beer. Amassing a stash of several dozen bottles, they were loath to sell right away, at least until a sailor named Jack Burge arranged a change in their market outlook.

Burge occupied a cubicle across from Strickland and Castro's, affording him a clear and tempting view of the fermented treasure trove. Apparently the temptation got to him. One day Burge said to George Detre, "Well, I think we're going to have a big sale on beer tonight." Detre didn't think so. He didn't sense the brewers were eager to sell just yet. "I think they will tonight," Burge offered. "Why?" "Because I just started a rumor that the Japs are going to raid the place." When he knew word had gotten around, Detre approached Strickland and Castro and asked how much they wanted for the beer. A bargain was struck and Detre took the whole supply. He tipped off Burge, and the two sailors spread a blanket under the fruit tree that night and drank until the sun came up.

Marine Sgt. James McCone's nickname was "Gunner" before his creativity and resourcefulness in Bicycle Camp earned him a new moniker. As Howard Charles wrote, "He'd see a tin can—'Oh my God, this is a container. This is not a tin can. This is a container. This can hold things, house things.' He'd see a bit of twine: 'We'll sew somebody up with this someday. This can be very, very vital.' " He was intense about it, became focused every waking moment, it seemed, on gathering useful things for himself and his fellow prisoners. His buddies started calling him "Pack Rat."

The Japanese were leery of McCone's eccentricities. "They'd look at him and kind of shake their heads a little bit and just leave him alone," wrote Charles. Pack Rat was hard to intimidate. He maintained a vacant, vaguely bemused posture somewhere between spaciness and menace. He walked with a bouncing lope that Charles suspected was phony and affected. "I don't know what there was in that man," Charles said. "I don't know what got him that way. He'd been a loner all his life. He grew up on this huge Montana ranch. His dad wasn't there. The Japs were scared of him. They were afraid of anybody who was crazy. And they thought he wasn't of sound mind." If the Japanese didn't know what to make of McCone, most of his shipmates didn't either when they learned he was the son of a prominent Montana politician, the late state senator George J. McCone, who had gotten a whole county named after him. They wondered: The kid could have gotten his card punched through family influence, and he joined the China Marines? In captivity, McCone was one of the most resourceful of survivors. He quietly assembled a crew he called "the Forty Thieves," whose ingenuity and generosity would keep many a man alive through the worst of the ordeal.

One day a *Houston* machinist's mate named Jack Feliz was thinking how much he'd like a mirror to help him shave when his wish wheeled right into camp. A Japanese soldier drove past the gate to deliver a load of rice. He parked his truck in the middle of the American compound before going in search of a work party, or *kumi*, to unload the rice. Feliz saw the truck's rearview mirror and recognized an opportunity. Pack Rat McCone saw a larger windfall at hand. He said, "Hey, Jack, you've got a real treasure there. Wait until I get my Forty Thieves, and we can work on that thing." McCone's buddies set upon the vehicle like a pit crew. Well equipped with tools, ever handy, and impeccably organized, they got right to work, lifting the truck and inserting concrete blocks under each axle, removing tires (for boots), the hood (for trays and plates), and the windshield (a card table). They stripped it for every piece that had a secondary use: metal, rubber, plastic, glass. In time only its chassis was left, picked like a buffalo carcass on a Cherokee plain. When they were through stripping the vehicle, Pack Rat called "Timber!" and the men pushed the chassis off the blocks and rolled it over to where some other junked vehicles sat. They got rid of the concrete blocks, used brush and bamboo to whisk away the vehicle's tire tracks, then hid in a nearby bamboo thicket.

When the Japanese driver returned, the sailors were rewarded first by the epithets the horrified soldier hurled at himself—translated loosely: "You dumb bastard! Where's your truck?"—then by the reaction of his superior, a sergeant, who received the missing vehicle report. A festival of brutality ensued as first a private and then a corporal appeared. Each heard the sergeant's story and each beat the driver in turn. When they looked around and failed to find the truck, the sergeant was forced to tell the camp commandant, Lieutenant Suzuki, who came over, lined the four of them up—driver, private, corporal, and sergeant—and hammered his doubled-up fists over the top of each head. Suzuki searched for the vehicle himself, at one point pausing and resting a hand on the bed of the very vehicle he was seeking, so thoroughly stripped as to be unrecognizable. Watching from the bamboo, Feliz, McCone, and the other Americans were "just choking ourselves to keep from laughing," Jack Feliz said. They were relieved the officer hadn't touched the hot radiator.

As audacious as he was, McCone was bound to get caught every now and then. Once he was collared borrowing a quart of Scotch from the docks. The guards knocked him to the ground and beat him with a bamboo stick, then made him kneel in the gravel with a thick bamboo pole wedged in the pit of his knees. He knelt in that gravel for some six hours with a sign around his neck that said: "This man stole many things." For about three days afterward, he could

CHAPTER 30

You took your chances challenging a system as rigidly hierarchical and ruthless as the Japanese Army. Most of the Americans found the courage on occasion to try. A successful challenge, either public or covert, could inspire. A failed one often stood as a morale-crushing cautionary fable.

In their dual accountability to the Japanese on one hand and to their own men on the other, the Allied officers occasionally walked the edge of a razor blade. The Japanese officers communicated only through them, holding them responsible for discipline, for cleanliness, and for turning out the *kumi*s that labored at the docks. Their men, quite inadvertently, frequently put them in a difficult position by waging a low-level campaign of petty sabotage against their captors.

Lanson Harris, the *Houston*'s enlisted pilot, was not the type to submit meekly to the prisoner's life. Though quiet and studious, he was unlikely to make, or to want to become, an officer because, as Red Huffman put it, he didn't have the capacity to swallow baloney. One day the guards sent Harris and some others into Batavia to fill trenches in a city park. Four or five hours on a shovel gave him some painful blisters. When the pilot complained to a guard, he instructed

Harris to hold out his hands. Out came the scissors, off came the top of his blisters, and back to work went Harris.

"Now when you get in a situation like that," Harris said, "you have to have something to think about. Most of the time we spent thinking about how in some small way we could get back at the guards. . . . Shortly after the blister-cutting episode some of us were assigned to a detail where we had to fill several fifty-gallon drums with water, build a fire underneath them, heat it, and then the guards would come in in the evening and use it for their hot bath. What they didn't know was that as we filled them up, all six or eight of us stood around and urinated in the water. When they got in the damn tub it was really nice to stand back and watch them splash this water all over themselves. It really gave you a lift to see something like that."

They put water into carburetors and generators, stole sugar not only to eat but to pour into oil drums or the gas tanks of vehicles. They loosened the caps on the drums and stacked them so they would leak. "If you had a chance to sabotage, this was uppermost in your mind," said Paul Papish. "Here again was an opportunity to— what you might say—keep your self-respect." Among the more dangerous acts of subversion were the efforts by several of the technically minded prisoners to build and operate radios. The twenty-three-year-old radio section chief in the 131st, Jess Stanbrough, had been collecting parts. Like Pack Rat McCone, he was adept at scavenging useful things, always on the lookout for copper wire down by the docks. Since copper's principal applications included radio construction, it was dangerous contraband to handle.

During the early weeks of captivity, a GE portable AM radio about the size of a small breadbox was smuggled into camp by a Lost Battalion sergeant named Jack Karney. He gave the radio, in a small leatherette case, to Stanbrough, who was proficient with a ham radio, a field transmitter, and Morse code. Stanbrough went right to work repairing the radio, rewinding its oscillator coil for shortwave reception. Before Java capitulated, he had noticed while riding in a command car that the island had no AM reception, so he looked farther afield and at 1,200 megahertz found a signal. On KGEI San Francisco, he heard the voice of William Winters, and Dinah Shore singing. The station, established by General Electric in 1939 for the Treasure Island World's Fair, would become the model for the Armed Forces Radio Service. It was a principal news source for U.S.

The USS *Houston* slides down the ways at her launching at Newport News, Virginia, on Sept. 6, 1929.

Passing under the Brooklyn Bridge, New York City, circa 1934–35.

President Roosevelt ends his world cruise at Charleston, South Carolina, March 3, 1939.

Reviewing the fleet at San Francisco, July 14, 1938.

Welcoming the President, by air and by sea.

Houston sailors hoist the President's catch off the Cocos Islands, August 1, 1938.

With Adm. Claude Bloch, commander of the United States Fleet, San Francisco, July 14, 1938.

Captain Rooks relieves
Capt. Jesse B. Oldendorf
as commander of the *Houston*,
August 30, 1941.

Adm. Thomas C. Hart, commander
of the U.S. Asiatic Fleet.

Capt. Albert H. Rooks, commander
of the *Houston*, at age 45.

Inspecting his crew.

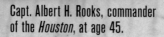

High spirits on the *Houston*, circa 1931.

The pleasures of China Station: *Houston* crewmen enjoy local entertainment during a prewar port of call.

Cdr. Arthur L. Maher,
the *Houston*'s gunnery officer.

Cdr. George S. Rentz,
the *Houston*'s chaplain.

Lt. Harold S. Hamlin,
as a Naval Academy midshipman.

Lt. Robert B. Fulton,
assistant engineering officer.

The ship's company,
circa 1941.

Ens. Charles D. Smith, turret two officer,
as a Naval Academy midshipman.

Ens. John B. Nelson, as a
Naval Academy midshipman.

Lt. Russel R. Ross, as a
Naval Academy midshipman.

Lt. (jg) Joseph Dalton, as a
Naval Academy midshipman.

Houston Marine
Sgt. Charley L. Pryor, Jr.

Pfc. Jim Gee.

S1/c Melfred L. (Gus) Forsman.

S1/c John Bartz.

Cox. James (Red) Huffman.

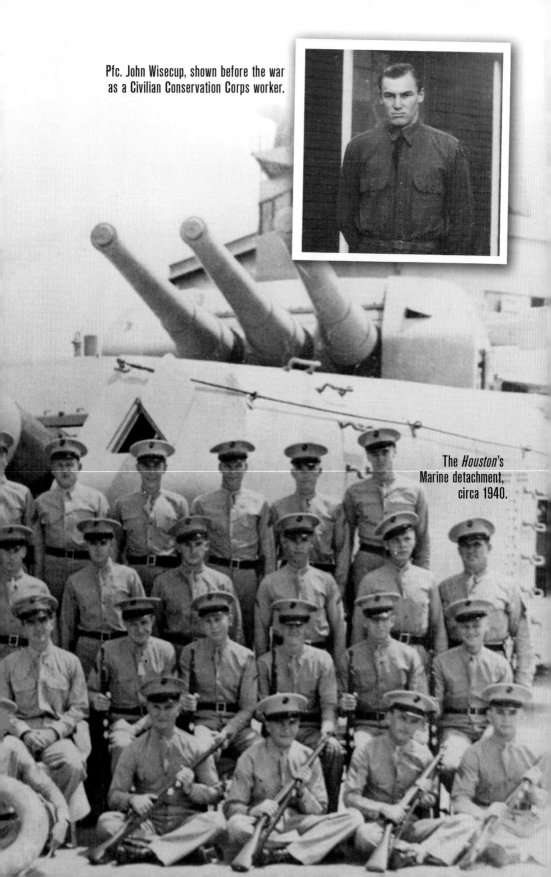

Pfc. John Wisecup, shown before the war as a Civilian Conservation Corps worker.

The *Houston*'s Marine detachment, circa 1940.

A catapult launch of an SOC floatplane.

Embarking President Roosevelt, the *Houston* passes through the Panama Canal, July 11, 1934.

AMM 3/c Lanson H. Harris, standing by his Curtis SOC Seagull float plane.

The HMAS *Perth*.

Turret One and Turret Two, the *Houston*'s forward eight-inch main battery, train to starboard in prewar exercises off Shanghai.

The gunners of the *Houston*'s 5"/25-caliber secondary battery, shown here off Chefoo, China, circa 1933.

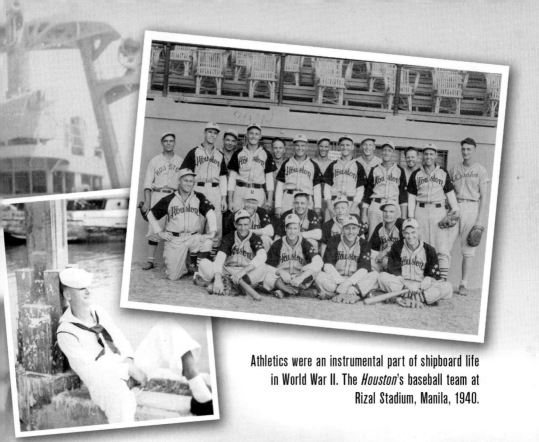

Athletics were an instrumental part of shipboard life in World War II. The *Houston*'s baseball team at Rizal Stadium, Manila, 1940.

Otto Schwarz kicks back.

Shore party heads for Tawi Tawi, circa 1941.

"She never struck her colors":
The battered *Houston* rolls over
and sinks, March 1, 1942.

Oil painting depicting Japanese
torpedo crew firing on the *Houston*
in the Battle of Sunda Strait.

Rear Adm. William A. Glassford, Hart's deputy and commander of the late Task Force 5, addresses the Memorial Day gathering.

THE WHITE HOUSE
WASHINGTON

May 30, 1942

On this Memorial Day, all America joins with you who are in proud tribute to a great ship and a gallant company of American men. That fighting ship and those fighting Americans shall live in our hearts.

I knew that ship and loved her. Her officers and men were friends.

When ship and men went down, still fighting, they did not go to defeat. They had helped remove at least two heavy cruisers and other vessels from the active list of the enemy's ranks. The officers and men of the U.S.S. HOUSTON were privileged to prove, once again, that free Americans consider no price too high to pay in defense of their freedom. The officers and men of the U.S.S. HOUSTON drove a hard bargain. They sold their liberty and their lives most dearly.

The spirit of those officers and men is still alive. That is being proved today in Houston, in all Texas, in all America. Not one of us doubts that the thousand Naval recruits sworn in today will carry on with the same determined spirit shown by the gallant men who have gone before them. Not one of us doubts that every true Texan and every true American will back up these new fighting men, and all our fighting men, with all our hearts and all our efforts.

Our enemies have given us the chance to prove that there will be another U.S.S. HOUSTON, and yet another U.S.S. HOUSTON if that becomes necessary, and still another U.S.S. HOUSTON as long as American ideals are in jeopardy. Our enemies have given us the chance to prove that an attack on peace-loving but proud Americans is the very gravest of all mistakes.

The officers and men of the U.S.S. HOUSTON have placed us all in their debt by winning a part of the victory which is our common goal. Reverently, and with all humility, we acknowledge this debt. To those officers and men, wherever they may be, we give our solemn pledge that debt will be paid in full.

Franklin D. Roosevelt

Enlistment ceremony for the Thousand Volunteers, Houston, Texas, May 30, 1942.

President Roosevelt's Memorial Day 1942 message, delivered at the induction of the Thousand Volunteers, Houston, Texas.

troops in the Philippines, who rebro...
region with their thousand-watt trans...
Before long, Stanbrough was getting BB... throughout the
even London.   ...n until its fall.
                                      ...om India and
Soon another radio turned up in camp,
Stanbrough rewired and concealed in a wooden ...ith, which
Though it had good reception, it was voltage-sensi...eese box.
noisy static—much more than a mere annoyance un...rone to
cumstances—and so he gave it to the Navy boys. Ra...se cir-
class Jerry J. Bunch Jr. kept it running, helped by his ol...first
ment chief, Harmon P. Alderman.   ...rt-

Stanbrough hid his radio inside the corner post of his bunk...
powered it by running a wire into the electric light socket overhea...
Knowing the danger the radio would pose were it discovered, he replaced the speaker with some earphones scavenged from the docks
and stashed an aerial antenna in the attic of the barracks. His dispatches were given to a POW who worked inside the Japanese camp
headquarters and thus had access to typewriters. He typed up the
news and circulated a clandestine bulletin that was sneaked into the
barracks, read aloud, and burned.

As the Japanese guards grew suspicious of the prisoners' improved
mood, Stanbrough became increasingly careful about sharing news.
When the news was bad, he paid a price from his own men too. They
often asked him how long he expected them to be in camp. Having
heard a broadcast that disclosed the disastrous final tally of the Pearl
Harbor attack, Stanbrough told them, "Oh, it looks to me at least
six months. We won't be home by Christmas." But the result was
that "some of the boys would not even speak to me with that much
bad news." Spirits rose when word came of the Battle of the Coral
Sea. The Japanese had been only too happy to describe the sinking of
the USS *Lexington* in that battle. But the radio brought them the rest
of the story: that a Japanese carrier too had gone down in the great
fight that saved New Guinea's Port Moresby from invasion and
blunted the Japanese drive to isolate Australia.

The prisoners bucked up their morale however they could. No one
knew what the future held, but the structure of the here and now
could be made to stand on a foundation of optimism and bracing
military routine. One day a *Houston* NCO brought a bit too much
gusto to these efforts, pushing things a step too far. Perhaps unsurprisingly, he was a U.S. Marine: 1st Sgt. Harley H. Dupler.

nd robust, filling his space like a steel beam
d. Feared and respected in equal measure, he
is rank and role seriously. Yet he could relate to
would share tales about his adventures during the
rvention, and in such idle moments he would allow
l him by his first name. He was always full of encour-
ang in there," he would say. "We'll make it." He knew
about team play, having starred on the Marine Corps
squad in the thirties. But when he was on the parade
ds leading them in close order drill, he was only ever Sergeant
ler. Because the officers were kept in separate barracks and lived
art from their men, his was a crucial leadership role. The two
Marine officers were no longer with the men. Lieutenant Gallagher
was in Japan, and Lieutenant Barrett was with the Navy officers.

One morning after *tenko,* in the dusty clearing between the barracks used by the Navy enlisted men and the one used by the Texas artillerymen of the 131st, Sergeant Dupler called his Marines to attention. He had decided to lead them in close order drill. It was a bid to buck up sagging morale at a time when the liberation he had long exhorted them to believe in was increasingly unlikely. On the dusty parade ground the *Houston*'s Marine detachment assembled, wearing a hodgepodge of U.S. Army fatigues and green Dutch army uniforms. Then Dupler began marching the men back and forth—"right *face*, forward *march*"—building a cloud of dust. "Had anyone else tried to instigate such a thing," Howard Charles said, "we would have told him to forget it. But we were eager to please Dupler."

The Japanese guards took immediate notice, but they were amused more than anything else. They laughed too at the 131st Field Artillery's commander, Colonel Tharp, who was said to carry a single-shot .22-caliber gun concealed in his walking stick. "The Japanese knew he had it and laughed at the fact that he had it," Seldon Reese said. Any of them who heard Dupler tell his Marines to stay fit and encourage them with empty promises—"Any day, now, our guys'll hit that beach out there"—surely laughed too. But if they did, it meant only that they didn't appreciate Dupler's deadly seriousness about keeping the proper frame of mind.

The other prisoners—the Texas artillerymen, the Brits, the Dutch, and the Australians, each in their separate barracks—noticed troops in the Philippines, who rebroadcast the signal throughout the region with their thousand-watt transmitter at Bataan until its fall. Before long, Stanbrough was getting BBC newscasts from India and even London.

Soon another radio turned up in camp, a small Zenith, which Stanbrough rewired and concealed in a wooden Velveeta cheese box. Though it had good reception, it was voltage-sensitive and prone to noisy static—much more than a mere annoyance under these circumstances—and so he gave it to the Navy boys. Radioman first class Jerry J. Bunch Jr. kept it running, helped by his old department chief, Harmon P. Alderman.

Stanbrough hid his radio inside the corner post of his bunk and powered it by running a wire into the electric light socket overhead. Knowing the danger the radio would pose were it discovered, he replaced the speaker with some earphones scavenged from the docks and stashed an aerial antenna in the attic of the barracks. His dispatches were given to a POW who worked inside the Japanese camp headquarters and thus had access to typewriters. He typed up the news and circulated a clandestine bulletin that was sneaked into the barracks, read aloud, and burned.

As the Japanese guards grew suspicious of the prisoners' improved mood, Stanbrough became increasingly careful about sharing news. When the news was bad, he paid a price from his own men too. They often asked him how long he expected them to be in camp. Having heard a broadcast that disclosed the disastrous final tally of the Pearl Harbor attack, Stanbrough told them, "Oh, it looks to me at least six months. We won't be home by Christmas." But the result was that "some of the boys would not even speak to me with that much bad news." Spirits rose when word came of the Battle of the Coral Sea. The Japanese had been only too happy to describe the sinking of the USS *Lexington* in that battle. But the radio brought them the rest of the story: that a Japanese carrier too had gone down in the great fight that saved New Guinea's Port Moresby from invasion and blunted the Japanese drive to isolate Australia.

The prisoners bucked up their morale however they could. No one knew what the future held, but the structure of the here and now could be made to stand on a foundation of optimism and bracing military routine. One day a *Houston* NCO brought a bit too much gusto to these efforts, pushing things a step too far. Perhaps unsurprisingly, he was a U.S. Marine: 1st Sgt. Harley H. Dupler.

Dupler was intense and robust, filling his space like a steel beam anchored in the ground. Feared and respected in equal measure, he had always taken his rank and role seriously. Yet he could relate to his men too. He would share tales about his adventures during the Nicaraguan intervention, and in such idle moments he would allow his men to call him by his first name. He was always full of encouragement. "Hang in there," he would say. "We'll make it." He knew something about team play, having starred on the Marine Corps football squad in the thirties. But when he was on the parade grounds leading them in close order drill, he was only ever Sergeant Dupler. Because the officers were kept in separate barracks and lived apart from their men, his was a crucial leadership role. The two Marine officers were no longer with the men. Lieutenant Gallagher was in Japan, and Lieutenant Barrett was with the Navy officers.

One morning after *tenko,* in the dusty clearing between the barracks used by the Navy enlisted men and the one used by the Texas artillerymen of the 131st, Sergeant Dupler called his Marines to attention. He had decided to lead them in close order drill. It was a bid to buck up sagging morale at a time when the liberation he had long exhorted them to believe in was increasingly unlikely. On the dusty parade ground the *Houston's* Marine detachment assembled, wearing a hodgepodge of U.S. Army fatigues and green Dutch army uniforms. Then Dupler began marching the men back and forth— "right *face*, forward *march*"—building a cloud of dust. "Had anyone else tried to instigate such a thing," Howard Charles said, "we would have told him to forget it. But we were eager to please Dupler."

The Japanese guards took immediate notice, but they were amused more than anything else. They laughed too at the 131st Field Artillery's commander, Colonel Tharp, who was said to carry a single-shot .22-caliber gun concealed in his walking stick. "The Japanese knew he had it and laughed at the fact that he had it," Seldon Reese said. Any of them who heard Dupler tell his Marines to stay fit and encourage them with empty promises—"Any day, now, our guys'll hit that beach out there"—surely laughed too. But if they did, it meant only that they didn't appreciate Dupler's deadly seriousness about keeping the proper frame of mind.

The other prisoners—the Texas artillerymen, the Brits, the Dutch, and the Australians, each in their separate barracks—noticed the commotion the Marines were causing. They were not amused at all. They were galvanized. They decided to follow suit.

As Howard Charles relates it, the British soldiers imprisoned on the other side of a fence were the first to line up and start their own close order drills. Then the men of the 131st Field Artillery came out, followed by the Dutch and the Australians. Confronted with a mass movement, the Japanese posture changed altogether. They feared losing control over the camp. "The guards poured out on the grounds to stop it then," said Charles. The immediate object of their wrath was the instigator of the exercise, Harley Dupler.

Two Japanese guards ran to Dupler and brought rifle butts down on his torso and head. He reeled and faltered and kept trying to rise, but the guards bore down and worked him over. It was a beating the likes of which the prisoners hadn't yet seen, certainly not to anyone who had survived. They beat Dupler until he couldn't stand, and then they battered him some more. The drill-field gathering dispersed. Quiet returned to the camp.

Dupler never led close order drill again. Afterward, something seemed to go out of him. The old lesson was driven home: tempting as it was, you didn't trifle with the guards. "There were times you'd just say, 'Well, I don't give a darn how it's going to turn out, but I'm going to take one good healthy poke and then let the chips fall where they may,' " Paul Papish said. "But then I guess you think real fast, and you say, 'There's really no reason for doing it. You're only going to bring nothing but grief on yourself.' The Japanese believe very strongly in force punishment." Most prisoners understood that their reckless pride might mean the death of a friend.

The idea that they *could* retaliate but chose not to in order to protect their friends was therapeutic in a way. "I never admitted that we were whipped," Gus Forsman said. "I think that was one of the things, too, that helped us—not admitting to ourselves that we were beaten."

*

At Bicycle Camp, suspicions flourished—along with budding resentment—that the officers of the 131st were keeping a stash of money for their own benefit. The rumors were correct. The officers had a bankroll of $150,000 intended for supplies and payroll. The Japanese never confiscated it. They allowed the artillery officers to

buy food in native markets outside camp, supplementing the modest pay the Japanese gave the soldiers for working: 25 sen per day
for officers, 15 for noncoms, and 10 for enlisted men.* The men
seized the opportunity to buy tins of corned beef, pinto beans,
meats, fruits, sweetened condensed milk—especially prized for its
concentrated calorie content—coffee, tea, and sugar. The twice-
daily main course of rice got a little more interesting with some
spicing up.

The inequality led to grumbling, and an every-man-for-himself
attitude was festering. The resentment grew intense enough that the
131st's noncoms designated Master Sgt. E. E. Shaw to take the com-
plaint to the officers. When Shaw threatened to pursue the issue after the war, he was summarily court-martialed and busted to private
for thirty days. Maj. Windy Rogers intervened to keep his punishment from being worse. But the confrontation had its intended effect. Thereafter the funds were used to benefit all Americans in
Bicycle Camp. They ate well for the duration of their stay there. And
despite the near rebellion, a number of officers—most notably Major
Rogers, Capt. Samuel H. Lumpkin, Capt. Ira Fowler, and Lt. Jimmy
Lattimore—won the wholehearted respect of the enlisted men.
Prisoners of other nationalities noticed the Americans' inexplicable
wealth and took to selling their own hoarded provisions to them.
The Australians were usually able to charge a considerable premium
and in this way the lifesaving wealth trickled down.

The source of the money was an officer who remained something
of a mystery to the men in the camp, 2nd Lt. Roy E. Stensland. He
was a Los Angeles native and a West Point man, a member of a team
of carefully selected junior officers dispatched to the Dutch East
Indies by General MacArthur's headquarters to buy food and charter
vessels to supply the Philippines through the Japanese blockade.
Stensland went to Makassar with an 800,000-guilder letter of
credit, but once the Japanese encroachment made it impossible to
requisition ships to break the blockade, the mission dissolved and
Stensland fell in with the 131st.

A well-funded liaison role was unusual for a second lieutenant,
but Stensland was no usual officer. He rated in the top one percent

---

*A sen, no longer used in Japanese currency, is 1/100th of a yen.

on the Army's scale for resourcefulness. More than a little hairy, with a thick frame and long arms, he was fearless and intimidating. "He'd remind you of a damn gorilla walking down the road," said Marvin Robinson. "I mean, that's his appearance. But he was all man." The Japanese called him "King Kong." His fellows in the 131st called him "Mr. Bear."

More intriguing than Stensland's physical stature was the fact that he seemed to live in an alternative dimension where the usual rules of offense and consequence did not apply. He liked the booze, but his drinking took nothing from him. He took from it. It seemed to give him strength and superabundant willpower. When a guard came down on a prisoner it was often Stensland who stepped in and took the beating. He was good at staying on his feet. Reportedly the Japanese guards even invited Stensland to drink with them on occasion. Once they allowed him to hunt pigs with them, although that time, reportedly, Stensland himself became the target of a few rifle shots. But nothing ever touched him while he was out front spotting artillery fire against the Japanese on Java. Why would a rifle shot from a drunken guard perform any better?

One day as he was heading to work on a dockyard *kumi*—he was one of the few officers regularly to do so—Stensland witnessed a Japanese guard beating a Dutch woman. She had ridden her bicycle to the camp that afternoon, stopping by the fence and holding high some bananas as an offering. Seeing this, the guard rushed her from behind and struck her. She toppled off the bicycle and hit the ground. "Lieutenant Stensland, before you knew what was happening, was over there, and he knocked that Jap down," Lester Rasbury of the 131st said. "The Jap went one way, and the rifle the other. The lieutenant helped the lady up, and, boy, that Jap picked up his rifle and ran. He got out of there, and he didn't do anything about it. It scared him, I think."

"I thought he was a dead man," said the Lost Battalion's Houston "Slug" Wright. "He came out of it because that Japanese was afraid to go to his superiors and say that an American beat him up. He was lucky as the dickens, and that wasn't the only time that he walked right into a situation and told the Japanese what they could do and walked away from it. If it would have been me, they would have killed me, but old Stensland was the type of man that had more courage and guts than anybody that I have ever seen."

What seemed to distinguish Lieutenant Stensland from Sergeant Dupler—at least what may begin to explain the diverging reactions the Japanese had to the two courageous leaders—may have been that Stensland had a little of Pack Rat McCone in him: a raging mind, mercury in the blood, and a visible unconcern with the personal consequences of rebellion.

CHAPTER 31

In June, the spirit of the Japanese darkened, and Jess Stanbrough, Jerry Bunch, and others in the secret radio news circle were first to figure out why. There had been a terrible collision between the American and Japanese aircraft carrier fleets. From the sound of it, the battle—fought near Midway Island, alarmingly close to Honolulu—dwarfed the Battle of the Coral Sea fought thirty days earlier. Something big had happened. A decisive battle had been won. But one didn't need a radio to know that something had displeased and disturbed the guards.

A prisoner had to keep his optimism closely guarded, like a secret straight flush. Their heightened energies seemed to draw directly from the reserves of their captors. Ens. John Nelson let his exuberance get the better of him when a Japanese guard tried to taunt him about the progress of the war. "This one day we were on a working party," said Lloyd Willey, "and Ensign Nelson was with us. This one Jap guard was sitting down with a stick in the dirt. He said, 'San Francisco—*boom boom boom boom!* New York—*boom boom boom boom!*'" Nelson, who was plugged in to the latest news courtesy of KGEI and had heard of Jimmy Doolittle's April raid on Japan, wasn't buying it. Willey said, "Nelson listened for a while, and then he said, 'Tokyo—*boom boom boom boom!*' That made the guard suspicious. He said. 'Radio? You have radio?'" There were innocent denials all around. The Japanese searched the barracks but did not turn up the radio.

If your ego got the better of you, if you gave in to the urge to fight back, you could get yourself—or worse, somebody else—killed. The Japanese said they would execute ten men for every man who tried to escape. That was at the heart of the moral dilemma that plagued the prisoners. U.S. military regulation imposed a duty to attempt to escape, and the Geneva Convention recognized that duty. Yet they were held by an enemy who believed in mass reprisals and punishment by proxy. Because only the seniormost officers appreciated these legalities, the enlisted POWs were often bewildered to find their officers variously encouraging and forbidding escape. On June 14, the Japanese solved the ambiguity for their Bicycle Camp guests when they gave the officers a legal document to sign.

It was a pledge not to escape. It read in part, "I will obey all orders from the Japanese." According to Ensign Smith, "We refused to sign this document and nothing more was heard of it for a short time." Lieutenant Hamlin tried to negotiate the language of the pledge to eliminate its conflict with American military law, which required prisoners to attempt escape. To the phrase "I will obey all orders from the Japanese" he proposed adding, "insofar as they are not contrary to my oath of allegiance to the United States." If it was a labor negotiation, management held all the cards. The Japanese were going to have things their way.

Shortly after the no-escape pledge was foisted upon the prisoners, they got the opportunity to take their subversive radio arts to new levels, not merely to receive news but to make it, to go international, to broadcast word of their survival to a nation that still wondered at their fate. One day the Japanese invited Allied officers to write letters and read them over Batavia's Japanese-controlled shortwave radio. Ever suspicious of propaganda, they refused, at least until cooler heads realized it might be a way to send word home and reassure family that there had been plenty of survivors of Java's collapse.

It fell to the Australian broadcast veteran Rohan Rivett to go to the Batavia studio each day to read a letter over the air. The first was written by an Australian army captain. The second correspondent, another Australian captain, described Bicycle Camp's conditions as "comparable to those of Dudley Flats." The Japanese, believing the reference to Melbourne's slum was a compliment, permitted the broadcast to go out. Quickly enough Rivett realized the value of the tool he had been given. On June 20 his own turn came and he sent the following broadcast, intended not to detail the fates of the *Perth* and the *Houston* but to offer the first indication of the damage they had inflicted and to narrate the path the ships' survivors had taken through Serang to the Batavia compound.

> At Serang were nearly all the survivors from the gallant Australian cruiser *Perth* and the American cruiser *Houston,* sunk in a terrific battle against superior Nippon forces at the entrance to Sunda Straits on the early morning of 1 March. I have heard the Nippon sailors on a destroyer which picked up some of the 300-odd *Perth* survivors pay a generous tribute to the wonderful fight put up by the two vessels, surrounded by great numbers of Nippon cruisers, destroyers, submarines and transports. Nippon officers themselves paid generous tribute to the deadly efficiency of *Perth*'s gunners, both in that last action and in the action on 26 February [sic] in the Battle of the Java Sea.

According to Rivett, "From first to last perhaps a hundred men of all ranks and nationalities had letters broadcast, while at the same time the Japanese were also transmitting the names of all those in the camp at a rate of twenty-five names every two days. It was a painfully slow business, but it was better than nothing, and those of us whose names were sent home were much luckier than tens of thousands of others in Japanese hands, whose people did not hear that they were prisoners until late in 1943."

The broadcasts soon rippled on American shores. In early July, the mystery of Captain Rooks's fate became what in 1942 must have passed for a minor media event. Japanese-controlled Batavia radio broadcast Rivett's first message, stating that a thousand survivors of the *Houston* and *Perth* were at a former army barracks at Batavia. The media began focusing on the question of the survivors of the USS *Houston* and its captain. Edith Rooks seemed able to withstand it. Speaking with reporters, she never sank into despair or pity. She only ever spoke of her admiration for her husband and her pride that her son was following in the bright wake of the Rooks family naval tradition. She would circulate widely in wartime Seattle, sponsoring the launchings of new warships out at the shipyard, working with

Navy Relief, and staying current with the traumas and bereavements in the network of Navy women around her. She was direct and brutally frank in discussing with her fellow war wives the pain that attended the long absences and occasional losses, confronting things no one wanted to talk about, and cleansing dark thoughts by exposing them to the light and air of forthright discussion. She was like a latter-day Unsinkable Molly Brown, steady and stalwart in the face of tragedy, headstrong as her ship began to sink. She had a rare ability to confront the worst in life without flinching and wrestle it to the ground. It was, after a fashion, a way of coping.

The War Department had duly notified the parents of soldiers in the 131st Field Artillery that their sons were missing. Drawn tight as a community in grief, they began meeting for mutual support. The battalion's five batteries were pulled from tiny towns throughout north-central Texas. Their sons might be lost, but the families had found each other.

Sgt. Crayton Gordon's mother wrote the *Ft. Worth Star-Telegram,* "I know many of the boys who are now in Java and particularly do I remember Sergeants Billy Joe Mallard and Wade H. Webb, both of Hillsboro. I was closely associated with these young men of the 'Lost Battalion.' I know the ability of those boys and know that they can meet whatever faces them like men. I am proud of the boys and of their brave parents." Reportedly it was a *Star-Telegram* writer who coined the nickname "the Lost Battalion." It stuck fast enough and became nearly official.

Until they became un-lost, the families would make do. The mother of Frank Fujita, a sergeant with the Lost Battalion who happened to be Japanese American, bucked up her courage and wrote a letter to the *Abilene Reporter News,* published in October 1942.

I am proud of my two boys and their volunteer service for our wonderful USA. I am not regretting their enlistment, and since it has come to war, and of course that means fighting, I only wish I had two more to go. I have three girls—Naomi, Freda and Patricia, and myself—all to give freely in whatever way we can serve. And also Mr. Fujita, who is an alien, but through no fault of his own. He has tried several times to be naturalized, but the law, of course, [says] no. But he is 100% American at heart, and has been so ever since coming to this country in 1914. He is willing to be used in whatever way

Uncle Sam can use him. He renounced all relations to Japan when coming to this country—even to writing to his mother. He would not teach his children the Japanese language, as he wanted them to always speak American. We are both proud to have two boys to give in defense of our country; and if they should lose their lives, it would be for a glorious cause. We would gladly do the same.

If any of the Navy company or the Texans of the Lost Battalion ever took their families for granted, if they ever assumed that the good meals they had enjoyed and the hopes they had nourished had been the natural result of their industry, foresight, and clean living, Bicycle Camp was there to set them straight. They escaped by talking about the convertibles they were going to buy, the college degrees they were going to pursue, the farms they would inherit and run. There was little talk of girlfriends. As hunger and disease got to them, thoughts of the fairer sex faded from the picture. When they slept, aromas from imaginary kitchens seasoned their dreams. Awake, they brainstormed menus, recited lists of ice cream flavors, made a competition of waxing eloquent on hamburgers they had known. They remembered the little things about home, once so familiar as to be unremarkable but like revelations now that they were impossibly out of reach. The hopeful among them learned to revalue their gifts and aspirations.

★

On July 4, Ensign Smith returned to Bicycle Camp with his dockyard working party. As they entered the gate and passed the guardhouse, Smith noticed that all of the camp's prisoners were lined up at the Japanese commandant's office. "As I marched my troops up and halted in front of the guardhouse the officers were called out separately and a note stuck under my face which said, 'If you do not sign the oath, your life will not be guaranteed.'" The prisoners' refusal stood. Smith wrote:

> I was then taken by the Japanese guard into the rear room of the guardhouse and put in a room where I found the senior officers and hut commanders all ready [sic] there. We were not allowed to talk or smoke and we stood there at rigid attention for about forty-five minutes. At the end of this period we were

lined up outside and marched under guard across over into the Japanese side of the camp and into a garage where we all found the officers from the camp waiting. The Japanese made a great show of loading their rifles and cocking their pieces as if they thought that they could bully us into doing things by force.

A guard held up a sign restating the ultimatum of a few weeks before: "If you do not sign the oath, we do not guarantee your lives." That the Japanese imposed written legalities on their prisoners was rather rich in view of their government's own refusal to ratify the Geneva Convention. It may seem absurd that the Japanese expected a duress-induced promise to trump a man's wartime instinct for survival. And it certainly seems quaint that the prisoners risked torture by refusing to sign a contractual nullity. But that is just what they did. After several weeks of reduced rations, restricted access to cooking facilities, and confinement of officers and senior NCOs, not to mention threats of death, the responsible officers of the various POW factions finally advised their men to sign the agreement. Extracted under duress, it would be void in any event.

There were just three holdouts. Two Australian army captains and Lt. Frank Gillan, the *Perth*'s engineering officer, refused to sign the oath. "You can always be sure that some Australians will go out of their way to aggravate the Japanese," said Jess Stanbrough. That morning the guards took the three protesters to the guardhouse, produced thick bamboo sticks and forced each to kneel on the gravel walkway with the bamboo behind his knees. They were kept in that agonizing position for six hours while half a dozen guards, including Lieutenant Suzuki, did Joe DiMaggio impersonations on them with their rifle stocks. Three or four times Suzuki unsheathed his saber and struck them with its flat side. The three men stayed conscious throughout.

Finally the senior officer in the camp, Australian Brig. A. C. Blackburn, together with Col. Albert C. Searle, the senior U.S. Army officer on Java, prevailed upon the men to sign the oath and the beatings ceased. "The three men were in obvious pain," observed Lieutenant Hamlin, "but bore the torture with great fortitude. The men were black and blue all over, and so remained for several days."

Signing that piece of paper meant something to the men. It hurt. "There ain't a one of us who didn't think we were traitors," said John

Wisecup. "All during the war, I thought of that. . . . We believed actually that we were selling our country down the road."

According to Jess Stanbrough, the dustup over the oath marked the beginning of the war. "After the Fourth of July, all hell broke loose," he said.

In mid-August, Lieutenant Suzuki and his contingent of Japanese guards left Batavia and were replaced by a company of Koreans under a Lieutenant Sonai. Abused by the Japanese, they vented their frustrations downstream on the prisoners. "The Brown Bomber was our first infamous one," Stanbrough said. "He'd go pick out somebody, and usually the taller you were the worse you'd get it."

As the prisoners would soon well understand, the Koreans' position in the Imperial Army pecking order was but a half notch above the captives themselves. Nicknames made it possible to discuss them in a common shorthand. The guard nicknamed "Snake Eyes" had a beady look. "Pock Face" was fighting eczema. "Hollywood" was busy with his hair all the time. His fastidious dress did not keep him from being one of the nastiest guards in Bicycle Camp. The "Brown Bomber" bore a certain resemblance to Joe Louis. The Korean named "Liver Lips" because of his heavy facial features was "the worst one that we ever ran into," said Charley Pryor. "He just went through there from one end to the other bashing and hammering and clubbing with his silly rifle. . . . I think he was just about the meanest and orneriest rascal that we'd ever run into. You didn't have to provoke him. He'd just see you, and he was provoked."

For a variety of reasons there was never serious talk of escape from Bicycle Camp. They could have managed it, could have scurried over the concertina wire, made it back into the jungle. But then what? As the crow flew it was five hundred miles to Australia. Java was Japanese-held, as were its skies and surrounding seas. The jungles were alive with unfriendly natives. The well-traveled men of the Navy company had a better handle on these realities than artillerymen of the Lost Battalion. "A soldier might tell you, 'Yeah, we'll get a boat and go,'" said George Detre, "but . . . not the sailors, no, we never seriously entertained escaping."

CHAPTER 32

In early October, seven months into the prisoners' tenure as guests of the Imperial Empire, an uneasy order had settled over Bicycle Camp. That was about to change. Rumors began surfacing that a move was afoot. The Japanese guards, in their guttural pidgin, spoke of vacations in a green, mountainous land full of sunshine.

On October 8, the first of several groups of prisoners was marched out of Bicycle Camp, taken down to the Tanjung Priok waterfront, and mustered in the shadow of an old freighter, a coal-burning five-thousand-tonner named the *Kenkon Maru*. Sprayed with disinfectant, the men were herded up the gangway and led to their stowage, hundreds upon hundreds packed in each hold.

Pack Rat McCone's reputation was well established by then. Having honed his talent at dockside requisition, he was, according to historian Gavan Daws, "the only man who could make five-gallon cans invisible to the Japanese." Up the gangway he strode, hauling a beggar's ransom in surplus: two tires, a gang of pipe, containers useful for capturing water, and several sacks of other valuables slung over his back. "Man, he had some gear," said John Wisecup. "The 'Gunner' was really loaded." The Japanese guards laughed out loud at the sight of it. "They seldom laughed," said Wisecup, "but they did this time." "He became a sort of hero, or whatever you want to name him, but he was the one who controlled an awful lot of water aboard that trip," Howard Charles said.

This first group, known as the "Black Force" after its senior officer, Australian Lt. Col. C. M. Black, consisted of 191 Americans and 600 Australian soldiers and sailors. Its senior U.S. officer was Capt. Arch L. Fitzsimmons, the commander of the Lost Battalion's Headquarters Battery, leading most of the Americans to call Black Force the Fitzsimmons Group. It included three of the 131st's superb second lieutenants, James Lattimore, David Hiner, and Roy Stensland, as well as nineteen members of the *Houston*'s Marine detachment, including Howard Charles, Jim Gee, Pinky King, Pack Rat McCone, Freddie Quick, Robbie Robinson, and John Wisecup. *Houston* sailors in this group included Gus Forsman, Otto Schwarz, and forty-one others.

The remaining Americans, including all of the Navy company officers and medical staff, and a few Marines who had been overlooked in the hasty first selection, including sergeants Harley Dupler and Charley Pryor, stayed behind as the *Kenkon Maru* departed on October 8. Nominally commanded by the Lost Battalion's leader, Lt. Col. Blucher S. Tharp, a second group of Americans, 477 strong, piled into the holds of the four-thousand-ton merchantman *Dai Nichi Maru,* fetid with the smell of animal waste. Joining hundreds of Dutch and Australians, under the overall command of Australian Brig. Arthur L. Varley, they left Batavia on October 11. Beginning with these two departures in the first half of October, at least five merchantmen made the run from Batavia northward by the end of 1942, largely emptying Bicycle Camp of Allied prisoners.

The saga of the so-called hell ships would become a grim chapter in the story of Japan's treatment of its POWs. Ens. Charles D. Smith wrote, "The Japanese method of shipping troops is one man per ton, so on a two thousand ton ship, they transport 2,000 troops or prisoners." There were three tiers of wooden platforms built all around the bulkheads of the hold. When the holds were jammed full, "the Japs made space," said Julius B. Heinen of the 131st. "They just took a rifle butt and jammed it at the guy who was closest. Well, his reaction was to try to get away from the rifle butt that was coming at him, so he moved backwards with as much force as he could generate. That left another space where another man could get in." They were packed in like farm animals, clothes soaked with their sweat and little liquid intake available to replace it. The crowding was so

bad that the Japanese merchant captain protested to Army authorities but was summarily overruled. When the rusty old *Dai Nichi
Maru* departed Batavia, it was stuffed with three thousand POWs.

The act of transporting prisoners in unmarked ships carrying war
matériel was against the Geneva Convention. As Rohan Rivett was
herded by screaming guards into a hold on the *Kenkon Maru,* he saw
that it was full of armored reconnaissance vehicles. Conditions on
the ship were unfit for humans. "There had been cattle hauled in
that ship, as I recall, and there was straw in the bilge," said Howard
Charles. The ship reeked of its earlier cargo. Down in the hold, the
temperatures approached 120 degrees. There was no circulation, no
air to breathe, nowhere for a dysentery patient to run ten times an
hour. If you opened a porthole, you got as much seawater as air.
Enterprising sailors got fresh water by bleeding steam from the engines of the ship's cargo crane. They had to duck and cover whenever
a perplexed engineer came looking to see why his steam pressure had
fallen.

The journey out of Batavia was a short one, just three days.
Fortunately for the prisoners, the Allied submarine offensive against
Japanese merchantmen had yet to reach full fiery bloom. When subs
roamed without hindrance later in the war, they would exact a terrible toll on these uniquely vulnerable human cargoes. By day the
men roasted inside the stinking enclosure of a hull heated by the un-
blinking equatorial sun. At night they thrashed through haunted
dreams. Those prisoners who had compasses said the ship was
headed north and speculated that their destination could be
Singapore or maybe even Japan itself. Because the *Dai Nichi Maru*'s
skipper didn't have charts of the waters north of Java, he sailed only
by day. Each sunset he dropped anchor. *Perth* survivor Ray Parkin
wrote, "It was a night of darkness and heat and drugged stupor; of
entangled bodies which flung unconscious arms and legs athwart
each other so that, on awakening, it was hard to tell which limbs
were your own. You were conscious of having far too many arms and
legs." Men with the slightest sense of claustrophobia had raging
breakdowns.

On the third morning, those few who got topside to relieve themselves could see all around them a rabble of islands and scattered
islets whose rocky shores were garnished with scraggy foliage. The
steep red slopes of the mainland lay ahead. The Japanese guards
didn't let them gawk for long. They chased them back down into

the hold. But the curious prisoners kept pushing topside, "like froth from a boiling saucepan," Ray Parkin wrote.

For the men on both ships, the common mystery of their destination ended when the chunking rumble of the coal-fired steam engines stopped, the hatches opened to sky, and the men stretched their legs and climbed on deck. As the breeze caressed them, they saw they had entered a large harbor. Descending the gangway under guard, they set their sore feet, at last, on land. They were the newest tenants of proud Singapore.

CHAPTER 33

The harbor was a ruin, littered with hulks of bombed-out British ships. All along the wharf lay huge piles of scrap iron—steel plates from dismantled oil tanks, automobile chassis squashed flat. "Once again," Rohan Rivett observed, "as in Batavia, one felt as if a blight were hanging over the city."

Both of the main groups had the same experience on arriving. Loaded on trucks near the dock, they were convoyed through Singapore's central city and then out into the countryside. Soon a fortresslike stone structure was visible, situated on scenic heights overlooking the city from the northeast. Known as Changi, this district of the island was the onetime home of a Royal Army garrison. The turreted gray stone edifice, the Changi Jail, was its signature structure. It was the most forbidding prison Charley Pryor had ever seen. When the trucks stopped in front of it, he asked himself, "Oh my God, what in the world have I done to deserve this?" But a mistake had been made. Before Pryor knew it, the Japanese were loading their prisoners back onto the trucks and taking them to the garrison barracks. These long barracks and smaller administrative buildings in the landscaped district were pleasant, picturesque even, with trees arranged in a neat layout. The barracks were mostly stripped bare, but there were a few bed frames and even some mattresses. The exhausted prisoners flopped down and sacked out.

Singapore was known as Great Britain's Gibraltar of the East before it collapsed and capitulated like the Batavia of the North. Now the Japanese, rudely ignoring propaganda about Singapore's invincibility, had imprisoned the British in their own fortress.

A total of about fifty thousand Allied prisoners were in Singapore, including thirteen thousand Australians and a small minority of about eight hundred Americans. Among them was a young British private named James Clavell, whose eventual novel *King Rat* would be based on his experience as a Singapore POW. "Changi was a school for survivors," he would write. "It gave me a strength most people don't have. . . . Changi became my university instead of my prison." Observing the landscaped idyll of their surroundings and the cock-of-the-walk sureness of the British officer corps nominally administering it, the *Houston* sailors could never quite fathom Changi. "It was the strangest thing I've ever seen in my life," said Otto Schwarz. "These guys acted as if they were on regimental maneuvers."

The British had had eight months since February 15, 1942, to acclimate themselves to captivity. Though their pride was wounded, they were on the surface still in charge, brightly so and with bucked-up spirits. Save for the daily *tenkos* and the occasional presence of Sikh soldiers who had turned coat and served the emperor, scarcely a Japanese soldier or guard was in sight. Howard Charles asked himself, "Why don't they make a run for the wall? They could make it; just by sheer numbers they could overwhelm these guards and go somewhere. . . . I remember asking a few of them that, and they just looked at me with a cold stare, like, 'You've got to be out of your head.'" Everyday life as prisoners at Singapore had the aura of an absurd dream: the posturing of the British, pretending at command; the Japanese, lurking unseen like puppeteers; the manicured enclave turning dingy under occupation; creeping hunger blanching any illusion of order and civilization; the future, clouded in doubt.

At Changi the Allied prisoners would learn to count their blessings. Contrary to myth, Changi was no death camp. There was time for leisure when the light work of clearing the district's rubber plantation and stevedoring at the docks was finished. There were some robust baseball games. Though John Wisecup, buckled by a knife-in-the-belly bout of dysentery, was unavailable to pitch, the Americans stood their ground against a formidable Australian team that boasted several cricketers whose talents readily crossed over to the chalk diamond. Charley Pryor put on a show, hitting seven home runs in the four games they played, making an indelible impression on the slap-hitting Aussies and winning them over thoroughly—"Lay on one, Yank!" Lieutenant Hamlin gave several lectures to the Brits on the late, great USS *Houston* and her wartime exploits. At a musical revue at the Changi parade ground, Marine Pvt. Freddie Quick, a practiced baritone, caused jaws to drop when he stood before thousands and delivered an a cappella solo of an Irving Berlin peace song that Kate Smith had turned into a sensation in November 1938. Though "God Bless America" had graced both the Democratic and Republican national conventions in 1940, it was still fresh to the ears of this audience. Quick nailed it. As Howard Charles recalled, "Everybody just sat there spellbound because he was a great singer, and he belted this thing out like you had never heard it sung before. The Japs standing along the wall had rather frightened expressions, because they were afraid that this was going to rally the men to some kind of action." Quick left the parade ground silent.

Mostly, though, the prisoners of different nationalities entertained themselves by comparing their grievances. They debated who had the more powerful claim to having been sold out. There was resentment to go around. The Americans noticed that the British fed their dogs better than their enlisted men. Australians were allied with the Americans in their dislike of the imperious British brass. According to Otto Schwarz, some Scottish Gordon Highlanders told the Americans that if any trouble started, "they'll be right at our sides." In the absence of the Japanese, the British were seen by default as the hand of the enemy.

Stealing from the British became a way of life. "They had their own stuff cached away . . . and we made it our business to find out where they were hiding it," said Howard Charles. The absence of good rations forced them to get creative with their menus. Stray cats—or "alley rabbits"—filled the bill. Some Australians took to ribbing the Yanks by slyly squeaking "meow, meow" whenever they walked by. Outside the perimeter of the Changi Barracks, beyond the coils of concertina wire, were some sprawling groves of coconut trees. Marine Cpl. Hugh Faulk was particularly adept at shimmying up the trees and knocking the fruits from their high perches, careful not to unleash a deluge lest it alert the guards. Once a British military policeman stopped some tree-climbing American thieves and informed them, "Those are the King's coconuts." The officiousness of his tone approached self-satire, though it had to be taken seriously: the penalty for stealing the King's coconuts was a jail sentence.

As John Bartz tells the story, one time some Americans raided a British general's chicken pen. The culprit, caught, was put in irons. Lieutenant Hamlin went to the jail and confronted the colonel in charge. "You have got to take that man out," Hamlin said. "We do not put our people in irons. *At no time* do we put our people in irons." Hamlin got his man back.

Lieutenant Hamlin was never shy about standing up to the British. One day he failed to salute a British colonel, who took umbrage at the disrespect shown by a Yank who was dressed in the ragged fashion of Serang and Bicycle Camp. The Brit declared, "Well, my man! Don't you know you should salute?" Hamlin just stared at him. "Don't you know who I am?" the colonel thundered. He announced his senior rank and station, whereupon Hamlin said, "Pleased to meet you. I'm Harold S. Hamlin, Acting Admiral for the American Pacific Fleet, Changi Area."

Strictly speaking, Hamlin was within his rights to claim temporary flag rank. He was the senior U.S. naval officer at the new Changi Station and thus its acting commander. On an empty chessboard, a pawn can be king, just as a king's royal coconuts, commandeered by an imperial emperor, can become fodder for slaves.

CHAPTER 34

The Japanese aroused suspicions when they sent around a questionnaire asking the prisoners about their technical backgrounds. Leery of disclosing anything their enemy might find useful, some of the Americans professed to be students or farmers or certified "peach-fuzz inspectors." Those who did disclose actual technical or mechanical aptitude were called to the Changi commandant's office and told how fortunate they were. They were going to be taken to Japan.

Most of the men in the *Houston*'s engineering department, as well as technically minded Lost Battalioners such as Jess Stanbrough, joined this "technical party" on the same miserable ship that had brought them to Singapore. On October 27 the *Dai Nichi Maru* got under way north. Stopping over in Formosa, the ship arrived at Moji in northern Kyushu on November 25. A few days later, on November 28, another group left Singapore for Japan. This party included Frank Fujita, the Japanese American whose mother had written with such pride of his service in the 131st.

Fujita had plenty to lose in his dealings with the Japanese. His father's countrymen, his captors, had no idea of his true heritage. Fujita didn't quite know why. He assumed they took him for a Filipino or a Mexican. Though his name was as Japanese as could be, no one paid him much attention. But his buddies did. "Hell, they are going to kill you," they would tell him. "Change your name. For God's sake, don't tell them you're half Japanese." Fujita was scared. He had no doubt they were right. Yet he could not quite pull the trigger on adopting a racial disguise. "If I change my name to Joe Martinez or something, well, when they kill me anyhow they might have me listed as Joe Martinez, and then my folks will never know what happened to me. So I figured hell, I was born with this name, and I might as well die with it."

On November 28 he found himself jammed with 2,200 other men aboard the *Kamakura Maru,* a 17,500-ton Japanese passenger ship. Each man had a single canteen to last him the ten-day voyage. The ship left Singapore and stopped at Formosa, where some POWs debarked. Continuing north, the ship reached Japan on December 7, 1942, and docked at Nagasaki, the home Fujita's father had left in 1914. The northern winds were cold on his face.

The POW camp known as Fukuoka #2 was situated about a mile from the port city's great Mitsubishi shipyard. The inland dry dock there was massive enough to hold four ten-thousand-ton ships simultaneously. The Japanese workforce was far less impressive. Whereas American shipbuilders at Newport News, Mare Island, Puget Sound, Seattle-Tacoma, Quincy Fore River, and elsewhere relied on professionals, the Japanese at Nagasaki employed children, the mentally ill, and starving and sick prisoners for its labor. Spread among the various yard crews, the Americans worked alongside Japanese civilian riveters, welders, and stage builders. Fujita's job was to build scaffoldings on the angle-iron frameworks that cradled the infant hulls of new ships. The yard's noise level was monstrous. The clangor of its overdriven riveters made speech communication impossible. Yard foremen used colored chalk to mark hull plates for different types of processes, such as bracketing, riveting, or cutting with a blowtorch. Fujita's work took him all over the yard. He soon understood that if he was discreet enough, he could get away with murder as a saboteur. He carried a piece of chalk tied to a long stick. Whenever he felt he could get away with it, he would furtively change the foreman's markings on randomly chosen plates and beams. "We carried on our own little war there," he said.

They were in this war whether they wanted it or not. An average of six prisoners a day died on the job in the Nagasaki shipyard, a dangerous gauntlet of high-voltage wires, high-pressure hoses, and toxic industrial substances. Heavy steel objects were hoisted with fraying cables, equipment was poorly maintained, and workers labored prone on high platforms, vulnerable to lethal human mischief. One day Fujita got hit in the head with a large rivet. It smarted badly and could have killed him. He looked upward in the direction of where it had fallen and saw a Japanese worker two stages above him, smiling nastily, fiercely pleased with his aim. Fujita took a long look at him, marking his features.

A few days later his opportunity for payback came when his task put him about six levels above where the rivet dropper happened to be working. Calmly Fujita found a big shipfitter's bolt, slipped a couple of heavy industrial washers over it, and twisted on two or three large nuts. It was about fifteen pounds of metal. Hefting his handmade iron bomb, Fujita aimed by eye, made a minute adjustment for the brisk wind, and let go. The blow to the top of the Japanese worker's head was direct and, according to Fujita, instantly fatal. "He never even kicked," recalled the artilleryman, who within sixty seconds had shuffled and quickstepped around the platforms and scaffolding to the other side of the yard. He was on his own, feeling his way in a brutal new world.

Japan had scores of POW camps, most located in major urban centers near shipyards, or in the mountains adjacent to mines. The senior *Houston* officers under Cdr. Arthur L. Maher, who had arrived at Shimonoseki on May 4 and moved to the camp at Ohuna, had long since acclimated themselves to the frigid climate. The hard work in the mines, the rough treatment by the guards, and the sparse rations "took us all down," Maher wrote. When dysentery and beriberi struck in the summer, the guards eased up on exercise, though no more food came. Meanwhile, every day brought more Japanese officers from Tokyo to pick out prisoners to interrogate. The *Houston*'s senior surviving officer faced questioning from as many as a dozen Japanese at a time.

"They were anxious to find out almost anything they could regarding our Navy," Maher wrote, "the operations of the ships, the officers in command, the number of men on board, the modern installations, radar and so forth." Because the barracks at the small Ohuna camp were within earshot of the guardhouse, prisoners spoke loudly so as to let the others overhear the questions and plan their answers. It was wise to keep one's evasions consistent. Inadequate answers brought a summons to the courtyard, where the offender was hauled before the POW company and beaten with clubs at the direction of a Japanese warrant officer.

*

On January 7, 1943, the *Houston*'s remaining officers at Singapore were loaded into trucks and driven to a train station, where they said farewell to the Allies' bastion of disgrace. This group included Colonel Tharp, Lieutenant Hamlin, and Ensigns John Nelson and Charles Smith, as well as 1st Sgt. Harley Dupler, Lanson Harris, Red Huffman, and Charley Pryor. Marching out of camp, they were led by a unit of Gordon Highlanders who groaned a haunting melody on their bagpipes as their lone drummer beat the cadence. "It was an honor, we understand, to be piped out, an old Scottish custom the Japs didn't like," pharmacist's mate Raymond Day wrote. "For the sound of the pipes, they say, were devils and was against civilization for such savage music. So we had the Pipers play all the more." Along the way, natives lined the city's thoroughfares shouting encouragement and tossing them food and cigarettes. The officers boarded filthy boxcars, found patches of personal space, and began a squealing crawl north.

Two days later, they arrived at the Malayan coastal city of Georgetown, also known as Penang, and two days after that were herded to the docks to board another merchant vessel. The Japanese, inveterate busybodies when it came to moving prisoners around, were economical with information. Their native language seemed to be hyperbole, allegory, and propaganda. "You're going to a health camp," the guards told them. "You're going to go to a nice place where the food is plentiful and the sun is shining." Where they went first was back into the steel confines of another hell ship. When Colonel Tharp's group boarded the decrepit *Dai Moji Maru* about fifty Americans stayed behind at Changi. John Wisecup, Paul Papish, and Robbie Robinson were among those kept behind for reasons of ill health and placed under the nominal command of the lone American officer left with them, Marine 2nd Lt. Edward Miles Barrett. On January 11, the rest of them headed for sea. A second ship, the *Nichimei Maru*, embarked fifteen hundred Dutchmen and five hundred Japanese engineers whose services were needed somewhere in the north. The two freighters were escorted by a small corvette that looked like a large pleasure craft with a three-inch gun mounted astern. The little convoy settled on a northwesterly course through the Straits of Malacca.

At daybreak on January 15, 1943, the ships neared the Gulf of Martaban near Rangoon. Up on the main deck, Sgt. Luther Prunty was bulling around with two other Lost Battalion sergeants, trying to figure out where they were headed. Rumors had it they were just a day or so from making port. Having judged that they were well clear of Malayan waters, Prunty said, "Well, we ought to be out of the danger zone." Sgt. Julius B. Heinen Jr. figured the exact opposite. The closer they got to India, he said, the closer they would be to Japanese airfields. Then Heinen said, "Just incidentally, if you'll look up in the sky right over there right now, you're going to see three planes, and I'm going to bet you that they're ours. Prunty, those damn planes are going to make a run on these ships!"

As the aircraft approached, Charley Pryor was in the *Dai Moji Maru*'s after cargo hold, directly below the open topside hatch, watching some guys play a card game they called "Stateside Poker." It was a variation common among prisoners. Bidding was vigorous but debts were deferred—kept careful track of, but not paid—until they returned to the States after the war. Under the circumstances it might as well have been called "Bright Side Poker." A series of deep, muffled explosions shook the ship, putting an end to the card game. "We heard this tremendous *whomp whomp whomp* and couldn't imagine what the Sam Hill it was," Pryor said, "but I just looked up through there, and I see this great silver airplane with four motors."

There were three of them. As the big B-24 Liberator bombers vectored in at about twelve thousand feet to make their bomb runs, hysteria gripped the *Dai Moji Maru*. Japanese soldiers up on deck fired their rifles at the planes and struggled to unlimber the two French-built, wooden-wheeled seventy-five-millimeter field guns tied down on wooden platforms fore and aft. Sergeant Heinen ordered all prisoners on deck to return to the hold. He told them to take off their shoes, tie them together and hang on. "Just don't panic. Don't get in an uproar," he said. He yelled down to Ens. Charles D. Smith and swapped places with him. Tracking these bombers from a ship called for a naval officer's talents. Heinen took charge of the men in the hold and Smith climbed topside.

The aircraft that found them early that morning were part of a flight of six B-24D Liberators operating from an Indian airdrome called Pandaveswar, well hidden in the countryside about a hundred miles northwest of Calcutta. Fanning out over the Gulf of Martaban hunting Japanese shipping, three of those planes found the POW convoy about fifty miles off the Burma coast, near Tavoy.

The *Dai Moji Maru* was an underpowered old bucket, saddled with a full load of coal and capable of only about six knots. With their limited elevation, her two field guns, one mounted fore and the other aft, were poorly suited to antiaircraft defense. But as the B-24s lumbered in, the Japanese gun crews untied their deck cables, tracked the planes, and opened fire. The old *marus* made difficult targets. Their captains began circling on contact with the bombers.

A Liberator nicknamed "Captain and the Kids," piloted by Capt. William A. Delahay, droned overhead and dropped four bombs on the first run, missing the *Dai Moji Maru* by about a quarter mile astern. Another B-24 targeted the lead prison ship, the *Nichimei Maru*. Its bombardier's aim was true. A stick of bombs walked right across the ship's fantail, killing most of the men in the after hold. She heaved up out of the sea and settled back again, broken at the keel. As fate would have it, the *Nichimei Maru*'s after hold was full of Japanese engineers. The men in the forward hold—Dutch POWs— suffered far fewer casualties.

Belowdecks on the *Dai Moji Maru*, Julius Heinen found Capt. Hugh Lumpkin, a medical officer, and two other Lost Battalion officers absorbed in a game of bridge. "What's the bid?" he asked. One of the officers said he'd bid four spades. Heinen took his own cards, looked at everyone's hands, and said, "If you play that hand correctly, you could make five spades, but I don't think you've got time to finish it. They're making a run over us with three bombers, and they've already sunk the ship ahead of us."

Cards flew. As the bombers headed for them, Ensign Smith stood at the edge of the hatch above, calling down ranges and angles of elevation: "Thirty degrees, forty, forty-five . . ." Zero degrees was a line to the horizon, ninety was straight overhead. The soldiers from the Lost Battalion were hazy on what all the Navy's aerial geometry meant, but understood well enough when Ensign Smith announced, "I can see them! *Jesus,* these are close!" The planes homed in on them again, approaching the drop point of fifty-five degrees. As the American bombers bore in high on the starboard hand of the undamaged *Dai Moji Maru,* gunners on the ship's forward mount tracked one of the twin-tailed bombers and carelessly closed their firing key just as the plane flew behind the ship's superstructure. The projectile slammed into the bridge, blowing its starboard portion clean away and raining shrapnel over the bridge and the forward deck. Still tracking the plane, the crew fired again. This projectile struck a guide wire directly in front of them and exploded, killing them all. Five bombs came whistling down and landed right across the *Dai Moji Maru*'s beam, straddling the ship, three to starboard and two to port.

Observing his target from twelve thousand feet through his Norden bombsight, the bombardier of the plane, 2nd Lt. Thomas B. Sledge, could see flames raging amidships on the vessel. Then he watched as his bombs splashed close aboard, the nearest barely twenty feet alongside. The blasts ruptured hull plates, lifted the ship's bow clear of the water, and turned her about fifteen degrees off her previous heading. As Sledge completed his run, he saw that the ship was stopped and the fire was out. He cursed, thinking that his hits had caused the fires and the towering spouts of his near-misses had quenched them. But the fires were from an altogether different cause: the incompetent zeal of the Japanese field gun crews on the *Dai Moji Maru*.

Charley Pryor figured it was the dense mass of coal filling the ship's hull that had kept it from collapsing below the waterline. "Up above the water line," Pryor said, "and above the coal bunkers, it just caved the whole side of the ship in. If we'd been an oil burner, it'd have torn all the seams loose and we'd have been sunk right there." The Japanese gun crew on the fantail seemed just as intent on scuttling the ship with their flak barrage. On one of their first volleys at the Liberators, they failed to lock the breech of their field gun properly and produced a back blast that set the gun's wooden platform and after magazine afire. At least thirty Japanese were killed. Flames engulfed the stern of the ship, threatening the aft hold, full of Australians. As those sailors fought the fire, the medical people on board, including Dr. Lumpkin, Staff Sgt. Jack Rogers of the 131st's medical detachment, the *Houston* ship's doctor Cdr. William Epstein, and pharmacist's mate second class Raymond Day, tended to more than a hundred wounded and dead on deck.

The B-24s turned and came around yet again. Spotting them at a distance, the Americans cursed, and asked the Japanese skipper to grant the *Houston*'s chief signalman, Kenneth S. Blair, permission to alert the planes that they were a POW ship. An Australian major, as it happened, just went and did it, blinking a message to the pilots with a flashlight. One of the planes returned the signal and, to everyone's relief, departed to the west.

The *Dai Moji Maru* stopped to rescue survivors from the *Nichimei Maru,* lingering until after dark to get the work done. There were 960 in all, the majority of them Dutch. Ensign Smith, who had seen the whole show while spotting the aircraft topside, wrote, "I will give credit to the Japanese merchant captain of the *Moji Maru,* who conducted himself in a thoroughly seamanlike manner and after the planes left he refused to leave the vicinity until all survivors from the other ship were picked up." It wouldn't occur to Charley Pryor till much later that what may have compelled the Japanese captain to save them was not mercy but necessity: The prisoners jamming his miserable holds were needed alive for a reason.

One *Houston* sailor who had traveled this path with the Fitzsimmons Group, Donald Brain, heard en route to the docks that they were headed for Burma. Uncommon among the *Houston*'s working-class enlisted men, Brain knew the remote country well from his father's prewar work in foreign oil fields. His dad's job had taken him all over the world: Kirkuk, northern Pakistan, Shanghai, Rangoon. From the age of twelve to seventeen Brain had lived in the last of these cities, Burma's great southern port. He learned the local commoners' language, knew the gentleness of the Buddhist mind, the communal style of child rearing, the quiet spirit of industriousness. And he knew the fractious country well enough to weigh its possibilities and risks as a home in captivity. He thought of the mines in the north, the oil fields in the Irrawaddy River Valley, and the rubber plantations in the south. If Burma was indeed the destination, all of these would be likely places to put prisoners to work.

In Singapore, there had been talk of a railway in jungles far to the north. They had seen the groups of British and Australian prisoners shipping out, to where nobody knew. Brain doubted the experience would live up to the guards' sunny billing. But what was this talk about a railroad? Don Brain wondered. The hearsay was never very specific. He knew enough about Burma to ask this: If that was indeed their destination, where in its godforsaken jungles was there a railroad to work on?

CHAPTER 35

The men on the *Dai Moji Maru*—dozens of them, mostly Dutch, were horribly wounded in the attack by the U.S. bombers—spotted land again on January 16. The coastline was broken by a wide sweeping delta where a powerful river dissipated into the sea. Mangrove forests and rice paddies surrounded them as the ship navigated the winding river channels and estuaries. Forty miles into the delta system, they came upon a city. Speculation flew about its identity. It was well familiar to at least one sailor. "Hell, I know where we are now," said Donald Brain. "This is Rangoon, Burma." He caught some flak for being a know-it-all, but he was right.

The Japanese Fifteenth Army invaded that country on January 16, 1942, rolling over two weak divisions of Burmese and Indian irregulars in less than two weeks and putting the imperial sword against Rangoon, the threshold to Great Britain's south Asian empire. When Japanese troops landed on March 7, taking the port city as the Dutch were surrendering on Java, the rout acquired epic proportions. Nearly a million Burmese became refugees, fleeing for their lives as the Japanese advanced northward. The British Army commander who yielded the city, Lt. Gen. Sir Harold Alexander, had already built a reputation as a steward of hopeless causes. Less than two years earlier, he had directed the British evacuation of Dunkirk. U.S. Gen. Joseph W. Stilwell's forces escaped into India in a withdrawal that would make "Vinegar Joe" too a hero for his exploits in retreat. By the end of April 1942, the Japanese had pushed north and seized Lashio, the western terminus of the Burma Road. When that supply link was severed, China was once again left to its own starved devices. The enemy's success provoked fear in Allied military councils that the Japanese might link up with the Germans in the Middle East, bringing the immediate collapse not just of China but of India too.

Almost immediately on arrival in Rangoon, the prisoners were transferred to smaller vessels and sent to sea again. Departing, they headed east, traveling all that afternoon and through the following day. At dusk they approached the shore again. From within the Salween River delta, a smaller town could be seen near the coast: Moulmein.

The name held vague meaning for them. Those who knew the Rudyard Kipling poem "Mandalay," popularized by the Robbie Williams song "The Road to Mandalay," had heard of the Moulmein Pagoda already. Before them now such a structure stood, an angular temple towering over the village like an ornamented gateway between jungle and sea. "We were still young and adventurous," said Jim Gee, who had arrived with the Fitzsimmons Group earlier, in October, "and at this time still had a lot of strength. We looked at things from the eyes of an adventurer." Scattered lights of settlements peeked through the palm-topped overgrowth. A red moon "lit the ground almost as though the sun was shining," he said. "And I shall never forget the beauty that surrounded us as we made our way by these small boats into the landing."

Unloaded at gunpoint, the healthy prisoners were taken up a narrow cobblestone street to a wooden building that seemed to date to the early 1800s. It was a jail. Its denizens—Burmese political prisoners and British army personnel—were moved out to make room for the newcomers, and they inspected the jail like curious ants. From conversation with natives—Donald Brain could still get by in the Burmese language—and from a few telling details, such as a mortician's slab in the midst of the prison, the Americans learned that the facility had been used to impound lepers. For a few panicked moments, some of them envisioned a disfiguring contagion overtaking them. Then they claimed real estate and ate a meal of hardtack and stew. From a Burmese prisoner they verified a lingering rumor: They had been brought there to build a railroad into the jungle.

Al Kopp, a *Houston* pharmacist's mate who landed in January with Colonel Tharp's newcomers, volunteered to stay behind at Moulmein as medical caregiver to forty-two Dutch prisoners gravely wounded in the air attack on their convoy. With no medicine or instruments to work with, Kopp would be forced to watch every last one of his patients die. Meanwhile, the rest of the prisoners milled through Moulmein's streets, where local people tossed fruits and vegetables to them, as well as a type of cheroot that was potent enough to knock you silly if you smoked it. Taken to an open field with a railway siding, they were loaded into cattle cars. The locomotive at the head of the train chuffed to life and was soon enough pulling them south.

Their journey to this point happened to be a virtual reverse tour of Amelia Earhart's itinerary five years before. The legendary aviator had flown her Lockheed Electra 10E from Rangoon to Bangkok, Singapore, and Bandung—fighting dysentery en route to an undocumented fate somewhere in the central Pacific. These locales, whose names were more or less familiar to some of them from their time in the Asiatic Fleet, were well-established way stations on the road to oblivion.

Their final destination—and the first stop in the new odyssey to follow—was the Burmese town of Thanbyuzayat. After unloading, they were taken to an open field ringed with guards who were busy burning brush. In the field, standing on a crate of some kind, was a stocky Japanese colonel, his sharp army uniform festooned with ribbons. The Americans would never forget the man's stagecraft: Col. Yoshitada Nagatomo, peacock proud, chest puffed up and the brim of his cap cocked low. Notwithstanding his Napoleonic stature, he had a well-cultivated air of pomposity—"very cocky, a king-of-the-walk type," recalled Howard Charles on witnessing the same performance when the Fitzsimmons Group arrived. Nagatomo's outfit was dominated by his tall brown leather boots, flashy and oversized, so much so that one *Houston* sailor thought "he could run and jump and land inside of them." Nagatomo stood before them on a sweltering field surrounded by an entourage of guards, and gathered himself to speak. With an interpreter turning his guttural roar into something

they could understand, he instructed the prisoners to listen intently.
They did. They would never forget his words.

It is a great pleasure to us to see you at this place as I am appointed chief of war prisoners camp obedient to the Imperial
command issued by His Majesty the Emperor. The great East
Asiatic War has broken out, due to the rising of the East
Asiatic nations whose hearts were burned with the desire to
live and preserve their nations on account of the intrusion of
the British and Americans for the past many years. There is,
therefore, no other reason for Japan to drive out the anti-Axis
power of the arrogant and insolent British and Americans
from East Asia in co-operation with our neighbors of China
and other East Asiatic nations, and to establish the Greater
East Asia Co-Prosperity Sphere for the benefit of all human
beings and establish everlasting peace in the world.

During the past few centuries, Nippon has made great sacrifices and extreme endeavors to become the leader of the East
Asiatic nations, who were mercilessly and pitifully treated by
the outside forces of the Americans and British, and Nippon
without disgracing anybody has been doing her best up till
now for fostering Nippon's real power.

You are all only a few remaining skeletons after the invasion of East Asia for the past few centuries and are pitiful victims. It is not your fault, but till your government do not
wake up from the dreams and discontinue their resistance, all
of you will not be released. However, I shall not treat you
badly for the sake of humanity as you have no fighting power
at all. His Majesty the Emperor has been deeply anxious about
all war prisoners and has ordered us to enable opening war
prisoner camps at almost all the places in the Southern countries. The Imperial Thoughts are inestimable and the Imperial
favors are infinite and as such you should weep with gratitude
at the greatness of them, and should correct or mend the mis-
leading and improper anti-Japanese ideas.

He asked them to look around them and see the sorry state of the
world. Its endemic poverty and filth, not the depredations of the
Japanese slave keepers, were the reasons they lacked medicine, food,
and supplies. Women and children could not eat; why should

prisoners or soldiers have other expectations? Nagatomo declared that they would live according to Japanese military law, that their possessions would be limited, and that anyone attempting escape would meet "the extreme penalty."

"If there is one foolish man who is trying to escape, he shall see big jungles toward the East which are impossible for communication. Toward the West he shall see boundless ocean." To the north and south lay the Japanese Army. Then Nagatomo referred to the "ill-omened matters which happened in Singapore," perhaps referring to the executions of prisoners who tried to escape, or to the thousands of Chinese who had been butchered on the beaches shortly after the Japanese seized control.

Then he got to the point.

> By the hand of the Nippon Army Railway Construction Corps to connect Thailand and Burma, the work has started to the great interest of the world. There are deep jungles where no man ever came to clear them by cutting the trees. There are also countless difficulties and sufferings, but we shall have the honor of joining in this great work which was never done before, and you shall do your best efforts.
>
> We will build the railroad if we have to build it over the white man's body. It gives me great pleasure to have a fast-moving defeated nation in my power. You are merely rubble but I will not feel bad because it is your rulers. If you want anything you will have to come through me for same and there will be many of you who will not see your homes again. Work cheerfully at my command.

Nagatomo's basic ethos was already emblazoned far more succinctly in German over the gates to concentration camps throughout central and eastern Europe: "*Arbeit macht frei,*" work brings freedom. Over the backs of the white man the Burma-Siam Express shall ride.

"Thanbyuzayat turned out to be the beginning of a real nightmare," Jim Gee said. It was the northwestern terminus of one of the most notorious engineering projects in history. The prisoners did not know what awaited them, but they were quick to grasp their isolation. "At that point we learned that life was going to be pretty rugged," Gee said. "It didn't take a very educated man to see that conditions in this part of the world were going to be very bad. We knew something about the climate. We knew it had a rainy season, and we knew it had a dry season. We knew that both were severe. And just the thought that we were going to be in the jungles, wearing as few clothes as we had, working under the conditions that we knew and could see the natives work, we knew that we were in for a spell of pretty rough living."

Howard Charles, who had to this point never really feared the Japanese, heard Nagatomo's words and felt a chill in his bones. "I knew this guy meant business. . . . I just had this sinking feeling that this was going to be a bad show, and if we lived through it, we were going to be very lucky."

Part Four

IN THE JUNGLE
OF THE KWAI

★

Ship me somewheres east of Suez, where the best
    is like the worst,
Where there aren't no Ten Commandments an' a
    man can raise a thirst;
For the temple-bells are callin', an' it's there that
    I would be—
By the old Moulmein Pagoda, looking lazy at the
    sea;
    On the road to Mandalay,
    Where the old Flotilla lay,
    With our sick beneath the awnings when we
        went to Mandalay!

                —Rudyard Kipling
                "Mandalay" (1892)

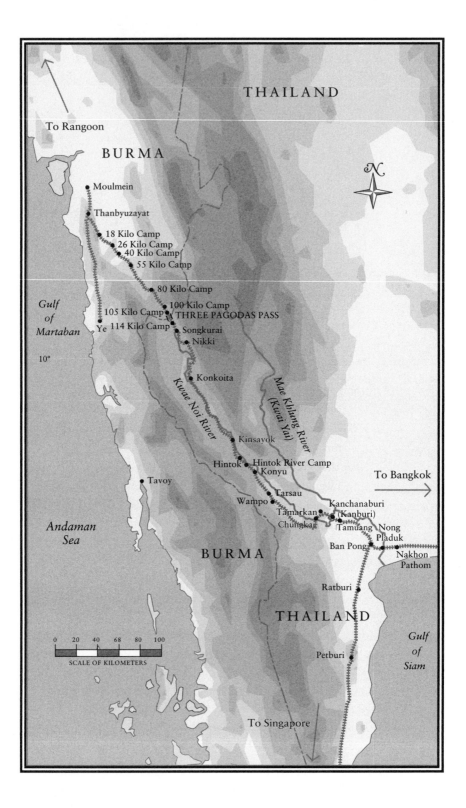

CHAPTER 36

It was all about China. A world war engulfed the Pacific because Japan had struggled to subjugate its mainland neighbor. Franklin Roosevelt's economic sanctions and oil embargo were punishment for Japan's assault on China, Asia's keystone in the economic world order. Japan's earliest offensives in the southwestern Pacific grew from its need for oil to pursue its war on the continent. Now Japan aimed to strangle China by cutting its essential lines of supply from India and Burma, kept open by threadbare British and American armies.

Japan's ability to fight in Burma was complicated by the predations of an increasingly assertive American submarine force. In the war's early going the best supply route to Burma was by sea, from the home islands south through the South China Sea, around Singapore, through the Strait of Malacca, and up to Rangoon. Even without a submarine threat the two-thousand-mile journey would have strained the capacity of Japan's thump-shafted merchant fleet. As the U.S. boats extended their reach, the sea lanes became a prohibitively dangerous gauntlet for the Japanese to run. By May 1942, they had lost sixty-seven ships to Rear Adm. Ralph Christie's Fremantle-based raiders. In short order Japan's struggle for Burma required a flow of arms and supplies far larger than its merchant marine could sustain.

The solution to the quandary had been drawn up years earlier: a new railway link between Bangkok and Rangoon. In Burma, well-developed lines already ran from Moulmein south to Ye. In Thailand, tracks extended from Bangkok west to Ban Pong, then turned south to the Malayan border. A great gap, held firm by the mountain ridges and impassable jungle that straddled the border between Burma and Thailand, stood between the two systems. The Japanese calculated that if a link could be forged through the 258-mile-wide gap separating them, a war might be won.

A 1939 report commissioned by the Japanese Army had concluded that two regiments of railway engineers would need a full year to connect the existing rail lines. Prepared by a civilian consultant, the study attracted new interest once Burma emerged as a theater against the Allies in India. With the demands of war sapping the availability of labor and matériel, newer estimates showed the project would actually take five or six years to complete. The sudden and unexpected surplus of Allied war prisoners and local coolies, or *romusha*, had changed that calculus altogether. An army of slaves would compensate for Japan's deficiencies in mechanization.

Though it had established its brutal pattern of treatment of POWs in China through the 1930s, Japan had haltingly committed itself to the principle that prisoners should not do work that was militarily useful to their captors. Japan had ratified the Hague Convention of 1907, and in 1928 it signed (but a year later refused to ratify) the more expansive 1929 Geneva Convention on the Treatment of Prisoners of War. The Imperial Army pressured the Japanese privy council not to ratify the convention because it was unlikely to bring reciprocal benefits: Bushido warriors did not become prisoners. Japan's refusal to ratify the Geneva Convention would provide the cover it needed to deny that its prisoners of war were entitled to legal protections.

In March 1942, the commander of the Southern Field Railway Group in Saigon ordered preparations to begin for construction of the railway. On June 20 came the Army's formal decision to proceed. Given the pressures of wartime, they needed it done fast—in twelve months. The job was assigned to the Fifth Railway Regiment in Thanbyuzayat, Burma, and the Ninth Railway Regiment in Ban Pong, Thailand. It would fall to a civilian engineer named

Yoshihiko Futamatsu, who worked for Japan's national railway, to bring to fruition the most ambitious and notorious of World War II's civil engineering projects.

Futamatsu, promoted to major in wartime, determined that the best route for the railway was to follow the Kwae Noi River west from Ban Pong. That plan would run headlong into nearly insuperable obstacles of terrain, not to mention weather. A landscape broken by rocky ridges and snaking jungle rivers and tributaries would require exhaustive rock cutting, bridges, and viaducts along sheer cliffs. Moving north and west from the rice paddy plains of central Thailand, the terrain grew jagged and steep. As construction bogged down in the spring monsoon season, workers' lives would be at risk from a mélange of tropical diseases and breakdowns in supply. Less difficult paths were available, but the route along the Kwae Noi had one surpassing advantage: The river, with its barge traffic, made heavy transport much easier. Large bridge trestles and heavy loads of ballast and other materials could be carried upriver from Ban Pong or cut or quarried locally. Heavy construction equipment was unavailable, but a swarm of manual laborers could more than make up the difference.

By the end of June 1942, the project's infrastructure was taking shape. Twelve hundred British prisoners from Singapore began building base workshops and storage facilities around the town of Nong Pladuk, on the Thai end of the line. With its foundries, forges, engine shops, power stations, and an oil refinery—much of it scavenged or pillaged from Malaya, Sumatra, and Java—the town of Kanchanaburi in Thailand, often called Kanburi, became the headquarters for the entire line. Meanwhile, plans were afoot to bring prisoners to Burma to begin work from the northwest. A huge workforce of Burmese, Chinese, Tamil, Indian, and Malay natives—as many as 350,000 of them would be lured into imperial servitude—had built a chain of work camps every three or four miles along the right of way. They were joined by sixty thousand Allied prisoners of war, who rounded out the workforce and constituted its trained and disciplined core. Under their captors' plan, they would build the railway simultaneously from either end, inland from coastal Burma and central Thailand, joining the two lines near the mountainous border with an imperial golden spike.

Such a trial had never confronted American fighting men before. Pressured to perform five years of work in twelve short months, they would be given over to the jungle and left to wrestle it toward civilization. They would contend with all its elements—its hardwoods, rocks, and vines, its predators both mammalian and bacterial, under the lash of their enemy and assault from the elements. The work would harden some and consume others. They would forget all but the most basic memories of home, picking their way through a life in captivity that would become the grist for sleepless nights ever afterward.

CHAPTER 37

How does one build a railway through an impassable jungle? How does one do it without industrial equipment, without hydraulics, steam, or mechanized tools? The task begins with an imperative: that it *will* be done. It will be done whether people go hungry, suffer disease, or are beaten to death with sticks. The imperative, enforced with martial ruthlessness, drives everything, but it comes with a cost. The Imperial Japanese Army was good at enforcing imperatives, if generally unmoved by the costs.

A railway begins with a survey, a right-of-way, and a cleared path. The path is staked out by engineers and cleared through forests and hills. In mountainous terrain such as the jungles of Burma, the challenge then is to tame that path, to make dangerous, jungle-draped elevations flat and level and passable by train. Long climbing stretches of earth must be leveled, ravines built up, hills knocked down, valleys filled. The railway must be squeezed through gaps between cliffs and rivers, carved as a channel through hard rock, bridged over a river system's innumerable feeders and estuaries.

Then the path is shoveled up into a raised earth embankment, a base for a layer of broken stones, known as ballast, that allows the embankment to bear a crosshatched layer of wooden ties, or sleepers, and steel rails, and ultimately the weight of the freight trains themselves.

Like a collective embodiment of fabled John Henry in the mine, the prisoners would do with thousands of hands what should have been done by machine. In Burma, those hands were Australian, Dutch, and American. In Thailand, on the southeastern end, they were predominantly British. The British had gotten started in June 1942, just as the Japanese carrier fleet was trounced in the Battle of Midway. By the turn of 1943, as the fight for Guadalcanal was shifting in the Americans' favor and General MacArthur was beginning the assault on New Guinea, work on the railway was in full swing. News of these victories would take months to reach the prisoners and kindle hope in their souls.

After the men in Fitzsimmons Group were marshaled at the leper's prison at Moulmein, they were loaded into trucks and driven twenty-six kilometers into the countryside to the site of their first work camp. Since the work camps in Burma were named for their distance in kilometers from the Thanbyuzayat headquarters, this camp was known as 26 Kilo Camp. The Burma half of the railway was loosely structured around these kilo camps, each with its own Japanese commander, sited on the rail right-of-way from Thanbyuzayat (0 Kilo Camp), all the way up to Three Pagodas Pass on the Thai border, or 114 Kilo Camp. It was at 26 Kilo Camp that the story of the Americans on the River Kwai Railway began.

The 191 men of Captain Fitzsimmons's group were loosely attached to a larger force of three thousand Australian prisoners under the leadership of Brig. Arthur L. Varley of the Australian Army. This group, who gathered at Thanbyuzayat in October, was the nucleus of the construction unit working on the Burma side of the line. The Allies would refer to it as "A Force." In the Japanese scheme of organization, it was known as the "Number 3 Thai POW Branch" or "Branch Three."* Its commander was Col. Yoshitida Nagatomo.

The Americans who arrived later, in January on the *Dai Moji Maru,* were greeted by Colonel Nagatomo and put under separate command in a unit known as Number 5 Thai POW Branch, or Branch Five, commanded by a Japanese army captain named Totare Mizutani. This group would work independently of, and have little

---

*The name was confusing insofar as most of the Americans would never work on the Thai end of the line. The Number 3 Thai POW Branch worked in Burma.

contact with, the prisoners of Varley's Branch Three. They began work at Alepauk, or 18 Kilo Camp. From the moment of their arrival, they leapfrogged their counterparts in Branch Three as expediency required, en route to their designated base camp at 60 Kilo Camp.

The kilo camps, built in advance by parties of *romusha*, were of primitive design, consisting of several long, open-sided bamboo huts roofed with interwoven palm leaves—nepa, sugo, or coconut; *atap*, they called it. There was no metal in their construction, no nails or other hardware. The bamboo joints were fastened with strips of bark. A door at one end opened into a dirt center aisle on either side of which was a six-foot-deep sleeping platform made from bamboo branches. There were about a hundred men per barracks.

Each man got a one-by-two-meter-long bamboo platform for personal space. They slept shoulder to shoulder, ate there, stashed their stolen possessions there. Rough-hewn though this life was, it was, at first, far more tolerable than the hell ships. A contingent of twelve to fifteen guards and Japanese Army engineers lived in their own hut across camp. The guards who oversaw the individual camps made it abundantly clear, as Colonel Nagatomo himself did, that death was the penalty for escape. The camps had no discernible perimeter. No walls were needed. The surrounding jungle was its own prison. The tall trees, dense bamboo undergrowth, and predatory animals were as confining as a concertina-topped fence with guard towers.

With the survey done and elevations calculated, the Japanese engineers stretched lines from tree to tree, marking sections of earth to be cut and others to be filled, and the prisoners got to work decapitating hills and filling ravines to lay the embankment of the railway. In the early going, cutting and filling were the principal tasks. The Japanese gave them all the work they could handle and more. The engineers set a daily quota of dirt for each prisoner to dig. At the beginning of the project it was one cubic meter per day. This turned out to be far more work than it might first have seemed. The men had not only to dig the dirt at the cutting site but also load it and carry it to a corresponding area needing a fill.

During the dry season, in the coastal foothills, the work was as easy as it would get. They shoveled and dumped, shoveled and dumped, loading sacks that were suspended from long poles and hauled to whatever depression or ravine needed filling. The poles, known as yo-ho poles for the rhythmic chants the native workers sang while working with them, were long bamboo rods from which hung a rice cloth sack large enough to hold several bucketfuls of earth. Each end of the springy pole, whose bounce seemed to make it easier to bear the loads, was carried by a prisoner. They would march several hundred yards with a fully laden yo-ho pole straining from their shoulders, spill and fill, and march back to do it again.

"You might spend a whole month making one fill in one place," said *Houston* sailor Howard Brooks. "There were relatively short distances. But there might be stones close by where you start breaking up stones and putting fill in, putting stones on top for the ties you're going to lay on it. You might do that and then you might do it in reverse another place. Then you might leave and go on down to the next camp and start the same thing over again."

The cuts could be 150 yards long and sixty to eighty feet deep. "There was a lot of rock—a tremendous amount of rock—that you had to go through, and this was all done by hand," Gus Forsman said. The scope of the work didn't bow them. There was almost always immediately to hand a smaller objective, a quota enforced with the rod, to concentrate their minds.

Their tools were primitive when they had tools at all. There were no bulldozers or bucket loaders, no graders. The prisoners were all those things. They were dump trucks. They were steamrollers. They packed the railroad embankment by the percussion of their bare feet walking over it. Their shovels, made from soft metal, bent and broke when struck too vigorously into the root-infested earth, "like a pork and bean can on the end of a stick," Howard Brooks said. "We got beat up more for bending a shovel than we did for not working at all." They learned, in other words, to rely not on their tools but on their own hands. And as they did so, extending the railway into the mountains, every so often they would notice what appeared to be old survey markings from some earlier effort to carve out a right-of-way. Rational minds had come before them, labored briefly, and declined to proceed. Now such discretion was no longer available. When the prisoners lost track of the old markers, they set their own course into the unsurveyed jungle.

CHAPTER 38

Staying mostly at his headquarters at Thanbyuzayat, Colonel Nagatomo kept a studied distance from the backbreaking exertions of his charges up the line. Brig. Arthur Varley's challenge was to build rapport with his counterpart and cultivate an ability to prevail upon him to treat his prisoners with as much humanity as possible. But Varley could see a hopeless situation settling in as the size of Branch Three swelled, en route to a number approaching ten thousand men later that spring—mostly Australian and Dutch, with a sampling of British and Americans in the mix. He had seen the worst of war's foul enterprise, having received two Military Crosses for conspicuous gallantry as a young lieutenant in World War I. But nothing he had seen during that earlier conflict could have prepared him for the ruthlessness of the Japanese now. Several months before the first Americans arrived, Varley's men had been working near Tavoy, constructing airfields for the Japanese. Eight Australians were caught trying to escape and were brought before Nagatomo. He coolly ordered them executed. Varley's pleas went nowhere. The death sentence was inflexible. The only thing that struck Varley more than the camp commander's cold-blooded allegiance to the Bushido code was the good-natured, downright cheerful way the Aussie "diggers" conducted themselves as they were led blindfolded to their graves. "They all spoke cheerio and good luck messages to one another and never showed any sign of fear. A truly courageous end," he wrote in a secret diary that he kept, at considerable risk to his life, from the beginning of his time in Burma.

Confronted with Nagatomo's murderous discipline, Varley pursued a continuous and ongoing negotiation with him and his deputies, Lieutenant Naito and Lt. Kititara Hosoda, bargaining to secure medical treatment for his weakest men and fair treatment from the guards. He monitored their treatments, provisions, and punishments, lobbied for the Japanese to make the payments they promised in exchange for work—a private got twenty-five cents a month, an NCO thirty, an officer forty—and pressed for the Japanese to allow the Red Cross to admit a ship into Moulmein, as the Geneva Convention provided.

Nagatomo remained relatively aloof in these parleys, insulating himself by communicating to Varley through a Dutch translator named Cornelius Punt, or through Lieutenant Naito, who knew some English. Varley and his medical officer, Maj. W. E. Fisher, the senior physician among all nationalities in Burma, wrote numerous letters to Nagatomo warning him of deteriorating health conditions. By the time the second group of Americans arrived in January, contagion was well established and various diseases had a firm foothold in the camps under Varley's purview. Nagatomo seemed to consider the growing number of dysentery and malaria patients in the Thanbyuzayat hospital as malingerers. With a thousand beds, Thanbyuzayat was a large hospital. But the medical staff there had barely enough equipment to staff a small rural clinic. They had three thermometers and perhaps half a dozen two-inch rolls of bandages at any given time. They reboiled mosquito netting and old rags to use as dressings, covering them with banana leaves taped down with strips of latex. Varley, in his diary, documented his every meeting with the Japanese, every request for drugs, beds, rice bags and canvas, drums for boiling water. He also documented the futility of such efforts.

There were signs of empathy and decency in several Japanese officers at Thanbyuzayat. Lieutenant Hosoda, who stood in as Branch Three chief during Nagatomo's occasional absences, wept at his first sight of dysentery's effects on the prisoners. He ordered guards to bring in, under the cover of darkness, fruit and eggs to the patients.

There was a second lieutenant named Suzuki, a surgeon in private practice, who, according to Dr. Fisher, examined the most serious of the sick at Thanbyuzayat "competently and sympathetically, talked intelligently about surgery and expressed the hope that the fellowship of medical practitioners need not be abolished by the exigencies of war." There were times when Nagatomo himself, having personally seen to the execution of escapees, seemed to draw close to sympathetic cooperation with Varley. "Were there any good Japanese?" Fisher asked in his diary. "The answer is yes, but so few as only to constitute an exception proving the rule to the contrary."

On December 7, 1942, Nagatomo traveled to Rangoon and from there on to Singapore for a conference of camp commanders. His relief was Lieutenant Naito. The Allied POW commanders were uneasy about the Japanese junior officer. Though he could fight his way through an English-language phrase, something in the glint of his eye struck them as not quite right. Six days after Nagatomo's departure, three Dutch officers were shot and executed, supposedly, Naito said, on the personal written order of the colonel from Rangoon. On January 10, Nagatomo returned to the base camp claiming to have spent twenty thousand yen on blankets, clothes, boots, hats, toothbrushes, toilet paper, and sporting goods for the prisoners. Nothing was ever seen of it on the railway.

The men exhibited the ravages of the bacterial war quickly. After Serang, Bicycle Camp, Changi, and several months with Branch Three, Gus Forsman had dropped from 145 to 80 pounds. The nutritional deficiencies invited beriberi, which revealed itself through sudden, painful swelling that if left unchecked could assault the heart. "If you poked your finger into your leg, the hole would stay there for twenty minutes to half an hour," said Otto Schwarz. "The soles of your feet were so swollen you couldn't stand up from the pain." Dry beriberi was severely painful, but it was the wet variety of the disease that killed you. "When it got to your heart, forget about it. It caused progressive swelling from outside into your core," Schwarz noted.

Mosquitoes spread malaria, leaving men with cold, sweaty, shuddering chills. In the worst cases of cerebral malaria, or malignant tertiary malaria, the body overheated enough to warm the brain and bring delirium. The prisoner felt as though he were encased in a sphere, looking out through fishbowl glass at the blurry world, an oscillating, electric ringing in the head. "You feel like your mind is a closed circuit, not quite making contact with the outside world," Ray Parkin wrote.

A number of Varley's countrymen were well over fifty years old—he himself was forty-nine—and could not afford to be placed on limited duty, because limited-duty workers were not paid and men who were not paid had trouble getting enough to eat. The extent of the danger to them was apparent enough. But the Japanese seldom acknowledged the medical crisis at hand. As Varley wrote in his diary, "The J's require absolute proof—not warnings of these dangers. Unfortunately the proof lies in the burial of a number of men who could have been saved if our warnings were heeded and necessaries supplied. It is so difficult and heartbreaking to fight for the lives of our men in all these matters and meet a brick wall on all occasions, by being told things are not available."

The jungle's contagions afflicted the Americans in Branch Three especially hard, because they had none of their own medics with them. When Drs. Epstein and Burroughs from the *Houston* and Captain Lumpkin from the Lost Battalion arrived in January and went upcountry with Branch Five, they had little contact with the other group. Treatments were seldom ever more elaborate than a damp cloth over the head. "A little quinine would have saved a lot of lives," said Otto Schwarz. "We were very rarely given it, just once in a blue moon." At Thanbyuzayat, Nagatomo's headquarters camp, was a reasonably well-equipped field hospital, but it was a prohibitive distance from the work sites where the weakest prisoners fell, far up the line.

The pace of work on the line was driven by many things that the Japanese could control—rifle butts on bones, the withholding of rations and medicines—and slowed by the never-predictable patterns of sickness. Looming behind all those variables was the knowledge that in a few short months, by April or May, the monsoon season was going to multiply the difficulty of every task. There was pressure to get the embankment laid quickly so that grass and other vegetation could grow through it before the seasonal torrents picked it apart.

*

The disease-ripe jungle would have posed a challenge to Western medicine even under ideal sanitary conditions. Without instruments and manufactured pharmaceuticals close at hand, the best Allied doctors were helpless. In the jungle, these shortages could turn even the smallest of wounds into death sentences.

Two Lost Battalion officers, Capt. Arch Fitzsimmons and Lt. Jimmy Lattimore, having heard that a group of Dutch physicians was based farther down the line, went to the Japanese and begged them to order one of them to join Branch Three. Just one would make the difference between life and death. They offered their watches as a bribe. As it would turn out, a gifted Dutch doctor had heard of their plight and was asking for them in turn. In April, a doctor whom some of the Americans in Branch Three had met in Singapore showed up at 40 Kilo Camp to join them as their on-site medical caretaker. His name was Henri Hekking.

Howard Charles remembered seeing Hekking back at Changi, gathered with Allied officers in one of the stucco barracks, rehashing the fall of the Dutch East Indies. Born in Surabaya to Dutch parents, Hekking felt indeed that they were *his* islands. It was his grandmother, a committed herbalist and healer, who set him on the path of studying native medicine. When he was sixteen, his father's work took him back to the Netherlands. Though he didn't want to leave, Hekking went there to study medicine on a Dutch army stipend, then paid for his training with a ten-year term of service that took him back to the East Indies as a medical officer in the colonial army. There Hekking continued pursuing his grandmother's art, first at Batavia, then at a hospital in the Celebes, and finally, before his capture, at the hospital on Timor. When the Japanese seized Timor and took him prisoner, it marked the end of his fulfillment of his promise to his *oma* that he would return and use his skills to help the natives of his homeland.

On his arrival at 40 Kilo Camp, Hekking introduced himself to the camp commander, Major Yamada. After exchanging niceties, the Dutchman told Yamada, "I wish to speak to you about food. The men will need meat."

"No meat," Yamada replied. "Later, Nippon kill water buffalo. Boom-boom. Understand-kah?"

Hekking was not bowed. "The men must have meat and citrus—fruit, any kind of fruit."

"No fruit," the major said.

The flat denials moved Hekking to appeal to the Japanese officer's self-interest. He knew Yamada had a tight deadline to complete his segment of the railway. He took a new tack. "As a doctor, I must warn you that if you do not provide protein and citrus, these men will soon become sick, and if they become sick, how do you build a railroad?"

Yamada darkened. He asked: "You warn me, Captain?"

"Yes, I—" Hekking offered, before he found himself reeling backward from the blow he never saw coming. As Hekking found his balance and clutched his face, Yamada shouted, "You do not warn me, Doctor! I warn you! You will speak no more of food!" Yamada ordered a roll call, mustering the prisoners before him. Then he began a speech that was an angrier, more threatening version of the address his superior, Colonel Nagatomo, had given the prisoners at Thanbyuzayat. As Charles recalled it:

> Prisoners were worthless driftwood washed ashore on the tide, he said. In Japan, one who surrendered to the enemy was worse than worthless, he was dead, for all practical purposes. He could never go home again, members of his family were disgraced, his offspring would suffer for many generations. But we were lucky: the railroad gave us the opportunity to redeem ourselves.

Yamada was just getting to the part about how his segment of the railway line would be built better and more quickly than any other when a voice began to sing. It was Freddie Quick, doing a reprise of his turn at Changi singing "God Bless America." His voice, Charles wrote, was "a beautiful baritone, challenging [Yamada], mocking everything he stood for."

The Japanese major's face went crimson as he scanned the ranks for the offender, found him, and shouted for him to stop singing. Two guards seized Quick and pulled him in front of Yamada. The guards tied his hands behind his back, then, wielding bamboo poles three inches in diameter, began pounding him over the head. On demand, the bleeding Marine repeated his name, rank, and serial number, each time weaker than the last. He was made to kneel, with another pole behind his knees. The guards kept working on him, lifting and pummeling, the thick bamboo shaft whistling down and cracking him atop the head, his legs numb and starved for blood. "Stop!" Henri Hekking shouted. "You will kill that man." The physician felt a crushing weight in his midsection—a rifle butt. The bamboo continued to fall on Quick. The guards relented only when finally he pitched forward, unconscious.

Jim Gee, Howard Charles, and some others hauled the unconscious Marine to a hut and laid him on the bamboo platform. "Is he gonna live?" someone asked. Examining the gash in his head, Hekking said, "Oh, yes. I would sew this up if I had some way to disinfect it." He said he needed a suture, some thread, and some cloth. Jim Gee volunteered to get some water boiled and, for a cloth, offered the shirt off his back.

*

The Lost Battalion's Lieutenant Lattimore, installed by Major Yamada as the food and supply officer at 40 Kilo Camp, confronted the Japanese officer one day about the inadequacy of their daily ration. The Japanese had informed Lattimore that working prisoners were to get a ration of five hundred to eight hundred grams of rice each day. In actuality, they were getting half that. The rice was "rotten and unusable, all of a grade the natives usually fed to cattle," Howard Charles wrote. Hekking realized that the prisoners were contributing to the problem by washing their rice. He insisted they stop. The "gray rice" they were served—dirty floor sweepings with a certain proportion of bugs and other foreign garnishments—was in fact an important source of vitamins and protein. They were supposed to receive 125 grams of meat. There was none to be had—and whenever there was a windfall, say if a water buffalo was killed, the guards always took the steak. Prisoners were supposed to get 250 grams of vegetables, but this came in the form of melon, full of water and with little caloric content to fuel a working man's metabolism. As the Lost Battalion's talented medical officer, Capt. Hugh Lumpkin, would tell an interpreter with Branch Five, based farther down the line, "Melons were only hog feed in the States."

Jimmy Lattimore was small of build and modest of mien, but he never had any trouble standing up for his men, no matter how many times his spectacles were sent flying. According to Howard Charles, Lattimore waved the food allocation order in front of Yamada's face and asked if he had ever planned to honor it. When the officer scoffed, Lattimore said, "You don't worry about a day of reckoning, because you think you'll win the war. Is that it? There's a day coming, buster. You'll see."

Assisted by two orderlies, Slug Wright from the Lost Battalion and Robert Hanley from the *Houston,* Hekking ran the most challenging kind of solo practice. He devised some innovative remedies out of the jungle's natural medicine chest. Certain types of leaves healed cuts. Long, saberlike legumes held beans that when crushed and boiled produced a tonic—"bitter as gall," according to Don Brain, but useful in reducing fevers. Hekking's knowledge of jungle ailments and natural remedies was encyclopedic. If Pack Rat McCone was resourceful in stitching wounds with safety pins and twine, Henri Hekking took lifesaving resourcefulness to the level of mysticism, if not near divinity. He knew that palmetto mold could be used like penicillin, that pumpkin could be stored in bamboo stalks, fermented with wild yeast, and used to treat men suffering from beriberi (it got them pleasantly drunk to boot). Tea brewed from bark contained tannins that constricted the bowels and slowed diarrhea. Wild chili peppers had all sorts of beneficial internal applications.

Hekking was supposed to report to British doctors who had been trained at the finest medical schools. Leery of native ways, they called him a witch doctor. Hekking had as little regard for their practices as they did for his. Because supplies of quinine were limited, he never prescribed it preventatively. He preferred to encourage the immune system to function, and administered the medicine only to fight an actual infection. He mixed beef tallow with acetylsalicylic acid to fight athlete's foot, distilled liquid iodine by mixing iodine crystals and sake, and ground up charcoal and mixed it with clay, a remedy that absorbed intestinal mucus. Assessing a skeletal patient squirting his insides out from dysentery, he could see beyond surface appearances and determine its underlying nature, amoebic or bacillary. When more potent medicines became available—Captain Fitzsimmons procured some sulfapyridine tablets once—Hekking would be miserly and economical, shaving the tablets down and administering the shavings directly into septic wounds. He used gasoline for alcohol, kapok for cotton, leaves for bandages, and latex for an adhesive.

Doc Hekking thought the classically trained physicians were hopelessly out of their element. "It was most distressing to him," Howard Charles wrote, "discovering how different their approaches were to the treatment of tropical diseases. . . . He was light-years ahead of these doctors." One of Branch Five's medical officers, Captain Lumpkin, who had practiced medicine in Amarillo before mustering for war, said that any doctor who trained in the jungle with the Dutch East Indian Colonial Army knew more about tropical diseases than the collective mind of the American Medical Association.

Hekking saw his patients as whole human beings and treated the whole man. "He was the first man that I ever heard of that treated a man as a unit," said Slug Wright. "He claimed that man had to be cured two ways: the body is only a small part of it; the mind is important as well. So he cured the mind and the body together. He was using psychosomatic medicine." Hekking sometimes turned around a patient in decline by intentionally angering him. He found that a rush of rage could be a lifesaving stimulant, even if the patient was in no shape to act out the impulse. Hekking inspired such confidence in his patients that even his placebos had powerful effects. He saved a different kind of placebo for the enemy. When Japanese soldiers came to him for help with venereal disease, he would send them to the native black markets to get the medicine he needed. When the medication was brought to him, he would set it aside for the prisoners and inject the Japanese with water. Sometimes he gave them a salve of plain acid and told them to apply it regularly. He didn't mind seeing them jump. He seemed fearless. Once he took a sulfapyridine tablet and made a mold from it. With the mold in hand, he was able to cast replicas using rice flour and plaster of Paris. He would trade the counterfeits to the Japanese for the quinine and other medicines his patients so urgently needed.

Hekking was the gatekeeper between the sick ward and the railway work parties. When the Japanese came around demanding workers, patients looked to him for a reprieve. Hekking would place the worst ones on the limited-duty or no-duty list. The next morning, if the Japanese couldn't fill their quota of workers, they would go through sick bay and grab the sick for duty on the line. It fell to the doctor to protest the selection. Many times, he got the hell pounded out of him for his audacity.

Henri Hekking worked one of his miracles on Jim Gee. The Marine was one of the first *Houston* men to go down with a fever, collapsing while digging a grave in the jungle out by 26 Kilo Camp. Taken to a medical tent, he lay unconscious for three days. His meltdown was so severe, his loss of fluids so pronounced, that he lost fifty pounds within a week. In the midst of his delirium, Gee remembered coming to and seeing a strange man speaking a strange

tongue. He didn't know if he was in heaven or hell. He heard someone say his struggle had been long and difficult, that he had nearly
lost his mind. It was Hekking, who for thirty-six hours straight had
sat by his bed, patiently enduring the Marine's rage. Hekking had
brought a large sack full of roots taken from a low-growing weed
known as *Cephaelis ipecacuanha*. Major Yamada, in a show of mercy—
or perhaps just impatience with Hekking's doggedness—had permitted him to go into the jungle, under guard, to gather the plants.
He boiled them into an herbal tonic and cajoled the Marine to drink,
encouraging him, touching his hand to his patient's clammy skin.
Gee struggled to sit upright and drank. Hekking got some people to
carry him outside and sat him in the sun. When Gee's strength came
back, the good doctor saw to it that he was taken back to the field
hospital at Thanbyuzayat.

CHAPTER 39

For Charley Pryor, working with Branch Five in the lowlands near 18 Kilo Camp, the work was hard but manageable. He found that the guards didn't bother him much if the work got done. They had food. They even had entertainment. One of the Dutch prisoners in Branch Five was a professional magician who had once worked on Holland-to-America cruise ships. For the Americans, his sleight of hand was a welcome diversion in a countryside that seemed immune to reason. The natives saw it differently. When he set a silk handkerchief prancing and fluttering, the few *romusha* brave enough to watch from the perimeter disappeared in terror.

The Americans could have learned from the natives' jungle wisdom. Clearing a right-of-way through some bamboo thickets, sweeping their picks back and forth, they were liable to disturb real estate claimed by all types of wild creatures. They found big blue-black scorpions with six-inch tails whose stingers were sharp enough to stick fast in a hickory-handled shovel. Charley Pryor said he caught a centipede that measured twenty-eight inches in length. Later he unearthed a nest of tiny snakes lying under a clump of bamboo. Curious, he put on a pair of gloves, reached down, and pulled one up, holding it by its head. He opened its mouth with a knife blade and noted two fangs deep in the cavity. When some natives saw what he was doing, they broke and ran. A safe distance away, they turned to Pryor again and began making frantic gestures. Pinching their forearms, they pointed to the sun in the west, then to the eastern horizon with a negating wave of the hand. The sun would go down, but another sunrise wouldn't come. Talking to a British prisoner later that day, Pryor discovered the serpent he had been toying with was a krait, more poisonous than a cobra.

They would start work at sunup and fulfill their quota by midday. Little did they appreciate at first that their efficiency would work against them. "The prisoners worked in a rather foolish fashion against the advice of the officers," Ens. Charles D. Smith wrote, "racing through their work to try to finish early so they could return to camp and have more time off for themselves." That might have been a good strategy so long as your overseers were U.S. Navy boatswains. On the Burma-Thailand Railway, the Japanese were not in the business of granting privileges or giving breaks. They just raised the quotas to match the prisoners' evident capacity: one and a half, two, three cubic meters a day. Because the Japanese relied on POW officers as go-betweens, they were exempt from the work details. When the enlisted men went out to the line, the officers stayed in their huts. Part of it was to be expected. They had earned the privilege not to work.

As the rail embankment stretched into the hills, the prisoners grew distant from the semblance of civilization that could be found at the Thanbyuzayat base camp. Brigadier Varley's diary refers to tennis and soccer tournaments being played there as late as March 1943. Colonel Nagatomo presented the prizes. Concerts were permitted after working hours and on rest days. Perhaps remembering Freddie Quick's star turn in Changi, and his defiance at 40 Kilo Camp, the Japanese required that the playlist be approved in advance, and they forbade nationalistic tunes.

Uncertain omens played at the prisoners' hopes and fears. On February 12, prisoners at Thanbyuzayat could hear a series of distant detonations. As the guard was increased and POWs confined to huts, rumors passed that Moulmein had been bombed, though drivers traveling up from the port town disputed it. There was speculation that Allied bombers might have attacked ships off the coast. Meanwhile, as the base hospital was filling with growing numbers of no-duty sick, the epidemiological picture took a dramatic turn for the worse. Word arrived that far up the line, as far out as 80 Kilo and

85 Kilo Camps, cholera had broken out. The news chilled the spine
of every thinking man. In the absence of the right treatments, the
disease could kill a healthy man nearly overnight. Near the end of
February, the *Houston*'s Dr. Epstein was sent up from base camp to
continue to look after Branch Five, and soon thereafter Brigadier
Varley asked that Epstein and six Australian and Dutch doctors head
even farther up-country to take over the new field hospital at 30
Kilo Camp. The monsoon season was coming, and when its rains began washing down it would become impossible to move the sick all
the way back to the base hospital.

As if the medical news were not bad enough, the first week of
March saw, for the first time, Allied aircraft over Thanbyuzayat. On
March 1, three twin-engine bombers appeared, circling the camp
and the railway yards at five thousand feet. The planes dropped flares
north and south of the camp, then unloaded their bombs on unknown targets to the north. The Korean guards panicked at the
sight of the planes. Fixing bayonets, they confined prisoners to their
huts once again and scrambled down into the slit trenches around
the camp, a privilege denied to the prisoners who had dug them.
The appearance of the bombers seemed to have an effect on the
camp's Japanese leadership as well. The next time a fresh group of
prisoners of war arrived at the base camp, Colonel Nagatomo was
there to greet them. This time, however, he read only portions of his
grand stump speech. It seemed to Brigadier Varley that some of the
pomp had gone out of his circumstance.

CHAPTER 40

Sinuous and halting, the emergent railway crept up the mountain, moving in contractions and dilations like a vast segmented worm. Alive with the movements of thousands of feet and hands, it grew from the earth, writhing across Burma's gentle lowland foothills and plains and entering a land of steep, jungled rises and rocky barriers around rivers.

By the end of March 1943, the mobile track-laying parties had spiked down meter-gauge rails as far as 18 Kilo Camp. Jim Gee, fully recuperated from his bout with malaria, rejoined his fellows at 26 Kilo Camp, where the work, far less advanced, involved laying sleepers atop the finished railway embankment. Brooking no delays and urgently pressed for time, the Japanese ordered 1,850 men from Branch Five to leapfrog from 18 Kilo Camp all the way up to 85 Kilo Camp, where the railway was little more than a surveyed right-of-way through virgin jungle. Against the wishes of the doctors, the sick moved with them. As commander of Branch Five, Captain Mizutani decided to move them to the hospital at 30 Kilo Camp. He took it upon himself to decide which of the no-duty sick at 18 Kilo would make the trip on foot and which would be driven. He unsheathed his sword, walked up to each man in turn, and struck him a swift, flat blow. If the prisoner got to his feet, he was ordered to march. If he didn't, he was borne on a stretcher and loaded onto a truck. Humping along the service road that paralleled the right-of-way, the healthy said goodbye to the lowlands and launched their forced assault on Burma's mountains.

Hastily built by *romusha* who doubtless had faced unimaginable suffering, the camp at 85 Kilo was filthy. The prisoners arrived to find pit latrines adjacent to the kitchen hut. Some of them had partially fallen in. Sour, mildewed rice was strewn about in piles. No boiled water was available. Touring the camps, Brigadier Varley noted a pig's carcass suspended from a tree near the kitchen, black with flies. Working in the field was in many ways preferable to languishing in that squalor. Still, wielding a pick under the hot Burmese sun, hacking out clumps of bamboo and their roots, was draining and dusty work. On March 30, some welcome showers cooled them, temporarily suppressing the dust. Up to then there had been only one rain in the past five months, totaling about an inch of water.

The 85 Kilo Camp was the real jungle. Here they faced dangers many and manifest. The root structures of the bamboo were alive with snakes: deadly bamboo snakes, tan in color, two to three feet in length; cobras; pythons. Without axes or hoes to root them out, Pryor used a small hand pick. "We'd get in there, and you'd hit one and sling him out there. . . . We were always conscious of snakes."

The hills and rocks slowed the work, introducing new engineering challenges. High in the hills, the prisoners worked far from their sources of food and medicine, the flow of which up into the mountains was restricted like blood flowing through a calcified artery. Already inadequate supply trains had a hard time keeping up. Once a prisoner of war had dragged himself far enough into the mountains, there was no getting food to him, and no getting his half-starved carcass out. The natives who ran the canteen stores near the base camp knew better than to set up shop that far upland. The prisoners were thus forced to subsist on the rations they got from their masters, unfortified by the private market. Adding to their isolation was an administrative quirk: Captain Mizutani's Branch Five was technically administered from Singapore, which seemed to give it a second-class status that slowed provisioning from base camp. Branch Five was going to conquer this mountain on its own.

Clearing work at 85 Kilo lasted three weeks, then the workers were moved back to 80 Kilo. The terrain there was cut through by several tributaries feeding the Zami River. Several of the cuts were so deep that something more than ordinary cutting and filling was required. Bridges would be necessary to span the gaps.

Bridges would become the signature feature of the Burma-Thailand Railway; indeed, Hollywood would define the very concept of Allied POW servitude in Asia around their construction. The largest and most famous of them would be built by British POWs in Thailand, far to the southeast of the Burma-Thailand border, the eastern limit for most Americans working on the railway. Though most of the American prisoners did not participate in the initial construction of the so-called Bridge on the River Kwai, as the long steel and concrete structure spanning the River Mae Khlung on the Thailand side of the line became known by way of the award-winning movie, their lives would become enmeshed with it, and the film a cultural shorthand by which their ordeal could be understood.

Or, as it happens, misunderstood. In David Lean's 1957 film, the bridge—and by implication the entire railroad—was a showpiece of British pride and know-how. It was premised on the idea that the British had engineering expertise far beyond that of the Japanese. Ripe with Western chauvinism, the film depicted the British as the teachers and contractors to the unsophisticated enemy. The reality was just the opposite. The real railway was driven from end to end by Japanese ambition and know-how. Though Japan lacked the machinery to construct it by state-of-the-art means, there was no lack of design expertise—or ruthless will. Japan would do with cold dispatch what Western colonialists had deemed impracticable.

The railway had far more than just one bridge. In had 688 of them—uncelebrated, remote, anonymous structures crossing ravines and tributaries along the way, the vast majority fashioned from timber. Only seven of these bridges were built from steel. And though the largest and most difficult bridges were on the Thailand side of the line—the rivers there would swell with runoff from the coming monsoon rains, requiring monumental efforts to span them—six of the railway's seven steel bridges were on the Burma end of the railway, between 45 and 85 Kilo Camps.

Hard timber for bridge construction was readily available in the jungle surrounding 80 Kilo Camp. The prisoners hauled the great trunks of wood from the forest, squared them with sharpened hoes, and drove them into the earth to make pilings. Charley Pryor, with

Branch Five, helped drive pilings, cut timber, and clear the service road too. Back home in Littlefield, Texas, he had gotten good with an axe hacking mesquite trunks for firewood. With three others helping him—Sgt. Hugh Faulk, an Idaho lumberjack, and an Australian—they could do four days' work in a day. The beauty of the detail outside camp was they could sleep in occasionally, because the guards never went looking for them in the jungle. When they were really feeling their oats, they would cut some buttery soft balsa wood and include it in the stacks too.

Once in a while, powerful machines were available to help them: elephants. One or two of the great beasts were on hand at 80 Kilo Camp to drag heavy logs out of the jungle, but they sometimes made more trouble than they solved. "An elephant's a smart bugger," said Pryor. "He tests these logs before he puts much effort into them, and if it seems heavy, well, he'd back off from it." No amount of beating the beast over the head with an iron hook seemed to persuade him otherwise. Faced with a recalcitrant elephant, the Japanese often had no choice but to require prisoners to do the hauling instead.

The pilings, virgin teakwood, were selected for length and breadth from the rich forests surrounding the camp. Pryor and his fellows brought them down with old crosscut saws, used picks and poleaxes to trim them to fit, then dragged them, by hand or by *elephas maximus,* to the bridge site, where they had dug starter holes in the earth. Wherever a bridge piling was needed, a derrick (or a scaffold) would be constructed from bamboo or tree saplings secured by wire twists. The piling would be raised and lowered through the derrick, then seated into the starter hole. Then atop the scaffolding would be erected a wooden pulley mechanism, holding up a heavy weight that could be raised and lowered like a hammer to drive the piling into the earth.

Pryor called them "spider rigs." Eight or ten men would pull on a web of ropes—"monkey lines"—fitted through a pulley atop the scaffolding. They kept rhythm by counting in Japanese—"*ichi, ni, san, shi, go*"—or by singing a song chosen by the engineers. For a time the engineers themselves stood atop the rickety derricks, directing the fall of the hammer. That arrangement lasted until some Australians found they could set the whole assembly swaying by deliberately falling out of sync on the count. Two engineers tumbled to their deaths that day, after which the prisoners got the job of climbing the tops of the derricks. When a piling had been driven to the proper depth in the ground, they would tear down the derrick, select a new piling site, and start all over again.

With pilings driven, trusses were next, installed from piling to piling, fastened with nails where possible but more often simply tied with vines, until the rail bed reached the opposite bank at the proper elevation. Bridges crossing the larger streams in hillier terrain sometimes required several decks of wooden pilings, one standing on top of the other. "It worked," said Luther Prunty of the Lost Battalion. "It seemed impossible, but it worked. . . . It wasn't so hard once you got the hang of it. It was just like marching. . . . There's nothing that manpower can't substitute for."

CHAPTER 41

The first American had yet to fall when the men of Branch Three, laying rails, reached 23 Kilo Camp. Up to that point, that camp had been home only to Burmese *romusha,* and the condition of the camp showed it. It was evident why scores of thousands of the native slaves would die. It had to do not with their constitution or their knowledge of the region, but with their lack of discipline in maintaining proper hygiene. Wholly unprepared to survive in a disease-ridden aboriginal wasteland, though they were natives, the throng that died was unmeasurably large. Many responsible estimates approach a hundred thousand. It would become a human tragedy whose intensity and scale grew as the rail reached toward the mountains from each end. If anything put the lie to the rhetoric of a Greater Asian Co-Prosperity Sphere, it was in the atrocious mass crime that Japan perpetrated on its workforce of conscripts.

In the native-type huts, lice infestation was rampant and there was never enough boiled water to scald the floors clean. For the prisoners, there was never any choice about attending to the vital business of sanitation. Otto Schwarz said, "As we would go into a new working camp, the first thing anybody did was dig a couple of fire pits, put in the fifty-five-gallon drums, fill them with water, and get the water hot. Before you got your rice, you had to get in line and dip your mess kit or coconut shell in the hot water. Blowflies were all over everything. And that's what carried dysentery.

"We kept our structure. We had our officers, our NCO's—our chain of command was kept intact. We always dug big ditches and put bamboo across the tops, so we could perch and do our business. . . . But if you went into a native camp, they'd have families of natives there on the railroad to work, but no leaders, no bosses, and no sanitation whatever. Feces were all over the place. They crapped wherever they stood. When they died, they lay there and rotted away. Disease ran rampant in those camps."

Faithful adherence to simple procedures—such as dipping mess kits in boiling water before eating—made all the difference. "If a passing fly chose to step into your rice ration as it was about to be eaten, there was no alternative but to throw the lot into the fire and go without," wrote Ronald Searle, a Royal Army sapper captured at Singapore. "Although such a gesture was dramatic for a starving man, there could be no hesitation." Survival meant continued deprivation. "There were times when most of us felt that perhaps those chums who had encountered The Curse of the Fly's Footprint were the fortunate ones."

Hygiene, health, and morale stood in symbiotic linkage. If the prisoners in a camp got careless with the first, the other two collapsed in turn. One sip from a tempting but bacteria-hosting wayside pool, a lack of religiosity in boiling one's mess kit, failure to see that upstream from one's bathing area was another pool used by the dysentery-prone—a single slip ensured that a bad life would grow far worse in a hurry. Dr. Fisher already had a surplus of patients to care for. In March he admitted 464 men from Branch Three and discharged 322. An additional sixty-five from Branch Five were there already too. With the monsoon season looming, work was slowing just as it should have been accelerating, and renewed pressure came from on high to complete the job. On April 7, Maj. Gen. Akira Sasa of the Japanese Army, the chief administrative officer of all branches in Thailand and Burma, arrived at the Branch Three headquarters to take stock of the growing crisis.

On his tour of camps up the line, General Sasa was driven by truck, with Brigadier Varley and Major Fisher riding in the back as it made the bouncing ride as far as 85 Kilo Camp. Varley appreciated that the condition of the service road made it impossible to use to transport the "heavy sick." "They would either die from the jolting about," he wrote, "or be so knocked about that it is far better to let them take their chances in outlying camps. Further with heavy rain it will be impassable. My previous fears voiced to Js months ago, were confirmed in my mind, i.e. that unless the rail was laid to outside camps we would not be able to maintain food supplies to these men." Sasa had no interest in the Allied officer's opinions. He never spoke directly with Varley and attached no value to the Branch Three commander's concerns. He looked at the rail and the mountains, considered the requirement that the railway be finished by August, and deemed the progress insufficient.

A Japanese medical officer, Dr. Higuchi, then called a conference with Varley, Fisher, and two other officers. The Japanese commandant of 75 Kilo Camp, Lieutenant Hoshi, appeared before a muster of sick personnel on April 13 and gave a speech.

> Major General Sasa has visited camp and expressed himself very satisfied with it, its order and cleanliness and conditions. But one thing he was not satisfied with was the number of sick who are far too many. There should be no sick here—all sick men were left behind. If men become sick they should not exceed twenty percent, a total of 380, this has been much exceeded. Some men who are sick I am trying to send them to Thanbyuzayat, but there is no transport and I am considering making them walk.

Hoshi repeated the rhetorical boilerplate blaming the Allies for Japan's aggressions. "The number of sick has got to come down— this is not Sasa's orders but from higher up. Japan is striving to build this railway by August. It must be finished by August. . . . If you die you are soldiers and dying is part of your job and you will be contributing to the greater glory of Japan. . . . You have sick only because you don't try. If you are sick you only lie down all day and if you lie down you don't need food. In future the sick will not get food even rice—the workers only will be fed. You will also be forced to go to work. Remember it is only four months."

The speech was steeped in the conviction that the emperor's divine will could command nature, defeat time and distance, and reach beyond the limitations of human endurance. The work would be done in spite of the vicious cycle that was whipping the prisoners from all sides: Survival depended on work, but disease conspired against both. The Japanese medical presence was a cruel joke. According to Ensign Smith, Higuchi's medical training consisted of a couple of years in dental school. Dr. Fisher, with the other Allied medical personnel, shared that assessment, stating that Higuchi "knew nothing of medicine and showed no evidence of clinical experience. . . . He was our bane in Burma." When the rains came, an out-of-balance equation would be tipped past the failure point. The men's dusty-mouthed pleas for water would be fulfilled with horrifying abundance. The rains would defeat the technology of medical transport, defy medicine, and overwhelm human will with bacterial scourges that have killed men since the dawn of time. The jungle would coil and strike back at the assault of the railway and road builders. The clouds would converge over the jungle and make survival itself seem an unreachable summit.

*

Charley Pryor, who had had no trouble with his health when Branch Five started work at 18 Kilo Camp, caught a blowtorch of a fever after the move to 85 Kilo Camp. It laid him flat for more than two weeks. When his fever first spiked, Captain Lumpkin took him off the duty list. The fever wouldn't break. A week went by, and another week. His temperature hit 107.5 degrees. The Dutch doctors at 85 Kilo, who hadn't a drop of medicine to give him, puzzled over the fever's persistence and diagnosed him with cerebral malaria complicated by jungle fever.

Burning up from within, Pryor begged for a wet blanket to be laid over him. With one draped across his body and another one over his head, he was still pushing the mercury to 105 degrees. He was so overheated that his vision blurred. He couldn't see the jungle canopy a hundred feet above him. He couldn't keep any water or food down. Once a robust 188 pounds, Pryor had by now withered down to no more than 75—"nothing but the skin stretched over the bones," he said. After the eighteenth day, the fever broke. The day after the fever left him the Japanese decided to truck him back to Thanbyuzayat. It was April 16 when he was put on a truck with four or five other litter patients and driven down the pothole-laced service road. The jackhammering of the truck bed against his spine had him cursing the driver in four languages. It was a good sign.

Pryor got back to Major Fisher's base hospital in time to witness the festivities attending the celebration of Emperor Hirohito's forty-second birthday. The Japanese marked April 29 by producing a propaganda film showing prisoners on the railway cheerfully working in the care of their most merciful captors. They circulated written instructions concerning the production, which was preceded by several days of setup and rehearsals. No-duty prisoners were turned out of the hospital to form an audience for a concert. They carefully rehearsed enjoying it. When Colonel Nagatomo realized the players weren't fully and properly dressed, he ordered clothing for them. Missing buttons were sewn on in a hurry. A curt order was passed to the prisoners—"You will be happy"—and then the curtain rose and the show began. Guards wheeled in tables laden with fruit and meat. All of a sudden the base hospital had new sinks, racks of real surgical equipment. "It looked like an Army field hospital in there," Jim Gee said.

Outside, a concert platform was quickly built. Trucks drove to the hospital gate unloading patients, who were then placed on operating tables surrounded by doting Japanese medical personnel. Stocks of food and medicines until now unavailable were piled everywhere, clearly labeled for the cameras. An International Red Cross team was filmed inspecting the camp. The Japanese had long been playing that organization for fools, commandeering rations mandated by the Geneva Prisoner of War Convention, seizing shipments of medicines, and dumping loads of morale-saving mail from home into open pits. The ubiquitous Dr. Higuchi, costumed in a white gown, was trotted out to examine sick prisoners for the cameras.

There were photo opportunities aplenty, with happy, smiling prisoners all around. As Otto Schwarz recalled, they were at one point instructed to sing for the cameras. Some Australians, insurgents to the end, struck up the popular tune "Bless 'Em All," but replaced the verb with a four-letter obscenity. The Japanese captured it on film and tape, pleased at their prisoners' happiness.

Production of the phony showcase lasted long enough for many of the prisoners to eat like kings for just one meal. Then the Red Cross departed and the fantastic dream evaporated. When the show was over, the food and the phony field hospital disappeared. The Japanese even took back their buttons.

*

It would be a puzzle of life on the railway, emerging in the midst of its horror and occupying survivors' thoughts ever after, why some men lived and others died. Conditions on the line were in a spiraling descent owing to the cumulative result of more than a year of starvation rations, the intensifying difficulty of the work in the mountains far from the logistical infrastructure that might save them, and the inevitable breakdowns in hygiene, momentary or systemic, that opened the door to disease. Charley Pryor's recovery from malaria, or whatever it had been, suggested the depths of his constitution. Others were not so fortunate. In March, April, and May the Americans discovered that they were not immune from the terminal consequences of life on the Death Railway.

The regular relocations of working parties put undue strain on prisoners already teetering in illness. When an Australian working party from 75 Kilo was abruptly moved up the line, a thirty-man *kumi* under Lieutenant Hamlin was called to fill the hole at that camp. It was an onerous commute. For four days straight they marched ten kilometers every day from 85 Kilo to 75 Kilo Camp to finish an embankment. Rising before dawn and making the three-hour march, they worked all day and marched back to 85 Kilo after dark. The special duty kept them away from their huts for sixteen to twenty hours at a time. Their exertions, coinciding with an increase in the dirt-hauling quota to 2.2 cubic meters, marked the onset of a brutal period in which Lieutenant Hamlin's *kumi* was hit with a series of deaths. After continuous protests by Hamlin, the Japanese discontinued that particular work detail. But the deaths of Lawrence F. Kondzela, James H. White, and Sgt. Joe Lusk at the makeshift hospital at 80 Kilo Camp opened a breach in the hopes of even the most optimistic of the Americans.

Lusk was Charley Pryor's closest friend, and Pryor was on the detail that buried him at a cemetery near 80 Kilo Camp. He spread rocks over the grave and marked it with a heavy cross fashioned from a teak four-by-four carved with Lusk's name. He measured the distance and direction to each of the other graves in the cemetery there and marked it on a map. When people came for them—and he had faith that someday they would—they'd find them all.

But it was the death of another sergeant from the *Houston*'s Marine detachment two weeks later that irrevocably changed the alchemy of the survivors' experience and left them with questions that linger to this day. First Sergeant Harley H. Dupler had been admitted to the Thanbyuzayat hospital with chronic bacillary dysentery. Prisoners of a less clinical mind have speculated that it was the psychological ravages inflicted by the guards that did in the *Houston*'s "poster Marine." Dr. Fisher had treated him once already for dysentery, releasing him in early April. "He went to a working camp," Fisher wrote, "and six weeks later returned, an almost unrecognizable skeleton." The physician encouraged Dupler, saying that with a transfusion, some food, and rest he would make a rapid recovery. It was soon clear to the Australian, however, that Dupler had wounds that went deeper than the merely physical.

The story goes that Dupler had gotten bashed by a guard up the line in the jungle sometime in April, and at that point decided to stop eating. As a sergeant, he believed in the transforming power of roles. So long as he was investing himself in the rigors and rituals of the Marine Corps, as he had defiantly and famously done at Bicycle Camp, he was First Sergeant Dupler. Now, as a prisoner, he was something else, something that after seventeen years in the service he could not tolerate or reconcile himself to. As one survivor told it, Dupler embraced his illness as a last route to honor. According to Sgt. Benjamin Dunn of the Lost Battalion, Dupler said, "I'm glad I'm sick because I'm not going to work for the Japanese and help them fight my country. I won't do it. I'll die. I'd rather die." Dupler was a dead man well before he landed in Dr. Fisher's care. The Australian physician's positive prognosis had cheered him for a day, "then he became depressed again," Fisher wrote, "thanked his attendants, but said he wanted to die." And that's exactly what he did.

Lt. Ilo Hard of the Lost Battalion tried to split his rations with Dupler for a time, pressing on him half a can of Eagle brand sweetened condensed milk that he had stolen from a Batavia dock and saved for an extreme occasion just such as this. Dupler wouldn't take it. Although he had the physical strength to take command of his own survival, his mind wouldn't permit it. On May 14, within twelve hours of that decision, he passed away. "He had tried to be tough with the guards at work and had been beaten into submission," Dr. Fisher said. "His spirit had been broken and life, to a man who prided himself on toughness, was no longer worthwhile." In Dupler's service records maintained by the Americans while on the railway, Dr. Lumpkin listed two causes of death in addition to chronic bacillary dysentery: The first was "psychopathia psychasthenia," a neurotic state characterized by phobias, obsessions, or compulsions that one knows to be irrational. The second was "anorexia nervosa."

Sergeant Dupler was buried on May 15 by six American pallbearers, with Dr. Epstein the only U.S. officer able to attend. Brigadier Varley's Australians presented a wreath made from jungle leaves and red flowers.

The deaths of Sergeants Dupler and Lusk showed that physical strength had limits set by the mind. "They were some of the biggest, strongest guys," said John Wisecup, who belonged to that class himself. "They should never have died. There's no way to explain it—why they did this. They just lost the will to live."

CHAPTER 42

After Sergeant Dupler died it was a short eight days before the heavens opened up and did not close. Anvil-shaped cumulus clouds had been seen over the mountain ridges now and again through April. In early May intermittent rains began. Locals called them the bamboo rains. "It is as if the Wet were a baying animal impatiently waiting over the horizon to be unleashed," Ray Parkin wrote. "Every so often now it has sprung over the mountains, snarled at us, and been hauled back again." Even from his headquarters at Thanbyuzayat, Brigadier Varley could sense the cataclysm soon to be produced by the collision of the Japanese will to complete the line with the onset of the monsoon and the rampant contagion he knew it would bring. "The J. will carry out schedule and do not mind if the line is dotted with crosses," he wrote in a long diary entry on May 18, 1943. Four days later the rains came at them with their full fury.

Even the Texans had no frame of reference for the violent meteorological manifestation of the southern equatorial winter, the South Asian monsoon. The zone of turmoil produced by the collision of the southern and northern trade winds meandered on a twice-a-year frequency between the Tropic of Capricorn and the Tropic of Cancer. The stretch of hemisphere from northern Australia to southern Asia became spectacularly volatile during the season the Australians called "the Wet." Starting in the third week of May, the rains came and didn't stop until the entirety of the railway, from Thanbyuzayat to Ban Pong, had been soaked through and nearly submerged by the weight of a storm that had no beginning, middle, or end but simply *was*.

The monsoon arrived and settled over them and simply stayed there, burying them in water. It was a driving deluge that would not relent until October, pouring without letup for fifty-four days and nights. Such a period of time takes discrete shape only in retrospect, and hindsight erases the demoralizing feeling of permanence that the monsoon carried with it during its peak. Rain was not an occasion. No one talked about the coming and going of storms, about Mother Nature's wrath. "I don't remember any storms," said Howard Brooks. "I just remember rain pouring down in torrents."

The monsoon season transformed the landscape. Creeks became streams and streams became rivers, their volume and velocity increasing alarmingly fast. "Within the first day and then with ever-mounting zeal," Rohan Rivett wrote, "it widened the muddy rivers until they began to spread prodigiously and climb their jungle-fringed banks; dominating and assertive, it intruded on every conversation and even on the privacy of your thoughts; it brought change of habit to every living thing. . . . Now for us there was to be a testing of moral and mental strengths such as battle danger and hot-blooded action had never brought."

The rains were a feature of the season, a steady state, like the sun's angle of elevation during summer, like summer heat itself. It rained all the time. The men ate, worked, rested, slept, and woke under continuous rain. They had to rise in the middle of the night to wring out their blankets. Back home, violent weather had its way with you briefly. Maybe a tornado tore up your neighborhood or took away your house. It always moved on. But the monsoon oozed overhead and settled in like tar over a pit. Thunder was rare. The most frightening sudden cracks and booms came not from lightning bolts but from great trees hitting the ground. The ground, loose and light in the dry season, could no longer hold the greatest members of its arbor. "It's awesome to hear a huge tree three or four feet in diameter fall that way in the jungle," said Ilo Hard. "It shakes the ground."

Here the rains caused mudslides that buried the railway. There they washed out wooden bridges, imperiling the prisoners' already scant supply of food. Bridges were replaced on the fly by flimsy rope-railed catwalks that the men used to haul their supplies across. "I remember on one occasion that a bridge had washed out," Gus Forsman said, "and we strung two lines that crossed this ravine. . . . The train could come up to this one side of the ravine, and then we would go over there and get the supplies and go across this little catwalk deal across the ravine. Of course, the water is rushing ninety miles an hour down below you, and you'd lose your balance. Of course, if you were carrying a rice bag, it'd go over into the water— just saving yourself—and then when you got to the end, well, you'd get a bashing for letting it go. It was a really treacherous feat."

Up at 105 Kilo Camp, the Japanese operated three vehicles captured from the English. The six-wheel-drive Studebaker, the four-wheel-drive Chevy truck, and the six-wheel-drive Reo truck had front-mounted winches, so they could hoist themselves out of most any jam. But they had limited mobility. Even with the winches, Don Brain and a number of other drivers were able to move just ten to twelve miles a day through the mud. With limited hauling capacity, corroding spark plugs, and fuel shortages, they had short range and moved only essential supplies. "Finally they gave up on this truck thing because it was just a farce," Brain said. "They would have been better off with a bull cart."

To get food, the prisoners had to march five or six miles on foot to the nearest spot a truck or train could reach. Their proficiency with yo-ho poles came in handy then. They'd sling a bag of rice or a box of meat and, in Jim Gee's words, "chug-a-lug down the road." But eventually the sodden ground was too impassable for efficient use of yo-ho pole teams, their soaked payloads too heavy. Up near the border at Three Pagodas Pass, at a far-from-alpine elevation of 925 feet, the grade was too steep at 2.9 degrees for even a single locomotive to reach the summit. The grade didn't do any favors either for the barefooted workers hauling the supplies.

The rains depleted the *kumi*s as men were taken back down the line to effect repairs. As they grew sick, the work parties grew smaller still, until the sick themselves were again called upon to fill the gaps. Otto Schwarz said, "You would work whatever they decided you would work—eight hours, ten hours, twelve hours or fourteen hours—then you'd drag your butt back into camp and lay down on those hard bamboo slats with the knots in them and the rain would be coming down and the thatched roof would be leaking like a sieve. Oh, God."

They slept soaked. They kept their feet dangling off the end of the bed, unable—or, more crucially to survival, unwilling—to pull their muddy paws under the blanket. "There seemed to be no bottom to the mud in this place," said Charley Pryor. "You just lived in perpetual wetness."

The Japanese engineers knew all too well what the rains would do to their plans. In response they launched what became known as the "Speedo" campaign, so called because of the merciless cries of the guards, who set round-the-clock working hours, abandoned quotas, and stepped up their campaign of brutality to get the job done. Laboring from before sunrise to well after dark, the reeling prisoners redoubled their efforts. By one estimate, two men were expected to dig enough earth during the Speedo campaign to fill a whole dump truck every workday. There was a draconian unwillingness to allow a prisoner to claim no-duty status for reasons of health. "That word 'Speedo,'" said Howard Brooks. "You went to bed at night with it ringing in your ears." At the end of May, the Japanese ordered Branch Five to move out, and on the twenty-sixth they pulled up stakes at 80 Kilo and began climbing again.

The push farther up into the jungle to 100 Kilo Camp reflected Captain Mizutani's fantastic indifference to the human life in his care. Mizutani told Colonel Tharp that the sick were of no use "to us or to themselves." Accordingly, they were abandoned and left on their own at 80 Kilo Camp while the able workers marched up the line. Anyone unable to march on his own power would be left behind. Though it was a place to await death, the Japanese would call 80 Kilo Camp a "hospital." With reduced rations and no medicine, it was less a hospital than a hospice where men too sick to work were sent to watch each other die.

The decision to establish the hospital was an act of utilitarian cruelty: With the sick segregated, it was easier to allocate food only to the fit. Though the camp was better drained than 105 Kilo, stood on higher ground, and lay adjacent to a stream that provided sanitation, its lack of food and medicine turned deadly. During its first few weeks in operation, there were no luxuries such as actual medical staff, medicines, or kitchen personnel. "The least sick of the stretcher cases had to get up and do these jobs. As a result there were many more deaths than were necessary," wrote Ensign Smith.

With supply roads impassable, a worker's full rice ration was cut to a hundred grams a day: half a canteen cup of rice twice daily. The no-duty sick, who needed it all the more, got half of what the workers got. Captain Mizutani seemed to consider his rations policy as an incentive to improved health. But the only way the sick survived at all was by the entrepreneurial grace of the healthy. Men stole for them, brought burnt scrapings from the kitchen and contraband sweet potatoes into the hospital. Anything extra that turned up found its way back to the hospital. The men who catered to that grim ward had strong stomachs in addition to stout hearts.

Having fought off his fever and afflicted now with a trophy-caliber tropical ulcer, which he kept dousing with steaming water and wrapping with old rags, Charley Pryor saw the pathetic state of care at 80 Kilo Camp and decided to do something about it. He started voluntary duty as its custodian and its cemetery keeper. For several weeks he worked alone, the only fit man in a camp of the dying, until Commander Epstein arrived to handle patient care, to the extent the dying could be called patients absent any care to give them. Ben Dunn of the Lost Battalion was the only patient in his truckload of souls who walked into the camp under his own power. Pryor helped him hobble onto his bamboo platform. "I looked in that hut, and I couldn't believe that those guys were still living. It was a horrible mess. I don't know how they managed, but Charley did a remarkable job," Dunn said. "When a man's lying there with beriberi or any of those other things, and he's so sick that he's about to die, a fly will land on his eyeball and he won't even blink," Dunn said. "You know he's not going to live very long. I couldn't believe that could happen, but I saw it." For his steadfast work in the morguelike squalor of 80 Kilo Camp, Charley Pryor earned the nickname "Padre."

For Lanson Harris, the dream was always the same. There was a fabulous pink marble hall, so palatial and long that it disappeared to a vanishing point in the indeterminate distance. Down its center ran a table, bejeweled and plated in silver and gold, loaded with every kind of edible thing one might dream of. "I would try to get to this table," said Harris, "and so help me God for three and a half years I never made it. Something would always happen. I never would get to this damn table."

Their time as sailors seemed remote and undefined. They worried about things they had taken for granted. They cursed themselves for having ever complained about Navy chow. Hunger spurred creativity. Harris had learned to watch the monkeys. What they ate a person could eat. "If they ate certain leaves, shoots, we'd collect these up, take them back to the camp, boil them up and eat them. It didn't always taste the best. But they helped us get nutrition we were missing." The tobacco available locally, known as "wog," so full of nicotine it produced a powerful buzz, had off-label uses. Harris couldn't remember who got the idea to use the wog as a fisherman's Mickey Finn, but it saved more than a few lives.

He said, "We'd take little bits of tobacco and make a rice ball out of it. When we camped down on the river we'd get five or six guys across river and we'd throw these rice balls loaded with tobacco into the water. Other guys would be waiting a hundred yards down across the river with big bamboo clubs. The fish ate the rice balls, they got sick, regurgitated, and filled up with air. They would float up to the surface, and the floating fish would come by, and the guys with the clubs would whack them and throw them up on the beach. You'd do almost anything to eat."

At 100 Kilo Camp one day, a fifteen-foot king cobra, fleeing the rains, had worked its way into the rafters of the hospital hut. It was spotted and turned into dinner for the guards. The jungle was "like a zoo without the cages," said Roy Offerle.

Prisoners used most anything on hand to flavor their rice. Minnows, fish heads, even toothpaste filled the bill. John Wisecup crushed Indonesian peppercorns and mixed them with water and drank it, finding that it suppressed his appetite. At least it burned his stomach lining so bad he lost the urge to eat.

One afternoon, loud shouts roused the men at 100 Kilo Camp. A prisoner had gone down to the river to fetch a bucket of water and had sat down on a log to rest. When the log shifted and slithered beneath him, he got a little excited. Led by a Korean guard, some prisoners ran to the noise. The guard shot the great python and it rose up, head swaying waist high. He shot again and it fell dead into the underbrush. They measured its length at nineteen feet, eight inches, then carved it into twenty-inch tenderloins as thick as a man's thigh. Everyone in the hunting party got a piece.

The rains were heavy and steady enough to form an actual stream running through the sick hut. The waters brought an unexpected windfall just as they ruined the livability. The hut's residents learned to shape a crooked piece of wire into a hook, hang a small piece of rice on the wire, and dangle it through the bamboo decking into the stream below. There was nothing at all sporting about using one's bunk as a fishing boat, but the occasional lungfish the men pulled from the raging gullywasher under the hut was a gift they would have been fools to refuse.

The daily routine at 100 Kilo Camp, which Charley Pryor called "one of the most unlikely campsites on the whole road," was not for the sick or the weak. It was a life of continuous work whose ritual was enforced by the fact that only working men ate. Most of the survivors found someone to lean on, to trust unconditionally, and would help him in turn along when his own prospects sagged. The relationships sometimes paid their dividends in death: to the dead came eternal peace, while the survivors got his gear. Red Huffman and a sailor named Guy Pye helped each other along for a while. When Pye's tropical ulcer ravaged him, he was sent to a hospital hut, where a doctor removed his leg. Huffman took possession of a few valuables that Pye had himself taken from another dead man—a silver spoon, a mess kit, and an extra canteen. Huffman did his best to keep the extra canteen full of native rice whiskey.

The conditions between 80 Kilo Camp and the Burma-Thai border near Three Pagodas Pass were the worst on the entire railway. Most of the 131 Americans who died during its construction gave up the ghost at 80, 100, or 105 Kilo Camp. What they faced there was a cumulative ordeal that drew from each of the sources of misery that had plagued them to date: cruel weather, hard work, scant rations, invisible disease, and engineers and guards indifferent to their plight. For too many of the sick, these were the last insults their besieged constitutions could take.

Brigadier Varley spent May 31 to June 4 inspecting camps with Colonel Nagatomo. The road between 100 and 108 Kilo Camps was nothing but a jungle clearing, "the worst I have ever traveled on," Varley wrote, with ruts two feet deep, miring axles and differentials in the earth. When that happened, elephants were called in to haul the vehicles, but the great beasts lacked the tenacity of the prisoners. "Elephants working in this area are worked all day pulling trucks along until they knock up as happened in our case between 102 and 105 K., which distance we walked," Varley wrote. In the driving rain and flowing mud, he saw a wonderland of horrors. Burmese coolies lurched along the service road. Mothers cradled children stricken with cholera. Every twenty yards along the swiftly decaying roadway there were men collapsed and buckled in pain. "These poor devils do not appear to receive any treatment and no wonder they die like flies," he wrote. "My fears expressed so often during the past three months to [Nagatomo] that they would not be able to get food and canteen supplies through to jungle camps have been realised. . . . With the prevalence of cholera plus all other diseases in a force which has gradually been weakened over the past 13 months, one is alarmed and apprehensive of the future."

According to Ensign Smith, 100 Kilo was "the worst camp we had been in. This camp was located under a mountain on marshy ground with springs bubbling up. It was necessary to build up the center sections of the huts so water would not wash completely through." The Lost Battalion's 1st Lt. Clyde Fillmore would write, "It got cold about five o'clock each morning and we tried to keep at least one fire going in each hut during the night. Shivering and cold the men crowded around the fire as the early morning chill drove them out of their beds. . . . We were now deep in the jungle, shut out from the world by heavy, grey rain clouds that hung tree-top high everywhere, and surrounded by a depressing, soggy growth of bamboo, tall trees, labyrinth of vines and lush vegetation, that fell from the sky like a green, gloomy curtain."

Red Huffman was a fighter like John Wisecup but a bit more careful about picking his spots. Though he stayed out of the *Houston*'s brig and kept a clean service record, by his own admission he was no stranger to trouble on liberty. "I went along with the tides and kept my nose as clean as I could," he said. He tackled life at 100 Kilo as he would a surly corporal in a Manila bar. Huffman remembers being at the head of the column when Branch Five reached 100 Kilo Camp. He was the last man to leave it. "Everybody died there," he said. "That was my station."

CHAPTER 43

A s hard as they worked, as much as they achieved, it gave them no pride. Some felt downright ashamed of their contributions to the Japanese war machine, as if they had a choice. Some kept their heads down and conspired to destroy what they had built.

The moral conflict that slavery imposed on the diligent military conscience had been too much for Sergeant Dupler to handle. What bothers the survivors most about David Lean's film about the bridge over the river near Tamarkan was the fictionalized dynamic that led Colonel Nicholson to see the bridge as an expression of British superiority. As survivors of the actual railway see it, Nicholson's self-satisfaction bordered on collaboration. The British prisoners in particular have taken umbrage at the suggestion that the judgment and integrity of the actual officer who oversaw work on the Tamarkan bridge, Lt. Col. Philip Toosey, was colored by a desire to fulfill Japanese wishes. As the actual prisoners on the Burma-Thailand Death Railway knew, the Japanese engineers understood full well how to build a bridge. As they also knew, there were indeed ways to strike back at the Japanese captors. But on the real-life railway, and all along this concatenation of 688 bridges, the striking back took on forms much more concrete and direct than the fictional Colonel Nicholson's hollow victory of ego.

As far as the Branch Three and Branch Five prisoners are concerned, the amount of attention that the "River Kwai" bridge commanded obscured the fact that the worst atrocities on the railway
occurred further up the line from it. Of the 3,500 men who built the
Tamarkan bridge, only nine died, reflecting their proximity to the
base camp at Kanchanaburi and the pre-monsoon construction time-
line during which most of the work was done. The atrocity was not
so much this bridge as the railway that stretched 250 miles into the
monsoon jungles to its northwest. And it was there that the subterfuge of prisoners bent on holding on to their dignity found its
more dramatic expression, sometimes taking an unexpectedly lethal
form.

"Any way you could slow the Japanese down, you tried to slow
them down," Gus Forsman said. "For a cutting, they'd want a certain slope, and if we could, we'd try to make the slope as steep as
possible, knowing that when the rainy season came, you'd get a big
mud slide down into it. Sometimes I don't know whether that paid
off because then we'd have to go back in and clear it out. Like I
say . . . if you could get away with anything, you did."

Sgt. Roy Offerle of the Lost Battalion recounted with glee the
time that his Branch Five *kumi,* while trying to move a three- or four-
story-tall derrick to drive a new bridge piling, managed to topple
the thing over, shattering it to pieces. That little caper was as good
as a perfectly executed bomber raid. The prisoners disconnected train
hitches and mastered the illusionist's art of appearing to work hard
while actually doing no such thing at all. Through scrupulous inat-
tention they left loose patches of dirt in vital stretches of embankment, laid rails a shade too wide, set aside weak timbers for the most
crucial links in bridge trestles, let scarce and valuable tools slip under an alluvial flow of monsoon mud. With the ratio of prisoners to
guards in most places on the order of thirty to one, it was not hard to
get away with subtle failures. A well-tailored apology rooted in a
façade of incompetence usually kept the recriminations from being
too brutal.

"I know we Marines had a code among us that you'd do everything you could to slow this railroad," said Howard Charles.
Relating his treatment by the Japanese to the beatings he had gotten
from his son-of-a-bitch stepfather, Charles had sworn to himself
back at Bicycle Camp, "I would let them get their kicks from beating me, and I would wait, and one day . . ." Late one night he and

Pvt. Frank H. "Pinky" King sneaked out of their hut with sabotage on their minds. Things went further than they expected, however.

It began in a hut, probably near 30 Kilo Camp, where Branch Three languished, when Pinky King crawled over to Charles's bamboo sleeping platform in the middle of the night. King's work detail was out at the camp supply depot, near a railroad siding where the rails and other supplies were unloaded for use at the construction site. King poked Charles, waking him. He whispered, "Follow me." "Where?" said Charles. King shushed him. "Be quiet. Follow me."

King led Charles outside to the tool shed and told him, "The wirecutters are right in there, right straight on that wall." *Wirecutters?* King directed Charles to get the tools while he went to the *benjo* so he could make a noisy diversion if a guard appeared.

Implements safely in hand, they saw two guards on the camp perimeter some distance away from them. As the guards paused to converse, King and Charles made their move, crawling under the barbed wire, running, staying low until the tree cover blocked the line of sight back to camp. Then, stepping softly, the two Marines went down to the roadbed and followed the line a quarter mile back to the depot, where they came upon a flatcar parked on a rail siding. Rails came into camps piled on flatcars, which rode the tracks as far as the prisoners had laid them. The heavy rails and cross ties were stacked alongside the rail bed.

Fully loaded with rails to be put down in the morning, this flatcar was attached to a caboose. "The idea," said Charles, "was that we'd crawl under there and cut the band on the front end of that flatcar so that when the train moved, those rails in the front would come down and hit the ground, and that would unload all of those rails up there a quarter-of-a-mile from where we had to work on them."

Though simple, the plan was dangerous, and Charles knew it. He asked King, "Why me? Why did you pick me for this?" King didn't have a special reason for selecting him for the job. Apparently he hadn't thought much about it. Good Marine that he was, he grabbed the handiest volunteer. "He was a quiet guy," Charles remembered, "but if something was to be done, and he got the idea to do it—you loved to be with him, because he never showed any signs of being afraid." King's tool-snatching co-conspirator didn't have quite the same amount of ice in his veins. Returning to camp, Charles executed what for him was the scariest part of the mission, returning the wirecutters to the tool shed. He slipped back into the shed without the guards noticing, returning the tools like a thoughtful neighbor. Then they slinked back into their hut. Jim Gee noticed them crawling back into their sleeping platforms and breathed, "Where the hell have you been?"

"Out," King said.

Charles added, "Of our *minds*."

"We agreed not to place the burden of secrecy on anyone," Charles wrote. "So we never revealed what we had done, particularly after what we learned the following day."

The next morning, the Japanese started a locomotive, backed it into the flatcar to hitch it up, and began hauling the load of rails out toward the prisoners' work site. The train had gotten up some speed when the metal bands the two Marines had cut gave out, letting loose the ends of the rails at the front of the car. They cascaded off the train in a rushing cacophony of metal and hit the ground. Digging into the earth, the rails were driven backward as the train rolled forward, the still fastened rear-end bands effectively aiming the rails straight back into the caboose. With a whine of steel on steel, and the crack of wooden caboose walls yielding, the rails penetrated the front of the car like lances, driving in amid the engineers and guards inside. According to Charles, five Japanese were killed by the thrusting of the rails. "I don't know how many it hurt or mangled," he said. "There were two or three guys who saw the results of it; I never saw it, but the word got back that we had really done some damage." The next day Pfc. Bert "Bird Dog" Page happened to see them cleaning up the mess, hauling off several covered stretchers. There were no interrogations, no reprisals. It was all an unfortunate accident.

As in previous camps, sabotage pitted ultimate questions of right and wrong against the more ambiguous morality of risking collective punishment for solo acts. Their own self-interest required cooperation with the enemy, but as Sergeant Dupler had understood, cooperation could be viewed as a kind of hostility to one's distant brothers in arms. The chain of causation was more than a little attenuated, but there could be no question that there was an Allied soldier fighting near Mandalay whose life would become much harder if the railway were successfully built. If you caused even a one-day delay in the railway getting finished, who was to say what the consequences might be? King, Charles, and Gee, and everyone else like them were like special forces operatives—starving, brutalized special forces operatives—working behind enemy lines, doing what they could on instinct and guts. They seized their opportunities in the theater of combat operations just as any soldier, sailor, or Marine would do.

CHAPTER 44

In May, as the Speedo period began on the Burma railway and the summer monsoon unleashed itself against the mountains, back at Singapore Japanese troops came sweeping through Changi's barracks and hospitals, combing them for healthy candidates to send up to the Thailand end of the railway to reinforce a beleaguered unit known as "H Force."

Not all of the USS *Houston* survivors on the Death Railway had gone north to work in Burma. Nineteen Americans, including John Wisecup and Robbie Robinson of the *Houston* and Crayton "Quaty" Gordon and Frank Ficklin of the Lost Battalion, had been left behind at Changi for health reasons. Now they joined a band of three thousand men marching to the Singapore central railway station, destined for what may well have been the most difficult phase of work on the Thailand end of the line, a half dozen work sites located from Konyu to Hintok, some 155 kilometers northwest of the Thai branch base camp at Nong Pladuk. The work sites there would acquire notoriety on par with the worst atrocities of World War II. Most who survived it would never want to talk much about it. "What we lost on that railroad made that death march look like a picnic," Wisecup would say.

The geologic challenges found on the Thai end of the railway were formidable. At Chungkai, a camp just a few kilometers south of the big bridge at Tamarkan, a long rock ledge had to be blasted through. At the high rock plateau at Wampo, 106 to 114 kilometers from Nong Pladuk, the river cut the narrowest of valleys through the rock, leaving no room for the railway. The only way through was to set the railroad precariously against a cliff face along the river. The prisoners were forced to cut a ledge in the cliffs more than four hundred yards long. Hanging from ropes to tap the blasting charges into the rock, they built two long viaducts against cliffs along the Kwae Noi. Great timbers sixty feet long were erected to buttress the gaps. Two thousand British prisoners from Colonel Toosey's group finished the Wampo project in seventeen days. Like a patch of tall grass concealing a colony of ants at work in its depths, the jungle was alive from Thanbyuzayat to Ban Pong with the labor of a hundred thousand men, two hundred souls every kilometer, hunkered down and slowly starving, hammering down a railway for the Japanese Army.

At Hintok, geology conspired with epidemiology to give prisoners a double dose of misery. Through one rocky hillside they blasted a narrow slash for the railway embankment. Around the Kwae Noi's next bend they attached the railway to the curving cliff face itself, building viaducts that were held high above the swelling river by great multitiered trestles constructed from hand-hewn timber. Though cuts and fills were needed here as elsewhere, digging was hardly possible. Dynamite did the work of shovels, but no more safely. After the explosions settled, after the rock chips ceased raining down on the men on the hammer-and-tap crews who had drilled the holes for the explosives, the men emerged to clear the shattered detritus of the rocky hills by hand.

As bad as Wampo and Hintok were, the line's cruelest earthmoving task was farther north, at Kinsayok. The embankment there was so large—thirty feet wide by thirty feet high and a quarter mile long—that it more resembled an artificial ridgeline than a railway bed. The towering trestles and viaducts and murderous cuttings through solid rock were the Thailand branch's unique and signature challenge. It was borne mostly by British, Australian, and Dutch prisoners. But the ordeal had a handful of American witnesses and participants too. As they were herded into boxcars at Singapore, bound north to reinforce H Force, John Wisecup, Quaty Gordon, Robbie Robinson, and their Allied mates would hammer at a mountain of stone in the driving rain.

They rode with the sliding doors of their boxcars wide open. What little water they had was supplemented with water stolen from the boiler. Disembarking at Ban Pong, they went on foot into the mountains. Kicked and beaten by guards the entire way, they marched to Kanchanaburi, over the great bridge at Tamarkan. As the macadam road turned into a muddy trail, the stragglers fell out of line and were left behind to die in the jungle. Soon, assaulted by the first torrents from the mountains, they realized they were marching straight into a trial not only by fire but by water. It took more than two weeks to walk the ninety-six miles from Ban Pong to Hintok. Ronald Searle, a British sapper headed for Konyu, recalled:

> The road had petered out as the undergrowth changed to forest and then into a vast cathedral of vegetation with a ceiling of unbelievable height that veiled the occasional light filtering through. The forced marches continued through the nights and memories of them have become a compression of smells and feelings; plodding along a glutinous track thick with pitfalls, faces and bodies swollen and stinging from insect bites and cuts from overhanging branches that whipped back at us. Now it felt and smelt as I had imagined the jungle would: encroaching, oppressive and rotting. We were very aware of it confining us, although we barely caught a clear sight of it at first. The frequent rainstorms became more violent and the approximate track turned into a quagmire of calf-deep black slime. . . . I can still recall the bizarre sucking noise made by hundreds of feet being put down and pulled out of the mud.

The news of the reinforcements struck the bedraggled slaves of H Force as a promising development. "This period of movement must mean something big. Perhaps it is the big push to get the railway through—but we can't see how they will be able to work when the Wet Season really sets in," Ray Parkin wrote in his journal at Hintok.

The Japanese insistence on speed required a greater number of slaves than the engineering needs of the project should have dictated. The timber trestlework for the viaducts was straight out of *The American Civil Engineers' Handbook,* long edited by Mansfield Merriman, a Lehigh University engineering professor who evidently had acquired a following in industrial Japan. Designed for heavier American freight trains, the Merriman trestles were overengineered for their purpose. The prisoners paid a heavy price for this indulgence in terms of exhaustion, disease, and injury. Had the Japanese done the prudent thing and tunneled through the rock at Hintok rather than cut straight down through its deep mass along its entire length, they would have spared their slaves hundreds of tons of rock to move. But unlike tunnels, which were made from two points, cuttings could be made simultaneously at every point along a given distance—like the railway itself. Cutting was far, far faster. And deadlier.

Over a three-and-a-half-kilometer stretch of railway they made six major cuttings from the heart of the rocky earth. One of these, between the last Konyu camp and Hintok, became known as Hellfire Pass. It took little imagination to coin that nickname, for Hellfire Pass was a chilling simulation of the underworld. Working deep in a rock gorge that they blasted deeper every night, the prisoners looked up at their guards standing atop its ridges, backlit by gasoline-dipped bamboo torches stuck into the earth all around the top. A couple of bamboo-burning bonfires put great volumes of smoke into the sky while the torches lit the rocky cutting like a harvest moon on a foggy night. Fearing untimely explosions and disease, the guards came no closer to the cutting area than necessary. When they were visible, it was at a distance, walking the edges of the stony ravine wearing hooded raincoats that silhouetted them like imps standing sentry. Meanwhile, in the shifting torchlight, the skeletal shadows of prisoners danced all along the cutting's stone face.

The hammer and tap crews tried, as much as their atrophying frames would allow, to avoid hitting a toe or breaking a buddy's finger with their heavy hammers. "The head of the man holding the drill is only a few inches from where the hammer strikes," wrote Ray Parkin. "If you wander, or relax those tired muscles, there can be a split skull." The Japanese engineers, who forced out to work scores of men with useless limbs and horrible sores, took considerably less care with their explosives. Their excited cries of *"Speedo, ah-hoiy-hoiy speedo, speedo!"* often came too late for prisoners to avoid the blasts. "The stones and fragments came ripping through the treetops, cutting branches and lopping bamboos like scythes," Ray Parkin wrote. For too many men, nearly including Parkin, the bombardment of shattered limestone had lethal consequences. Any break in the skin could easily metastasize into a flesh-rotting tropical ulcer.

Every morning, before dawn, the prisoner-patients of the morning shift made their way down to the mist-shrouded cutting site at Hintok Mountain Camp. "Occasionally we caught glimpses of far-away sunlit peaks of other mountains, rising out of the cloud that concealed the thousands of miles of jungle between us and freedom," Ronald Searle wrote. The night shift worked by artificial light. Sleeping till noon, they awoke, prepared their bamboo torches and went out to work all night once again. The blasts and percussion of hammer on stone made for a constant din. "The daily blasting along this section is terrific," Ray Parkin wrote, "like a war approaching."

CHAPTER 45

The war *was* approaching. All of the prisoners knew it at some level of fact or faith, at least in its broad outlines. Rumors of its progress were whispered up and down both branches of the line, originating reliably with the stalwarts who managed to operate shortwave sets, even in the deprivation of the jungle. With the Lost Battalion's radio whiz, Technical Sgt. Jess Stanbrough, long since shipped away to Japan, it fell to Capt. Windy Rogers of the Lost Battalion and Gus Forsman of the *Houston* to run the radios while keeping the lowest of profiles, even among their closest peers. "The radios were dismantled and smuggled into camps all the time, all the way along the line," Forsman said. The prisoners fashioned components in camp, making vacuum tubes from test tubes. The origins and deployments of the equipment were closely held secrets. Still, Forsman said, "I don't believe we were ever without a radio at one time or another in the camp." The identity of the radio keepers was kept strictly secret too, not because friends couldn't be trusted but because fevers couldn't be. One never knew what a man might blurt out when racked with malarial tremors.

The war news didn't turn broadly favorable until about January 1943, and then it spread through the camps only in the most general terms: the Allies had landed in North Africa, various Pacific island campaigns were under way. The men tried to keep a utilitarian perspective on news: "You hear it but you're still here, so you forget about it," said Roy Offerle of the Lost Battalion. "I lived day by day. I didn't worry about yesterday or tomorrow. Really, to me that was the best way to keep your sanity and your wits about you—just what's going to happen today and nothing else."

Survival required close attention to the here and now, not to pipe dreams about great victories on distant battlefields. Near Konyu, some Australians dammed a stream and made a reservoir. Two hundred yards downstream they built a thirty-by-forty-foot system of perforated bamboo pipes held aloft on a trestle. In this way prisoners there could actually shower. Since the water was infested with cholera bacteria, they learned to shower with their mouths closed. But the path to life on the Death Railway was cleared by small victories such as this. If you kept your water boiled and your mess kits hot-dipped, if you stayed upstream of the dysentery pools and showered with your mouth closed, you might be all right.

Whether they were all right or not, the prisoners never revealed the truth when the opportunity came to send their first postcards home. The 1929 Geneva Convention provided in Article 36 that every prisoner be allowed to send a postcard to his family "within a period of not more than one week after his arrival at the camp" and that "said postcards shall be forwarded as rapidly as possible and may not be delayed in any manner."

With Japan having declined to ratify the convention, the least of the worries occupying Colonel Nagatomo, Captain Mizutani, or anyone else in the Fifth and Ninth Railway Regiments was the timeliness of their prisoners' personal correspondence. Reflecting their regard for the International Committee of the Red Cross, whose parcels and provisions, meant for prisoners, they were well known to have plundered, the Japanese authorities dallied in delivering the prisoners' later mailings via the Red Cross and the Swiss Consulate General. Luther Prunty, out in the jungle one day gathering wood for the 80 Kilo Camp kitchen, turned over a log and found a whole stash of completed postcards rotting in the sodden earth.

*

If news was vital for the prisoners' morale, information about them was no less vital to loved ones back home. The absence of word concerning the fate of their men kept alive an agonizing mystery and extracted a heavy psychic cost. With her husband missing along with his ship, with hard facts of the where and how so damnably few, Jane Harris, at home in Los Angeles, restored her emotional equilibrium by filling her life with denial and distraction. These provided a layer of insulation between her imagination and her subconscious. It kept them from colluding in their corrosive, whispering work.

She denied the thought that a new wife's worst fear—sudden, unforeseen widowhood—had probably already been realized. Since she could not know for sure, she went to work to keep herself productively focused, to avoid losing her mind. But at her desk in the payroll department at Bullock's department store, she could never for long avoid thinking of Lanson Harris or the *Houston,* the ship he had called home for more than a year. Until that day came, she would suffer with a monthly reminder of the misery in her life when the allotment of her husband's salary showed up in the mail.

She quit Bullock's after a year, took a job with some friends at a company that made window blinds, then moved to the Continental Can Company as a contometer operator. That rudimentary computer was useful for keeping the books, but it could not begin to help her figure the unknowable odds of her husband's safe return.

Anything less than a letter or a call from Lans himself would not satisfy her. She drove down to San Diego periodically on weekends to see old friends and to visit other wives who stood on the brink of widowhood with husbands missing in action on Bataan or Corregidor. One of her friends was married to a pilot who had flown General MacArthur out of Manila. The women all had plenty of time to contemplate the permutations of fortune that might have befallen their men.

She wasn't forced to confront her subconscious assumptions until her friends started urging her to visit the Army hospital and file a life insurance claim. "They said, 'You might as well go over and they'll settle with you and you'll get your insurance started.'" But she wasn't ready to give up on the man she had last seen more than two years before. "I said, 'No, because he's not dead yet.' They said, 'You're crazy. You should go over there and get the money.'"

She settled into the role of widow-in-waiting, trying to be a rock of strength for her grief-stricken family. Finally it caught up with her. She clung to her job to the detriment of her health. Saddled with sudden abdominal pains, she saw her doctor and learned she needed an exploratory procedure. But the idea of taking off work and submitting to hospitalization was intolerable to her. "I've got to work, keep my mind going," she said. She needed that contometer more than the managers at Continental Can did.

Had she known that she suffered from severe appendicitis, she might have beaten her fear of sitting in a silent hospital room where dark thoughts could emerge unsuppressed. Only when she was delirious with pain and on the brink of physical collapse—her doctor found that her appendix had burst—was she finally rushed into surgery. The ether and the anesthetic did what bromides from friends and family seemed never to do. They set her apart from the troubled earth. From within the gauzy shroud of medication she told the doctor, "Don't let me come to." She felt good. The weight was gone. They told her she had to wake up. She refused. She refused for three full weeks and stayed right there at White Memorial Hospital, clinging to sedation.

The emotional insulation of the work routine was finally pierced shortly before Christmas 1943 when the postman showed up and said, "Jane, you've got a funny-looking thing here." It was a postcard from her husband.

The three-by-five piece of weathered cardstock was stamped with an alien-sounding name: Moulmein, Burma. It carried no date. "How it got through the censors, I don't know," she said. How it had gotten from the Japanese to the Americans was equally a mystery. She took it to the Navy Department, showed it to a chaplain, then to an administrator. They wanted her to turn it over to them. She gave them a copy but retained the original.

With her husband's status indisputably converted from MIA to POW, Jane began going to the Red Cross, putting together little packages of toothpaste and other sundries and writing banal letters designed to clear the censors and reach this place, Moulmein, by whatever magical means the International Red Cross had devised to bridge the gap between warring enemies. But even as the news relieved some anxiety and made possible proactive courses of action, it raised other worries. The terse, preprinted multiple-choice messages on the card—"My health is (good, usual, poor). I have/have not had any illness" and so on—also seemed to worsen the anguish felt by Lanson's grandfather. When he read the postcard he sat down and cried, because the confirmation of Lans's survival also meant that his grandson was languishing in captivity. The older man passed away a few months later. "The only thing we could figure was that he died of grief," Jane said.

During the war, self-help books and magazines such as *House Beautiful* and *Good Housekeeping* were catering to the needs of wives whose husbands were off to war. "You come home from the station or airport or the little gray ferry and it seems like a farewell to everything about life you love. The everybody's-home-now feeling of a man in the house. The solid companionship of two big bath towels in the bathroom, two pairs of slippers under the bed, two people talking in the privacy of their souls," one article read. The slicks were full of coping tips for soldiers' and sailors' wives. It was all so clean and sane and sound. Alleta Sullivan, a mother from Waterloo, Iowa, who lost all five of her sons in the sinking of the cruiser USS *Juneau* and thereby became America's eternal symbol of wartime grief, counseled readers of *The American Magazine* that they should discount rumors of their loved one's death, even though it was by just such a rumor that she found out the worst had befallen her boys. She described her work touring the country visiting shipyards and factories, exhorting the workers to greater efficiency. But there was closure and finality in the brand of grief that Mrs. Sullivan had experienced. It required people to regroup and move on. Jane Harris couldn't do that. Her husband's survival had been established as of a certain date. But what of the intervening time? What of the future? No doubt the well-intentioned magazine editors had a bargeload of good advice for her. Still, the chemical comfort of a White Memorial recovery room was the most peaceful of all sanctuaries.

A Portland man named Fred G. Hodge, the brother of the *Houston*'s communications officer, Lt. Ernest D. Hodge, invested years in tracing not only the fate of his brother, but the rest of the crew as well. His work was rooted in his supposition that, statistically speaking, there *had* to be many survivors. He had seen a Melbourne newspaper report of Rohan Rivett's July 1, 1942, broadcast over the Batavia radio station referring to three-hundred-odd survivors of the *Perth* at Serang, Java. In that dispatch the *Houston* was not named, but there had to be some American survivors there too, Hodge thought. The Navy's communiqués had already detailed the parallel fates of the two ships. It complicated things that the Navy, still deeming the *Houston*'s crew roster a military secret, would not release it until after the war. Still, working with a network of sleuths—including the family of chief radioman Harmon P. Alderman in Dayton, Ohio, who, using their own shortwave radio sets, received propaganda broadcasts from Java that disclosed the names of at least forty-seven of the ship's survivors—Hodge made great progress.

Starting with just six names, Hodge would network aggressively among the community of USS *Houston* family members. As news about prisoners reached Washington via the International Red Cross in Switzerland, he collated it all, pursuing every conceivable link between shipmates as he found them, triangulating offhand mentions of this sailor's "buddy" or that one's "pal," contacting families with sons in the same division or with similar ratings to determine whether they knew who that buddy might be. Through the good offices of his congressman, Sen. Guy Cordon (R-Ore.), he tried to get the Navy to release the ship's roster. He was tireless, and even though he failed to determine whether his own brother had survived, the work gave him something to do with his days besides worry.

The experience filled Fred Hodge with disgust at the dilatory and opaque state of the Navy's bureaucracy. Agents from the Office of Naval Intelligence and the FBI, concerned that he might be running some kind of perverse con game on bereaved families, investigated his activities. Hodge used the results of the investigation, which cleared him of any suspicion, to encourage recalcitrant families to cooperate with him. He saved his anger for the Navy Department's stubborn refusal to provide a crew list. When the Navy wrote Senator Cordon that a final list of officers and crew killed in action had not been compiled, Hodge wrote to his constituency of *Houston* kin, "Such a statement is either a deliberate evasion or further proof that the Navy Department has returned to its Pearl Harbor status wherein one department wasn't supposed to know what went on in another department." Nevertheless, Fred Hodge, as champion of the *Houston* families' interests a generation before the Freedom of Information Act went to its first legislative committee, did immeasurable good. As a journalist would write after the war, "It is impossible to estimate the value of Mr. Hodge's work to home morale. There are thousands of questions in the minds of relatives who have heard nothing beyond the 'missing in action' announcement by the navy." Such was a brother's love that it could embrace the entire family of the ship and endure long past the time that he learned that

Layout of Bicycle Camp, in Batavia, where the *Houston* survivors were held.

Hintok Camp, Thailand, as sketched by John Wisecup.

Lt. (jg) Harold R. Rooks, son of the *Houston* skipper, went to war in the gunnery department of the USS *New Orleans* (CA-32).

Albert H. Rooks, Jr., and Edith Rooks, sponsored the USS *Rooks* (DD-804), launched at Seattle on June 6, 1944.

Lt. Col. Blucher S. Tharp, commander of the 2nd Battalion, 131st Field Artillery, a/k/a The Lost Battalion.

Capt. Winthrop H. Rogers.

Sgt. Luther Prunty of the Lost Battalion.

Lt. James Lattimore.

The new *Houston* (CL-81), struck by an aerial torpedo and heavily flooded, gave her own dramatic turn off Formosa in October 1944.

Tech. Sgt. Jess Stanbrough of the 131st Field Artillery, shown here in November 1941, maintained a secret camp radio while in captivity.

Capt. Samuel L. Lumpkin, Lost Battalion medical officer.

Brig. Arthur L. Varley, Australian Imperial Forces, the commander of A Force in Burma.

Sgt. Frank Fujita.

At the Newport News shipyard, a deckplate finds a home on the new USS *Houston* (CL-81).

The submarine USS *Pampanito* torpedoed a POW-laden Japanese merchantman, then rescued the victims.

The railway base camp at Thanbyuzayat, Burma.

Interior of typical atap hut, Burma-Thailand Death Railway.

55 Kilo Camp, Burma-Thailand Death Railway.

Pfc. Jim Gee as a POW.

Unidentified
Burma prisoners.

Postwar photograph of a massive wooden railway trestle south of Hinktok Station, Thailand.

Cutting near Konyu, Burma-Thailand Death Railway.

The finished railway near Kanchanaburi, Thailand.

Railway cutting near Chungkai, Thailand.

Aerial view of the wooden and concrete bridges at Tamarkan under attack.

A U.S. B-24 Liberator flies over the wreckage of the wooden bridge at Tamarkan.

A collapsed span of the concrete bridge at Tamarkan. The buttresses show the ravages of repeated bombing.

The concrete bridge at Tamarkan, made famous in *The Bridge on the River Kwai* (1956).

INCOMING   TOP SECRET

ORIGIN: TRINCO	TCO NR: 601
FROM: PATTERN	FIELD NR: 119
TO: OPERO	27 July 45 1210

I HAVE TWO PRISONERS OF WAR WITH ME. NAMES ARE
JAMES W. HUFFMAN NAVY AND LANSON H. HARRIS. BOTH ARE IN
GOOD CONDITION. HUFFMAN'S PARENTS LIVE AT 17729 SUPERIOR
STREET NORTH RIDGE CALIFORNIA. HARRIS' WIFE LIVES AT
705 SOUTH WOODS AVENUE LOS ANGELES CALIFORNIA. PLEASE
SEND FOLLOWING. ONE PAIR 9-B SHOES. 12 SIZE 32 SHORTS.
FOUR PAIR SIZE 32 PANTS. 4 SIZE 15 SHIRTS. 12 PAIR
SIZE 11 STOCKINGS. PLEASE NOTIFY THEIR FOLKS. THESE
MEN WERE ON THE USS HOUSTON WHICH WAS SUNK. I HAVE
NAMES AND LIST OF MEN WHO WERE ABOARD, WHO WERE KILLED
AND ALSO LIVING. WILL SEND THE DEAD NAMES LATER. THESE
MEN WERE POW AT TAYANG AIRFIELD. WILL GIVE INTELLIGENCE
OF AIRFIELD LATER. PLEASE SEND PX AND SMOKES SOONEST.

TOP SECRET

The founder of the
Office of Strategic Services,
Maj. Gen. William Donovan,
at OSS headquarters at
Kandy, Ceylon, in 1945.

TOP SECRET

INCOMING   TOP SECRET

ORIGIN: TRINCO   TCL NR: 646

FROM: PATTERN   FIELD NR: 123

TO: OPERO   28 July 45 1945

     1. HUFFMANS ADDRESS IS 17729 SUPERIOR STREET NORTH RIDGE CALIFORNIA. HAVE TOLD THEM THAT THEY WOULD BE INFILTRATED SOONEST. THEIR OWN WORDS QUOTE LETS US STAY HERE AND HAVE A CRACK AT THOSE GD JAPS UNQUOTE. THIS FEELING EXISTS WILL ALL FIVE AND THEY ALL ARE STUDYING OUR WEAPONS.

     2. AIR STRIPS WILL BE READY WITHIN 2 WEEKS. YOU COULD LAND NOW BUT I AM LEVELING A FEW PLACES WHICH WILL MAKE IT BETTER FOR A LIGHT PLANE. 5 DETAILS NEXT SKED.

OUTGOING   TOP SECRET   TOP SECRET

DEST.:   TRINCO   KDY TCO NR: 893

TO: PATTERN   FIELD NR: 76

FROM: OPERO   28 July 45 1835

FOLLOWING IS PRIORITY OF INFO TO BE OBTAINED FROM POW'S.

    1. NAMES OF SURVIVORS OF HOUSTON CREW.

    2. GENERAL PHYSICAL CONDITION.

    3. LOCATION OF POW CAMPS. NUMBER IN EACH.

    4. ANY NOTORIOUS INSTANCES OF CRUEL TREATMENT SUPPLY FULL NAMES OF JAPS RESPONSIBLE.

    5. HOW DO JAPS GUARD POW'S? WHAT ARMS DO THEY HAVE? HOW MANY GUARDS? HOW OFTEN CHANGED?

    6. GIVE FULL NAMES OF ANY JAP OFFICERS PLUS DUTIES AND ASSIGNED UNITS YOU MAY KNOW. ALSO MISCELLANEOUS INFO ON ORDER OF BATTLE SUCH AS CODE NAMES OR CODE NUMBERS. SEND ANY INFO OF MILITARY NATURE THAT YOU CONSIDER IMPORTANT.

    7. PHYSICAL CONDITION OF JAPS. ARE MEDICAL SUPPLIES LACKING?

    8. JAPS ATTITUDE TOWARD WAR WITH SPECIFIC REFERENCE TO INTERROGATIONS OR CONVERSATIONS BETWEEN JAPS AND POW'S.

    9. POSSIBILITY OF USE OF SECRET WEAPONS. GAS, BACTERIA WARFARE?

    10. IN WHAT WAYS IF ANY HAS JAP TREATMENT OF POW'S IMPROVED SINCE FALL OF OKINAWA?

    11. HOW CAN JAP MORALE BE MOST EFFECTIVELY LOWERED

Major Bartlett, (l.), huddles with OSS colleagues in Calcutta, planning their parachute infiltration into the Thai jungle. Capt. Roger C. L'Hereault (rear) would join him later to exfiltrate POWs from Petburi.

1305ᵀᴴ AAF BASE UNIT INDIA CHINA DIVISION

Liberated railway POWs deplane from a C-47 at Calcutta. *Houston* survivor Lloyd Willey, USMC, faces front at far right.

Col. John Coughlin (l.) ran OSS clandestine operations in Thailand from Kandy, Ceylon. Lt. Gen. Raymond A. Wheeler (r.), Deputy Supreme Allied Commander of Southeast Asia Command, was a logistics specialist who orchestrated the supply drops to secret camps in Thailand.

Cdr. William A. Epstein, Lt. Harold S. Hamlin, Cdr. Arthur L. Maher, after liberation.

Railway survivors in Calcutta.

Medical personnel tend to survivors in flight home.

Houston aviator Lanson Harris, at the controls of the C-47 evacuating him from Rangoon to Karachi.

A U.S. Air Transport Command C-47 Skytrain lands in Rat Buri, Thailand to evacuate Allied POWs.

TO ALL ALLIED PRISONERS OF WAR

THE JAPANESE FORCES HAVE SURRENDERED UNCONDITIONALLY AND THE WAR IS OVER

WE will get supplies to you as soon as is humanly possible and will make arrangements to get you out but, owing to the distances involved, it may be some time before we can achieve this.

YOU will help us and yourselves if you act as follows :—

(1) Stay in your camp until you get further orders from us.

(2) Start preparing nominal rolls of personnel giving fullest particulars.

(3) List your most urgent necessities.

(4) If you have been starved or underfed for long periods DO NOT eat large quantities of solid food, fruit or vegetables at first. It is dangerous for you to do so. Small quantities at frequent intervals are much safer and will strengthen you far more quickly. For those who are really ill or very weak, fluids such as broth and soup, making use of the water in which rice and other foods have been boiled, are much the best. Gifts of food from the local population should be cooked. We want to get you back home quickly, safe and sound, and we do not want to risk your chances from diarrhoea, dysentry and cholera at this last stage.

(5) Local authorities and/or Allied officers will take charge of your affairs in a very short time. Be guided by their advice.

Leaflet air-dropped on the
POW camp at Changi, Singapore,
on August 28, 1945.

USS *Houston* survivors are honored in Houston.

In Galveston for a Navy Day ceremony, *Houston* survivors pose on the deck of the new USS *Houston* (CL-81), Oct. 25, 1945.

Edith Rooks, with her husband's portrait.

Reunion of *Houston* Marines, 1956, with guest of honor Dr. Henri Hekking. Back row, from left: Jim Gee, Frank (Pinky) King, Hekking, Howard (Bob) Charles, Charley Pryor, James (Packrat) McCone; front row, from left: Marvin (Robbie) Robinson, Bert Page, Lloyd Willey, Walter Grice

John Wisecup, circa 1989, wearing a shirt he earned.

Jane and Lanson Harris, Irvine, California, December 2003.

Otto Schwarz, addressing the memorial service gathering at the 1997 USS *Houston* reunion, Houston, Texas.

James W. (Red) Huffman, Santee, California, December 2003.

Gus Forsman, 1994.

Frank Fujita, 1994.

John Bartz, San Diego, December 2003.

Wisecup in repose, near the cutting at Konyu, Thailand, 1989.

Lieutenant Hodge, once spotted alive and well and in command of a life raft drifting in Sunda Strait, had never been seen again.

Edith Rooks remembered her husband's portentous farewell in Honolulu. "One thing that has always discouraged me in counting too much on Harold's being a prisoner," she wrote Admiral Hart, "is that before he left me he urged me to accept the fact that the *Houston* would be one of the first ships to fight the Japs and that if I heard it was sunk to remember that literally he would be the last man to leave the ship."

It galled her that she couldn't find anyone with first-hand knowledge of the *Houston* and the fate of its captain. On December 7, 1942, she had received a letter from the War Department's Office of the Provost Marshal General stating that the International Red Cross had officially confirmed through interviews with *Houston* officers in captivity that her husband was presumed dead. When she pressed for details about this "official" information she received a reply that epitomized bureaucratic incompetence. It urged her to hope that the Merchant Marine would soon be able to reveal more about the loss of the "SS *Houston*."

Admiral Hart, in Washington, kept up a heroic correspondence that cultivated Edith's hope even as it eased her toward acceptance of her husband's loss. But as she learned of the Navy's halting progress in investigating rumors concerning her husband, the uncertainty took a toll on her. Hart had shared a hopeful rumor, mentioned in a letter from Lt. Joseph Dalton, placing Captain Rooks in Formosa. He realized that he might have stoked her hopes too vigorously. On May 5 he wrote,

> Probably I should not have passed to you that rumor which was contained in my last letter. I knew that it would very well amount to nothing whatever but decided that you, being the kind of person that I know you to be, should be given it for such as it might be worth. In fact I rather felt that you simply would not forgive me if I withheld it from you and you ever found out.

In this letter he went further, dispensing once and for all with the tortuous hopes that the both of them had held open for the *Houston*'s commanding officer.

Edith, though there is always at least a vestige of hope I suppose that we must accept the situation which is that there is not really much to cling to and that lives should be ordered on the basis that Rooks is not ever really coming back. Those words are very hard to write and if I were face to face with you I probably would not have voice enough to say them.

Yet Edith's response to Hart's attempt to close the door on hope just pushed her the other way on the seesaw of denial. In the same letter in which she mentioned settling her husband's affairs, apparently convinced of the finality of his loss, she also wrote, "I must say more and more I feel the promise of Harold's death seems based on flimsy proof."

In May 1943, the Navy's first prisoner list named 1,044 men held by the Japanese. The report at once kindled hope and sowed doubt. There were survivors. But only seven from the *Houston* were named. Family members joined all their countrymen in wondering about the survivors from the U.S. Asiatic Fleet's flagship. But they would not get the whole story until a disastrous world war had been set right and won.

CHAPTER 46

The Pacific Ocean's vastness was an irreducible impediment to planning, to communications, to every measure of effectiveness given to man and to machine. If the entire European combat theater was a triangle of land and sea formed by lines connecting Murmansk, Gibraltar, and Tobruk, six such triangles could fit like puzzle pieces inside that portion of the Pacific within which America and Japan fought. One story in particular brought home the gulf of distance that separated the men from their home and the inscrutable way that fate at least occasionally allowed some news through.

Grievously wounded when the *Houston* was sunk, Lt. (jg) Francis B. Weiler had died of his wounds on March 26, 1942, at a small Dutch hospital near Pandeglang after guiding his raft of survivors ashore. Less than one year later, a Marine courier showed up at the home of Dr. and Mrs. George Weiler, in Germantown, Pennsylvania, to give them their lost son's U.S. Naval Academy class ring.

Entrusted by Lieutenant Weiler to a Dutch nurse just before he died, it found its way to a Dutch doctor, who surrendered it to a Japanese officer, presumably at the Pandeglang hospital. It should have remained an untraceable loss, like any of the million other workaday lootings perpetrated by victors on the vanquished. Except Lieutenant Weiler's ring was different.

A world away, eight months later, U.S. Marines were in the fight of their lives on Guadalcanal. In the midst of a firefight, a Marine captain named Gordon Gayle was approached by a party of stretcher bearers, one of whom handed him a Naval Academy ring, saying it had been taken from a dead Japanese soldier. The Marines must have figured a Naval Academy graduate such as Captain Gayle would know what to do with the keepsake, and they were right. Looking at the ring later, Gayle saw the engraved name of Francis B. Weiler, his Annapolis classmate and the chairman of the class ring committee.

Gayle gave the ring to an artillery officer, a Captain Swisher, who was due to return to Henderson Field. Gayle asked him to get the ring to the division quartermaster so it could be returned to the States. But before Swisher could leave for the rear area, he got new orders to go to the front and spot artillery for an Army infantry unit in the thick of the fight. Swisher probably never heard the scream of the mortar round that killed him.

The ring passed next to an Army private named Charles Stimmel, a radio specialist with the 164th Infantry Regiment, the unit that Captain Swisher had gone to help. When Stimmel in turn was mortally wounded by shrapnel, on November 23, 1942, his dying request, made to his closest battlefield friend, was to return all his personal effects, which included the Naval Academy ring, to his parents in North Dakota. That is how by March 1943 the ring had made its way through the hands of nine different people, over 3,000 miles of ocean to Guadalcanal, and across another 5,500 miles to the Weiler household in a suburb north of Philadelphia.

*

If Fran Weiler's ring could find its way home, there had to be hope for a prisoner of war, even one in the middle of the monsoon at Hintok Mountain Camp who had every good reason to abandon hope.

"There has got to be another way out, if we are to live," wrote Ray Parkin, survivor of the HMAS *Perth,* who was gifted with an extraordinary ability to rise above his circumstances. "I am believing, more and more, in my Psychic Inductance theory. I am trying to find out how many vitamins there are in beauty. I am beginning to understand, as a purely factual statement, *man shall not live by bread alone.*

The bush is full of 'every word of God.' I think, perhaps, that faith and hope are a couple of unclassified vitamins. I don't mean faith in any dogma—but in what I see in the life of the heart of the bush."

Though the imperturbable teak forest was itself unmoved by human struggle, it had enough heart to inspire poetry by Kipling and even bring a man on the edge of death to a naturalist's reverie. Even as it tried to kill him, Ray Parkin was enthralled by the wilderness all around him, by the cool blue-green bamboo, by the slapping wings of Asiatic nightjars and hornbills, by the swarms of brownish butterflies, by "hooded lilies, several iris-like orchids, wild ginger, and banana (which bears no edible fruit), clumps of orchids in the branches of trees like corsages of yellow jonquils. There are waves of perfume in the bush which we sometimes walk into. Cinnamon, chocolate, and one honey-sweet like clematis. Sometimes the early morning dew on the dry bamboo leaves smells like the Australian bush—or is it just nostalgia?"

Parkin's "unclassified vitamins" were all around him, and his obsession to catalog them was the kind of force that gave a man a reason to stay alive. "Vines are leaping with bright new green leaves a foot or so across. They are heart-shaped—some are like two hearts alongside each other. Trees are blossoming. One purple like lilac, and growing like a giant ti-tree. . . . There are more bird calls; monkeys call like Swannee whistles—flutelike on a slurred scale. All nature moves and has its being, and we seem to sit on it like a scab."

John Wisecup or Charley Pryor or Red Huffman or Lanson Harris wouldn't have waxed poetic about Death Railway flora even if it had blossomed in their hair, hauled them aloft with the winds, and winged them clear to Pearl Harbor. They found strength in other things. Most mornings, before they began a new day of labor, Wisecup, Gordon, and the rest of the men at Hintok Mountain Camp awoke to the commotion of baboons, savage and frightening, making a racket on the cliff top southwest of the camp. The men had the idea now and then to hunt one for dinner, but few such plans survived the first sight of the savage animals. They settled for less-dangerous prey. Cobras offered pinkish meat that tasted like fish or chicken. A four-foot iguana was a delicacy.

As bad as the diseases in the mountain camps were, tropical ulcers were dreaded more. Slow, decaying killers, they started with a breach in the body's outer defenses—a small cut from a saw blade, a nick from a flying fragment of rock—and in time were gnarled caverns of necrotizing flesh. "The thing eats faster than a cancer can even think of eating," Charley Pryor said. Swelling out and turning up at the edges, the wound unfailingly drew a cloud of blowflies seeking a chance to lay eggs. The only remedy Pryor used was boiling water. It was too hot to touch, but it felt fine on the ulcer. He spent every free minute pouring it over a rag spread over his wound.

Some put maggots into the wounds to eat away the dead flesh. In Burma, the medical staff in Branch Five tore blue cloth from mosquito netting and used it as bandaging. But natural healing was nearly impossible under the circumstances. The best treatment involved outright removal of the gangrenous tendons and muscle—Dr. Henri Hekking favored curettage with a sharpened mess-kit spoon—followed if possible by local treatment with phenol or Lysol and a sprinkling of iodoform powder. His orderly, Slug Wright of the Lost Battalion, called this "the dry method." It used no water, no soap, no ointment, no mud. You scraped and you sealed and counted on healthy flesh to scab over and heal by itself. Progress was evident after just three or four days. A man usually didn't survive amputation. Dr. Hekking did not lose a man to a tropical ulcer.

One day when John Wisecup was working at the Hellfire Pass cutting site, the Japanese engineers detonated a load of TNT unannounced and caught him in a crossfire of limestone chips. He expected the wound to heal, but it festered and grew. There were good medical people around, but at Hintok they had nothing to work with, not even bandages. Wisecup covered his ulcer with mud and washed it with a hot salt-and-water solution. More ulcers opened up on his feet and legs, then beriberi swelled his belly to the point that the several-mile walk out to Hellfire Pass was too much to take. He was put on light duty: digging pits. The dying buried the dead, most of their graves unmarked. Fighting through roots and mud, Wisecup and Crayton Gordon put as many as seventeen men in a single flooded hole.

In the beginning, they valued life above all else. They dragged their sick and dying on the boxcars and on up from Kanchanaburi into the jungles around Hintok to work with them until they died. "Had we known . . . that they'd wind up in a damn slop-hole grave, [we would have] let them die on the trail," Quaty Gordon said. "It would have been far better not to have carried the man, to let him stop on the side of the road, and let a Jap either put a bayonet through him or a bullet through his head, and that would have been the end of it. You carried him and let him go through all the agonies of hell in that jungle. But that was *clinging to life;* that's what it amounted to."

At Hintok they died without drama or ceremony. "We'd find them laying out there outside the tents," Wisecup said. "At first we made individual graves, and then there were so many of them that we just couldn't keep up with it." One rainy morning he and another man were hauling a corpse on a stretcher through the rain. Wearing khaki pants torn across the rear, the Marine was sloughing through six inches of mud, bare feet bleeding with every step over the sharp bamboo shoots growing beneath the mire. As he walked, the swaying of the stretcher caused the dead man's feet to keep bumping into his exposed buttocks. Lice were all over Wisecup. He bit off curse after curse. The jungle was working on him. "I never will forget this. I never will forget this to the end of my days," he said. "I stopped and turned around, grabbed hold of the stretcher, and threw the whole bunch into the jungle."

The other man with him on that grave detail was a very religious young Dubliner. To him, it was bad enough that there was never time for last rites. It was bad enough that sometimes people delayed reporting a prisoner's death just so they could get his ration. Sometimes they simply failed to notice a death until the stench reached an appreciable level. But the Irishman considered Wisecup's act a sacrilege. He protested to the Marine, told him he was going to retrieve the body. Wisecup snapped at him to leave the body alone.

"John, we can't do that, lad. No good will come of it. You can't blaspheme the dead."

Wisecup roared that the dead man was free at last. "Goddamnit, he's out of the son of a bitch!" he shouted. "Leave that bastard laying over there."

The Irishman said nothing. After a few minutes, Wisecup cooled down and went and retrieved the corpse. "I can remember that just so plain—them cold feet hitting me in the ass. I was thinking, 'Look at him! He's out of it! He ain't got to put up with this shit no more!'"

CHAPTER 47

B_y the middle of 1943, the industrial base of the United States was at full wartime tilt. As silt, corrosion, and sea creatures were having their way with the old *Houston,* roiled by bottom currents off St. Nicholas Point, new ships were rolling off the line. The new light cruiser *Houston* was nearing completion, sliding off the ways at Newport News on June 19. The coming of that ship and so many others like her had been foretold to the Japanese slave drivers. It was the Australian doctor Weary Dunlop who did it in the spring of 1943, in the midst of the cutting project in the stony ridgelands of Hintok and Konyu.

Like every other doctor on the railway, Dunlop had been waging a war to keep the Japanese from forcing his sickest men out to work. After days of argument, which usually resulted in a sound beating for the doctor, a Japanese officer evidently tried to improve relations with Dunlop by inviting him to the screening of a propaganda film. The Australian agreed and that night was trucked up to the camp at Kinsayok and seated front and center beneath the projection screen with hundreds of Japanese on mats behind him. A sequence of propaganda pieces flickered on the screen, including a news review that depicted, as Dunlop wrote, "Nippon tearing Asia up into strips by the employment of every conceivable arm of the service." The film highlighted the unpreparedness of the U.S. Navy and featured plenty of footage of Pearl Harbor burning.

The reaction from the Japanese audience was the predictable lusty chorus of *"Banzai!"* At one point they were doubtless startled to see Dunlop himself jumping to his feet, right there under their movie screen, and shouting *"Banzai!"* along with them.

"You think good? Nippon bomb-bomb, sink American and British ships?" someone asked him.

"Yes!" Dunlop roared. "Old ships no good—*taksan* [many] new ships now built—better!" he said. He could have known little about the naval forces marshaling to retake the Pacific's far-flung realms, but his exuberant defiance would prove to be prophecy itself.

Ships were one thing; people were another. This was the first American war in three generations large enough to subsume entire families in the regular course of events. Thirty-seven sets of brothers, seventy-seven men, had served in the battleship USS *Arizona*. Fifty-two of them died. Off Guadalcanal the Navy lost the USS *Juneau* and five members of the Sullivan family, whose outsized legend would match that of the eventual flag raisers on Iwo Jima. Cdr. Al Maher's brother James was for a time the captain of the light cruiser USS *San Juan*, launched the same day the *Houston* was sunk. The *Houston*'s Howard Brooks had three other brothers in the Pacific when he was working in the Burma jungle. His older brother was a Navy medic on Iwo Jima and Okinawa. Another brother was killed in Luzon. The third Brooks boy was on the destroyer escort USS *Bright*, struck by a kamikaze off Iwo Jima. Captain Rooks's own younger brother was Maj. Gen. Lowell W. Rooks, of Tucson, Arizona, who served on the staff of Gen. Mark Clark and headed the planning group that had drawn up the North African offensive in 1942. An article in *The Oregonian* newspaper carried the headline, "Where Is the Crew of the Ghost Cruiser 'Houston'?" It reported on Fred Hodge's ongoing quest to determine the fate of his brother, and the rest of the crew of the *Houston*.

In the midst of another severe bout of malaria, Jim Gee languished in 114 Kilo Camp. Splayed out on what he was convinced would be his deathbed, "out of his mind" with the tremors, he saw his sister, Johnnie Gee, appear, looking down on him from a tree outside the sick hut. In his hallucination she had joined the service and had come looking for him. Her mouth was moving and they talked for a time. He had yet to learn of women in the military—in mid-1940, when Gee, then nineteen, had left the States, he hadn't heard of the women's auxiliaries—but the oddity of it would not occur to him until later. When he shook off the fever and came back to his senses, Jim Gee was the most disappointed Marine on the Burma-Thailand Railway. But the vision renewed his hope, for the clarity and immediacy of the image of his sister searching for him told him that people were out there coming for him. "This dream gave to me the strength, again, to know that, gosh, they're really looking for us," Gee would say. "They're getting pretty close, and they can't be far away because this was too realistic."

One possibility might have struck him as a fantasy as outlandish as Johnnie floating in the trees: Less than two years after their ship's loss, a new USS *Houston* was with the American fleet leading the way across the Pacific to reckon with their captors. If the new *Houston* was not strictly speaking a sister to Captain Rooks's old heavy cruiser, there was certainly something of a blood relation there. Surging westward in the same task force as the new light cruiser *Houston* was the heavy cruiser USS *New Orleans*. Like the old *Houston,* she had felt the sting of Japanese torpedoes. In the Battle of Tassafaronga near Guadalcanal on the night of November 30, 1942, the *New Orleans* had taken a Long Lance torpedo that blew away her bow, forecastle, and a turret—everything forward of its number-two turret. The ship's exposed cross-section of compartments was sealed over, and she was taken to Sydney for temporary repairs. Then CA-32 returned to Puget Sound Navy Yard in April to receive a new bow— and a new young officer. Ens. Harold R. Rooks, fresh from Harvard's ROTC program, joined the ship on June 14, 1943. A year earlier, Secretary of the Navy Frank Knox had summoned Ensign Rooks to Washington and presented him with his father's Medal of Honor. Now Rooks joined the *New Orleans* gunnery department.

Her son's assignment doubtless filled Edith Rooks with a mix of pride and fear. When Secretary Knox wrote her in November 1943 to invite her to come to the Seattle-Tacoma shipyard to smash a champagne bottle across the stem of a new destroyer named in her husband's honor, the last ship in the famous *Fletcher* class, the opportunity to reflect on the full weight of the Rooks family naval tradition must have come bearing down on her. It compelled her, on the second anniversary of the Pearl Harbor attack, to sit down and write Secretary Knox a letter:

Thank you for asking me to sponsor the USS *Rooks,* DD-804. It is a privilege. I am very grateful for this memorial to Captain Rooks.

Our older son Harold graduated May 27th, 1943 from Harvard [and] was commissioned Ensign U.S.N.R. the same day and in 2 weeks joined the U.S.S. *New Orleans.* Like his father, he is the first of his classmates to fight at the front. I hear from his superior officers the highest praise of his capability and devotion to duty.

If there were a time limit on his duty in the Battle area I feel I could bear even this.

Though her last sentence only implied what many other mothers would have beseechingly implored, it failed to mask the idea that even an iron soul such as Edith Rooks was willing to risk only so much personal grief.

But to a young Marine 7,500 miles away, suffering the rigors of malaria at a place called 114 Kilo Camp, her son had an important charge to keep. The forces the prisoners envisioned coming for them had long since gathered and set sail. Among the swarm was the USS *San Jacinto,* the light carrier built with the $49 million surplus from the Harris County War Bond Drive, a ship that counted among its hard-hitting air group a future president, George H. W. Bush. As Lieutenant Bush and the other aviators of VT-51 were flying strike missions against the radio installations at Chichi Jima in the first week of September 1944, the USS *New Orleans* moved in close to bombard that island with her guns. It was the son of the old *Houston*'s late captain, deep in the plotting room, who was laying the main batteries on target.

CHAPTER 48

When the war reached the American POWs, they rather wished they could have stayed hidden and been spared its fury. There were no liberating armies, no waking fulfillment of the dreams falsely spun when the troopers of the Lost Battalion first arrived at Bicycle Camp. Rather, it took the form of large bombers flown by pilots who had no earthly idea that their bombs would terminate their parabolic plunges among American captives.

Flying from bases in India in indirect support of General Stilwell's Burma Raiders, the bombers of the Tenth Air Force ranged up and down Burma's western coast, hitting dockyards, shipping, bridges, and railway centers. They spread a steady rain of iron on Japanese targets in Burma from before Christmas 1942 clear through 1943. Their success against shipping was partly why a railway had to be constructed in the first place. Nowhere were Japanese supply lines safe, not by land, air, or sea. But the wings of freedom were, for the prisoners, wings of death.

On June 12, 1943, the jungle's peace yielded to a symphony of radial aircraft engines. Six planes—B-24 Liberators—approached from the southeast, circled the camp, and made their bomb runs in two waves of three. The Japanese raised no air alarm. Once more, they confined the prisoners to their huts and refused them access to the slit trenches. Though the bombers' targets appeared to be the railway lines and workshops east of the camp, two bombs fell within the camp perimeter. There were deep percussive thuds, the closest of them sending shrapnel through the *atap* roofs. One of these bombs struck a well inside the camp that from the air might have looked like a gun emplacement. Twelve prisoners were killed and fifteen wounded. Losses among the Burmese camped outside the fence were doubtless heavier.

The next day Brigadier Varley was called to the Japanese head-quarters and met some Japanese officers he had never seen before. One of them spoke perfect English and identified himself as a repre-sentative of the propaganda department at Rangoon. He asked Varley what he thought about the bombing and the deaths of the prisoners. Varley replied that the camp's illegal proximity to the rail yards, a military target, was bound to bring tragedy. He said that Japanese antiaircraft fire from within the camp not only brought re-turn fire from the bombers' window and turret gunners but was sure to void any protection the Red Cross might have guaranteed the hospital and the prison camp.

On June 15, bugles sounded as the Liberators again appeared. Though there were just three planes on this raid, the results were far worse. Thanbyuzayat's fourteen huts, which must have looked like a military barracks from the air, were in the crosshairs now. Though the new hospital was not hit, bombs fell inside the camp, collapsing several slit trenches and setting several roofs afire. Nineteen Australian and Dutch prisoners were killed, with about thirty wounded. Varley himself was injured in this attack, receiving shrap-nel in his legs and back, bruises from head to toe, two black eyes, and punctured eardrums.

Adorning the top of the camp's center hut was a red cross impro-vised from red blankets but with no white background to make it recognizable. It had faded under the elements and had been blown partly out of position by the wind. When the Japanese finally let Varley's men construct a more visible cross out of red sand, the B-24 bombardiers still did not get the message. They put a bomb right in the center of it. According to Slug Wright, the aviators came over low enough to see them, but thought the prisoners, with their deeply tanned skin, loincloths, and panicked tendency to flee for cover in the perimeter jungle, were natives working with the enemy. The Japanese refused Brigadier Varley's request to broadcast the hospital's location from Rangoon.

On June 18, Colonel Nagatomo had to acknowledge that his headquarters was no longer tenable. Rail yard operations at Thanbyuzayat ceased. Nagatomo's men broke down his headquarters and began moving it, along with all personnel and prisoners, from Thanbyuzayat up the railway line to 4, 8, and 18 Kilo Camps. They moved just in time. Over the next few weeks the Liberators came with a vengeance, hammering the Thanbyuzayat railhead, the old workshops, the camp, and the line, rolling up track like wire with their blasts.

The last five months of the railway's construction, from June to October 1943, were the hardest for each of the nationalities out on the line. In June, on the Thailand side of the Dawna Range's borderland ridges, through a short chain of camps around a place called Songkurai, there was a frightful cholera outbreak. The railway had no horror more lurid than what the British and Australians in F Force confronted just southeast of Three Pagodas Pass. The men were force-marched from Nong Pladuk 185 miles into the mountains, arriving seventeen days later at Songkurai No. 2 Camp, where they went to work on a major bridge. There, in the midst of cholera-laced waters, thousands of British and Australian prisoners died, as many as fifty a day at its peak. Some of the subgroups in F Force faded away nearly to a man. According to a British chaplain who gave last rites to a great many of these dead, "No medical officer or orderlies ever had to contend with such fantastic, sickening, soul-destroying conditions of human ailment." Hundreds were cremated in a large open fire outside the camp. As the heat cooked the sinews, the pile came alive with limbs stretching and gesturing momentarily before returning to peace. "I thought at first they were trying to climb out," the chaplain wrote.

*

Inspecting 105 Kilo Camp, Brigadier Varley discovered a Japanese sergeant "blitzing the sick parade," forcing the sick to grab shovels and shuffle off to the embankment. When Varley confronted him, the sergeant said Colonel Nagatomo had ordered it. Varley responded by calling his own muster and asking Nagatomo to make an inspection in his presence.

When the colonel showed up, he was confronted with hundreds of prisoners with suppurating tropical ulcers, drawn and enfeebled by dysentery, skin clinging to bones like loose tent canvas. "Nagatomo was astonished," Varley recorded in his diary. The Japanese commander seemed to have a change of heart. "He ordered that numbers going to work be left to [the doctors] and he asked what medicines and drugs &c were required." That night, arrangements were made to transfer the sickest patients all the way back to 55 Kilo Camp, within reach of the camp supply train. During the first week of July, 7,824 patients moved to what became the Burma branch's principal base hospital, Otto Schwarz among them. Flooded immediately with 1,500 patients suffering advanced pellagra, dysentery, malaria and tropical ulcers, 55 Kilo was, according to Fisher, "one of the worst, if not the worst camp dignified by the name of hospital on the whole length of the line." The death toll for July would be the worst yet on the Burma side of the railway.

In his continuing parleys with Japanese officers, Brigadier Varley noticed more than once that they were referring to a document written in Japanese. From what Varley could tell, it was a fresh copy of the pertinent articles of the Geneva Convention. If Colonel Nagatomo came around to embracing international law, it is doubtful that his superior, General Sasa, ever did. In any case, by July 1943 it was far too late for a sudden embrace of prisoners' rights to make any difference. The Wet had hold of them and disease was raging throughout the camps.

It was in July when Allied airpower began making its presence felt farther up the line. On July 11, Varley saw reconnaissance aircraft of "a type not seen before." They were "twin-engined and dual body and appeared to be fast." Every day just before noon a plane believed to have been a P-38 Lightning would range down the length of the railway at high altitude taking pictures. Jim Gee said, "He was as regular as clockwork, and he flew down and we'd get outside and we would wave to him and holler at him, and he, of course, was 32,000 feet high . . . That old boy will never know how much courage he gave us."

The trick to preserving hope was to parcel it out in packages no larger than necessary to sustain yourself for three months at a time. The ninety-day interval was long enough to contain visions of significant progress in the war, yet short enough for the imagination to cycle around and revise or extend. The stoutest prisoners were

CHAPTER 49

In Japan, near Nagasaki, at Fukuoka #2 Camp, the Japanese guards realized as early as February 1943 that one of their American captives was a son of Nippon. Somehow the issue didn't come to a head until the guard who ran the *tenkos* at Frank Fujita's barracks got the inkling to show off his language proficiency by reading the barracks roster.

Fujita presumed that he had gotten by up to that point because his olive skin, high cheekbones, and angular facial structure looked like the product of Filipino or Mexican heritage. But as his crewmates had warned, eventually there was no disguising the pedigree of his surname. Encountering it on the muster roll, the guard puzzled over it, then looked up, demanding: "*Fu*-ji-ta. Where is this *Fu*-ji-ta?" He approached the American artilleryman and began pawing him, running his hands over his face, inspecting the texture of his skin and hair. "Oh, this is fantastic," the guard exclaimed. He disappeared and returned with the sergeant of the guard, abuzz about his discovery.

The next day they let Fujita off work and the camp commander brought an interpreter with him to help question the unusual captive. Why had he joined the U.S. Army? Had the Americans conscripted him against his will? They showed more pity than out-rage. "A Japanese who can't speak Japanese—how terrible," they seemed to think. In an apparent effort toward rehabilitation, the commandant made Fujita his private servant. As he went about preparing the commandant's meals, an English-speaking corporal was assigned to teach him Japanese.

Fujita used his position to scrape up leftovers for the sickest men in the POW barracks. Meanwhile, the Japanese continued to coax him to switch sides. In exchange for his loyalties they offered him the rank of captain and as many geishas as he could handle. "They got mad as hell when I laughed at them and told them they were doomed." Fujita asked them why anyone would want to join a mili-tary that was busy losing a world war. That kind of talk got him well acquainted with their rifle butts.

Fujita saw trouble in learning the language of his father's home-land. "I figured my best bet is to keep my head where it belongs—on my shoulders—and not to learn anything. So I kept playing stupid." When the corporal assigned to tutor Fujita began to receive beatings from superiors for failing in the task, he began to threaten his understudy in turn. He would rush the American in a rage, back him up against a wall, and furiously whip his saber in front of his face, so close that Fujita could feel the breeze. Fujita was fearless and defiant, boasting to his captors how with E Battery of the Second Battalion, outside Surabaya, he had killed Japanese soldiers in bat-tle, five of them, and had helped shoot down a Zero fighter plane. The daily threats of death inoculated him to fear and deadened the impact of physical abuse.

The Japanese must have realized this, because they responded to his bragging with renewed entreaties and protests. "You're Japanese," they would say. "No, I'm *American*," Fujita replied. "No, the Americans are enemies." "No. *You're* the enemy," the Texan said. The Japanese of-ficers listened to the words coming from the mouth of the son of a Nagasaki native and shrugged. What could be done about this way-ward samurai?

In time Fujita was something of a sideshow, if not a celebrity. When dignitaries visited camp, the commandant would bring him out and put him on display. "Look what we have here. A Japanese who doesn't want to be a Japanese." Meanwhile, the enlisted men—most of them were Koreans, eager to settle scores with Nippon on the best of days—seethed, cherishing the thought of getting Fujita alone one day, a Japanese whom they would have license to beat.

It happened on August 6, 1943, when the officers and the sergeant major were away at a meeting in Nagasaki. The guards seized their chance. Word went out to get Fujita. Two guards grabbed him and took him out to the guardhouse. A guard known as "The Jeep" pulled a large club from a rack of clubs the guards kept handy for setting prisoners straight. He bashed Fujita for all he was worth. They hit him with fists and rifle butts, from all sides, from front and back. Fujita fought to keep on his feet. "I was bound and determined those sons of bitches weren't going to get me on the ground," he said. Beatings could turn lethal if a prisoner fell. They beat him from the guardhouse, forcing him to stagger outside toward a fifty-foot cliff. He held his head high as the blows rained down. Somehow he avoided going over the cliff into the bay. The Koreans beat him back in the direction of the guardhouse. Finally tiring, or perhaps growing bored, they stopped, shoved him to the ground amid a throng of POWs who had gathered in witness, and disappeared. The American sergeant missed the next three days of work at the shipyards because he could not see through the swelling in his face.

★

Prison life in Japan was static. Prisoners worked in fixed locations, in mines or at shipyards. In contrast, the fluid nature of the Burma-Thailand railroad kept prisoners on the move. A lifetime ago, at Changi, the Australians had taken to calling themselves the "Java Rabble." Colonel Nagatomo picked up the phrase at his welcoming lecture in Thanbyuzayat—"the rabble of a defeated army." They witnessed the rabble gathering and moving, slogging up the line in loincloths, strung out on the march, skeletal from hunger. Proud British units—Argyll and Sutherland Highlanders, Gordon Highlanders, and First Manchesters—traveled with tough Australians, veterans of the Syrian campaign, the Texas artillerymen, and the men of the *Houston,* the few men who actually put up a fight for Java.

From time to time, Japanese used the road, marching toward the front in Burma. Timor ponies pulled carts full of their gear. Sometimes it was the soldiers who did the pulling. Word passed that they had eaten their ponies as their rations failed. Clyde Fillmore saw a platoon of young Japanese infantrymen, "small, illiterate, absurd little creatures" marching along to the front near 83 Kilo Camp. "Ragged, hungry and bewildered we saw them pass, part of a drama they neither desired nor understood." They would ask for drinking water from time to time from the staff in the Japanese camp kitchen, and whenever they were refused, the imperial soldiers approached the prisoners. Sometimes the POWs shared the precious fluid. "They thanked us with bows and soft Japanese words, which we were not accustomed to," Fillmore wrote.

*

At 100 Kilo Camp, Luther Prunty, suffering from tropical ulcers, tore a page from his Bible and rolled himself a nice cigar. He and a soldier named Worthington "had a testament each." Prayers took many forms on the Death Railway: spoken, read, thought, puffed through the lungs. When faith failed, death almost always followed. Death seemed to be a by-product of collapsed moral strength, a slow decline, as if the patient were acclimating to the idea before the final surrender. Time and again at the 80 Kilo Camp hospital, Charley Pryor witnessed the slow atrophy of the will to live. One *Houston* sailor, in his final forty-eight hours, complained that he was having just endless trouble getting his leave arranged. He'd signed the papers but now they couldn't find them. He needed to find them because he'd bought a bus ticket back to Arkansas and if they didn't find them, he couldn't go, and there was a good chance he'd get on the wrong bus anyway. He'd never get home. To top it all off, someone had swiped the dress whites he was planning to wear home. The sailor had had them pressed and laid out just so. He wanted Pryor to go to the master-at-arms and help him solve the mystery of their disappearance. It's the kind of thing the Padre would do. No doubt the Marine sergeant told him he would.

According to Pryor, one prisoner, having seen how the Japanese sometimes excused the worst tropical ulcer patients from work, thought he'd go get himself one. He found a piece of bamboo—the stuff seemed poisonous; its scratches festered almost immediately—and began scratching a sore on himself. He worked at it over a period of days, picking at the wound with bamboo slivers, rubbing mud in it. When Pryor was working as steward, custodian, and chief gravedigger at 80 Kilo Camp, this man was among one day's incoming litter patients. He lasted about four days.

It was usually apparent when a man was preparing himself to die. Often he would stop eating. Sometimes he would announce his despair to the world. One remedy, surprisingly effective, was tough love. Actually, it more resembled hazing. This kind of therapeutic ball busting came naturally to a guy like John Wisecup, who seemed to have a talent for getting inside people's heads. "They'd tell you, 'I'm finished. I'm gone. . . .' So you'd slap them around or something like that. Make fun of them. That was the best way, to ridicule the guy. Curse him. Call him all kind of names. That's the best way. Really, it's the old Prussian system, you know. . . . What you've got to do is make a guy mad. As long as he's feeling sorry for himself, he's dead." Unhealthy thoughts had to be confronted and conquered immediately. It was like scraping an ulcer, like laughing at a friend getting beaten by a guard just to prevent a necrosis from infecting the group psychology.

Paul Papish, who was laid up with dysentery and beriberi at Changi and later reunited there with the returnees from H Force, said, "It was Wisecup, I guess, who would stand back there and just berate us: '*Go ahead and give up! Die! I'll get your shoes!*' I told him one time that, by God, I was going to get out of there, and I was going to get well enough and strong enough to punch him right in the nose." They learned to read the subtle signs that they were stoking somebody's will to live. If a guy started trimming his beard again, it was a hopeful sign.

When Gus Forsman was on the brink of surrender, gripped by dysentery, wet beriberi, jaundice, and malaria, an old friend from the gun mount on a ship that seemed like a ghost from a lost time stepped up and saved his life. In another life, Elmer L. McFadden had been a gunner's mate and first loader on the flight deck five-inch gun on which Forsman was a pointer. McFadden knew him well enough to threaten that if he died, he would go to Forsman's hometown, Iowa Falls, and tell his family how he had lain down and given up. It angered Forsman so much that he got out of bed, went into the jungle, and traded his shorts for six duck eggs and some brown sugar. Properly fed, he recovered in a hurry.

Jim Gee helped bring Howard Charles around from dysentery by teaching him to play chess. "Look, Charlie," he said, "your mind is like the muscle in your arm. Either you use it or it gets flabby and useless." Gee described survival as a kind of dialectic. "There are three forces at work here," he told Charles. "Like legs of a triangle.

First food. Either we have enough or we're dead. Second, health. That needs no explanation. Third, attitude, which is probably the best medicine. Food, health, attitude. They're interlocked, each totally dependent on the other. We have to have all three. No food, no health. Bad attitude: the triangle collapses. . . . Those guys who turn in early, they're the ones I worry about."

Capt. Hugh Lumpkin knew how to deal with them. The Branch Five medical officer knew how to give the tough kind of love that hurt initially but saved lives. Once a demoralized soldier told him he didn't have the strength to walk to the mess line. When Lumpkin suggested the kid have a friend do it for him, he responded, "I don't have a friend." Sensing a potentially fatal case of self-pity, Lumpkin said, "If you haven't made a friend, you deserve to die." It was enough of an emotional spark to help the kid fight his way to survival.

Sometimes no psychological tricks were needed. Straight-up Samaritanship saved lives too. Two soldiers, Jesse Webb and Lester Fassio, came to Dan Buzzo, who was sick and near death, and asked him how he liked his eggs. Buzzo knew eggs were a luxury worth four days' wages on the line, and he said, "Don't kid me. There are no eggs within a hundred miles." But Webb and Fassio weren't kidding, and their bruised bodies were the receipt for the price they had paid to bring the eggs into camp. A Korean guard had caught them and gave them the de rigueur bashing, but inexplicably let them keep the eggs. Buzzo had them sunny side up, but required his benefactors to have a bite too. "I guess that was my turning point," Buzzo would say, "those two eggs." According to Major Fisher, the senior Australian medical officer, "Probably no single factor in the whole of P.O.W. existence saved more lives than the humble duck egg."

People who died did so out of despair. They died cursing God. They died in a dissociating madness, protesting their circumstances then shutting themselves down like zombies. *Perth* survivor Ray Parkin captured the specter of a prisoner's death rattle with images that do not easily leave the mind:

> A figure of six foot three inches emerges from between the gleaming wet tents. He is so thin that every bone in his body shows. The two bones of his forearm stick out painfully at his wrists, and the two rows of carpals and metacarpals in the

backs of his hand. His fingers hang long and thin, punctuated by the knobs of articulation. Swinging at the end of stiff, bent arms, with sharp protruding elbows, they look like two small stiff faggots. His shoulders are sharp with emaciation and the studs of the acromium process, where the collarbone meets the shoulder blade, stick up like bollards on a wharf. His collar bones jut out, like bent iron bars, over a chest cage which might be that of a dressed fowl in a delicatessen. The navel sits on an odd little hemisphere low in front. On either side bony hips flare like the rim of a jug. His thighs are bones, with strings of haunches running down the back, from the shriveled knot that was once a round buttock. A knee cap sticks out in front like a piece of spiked armour. Below this, the long thin knife-like shin: it too, has strings instead of muscles. Legs not unlike those of a fowl. Long, bony feet, right-angled, are splashed past the ankles with the mud and excrement through which they walk.

This is a man. This is a man who walks naked in the rain to the latrine. Side by side with other wretches, yet alone, he crouches like a dog with a kennel in a bitter wind. He is helpless and racked with violent spasms. Dysentery reduces both body and spirit. In the rain he must crawl there and return to soiled blankets, to lie weak and helpless, without removing the mud of his beastly pilgrimage.

This comes to us all in turn. Men watch each other in silent understanding. What they see is ludicrous, but they don't laugh.

Sacrifices were made on the railway that were every bit as dramatic as Chaplain Rentz giving up his life jacket in the Java Sea. According to Robbie Robinson, it could be "as small a thing as hiding, from yourself, let's say, a can of condensed milk—even have the guts to hide it from yourself for that period of time until you reach it in the jungle when your buddy lay there, and you know that he was probably gone. Then you would break it out, and it would go to him—after all of the temptations that you, in possession, had. I call that a pretty good sacrifice." They spent their scant reserves of energy hauling their buddies from one camp to the next on stretchers fashioned from yo-ho poles.

The men of the Lost Battalion were helped in captivity, as many of the *Houston* and *Perth* survivors were helped, by their parochial closeness. "It's people you've known, gone to school with, you know their families. As long as you've been together, you know their families intimately—everything about them. Well, they just look at you different," the Lost Battalion's Sgt. Luther Prunty said. They could see through the distractions—the bloody leakings of amoebic dysentery or the ripeness of beriberi or a seeping tropical ulcer—and see the person they knew, a buddy in need of a meal.

Courageous and selfless though so many of them were, few ever dared try to escape. The thought was often on Charley Pryor's mind. He realized how easy it would be. At 80 Kilo Camp he was largely free of supervision. For a while the guards came to verify the deaths claimed by Dr. Epstein, but once they got wind of the conditions there, they stopped coming altogether. Pryor realized it would be easy enough to fake his own death—to prevail upon Epstein to sign his death papers, then dig a hole, decorate it with a phony grave marker, and become a ghost. He could float away into the jungle. It was tempting, but the obstacles beyond the camp perimeter were still formidable. Pryor never rolled the dice.

Another trio of Americans had to learn the hard way. Gus Forsman, Roy Stensland, and Jimmy Lattimore made a bid to escape after *tenko* one night. Stensland had long ago learned to cultivate risk and exploit it through audacious, sudden action. He'd pounded a Japanese private on Batavia, had even drunk with his captors. How hard could it be to walk to freedom? The damnedest things were possible if only you tried. They thought they might make the coast and signal a submarine for assistance.

One night around ten P.M. they left the camp boundaries and set out into the nighttime jungle. They crossed hills and steep ridges, traversed cliff facings, and hacked through heavy scrub. They quickly ran out of water, but knew they couldn't risk contact with Burmese hillmen, who stood to profit richly from their capture. Two hours into their flight they looked back toward camp and saw the watch fires burning. How far had they come? How far was there yet to go? From what they could tell, there lay ahead of them unimaginably dense and imponderably long stretches of jungle. Trying to penetrate it by night was more than they were up to. They weighed their chances and finally elected to cut their losses and return to camp before anyone knew they were missing.

CHAPTER 50

On August 1, at 100 Kilo Camp, the men in Branch Five suffered their most devastating blow to date. Hugh Lumpkin, the Lost Battalion's twenty-nine-year-old medical officer, "had the weight of the whole camp on his shoulders, because he was about the only officer capable of controlling the Japs and the Koreans," one of his battalionmates would write. Overworked and underfed, he got careless. He obtained some native sugar and ate it without sterilizing it. From that point on, racked with dysentery and charged with caring for 1,800 men at 100 Kilo Camp, where by this time only 97 of the 410 Americans on hand were able to work, Lumpkin struggled to deal with the maladies that surrounded him. "It was hard to find anyone with such disregard for his self and such devotion to duty as this man from Artillery," wrote a friend. "He was on the go all day and night, every day and night; nothing was too much trouble for him. His manner towards the patients never altered, always a smile and a cheering word."

As another railway survivor tells it, Lumpkin couldn't shake his fear of cholera. He was terrified by the news that an outbreak had ravaged one of the British camps not too far away, killing good men by the hundreds. Fear of it overwhelmed him. "Once the dysentery took a hold of him, he was so run-down from worrying about this cholera case and trying to keep everybody alive . . . he went real fast," said Roy Offerle. He refused hospitalization, asking, "What about my men?" When he did finally stay in bed it was only because he had no strength to rise. At that point he just allowed himself to die. "It was almost like a death blow to all of us," said Dan Buzzo. "It really tore us up. He was a great man." Ben Dunn of the Lost Battalion said it was not just fear of cholera but the disease itself that had killed Lumpkin. According to Gus Forsman, "He didn't have it left in him because he had expended so much energy and everything toward the health of the POW's." After Doc Lumpkin was dead and gone even the Koreans saluted his grave.

Dr. Lumpkin's fears were rooted in dark reality. As the Speedo campaign continued through August 1943, driving the prisoners to their limits and the railway toward completion—by the middle of the month the embankment would reach the 112 Kilo marker, with the rails laid to 83 Kilo Camp—prisoners were shuttled back and forth between the hospital camps at 80, 55, and 30 Kilo Camps, within closer reach of foods and medicines, and the work site at 108 Kilo, ever closer to the dreaded "cholera camps" on the Thailand branch of the railway.

*

In the jungle, a strain of bacteria known as *Vibrio cholerae* runs rampant where hygiene is lacking, coursing through river deltas and waterways contaminated by human waste, attaching itself to small animals living in the water. When the cholera reaches a human body, it finds a home in the small intestine, stimulating it to secrete fluid until severe dehydration sets in. In its worst form it causes profuse watery diarrhea, vomiting, and leg cramps. It seizes hold of a man in an instant and wrings him dry. Victims lose body fluids so fast that they lapse into shock. Without treatment, death can occur within hours.

Rumors of cholera's presence was perhaps the only talisman the prisoners had against the guards. The Japanese and Koreans were terrified of it and did what they could to make the scant supply of inoculations available where conditions were threatening. The disease was rare in the Burma camps. There were several cholera deaths at 60 Kilo Camp in the end of May, and Burmese *romusha* suffered an outbreak at 75 Kilo at around the same time. But its most horrifying predations were in Thailand—at Hintok, Konyu, and later at a place called Songkurai.

A handful of Americans saw firsthand what the jungle had wrought upon the British prisoners in the camps around Three Pagodas Pass. Dr. Hekking asked Slug Wright to lend a hand at a cholera camp near 114 Kilo Camp, hit heavily by a fresh scourge. According to George Detre, 2,500 prisoners were said to have died there. When he saw it for the first time, "it was like a ghost town," Detre recalled. "They walked everybody out of there that could walk, and the rest of them set the camp on fire. The guys that were laying there sick, they burned. . . . There was clothing waving in the wind, and we saw these partially burned barracks and canteens hanging there. . . . It was eerie. Believe me the Japanese cut a wide swath around the place." Only a handful of Americans were witnesses to this horror. Slug Wright saw a British major shooting his own men infected with the disease. Word of the cholera-afflicted camp reached up and down the line. Soon it announced itself: "You could smell that camp for miles," said Eddie Fung of the Lost Battalion.

*

One struggles to grasp how some of the POWs did it, survived the round-the-clock physical and psychic assault from man and from nature. Part of the reason lies in the way they framed the experience. Those who used language carefully distinguished between suffering and enduring. "*Suffer* is a dangerous word here just now—it can induce self-pity," wrote Ray Parkin. "*Endure* is a better word, it is not so negative. Enduring can give an aim, a sense of mastery over circumstance. I have seen so much self-conscious suffering and men dying from self-pity."

In the midst of his ordeal in Japan, Frank Fujita kept an unshakeably positive outlook. "I find beauty in everything, even in death, you know. I always find something that's worthwhile. And even when we were starved to death—most of us down to eighty or ninety pounds or walking skeletons—then instead of me sitting around thinking how horrible a shape we were in and 'Oh, woe is me,' I thought this was an absolutely marvelous opportunity to study anatomy."

"There is a lot to grumble about; a lot to be disappointed about; a lot to lose our tempers over; but there is also much to marvel at," wrote Ray Parkin. "For instance, the loyalty of a man's body—to watch a sore heal itself—to feel that pain is not so much a tragedy but a process. There is a fascination in trying to help it consciously, to try to break down any internal resistance to recovery by trying to quell devastating emotions like bad temper, hatred, fear, lust, envy." There was enough of an enemy in nature. There was no need to allow a psychological fifth column to form up from within.

The Japanese had their own way of motivating. When the officers weren't raiding the sick parade and the guards weren't bashing with rifle butts, they encouraged the prisoners to sing to keep up their spirits. "It has become quite an institution," Ray Parkin wrote of the bandstand brigade that worked at Kinsayok in September. The battalion bugler blew military marches on his cornet, at least until the workers were out of earshot of camp. The favorite of the Japanese was "She'll Be Comin' Round the Mountain," except that the Aussies didn't use the traditional lyrics. They substituted their own, better suited for the circumstances: *"They'll be droppin' thousand-pounders when they come. . . ."*

CHAPTER 51

Colonel Nagatomo had doubtless been well briefed on the progress of the two threads of the railway, rising out of the jungle in two simultaneously constructed halves that would join near the Burma-Thailand border. On September 21, 1943, forward elements of Branch Three began arriving at 85 Kilo Camp, meeting up for the first time with their countrymen in Branch Five. A few days later, with the railway's completion evidently within view, Nagatomo told Brigadier Varley that within a month, half of the prisoners in Branch Three would be shipped to Kanchanaburi, Thailand, including all of the sick. Was the end of the project upon them? Though few had a broad enough perspective to know, it seemed that it was. And when it came to pass, the final linking of the two railway branches about thirty-four kilometers southeast of Three Pagodas Pass was a surreal anticlimax to the Americans' frightful twelve months in the jungle.

On October 17, the two ends of the line met on the Thai side of Three Pagodas Pass. History records no moment akin to the Russians and the Americans joining hands at the Elbe River. There was no joy in the railway's completion, no feeling of shared achievement. As the collision of the north and south trade winds expended the last of their drenching energies, as the belt of equatorial monsoon rains collapsed into the mountains and receded south toward the Tropic of Capricorn, the Burma-Thailand railway's final stake was driven near the waterfalls at Nikki, the source of the iconic river that would become known as the River Kwai. At that point the sharp cries of "Speedo!" surrendered to the quiet of the jungle, and the *kumi*s of Branch Three and Branch Five were disbanded, their membership dispersed.

From August through November, 226 men were buried at 100 Kilo Camp, and 225 more at 80 Kilo Camp. In the absence of a chaplain, Lieutenant Hamlin read the burial services at 100 Kilo. Funerals became anticlimactic and were usually sparsely attended by the three- or four-man gravedigging crew, a few friends, and an officer. The *Houston*'s bandmaster, George L. Galyean, was often on hand to blow taps on an old German flugelhorn he had scavenged at Batavia. "They had the bugle going all of the time. Somebody was dying all the time—all the time," said Roy Offerle, whose older brother Oscar, afflicted with a bad tropical ulcer, died in his arms at 80 Kilo Camp on November 18.

The horrors of 80 Kilo Camp came to an abrupt end when the camp was abolished on December 4 and its sick moved to 105 Kilo Camp, where some Australians were said to have medical supplies. The shifts between railway camps had been so routine that the thought of a final move out of the jungle seemed fantastic. Until transportation could be arranged, the prisoners camped in the sodden deathscape between 84 and 122 Kilo Camps, working as railway maintenance crews. The guards could be heard talking about the move. The prisoners, they said, were once again bound for the "land of milk and honey" promised back in Singapore. The prisoners had long ago learned to be skeptical of the guards' pronouncements, vague and suspect on the best of days.

While some were chosen to stay in the mountain camps and maintain the railway against erosion and bombing and the varied sabotages of a defiant jungle, most were shipped to camps in western Thailand. Boarding boxcars to ride the narrow-gauge railway themselves, the evacuees thought of their efforts at sabotage, of the soft pilings they had bolted in place and the weak spots in the embankments they had cultivated, and worried those might be the instruments of their own demise. "It was more or less like a Toonerville trolley," said Gus Forsman. "The boxcars swayed an awful lot, and

you wondered—especially when you went across a bridge or something like that—whether it would hold, or whether you were going
to go crashing in."

But Jim Gee, for one, felt blessed. As his train rumbled and
squealed its way across the railway's Thailand branch, he surveyed
the starker terrain there and felt fortunate he had worked in Burma
rather than Thailand. The other prisoners must have had a horrendous time of it. There were longer and deeper valleys to fill, breath-
taking viaducts squeezed onto cliffside shelves along the River Kwae
Noi, itself far faster, more voluminous, and treacherous than Burma's
monsoon-fed cataracts. "I think we all came to the conclusion that
they had probably the rougher part of it," Gee said. He took it all in
and reflected on his experiences and arrived at a conclusion that only
a humble man would make: "We were lucky." Some of the trestles
stood in three tiers, as much as ninety feet high. To the surprise of
the passengers, they held. Against all expectation, the hand-made
railway functioned.

*

On November 20, 1943, at 60 Kilo Camp, the steward of Branch
Three, Col. Yoshitada Nagatomo, delivered a salute—a pathetically
self-justifying one—to the men whose deaths he had presided over
during the course of the railway project.

> In my opinion it is a virtue since ancient times to pay hom-
> age to the souls who have died in war, even though they may
> be enemies. Moreover, you were under my command, and
> have endeavoured to work diligently in obedience to my or-
> ders, while always longing for the final repatriation to your
> countries once war is over and when peace is restored. . . .
> Now you have passed on to the other world, owing to un-
> avoidable prevailing disease and epidemics and to the indis-
> criminate enemy bombings, I cannot see you in this world any
> more. Visualizing your situation, and especially that of your
> relatives and families, I cannot help shedding tears, sympa-
> thizing with your unfortunate circumstances. This tragedy is
> the result of war. However, it is owing to fate that you are
> in this condition, and I consider that God has called you here.
> However to-day I will try to console your souls and pray for

you in my capacity as your commander, together with the other members of my staff by dedicating a cross and placing a wreath in your cemetery.

In the very near future your comrades will be leaving this district; consequently it may be impossible to offer prayers or place a wreath in your cemetery for some time to come. But undoubtedly some of your comrades will come here again after the war to pay homage to your memory. Please accept my deepest sympathy and sincere regards, and may you sleep peacefully and eternally. <s> Yoshitada Nagatomo, Lieut. Col., Chief of Branch Three of Thai War Prisoners' Camp. November 20, 1943

The next day Colonel Nagatomo had some thoughts for the living too:

We have exploited untrodden jungles. Under the burning heat of the tropical sun and the daily torrential downpour of rain we have achieved this epochal and brilliant feat in this period of time, with the inflexible and indefatigable energies of those who have wielded the pick and shovel. This achievement reflects great credit on us, and must be attributed to the fact that each of you has been zealous in doing your own respective work, grasping my mind and aims, observing my instructions of various times and many rules since the establishment of Branch Three. I extend to you my thanks for your labor with the deepest regards. . . . Happily let us celebrate this memorable day by having a very pleasant and cheerful time to everyone's heart's content. Let this occasion be chiefly one of looking to the future and reflecting on the memories of the past year.

For most any Death Railway prisoner it would have been easy to reflect on the memories of the past year and strip down one's thinking to its vindictive, spiteful core. Of the people prone to seeing the world through such a lens, who could have been more likely than the Lost Battalion medical orderly who had seen it all, Slug Wright? As he was being shuttled by railcar to Thailand from the cholera wasteland around 114 Kilo Camp, he saw a Japanese train that had come up from Burma. When his train stopped and he was ordered to get off, Wright could hear the miserable moaning of the occupants of one of the boxcars. It was full of wounded Japanese soldiers, amputees among them. A Japanese nurse saw that Wright had a bunch of bananas and a big bamboo stalk containing about a gallon and a half of water. She approached him and asked in flawless English: "Do you have anything to eat or any water? These men haven't had anything to eat and nothing to drink?" The woman's nerve was extraordinary, for Wright wasn't inclined to be helpful. "I almost said, 'Big deal! Neither have we!' But I didn't. I hadn't talked to a woman, especially a woman that could speak English. . . . She was a nice-looking lady and everything like that. . . . So I handed her the bamboo, and I gave her my damn bananas." The woman, who seemed to be a trained opera singer, rewarded him with a rendition of "Columbia, Gem of the Ocean." After everything Wright had been through, the beauty of the solo was staggering. "I stood there and bawled like a baby," he said. "I didn't dare tell my fellow POW's what had happened, because they would be ashamed of me. But there is one time in my life that I am not ashamed of what I did. That was the enemy, but I just couldn't do to them what they had done to me."

CHAPTER 52

In the end, the railway of death was its builders' route to salvation. The ghost sailors of the *Houston* and the *Perth* and the vanquished defenders of Java and Malaya rode its meter-gauge track out of the mountains toward new camps in Thailand's central lowlands— places like Kanchanaburi and Tamarkan, Tamuan, Chungkai and Nakhon Pathom, home to a massive hospital with eight thousand beds. The most notorious engineering project of World War II was finished. At turning points such as this, there must be numbers to assess, but numbers do nothing to account for the varying traumas of individual experiences. Nonetheless:

In Branches Three and Five, there were 1,845 dead from an original strength of 11,824, for a death rate of 15.6 percent. Overall, of 61,806 Allied prisoners forced to work on the Burma-Thailand Railway, 12,399 died, including 6,904 British, 2,815 Australians, more than 2,000 Dutch, and 131 Americans. A full 45 percent of the men in F Force at Songkurai died. Of the 525-man group known as H Force, which John Wisecup joined at Hintok and Konyu, only 116 returned. The train that carried them back had about the same number of boxcars as before, but this time there was plenty of room for all.

The railway's overall mortality rate of 20 percent is horrendous relative to that of Allied prisoners in other theaters. But it positively pales beside the numbers measuring the ordeal of the local Asian conscripts or *romusha*. Estimates of their deaths are conflicting but appear to approach 100,000, about one-third of the estimated 300,000 ordinary Asian civilians forced into service on the Death Railway.

The Allied survivors trickled down out of the mountains as if washed out by the last runoff of the 1943 summer monsoon. In Brigadier Varley's A Force, about a thousand men, the "heavy sick," went to Bangkok for hospitalization. Six thousand less severely ill found a new home at Kanchanaburi. Most of the survivors of the Burma branch were taken there in groups of two hundred and three hundred, joining thirty thousand men in a huge prison camp at Tamarkan near the River Kwae Noi, near Kanburi, where the railway's largest steel trestle bridge stood. Some of them would go on to Saigon or Singapore for transshipment to Japan. The remaining three thousand men of A Force stayed on the railway line between 105 Kilo Camp and Konkoita, doing maintenance work, cutting firewood for locomotive fuel, and building military fortifications.

As the prisoners moved into Thailand following the railroad's completion, the Japanese "seemed to indulge in a system of competitive bidding at the railroad station for every new group of prisoners as it arrived," wrote Lieutenant Hamlin. The *Houston* men kept track of one another through an active news grapevine. They accounted for each other, keeping forbidden lists under floorboards in huts. Some of the men dared imagine that the ordeal would one day end. When that day came, careful records on each man's whereabouts would be essential to a final reckoning of who had lived and who had died.

At Kanburi in January or February 1944, the first parcels from the International Red Cross reached the prisoners, courtesy of the Swiss consulate in Bangkok. There were shoes, cigarettes, field rations, chocolate, cheese, hardtack, powdered milk, tins of beans and beef stew. The sudden availability of provisions may have been driven by the progress the United States was making in the Pacific. The Japanese seemed increasingly aware that they would be called to account for their treatment of their prisoners.

"This camp was much better than anything we had seen before, because the Chinese and Thais did everything possible to get through information to us and also to bring in canteen supplies in the form of fruit, peanuts and meat," wrote Ensign Smith, who came down to Kanburi from 105 Kilo Camp in April. Robbie Robinson called the Thailand camps "opportunity camps" because of their ready opportunities to make a buck or improve one's circumstances through enterprise. Charley Pryor noted that since the country's economy depended on agricultural exports, the diet improved markedly. Slug Wright was invited to a private dinner with Henri Hekking, who had purloined some fried fish and eggs to put over his rice. To Wright it was "like dining at the Savoy in Hollywood." Assigned to tend gardens or herd livestock along the river, they came into daily contact with native boatmen selling fruits and eggs, medicines and supplies. Pack Rat McCone, unsurprisingly, was as resourceful as any of them. He made good money trading on the river and was in turn generous in loaning out his earnings to those in need. "He lost no telling how many dollars," Robinson said. "But that's the type of guy he was."

John Wisecup was put to work in Kanburi's sick hut taking care of tropical ulcer patients. There were scores of them. He carried them in and out of surgery and assisted with amputations, the majority of them fatal. The operating table was a stretcher laid on a stack of crates out between the sick huts. When no anesthesia was available, Wisecup applied his strength to holding patients down while the sawbones went to work. "They'd chloroform the guy. We'd stand and hold him until he went out. Then they'd scrape these leg ulcers or cut off the leg or whatever they had to do, and then we'd haul him back in." Slug Wright witnessed at least one case of bubonic plague there.

*

The diseases and the amputations were the legacy of the monsoon and the railway and the jungle. All those things belonged to the past now. But one new obstacle loomed: the bridge. This particular bridge was larger than anything they had built in Burma. In the ensuing decades it would grow much larger, large enough to span oceans and continents, to outgrow the facts of its creation and emerge as a legend itself. Spanning a river swollen by the monsoon season, it was big enough to invite attack from the American bombers that were swarming over the Burma and Thai junglescape in numbers that grew daily.

Following Major Futamatsu's design, the railway traces the River

Kwae Noi for several hundred kilometers. During the monsoon season, the mountains of the Dawna Range require the river to do monumental work, draining the hills of their torrential runoff and channeling it into the Gulf of Thailand. The name "Kwai" is redolent of the misery the POWs suffered, far more so than the fictionalized movie that bears it. For starters, the bridge does not cross the River Kwae Noi. It crosses the River Mae Khlung, which joins the Kwae Noi between Kanburi and Tamarkan.*

Colonel Toosey, who arrived at the bridge site in October 1942, just as the Americans of Branch Three were seeing the first of Burma, had overseen the construction of two structures that crossed the quarter-mile-wide stretch of river. A wooden bridge was built first to enable the movement of supplies and equipment across the river for the construction of its larger concrete and steel neighbor. Known to the Japanese as the "Mekuron permanent bridge," the concrete and steel span was large, though its structure was simple compared to the multitiered timber bridges the prisoners had built farther up in the jungle. What it lacked in complexity it made up in bulk. Eleven twenty-meter steel trusses sat on concrete abutments, plus nine five-meter wooden spans on the northern end.

Building the massive concrete piers in midstream had been a technical challenge. First, temporary cofferdams were dug into the river bottom, then filled with ballast. Prefabricated concrete rings were then dropped one by one into the cofferdams, and the earth dredged from inside by hand. The work required prisoners to don old-fashioned diving helmets and work underwater inside the cofferdams, clawing the riverbed so the pillars would sink. The steel trusses themselves were reportedly salvaged from Java. The Japanese recycled them to good effect here.

Most of the British prisoners who had built the great concrete and steel structure over the River Mae Khlung at Tamarkan were no longer present when the Americans began arriving in late 1943. Colonel Toosey was sent to Nong Pladuk in December 1943, apparently under the Japanese policy that segregated officers from enlisted

---

*According to a leading Australian authority on the railway, Lt. Col. Terence R. Beaton, in 1960 the River Mae Khlung was renamed the River Kwai Yai at least in part to mold life to art and accommodate the bridge's association with the famous movie.

men. His men were dispersed to other camps from Saigon to Singapore, making room for the newcomers washing out of the mountains.

Though their working days were not over, conditions here were much better than they had been in Burma. John Wisecup was amazed at the things prisoners had hung on to through the ordeal at Hintok. A Scotsman still had his bagpipes, a boxer his gloves. Out on burial detail, Wisecup traded odd items with Thai locals for duck eggs—watches, Ronson lighters, flints, Parker pens. Most of the survivors of the mountains were sick, awaiting transport to better hospitals. One day the Japanese raided the sick hut at Kanburi and organized a *kumi* of its fittest men to work the Tamarkan railroad bridge. John Wisecup joined the workers who put the finishing touches on the "Bridge on the River Kwai." With the concrete piers finished, and with trains already using it, their work was limited to putting up braces, side stays, and sleepers. "They were in a hurry to finish it," he said. "Boy, they were really rough on us."

The bombers were rougher. As it happened, the Australians had been right: they *were* dropping thousand-pounders when they came. What none of the songsters had anticipated was that more than a few of those bombs would fall on them. Tragically, the bridge would prove most lethal not in its construction but because it attracted the full power of the United States Army Air Forces, and because the Japanese chose to locate one of the largest prisoner of war camps in central Thailand mere yards from this strategic target. When the men of the *Houston* were looking longingly to the skies for protection, Allied airpower had let them down. Now the airplanes fulfilled the sailors' hopes all too thoroughly. They flowed over them like storm fronts.

Freedom was heralded by airpower, by multiengine planes the likes of which they had never seen before—B-24s, B-25s, B-29s, Mosquitos, Beaufighters, P-38s, and later shorter-ranged single-engine planes whose appearance suggested the proximity of friendly bases and renewed the POWs' faltering hope. Tipped off by Allied intelligence agents that Bangkok's dockyards had been expanded and that the Japanese were building a railway to link the port with Moulmein, Allied air forces escalated and extended their campaign to bomb Japanese railheads and bridges and rolling stock, destroying with impunity what prisoners had risked death to sabotage. The lifting of the monsoon opened the way for a new torrent of bombs. It was the nature of war, and the nature of the Japanese practice of exploiting their prisoners as military chattel, that victory, when it came, would not be antiseptic or painless. The success of the bombers would come at the prisoners' expense. As the bombs fell on the bridges and their approaches, the Japanese organized *kumi*s to repair them. More than occasionally, the bombs went astray and took a horrible toll from the prison camps. For survivors who had come this far on fatalism, there was little cause to care.

CHAPTER 53

The U.S. Tenth Air Force had grown from a skeleton organization in 1942 to a powerful aerial striking force operating out of bases in India. The primary mission of its B-24 Liberators, B-25 Mitchells, P-40 Warhawks, P-38 Lightnings, P-51 Mustangs, and A-36 Apaches was to keep open the supply routes to China, including a legendarily difficult airlift corridor over the Himalayas known to history as "the Hump." Secondarily, it was charged with blocking Japan's supplies flowing into and across Burma. As with ABDA at the outset of the war in the Dutch East Indies, it took months of political upheaval before the varied American and British air assets came under unified command. At the end of 1943, the Tenth Air Force and the RAF's Bengal Air Command were joined as the Eastern Air Command under Maj. Gen. George E. Stratemeyer. Stratemeyer appreciated the challenge at hand. "A resourceful, able and wily enemy must be blasted from the jungles of Burma and driven from the skies in days to come," he wrote to his men. "We must establish in Asia a record of Allied air victory of which we can be proud in the years to come. Let us write it now in the skies over Burma."

He was referring to all of Burma, principally its strategic central region, the wedge between India and China. But he did not neglect the realm of the Death Railway. Over southern Burma and central Thailand, whose corduroy ridgelines gave false verdant beauty to the deathscape of the POW railway, it was his longest-range aircraft that carried the load. The flight from India was a challenge for even the best pilots and navigators. Burma featured some of the worst flying weather in the world. The mountains and valleys disturbed the circulation of the monsoons, leading to unpredictable weather. The Tenth's Liberator pilots needed every bit of their plane's famed endurance to make the three-thousand-mile round-trip to Tamarkan and back.

The Liberators of the Tenth Air Force's Seventh Bomb Group flew their first reconnaissance missions over the railway in January 19, 1943, when Col. Conrad F. Necrason, the same pilot who had led the attack on the *Nichimei Maru* and the *Dai Moji Maru,* photographed the entire length of the line, unaware that the slaves hacking the right-of-way through the jungle were Allied prisoners. Because the bomber command gave priority to targets far closer to India, the B-24s did not make their first concentrated effort to destroy the bridges, rail junctions, and marshaling yards along the Kwae Noi until the latter part of 1944.

The September 6–7, 1944, strikes on Nong Pladuk turned out to be tragic miscues. As at Thanbyuzayat the previous June, the Japanese placed their prison barracks in harm's way. The campaign of aerial bombardment to follow would all but destroy Nong Pladuk's vital rail facilities. But they also commenced a terrible phase in the war in which American forces—bombers and submarines— inflicted grievous numbers of deaths on their own countrymen and allies. The B-24Js that pasted Nong Pladuk killed more than a hundred prisoners. At sea the toll was even higher. The railway survivors had heard enough war news to dread the thought of sailing between Luzon and Formosa in the South China Sea, well known as a torpedo gallery for the increasingly bold U.S. submarine wolf packs. Called "Convoy College" by the Americans for its status as a rendezvous area for Japanese merchant shipping, it was a harrowing journey. Like their counterparts in the Tenth Air Force, the submariners had no way to know that some of the ships they hunted were full of friendly POWs.

On June 24, 1944, the Japanese transport *Tamahoko Maru* had been torpedoed by the USS *Tang* (SS-306). Among the dead were

560 Allied prisoners of war, including two survivors of the USS *Houston* and fifteen members of the Lost Battalion. The survivors were bound for prison in Japan. Imprisoned at Camp Omori, also known as Tokyo Main Camp or Tokyo Base Camp No. 1, the *Houston's* Cdr. Al Maher was joined by fellow prisoners such as Maj. Gregory "Pappy" Boyington, the legendary Marine fighter ace, and later, by Cdr. Richard H. O'Kane, the celebrated captain of the *Tang*, who had no way to know that it had been his own torpedoes that had killed some of Maher's men on June 24.

Every aspect of Japanese national life was suffering under the tightening chokehold that O'Kane's brothers in the Silent Service were applying to Japan's oceanic lifelines. On September 6, the same day as the tragic bomber raid on Nong Pladuk, a convoy of unmarked passenger-cargo vessels laden with Allied prisoners departed Singapore and was soon beset by American submarines. In the predawn hours of September 12, the USS *Pampanito* (SS-383), under Lt. Cdr. Paul E. Summers, the *Growler* (SS-215), and the *Sealion II* (SS-315), stalking Japanese merchant traffic in Convoy College, located and attacked the Japan-bound convoy of seven transports and two oilers, escorted by six destroyers.

Caught on the surface at one point, the *Growler* made a bold head-on surface attack on a Japanese destroyer charging her. Struck by two of the *Growler's* torpedoes, the *Shikinami*—which had helped sink the *Houston* in the Battle of Sunda Strait—burned so furiously that her fires blistered paint on the submarine's conning tower as she passed by, sinking just two hundred yards away. The *Pampanito* torpedoed and sank the 524-foot transport *Kachidoki Maru*. Cdr. Eli Reich's *Sealion II* put two torpedoes into the *Rakuyo Maru*. It took about twelve hours for the old ship to sink, for its full payload of rubber absorbed much of the force of the blasts and provided some buoyancy. As Reich took his boat deep to avoid the depth charging that followed, the convoy fled, zigzagging on a new course for Hong Kong.

The tragedy of the POWs on the doomed hell ships *Rakuyo Maru* and *Kachidoki Maru* must rank among the saddest of the Pacific war. Unknown to the subs that hunted them, they embarked thirteen hundred and nine hundred Allied prisoners, respectively. As the *Rakuyo Maru* took on water, her decks became a battlefield of sorts. Panicked prisoners rushed the ladders. The Japanese crewmen, holding them at bay with makeshift weapons, took all ten of the ship's lifeboats and made good their escape. The unlucky crew remaining on the sinking ship were left to contend with their prisoners. As a tanker in the convoy erupted nearby, brightening the predawn darkness, the prisoners seized the opportunity to settle old business. They set upon the Japanese crewmen and beat many of them to death by hand in one of the uncommon instances in the Pacific war when Allied prisoners rose up en masse against their captors. The ship disappeared beneath the waves around 5:30 P.M. that afternoon.

In the water as on board the ship, the Australian and British survivors were left to their own devices once again when Japanese ships—two frigates and a merchantman—apparently responding to an SOS, reached the sinking site and organized the rescue of their countrymen in the lifeboats, leaving the Allied survivors behind. The *Growler* and *Pampanito* chased down the remaining ships that night. The *Growler* torpedoed and sank a Japanese frigate, the *Hirado,* incidentally killing a number of prisoners in the water with the explosions. The stunned survivors piled into some abandoned lifeboats and began paddling west toward the China coast, some 220 miles distant, splitting into two groups on the way. Three days into their race for shore, the men in the smaller of the two groups—four boats commanded by an HMAS *Perth* survivor named Vic Duncan— could see the other group of six boats hauling along nicely about six miles away. Then a sailor called out to Duncan, "Smoke on the horizon."

It was a trio of Japanese corvettes. The men in Duncan's group watched as the other group was surrounded by the corvettes. Then, in helpless horror, they listened as the mad-woodpecker sound of distant machine-gun fire reached them over the water. The men in Duncan's group were approached next and asked if they were Americans; responding negatively, they were not shot but were taken prisoner and held in various camps in Japan.

What precipitated the slaughter of the other lifeboat group is beyond knowing. What is certain is that after leading A Force through the worst of the Burma railway construction, after parleying nose to nose with Colonel Nagatomo through every abomination his men were forced to endure, after keeping a secret diary that would document the story of his men's experience in intimate detail, the commander of the doomed lifeboat flotilla, Brig. Arthur Varley, had well earned a fate other than this. After the three Imperial corvettes finished with them and moved on, none of the men on those six boats, including Varley, were ever seen again.

*

For the American wolf packs operating in Convoy College, September 12 appeared to be a banner day. Three days later, however, the mood changed. When the *Pampanito* surfaced on the afternoon of September 15, the crew was stunned to find themselves in the midst of a large debris field dotted with men clinging to wreckage. Some were ill and many were wounded; all were fouled by bunker oil and ravaged by more than three days adrift without rations or water. They were friendlies, survivors of the *Rakuyo Maru*. As the submarine's crew set about pulling the men from the water, Commander Summers radioed for help, summoning the *Sealion II* as well as the nearby subs USS *Queenfish* and USS *Barb*.

The extent of the disaster became quickly manifest as Summers's crew hauled aboard survivor after survivor, seventy-three in all. According to the *Pampanito*'s patrol report:

> As men were received on board, we stripped them and removed most of the heavy coating of oil and muck. We cleared the after torpedo room and passed them below as quickly as possible. Gave all men a piece of cloth moistened with water to suck on. All of them were exhausted after four days on the raft and three years imprisonment. Many had lashed themselves to their makeshift rafts, which were slick with grease; and had nothing but lifebelts with them. All showed signs of pellagra, beri-beri, immersion, salt water sores, ringworm, malaria etc. All were very thin and showed the results of undernourishment. Some were in very bad shape. . . . A pitiful sight none of us will ever forget. All hands turned to with a will and the men were cared for as rapidly as possible.

The seas were whipping up, and by the time a typhoon passed through the area, making further rescue operations pointless, the four submarines had saved just 159 of the *Rakuyo Maru*'s 1,318 prisoner-passengers.

According to Clifford Kinvig, these Australians and Britons, taken to Saipan and then dispatched for rendezvous with their home governments, "provided the first 'open source' information on conditions in the railway camps." Their astonishing reports had almost immediate international repercussions. In October 1944, the pilots of the Seventh Bomb Group began receiving briefings about the disposition of Allied prisoner of war camps along the railway. On November 17, British and Australian representatives released coordinated statements describing the atrocities of the Burma-Thailand Railway. But they were powerless to stop what was happening to their men in Japanese custody. There was nothing to be done for them but finish the war as swiftly and decisively as possible.

CHAPTER 54

The barbed-wire perimeter of the Tamarkan prison camp was just a stone's throw from the point where one end of the great bridge touched land. A large concentration-camp–like complex that covered six or seven city blocks, Tamarkan was home to several thousand Allied prisoners. Pinky King was cleaning up the evening meal for some Japanese at their cookhouse outside the camp near the river when, from the north, he heard the drone of engines in the sky. There were aircraft, nineteen or twenty of them, big ones, coming right down the river at an altitude so high he had trouble identifying them. "Look at the mighty Japanese air force," he said. Among the prisoners, a debate ensued as to their origin. No one had seen such a demonstration of Japanese airpower before. Doubts arose when a Japanese antiaircraft battery near the bridge opened fire on the formation. As the bombs rained down, the prisoners went wild. So did the guards. Koreans ran. Prisoners ran. "They just went wild running," recalled King.

At the end of November, B-24s from the Seventh Group, flying from India, launched a serious effort against Tamarkan's great railway bridge. From high altitude, they failed to bring down the steel spans. Their inefficacy was no surprise to anyone aware of their scant record against central Burma's bridges in 1943. The big bombers' high-volume mode of iron slinging proved to be ill suited to knocking bridge spans from their concrete piers. It took not only tremendous accuracy but also fuses timed with hairsbreadth precision—and not a little luck. Bomber commanders experimented with different angles of attack, aiming points, and aircraft formations. Against one especially heavily targeted bridge south of Mandalay, Tenth Air Force B-24s and B-25s flew 337 sorties during the year, dropping 1,219 bombs but scoring just eighteen hits. That 1.5 percent rate actually overstated the accuracy of the big B-24s: In their eighty-one sorties they accounted for just one of those hits. The skip-bombing tactics used successfully by medium bomber pilots against Japanese shipping were less useful against much narrower targets such as bridge abutments. Low-level attacks were problematic too because the bombs, with no time to orient to a vertical trajectory before they hit, seldom detonated. All manner of mechanical modifications—heavy spikes in the bombs' noses, air brakes on the fins, and even parachutes—made little difference.

Swollen by the summer monsoon, the River Kwae Noi flowed south beneath the two east-west bridges, then turned in a sweeping bend east, tracing the southern edge of the Tamarkan prison camp, where a pier lay thick with barges full of supplies and equipment. North of them was a network of tracks and switches, beyond which three flak batteries were positioned. The prison camp was precariously situated, well within an antiaircraft shell's burst radius of the bridge. When the bombers came over, the shrapnel from the flak landed in the camp. "When we protested the camp being located in the very center of military objectives the Japanese blandly replied that they knew it, but had not they placed the three ack-ack batteries about the camp to *protect* us?" Lt. Clyde Fillmore of the Lost Battalion would write. If there was any ambiguity about the threat posed by the flak batteries, it applied doubly to the bombs themselves. "You cussed the planes and everyone in them; you hated to see them come and then somehow you hated to see them leave, but you could not hold down a surge of pride that these planes were American planes and that we were carrying the war to the Nips," Fillmore wrote. "You want to cheer them for tearing up the bridge, and you want to cuss them for trying to kill you," said Roy Offerle. Their exuberance chafed their captors. At Tamarkan the order came down, "Prisoners will not laugh at Japanese guards during air raids."

The big B-24s generally targeted the main bridge spans, while the smaller B-25 Mitchells, as well as Royal Air Force Beaufighters and Mosquitos, swift and light, targeted the bridge's approaches. Later, higher up, visible by their contrails, came B-29 Superfortresses. The prisoners had never seen their like before, four-engine bombers with long tubular fuselages. From their altitude and size, they knew it was a new kind of aircraft. There were rumors that these futuristic bombers were hitting Singapore and Bangkok, and that even Tokyo itself was under assault. When fighter planes began showing up escorting the bombers, they knew friendly forces had to be close. "That little P-51 came down with the B-24s there one day—goodness!— we didn't know what it was, but we knew whose it was," Luther Prunty said.

And sometimes they left behind a taste of things to come. At Kanburi, right next to Tamarkan, Slug Wright was watching some bombers at work when he spotted a different sort of object falling with the payload. It hit the ground about fifty yards away from him. It was a one-gallon can with the top shorn off. He went over and picked it up, reached his finger in, and tasted the residual liquid inside—peach syrup, cold and sweet. "My friends, American airmen, flying right over, by golly, threw the damn peach can out of the damn plane after they had eaten all the damn peaches. That's how close I was to America—tasting that peach syrup."

Red Huffman, working to repair the damaged bridges at Tamarkan, remembered the bombers leaving a different kind of calling card. One day he was huddled in an air-raid trench when he heard the roar of engines, looked up—he could never keep himself from looking up—and saw the metal skin of an aircraft so close overhead that he could make out its rivets. When the plane had gone, he got to his feet, looked around, saw something bright and small in the dirt, and said, "I don't believe it." It was a Juicy Fruit gum wrapper. "I picked it up and it smelled just like chewing gum. I hadn't smelled anything like that in three years."

After the bombers departed, there was always work to do repairing the bridges. The Japanese engineers would buck up their wounded pride and whip together a *kumi* to head out and undo the damage. According to Huffman, "When the all-clear would go and the bombers went away, we'd get a work force together, go over there, find out what was wrong from the Japanese engineers, and do the job. We did wooden patches mostly. We'd lay spare tracks in.

I don't know how many times the bridges, the wooden and steel bridges, were repaired."

One time after the all-clear sounded Huffman and some others who had emerged to undertake repairs heard muffled shouts from below the earth. They found a man buried in the rubble about ten feet under. He had kept himself alive by using a handy piece of hollow bamboo as a snorkel. "He was breathing under the ground through the bamboo coming to the surface, and hollering through it, too. That's how we knew he was there," Huffman said. The Japanese gunners defending the bridges had their innovations too, mounting antiaircraft guns on mobile flatcars and planting mines on bridge abutments or railway embankments and detonating them by remote control as bombers flew by. These tactics were throwbacks to the days of Richthofen's barnstormers, but within a very short time technology would show the way to an even more destructive future.

It was a largely uncelebrated technical achievement—the Allied nations' first smart bomb—that made it possible finally to destroy the great bridge over the River Kwae Noi. The newfangled bomb known as the VB-1 AZON was delivered to the Seventh Bomb Group's 493rd Squadron in late 1944. It was a thousand-pounder equipped with a gyro, solenoids, and moveable fins to hold it steady in free fall, and a radio receiver and servomotor to steer it left or right. The acronym "AZON" stood for "azimuth only," indicating the limited (though revolutionary) extent of steering control the bombardier had over the weapon in flight. There was no way to adjust its range in free fall, no way to flatten or steepen its trajectory. But it could be guided left and right by visual means, as a powerful flare burned in its tail fin. Against a long, narrow target such as a bridge, control over one dimension of the trajectory was usually enough to greatly improve the chance of a hit.

On February 5, 1945, a raid by B-24s missed the bridges but took out some of the gun positions and tracks near their approaches. Four days later Seventh Group bombers hit two sections of the wooden bridge. On February 13, another raid finally succeeded in bringing down several spans of the main concrete and steel structure over the River Kwae Noi, known as "Bridge 277" to the men who bombed it.

The end of the bridge heralded the end of the war, and the status and security of all Allied prisoners of war entered a tenuous and uncertain new phase.

At Kanburi, the new camp commandant, Captain Noguchi, and his sergeant-major, Sergeant Shimoso, were insistent disciplinarians. But the bombing seemed to unnerve even them. "You could see they were worried. They showed it," said John Wisecup, who was there briefly before returning from Thailand to Singapore with the rest of H Force. "We started worrying too as to what they're going to do with us. But you threw it off in the back of your mind. You're so goddamned tired and hungry and disgusted that, I don't know, it didn't worry you that much. You knew that it was in the cards for them to do you in."

Talk among prisoners was alarmingly persistent that a landing by Allied troops would force the Japanese to kill all the prisoners in their care. According to Pinky King, the guards often threatened that if they were going to die, they would take their prisoners with them. At Kanburi, Eddie Fung noticed the machine gun emplacements around the camp, ostensibly installed for antiaircraft defense. "They had been very casual about guarding us. We began hearing rumors that there might be a wholesale slaughter." At Tamarkan, too, prisoners noticed one day that the Japanese seemed to have turned their antiaircraft guns in toward the camp.

According to documentation produced after the war, the commanding general of the Sixteenth Imperial Japanese Army instructed his troops that prisoners of war were fair game for killing. Troops were advised to kill "cautiously and circumspectly, with no policemen or civilians to witness the scene, and care must be taken to do it in a remote place and leave no evidence." Orders traced to a Kempeitai unit and dated April 3–21, 1944, stated, "When prisoners are taken, those who are not worth utilizing shall be disposed of immediately. . . . Surrenderors found to be malicious after the interrogations performed on them . . . will be immediately killed in secret and will be disposed of so as not to excite public feeling." A secret Imperial Japanese Navy document dated March 20, 1943, read, "Do not stop with the sinking of enemy ships and cargoes; at the same time that you carry out the complete destruction of the crews of the enemy's ships, if possible, seize part of the crew and endeavor to secure information."

Unbeknownst to the POWs, on August 1, 1944, a declaration

had been issued by the Japanese War Ministry granting local camp commanders discretion to execute all Allied prisoners of war. Throughout their tenure on the Death Railway, the men had acclimated themselves to the risk of death as an element of daily living. Any number of offenses could get a man executed in the struggle to stay alive. Now the act of survival itself could be an offense that carried a death sentence.

The written document referencing a liquidation of the POW population was not a direct order but a clarification of some earlier policy guideline issued at the request of a prison camp commander in Formosa. According to author Linda Goetz Holmes, the war minister who wrote it did not actually have the authority to issue orders. Nonetheless, the chilling implications of the memo evoked the worst horrors of the worldwide Axis rampage. It stated, "Although the basic aim is to act under superior orders, individual disposition may be made in the following circumstances." It allowed a commander to make a "final disposition"—that is, "to annihilate them all, and not to leave any traces"—if there was an uprising, or if he feared prisoners might escape and become a hostile fighting force. This falls short of proving an actual order to kill Allied prisoners, but in the context of what the POWs were hearing from their own camp guards, it supports the idea that the possibility of a mass slaughter was more than idle chatter.

CHAPTER 55

The spirit of the *Houston*—the faith of the city's people, the fruit of their finances, and the volunteer gusto of their adult sons—was making rapid progress toward saving the vessel's lost crewmen. The U.S. Fifth Fleet, including the new *Houston* and the *New Orleans,* embarking Lt. (jg) Hal Rooks, liberated the Mariana Islands in mid-June, taking down most of Japan's carrier airpower in the so-called Great Marianas Turkey Shoot. Three months later the two cruisers supported the landings in the Palaus as the Marines seized Peleliu. In October they joined Adm. William F. Halsey Jr. in the Third Fleet's audacious carrier raids on Formosa. In the counterattacks by Japanese land-based planes that followed, the new *Houston* joined both her lost namesake and the *New Orleans* in their terrible acquaintance with Japanese torpedoes.

Like the heavy cruiser USS *Canberra* (CA-70) the day before, the *Houston* was struck by an aerial torpedo and left dead in the water, in grave danger of sinking. Taken in tow by other warships, a risky proposition so close to enemy air bases, the two cruisers were towed to rear areas at a gingerly four-knot pace, on the verge of sinking the whole way. With their ships playing the unwelcome role of magnets to further attacks, Third Fleet wags called the damaged cruisers "BaitDiv," a play on the Navy shorthand "BatDiv" for a battleship division. The joking ended on October 16, when Japanese planes hit the *Houston* again. With the ship staggered by a second aerial torpedo, only her crew's determined damage-control work kept her from joining old CA-30 below the waves. Nearly two weeks later, against all odds, she reached the fleet base at Ulithi.

Though the fate of prisoners would remain an open question until surrender was secured, the war between navies was essentially over. In 1943 and 1944, American industry built 25 cruisers to Japan's 5, 202 destroyers to Japan's 36, and 22 fleet carriers to Japan's 7. In merchant ship construction, the disparity was even more pronounced, with U.S. factories turning out nearly ten times Japan's tonnage in that same two-year period. By the end of 1944 American factories had produced a total of 300,000 planes during the war. Japan had managed about one-sixth of that.

It was the gross mismatch in aircraft production that enabled John Wisecup, convalescing at Changi after his ordeal in Thailand, to pull a morsel of hope from the air and keep up his struggle of will against his captors. He was working outside splitting logs when someone told him to hit the ground. "And you know, *whoosh!* We look up and, Christ, here they come—about four of them. They're not more than a hundred feet high, and they buzzed us. . . . I said, 'Boy, it ain't going to be long.'"

That feeling was becoming evident all through Japan's faltering Pacific imperium. The first B-29 flew a reconnaissance mission over Tokyo on November 1, 1944, heralding far worse to come. Weekly, then daily, then three and four times daily, bombers of the American Twentieth Air Force ranged freely through Japanese skies, each loaded with more than seven tons of explosives, high explosive and incendiary alike. From November to the war's end, they would drop 157,000 tons of bombs on the home islands. By optimistic estimates, the Twentieth would by the end of 1945 have built the capacity to deliver over half of that ten-month expenditure of bombs within a single month.

Duly nervous, the guards taunted prisoners with boasts of Japan's supposed triumphs. But the falsities were easy to tease out, and thus too the desperation that underlay them. "Bombed San Francisco," a guard would assert. Knowing the provenance of his captives, he would continue, "Bombed Amarillo," or, "Bombed Decatur." In the end language barriers and a poor sense of North American geography betrayed the lie. The absurdities mounted. When one of the

Americans finally responded, "Oh, bullshit!" a guard said, "Bombed Bullshit!"

★

After a year in the Burma jungle, Otto Schwarz, Howard Charles, Robbie Robinson, and more than a hundred other Americans were shipped to Saigon, which they all expected to be a way station for an eventual shipment to Japan. There they enjoyed the relatively light, opportunity-laden work of unloading barges on the city's vast waterfront, among many other assignments at airfields, railways, and radio stations. North of Saigon, in a resort area once popular with wealthy Frenchmen, the Japanese were digging a tunnel network similar to the defensive system they had built in Mount Suribachi on Iwo Jima. But with American B-24s on the prowl, the trains that hauled the prisoners to work sites had to move in fitful sprints, racing from tunnel to tunnel trying to avoid air attack. "There wasn't an engine on that railroad that wasn't filled with bullet holes," Schwarz said.

One day down at the docks, the guard in charge of a dock party unloading a barge called a break and marched down into the barge and stood among the prisoners. He sat down on a crate and told everyone to relax. He spoke excellent English, and he had a message for his charges. "You know, you Americans think you're smarter than the Japanese, but we watch a lot of your gangster movies, and we know just how you people operate. Now I'm going to show you what you look like to us." He went into a little act, a comic improv portrait of an American prisoner casing the waterfront, peering hither and yon as if keeping a lookout for the guards. Then he went to a crate and opened it, removing a can of condensed milk. He looked around, removed his hat, and covered the can with it, then set it down and raced to the other end of the barge as if to make sure the coast was clear for his getaway. When he returned to pick up the covered stash of contraband, though, he found nothing underneath the hat. In the seconds he had left it alone, one of the POWs had swiped the milk, writing another ending to the guard's little performance.

He flew into a rage, called a *tenko,* and summoned more guards. In the lengthy ordeal of searches that ensued, the can never turned up. Finally, the guards conceded defeat. The prisoners marched out of the dockyard back across the street to their camp. As they passed through the gate to the street, the guard was standing there, glowering stonily, still fuming at his humiliation. Then, as the Americans filed past him, spinning out from within their marching ranks came the missing can, rolling over the ground and swiveling to a stop right at his feet. Otto Schwarz said, "That was the American answer to him for telling us how we looked."

*

Commander Al Maher and the rest of the prisoners at Camp Omori in Tokyo ushered in 1945 with a fireworks display to remember, and even the terror at being within the radius of the escalating B-29 strikes couldn't keep some jubilation from leaking through. Frank Fujita, transferred to Omori in October 1943, wrote in his diary, "Most of us stayed up to see the new year in and it came in with a bang! Just as the clock struck 12:00 mid-night one B-29 dropped incendiaries that burst directly above the camp, scattering chemical incendiaries in all directions. That's what I call a Happy New Year." He noted that had the bomb been a high explosive model he would not likely have survived.

On February 25, the air commands on Saipan and Tinian sent against Tokyo a daylight raid comprising 170 Superfortresses, the biggest thus far. Within a few short weeks, the bombing of the imperial capital city entered the realm of phantasm. In an incendiary perfect storm on the night of March 9, Tokyo ignited like metropolitan-scale tinder. Fujita seemed to relish the spectacle of Hades arising to swallow him. He had lost the capacity for terror, chronicling the horror as one might recount a baseball box score: "The Saturday morning raid was sure a rooter—over 250,000 family units destroyed—over 50,000 casualties and over 1,000,000 people left homeless— Big raid on Nagoya last night and over 20,000 homes burned—here in Tokyo we see it all—action on all sides almost to our very walls—it's just a matter of time until they burn us out— Come on Boys! Come on!" Before the night of March 9, fewer than 1,300 of the city's residents had died in air raids. In that one attack, however, fatalities numbered some 100,000 people. It was a disaster that compared to the 1923 Tokyo earthquake. Huge swaths of Tokyo, as well as of Nagoya, Osaka, and Kobe, were left in cinders.

In Japan's frozen north, at an iron ore mine in Ohasi, Jess Stanbrough, Pops Early, Red Reynolds, and Jack Feliz smelled smoke on the breeze. They had overheard a Japanese guard returning from Tokyo saying that he couldn't find his family, couldn't even find his neighborhood. Judging by the terrible smell in the air, the neighborhood might well have found him. "It smelled like a fireplace burning pine wood, and it just darkened," Stanbrough said. "The sun became a dark orange, like it does when you look at it through a smoked glass filter." Japan was choking to death on the fumes of the hemisphere-wide wildfire it had started three and a half years before. One day at Ohasi the Japanese decreed that the big motors that drove the ore-crushing machinery were to be operated without oil in their journals. They didn't seem to grasp the consequences of their conservation effort. Anyone who had ever driven a car knew that unlubricated bearings would run only briefly before they overheated, smoked, and seized.

At Camp Omori, Commander Maher saw signs of the aftermath of Tokyo's incineration: a clot of big logs floating down the river into Tokyo Bay. Meant for shipbuilding in a city that could no longer sustain the trade, they found alternative uses as reinforcements for bomb shelters. With their railroad work sites incinerated, the prisoners filled their days building structures to protect their captors from the attacks. Maher seemed to understand that a war as terrible as this had to end with such a grim reckoning: "We more or less accepted it philosophically."

In Thailand, rumors flew that American secret agents were trying to incite an insurrection among the rebel paramilitaries. The war was moving into the shadows now, like a preview of asymmetric campaigns to come. And in the volatile political climate of wartime Thailand, a war of ideas was beginning, a complex mix of nationalism and communism that began to play out as the Japanese stranglehold over the country gave way. As Lloyd Willey remembered it, that war flared every Wednesday when a B-24 flew over Phet Buri, known as Cashew Mountain Camp, dropping leaflets. "I imagine they had an air gun up there," Willey said. "You'd hear a boom and you'd just see a cloud of leaflets coming down and the Japs were running everywhere in the confusion trying to track down these leaflets and confiscate them." Captioned in Thai characters, the illustrations told the whole story: pictures of Mount Fujiyama with American bombers flying by, or pictures of a sinking Japanese ship in a submarine's periscope. Everywhere they rained down, POW morale rose. The prisoners could save their Bibles for praying now. They rolled their cigarettes using the leaflets instead.

Unlike Java, where natives were hostile, even murderous, the local

Thai population had a deep distrust of the Japanese. As early as September 1942, curious civilians were probing the edge of the fence line at the Tamarkan camp, exploring rumors of prisoner abuse. The industrious, conscientious Thais could not tolerate the predations of the Japanese. Several courageous individuals—K. G. Gairdner, who worked for the Siam Architects Imports Co. until the Japanese interned him in Bangkok, E. P. Heath of the Borneo Company, and R. D. Hempson of the Anglo Thai Corporation—formed the core of a black market in pharmaceuticals and foodstuffs that gave thousands of prisoners a chance at life. Gairdner's secret weapon was his wife, Millie Gairdner, who as a Thai national enjoyed the freedom to move and develop familiarity with the camps along the railway. Her web of contacts matured into a humanitarian network that brought food, medicine, and information into the camps. The move into Thailand was a huge relief in this respect. It was a return to civilization.

The former mayor of Kanchanaburi, Boonpong Sirivejjabhandu, turned his Japanese-sanctioned franchise supplying camps with canteen goods into a goodwill effort. As his fleet of river barges ferried food, medicine, and cash to camp commandants all through the River Kwae Noi's lowlands, his store in Kanburi became a principal black-market trading post for prisoners. His political savvy kept him square with the Japanese, though the dreaded Kempeitai secret police operated constantly in the shadows, setting stings for suspected black marketeers.

Interred at Tamuan, Charley Pryor got wind of a Kempeitai entrapment operation. They were smooth operators, dressing like natives and conversing easily with locals. Pryor recognized them as Japanese, but what were they doing? Caution was the word of the day. In dealing with black marketeers, you learned to keep your exposure limited and your contacts personal. Direct contact with prisoners was terse, broken off altogether whenever a suspected Kempeitai loomed near.

"The Kempeitai spent the day seeking excuses for bashing the troops," wrote Dr. Fisher. Their methods reached from mundane punching and kicking to assault with rods and swords to exotic and creative techniques of torture that led frequently to death. The Kempeitai would take hoses, turn them up to full pressure, and force them into the victim's mouth. As the prisoner's stomach bloated with water they would kick him in the abdomen. At Phet Buri,

Lloyd Willey witnessed the "Kempeis" try to impress some Indian prisoners into the Imperial Army. When they refused, they were taken to the jungle, buried up to their necks in the earth, and doused over the head with sugary syrup to draw carnivorous ants.

In 1938, after its nationalist movement forced Siam's king to abdicate, the country had become known as Thailand, or Muang Thai. The name Siam had a mythic allure that harked back to ancient empires. But it also had racial connotations—deriving from the word *sajam,*" meaning "the dark race"—that this proud people found pejorative. The new name, though derived from the native name from the kingdom, was far more modern. Muang Thai meant "the kingdom of the free."

Freedom came to the country on the strength of its proud nationalists and on the wings of aircraft braving enemy airspace on moonlit nights. Pryor remembered hearing the hum of well-tuned radial engines as he lay in his hut before sleep. It was clear they were American planes, but he couldn't fathom their mission. They never dropped any bombs, and reconnaissance flights were only ever flown in daylight. Their mission remained mysterious until Pryor got his first inkling that some kind of clandestine military operation was percolating out in the jungle. Perhaps the nighttime flights had some relation to it.

One day Pryor was startled to find that barely an hour after the bombers had come over dropping their pamphlets written in Thai, they had been translated into English and distributed within the camp. He learned from a British prisoner that a suspicious-looking Thai had approached a work party near the edge of the camp, reportedly saying to the POWs, "I am your friend. I am with your friends. Your friends are not far away. Your friends are within fifty-three kilometers." The Thai said he wanted a prisoner of each nationality to attempt an escape with his aid. The Brit, Pryor recalled, was skeptical. He told the Thai that the Japanese would undoubtedly kill them all if such a reckless plot were discovered. The Thai said he didn't think so. Motioning to the edge of the jungle, where a squad of heavily armed Thais appeared, he said, "If we run into Japanese, it will be bad for Japanese."

CHAPTER 56

When the *Houston* and Lost Battalion men were moved into Thailand, they found themselves in the midst of a political struggle for the postwar soul of Asia. The Thai nationalist movement, well armed and broadly supported, had forced the collaborationist junta running the country to the precipice. On July 22, 1944, the militarist Pibul government, which had declared war on Britain and America, fell. The overthrow was in part occasioned by the fall of the Tojo cabinet in Japan. The Japanese were losing their grip on the Kingdom of the Free. As 1944 passed, an audacious covert American plan was under way to kindle an anti-Japanese insurgency.

The effort was the brainchild of Gen. William J. Donovan, a Columbia Law School classmate of Franklin D. Roosevelt, a former Wall Street lawyer, and the founder of the U.S. Office of Strategic Services, the organizational forerunner of the Central Intelligence Agency. In 1919, as assistant secretary of the Navy, FDR had tapped Donovan, a returning World War I hero and Medal of Honor recipient, to head the Office of Naval Intelligence. The president grew to rely on the savvy aide, employing Donovan as his own secret eyes and ears, sending him to report on events in hot spots around the world. An internationalist like FDR, Donovan believed the United States needed to engage itself with the political life of Southeast

Asia. He feared that Thailand was an "intelligence blind spot" in the midst of Japan's mainland empire. Correcting that would have any number of benefits: General Stilwell in Burma needed to know about Japanese forces heading his way through Thailand; the Tenth Air Force wanted data on targets from Burma to Bangkok to Saigon; diplomats in Washington aimed to gauge the mind of the Thai people and their willingness to take up arms against Japan. A couple of radio-equipped agents in the right places could make a difference. The capital city of Bangkok, a communications center large enough to have strategic targets worth bombing and strategic intelligence worth stealing, topped the list of espionage priorities.

The agency's ambitions went beyond mere espionage. General Donovan's planners were aiming to set up a network of secret guerrilla bases situated all through the Thai backcountry. They would free Thailand of Japanese oppression and, in Donovan's vision, serve as "the opening wedge for postwar American economic and political influence in Southeast Asia." To that end in late 1942 a cadre of 214 American field officers, working with 56 hand-picked Thai agents, began recruiting and training guerrillas. The goal was to develop a dozen battalions of Thais, each five hundred strong. The OSS was not authorized to deal with the Thai government on behalf of the United States. But because the State Department had yet to formulate an official policy with regard to the tumultuous state, Donovan's men were turned loose to fill the void.

The OSS officers had trained at President Roosevelt's retreat near Hagerstown, Maryland, practicing their spycraft by penetrating and observing U.S. war production centers. Slipping into factories, they mapped them as an enemy agent would. It was hard to find native Thais with such covert skills in their occupied homeland, in part because of the competition for recruits posed by British and Dutch intelligence services. The OSS focused its recruitment effort domestically, hand-selecting the best of the Thai students pursuing postgraduate studies in the United States. In January 1943 the first class of Thai agents was placed under the command of the Thai military attaché in Washington, Col. Khap Khunchon (also referred to as Kharb Kunjara). He took their oath of allegiance at the Thai Legation, holding a ceremonial Confederate sword bought at a costume shop, and heard each man pledge to overthrow the Japanese tyranny that gripped his homeland. Sent to a secret training center near Orange, Virginia, within twenty miles of the battlefields of

Spotsylvania, The Wilderness, and Chancellorsville, they prepared for a very different rebellion, training to become officers in the Free Thai Army.

The presence of so many Asian nationals in the middle of Dixie's northern frontier would have attracted unwanted notice in the absence of a good cover story. But since Orange boasted a hosiery mill of some consequence, they passed as a traveling group of Asian manufacturing representatives. The cover held up through their training, in which they learned communications, demolitions, weapons, and a type of "stream-lined ju-jitsu" used by the Shanghai police. Seeing their progress, Capt. Nicol Smith, the OSS officer in charge of their training and eventual infiltration into Asia, was impressed. "They can throw their weight in wildcats," he said.

By June 1944 they were in the field, flying from India to Kunming, then riding ponies down to China's southern frontier. They infiltrated on foot through French Indochina and into northern Thailand, whereupon their radio signals went dark. In deep suspense, Captain Smith listened ten times a day to the radio, hoping to hear a signal from the field.

The infiltration was dangerous business. On July 1, Smith heard from an agent code-named "Charlie" that two of the Virginia-trained agents had been compromised, caught, and killed. It was a disaster on its own terms, but no doubt the Japanese were also now alert to the insertion of agents into their midst. Finally, on October 5, after nearly four months of waiting, Smith received news of an agent's safe landing. From deep within occupied Thailand came word that an agent code-named "Pow" had set up shop in Bangkok.

The best minds in the OSS could never have imagined the intelligence bonanza Pow would produce. He had been told that an indigenous Thai underground existed and that its leader was a "big shot." But he had no idea who actually ran it. Arrested and taken to the police headquarters in the capital, Pow reported to Smith that the number-two man in the anti-Japanese underground was actually the head of the Thai national police. Pow's message, Smith discovered to his delight, had been sent from within Bangkok's police headquarters. The OSS was even more stunned to realize that the number-one man in the underground was none other than the leader of the government: the regent of Siam, Pridi Phanomyong, also known by his title, Luang Pradit Manutham. As Nicol Smith would write, "A lamp had been lighted in the capital of Siam."

Given the OSS code name "Ruth," Pridi was a forty-four-year-old Paris-trained attorney who had risen to fame in the summer of 1932, leading a bloodless coup that unseated the ruling monarchy. He was, in Smith's words, "a revolutionary whom success had not turned into a conservative." He stood for universal education and work, for the common man over the monarchic elite. He was the ideal candidate to lead a democratic rebellion. And given that his deputy was the chief of the Thai national police—Gen. Adun Adundetcharat, given the OSS code name "Betty"—the climate could not have been more favorable to start the clandestine movement that General Donovan's group had long envisioned.

"A double life is not an easy one," Ruth would tell Captain Smith. "By day I sit in my palace and pretend to busy myself with the affairs of His Majesty. In reality the entire time is taken up with problems of the underground—how we are going to get more guerrillas; how we are going to feed the ones we have; how we can, without causing suspicion, replace governors from provinces where we are putting in American camps." It was the unique and defining characteristic of the Thai insurgency that it was led by sitting heads of state working as double agents against their own quisling administration.

With help from Ruth and Betty, Col. John Coughlin, the chief of Office of Strategic Services Detachment 404, which ran operations in Burma and Southeast Asia, oversaw the creation of a guerrilla network across Thailand. Near the OSS headquarters at Kandy, Ceylon, by the seaside town of Trincomalee, Capt. Nicol Smith set up a training base where volunteers brought in by his Free Thai Army advance men rehearsed small-boat tactics, weapons training, unarmed combat, junglecraft, wireless communications, mapmaking, demolitions, and intelligence gathering. By the close of January 1945, the first two American field agents had followed Pow into Bangkok. During the next few months more U.S. agents, assisted by the Free Thai Army liaisons trained in the States, parachuted into other locations with the goal of creating a rebel force ten thousand strong. A world away, deep in the jungle of a country officially committed to the wrong side of the Pacific war, Allied prisoners of war prayed for a deus ex machina to rescue them, and a rebellion awaited its spark. With the OSS network spreading through Thailand's tropical wilderness, both were coming to fruition.

CHAPTER 57

Outside the Kanburi camp, Gus Forsman was working as a goatherd along with a one-armed Australian who helped him with the herding and milking and the hauling of the milk to the Japanese cookhouse. They took full advantage of the opportunities that came their way, bartering with natives and watering the milk after they had taken some for the hospital. Forsman learned to procure medicines from the Japanese—sulfa, iodine—putatively for the benefit of his goats, and give it to the hospital. A thought began tickling the back of his brain: Could he escape? He had no connections—all around him lay a yawning cultural divide. But with the bombings well under way, Forsman had read fear in the eyes of his Korean guards. Engaging them in conversation, he got the sense they no longer believed it was their war, that they wanted it to end. The feeling was revolutionary. It opened a world of possibility.

One day while he was out working with the goats, Forsman met a man who claimed to be a Portuguese doctor. He said he had links to the resistance in French Indochina. The doctor asked Forsman for information on the camp, the number of prisoners, the preparedness of the guards. Against his better judgment Forsman cooperated, and in turn received as his reward copies of the Bangkok newspaper, which he passed up the chain of command to the Lost Battalion officer in charge of the Americans at the camp, Capt. William "Ike" Parker whom the Navy guys called "skipper." The Bangkok paper was an improvement on the English-language news the Japanese fed them every now and then, which was laced with uproariously funny propaganda. "We learned, from these sources, that the Japanese invented the Ford car, gave the world the telephone and begot the first electric light," wrote Clyde Fillmore. Gus Forsman continued meeting weekly with the Portuguese, returning with the news and whatever medicine had been for sale too: sulfathiazole, Atabrine, quinine tablets.

One morning the doctor didn't show up. In his place came a native with a mouth full of silver-capped teeth. He said he wanted to buy something. An instinct told Forsman to play dumb. It was no secret that the Kempeitai was after the biggest operators on the growing black market. Robbie Robinson and Dan Buzzo had built relationships with the captains of the small river boats, trading goodies from their ditty bags for anything the hospital might need. One day Robinson and Buzzo had come to the river ready to trade and noticed that the captains were hesitating to approach them. Sensing a dark presence, the two men dumped their entire load into the river. Buzzo had a valuable ring, which he refused to deep-six. He wrapped it in a leaf and put it in his rectum. They narrowly avoided a Kempeitai trap. When the Japanese secret police made their move and rounded them up for search, there was nothing on which to hang them. Mindful of this, Forsman cautiously told the man he had nothing to sell, and left the scene. When the *Houston* sailor returned to the river the next day, two Japanese soldiers were waiting for him. They put him in handcuffs and marched him back to what they called Kempeitai headquarters. There he had his second encounter with the man with the silver teeth.

In the interrogation, they had no patience for his evasions. They screamed and ranted, made him kneel by a big teakwood table, chained him to one of its thick carved legs, and broke stout bamboo canes over his back. They lashed him with electrical wires. One of them said something ominous about taking him down to the river, but they returned him to his cell instead.

The next day the Japanese took Forsman, along with his superiors, Windy Rogers and Ike Parker, to Bangkok to commence court-martial proceedings. The use of actual legal process seemed extravagant given the summary nature of justice on the railway. Some say the Japanese were fast discovering the merits of legalities, knowing that the day was coming when they would be called to account. It still wasn't much of a trial. No evidence was presented, no questions asked. The handcuffed defendants filed into a large house, faced a panel of Japanese officers, and were given their sentence: six years in solitary confinement. Major Rogers, thinking it all a joke, said, "Six years hell. We'll be lucky if we serve six months," whereupon a guard hammered him to the floor. The war effort did seem to be falling in around the Japanese. But who was this Yankee to tell them what they could do with their slaves?

Locked in a civilian jail in Bangkok, Forsman recognized one of his cellmates: the Portuguese doctor he had first met at the goat farm. The Japanese beat him so regularly and severely that the sailor doubted he ever survived. Before Forsman knew it, he was being loaded into a cattle car for a train ride to Singapore. To avoid Allied bombers, the train traveled at night. When they had to leave the train in the freight yard by day, the engineers camouflaged it with palm fronds. From within the leafy concealment Forsman could look out and see enough of the wreckage to know the bombers had been doing their job.

When the train reached Singapore, Gus Forsman began an ordeal above and beyond what most of the railway prisoners had to endure. Brought to the Outram Road Jail, several miles from Changi, their residence on the first pass through the city three years earlier, he was taken to a cellblock, where he was shown a thick oak door and introduced to the new life of misery that lay behind it.

The name Outram Road is synonymous with inhumanity to those aging few who know what the name represents. It is a footnote to the larger railway ordeal, but one that seems important to relate as an object illustration of the arbitrary nature of Japanese wartime cruelty. They shipped Gus Forsman nine hundred miles for an infraction that held no meaning, posed no threat. It was an experience he never should have survived. Outram Road was reserved for the recipients of the worst punishments the Japanese garrison at Singapore meted out. Formerly the main civil prison in Singapore until the new jail at Changi was opened in the 1930s, two of its main blocks were run as a military prison reserved for those who had committed "anti-Japanese offenses." A survivor described it as "a vast tomb" whose dominant feature was a suffocating, strictly enforced culture of silence. "There could be a sick, deadly hush throughout the entire prison, so quiet that you could hear the metallic twisting of a key in a lock echoing up the levels to the long roof," a Scottish prisoner named Eric Lomax would write. "A warder's boots would make a booming sound on the stone floor, and I would be afraid that the sound of a whisper would carry all the way along to him.

"This was a place in which the living were turned into ghosts, starved, diseased creatures wasted down to their skeletal outlines."

There Gus Forsman would languish, stripped naked, washed down, and sent to live for six years in a four-foot-wide, ten-foot-deep concrete cell with only a bucket for a latrine. At the top of the fifteen-foot ceiling was a small metal grate to the outside. For a bed he was given two planks of wood laid side by side, with a wooden block for a pillow. Twice a day he received a demitasse cup of rice and a cup of tea. This ordeal was very different from the screaming fervor of the Speedo campaign on the railway—Outram Road was a regime of torture by silence. He had only himself to talk to. He asked himself questions and answered them; counted the bricks and counted the cracks in the bricks. For amusement he caught flies and pulled off their wings so they would stick around and keep him company. His only human contact was when a guard replaced his fouled "honey pot."

He paced and he cursed, unleashing on the cold walls the full vocabulary he had acquired manning a gun on Captain Rooks's late Asiatic Fleet flagship. He had plenty of time to ponder the existential mysteries surrounding him. For instance, there were 437 bricks in one wall of his cell, but just 435 in the other. He'd count them again—a *tenko* for the pavers—and get 433. He sang. He tried to remember books he had read, the sequence of their scenes. He took apart carburetors in his head. He reconstructed the agenda of the confirmation and catechism classes he had taken at the Lutheran church at his hometown in Iowa. For no obvious reason except to keep his nerve circuits alive, he would go to the corner and stand on his head until his head hurt so much he couldn't take it.

The tea and rice diet evolved into a tyranny of repetition. The good days were days when a couple of kernels of corn came mixed in with his rice. He set them aside and cherished them like the rarest of truffles, sucking their juice and chewing them to nothing before swallowing. Through it all, Forsman could not push from his mind the absurdity of his situation. Having survived forced labor building a goddamn railroad through impassable hills and disease-ridden jungle, this son of a railroad worker was to starve to death like a stock cartoon prisoner languishing in a forgotten dungeon cell. He understood the stupidity of the risk he'd taken in trading with the locals. More compelling to him than anything his subterfuge with the outsiders might ever have gained—and the drugs he had obtained were not trivial benefits—had been his need for contact with the free world. He longed to breathe that air again, to seize hold of the hand of that aircrewman, safe on high, destroying his and his shipmates' hard-built handiwork with payloads of empty peach tins and steerable bombs and fragrant chewing gum wrappers. But until victory came crashing down around him, he would take a breather from the real world of men and play with flies. He found that if he picked the wings just right, he could get two or three hours entertainment from a single one.

*

In February 1945, a photo of five Marines and a Navy corpsman planting a flagpole on a western Pacific mountaintop graced the front pages of hundreds of newspapers worldwide. After a month more of bitter fighting, Iwo Jima finally fell. In April, as troops were going ashore on Okinawa, the bombing of the Burma-Thai Railway reached its peak and Allied aircraft began to tip the balance in their race to destroy the bridges faster than the Japanese could force their slaves to repair them. With their weak air defenses and lack of appreciable aerial striking power, the Japanese garrison in Southeast Asia resembled nothing so much as the Allies in Java in February 1942.

On April 13, news began circulating that would touch the heart of every *Houston* sailor wherever he was and whenever he received the news. That day the joint Army-Navy casualty list was led with a prominent name: "Roosevelt, Franklin D., Commander in Chief," who had died the previous day. In May, a world away, Germany surrendered. As fate would have it, a member of the Rooks family was involved with the negotiations with the Nazis at the highest levels. On the morning of May 12, 1945, Maj. Gen. Lowell W. Rooks, fresh from his assignment as commander of the Ninetieth Infantry Division in the Ardennes, was sent to Flensburg in his new capacity as head of General Eisenhower's SHAEF* Control Party, the job of which was "to impose [Eisenhower's] will on the German High

* Supreme Headquarters, Allied Expeditionary Force.

Command." On a passenger ship in Flensburg's harbor General Rooks interviewed Admiral Doenitz and his *Oberkommando der Wehrmacht* braintrust. According to a U.S. Army colonel who witnessed the events, "If ever a man with a field marshal's baton looked unhappy, Doenitz did (after he came out). Rooks must have taken almost no time to deliver his message. The Germans were marched off and put into cars to take them home to pack."

Freedom was in the air. In June, the prison camp at Kanburi closed. Officers were segregated from the enlisted men and sent to Nakhon Pathom, forty-five miles west of Bangkok. The Japanese seemed to be concerned that prisoners in camps along the railway, lying in the likely path of invading forces, might form a fifth column against them. If the prisoners were held in a conspicuous place, it might make it difficult to hold them hostage, use them for blackmail, or carry out the "disposition" that the army command was preparing for.

The Japanese struggled to raise their battlements against the bombers. In the spring, a large number of *Houston* and Lost Battalion men were transferred from Kanburi and Tamarkan to the town of Phet Buri in Thailand's south. Their job there was to construct an airstrip, as if the starving empire could do anything against the silvery fleets of bombers now crossing the skies at will. Phet Buri's Cashew Mountain Camp was a huge concentration camp on southern Thailand's agricultural coastal plain. About a dozen large *atap*-roofed barracks each accommodated about two hundred men. Red Huffman was part of the large group of prisoners there whose job was to break rocks and move earth to make a serviceable landing strip. Since boarding a cattle car at 114 Kilo Camp and leaving the cholera-infected jungle behind, Huffman had mastered the art of the cushy work detail. At Tamarkan, one of the *Houston*'s Chinese mess cooks, Marco Su, had gotten him a job in the guards' cookhouse, where he showed up to find Pinky King and a number of other familiar faces already at work. When the bombing attacks forced Tamarkan to close, Huffman had been sent next to Chungkai, where he maneuvered himself into another cookhouse detail.

When he arrived at Phet Buri, he had to find a different skill set to exploit. Opportunity knocked when a Japanese soldier approached Huffman and asked him if he knew how to drive a bulldozer. The fact that he had never touched a bulldozer before didn't keep him from answering, "Hell, yes." The Japanese had brilliant engineers but a severe shortage of men with daily experience in practical mechanics. They had a Caterpillar tracklayer but no idea how to start it. It took Huffman only a few minutes to see that the vehicle used a separate gas engine to start the main engine. Thus did a farm boy become an airfield grader. Setting to work patching over holes in the earth caused by the removal of trees, Huffman, joined by his shipmate Lanson Harris, who as a pilot and aviation machinist's mate was also technically adept, helped them build one fine airfield, which was referred to as Tayang.

When they weren't working the tarmac, the two Americans were detailed to a truck depot near the camp's perimeter. Because the guards seemed to consider the two men reliable, they were allowed to work with minimal supervision. About a half mile outside the main camp, the Japanese had gathered a dozen old vehicles in poor repair. Huffman and Harris cannibalized six of them so the other six could run. Flat tires were patched with tree gum. Though there was a guardhouse about four hundred yards from the truck depot, whenever Harris was feeling brave and the guards were occupied with their lunch, he would sneak out and explore the perimeter. "Anything to get the hell out of camp and scrounge around for something to eat," he said. He found a grove of banana palms near the fence and took to raiding it as often as possible.

His second or third week at Tayang, Harris was in the banana grove when he noticed a trio of strangers on the other side of the fence. He wasn't sure what to make of them. They were wearing sarongs and looked like Thai locals, but he knew that didn't prove anything. The Japanese were known to recruit natives as collaborators, tempting their prisoners to break military law. Harris thought, *Oh God, I'm going to be caught by these damn* Kempeis. His alarm intensified when one of them approached him and pulled out a weapon that looked a lot like a Japanese service pistol. The man handed the weapon to him to examine. It turned out to be a German Luger. Harris was befuddled. "These guys were trying to communicate with me, but couldn't speak the language," he said. "I assumed he wasn't a Kempei policeman, but I didn't know who the hell he was." Harris returned to camp full of questions and uncertain of the wisdom of treating the strangers as friendlies.

Harvesting bananas a few days later, Harris again encountered the trio, but this time they were accompanied by a fourth man. The man conveyed the idea to Harris that he wanted him to go with him. When or where or how was beyond Harris's grasp. Then the man unfolded a piece of paper from his coat and showed the American a drawing of a box hanging from a parachute. "This didn't mean a damn thing to me," Harris said, "but he kept pointing to this picture of the parachute and pointing out in the jungle, like he wanted me to go somewhere where there was a parachute. Well, I had enough smarts to know there were no parachutes out in the damn jungle anyplace.

"When you're associated with people under these conditions, never, *never* do you trust anybody. If you're gonna do something you never say anything about it, because there are guys who would turn you in for damn near nothing, and all kinds of problems can result from this." Still, he felt he could trust Red Huffman. "I knew Red very well. So I told him what had happened. He couldn't figure it out and I couldn't figure it out.

"I said, 'Red, tell you what you do. Tomorrow morning when we go on that working party, you come with me and we'll see if we can find those guys out in that banana grove.'" That's what they did. And once again, the strangers were waiting for them. The mysterious Thais gave the Americans pause. They looked young, in their thirties perhaps. They also looked to have quite a drug problem. They would put a grayish powder in a little U-shaped tube, put it in their nose and inhale. "Every hour and a half they'd do it. Their eyes were blood-shot. They were higher than hell," said Huffman. "They would get all calmed down and squared away when they'd snort."

They were slipping Huffman and Harris handwritten notes with messages like, "Come with us and we will take you to your friends," or "Anytime you want, run away and we will grab you by the hand." From the strangers Harris got the idea that they were planning to infiltrate one of their men into the prison camp. They managed to get across to the American that if their man was carrying a large saw over his shoulder, that would be the signal to make their move and escape. The plan seemed deeply suspect to the Americans, but they were hard pressed to think of better alternatives. They knew the price of loose lips. Still, the plan leaked within a very small circle of prisoners.

They entrusted their secret to yeoman John C. Reas, who with another yeoman, John A. Harrell, had been faithfully keeping a forbidden register documenting the whereabouts of the *Houston's* men. Such a list would be as valuable as gold when the final reckoning was made. Harris and Huffman saw that if they could get that list out of camp and give it to American authorities, their shipmates might be saved all the faster. "We brought Reas into our confidence and he agreed to give us this diary," Harris said.

The *Houston* men knew the risk they were running in letting word of the plan spread. "You never tell anybody you're gonna escape," Huffman said. "In all the time we were there, to my knowledge, nobody had ever made a successful escape." Any number of prisoners had gone gallantly to their deaths for attempting it. More than a few Americans at Phet Buri witnessed what the Kempeitai did with escapees. It went beyond simple execution. Lloyd Willey had seen the Japanese secret police tie up natives, jam hoses into their mouths and flood their innards with water. They shot them, poured scalding water on the tender skin behind their kneecaps, drenched them in gasoline and hit them with lit matches. Once, looking on dumbfounded with Huffman as a Kempeitai agent poured scalding water into a man's nostrils, Willey asked, "What are they trying to do, burn him to death?" Huffman said, "Hell I don't know, but we're going to have to get out of here." Yet even stout hearts such as Roy Stensland, Jimmy Lattimore, and Gus Forsman had gone under the wire, entered the jungle, then thought better of it while the opportunity for a second thought still existed. At the very moment Harris and Huffman were struggling to figure out their destiny, Gus Forsman was languishing at Outram Road, enduring solitary confinement for a far lesser offense.

One day in the second week of June, Lanson Harris and Red Huffman were working out at the truck depot installing a radiator. Harris was sitting on one fender of the truck, Huffman on the other. Harris, cut off from news and living with a three-year-old worldview, thought Hitler and Tojo probably owned the world. He considered what they were about to do and said to Huffman, "This is really stupid." On the face of things, it was. But what were the alternatives? Huffman replied, "You know, it's been three years. We could die in here." The willingness to take death-defying risks often arose from having nothing to lose. Here was a chance, for the first time in years, to take charge of their fate. Huffman realized that these strangers might be offering him the only chance at life he was going to get.

From several individuals they learned that word of the escape plan had leaked beyond their immediate circle of confidants. A U.S. sailor with a lower tolerance for risk had talked about informing the Japanese. When Huffman discovered the threat, he considered terminating the plan. But then he learned that another shipmate, chief water tender Archie Terry—a dependable, "4.0" guy, Huffman said—had pledged to kill the would-be informant if he didn't keep his mouth shut. That seemed to recalibrate the wavering sailor's assessment of risks, and nothing was ever said to the Japanese.

Harris and Huffman were debating how to play their hand when they received an omen. The rains were frequent on the coastal fringe of the summer monsoon, but that day out of the clouds fell a driving rain of fish. Red Huffman has never been able to forget the moment when the heavens turned loose the silver-scaled torrent. "I don't think you could see the ground, there was that many of them," he said. "It poured down." Outside the camp's perimeter, kids ran around picking them up and impaling them on bamboo sticks to dry and eat. At least one rationalist found a ready explanation for the phenomenon. Dr. Epstein, the senior American officer at Phet Buri, said it must have been the product of a waterspout off the coast. In a Christian's worldview, it might have seemed downright apocalyptic. But the Chinese had several centuries of lore that told them otherwise.

"You ever seen it rain fish?" Huffman asked Marco Su, the mess cook. Su said that the fish storm was a sign of the arrival of the dragon. In the annals of Chinese serpent-worship the species of "spiritual dragon" known as the *shen lung* is the god of rain and water, a common man's deity who responds to prayers by exhaling clouds over farmers' fields and sprinkling them with fertilizing moisture. In some versions of the legend, the dragon—half animal, half divine—rains its own scales, like those of a carp, over the fields, heralding the coming of better days.

Unexpectedly blessed with the piscine shower, the prisoners turned out and gathered as many of the fish as they could. In the camp kitchen that day, the cooks made a fine stew. Three and a half years of submitting to foreign laws of war may have predisposed the Americans to accept alternative laws of nature, and hear their messages too.

Shortly afterward the prearranged signal came from the mysterious Thais. "All of a sudden we looked up and here comes this clown walking through the camp with this big grin on," Harris said. It was a Thai guerrilla. He was carrying a saw over his shoulder. It was their signal. Harris said to Red, "Damn it, it's now or never."

They chose their moment carefully, waiting until the nearest Japanese guard had retired to his hut, finished lunch, and fallen asleep. As a prostitute stood by him, fanning away flies, the Americans bolted. Harris found the small tunnel they had prepared under the fence some days before, and he scurried through; Huffman followed.

Outside the perimeter, the two USS *Houston* sailors ran. Sprinting through the banana grove north of camp, alive with adrenaline, they encountered four more Thais. One of them grabbed Huffman by the hand, saying, "Come, friends, come." As they ran, the Americans saw the smoking embers of campfires outside the camp and realized that their guides had been patiently waiting for them, perhaps for days.

Thirty-nine months after a Japanese projectile struck the faceplate of the *Houston*'s Turret Two, forcing him to dive blindly through a hatch to escape the inferno, 880 days after he listened to a war criminal on the edge of Burma's carnivorous jungle grandly welcome him into a life of servitude for the glory of Imperial Japan, Red Huffman sprinted through a grove of banana palms hand in hand with strangers whom he had no choice now but to trust. He prayed for the jungle to swallow him.

INCOMING   TOP SECRET

ORIGIN:	TRINCO	TCO NR:	601
FROM:	PATTERN	FIELD NR:	119
TO:	OPERO	27 July 45	1210

       I HAVE TWO PRISONERS OF WAR WITH ME. NAMES ARE JAMES W. HUFFMAN NAVY AND LANSON H. HARRIS. BOTH ARE IN GOOD CONDITION. HUFFMAN'S PARENTS LIVE AT 17729 SUPERIOR STREET NORTH RIDGE CALIFORNIA. HARRIS' WIFE LIVES AT 705 SOUTH WOODS AVENUE LOS ANGELES CALIFORNIA. PLEASE SEND FOLLOWING. ONE PAIR 9-B SHOES. 12 SIZE 32 SHORTS. FOUR PAIR SIZE 32 PANTS. 4 SIZE 15 SHIRTS. 12 PAIR SIZE 11 STOCKINGS. PLEASE NOTIFY THEIR FOLKS. THESE MEN WERE ON THE USS HOUSTON WHICH WAS SUNK. I HAVE NAMES AND LIST OF MEN WHO WERE ABOARD, WHO WERE KILLED AND ALSO LIVING. WILL SEND THE DEAD NAMES LATER. THESE MEN WERE POW AT TAYANG AIRFIELD. WILL GIVE INTELLIGENCE OF AIRFIELD LATER. PLEASE SEND PX AND SMOKES SOONEST.

Part Five

RENDEZVOUS WITH FREEDOM

★

"Those are our boys! Go get them!"

—Adm. William F. Halsey,
on board flagship USS *New Jersey*,
approving directive to medical
rescue teams, August 1945

CHAPTER 58

Harris and Huffman ran for a good four hundred or five hundred yards, through the banana grove, over a streambed, into a cornfield, and into thicker woods before one of their Thai escorts showed them to a shelter and they allowed themselves to rest and take stock of the new world they had entered. Their shelter was a spectacular natural refuge: the crown of a great banyan tree. With its network of aerial roots thickened into a rotunda of limbs, garnished by an eight-feet-high coppice of undergrowth, it provided the runaways with a nest of concealment nearly thirty feet around. Their escorts showed the Americans how to disappear into it, and told them to wait. "About twenty minutes later," Harris said, "here come these Japs, running through the jungle with their bayonets, stabbing bushes and screaming and hollering and raising hell. I'm sitting there thinking, *Oh my God.*"

The dragon was watching over them, for the soldiers moved on. But the Americans quickly realized there was no point taking the risk of traveling by day. "We stayed under that bush until nightfall," Harris said, "until a guide picked us up and took us to what we call a *kampong,* nothing more than a small village in the middle of the jungle. We walked to this *kampong,* and there we rested and had something to eat. Then we picked up and went to the next *kampong.*"

Moving by night, they trusted their escorts to know where to go and when to stop. Their faith was well placed. One night they stopped at a hut of some kind. The woman who inhabited it was duly awakened, and before they knew it they were being served a meal. In the dark, Huffman had no idea what he was eating, but Harris's taste buds had a longer memory. He told Huffman that it was freshwater shrimp. Wherever they stopped to rest, the Thais piled up green leaves and set them afire, producing smoke apparently meant to drive away the mosquitoes. "They would nearly kill you with the smoke. You couldn't get any sleep," Huffman said. But soon he would find himself fearing larger predators.

One afternoon Harris heard a commotion outside the jungle hut he was staying in. Three or four Japanese soldiers appeared and accosted the Thais, making demands. Harris had no idea where they had come from. He couldn't hear the conversation but saw the guerrillas point up the road into the jungle. The Japanese stormed off in that direction. When they got under way again, the escapees hadn't gone more than half a mile before they had their first glimpse of the formidable capabilities of their escorts: Around a bend in the path they came upon the Japanese again, their bodies sprawled limp beside the trail, clothes and heads gone. There was no going back now.

Days passed in flight, a week, maybe more. One day they were tracing the route of a small but deep stream through the jungle, seeking a way across—Harris in the lead, followed by Huffman and three armed Thais bringing up the rear—when they came to a place where a fallen tree bridged the stream. Crossing it, they marched up the path on the other side when out of the bush emerged a squad of men, olive-skinned and small of frame, but well armed and "painted like Comanche Indians," Huffman recalled. They were carrying Japanese rifles, which they leveled and aimed at the Americans' guts. Huffman was bare-chested, with a tattoo of an eagle and an American flag all but screaming his status as an escaped prisoner. One of the newcomers stuck a big pistol right in his face. It looked like a .45, but it was no make or model the sailor had ever seen before. Harris thought, *After all this . . .* With unintelligible grunts and stark gestures, the Americans were ordered to fall in and follow.

Wholly uncertain of their status, they marched another two or three hours into jungle, finally coming to a clearing that was the site of a camp of some kind. Harris didn't get a good look at it because he and his shipmate were quickly ushered to a bamboo shed and locked inside. That evening, one of their captors opened the door and told them to come out. He took them down to a river. He reached into a bag and produced something. It was a bar of soap. "He told us to take a bath," Harris said. Soap hadn't touched their skin in more than three years. They rinsed the detritus of Thailand and Burma from their filthy hides. The two Americans spent that night locked up again in the shed.

Early the next afternoon they heard a commotion outside. Peering out through narrow gaps in the bamboo wall, Harris saw a dozen or so young natives—they looked like just kids—enter the compound. Wearing green uniforms and carrying sidearms and short rifles of an unfamiliar type, they were led by an older Thai man wearing a cowboy hat and carrying a .38-caliber pistol in his belt. It was this man who opened the shed, saw Harris and Huffman, drew his pistol, removed his hat, and announced, "I'm gonna take you to your friends from Texas." Another man approached the Americans and handed them a box of Hershey chocolate bars and a carton of Camel cigarettes. Harris, partaking of the gifts, said to Huffman, "By God, there's gotta be Americans around here *some*place."

Of all the far-flung outposts that the OSS operated across the Asian mainland, it fell to the crew in the guerrilla camp code-named "Pattern" to be the first friendlies to lay hands on survivors of the ghost cruiser *Houston*. It was July 25, 1945, when Red Huffman and Lanson Harris, their bellies full of Hershey chocolate and their blood charged with nicotine, were taken from their bamboo hut and marched through the jungle to their rendezvous with freedom. Harris remembered hearing a motor running, then seeing in the moonlight the silhouettes of bamboo structures ahead. The door of a nearby hut opened, and two figures emerged to meet them. One was wearing U.S. Army fatigues. The other man was taller, clean shaven, and dressed in fatigues that looked foreign to Huffman.

The taller man approached the exhausted, mostly naked sailors and said, "Welcome aboard. Isn't that what they say in the Navy?"

Huffman said, "Yes, sir."

"Where in the hell have you guys been?" the American asked. "I sent these guys to pick you up three weeks ago."

Their savior was Maj. Eben B. Bartlett Jr., a thirty-three-year-old OSS field operative from Manchester, New Hampshire, and the commanding officer of the Pattern guerrilla camp outside Phet Buri. A qualified parachutist, Bartlett had proven his mettle in Europe as a Third Army liaison to the French underground. In August and September 1944 he had worked hand in hand with the French Forces of the Interior, ensuring their cooperation with advancing American units and even leading them in attacks on the Germans. The citation of the Certificate of Merit that Gen. Dwight D. Eisenhower awarded him for that period mentioned an incident where Bartlett and his interpreter "captured fifteen armed German soldiers and persuaded eighty-five others to surrender."

Major Bartlett's record of initiative in Europe suited him for the freelancing nature of OSS service in Thailand. As part of Col. John Coughlin's operation run from Kandy, Bartlett was flown from Ceylon into Calcutta on May 19. Joined by members of his field team—Cpl. Verlin (Pete) Gallaher and a Thai radio operator known as Art—he went to Jessore, northeast of Calcutta, and on May 26, climbed into a B-24 Liberator for the seven-and-a-half-hour flight to the Pattern camp's drop zone in a remote jungle clearing.

In the middle of June, Bartlett's guerrilla force began gathering. Each week about thirty Thais arrived for field training. They learned to field-strip weapons, shoot, use demolitions, make maps, communicate, navigate, patrol, and scout. Bartlett lacked the tools and medical personnel to fight the maladies the newcomers brought. But he made do with what he had, fashioning bandages from parachute fabric while waiting for the nighttime supply drops to start.

Though the State Department was understandably leery about sending large caches of arms into a country that was officially at war with the United States, upon the Joint Chiefs of Staff's approval of the operation, Lt. Gen. Raymond A. Wheeler, a logistics specialist, authorized a dozen transport aircraft to begin dropping supplies and munitions to the six OSS camps then in operation. Organized by Detachment 505 in Calcutta, Operation Salad, as the supply operation was known, used Tenth Air Force C-47s to drop more than seventy-four tons of ammunition, weapons, supplies, medical supplies, and matériel in late June. On June 21, Wheeler's fliers floated the first crates into Bartlett's drop zone.

Despite the fact that it was monsoon season, some nights were dry and clear. On those nights the moonlight illuminated the scattered high cirrus clouds as the planes made their runs near Phet Buri, Kanburi, and elsewhere. Prisoners in those locations, curious, puzzled, and hopeful, had dared not pray for the arrival of these aerial messengers. They had not envisioned this clandestine war, pursued at night by men out of uniform, foreign nationals, daring aviators hauling crates, and covert Yankee entrepreneurs such as Eben Bartlett.

When a warning came from Ruth that the supply drops had been detected by the Japanese, coupled with a recommendation that they cease, Bartlett was not at all bothered. "THE WAY I FEEL ABOUT THIS BUSINESS IS YOU HAVE TO BE A LITTLE BOLD OTHERWISE IT WILL BE TILL DOOMSDAY BEFORE YOU COULD GET IN ENOUGH SUPPLIES," he radioed headquarters. "ONE HAS TO TAKE A FEW RISKS IF WE ARE TO ACCOMPLISH OUR MISSION." To conceal the nature of the supply effort, he recommended that bombers, which were more frequently seen in this airspace, fly the missions instead of C-47s. But Colonel Coughlin felt the need to mollify his courageous Thai patron. On June 30, he radioed Bartlett that he was suspending the drops.

Pattern camp was armed for war. Bartlett presided over a cache of arms large enough to equip a light infantry battalion: 388 carbines, 317 Thompson submachine guns, 90 M3 carbines, 50 M1 Garands, 8 Springfields, 218 .45-caliber pistols, 14 Browning automatic rifles, 825 hand grenades, 2 sixty-millimeter mortars, and a bazooka. He wondered if he might need to tap that terrible potential. "IF JAPS COME IN HERE," he radioed on July 3, "SHALL WE FIGHT IT OUT OR TAKE TO THE HILLS OR IS THE DECISION LEFT UP TO ME ACCORDING TO THE SITUATION?"

But headquarters wanted them to lie low. Kandy radioed Bartlett, "PRESENT POLICY IS NOT TO HAVE ANY OF OUR GROUPS FIGHT IT OUT UNLESS RUTH SO ORDERS. MEANWHILE YOU SHOULD HAVE ESCAPE PLAN AND SUPPLY CACHE THAT WILL ENABLE YOU TO GET AWAY."

Bartlett had plenty else to do. All through June, his native right-hand man, Pow Khamourai, had been watching the Phet Buri camp and its nearby Tayang airfield and radioing reports of its assets and personnel directly to Ceylon. Much of the reporting by other Thai agents was deemed "lamentable." Although the OSS had to risk operational security by transmitting instructions to Pow—explanations of what radar was and what the installations looked like—his detailed reporting was considered excellent. In early July, he discovered and reported the presence of Americans among the prisoners at Tayang. Rumors of American prisoners nearby had been circulating for a while. Some of Betty's men found an Australian

POW who mentioned having been with survivors of the USS *Houston* out in the jungle somewhere. He described how bombers attacked the big bridge, and how the Japanese drove the prisoners under it for cover.

In Bangkok, Pow visited Nicol Smith and told him about his discovery outside Phet Buri: "Things are getting hot down there. Lots of Japs." Though Operation Pattern hadn't yet been compromised, there had been scares. Once, Pow was confronted with a pair of Japanese soldiers near the camp, "heading straight for it like a couple of homing pigeons," he said. "If we hadn't ambushed them, nothing could have stopped them from blowing the show." Smith asked him what he had done with the bodies. "Buried them in the woods," Pow replied. "The only trouble is that several others have dropped out of sight lately in the same way, and we're afraid the Jap commander suspects why."

When Bartlett learned of the U.S. prisoners so close to his camp, he ordered two of his men to try to contact them, to encourage their escape and arrange a rendezvous. When Huffman and Harris made their break, it was a Free Thai Army patrol from Pattern camp that led them through the jungle to the OSS major. "Upon their arrival," Bartlett wrote, "a runner came and informed me that they had two Americans. I sent an armed guard of four men to pick them up and bring them to camp." At midday on July 27, the Morse transmitter at Bartlett's field station sent the following high-pitched stutter into the ether: "I HAVE TWO PRISONERS OF WAR WITH ME. NAMES ARE JAMES W. HUFFMAN NAVY AND LANSON H. HARRIS. BOTH ARE IN GOOD CONDITION. . . . PLEASE NOTIFY THEIR FOLKS. . . . PLEASE SEND PX AND SMOKES SOONEST."

With escapees to look after, the difficult supply situation Bartlett faced couldn't have come at a worse time. Since arriving in-country Bartlett hadn't received a single package of food. The airlift embargo angered him, especially because he had seen with his own eyes the drops B-24s were making to a Thai army camp nearby. Not that Huffman and Harris much noticed the shortage of rations. They were glad to be put to work in the mess, taking turns directing the preparation of whatever the Thais brought in from the jungle. It was the best duty they had had in more than three years.

Bartlett interrogated them, but gingerly. "He would get us apart," Red Huffman said. "You'd never know when he was going to ask a question. All of a sudden he'd turn around and ask you something. We gave him more information than he had ever had. We told him everything we knew. He was making sure he was getting the truth. Then he would have his radioman radio it to India." Soon after their arrival, Huffman and Harris were joined at Pattern camp by two English prisoners and an Australian. A much larger catch was in the offing. Bartlett informed Kandy that Tayang held 1,500 prisoners, had no planes, stored 25,000 gallons of gas, housed three radio stations but no radio direction-finding equipment, and had heavy machine guns but no larger antiaircraft emplacements. The information coming from the two Americans was voluminous. "WHAT PARTICULAR INFORMATION DO YOU WANT ME TO FIND OUT?" Bartlett asked headquarters. "WOULD TAKE A DAY TO SEND ALL THEY HAVE TOLD US."

Kandy responded the next day that it wanted the names of the *Houston*'s survivors, information about their condition, the location of prison camps, the total numbers of prisoners, how the Japanese guarded them, evidence of their cruelty, information about their attitudes toward war, specific conversations between POWs and guards, how the fall of Okinawa was influencing Japanese treatment of POWs, and how enemy morale might be lowered through propaganda.

One time Bartlett turned to Huffman and asked, "Would you sneak back into camp and warn them and tell them I'm coming?" It was a preposterous suggestion. Huffman refused the request in no uncertain terms. "Neither one of us would go, because we'd been prisoners for three and a half years almost," he said. Nevertheless, Harris and Huffman and their three Allied friends seriously weighed the option of reengaging with their enemy. In a July 28 radio transmission, Bartlett reported to Ceylon: "HAVE TOLD THEM THEY WOULD BE [EXFILTRATED] SOONEST. THEIR OWN WORDS QUOTE LET US STAY HERE AND HAVE A CRACK AT THOSE GD JAPS UNQUOTE. THIS FEELING EXISTS WITH ALL FIVE AND THEY ALL ARE STUDYING OUR WEAPONS."

They did some celebrating too. After the sailors' safe arrival at Pattern, there was a jungle feast in their honor. The main dish was monkey. Though the Americans declined the proffered plates, they had their fill of Hershey bars. Huffman broke out his two canteens and the ex-prisoners got "all hooched up" on the stout rice wine.

Huffman offered Bartlett a shot of it, but it seems the OSS man preferred scotch.

The most coveted treasure that the sailors turned over to Bartlett was the roster of *Houston* personnel, living and dead, kept by John Reas and John Harrell. With the disclosure of this priceless record, scores of families would finally know their loved ones' fates. On July 29 the information that Fred Hodge and so many others had tried for years to ferret out began flowing as beeps from a portable transmitter hidden deep in the Thai jungle. The bursts of secret knowledge—a roster of lost names, from "AGIN, G. L." to "ZABLER, W. E."—filled Pattern's outgoing Morse bandwidth for nearly a week. It was not until August 5 that Major Bartlett's radioman hand-keyed the last of the dots and dashes representing the 301 names on the list. Two days later he started sending a shorter list: the names of sixty-three of the seventy-seven *Houston* men who had met their end as prisoners of war. From that point on, Bartlett's mission was to ensure that as few names as possible were added to the roster of fatalities. The resourceful commander of Pattern camp began to figure out what he could do for the rest of the prisoners at the Tayang airfield.

CHAPTER 59

All our men are bang-happy and would give their eyeteeth to begin an extensive sabotage campaign against the Japs." So said Capt. Bud Grassi, head of the OSS base near Kanchanaburi, to Nicol Smith. He was chafing under the firm policy that blocked him from conducting overt actions of his own and forced him to rely instead on native proxies. "It's damned hard to take when Thais come to us with explosives that they have slipped out of Jap supply dumps. I can't help thinking how easy it would be to leave a few time pencils in these dumps, and no one would ever know what caused the explosions. We can also cut the Burma-Bangkok Railroad at innumerable places.

"Another thing the fellows are anxious to get at is rescuing the two thousand American, British, Australian and Dutch prisoners in the POW camp near Kanburi before the Japs kill them all off."

The people who ran OSS Detachment 404 channeled the joy they felt on locating survivors of the Houston into planning their exfiltration and eventual homecoming as soon as possible. There were several possible avenues—by PBY Catalina flying boat from the southern coast of Thailand near Prachuab; by boat from the coast up to Bangkok, then up to the OSS main airfield at Pukeo; or via a single-engine Lysander flown directly from Tayang to Rangoon, then to Kandy or Calcutta. Bartlett's men reconnoitered Tayang in case the last option was chosen. Evaluating the airfield's security level and obstacles to approach, the major recommended a dawn or dusk landing.

"The only difficulty anticipated in the arrangement to date has been the openly expressed preference of the two rescued seamen to 'stay here and have a crack at those GD Japs,'" Bartlett wrote. "It is probable that circumstances will compel this wish to be denied them."

If the British were to be believed, the Royal Army was planning an invasion of Thailand in November. Accordingly, Washington had urged the OSS leadership, "Keep cautioning [your agents] against overt action before Mountbatten strikes."

Inexorably the course was set for the war in the Pacific to end. By the middle of 1945, Okinawa had been taken, the last of the Japanese navy's strength extinguished. American aircraft ruled the skies. Grand plans were afoot to combine all of America's combat forces—almost everything already in the Pacific and whatever else could be brought over from liberated Europe—and throw it all against the Japanese home islands in a final strategic offensive, known as Operation Downfall. Free Thailand would contribute what it could. At Sattahip Bay, southeast of Bangkok, its small coastal fleet stood at the Allies' disposal. There were ten torpedo boats, four large gunboats, four submarines, and fifteen seaplanes. Several of those craft could operate as far south as Singapore, or even east to the Philippines. Though the supply of oil limited their radius, more was available on a black market fed by Japanese soldiers more than willing to steal it from their depots.

But a more imposing exhibition of naval power had already struck Japan's home islands. On the morning of July 14, as Lanson Harris and Red Huffman were slipping through the jungle toward their rendezvous with the OSS, the fast battleships *South Dakota, Indiana,* and *Massachusetts,* with the new heavy cruisers *Chicago* and *Quincy,* took station off Kamaishi, site of a great iron and steel works that adjoined the prison camp at Ohasi, where many *Houston* men were imprisoned, and trained their turrets inland. At 11:00 the *South Dakota* signaled to her sisters, "NEVER FORGET PEARL HARBOR."

At 12:10 P.M. the main batteries of Rear Adm. John F. Shafroth's task unit thundered out, hammering the coke ovens, hearths, and foundries near the prison camps for two hours. It was the first time that American naval gunfire hit the home islands. Over the next few days the bombardment would be joined by five more U.S. fast battleships, plus a British dreadnought, HMS *King George V*. Planes from the Third Fleet swarmed northern Honshu and Hokkaido, striking rail yards, harbors, and ground installations.

Jess Stanbrough was working at the power plant in Ohasi when the American sixteen-inch projectiles began raining down on the nearby camp. After the Tokyo fire raids, he had smelled the incinerated pine. When the bombardment of the Kamaishi ironworks started, he heard the low rumble down the coast. The guards explained that the imperial fleet was conducting gunnery practice. Having acquired a Japanese vocabulary of about five hundred words, Stanbrough and the others weren't fooled by the bid to save face. They had overheard mine workers conversing over morning tea: "Where were our planes?" "Well, we didn't see any. All we saw was the Americans." The Japanese always seemed to be talking about the bombers. Like the Allied attacks by air and from under the sea, the bombardment of Kamaishi claimed Allied lives. According to Stanbrough, "There was a lot of people that had been captured down on Wake Island and so forth in that camp that lost their lives. We had some eighteen or nineteen burn victims out of that. They brought them up to our place to try to do something. . . . Our medical boys—Navy guys—were over there pulling flesh off of them."

A season of fevered diplomacy was under way as the Allies stepped up pressure on the Japanese to surrender. On July 26, at Potsdam, Germany, Harry Truman, Winston Churchill, and Josef Stalin put forward a final demand for Japan to end the war via unconditional surrender.

> The prodigious land, sea and air forces of the United States, the British Empire and of China, many times reinforced by their armies and air fleets from the West, are poised to strike the final blows upon Japan. This military power is sustained and inspired by the determination of all the Allied Nations to prosecute the war against Japan until she ceases to resist. . . . We do not intend that the Japanese shall be enslaved as a race or destroyed as a nation, but stern justice shall be meted out to all war criminals, including those who have visited cruelties upon our prisoners.

The Japanese would invest some hope in the odd absence of reference to the Soviet Union in the Potsdam Declaration. Soon enough, however, what the Soviets were or were not doing would be of secondary significance. On August 6, a B-29 Superfortress with the name *Enola Gay* stenciled on her fuselage took flight from Tinian and released its epochal payload over the city of Hiroshima. Three days later another atomic device fell on Nagasaki. That same day Admiral Shafroth's battleships closed with the Japanese mainland and let Kamaishi have it again.

CHAPTER 60

At Tayang, near Phet Buri, Lloyd Willey saw a peculiar cloud move across the sky one day. It was like nothing he had ever seen before, streaked with multiple hues—purple, red, and yellow—and moving, it seemed, with unnatural swiftness. One of the Australian prisoners with him, who had taught at Melbourne University, told him that only a godawful explosion could have produced something so exotic.

A marked change had come over the guards. The Japanese ceased their daily routine of raising their flag and gathering in ceremony to bow to the emperor. One day they just stopped doing it. Willey had premonitions of what lay ahead as he joined a work party digging a six-feet-deep moat east of the airfield. "The Japs were very touchy about that moat. They wanted every side to be perfect. . . . All the dirt that was piled up, they put machine guns on each corner and they told our officers that the moat was to keep the Thais out. They said it was to defend the camp, but we knew the Japs were masters of deceit."

The Japanese willingness to kill prisoners was exhibited any number of times, perhaps most powerfully on December 14, 1944, when 150 U.S. POWs held on Palawan in the Philippines were ushered into an air raid tunnel and burned alive. Several of the doomed prisoners begged their captors to shoot them in the head, but the guards laughingly shot or bayoneted them in the stomach instead.

As fissures spread in the very core of Japan's great Pacific empire, the fate of prisoner and emperor alike lay shrouded in doubt. The atomic bombings reverberated within the halls of the imperial command long after their thermo-atmospheric effects had drifted southwest and bruised the skies over Thailand. According to an observer, a mood of "impatience, frenzy and bewilderment" gripped the Supreme Council for the Direction of the War when it convened on the morning of August 9. A rumor arose that Tokyo would be the target of the next atomic strike. This rumor, it appears, was the product of the desperate imagination and audacity of an American fighter pilot shot down over Osaka on August 8. Captured and tortured by a Japanese officer who demanded details about the new U.S. weapons program, the pilot said that the United States had a hundred more such bombs and that Kyoto and Tokyo would be struck within days. The short period between the two atomic attacks already carried out suggested all too powerfully that America might indeed have been able to continue them at will.

Yet as intercepts of Japanese military traffic revealed, a stubborn faith in Nippon's invincibility ruled the thinking of three of the six men who held the nation's fate in their hands. Army Minister Gen. Korechika Anami, Chief of the Army General Staff Gen. Yoshijiro Umezu, and Chief of the Naval General Staff Adm. Soemu Toyoda insisted that any terms of surrender carry four conditions: preservation of the sovereignty of the imperial throne, self-disarmament, Japanese control of war crimes proceedings, and no Allied occupation of the home islands. The conditions, if granted, would have given cover to Japan's militarists, who wanted to deny that they were ever actually defeated. Cooler heads feared that the aggressive demands would be seen as defiance and lead to further atomic bombings and fire raids. What conditions should be attached to the surrender papers was the subject of a clean deadlock, with three members of the War Direction Council supporting acceptance of the Potsdam Declaration with all four conditions, and three, led by Foreign Minister Shigenori Togo, favoring surrender with the sole assurance that the imperial system would be retained. The verdict breaking the impasse would be formally and finally given that night by Emperor Hirohito himself.

Japan's diplomats had tried to divide the nascent superpowers, confronting them by brokering a separate peace with Moscow. In the middle of July, Japan's ambassador to Russia had been informed that since Stalin and his deputies were away at Potsdam, the answer would follow on their return. On August 8, the Soviets had delivered that answer by breaking off diplomatic relations with Japan and sending their mechanized forces into Manchuria. Shortly before midnight on August 9, Emperor Hirohito joined his advisors in the air raid shelter in the basement of the imperial library. Noting the poor state of readiness of his defensive forces and the grotesque effects of the atomic blasts, he asked, "Since this is the shape of things, how can we repel the invaders? It goes without saying that it is unbearable for me to see the brave and loyal fighting men of Japan disarmed. It is equally unbearable that others who have rendered me devoted service should now be punished as instigators of war. Nevertheless, the time has come when we must bear the unbearable."

But as the intercepts revealed, the army remained unbroken in its defiance. On August 11, Field Marshal Terauchi, the commander of the Imperial Southern Army, which included Burma, among other regions, stated, "The plans of the Southern Army have changed in no way whatever. Each Army . . . will go ahead to strengthen its war preparations more and more." That same day, the chief of the Army General Staff announced, "The Imperial Army and Navy shall by no means return the sword to the scabbard."

On August 13, the U.S. Twentieth Air Force took the war of persuasion directly to the Japanese people when B-29s rained on Japanese cities not bombs but leaflets with transcripts of the surrender negotiations. The air in Tokyo was thick with intrigue and the latent energy of rebellion. It seemed possible that either domestic opposition or a military coup might overthrow the emperor. Fear of the latter was well grounded and immediate. Any number of high-ranking army officers had serious doubts that field commanders would comply with the terms of surrender. In the hidden depths of the Army Ministry's air raid shelter, a plot was taking shape to ensure that the rest of Japan did not either.

The field-grade officers who led the putsch pledged their allegiance not to the faltering emperor but to "the wishes of the imperial ancestors [which] constitutes a wider and truer loyalty to the Throne." There is evidence to suggest that their ranks included not just younger officers but at least one central figure in the army's planning and policy hierarchy. Like the twisted vision that seized the mind of Adolf Hitler as Soviet armies overran Berlin, the plotters saw the final immolation of the Japanese populace as a lamentable but just result of their failure in the war.

As the plotters tried to widen their circle, senior officers loyal to Hirohito unmasked their plan. On August 14 the plotters panicked and made their move. Lt. Gen. Takeshi Mori of the Imperial Guards Division was slain in a confrontation with one of the leaders of the revolt, Maj. Kenji Hatanaka. As Emperor Hirohito watched through the armored shutters of his palace quarters, the rebels occupied the Imperial Palace, winning the temporary cooperation of the Imperial Guards by presenting orders with the forged seal of General Mori. They tried to confiscate the phonograph recording that the emperor planned to broadcast that day, declaring the end of Japan's resistance. But the timely intervention of officers loyal to the emperor brought the Imperial Guards back to the side of law and order and stilled the rebellion that could have changed the fate of the world.

It took as long as two days for Emperor Hirohito's order to reach his commanders. As it descended upon them out of the blue, it induced disbelief, and doubtless led more than a few to contemplate mutiny by way of slaughter. Despite the horrors wrought by the U.S. bombing campaign, General Anami all along clung to a near-mystical belief that if the army summoned the will to continue fighting, "a road to success will somehow be revealed to us."

In Washington, concerns mounted over the fate of the estimated 15,000 American prisoners of war in Japanese custody (among an Allied total of 168,500). The instability of the political crisis gripping Tokyo, revealed to the Allied leadership via their code-breaking operations, created a chilling spectrum of possibility. Gen. George C. Marshall, the Army chief of staff, urged that any surrender negotiations with the Japanese require that Japan "immediately forthwith and without delay" transfer all POWs to staging areas for liberation by the Allies. The Allied governments that same day declared the Japanese people "individually and collectively" responsible for any harm that might come to prisoners of war. August 1945 was suffused with wrenching uncertainty as warring nations still numb from the pain of four years of total war lurched toward a final reckoning.

CHAPTER 61

What would Japan do with its prisoners? The question was in the mind of every POW. It concerned the White House, and even the Imperial Army's high command, who understood that their treatment of prisoners would affect Washington's handling of the postwar transition, even as their Bushido convictions protested that the surrendered rabble were worthless and might even pose a threat as a reconstituted military force during an invasion.

On the brink of liberation, prisoners in Saigon noticed that the guards no longer cared whether they worked or not. The guards asked them what this new secret weapon was that took the flesh off people, burned them to cinders, and razed whole cities. Visibly frightened, one of them asked Lost Battalion member Garth Slate, "Will they drop one on Saigon?" Then came the long-awaited news, spreading throughout the POW diaspora. It struck so many prisoners as a hollow anticlimax. The war was over.

Thailand had a great deal to lose from any last burst of Japanese rage. Ruth, as the country's regent and resistance leader, did not approve of anything that might put the tenuous truce at risk. He feared that the sudden appearance of C-47 transport planes at Tayang would be an aggravating incident that could be a prologue to tragedy. He declined to approve an exfiltration effort until conditions settled. Finally, approval was granted and OSS headquarters radioed Major Bartlett on August 16: "PRESENT PLAN TENTATIVELY APPROVED ON HIGHEST LEVEL INCLUDES COMPLETE EXFILTRATION ALL POWs IN PETBURI [sic] AREA BY AMERICAN C-47 AIRCRAFT. OUR INFO INDICATES 1500 POWs THERE INCLUDING 500 TOO WEAK TO WALK. TASK IS TREMENDOUS. . . . . POW EXFILTRATION BIGGEST OSS JOB TO DO AND HAS VERY HIGHEST PRIORITY. LET'S DO IT UP RIGHT. WE FURNISH EVERYTHING YOU HELP ORGANIZE POWs AND ASSIST MEDICS. ADVISE AS SOON AS FIELD READY TO TAKE SIXTEEN SORTIES PER DAY, SIXTEEN TO A PLANE."

The OSS parachuted in four more men to support Major Bartlett in the effort to retrieve the men at Tayang: Capt. Roger C. L'Hereault, Lt. W. B. Macomber, BM2/C Louis Pulgencio, and PHM2/C Van W. Pressley jumped from an aircraft making a food drop on the night of August 17–18. "COVER IS TO BE MAINTAINED UNTIL CODE WORD GOLDFISH RPT GOLDFISH IS GIVEN," Kandy radioed him. "AT THIS TIME YOU WILL PROCEDE [SIC] TO POW AREA BUT NOT BEFORE CODE WORD IS WIRED." Bartlett and L'Hereault received a transmission from a colleague: "SEE YOU AT THE MAYFLOWER."

Although Allied recovery teams for the Repatriation of Allied Prisoners of War and Internees (or RAPWI) were busily working under the auspices of the Southeast Asia Command, the OSS struck a secret agreement with their British clandestine counterpart, Force 136, to put Major Bartlett in charge of the Phet Buri area under the code name Operation Mainland. All Americans in Thailand west of the Bangkok River would be sent to Phet Buri for evacuation. Everyone else would go to Bangkok.

*

When the age of atomic weapons entered its third day, Jim Gee was thirty miles from Nagasaki, in a coal-mining camp in the mountains. He didn't notice the blast that leveled the city—by the latter half of 1945 explosions were so common around the besieged shipbuilding center that it was hard for him to tell one from another. But one day something very out of the ordinary happened. He and his fellow prisoners were called to the parade ground where just a few days before they had been exhibited to and scolded by the populace. A formal ceremony was under way. The Japanese apologized for the hardships inflicted on the prisoners and said they and the Americans were now friends. The Japanese turned over their weapons, and the camp commander ordered his people to surrender to the nearest dumbfounded American. "As soon as we found out in this camp that the war was over," the *Houston*'s Ens. Charles D. Smith wrote, "we kicked the Japanese out of their jobs, took their guns away from them and isolated them over in one side of the camp out of harm's way, so that we could go and come from the camp into the town at will."

The role reversal induced vertigo. A prisoner who had kept an American flag hidden in his effects fastened it to a flagpole and hoisted it over the camp. They set out into the countryside to forage. For every piece of food they received from locals, an item of commensurate value was given in return. They bartered their extra clothing for eggs, greens, and vegetables. They took no revenge. Within a few days the roar of Wright radial engines filled the valley, planes appeared overhead, and suddenly the skies were wondrously full of crates swinging from parachutes. Rocking to the ground came a bountiful harvest: candy bars, powdered milk, medicines, clothes. What they did not use immediately they took to the newly familiar countryside and traded for livestock, which they slaughtered on the spot.

"Hollywood couldn't have written a better ending," Jim Gee said.

*

The serenity that fell over the prison camps from Thailand to Indochina belied the racking implosions that at last stilled Japan's war machine. In Tokyo, some pilots were planning an unauthorized kamikaze reception for the U.S. ships gathering in the harbor. Tipped to the plot, the Imperial Army impounded their ammunition and fuel. At Atsugi Airfield, where General MacArthur was to arrive to direct the occupation, soldiers loyal to the throne subdued a navy captain who was furiously inciting a revolt, and removed the propellers from all the planes.

American aircraft littered the countryside with pamphlets printed in nine languages, instructing former prisoners: *Remain where you are, disarm the Japanese, show restraint, do not punish them.* The pamphlets also warned the Japanese that they were responsible for the prisoners. The prisoners seemed less interested in confiscating their captors' weapons than in drinking their sake.

On the morning of August 29, Lt. Col. Amos D. Moscrip from OSS headquarters flew to Tayang and joined Major Bartlett on the ground. Thirty-five American prisoners were already there, and fifty-eight more arrived by truck that afternoon. Moscrip wrote:

> I gave them a short talk regarding why we were there and where they were to go, how and when, and then we fell to in a huge party where generous supplies of cigarettes, gum, candy, razors, tooth brushes and paste, combs, mirrors, matches, Yank magazines, fruit juice, toddy, etc. were issued to all American POW's. The party lasted until 0200 the next morning, 30 August, during which time my team was very busy answering a multitude of questions for those news-starved Americans. Their physical condition seemed to be fair, from a layman's point of view, but they bore scars and marks of much suffering. . . . The American POW's presented me with an American flag that two of them had made in the POW Camp over a period of 8 months from scraps of material such as they could filch. This flag was about 4 × 6 feet and had been kept secret from the Japanese at all times. I promised them that the flag would fly until every American had left Tayang. I had a flagpole erected the first thing the next morning and the flag was raised in the presence of 5 Japanese officers and about 8 Japanese enlisted men. Through an interpreter, the ranking Japanese officer stated that he was very sorry but he did not wish the American flag flown at this time over the Japanese airfield. I explained that I wasn't interested in his wishes and after several exchanges of American and Japanese phrases via the interpreter, the Stars and Stripes whipped gaily in the breeze.

The first C-47 from Rangoon landed at Phet Buri bright and early the next morning.

The reality of freedom dawned slowly over them. Modern diagnosticians have ready labels for the psychological syndromes that beset them. But those labels didn't exist in 1945. "While the pictures may show the men to look fairly healthy, they weren't," Moscrip wrote. "It will take many of them months of good care and doctor's treatment to be able to regain their mental balance. It must also be remembered, and I think the narrative should bring out the fact, that these men were *the* survivors, that they were the fittest, and that many of the dead were left along the Burma-Siam Railway which they were compelled to construct. There wasn't a single POW among all of those who were evacuated from Petburi [sic] who were not at one time or another beaten by the Japanese." Operation Mainland's haul from Thailand and French Indochina was 530 Americans among a total of 2,013 Allied prisoners.

Over Tokyo, Navy planes were dropping food over the prison camps, the pilots revealing their exuberance through their ailerons and rudders as they showed off their combat-honed talents in low-altitude aerobatics. At Ohasi, Red Reynolds, the chronicler of the late president's 1938 tour on the *Houston,* was among the throng of prisoners marveling at an impromptu air show put on by a dozen or so U.S. dive-bombers. "They circled out and dived and wig-wagged," he wrote in his diary. "My God, grown men looking up, waving and shouting with tears running down their cheeks. I too was a big baby, but I'm proud and not ashamed. I've waited three-and-a-half years for this." As Reynolds recorded in his diary, one of the pilots zoomed in low and dropped a pack of Lucky Strikes, a book of matches, and a note reading, *Cheer up, boys, only a few more days—Ens. W. F. Harrah, 2221 East Newton St., Seattle, Washington.* "Boy he rates a bottle of Scotch from each man here," Reynolds wrote.

In Washington on August 28, OSS field agent Nicol Smith appeared at a press conference, declaring: "Anyone having relatives on the crew of the *Houston* can be very optimistic." That same day, American prisoners throughout southeast Asia began greeting their liberators, for out in Tokyo Bay a sight like no other greeted the residents of the capital city's prison camps. Gliding into view came the sleek gray hulls of U.S. warships, camouflage paint schemes bright and angular. As lead elements of the U.S. Third Fleet approached, led by the battleship USS *Missouri,* other ships came for the prisoners. Commodore Rodger W. Simpson's Task Group 30.6 happened to be led by the light cruiser USS *San Juan,* commissioned the day the *Houston* was lost and commanded in its early days by Capt. James Maher, the older brother of the *Houston's* Arthur Maher.

Several LCVPs from the *San Juan's* evacuation group, embarking medical parties, motored to the docks and tied up near Omori Camp No. 8. "The appearance of the landing craft in the channel near the prisoner of war camp caused an indescribable scene of jubilation and emotion on the part of hundreds of prisoners of war who streamed out of the camp and climbed up over the piling," Simpson wrote. "Some began to swim out to meet the landing craft."

Simpson was powerfully affected by conditions in the hospitals that his medics located. While he noted in his report the "almost universally helpful and outwardly polite" attitude of the Japanese, his outrage was nearly universal at the time: "With the end of the war, history started immediately to repeat, but we shall not be deceived again by the superficial friendship of this cruel race."

Thus began an eighteen-day evacuation process that would mark an official end to the ordeal. That day an Associated Press reporter was moved to poetry in his wire dispatch: "The hand that fills in the blank pages in the book of war began to write again today. It began on a page bearing the title 'USS *Houston*.' And as it started its journey across the paper, hope, like a swiftly-flaring spark, burned brightly again in hundreds of hearts in homes scattered across America."

Omori Camp No. 8, where Commander Maher was senior officer, was the first camp liberated. Its occupants were safely transferred to the hospital ship *Benevolence* in Tokyo Bay by the night of August 30. Before Maher received treatment, he requested to visit and personally thank the skipper of his brother's old cruiser, Capt. George H. Bahm. Shortly thereafter, the *Houston*'s senior surviving officer found himself with an invitation from Fleet Admiral Chester Nimitz himself to board the *Missouri* on September 2 and watch the Japanese sign papers of surrender. When Maher was taken to the ship and went aboard, he was greeted by a Naval Academy classmate. Rather than salute him, shake his hand, or embrace, by reflex of habit Maher bowed from the waist.

*

Word of the surrender took a while to trickle down to the men still imprisoned in Singapore at Changi. Sixty-nine Americans were held there. For varying reasons, mostly related to their health, most of them had stayed behind when the rest of the Americans were shipped to Burma or Hintok. When the railroad was done, the paltry few survivors of F and H Forces returned to Singapore. At Changi they enjoyed a comparatively lavish lifestyle, though the work of dismantling industrial machinery as quickly as possible and shipping it back to Japan had its expected share of anxiety, pain, and crisis.

To 2nd Lt. Miles Barrett, the highest-ranking USS *Houston* man in Singapore, the dramatically changing fortunes had been hard on the nerves. The possibility of liberation gave the prisoners a degree of hope that made fear possible again. "In many ways these weeks have seemed the most difficult of the whole war," Barrett confided to his diary. All along they had been scrapping for their survival. Then a ball of plutonium was crushed over Nagasaki, and six days later word arrived that Japan had accepted the Allied terms of unconditional surrender. The war over, the prisoners endured a few last *tenko*s, trying to hold down their excitement. Finally, on August 19, the prisoners' representative at Changi, an Australian colonel from F Force named Dillon, decided to press his luck, insisting on the immediate delivery of Red Cross supplies and the immediate release of prisoners known to be suffering in solitary confinement at the Outram Road Jail.

For Gus Forsman, the mind-wrecking routine there had never changed. Entombed in his routine of silence, he was not allowed to lie down during the day. He could only put down his board and sleep when the guard came by in the evening and issued a one-word command to turn in: *"Yasume."* Only once had the rigid routine ever deviated, about three months into his confinement, when he was allowed to take a walk outside the prison. It was a strange thing. The guards took six prisoners outside to water a garden. It had been their first contact with fresh air until that time. Forsman didn't understand the point of it. He knew only that everything the guards did was toward the purpose of what some psychiatrists would later call *menticide:* the killing of the mind.

But now faraway events had remade Forsman's world. There was light—the door to his cell opened and it flooded in, blinding him. He was ushered out and as his eyes adjusted he saw Capt. Ike Parker and Maj. Windy Rogers, considerably bonier and dirtier than he had known them before. They cringed at each other's stench.

Escorted by guards, they were taken to a well and instructed to draw from it. Forsman, who would have paid a thousand dollars for a Dixie cup full of water just moments before, drew three or four whole buckets, drank deeply—he would have jumped in had he found the strength—and began the long process of getting himself clean. He was guided to a stack of clothing and got dressed.

As the guards marched them toward the prison gate, Rogers was seized by a flash of horrible recognition. "They're going to shoot us

in the back," he said. "They're going to say we were escaping. By
God, let's give them a run for their money!" The frail men started
running. They tottered down the hill, trying to zigzag in order to
elude the expected hail of bullets. It never came. Perhaps the guards
couldn't draw a bead on the skeletons through the convulsions of
their laughter. The three Americans stopped at the bottom of the
hill and stood there, marveling at their survival, wondering what
was next.

A Chinaman rode by on a bicycle. Windy Rogers said something
to him, and he stopped to talk to the Americans. "The war is over."
"That's impossible," said the prisoners. "No. They boom-boom one
time. Japan finished." He urged them to head for Changi. Joined
momentarily by some other survivors of solitary confinement—
bomber crewmen, worn out from the special brand of torture the
Japanese reserved for "air pirates"—they set out on foot. After a
march that seemed like ten miles to Forsman, they reached the compound that three years earlier had been the portal to their ordeal as
guests of the Imperial Army. The guard at the gate didn't say a word.
Forsman noticed in passing that he was armed with a wooden rifle.

Up the road ahead, he saw a crowd of men coming toward them.
Since July 4 rumors had been circulating among the prisoners kept
at Changi Jail that ten prisoners had been executed at Outram Road,
possibly including some Americans. The rumors were never sorted
out, but that evening Miles Barrett, Crayton Gordon, John Wisecup,
and others saw how much worse life in captivity could have been.
Fourteen lost souls representing a hidden piece of the war's horrible,
slow-to-emerge truth came limping in their direction. There was a
mass embrace as they got introduced all over again.

Gus Forsman would not be convinced of his liberation until those
aptly named four-engine Liberator bombers were visible overhead,
this time dropping more than just Juicy Fruit wrappers. Crates of
C-rations, cigarettes, and candy, the bounty of a victorious nation,
spilled out and spouted parachutes. The volume was impressive, but
what moved Forsman most was seeing on the ground, amid the
windfall, a scattering of individual items, off-brand and different
from the bulk. Apparently some of the individual aircrewmen had
made their own personal contributions to the cause.

On September 7 an American flag flew over Changi Prison. "The
last time that I had seen that flag was when that ship went down,"

said Paul Papish, "the Stars and Stripes fluttering there at the mainmast." Prisoners broke out their own hidden stashes of goodies, reserve stocks of condensed milk and tins of sardines and rusty cans of
peaches and meat and vegetables, some of it hoarded since the innocent, early days at Batavia. They rooted through their bags, traded
this and that, exchanged home addresses, set their mattresses afire,
and raised hell, mostly because they could. Great and optimistic
promises flowed from their joy. The Americans would visit Australia,
see their Aussie friends, go into business together, start a chain of mo-
tels or something. At the end of the line, the men of the *Houston* and
the men of the *Perth,* soldiers of the Lost Battalion and sailors alike,
were bound as one crew.

★

The exodus led all of them home through Calcutta. John Wisecup
and Robbie Robinson were flown there in a C-47 from Singapore.
The ride by "gooney bird" over the Himalayas was an adventure. In
the thin, volatile air the plane pitched and yawed and soared and
plummeted, wings scarcely able to hold the sky. Down the center-
line of the passenger compartment a line was strung tight so that a
bucket could be slid to anyone who needed relief.

Wisecup and Robinson were in the air an hour when curiosity
seized them and they explored their aircraft. In a small galley area
between the passenger space and the cockpit, the two Marines found
a box of Butterfingers. They ripped into it, gorged for a while, then
returned to their seats. They couldn't stop themselves from expecting a Korean guard to materialize somehow and punish their thiev-
ery with a bashing. When an authority figure did approach them,
she was bringing even better fare. They had never seen canned rations before. They tore into them. A few minutes later, one of the
aircrew returned to them and handed them a first-aid kit. They
didn't understand why until they looked at their fingers and realized
they were dripping blood, split and slashed by the sharp edges of
the tins.

At Calcutta, they shambled down the ladder, still somehow afraid
that the rations hidden in their clothes would spill out and betray
them. They expected to be searched, the contraband confiscated. But
they got away with it; they were survivors, which meant they always
had. Shown to the relative opulence of the 142nd General Hospital,

they unloaded the rations and slid them under their mattresses. Someone came for them, saying they were wanted in the mess hall. They went there and found awaiting them a dinner of ham, steak, and eggs.

At Calcutta, most of the exfiltrated prisoners ate like fiends. Some of them, their metabolisms still calibrated to starvation, couldn't handle the rich fare. Given their back pay, they immediately found the chance to spend it on liberty. They went AWOL if they felt like it. They weren't taking orders from anybody. But the trouble they spent ducking the MPs was generally wasted. The authorities avoided ordering the fragile evacuees to do anything. They *asked* them instead. "They learned right quick not to come out with all these orders," said Garth Slate. " 'You do this now' and 'You better do this' and 'You've got to do that' and 'Oh, you got to do this' went out the window." That appears to be the extent of the psychological accommodation most of the ex-prisoners received from the military.

Some of them went outside to play baseball. John Wisecup had some work to do to get his fastball back, but at least there were no guards on hand to tell him how to do it. A well-meaning nurse rushed out to warn them that if they didn't put their shoes on, they'd be liable to get sick, not to mention lose face with the natives. There was laughter all around.

One night Gus Forsman huddled with Crayton Gordon, just talking about everything, coming to grips with the anticlimactic reality of freedom. Forsman smoked Chesterfields until his tongue swelled, racing with his Army friend to close the circle of the story of how a great U.S. warship had gone down in battle and released its survivors into a horrible and deadly, yet sometimes unforgettably life-affirming, ordeal that led them to this place in the heart of the unlamented Greater East Asia Co-Prosperity Sphere and the once and future Asiatic Station. Injuries to the body were fast-healing. The wounds to the psyche bled freely. They would for a while. It would be more than a few decades before he would ever speak comfortably of the experience again.

CHAPTER 62

Red Huffman and Lanson Harris were flown on a British Lysander directly from Pattern camp in the Thai jungle to Rangoon. On the tarmac there, they boarded a C-47. Huffman mentioned to the pilot that in better days Harris had done a little flying. The pilot seemed to appreciate what it meant and offered him the controls. For the first time since SOC floatplanes last flew from the *Houston,* Harris stretched his wings. Hands on the yoke, he turned and looked back into the passenger compartment. Somebody snapped a photograph. Then the two engines roared, the plane rolled and rose, and the former residents of Serang and Bicycle Camp and the *Dai Moji Maru* and Changi Jail and Thanbyuzayat and 80 Kilo Camp and Tamarkan and Phet Buri and Pattern camp set out for a world of more hospitable names, from Rangoon to Karachi and from Karachi to Calcutta.

At the 142nd General Hospital, they were given physicals and medication, then shown to a truckload of khakis and told to help themselves. They got showers and were deloused and fed. They were told that as soon as their worms got cleared up, they could go home. Every morning Harris went to the lab to have his stool looked at, and each time was told he had to stick around for treatment of his parasites. One day after a few weeks of failure, Red came hurrying over to him. "He had a piece of paper, like a government check, same color, same shape," Harris recalled. *"Good for one priority passage to the USA,* it said. 'I got rid of my worms!' Huffman announced.

"I said, 'Goddamn it, Red, you're not leaving me here. You go over there and crap in a box and tell them you're Harris.'" And that's what Huffman did.

They flew to Cairo and to Casablanca and to the Azores before beginning the final leg to Washington, DC. On that cross-oceanic flight, Huffman said to Harris, "You know the first thing I'm gonna do when I get home? I'm gonna take my girl down, and I'm gonna give her a tetanus shot."

"A tetanus shot? What the heck for?"

"Well, I'm so rusty, I'll probably give her lockjaw."

★

In Los Angeles, Jane Harris had received a Navy Department telegram saying that her husband was safe in American hands. The news came with a demand for strict secrecy, but Jane was not about to keep the news from family. A newspaper article appeared soon thereafter, describing how two unnamed USS *Houston* men had escaped from a Thai prison camp. "I put two and two together with the telegram I got, and I said, well one of those has got to be Lans."

He called her as soon as he landed in Washington. With no public transportation available thanks to the rush of postwar traveling, they settled for a few hours on the telephone. "We talked for a long time," Jane said. "It was unbelievable to hear his voice, that was for sure."

America's veterans of Asia Station came home to a nation in fervid celebration. But the jubilance was the flip side of an equally widespread ignorance of the costs. It would be decades before the culture of therapy took root and debriefings and psychological counseling became standard practice for men returning home from war's bloody funhouse. "This was all so new to everybody," said Jane. "The U.S. had had no experience with POWs. What do you do with them? Doctors at the veterans hospital didn't know how to cope with it."

In Washington, Howard Charles, John Bartz, and John Wisecup were ordered to the Marine Corps headquarters building at 8th and I Streets. "They treated us like real psycho cases," Wisecup recalled. "They didn't put us in the hospital. What they did was put a corporal to stay with us all the time." For the few days they were there, that corporal shadowed their every move. He explained once, "I'm told you aren't responsible. I'm told to stay with you. You guys are *Asiatic*." The Marines were offered either a hospital stay, a ninety-day leave, or a return to duty. They were interviewed not by psychiatrists but by prosecutors. War crimes tribunals were gathering. They wanted names, descriptions, affidavits, depositions.

Returning to duty briefly, Wisecup had no great expectations. He wanted two things: his promotion and his back pay. He got promoted to corporal for his six and a half years in the service, but when he asked for his private's back pay the topkick at the headquarters told him that no Marine, private or corporal, had any business walking around with two thousand dollars in his pocket. Wisecup didn't disagree and it appears he didn't take the money.

He had a run-in with a mail clerk who refused to turn over his squad's mail to him unless he was wearing an NCO insignia. Wisecup erupted and nearly punched the kid's lights out. The incident got him a meeting with the post sergeant major—and convinced him that there was no place for him in an organization that required adherence to such Mickey Mouse rules. He told the sergeant major he was through with the Corps. "What are you going to do when you get out?" he was asked. "You don't know how to make a living." Wisecup told him he had all kinds of experience. He had, in fact, worked on a railroad. "I can work in the mines," he offered. "You'll be digging ditches," the sergeant major responded. "Maybe so," Wisecup told him. "But I'm going out."

The trick was to go somewhere. The trick was to do something, keep your mind busy with movement and learning and activity and happiness, faked if necessary, just to keep it from settling in on and picking over the details of the previous four years. But the details were exactly what the U.S. government needed as they were preparing for the war crimes tribunals.

In Washington, Harris and Huffman collected their back pay and bought new uniforms. At the Navy Department of Records building, Huffman was approached by a commodore, who asked him, "Do you know where the *Houston* was sunk?" Huffman said he did, and the officer showed him to a huge room with a two-story-high map. Huffman climbed a moveable ladder and put a star near St. Nicholas Point. The commodore expressed surprise, saying they thought the ship had gone down two hundred or three hundred miles from there.

Their first challenge on survivor's leave was finding their way back

to the west coast. With no mass transportation available, they hired
a cabbie with a seven-passenger DeSoto for ten cents a mile plus two
hundred dollars for the return trip. Seventy-two hours later they
were in LA. Reunited with his wife and his father, Harris told most
of his whole horrible tale. After the suffering and uncertainty his
folks had endured on the home front, they were entitled to it. No
one else, Harris seemed to think, was. The rest of the world would
never understand. "That was bad for him," Jane Harris said. "He
kept all this inside. When he came home, everybody wanted to
know something. I said to him he ought to write a book. But he
would tell just the funny things that happened, things that they
would do to the Japs in the camps—urinating in the baths and so
on." Adventure. Hilarity. End of story.

Lanson Harris was home in Los Angeles when the FBI summoned
him and asked him to look at some pictures. They wanted him to
identify some guards. Accusations had been made. Charges had been
leveled. "They asked me questions like, 'Did you see this happen?
Do you know if this happened? Is there anything else you can tell us
that happened?' I said, 'No, no, no.' I didn't tell them anything. If
they asked me a question—'Did you do this or that?'—I'd say, well
I guess we did, or I guess we didn't. I never gave any positive answers."

"You had a period of exuberance and then a sort of a pall comes on
you," John Wisecup said. "For four or five months, nothing could
make you mad. But after that, gee whiz, I had trouble." Back in the
Burma jungle Dr. Henri Hekking, farsighted and wise, had warned
his patients of the fresh ordeal that would confront them on returning home after the war. There would be consequences for those who
failed to take good care of themselves. "He told us the importance of
exercise, of the mental attitude of living," Jim Gee said. The transition was strenuous. Howard Charles wrote:

> I remembered the little amenities people in civilized circles
> took for granted, but I was not comfortable using a knife and
> fork, trying to remember that pants were to be zipped, that
> toilets were to be flushed, that car doors and doors to build-
> ings were to be opened for females, that money was to be kept
> in checking accounts which one had to know how to balance.
> I was awkward with all those things, and it bothered me. My
> body was loaded with hookworms and I could not gain

weight. I was fleeing from something, I knew not what, although there was no longer anything to fear or run from. I was nervous because I was nervous.

Slug Wright had trouble adjusting to the sound of a woman's voice. "We watched these pretty-looking girls coming to work with red lipstick," Jess Stanbrough said, "and we hadn't seen that in about three and a half to four years. . . . If you hadn't seen painted lips, it looked so strange, and we sat there and marveled at that." After his wife picked him up to bring him home from the naval hospital in Van Nuys, she told him she wanted a divorce. Such cruelty had never been devised at Outram Road. "Why didn't you let me know when I called you, or why didn't you let me know when I was in the prison camp?" he asked her. "You wrote. Why didn't you tell me then?"

"She said she just couldn't do that because she'd heard about all these other problems that we were supposedly having. I said, 'Don't you know that when you're in a bad situation, a little more trouble doesn't hurt?' " Stanbrough got his revenge by living well. After returning to Austin and continuing his studies, he and three other men founded a firm in 1955 that became the defense contractor Tracor, a Fortune 500 company that at its peak employed eleven thousand people.

Revenge was on Howard Charles's mind when he returned to Kansas "with the thought of finding my stepfather and dealing with him once and for all—possibly giving him a dose of his own blacksnake whip." He found Jim Evans and took him for a drive. They cruised out to a field near Partridge, where the older man had once left the soon-to-be Marine for dead after beating him with a whip. Charles stopped the engine, fixed his stepfather with a cold stare, and said, "I've waited a long time." It was then that the strength he had acquired through adversity, the seasoning by abuse that helped him fight through long years as a prisoner, enabled him to see his stepfather for the sorry, aged weakling he really was. Evans cowered, seeming to fear for his life. But Charles had said everything he needed to say with the icy stare. He resolved then and there that he would no longer go by the name his stepfather called him, Howard, that he would thereafter take the name Bob. He told his stepfather to just drive on home. Given the reprieve, Evans breathed a sigh, offered Charles a job, and hinted that he might let him inherit the farm. "Go to hell," came the reply. This war was over. All wars were over. And Bob Charles, like America, had won.

John Bartz returned home to Duluth and confronted demoralizing disbelief within his own home. "When I first came back my mother and all of us got together, the whole group, about forty of them, relatives and all. They wanted to hear the whole story. I started, and you could see skepticism come on people. I guess it's hard to believe that somebody would take a hose and shove it up your ass and down your throat and pour water up both ends. It's hard to believe that. You don't want to believe it. So I just quit."

He quit talking, but he could never quite keep his mind from sorting it through. "I couldn't sleep," Bartz said. "I'd wake up at night screaming." He found a way to fight through it. He would leave the house in the middle of the night, get in his mother's car, and "drive it like a son of a gun." A few times he got pulled over by the police. The local cops learned who he was pretty quickly. "Oh, you're that Bartz kid, prisoner of war?" they would say. "Well, I'm not gonna give you a ticket, but you'd better slow down. There are other people on the road."

Slowing down was the last thing Lanson Harris needed. He came back from the war, reenlisted, and attended flight school at Pensacola and Corpus Christi. "I was flying for five or six years, and I was feeling pretty good." His career kept him moving. He kept going until it came time to stop. Jane Harris said, "It came time when he was in twenty years, and we had our daughter then, and she was ten. And he said, 'Well, I'd better get out of the Navy before I kill myself.'" He got an engineering degree. Working for Northrop, he tested parachute recovery systems for the Apollo program. In the sixties, tired of government waste, he turned to a line of work he found much more rewarding: teaching junior-high wood and metal shop.

"I was absolutely lost, like a fish out of water," Otto Schwarz recalled. "I'll never forget. I arrived in Newark late in the evening. I had taken the five o'clock from Washington. I was all alone. Now I hadn't been home in seven years. Washington had gotten a call through the day before to tell my parents that I'd be coming home. I stood in the railroad station absolutely alone. I didn't know what to do, but I knew that I didn't want to be alone." And yet going home meant returning to the broken home he had been only too happy to leave in the adventurous blush of 1941. That adventure was over, and 1945 showed him a bleaker, less certain vista.

"I spent the next three months just drinking my way from one bar to another," Schwarz said. "Most of my old friends from the neighborhood were still overseas. I went back to Washington twelve days early because I was broke. I had to go back and get more money. Really, really absolutely lost! We should never have been left and released like that, you know. It's a really strange feeling because you really don't feel like a human being anymore after coming out of those jungles."

Wisecup retrieved his manhood quickly enough by joining the Merchant Marine and going back to sea, where he stayed for seventeen years. His postwar career took him to Japan, where he met and married a Japanese woman, his third wife. She would outlive him, but his long correspondence to friends after the war reveal a man at peace with what war had forced him to suffer. John Wisecup died in Tokyo in 2001.

The habits of a prisoner languished and rattled but never seemed to die. They drank their tea extremely hot, having learned in camp to gulp the brew fast so they could go back quickly for more. They preferred burnt-rice coffee to Maxwell House, and slept better on hard floors than plush mattresses. They prepared the meals they had fantasized about on the railroad and savored them. They met their wives or married their girlfriends, had children who would have to sate their curiosity about the Death Railway from sources other than Dad, flailed at ghosts in their sleep. There were mixed feelings about rice. Some never lost their taste for it; others, when they left the chapel after their weddings, insisted that their guests throw cornflakes. Charley Pryor craved sweets in the jungle camps but seldom ate them after his freedom. More than anything else, he craved fresh lettuce. To Don Brain, a good meal was a quart of milk and a head of lettuce held and eaten like an apple. They caught up with world developments—atomic bombs, helicopters, ballpoint pens, kidney dialysis, aerosol sprays, as well as the new faces suddenly prominent in the culture. They had never heard of this newcomer Harry Truman, but boy, had that youngster Bing Crosby become big stuff. CBS Radio was featuring a sensational new singer named Sinatra.

Jess Stanbrough did well enough in life, but the lesson he took from his POW ordeal had nothing to do with wealth. "I resolved that although I might never be rich, I'd never be poor or hungry. If you come to my house at Cape Cod . . . if anyone hears this, and they come visit, they'll see a nice freezer filled up with food. They'll ask me, 'Well, you're a bachelor. Why do you have all that?' I have a nice big house on a one-acre lot and a big freezer. I'll say, 'Well, that's called POW syndrome.'"

Dentists would marvel at how their tree sap fillings had held up over the years. Doctors would wonder at the dead spots on their legs where tropical ulcers had once rotted the nerves out from beneath their flesh. They cultivated deep religious faith, learned Oriental cooking, went to pieces at the first echo of taps.

In 1978, in Coldwater, Michigan, Bob Charles was immersed in his business interests, running a printing company, resolvedly avoiding Otto Schwarz's reunions, "determined that the war would not be the biggest thing that had ever happened to me." One day the war found him, in the person of Pack Rat McCone standing on his stoop. It didn't take Charles more than a second to see the twinkle in the old Marine's eye. He showed him around his plant. At once McCone was on his game, casing the facility like a warehouse in Batavia. He thought for a minute, then said, "Charlie, you've got thirty windows in this place. You've got guys running very expensive and dangerous printing presses, and they're looking out the window. Not only that, you're losing heat in the wintertime and losing cool in the summer. Why don't I cover them for you?"

Ever resourceful, famously adept at odd jobs using odder tools, McCone stayed for dinner and convinced Charles to let him stick around for a while. Before McCone retired to the cot that Charles had set up on his enclosed back porch, the businessman told his wandering shipmate, "When you go down to the lumberyard, mention who you're doing it for. Charge the company. Get what you need. By the way, you're on my payroll."

"Oh, no I'm not."

"Yes you are. Either that, or you quit right now."

"I'm not going to quit," McCone said, "and you're not putting me on any payroll."

"Why?" Charles countered.

"Charlie, if you don't know why, I can't tell you."

They knew each other as few other beings can know each other. And they had confronted ordeals few innocents could summon in their most fraught nightmares. In 1980, troubled by the seizure of the U.S. embassy in Tehran, Fred Quick, at the age of fifty-nine, seriously considered putting that experience to work. "If I had my way about it, I'd find forty-nine other ex-POWs and we'd go over there and relieve those folks," he told a reporter. "Anyone who's been through the torture I have can take what these Iranians are handing out standing on your head." But it would be gilding the storm clouds to pretend the Death Railway was always a source of strength. One day in 1996, more than twenty years after he retired, Lanson Harris got a letter from the Long Beach Veterans Hospital calling for a physical. When he went in, and he saw some patients getting examined by the medical staff, and the doctor closed the door, it seemed to pop some kind of a psychological membrane. "I don't know why, but all of a sudden I see these POWs. . . . Oh God, I was crazy. Next thing I knew the doctor had me and two guys were holding onto me. They put me in the hospital to keep me from committing suicide," he said.

Red Huffman lives in Santee, California, outside San Diego, as this is being written, seldom venturing into the traumatic territory of memory that might have defined his life had he allowed it. Like John Wisecup and so many others, he stayed busy with challenging work. After the war he signed on for service in the Navy's underwater demolition teams, seeing action in Korea. Like his Marine shipmate from New Orleans, he looked to the Orient to find a bride. Though his right arm is no good, his mind is sharp. Only recently, though, has he taken to sharing with his wife, Mary, the details of his war experience. They sit together and read out loud to each other what little has been written about the *Houston* and the ordeal of her crew. Huffman has little to do with the USS *Houston* Survivors Association anymore. Though it has held reunions faithfully since about 1948, Huffman has found it painful territory to tread, and if you don't feel the need for the powerful bond of love and brotherhood available there, what's the point? His partner in flight from Phet Buri, Lanson Harris, who is Huffman's equal in independence of spirit, lives just up the highway from him, in Irvine. They haven't seen each other in many a year and it seems they might never again.

The Association's guiding light has been Otto Schwarz. Second only to the heavenly spirit of Captain Rooks in his stewardship of the *Houston*'s legacy, the retired chief boatswain's mate and postal worker has organized most every significant event on behalf of the ship's memory. Anything that has touched on the old cruiser, its history, its traditions, or its people has gone through Schwarz in Union, New Jersey. "I always had the philosophy that whenever I have the opportunity, no matter how I have the opportunity, either newspapers or television interviews or anywhere, one-to-one meeting with people, I don't want the world to forget this. I don't want them to forget the *Houston,* first of all, because it was an absolutely gallant ship with a courageous crew. I don't want people to forget what men can do to men."

Schwarz has run the reunions long enough, and published the *Blue Bonnet* newsletters regularly enough, that no gathering ever really takes place in his absence. Even when he's not there, you sense his presence in things. He has donated his entire personal collection of artifacts to the University of Houston Libraries, whose Cruiser *Houston* Collection houses sixty-eight boxes of documents, artifacts, and memorabilia pertaining to the ship and grows with the passing of every survivor. With the actual survivors aging fast and traveling less, the survivors' children, grandchildren, nieces, and nephews are taking over under the auspices of the USS *Houston* Next Generation Organization, under the energetic leadership of Val Roberts-Poss, daughter of survivor Valdon Roberts. The Lost Battalion Association holds its own events in Dallas every August, and the children are well in attendance there too. They're animated by the spirit that drove their fathers, but so long as a half dozen veterans still show up at the reunions, they don't need to look too far for a hero.

CHAPTER 63

On September 22, 1945, a field party of sixteen British and Australian troops from the War Graves Commission, accompanied by a Japanese interpreter named Takashi Nagase, a veteran of the Kempeitai's counterintelligence branch at Kanchanaburi, left Bangkok in a caravan of *atap*-roofed wagons and began a three-week journey up and down the full length of the railway searching for the dead. By the time they reached Thanbyuzayat and returned to Bangkok, they had located 144 cemeteries, innumerable scattered roadside graves, and more than 10,000 bodies.

The Allied War Graves Registration determined in 1946 that the total deaths among Allied POWs in the Pacific numbered 12,399. Of the 270,000 native laborers or *romusha* on the line, 72,000 were counted as fatalities, although the actual number of deaths may be three times that high. More recent estimates put Allied POW deaths at 16,000 and *romusha* deaths at more than 200,000.

If the scale of these numbers does not approach, say, Russian losses in World War II or the number of Jewish victims murdered in the Holocaust, the horror that underlies them matches anything in human annals. When the war was over, a sweeping effort was made to gather evidence and bring to justice those responsible.

The proceedings of the International Military Tribunal for the Far

East began on May 3, 1946, in Tokyo. The indictment brought fifty-five charges against twenty-eight defendants, all of them high-level generals and ministers, including Prime Minister Hideki Tojo. Absent from the indictment was the very figure who seemed to animate Japanese wartime decision making with a divine imperative, Emperor Hirohito himself. Though Pulitzer Prize–winning historian Herbert P. Bix has inferred the emperor's personal approval behind Japan's use of poison gas in China, the experimental use of bacteriological weapons in China in 1940, and the annihilation campaigns against Chinese communists in 1941, General MacArthur lobbied that the first grandson of Emperor Meiji be left out of the indictment in order to stabilize the delicate process of postwar reconstruction and reduce the risk that Japan might look to the Soviets for friendship after the war.

With Prime Minister Tojo left as its highest-ranking target, the indictment accused the defendants of conspiring to wage aggressive war and "murdering, maiming, and ill-treating prisoners of war [and] civilian internees . . . forcing them to labor under inhumane conditions." Chief U.S. prosecutor Joseph B. Keenan said to the press: "It is high time, and indeed was so before this war began, that the promoters of aggressive, ruthless war and treaty-breakers should be stripped of the glamour of national heroes and exposed as what they really are—plain, ordinary murderers." The earliest American articulation of the legal-moral basis of Keenan's vigor had come from Secretary of State Daniel Webster, who said in 1842: "The law of war forbids the wounding, killing, impressments into troops of the country, or the enslaving or otherwise maltreating of prisoners of war, unless they have been guilty of some grave crime; and from the obligations of this law no civilized state can discharge itself." These principles were codified in the Hague Convention II of 1899 in an annex entitled "Laws and Customs of War on Land," and supplemented by the Hague Convention IV of 1907, signed by forty-one nations, ratified by twenty-five including Japan. During World War I, in 1917, the U.S. Department of State held that Hague was not contractually binding because all warring nations were not signatories to it, but that "in so far as the rules set forth in the convention are declaratory of international law, they are of course obligatory as being part of the law of nations." This would be the legal interpretation that made Japan's calculated refusal to ratify the Geneva Convention of 1929 a moot point.

As the Allied prosecutors argued at Tokyo, Japan had committed itself to the Geneva Convention of 1929 on January 29, 1942, when Foreign Minister Shigenori Togo responded with these words to American and British inquiries on Japan's intentions: "Japan strictly observes the Geneva Convention of July 27, 1929, relative to the Red Cross, as a signatory of that Convention. The Imperial Government has not yet ratified the Convention relating to the treatment of prisoners of war of 27 July 1929. It is therefore not bound by the said Convention. Nevertheless it will apply *mutatis mutandis* [meaning 'with suitable or necessary alterations'] the provisions of that Convention to American prisoners of war in its power." What was a suitable or necessary alteration would be dealt with at trial.

By the time the last of 419 witnesses were heard and judgment made, the trial transcript filled 49,858 pages. The verdict came in the form of a 1,218-page opinion, which was signed by nine of the eleven justices assigned to the tribunal and rendered on November 12, 1948. It sentenced seven defendants to death, sixteen to life imprisonment, and two to shorter prison sentences. Two defendants died during the trial, and one was removed to a psychiatric hospital for treatment. Those condemned to die were dressed in U.S. Army salvage work clothing and hanged on December 23, 1948. These included Prime Minister Tojo and Lt. Gen. Heitaro Kimura, who as chief of the Burma-area Japanese Army in August 1944 approved orders to use Allied prisoners on the railway project.

According to the testimony of Tadakazu Wakamatsu, the head of transportation and communications for the General Staff, the decision to build the railway was made in the summer of 1942 by Chief of Staff Hajime Sugiyama, Minister of War Hideki Tojo, and Vice Minister of War Kimura in response to a request from the Southern Army.

United Press Tokyo war crimes trial correspondent Arnold C. Brackman wrote, "To observers in daily attendance at the tribunal, the prosecution's evidence always appeared to sink from bad to worse. Whenever I thought we had hit rock bottom of Poe's indescribable pit, we descended, to our shock, to a lower level of depravity."

Gen. Ryukichi Tanaka, the former chief of the Military Affairs Bureau, testified that Tojo had ordered "all prisoners of war to engage in forced labor" at a meeting of War Ministry officials in 1942 at Ichigaya, in the very building where the Tokyo tribunal sat. There was British testimony of coolies being forced to wear weights tied to their privates to amuse their captors; Chinese patients had glass rods inserted into their vaginas; "sick coolies were used for the practice of judo and thrown over the shoulders of Japanese."

On March 26, 1946, Prime Minister Tojo testified under cross-examination: "The Japanese idea about prisoners is very different from that in Europe and America. In Japan, it is regarded as a disgrace [to be captured]. Under Japanese criminal law, anyone who becomes a prisoner while still able to resist has committed a criminal offense, the maximum punishment for which is the death penalty."

A document from a Japanese agency known as the Central Investigating Committee Concerning Prisoners of War detailed the chain of responsibility on the Death Railway that ran from the NCOs and junior officers who ran the work camps to the Fifth and Ninth Railway Regiments, the Railway Inspection Office, the South General Army, the Imperial General Headquarters, and the Ministry of War itself. Sir Arthur Comyns Carr, the associate prosecutor for the United Kingdom, stretched rhetoric only slightly in calling this unofficial document "the confession of the Japanese Army with regard to the Burma-Siam railway." If it fell short of that, it certainly at a minimum revealed that Prime Minister Tojo's high command, and perhaps even the emperor, was in the loop regarding the use of prisoners as slave labor.

Some justice had been meted out privately, by the ex-prisoners themselves, after hostilities ceased. In Saigon, some Australians caught up with a guard who had been particularly cruel on the railroad, killing several of their countrymen in cold blood. They found him in civilian clothes, his distinguishing scar visible on the back of his neck. Afterward, all they would say was, "Well, he ain't going back to Korea. He's not going back."

An American survivor of the Death Railway told an interviewer:

> I had a debriefing by a lieutenant colonel who was an attorney, and he wanted to know about atrocities. When I told him some of the things that we had done against the Japanese, he threatened me that if I ever told it, he would have me court-martialed. We did some terrible things to those people, and I'm not going to tell you some of the things I did. But I did

some terrible things. I killed some people in prison camp. We poisoned them—not with poison but with bamboo arrows. I better shut up. Anyway, that's the end of that. But some of the other guys did some terrible things, too, as well. They were trying to get the Japanese, and we were, too. But mine was selective, and I'm sure the others did, too. We did not go out indiscriminately to do anything bad.

What was done in the jungle stayed in the jungle. More than a few guards who probably deserved it were given railway justice and left to rot. Either the U.S. Army lawyers didn't like what they were hearing or the Americans didn't like what they were asking. The Tokyo proceedings featured no American witnesses to the Death Railway atrocities. That work fell to Australians and Britons, notably Lt. Col. John M. Williams, commander of the 2/2 Pioneers, alongside whom the Lost Battalion had fought on Java, Lt. Col. Albert E. Coates, the superb doctor who ran the hospital at 55 Kilo Camp and later the larger one at Nakhon Pathom, and Col. Cyril Wild, a British survivor of F Force and war crimes investigator. They etched into the trial record—and doubtless into the minds of all in attendance—the rank horror of the three-year struggle to survive in the jungle.

While the Tokyo tribunal was the main event, the Pacific counterpart to Nuremberg, a total of 2,200 trials were conducted by U.S., Australian, British, Chinese, Dutch, Filipino, and French authorities in forty-nine locations between the end of the war and April 1956. The proceedings in Manila, Shanghai, Yokohama, Guam, Kwajalein, Rabaul, and elsewhere produced more than 4,300 convictions, 984 death sentences, and 2,519 prison sentences.

The Singapore proceeding, run by the Australian Army, targeted several lower-level commanders of the railway, including Lt. Col. Yoshitada Nagatomo of Branch Three, Maj. Totare Mizutani of Branch Five, and Col. Hirateru Banno, who nominally presided over F Force's evisceration by disease. The indictment charged Nagatomo with the executions of five Allied prisoners at Thanbyuzayat, as well as the broader accusation, leveled at him and his fourteen co-defendants, of killing and harming prisoners in the construction of the railway.

The voice of a ghost came back to haunt them. It was that of

Brig. Arthur Varley, who had buried his meticulously kept diary in a grave plot at Thanbyuzayat before he left for Singapore to board the *Rakuyo Maru* for his fatal rendezvous with U.S. submarines in Convoy College. Per his instructions, the diary was recovered in July 1946 and entered as evidence at Singapore. Nagatomo's own famous speech evidently came back to haunt him too. *We will build the railroad if we have to build it over the white man's body. You are merely rubble . . . and there will be many of you who will not see your homes again.* Those words spoke for themselves. "Those words hung him," Lloyd Willey said. At nine A.M. on September 16, 1947, at Changi Jail, Colonel Nagatomo swung from the gallows.

A regime was found liable for the acts of its officers. Individual commanders were found liable for the conduct of their underlings. It was the reverse of the U.S. experience in the 1930s Mafia prosecutions, where the bosses went free while the soldiers did time. Reflected in the three dissenting voices on the Tokyo tribunal and in legal commentary that continues to this day, there was no small degree of controversy over the standard of liability used to convict Japanese officers such as General Yamashita, the "Tiger of Malaya," who was held culpable for the acts of his men. Save Emperor Hirohito himself, as well as any number of unnamed and unknowable individual guards, the men responsible for the ordeal of the Death Railway were dealt with by the long arm of international law.

The question of reparations and individual compensation proved equally tricky and frustrating to the ex-POWs who sought it. The War Claims Act of 1948 created a fund to pay out lump-sum compensation to ex-prisoners of war and civilian internees. From seized and liquidated Axis assets of $228 million, a prisoner was entitled, under the 1952 amendment to the act, to $1 per day if he could prove that the enemy failed to feed him as required by the 1929 Geneva Convention. An additional $1.50 per day was payable if he was subjected to "inhumane treatment." The full $2.50 per diem stood to bring the average railway survivor a total of about three thousand dollars. If he failed to claim his piece by the statutory deadline, March 31, 1955, he received nothing. The 1951 Multilateral Peace Treaty with Japan, meanwhile, permanently blocked his right to sue for anything more.

The peace treaty repeatedly thwarted lawsuits and legislation aimed at extracting money from either the Japanese government or

its corporations, which, POW advocates say, had been unjustly en-
riched by the slavery of Japan's war prisoners. The absence from the
Tokyo indictment of corporations such as Mitsubishi, which ran the
huge prisoner-staffed shipyard at Nagasaki and sold the crossties
that the army used to build the railway, was an outrage to POW
groups. It led to the passage by the 107th Congress of the Justice for
United States Prisoners of War Act of 2001, which tried to revive
World War II–era claims against Japanese nationals that were barred
by the 1951 treaty. But since the State Department considered that
treaty "the cornerstone of U.S. security policy in the Pacific region,"
a position that most courts found persuasive, those suits went
nowhere. "A great nation does not repudiate its treaties," said State
Department legal counsel William H. Taft IV at a House hearing on
the bill. At a time when a litigation-conscious U.S. Congress was
granting individually tailored multimillion-dollar awards to families of victims of Islamic terror attacks, Taft seemed content to require veterans to look to that same body, not overseas private
defendants, for recompense, even if in granting a $2.50 per diem to
prisoners our legislature had long ago exhibited its essential disin-
terest in the men who lived and died to build the Death Railway.

*

The war over World War II continues, with some states such as
California permitting lawsuits against Japanese defendants, and
with some courts in Japan ruling in favor of plaintiffs with restitu-
tion claims. It was a Mitsui executive who predicted that if the
zaibatsu—Japan's great banking and industrial combines—were destroyed by war crimes tribunals or private litigation, Japan would be
fertile ground for communism. Yet it was Mitsui Mining that in
2002 was ordered by the Fukuoka District Court to pay 165 million
yen ($1.45 million) in restitution to fifteen Chinese nationals who
worked as slaves in the prefecture's mines during the war. Un-
avoidably the wheels of time move faster than the wheels of jurispru-
dence. By the time the appeals are exhausted, few of the survivors
will be left to savor any victory. They are living to see, however,
Japan finally apologize for its well-documented atrocities. In May
2005, Prime Minister Junichiro Koizumi, in Amsterdam to meet
with his Dutch opposite number, Jan Peter Balkenende, said,
"Humbly accepting the fact that Japan inflicted grave damage and

pain on people of many countries including the Netherlands during World War II, we would like to deeply reflect on this and offer heartfelt apology."

More than a few *Houston* men resolved to get justice on their own terms. When Charley Pryor was in South Korea during the Korean War, he kept an eye out for targets of opportunity unrelated to the current needs of the U.S. Marine Corps. He meant to get even with his onetime Korean guards. "If I had ever seen three or four of these guys, I'll tell you they would have suffered unusual consequences. . . . I would have made a horrible example out of four or five of them that I can name right now." But some mellowed in the knowledge that bitterness and vigilante fantasies took a price. "When you harbor something like that over a period of years, it hurts you as much or more than the people you have these feelings against," said Roy Offerle, who buried his brother in the jungle. "There's no use in it. Really. There was a war. They did things wrong. Maybe other people had done things wrong. But I have no animosity, really."

Once upon a time, Gus Forsman dreamed of revenge. Returning home to Iowa, he was eager to have another assignment, but the Navy couldn't find his records. He restlessly tolerated the bureaucratic stasis for a while before demanding and getting a discharge, whereupon he enlisted in the Army. "I wanted to volunteer to go to Japan for one thing. I planned on beating some heads over there," he said. The Navy knew his history in Asia and wouldn't have let that happen. When the Army discovered his status as an ex-prisoner of war, it decided to keep him from getting into a situation that both he and Uncle Sam might regret. "They figured I'd go over there on a revenge deal," he said. He wound up quietly retiring in 1964 before getting a recall four years later to go to Vietnam with the 269th Aviation Battalion, an assault helicopter outfit. Though he had a well-rooted case of post-traumatic stress disorder when he arrived in theater, it never kept him from doing his job. He earned a promotion to first sergeant.

Sixty years after the war, revenge was the farthest thing from Forsman's gracious mind. At the USS *Houston* reunion in 2005, the final year of his life, he rolled through the halls of Houston's Doubletree Allen Center just radiating warmth and cheer, happy to talk about what he had seen, endured, and done, and not in the least held back by the wheelchair he used or the oxygen cannula he wore.

The hospitality room buzzed with shared memories, small talk between big hearts. A television set ran the latest documentary of interest, people poring over a large conference table full of rare historical documents, photographs, books and manuscripts. At the previous year's gathering, the centerpiece on that table was a large transparent case holding a six-foot scale model of the *Houston*. The father and son who built it had no personal connection to the ship. They hauled it down from Ohio to show off their labor of love. Like all visitors who show up with a sincere interest, they are welcomed as family. Like the state of Texas itself, the *Houston* veterans and the "Next Generation" of their kin adopt new friends without formality.

The last veterans of the American Civil War were passing away as the veterans of World War II sank their roots into postwar life back home, beginning a new cycle of trauma and recovery. As this book nears publication, America is not far from looking at World War II just as it does at its Civil War—that is, without living participants to learn from. Too soon, the only available sources to study will be the written and recorded ones. No voices will be left, except those that are preserved on audio recordings by relatives with enough foresight and nostalgia—a rare combination of virtues—to do this service to history.

Historian Ronald Marcello's three-decade quest to record and preserve the stories of the Death Railway while the memories that housed them were still fresh has produced a sprawling collection of interview transcripts that resides at the University of North Texas in Denton, the home turf of the old 131st Field Artillery. To immerse oneself in these stories of witness, most of whose tellers are long dead, is to touch the sentiment that moved Stephen Crane to write his 1896 short story "The Veteran," about the gallant death of a Civil War veteran who, long after his war, ran into a burning building to save a pet:

> When the roof fell in, a great funnel of smoke swarmed toward the sky, as if the old man's mighty spirit, released from its body—a little bottle—had swelled like the genie of fable. The smoke was tinted rose-hue from the flames, and perhaps the unutterable midnights of the universe will have no power to daunt the color of this soul.

After the war, Thailand bought the concrete bridge at Tamarkan from the Allies for $2.5 million. It has been big business for the

tourist bureau ever since the movie came out, with tours and
T-shirts and bumper stickers and vendors' booths standing in com-
mercial tribute to one of the Pacific War's darkest episodes. The
"River Kwai" today buzzes with motorboats and the kinetic pursuits
of water sports enthusiasts under the steel bridge, which still stands
against the glittering backdrop of a tourist bazaar that efficiently
monetarizes the area's sad past. At the annual fall festival, organizers
pipe in sound effects to simulate bombing and antiaircraft fire. The
kickoff of the 1990 event was marred by the discovery of a mass
grave of *romusha* at Kanchanaburi. But the show went on. It always
does. The bumper stickers and T-shirts sell briskly.

The privately funded Thailand-Burma Railway Centre does the
more solemn work of remembrance. Founder and curator Rod
Beattie has built a library, memorial, and gallery devoted to educat-
ing the public about the railway. Though it opened only in January
2003, it is the product of Beattie's decade-long quest to walk the
right-of-way, map it, capture its history, and teach it to others. A
Buddhist shrine erected by the ex-Kempeitai interpreter Takashi
Nagase in 1986 can be found near the bridge site as well. In 1976,
Nagase organized a reunion of Japanese and American veterans of
the railway.

Twelve hundred miles to the south, the wreck of the *Houston* slumbers off Panjang Island, its crew still standing watch in Sunda
Strait, as her survivors like to say. The wreck, untouched by the cataclysmic tsunami of 2004, is disturbed only by the currents, which
keep a churning cloud of sediment roiling around her, warding off
all but the most determined intruders. In August 1973, Indonesian
salvage divers recovered the ship's bell and presented it to the
American embassy in Jakarta. Today it stands in downtown Houston,
in Sam Houston Park at Bagby and Lamar, atop a pink marble
obelisk memorializing the reciprocal sacrifices of the cruiser and its
city.

Edith Rooks and Fred Hodge got the answers they were seeking
and resolved themselves, as all bereaved relatives do, to living with a
hole in their hearts. But as the honors came and the encomia were
delivered, the hole filled with pride. In Walla Walla, a sweeping
park was named in Captain Rooks's honor. On June 29, 1983, at
Little Creek Naval Amphibious Base, in Norfolk, the Albert H.
Rooks Center for Tactical Development was dedicated as the new
headquarters for Commander, Surface Warfare Development Group.

Even as they are embraced by the Navy community—every officer and crewman on the submarine USS *Houston* (SSN-713) knows this story—they stand apart from it, for no ship's company ever endured an ordeal quite like the *Houston* men did. They stand apart from the POW community too because their brotherhood was forged at sea, aboard Franklin Delano Roosevelt's fishing yacht and the flagship of the Asiatic Fleet, where they fought the first major surface actions of the Second World War. Their closest brothers in the naval fraternity live halfway around the world. The Australians got on with their lives too—Lt. Frank Gillan as a marine engineer, H. K. Gosden as a rubber worker. The Americans have forged enduring friendships with them. Arthur Bancroft, head of the HMAS *Perth* Association, calls Otto Schwarz every Fourth of July to wish America a happy birthday.

They are running short on birthdays, and the world looks so different with each passing year. It is history's nature to be forgotten. As politics trumps geography and tradition, names change, conspiring against memory and lived experience. Burma is now Myanmar. Siam is Thailand. The Dutch East Indies are Indonesia, Batavia is Jakarta, Bangkok is Krung Thep. So many small places of outsized importance can no longer be found on the face of a map. History flees us. But entertainment is an edifice that never rusts.

If we are to believe David Lean's vision of Pierre Boulle's novel *The Bridge on the River Kwai,* the prisoners took fierce pride in building the best railway they could and developed a sporting competition with the Japanese who were working alongside them. There were no tropical ulcers or kneeling prisoners taking headshots and toppling into graves they had dug for themselves. There were no cholera camps, no afflicted wretches lurching through the monsoon to drain themselves into disease-ridden pits. If you believe what you read in James Clavell's *King Rat,* the British-run facility at Changi was the most notorious prison in Japanese-held Asia, not Outram Road or Kempeitai headquarters at Kanburi or 100 Kilo Camp or Hintok.

Time and again, the demands of entertainment have taken an essential aspect of historical reality and driven it so far as to outrun the truth. In *King Rat,* an American prisoner acquired vast personal power by breaking rules, accumulating contraband, and engaging in petty subversions that built a legend. Truth is different, more practical, and less or more interesting, depending on how much someone like John Wisecup or Pack Rat McCone intrigues you. Rules were there and opportunity was there. Survival was the product of one's ability to balance the two. "The fact is, the ones that obeyed the rules are the ones that are still there," said Seldon Reese of the *Houston*. "Now a few of us guys that did the stealing and swapping and trading, we got back home. Some of us got shot, but some of us got back home."

Frank Fujita had seen, somehow, a glimpse of everyone's future. On August 11, 1945, under skies droning with Wright radial engines, B-29s seeding the air with black specks whistling earthward, he pulled out his diary, put pen to paper, exuberant, and waxed Solomonic:

> Well after almost 4 years our fate is to be decided within the next few hours. We become free men or dead men in two days. If we are to be free we will emerge emaciated, weary fragments of humanity into a strange world, endowed with nothing but a few measly dollars, an unsurpassed knowledge of human nature and such a morbid philosophy on life that it will serve to ostracize us from society should we put it to use. We will be easy to please and hard to fool. We will be products of 1941 coming into a world five years in advance of us, the world of *Buck Rogers*.
>
> Most of us will be utterly lost, bewildered and cannot or will not fit into the new way of life and thus become the next generation of criminals, human derelicts or philosophers. Yet on the other hand a small percentage of the "horios" shall fit into society sufficiently enough to enable them to live out their span of life as the bourgeois. And yet a still smaller percentage, in years to come, will join the ranks of America's foremost men; men of medicine, men of science and government; men to become world famous in the aesthetic arts.— OR—we shall end our "horioship" as we would have been better off to have begun it,—in death.

He was right. Among the survivors—the resurrected ghosts of Captain Rooks's ship's company, the wayward Texans of the Lost Battalion—there was enough variety in the endgame of destiny to fulfill the breadth of the bomb-raid prophecy. Though every day thereafter they would fight their way through a monsoon-laced jungle of memories, and though they and their loved ones would wrestle with the legacy of an ordeal that claimed some four hundred lives per mile of track set down, most of them kept the memories where they belonged, boxed up, stored for exploration only when the time was right, held down and ignored at all other times. Most of them, in spite of it all, managed to do all right.

ACKNOWLEDGMENTS

Telling the story of a ship populated by more than a thousand souls is an exercise in arbitrary selection and undeserved exclusion. Confronted with the risk of overgeneralizing from unusual experiences, or missing the drama of a particular viewpoint in the rush of diverse stories, an author can only hope that his choice of narrative threads is faithful to the whole and that nothing in that selection leads to distortion or misemphasis. This version of the USS *Houston* story is the best I could do given the deep-piled source material and the unavoidable limitations of a single book.

My partner in this mission was Bantam Books senior editor Tracy Devine. As she did with our first collaboration, *The Last Stand of the Tin Can Sailors,* she invested innumerable days, nights, and weekends bearing down on several drafts of this manuscript, reading with a close eye and a well-tuned ear to craft the best possible reading experience. All surviving ambiguities, contradictions, non sequiturs, and overrenderings are mine. I am indebted to all the pros at Bantam who make publishing with that powerhouse imprint a pleasure, including Irwyn Applebaum, Nita Taublib, Chris Artis, Kerri Buckley, Loren Noveck, Glen Edelstein, Dina Katz, and Susan Hood. Thanks to Sue Warga for a keen copyediting performance, and to my friend and literary agent, Frank Weimann.

In capturing the wartime experiences of an inevitably thinning generation, I was saved more than once by the foresighted diligence of people—historians and loved ones alike—who years ago thought to document the ordeal of their elders. In taping their speeches, transcribing their reminiscences, and writing their own accounts of their lives, they enabled me to glimpse livelier incarnations of men who could give me only so much in person. The Oral History Program at the University of North Texas in Denton is a priceless repository of testimony from veterans of the *Houston* and the Lost Battalion, most of them long deceased by the time I began my research. This book grew from the dedicated work of Ronald E. Marcello and his colleagues, who have been doggedly gathering the witness of these men since about 1970. Julie Grob, the devoted keeper of the Cruiser *Houston* Collection at the University of Houston's M. D. Anderson Library, was an expert guide to the magnificent archival riches in her custody.

The members of the USS *Houston* (CA-30) Survivors Association, as well as its offshoot organization and eventual successor, the USS *Houston* Next Generation Association, have been kind in welcoming me into their society and friendship. Each of the four annual reunions and memorial services that I attended prior to completing work on this book was a lesson in humility and grace. Their love of their brethren and fathers, here and gone, is powerfully inspiring, and I am proud to be an adjunct member of the family. I appreciate the help of Steve Barrett, Ron Bennett, Vic Campbell, Dana Charles, Lin and Ron Drees, Joe Kollmyer, Larry Krug, Dawn Lodge, Sharron Long, Diane McIntosh, JoAnn Wychopen, Sherry Sylvester Ramsey, and especially Val Roberts-Poss, the Next Generation Association's *force majeure*. Otto C. Schwarz was a source of good sense and perspective throughout the project. He has been instrumental in sustaining the *Houston* survivors organization since he returned from the war.

Harold R. Rooks was most generous in sharing with me the vital materials in his personal collection, including his gallant father's papers and the correspondence between Captain and Edith Rooks. And special thanks to USS *Houston* wives, who kept an important charge in anchoring the lives of their husbands well after the world had largely forgotten their pain: Sylvia Brooks, Marti Charles, Shirley Gee, Jane Harris, Mary Huffman, Betty Maher, Jimmie Pryor, and Trudy Schwarz.

My friend Don Kehn Jr. shared with me valuable information, insight, and an infectious passion for all things relating to the *Houston*. Richard B. Frank and Paul Stillwell reviewed the draft manuscript and each saved me from a variety of embarrassments. Rod Beattie, Gordon Birkett, Robert J. Cressman, Roger Mansell, James McDaniel, Arthur Nicholson, Jonathan Parshall, Col. Tom Sledge, Barrett Tillman, Anthony Tully, Donovan Webster, and John Wukovits offered support, information, and encouragement. I thank Patrick Osborne at the National Archives in College Park, Evelyn M. Cherpak at the Naval War College's Cushing Library, and Mark Renovitch at the FDR Library. Thanks, too, to Linda Douglas, Bill Morgan, James Mullins, and Renichi Sugano.

My admiration for the veterans of the last flagship of the Asiatic Fleet knows no bounds. I am indebted to all of the *Houston* men who shared with me their harrowing sixty-year-old memories, as well as those I met at the various survivors reunions from 2003 to 2006: John E. Bartz, Howard E. Brooks, H. Robert Charles, Jack M. Feliz, David C. Flynn, Melfred L. (Gus) Forsman, Robert B. Fulton II, Frank E. (Ned) Gallagher, Ray Goodson, Lanson Harris, John E. Hood, James W. (Red) Huffman, William M. Ingram, Alois (Al) Kopp, Paul E. Papish, Eugene Parham, Clarence H. "Skip" Schilperoort, Otto C. Schwarz, Jack D. Smith, George D. Stoddard, and Lloyd V. Willey— all are men of grace and strength who inspire by their simple, mute example. I wish I could have known them sooner, and their shipmates long passed.

BIBLIOGRAPHY

Key:

CHC: Cruiser *Houston* Collection, Special Collections and Archives, University of
Houston Libraries, Houston, Tex.

HRR: Personal papers of Harold R. Rooks.

NARA II: National Archives and Records Administration II, College Park, Md.

UNT: Interviews conducted by Dr. Ronald E. Marcello for the Oral History
Collection at the University of North Texas (previously North Texas State
University), Denton, Tex.

OFFICIAL REPORTS

Commander, Destroyer Division 58, "Report of Action with Japanese on February
27, 1942. Events before and After" (by Cdr. Thomas H. Binford), Serial CF-05,
March 4, 1942. NARA II, Record Group 38.

Commander, Destroyer Squadron 29, "Notes on Night Actions" (by H. V. Wiley),
March 4, 1942. NARA II, Record Group 38.

Commander, Task Group 30.6 (Commander Task Flotilla 6), "Action Report
Covering Evacuation of Prisoners of War During Period 29 August 1945 to 19
September 1945" (written by Commodore Rodger W. Simpson), Serial 0024,
September 22, 1945. NARA II.

Commonwealth of Australia, Department of the Army, Military Court, Trial of
Japanese War Criminals, including Lt. Col. Yoshitada Nagatomo and others,
Singapore, August 5–September 16, 1946. National Archives of Australia,
http://naa.gov.au.

———. Trial of Japanese War Criminals, Major Totare Mizutani, Singapore, Case
No. 235/911, May–June 1946. University of California–Berkeley War Crimes

Studies Center, http://ist-socrates.berkeley.edu/~warcrime/Japan/singapore/Trials/Mizutani.htm.

———. Trial of Japanese War Criminals, Maj. Gen. Akira Sasa, Singapore, Case No. 235/1109, January 1948. University of California–Berkeley War Crimes Studies Center, http://ist-socrates.berkeley.edu/~warcrime/Japan/singapore/Trials/Sasa.htm.

"Convention Between the United States of America and Other Powers, Relating to Prisoners of War," ratified by the United States in January 1932. The Avalon Project at Yale Law School, www.yale.edu/lawweb/Avalon/lawofwar/geneva02.htm (last viewed by the author on February 27, 2006).

Glassford, Rear Adm. William A. "U.S. Naval Forces in Southwest Pacific, operations of," March 12, 1942. NARA II.

———. "Enclosure Accompanying Secret Letter," Vols. 1 and 2, Records of the Office of the Chief of Naval Operations, May 16, 1942. NARA II, Record Group 38, Box 1725.

Hamlin, Lt. (jg) Harold S., Jr. "USS *Houston* in Battle of Java Sea" (personal narrative), recorded September 14, 1945. NARA II.

———. "Statement of Lt. Cdr. Harold S. Hamlin," undated ca. October 1945. NARA II.

———. "Report of Service as Prisoner of War, March 1, 1942, to August 29, 1945," August 30, 1946. NARA II.

Hart, Adm. Thomas C. "Events and Circumstances Concerning the 'Striking Force,'" February 6, 1942 (with supplement dated February 17, 1942). NARA II.

———. "Narrative of Events, Asiatic Fleet, Leading up to War and from 8 December 1941 to 15 February 1942," June 11, 1942. NARA II.

———. "Supplementary of Narrative," undated, sent by Hart to Secretary of the Navy James Forrestal on October 8, 1946. NARA II.

HIJMS *Atago,* "Tabular Record of Movement," by Bob Hackett and Sander Kingsepp, www.combinedfleet.com/atago_t.htm.

HIJMS *Haguro,* "Tabular Record of Movement," by Bob Hackett and Sander Kingsepp, Revision 1, www.combinedfleet.com/haguro_t.htm.

HIJMS *Nachi,* "Tabular Record of Movement," by Bob Hackett and Sander Kingsepp, Revision 3, www.combinedfleet.com/nachi_t.htm.

HMAS *Perth,* "Action Narrative—Day and Night Action off Sourabaya, 27th February, 1942" (by Capt. Hector M. L. Waller), undated. www.fepow-community.org.uk/Research/London_Gazette/java_sea/html/body_enclosure_1.htm (last visited by the author on February 23, 2006).

HMS *Electra,* "Report of Action, February 1942, by Senior Surviving Officer" (by Lt. Cdr. T. J. Cain), undated. www.fepow-community.org.uk/Research/London_Gazette/java_sea/html/enclosure_2.htm (last viewed by the author on February 23, 2006).

HMS *Exeter,* untitled dispatch on the Battle of the Java Sea (by Capt. Oliver L. Gordon), October 1, 1945. www.fepow-community.org.uk/Research/London_Gazette/java_sea/html/appendix.htm (last viewed by the author on February 23, 2006).

International Military Tribunal for the Far East. Proceedings of the Tokyo War Crimes Tribunal. May 3, 1946–November 12, 1948.

Maher, Arthur L. "Jap Prison Experiences," recorded December 5, 1945. NARA II.

National Institute for Defense Studies (Japan), *Senshi Sosho* (War History Series), "Batavia Battle" (Battle of Sunda Strait), excerpt from vol. 26, *Ran'in Bengaru wan homen kaigun shinko sakusen* (Naval Invasion Operations in the NEI and the Bay of Bengal), pp. 483–487. Tokyo: Asagumo Shimbunsha, 1969. Excerpt translated to English by Akio Oka, courtesy of Vincent P. O'Hara and Don M. Kehn Jr. (What appears to be an alternative translation of this account, titled "Rough Translation of Official Japanese Account of the Battle of Sunda Straits," translator unknown, is in the collection of the USS *Houston* (CA-30) Survivors Association, Val Roberts-Poss, president, Round Rock, Texas.)

Reynolds, Gary K. "U.S. Prisoners of War and Civilian American Citizens Captured and Interned by Japan in World War II: The Issue of Compensation by Japan," Library of Congress, Congressional Research Service, July 27, 2001.

Rockwell, Rear Adm. F. W. "Supplementary of Narrative" (letters, reports, dispatches, photographs concerning activities in Luzon area, December 1, 1941, to March 1942), July 29, 1948. NARA II.

Royal Navy, Commander-in-Chief, Eastern Fleet. "The Battle of the Java Sea" (by Commodore J. A. Collins), March 17, 1942. www.fepow-community.org.uk/ Research/London_Gazette/java_sea/html/commodore_commanding_china_ for.htm (last visited by the author on February 23, 2006).

Royal Navy, Tactical, Torpedo and Staff Duties Division, Historical Section. *Battle of the Java Sea, 27th February 1942* (Battle Summary No. 28), 1945.

Smith, Ens. Charles D. "USS *Houston* (CA-30) and Experiences in Jap Prison Camp" (personal narrative), recorded September 18, 1945. NARA II.

Stivers, Ens. John B. Untitled statement. NARA II.

U.S. Army Air Forces, Historical Office. *The Tenth Air Force, 1943* (Short title: AAFRH-17), U.S. Air Force Historical Study No. 117, July 1946.

U.S. Department of the Army, Office of the Chief of Military History. *Political Strategy Prior to Outbreak of War*. www.ibiblio.org/pha/monos/150/ (last viewed by the author on February 27, 2006).

U.S. Department of the Navy. "Yangtze River Patrol and Other U.S. Navy Asiatic Fleet Activities in China," in *Annual Reports of the Navy Department*, 1920. Naval Historical Center.

———. Communiques No. 36 (February 1, 1942) through No. 57 (March 18, 1942). www.ibiblio.org/pha/comms/1942-02.html (last visited by the author on February 23, 2006).

———. "President Awards Congressional Medal of Honor to USS *Houston*'s Commanding Officer," June 24, 1942. CHC.

———, Office of Naval Intelligence. *Combat Narrative: The Java Sea Campaign*, 1943. http://ibiblio.org/hyperwar/USN/USN-CN-Java/index.html.

———. Bureau of Naval Personnel. "Service Record of Capt. Albert Harold Rooks," Pers. 2224b-RCA, April 7, 1943. HRR.

———. Office of Naval Records and History, Ships' Histories Branch. "History of

USS *Houston* (CA-30), compiled October 7, 1948. William A. Bernrieder Papers, CHC.

———. Office of the Chief of Naval Operations, Division of Naval History, Ship History Branch. "History of Ships Named *Houston*," compiled May 25, 1959. William A. Bernrieder Papers, CHC.

U.S. Department of State. "Postwar Status of Thailand," January 10, 1945. National Archives and Records Administration, Record Group 59. NARA II, Record Group 38.

U.S. Naval Liaison Office, Calcutta, India. "Loss of USS *Houston*" (summary submitted to Director of Naval Intelligence by Lt. (jg) Harold S. Hamlin and Lt. (jg) Leon W. Rogers, with personal statements taken at the 142nd General Hospital from Lieutenants Hamlin and Rogers, Cdr. William Epstein, Ens. Charles D. Smith, yeoman third class John Allison Harrell, Ens. John B. Nelson, Ens. Preston R. Clark, and seaman first class Charley L. Thomas (of the USS *Stewart*, DD-224). Serial 01143, September 11, 1945. NARA II, Record Group 38, Box 1721. See also www.ibiblio.org/hyperwar/USN/ships/logs/CA/ca30.html (last visited by the author on February 23, 2006).

U.S. Office of Strategic Services, India-Burma Theater. Planning documents for operations in Thailand, 1945. NARA II, Record Group 226, Entry 154, Box 157.

———. Records of Operation Pattern (guerrilla base near Phet Buri, Maj. Eben B. Bartlett Jr., commanding), June–September 1945. NARA II, Record Group 226, Entry 154, Box 153.

———. Records of Operation Mainland (repatriation of Allied POWs), September 1945, NARA II. Record Group 226, Entry 154, Box 151.

U.S. Strategic Bombing Survey. "Interrogation of Admiral Soemu Toyoda," USSBS No. 378, Nav. No. 75, November 13–14, 1945.

———. "Interrogation of Rear Adm. Akira Shoji (commander of IJN *Mogami*), USSBS No. 459, Nav. No. 101, November 17, 1945.

U.S. War Department, Office of the Assistant Secretary of War, Strategic Services Unit, History Division. *The Overseas Targets: War Report of the OSS,* Vol. 2. New York: Walker & Co., 1976.

USS *Alden* (DD-211). "Engagement with the Enemy, 'Battle of the Java Sea.' February 27, 1942" (by Lt. Cdr. L. E. Coley), March 7, 1942. NARA II.

USS *Houston* (CA-30). "Operations for December 21, 22 and 23, 1941," December 23, 1941. Prepared by Capt. Albert H. Rooks Jr. CHC.

———. Ship's Log, August 1941–January 1942; Ship's Log for February 1942 reconstructed in captivity by Harold S. Hamlin and given to Bureau of Naval Personnel in September 1945. NARA II, Record Group 38.

———. "Action Report—USS *Houston* (CA-30) on the Battle of Sunda Strait, 28 February 1942," November 13, 1945. NARA II, Record Group 38.

———. "Action Report—USS *Houston* (CA-30) on 25, 26 and 27 February, 1942 against aircraft only," November 13, 1945 (prepared by Capt. Arthur L. Maher). NARA II, Record Group 38.

———. "Action Report of the USS *Houston* (CA-30) in Defense of Convoy off Darwin, Australia, 16 February 1942," November 14, 1945. NARA II, Record Group 38.

————. "Action Report—USS *Houston* (CA-30) on 4 February 1942 against enemy aircraft," November 15, 1945 (prepared by Capt. Arthur L. Maher). NARA II, Record Group 38.

————. "Action Report of the USS *Houston* (CA-30) in the Battle of the Java Sea, 27 February 1942," November 16, 1945 (prepared by Capt. Arthur L. Maher). NARA II, Record Group 38.

————. "Zentsuji Report" (prepared by nine officers of the *Houston* in captivity at Zentsuji, Japan), undated. Courtesy of Rear Adm. Robert B. Fulton.

USS *Houston* (CL-81). "Report of Actions Occurring 12, 13, and 14 October 1944," Serial 0134, October 20, 1944. NARA II, Record Group 38.

————. "Report of Actions Occurring 16 October 1944," Serial 0135, October 29, 1944. NARA II, Record Group 38.

————. "Report of Salvage of USS *Canberra* and USS *Houston*," Serial 0032, November 30, 1944. NARA II, Record Group 38.

————. "USS *Houston* (CL-81), Battle Damage, Report of," Serial 003, January 20, 1945. NARA II, Record Group 38.

————. "Roster of the Fitzsimmons Group" (USS *Houston*/Lost Battalion POWs), undated. USS *Houston* (CA-30) Survivors Association.

————. "Deceased List," 1942–1944. USS *Houston* (CA-30) Survivors Association.

————. "Roster of Deceased Americans in Capt. Fitzsimmons' Party, 1943–1944." USS *Houston* (CA-30) Survivors Association.

USS *Houston* Marine Detachment. Service Records, through August 1945. USS *Houston* (CA-30) Survivors Association.

USS *John D. Edwards* (DD-216). "Battle off Bawean Island—Report of Action; events prior and subsequent thereto" (with track charts), March 4, 1942. NARA II, Record Group 38.

————. "General Conclusions and Recommendations Based on War Operations to Date" (by Cdr. Henry E. Eccles), Serial CF-0018, March 4, 1942. NARA II, Record Group 38.

USS *John D. Ford* (DD-228). "Night Attack on Japanese Ships at Balik Papen, Morning of January 24, 1942—Report of" (by Lt. Cdr. Jacob E. Cooper; with executive officer's report by N. E. Smith), Serial CF-1, January 25, 1942. NARA II, Record Group 38.

————. "Report of Action of Allied Naval Forces with Japanese Forces off Sourabaya, Java, NEI, February 27, 1942," March 6, 1942. NARA II.

USS *Pope* (DD-225). "Night Destroyer Attack off Balikpapan, January 24, 1942," January 25, 1942. www.ibiblio.org/hyperwar/USN/ships/logs/DD/dd225Balik papan.html (last visited by the author on February 23, 2006).

————. "Action Report—USS *Pope* (DD-225), 1 March 1942," undated. www .ibiblio.org/hyperwar/USN/ships/logs/DD/dd225-Java.html (last visited by the author on February 23, 2006).

INTERVIEWS

Interviews denoted "UNT" were conducted by Dr. Ronald E. Marcello for the Oral History Collection at the University of North Texas (previously North Texas State University).

Bartz, John E., interviewed by the author, December 12, 2003.

Brain, Donald, UNT No. 546, March 11, 1981.

Brooks, Howard E., interviewed by the author, September 23, 2003.

Buzzo, Dan C., UNT No. 1245, February 11, 1998.

Charles, H. Robert, interviewed by the author, February 19, 2004, and September 22, 2004; see also UNT No. 1243, March 25, 1998.

Chumley, Horace, UNT No. 199, April 3, 1974.

Detre, George, UNT No. 475, August 17, 1978.

Douglas, Griff L., UNT No. 425, April 18, 1978.

Dunn, E. Benjamin, UNT No. 1329, November 16, 1999.

Evans, Pete, UNT No. 624, February 15, February 19, and March 7, 1984.

Feliz, Jack M., UNT No. 1373, February 28, 2000.

Flynn, David C., interviewed by the author, April 18, 2004.

Forsman, Melfred L., interviewed by the author March 5, 2005; see also UNT No. 521, July 28, 1980.

Fujita, Frank, Jr., UNT No. 59, November 9, 1970.

Fulton, Robert B. II, interviewed by the author, various contacts.

———, interviewed by Joseph Kollmyer, June 22, 2002, tape transcript provided courtesy of Rear Adm. Fulton.

Fung, Edward, UNT No. 404, December 21, 1977.

Gallagher, Frank E., interviewed by the author, 2004.

Gee, James W. UNT No. 110, March 13, 1972, and March 19, 1972.

Goodson, Ray, interviewed by the author, 2004.

Gordon, Crayton R., UNT No. 383, January 31, 1977.

Hard, Ilo B., UNT No. 510, March 26, 1980.

Harris, Jane, interviewed by the author, June 4, 2005.

Harris, Lanson, interviewed by the author, December 11, 2003.

Heinen, J. B., UNT No. 174, October 19, 1973.

Hood, John E., interviewed by the author, February 28, 2003.

Huffman, James W., interviewed by the author, December 10, 2003.

Ingram, William, interviewed by the author, December 10, 2004; see also interview transcript dated March 1, 2002, interviewed by Floyd C. Cox, Center for Pacific War Studies, National Museum of the Pacific War, Fredericksburg, Texas.

King, Frank H., UNT No. 468, December 12, 1978.

Knight, Douglas F., UNT No. 413, March 12, 1978.

Kopp, Al, interviewed by the author, March 30, 2005.

Minshew, Cecil T., UNT No. 597, February 18, 1983.

Offerle, Roy M., UNT No. 457, August 14, 1978.

Papish, Paul E., UNT No. 781, January 30, 1989.

Prunty, Luther, UNT No. 689, October 20 and 27, 1986.

Pryor, Charley L., Jr. UNT Nos. 139 and 723, November 4, 1972, January 22, 1973, and February 20, 1973.

Rayburn, Eldridge, UNT No. 499, January 16, 1980.

Reed, Raymond D., UNT No. 486, March 13, 1979.

Reese, Seldon D., UNT No. 426, June 21, 1978.

Robinson, Marvin, UNT No. 580, May 25, 1982.

Rooks, Harold R., interviewed by the author September 9, 12, and 13, 2004; various other correspondence and conversations.

Schilperoort, Clarence H., interviewed by the author, September 24, 2004.

Schwarz, Otto C., interviewed by the author, September 23–24, 2003; various telephone contacts.

———. UNT No. 497, August 7, 1979.

———. Interviewed by Floyd C. Cox, February 28, 2002, Oral History Program, National Museum of the Pacific War.

Slate, Garth W., UNT No. 528, August 13, 1980.

Sledge, Tom, interviewed by the author, February 18, 2005.

Smallwood, P. J., UNT No. 166, October 11, 1973, and October 25, 1973.

Stanbrough, Jess, UNT No. 658, April 15, 1985.

Stewart, William J., UNT No. 544, June 11, 1981.

Visage, William A., UNT No. 698, July 15–16, 1987.

Webb, Wade H., UNT No. 1181, February 7, 1997.

Weissinger, William J., Jr., interviewed by Samuel Milner, August 12 and 19, 1959, Corpus Christi, Tex. Papers of Samuel Milner, CHC.

Willey, Lloyd, interviewed by the author, December 9, 2003; see also UNT No. 1295, March 3, 1999.

Wisecup, John H., UNT No. 704, July 28, 1987.

Wright, Houston Tom, UNT No. 466, August 15, 1978.

UNPUBLISHED EYEWITNESS ACCOUNTS

Bancroft, Arthur (HMAS *Perth*). Diary, March 1942–January 1943. CHC.

Barrett, Edward Miles. Diary, June 25, 1940–September 1, 1945, transcription October 26, 2004, by Michael Barrett. Courtesy of Michael Barrett.

Fujita, Frank Jr. Diary, 1941–1945. Oral History Collection, University of North Texas.

Harris, Lanson H. Speech, Long Beach Yacht Club, Long Beach, Calif., March 11, 1983, tape transcript courtesy of Lanson and Jane Harris.

Lamade, Cdr. John D. *USS Houston: December 8, 1941, to February 28, 1942*, privately published, undated (circa 1944). HRR and collection of Joe Kollmyer.

Madson, Quentin C. Diary, November 27, 1941–May 14, 1942. CHC.

Norwood, Gus. "Twelve Careers," unpublished, 2005. Courtesy of Joe Kollmyer.

Parham, Thomas Eugene. Untitled statement, April 29, 1947. USS *Houston* (CA-30) Survivors Association.

Reynolds, Red (James E.). Diary, March 1, 1942–September 15, 1945. CHC.

———. "Presidential Cruise, 1938," undated (circa 1988). CHC.

Schwarz, Otto C. "One Man's Story: A Crew Member of the USS *Houston* (CA-30)," December 28, 1999. CHC.

Stoddard, George D., as told to Loyal Martin Griffin Jr. "The Sinking of the USS *Houston* and Life in Japanese Prison Camps," 1946. CHC.

Varley, Arthur. Diary, May 12, 1942–March 26, 1944 (typed transcription). CHC.

Wilkinson, Eugene T. "POW Wilkinson Remembers," undated. CHC.

Wisecup, John H. "After the Battle—Hintok!" (verse, sketches, and drawings, circa 1943–1944). CHC.

PRIVATE PAPERS AND CORRESPONDENCE

Bernrieder, William A. Papers. CHC.

Davis, Nathaniel P. (Chief, Division of Foreign Service Administration, U.S. Department of State). Letter to Lawrence T. McCarthy, June 29, 1940. NARA II, Record Group 59.

Day, Raymond. "Saga of the *Houston*, March 1942–August 1945," given May 24, 1946, to BuMed, Hospital Archives, Navy Department, Washington. USS *Houston* (CA-30) Survivors Association.

Eccles, Henry E. Papers. Cushing Library, Naval War College, Newport, R.I.

Eddy, M. V. Letter to Otto C. Schwarz, June 20, 1988. CHC.

Fisher, W. E. "Medical Experiences with Ps.O.W. in Malaya, Burma and Siam, 15 February 42 to 16 August 45." CHC.

Fulton, Robert B. II. Papers. CHC.

Hart, Thomas C. Papers. Naval Historical Center, Washington, D.C.

Hekking, H. "Affidavit and General Statement," December 25, 1978. CHC.

Hodge, Fred G. "Exchange of Information Sheet for Relatives of Personnel on USS *Houston* Lost in Sundra Straits [*sic*], February 28, 1942" (KIA/MIA roster and bulletin), first edition, January 15, 1944; second edition, May 10, 1944; fourth edition revised August 15, 1945; fifth edition revised to V-J Day, 1946. CHC.

Kollmyer family. Papers and correspondence. Courtesy of Joe Kollmyer.

Lumpkin, Samuel H. Papers, Texas Military Forces Museum, Camp Mabry, Austin, Texas.

Maher, Arthur L. Papers. Naval Historical Center, Washington Navy Yard.

Milner, Samuel. Papers (including drafts of the unpublished manuscript, "The Undefeated"). CHC.

Mintzer, Jack Weiler. "The Story of Lieutenant (j.g.) Francis Weiler's U.S. Naval Academy Class Ring," undated narrative. CHC.

Peterson, R. E. Correspondence (1941). CHC.

Pistole, Frank. Correspondence (1941–42). CHC.

Pryor, Charley L., Jr. Papers. Courtesy of JoAnn Pryor Wychopen.

Rooks, Albert H. Correspondence (1941–1942). Courtesy of Harold R. Rooks.

Rooks, Edith. Correspondence. Courtesy of Harold R. Rooks.

Schilperoort, Clarence. Papers and photographs. Courtesy of Clarence Schilperoort.

Smith, Jack D. Narrative sent to the author, September 2, 2003.

Stewart, William J. Correspondence (1981). CHC.

Weissinger, William J., Jr. Correspondence (circa 1977). Courtesy of Robert J. Cressman.

Willey, Lloyd. "Poems of the USS *Houston*, Her Crew, and the Men of the 'Lost Battalion.'" Prepared by Christy Willey-Larivee, January 1984.

Wisecup, John H. Correspondence. Courtesy of James McDaniel.

Wisecup, John H. Papers. CHC.

Secondary Sources

BOOKS

Aldrich, Richard J. *Intelligence and the War Against Japan: Britain, America and the Politics of Secret Service*. Cambridge, U.K.: Cambridge University Press, 2000.

Bartsch, William H. *December 8, 1941: MacArthur's Pearl Harbor*. College Station, Texas: Texas A&M University Press, 2003.

Bee, W. A. (Bill). *All Men Back—All One Big Mistake*. Carlisle, West. Aus.: Hesperian Press, 1998.

Bernstein, Mark, and Alex Lubertozzi. *World War II on the Air: Edward R. Murrow and the Broadcasts that Riveted a Nation*. Naperville, Ill.: Sourcebooks, 2003.

Bix, Herbert P. *Hirohito and the Making of Modern Japan,* New York: HarperCollins, 2000.

Blair, Clay, Jr., and Joan Blair. *Return from the River Kwai*. New York: Simon & Schuster, 1979.

Boulle, Pierre. *Bridge on the River Kwai* (originally published as *Le Pont de la Rivière Kwái*). London: Secker & Warburg, 1954.

Brackman, Arnold C. *The Other Nuremberg: The Untold Story of the Tokyo War Crimes Trials*. New York: William Morrow & Co., 1987.

Brown, Anthony Cave (ed.). *The Secret War Report of the OSS*. New York: Berkley, 1976.

Burchell, David. *The Bells of Sunda Strait*. Adelaide, Aus.: Rigby, 1971.

Byas, Hugh. *The Japanese Enemy: His Power and His Vulnerability*. New York: Alfred A. Knopf, 1942.

Cain, T. J., with A. V. Sellwood. *HMS Electra*. London: Futura Publications, 1959.

Chalou, George C. (ed.). *The Secrets War: The Office of Strategic Services in World War II*. Washington: National Archives and Records Administration, 1992.

Charles, H. Robert. *Last Man Out*. Austin, Tex.: Eakin Press, 1988.

Coates, John Boyd, Jr. (ed.). *Preventive Medicine in World War II*, Vol. III: *Personal Health Measures and Immunization.* Washington, D.C.: Office of the Surgeon General, Department of the Army, 1955.

Cook, Haruko Taya, and Theodore F. Cook. *Japan at War: An Oral History*. New York: New Press, 1992.

Craven, W. F., and J. L. Cate (eds.). *The Army Air Forces in World War II,* Vol. I: *Plans and Early Operations, January 1939 to August 1942.* www.ibiblio.org/hyperwar/AAF/I/AAF-I-10.html (last viewed by the author on February 27, 2006).

Cressman, Robert J. *The Official Chronology of the U.S. Navy in World War II*. Annapolis, Md.: Naval Institute Press, 2000.

Davies, Peter N. *The Man Behind the Bridge: Colonel Toosey and the River Kwai*. London: Athlone Press, 1991.

Daws, Gavan. *Prisoners of the Japanese: POWs of World War II in the Pacific*. New York: William Morrow & Co., 1994.

Day, Clarence Nixon. *Hodio: Tales of an American P.O.W.* Merrillville, Ind.: ICS Books, 1984.

Dull, Paul S. *A Battle History of the Imperial Japanese Navy, 1941–1945*. Annapolis, Md.: Naval Institute Press, 1978.

Dunlop, E. E. *The War Diaries of Weary Dunlop: Java and the Burma-Thailand Railway, 1942–1945*. Ringwood, Vict., Aus.: Penguin Books, 1986.

Edmonds, Walter D. *They Fought with What They Had*. New York: Little, Brown, 1951.

Evans, David C., and Mark Peattie. *Kaigun: Strategy, Tactics, and Technology in the Imperial Japanese Navy, 1887–1941*. Annapolis, Md.: Naval Institute Press, 1997.

Ewing, Steve. *American Cruisers of World War II: A Pictorial Encyclopedia*. Missoula, Mont.: Pictorial Histories Publishing, 1984.

Feliz, Jack M. *The Saga of Sailor Jack*. Lincoln, Neb.: iUniverse, 2001.

Fenn, Charles. *At the Dragon's Gate: With the OSS in the Far East*. Annapolis, Md.: Naval Institute Press, 2004.

Fillmore, Clyde. *Prisoner of War*. Wichita Falls, Tex.: Nortex Press, 1973.

Findlay, Alexander Geo. (ed.). *A Directory for the Navigation of the Indian Archipelago, China and Japan, from the Straits of Malacca and Sunda and the Passages East of Java, to Canton, Shanghai, the Yellow Sea, and Japan, with Descriptions of the Winds, Monsoons and Currents, and General Instructions for the Various Channels, Harbours, Etc.* London: Richard Holmes Laurie, 1870.

Flower, Desmond, and James Reeves (eds.). *The War, 1939–1945: A Documentary History*. London: Cassell, 1960.

Frank, Richard B. *Downfall: The End of the Imperial Japanese Empire*. New York: Penguin Books, 1999.

Friedman, Norman. *U.S. Cruisers: An Illustrated Design History*. Annapolis, Md.: Naval Institute Press, 1984.

Fujita, Frank, Jr. *Foo: A Japanese-American Prisoner of the Rising Sun*. Denton, Tex.: University of North Texas Press, 1993.

Glusman, John A. *Conduct Under Fire: Four American Doctors and Their Fight for Life as Prisoners of the Japanese, 1941–1945*. New York: Viking, 2005.

Goodwin, Doris Kearns. *No Ordinary Time: Franklin and Eleanor Roosevelt: The Home Front in World War II*. New York: Touchstone Books, 1994.

Gordon, Ernest. *Through the Valley of the Kwai: From Death-Camp Despair to Spiritual Triumph*. New York: Harper & Bros., 1962.

Gordon, Oliver. *Fight It Out*. London: William Kimber, 1957.

Grove, Eric. *Sea Battles in Close-Up: World War II*, vol. 2. Annapolis, Md.: Naval Institute Press, 1993.

Haley, William F., Jr., and Bryan III. *Admiral Haley's Story*. New York: McGraw Hill, 1947

Hara, Capt. Tameichi, with Fred Saito and Roger Pineau. *Japanese Destroyer Captain*. New York: Ballantine, 1961 (original Japanese edition published 1956).

Hardie, Robert. *The Burma-Siam Railway: The Secret Diary of Dr. Robert Hardie, 1942–1945*. London: Imperial War Museum, 1983.

Henderson, Lt. Col. W. *From China Burma India to the Kwai*. Waco, Tex.: Texian Press, 1991.

Holbrook, Heber A. *U.S.S.* Houston: *The Last Flagship of the Asiatic Fleet*. Dixon, Ca.: Pacific Ship and Shore, 1981.

Holmes, Linda Goetz. *Unjust Enrichment: How Japan's Companies Built Postwar Fortunes Using American POWs*. Mechanicsburg, Penn.: Stackpole Books, 2001.

Hoyt, Edwin P. *The Lonely Ships: The Life and Death of the Asiatic Fleet*. New York: David McKay Company, 1976.

Hughes, Capt. Wayne P., Jr. *Fleet Tactics*. Annapolis, Md.: Naval Institute Press, 1986.

Hymoff, Edward. *The OSS in World War II*. New York: Ballantine Books, 1972.

Imamura, General Hitoshi. *Memoirs of General Imamura* [*Taishō Kaisōroku*], vol. 4: *Cessation of Hostilities* [*Tatakai Owaru*]. Tokyo: Jiyū Ajia-sha, 1960. Partial English-language translation in *The Japanese Experience in Indonesia: Selected Memoirs of 1942–45,* edited by Anthony Reid and Oki Akira. Athens, Ohio: Ohio University Center for International Studies, Center for Southeast Asian Studies. Monographs in International Studies, Southeast Asia Series, No. 72, 1986, pp. 31–77.

Ingersoll, Ernest. *Dragons and Dragon Lore*. New York: Payson & Clarke, 1928.

Ingram, Cecil B. *A Worm's Eye View: Diary and Memories of World War II and the Pacific Theater*. Longview, Tex.: self-published, 2000.

Johns, W. E., and R. A. Kelly. *No Surrender: The Story of William E. Johns, DSM, Chief Ordnance Artificer and How He Survived after the Eventual Sinking of HMS Exeter in the Java Sea in March 1942*. London: George G. Harrap, 1969.

Karig, Walter, and Welbourn Kelley. *Battle Report: Pearl Harbor to Coral Sea*. New York: Farrar & Rinehart, 1944.

Kehn, Don. *Upon a Blue Sea of Blood: Deciphering One of the Great Mysteries of World War II: The Obscure Fate of USS* Edsall *(DD-219), 1 March 1942*. Work in progress.

Kelly, Darryl. *Just Soldiers: Stories About Ordinary Australians Doing Extraordinary Things in Time of War*. Queensland, Aus.: ANZAC Day Commemoration Committee. www.anzacday.org.au/history/ww2/anecdotes/survivors.html (last viewed by the author on February 27, 2006).

Kinvig, Clifford. *River Kwai Railway: The Story of the Burma-Siam Railroad*. London: Brassey's, 1992.

La Forte, Robert S., and Ronald E. Marcello (eds.). *Building the Death Railway: The Ordeal of American POWs in Burma, 1942–1945*. Wilmington, Del.: SR Books, 1993.

Lacroix, Eric, and Linton Wells II. *Japanese Cruisers of the Pacific War*. Annapolis, Md.: Naval Institute Press, 1997.

Lael, Richard L. *The Yamashita Precedent: War Crimes and Command Responsibility*. Wilmington, Del.: Scholarly Resources, 1982.

Larrabee, Eric. *Commander in Chief: Franklin Delano Roosevelt, His Lieutenants, and Their War*. New York: Touchstone Books, 1987.

Lee, Bruce. *Marching Orders: The Untold Story of World War II*. Boston: Da Capo Press, 1995.

Leutze, James. *A Different Kind of Victory: A Biography of Admiral Thomas C. Hart*. Annapolis, Md.: Naval Institute Press, 1981.

Lewin, Ronald. *The American Magic: Codes, Ciphers and the Defeat of Japan.* New York: Farrar, Straus & Giroux, 1982.

Lilley, James, with Jeffrey Lilley. *China Hands: Nine Decades of Adventure, Espionage, and Diplomacy in Asia.* New York: Public Affairs, 2004.

Lomax, Eric. *The Railway Man: A POW's Searing Account of War, Brutality and Forgiveness.* New York: W. W. Norton, 1995.

Lundstrom, John B. *The First Team: Pacific Naval Air Combat from Pearl Harbor to Midway.* Annapolis, Md.: Naval Institute Press, 1984.

————. *The First Team and the Guadalcanal Campaign: Naval Fighter Combat from August to November 1942.* Annapolis, Md.: Naval Institute Press, 1994.

MacArthur, Brian. *Surviving the Sword: Prisoners of the Japanese in the Far East, 1942–45.* New York: Random House, 2005.

Maga, Tim. *Judgment at Tokyo: The Japanese War Crimes Trials.* Lexington, Ky.: University Press of Kentucky, 2001.

Manchester, William. *Goodbye, Darkness: A Memoir of the Pacific War.* Boston: Little, Brown, 1979.

Marston, Daniel (ed.). *The Pacific War Companion: From Pearl Harbor to Hiroshima.* Oxford, U.K.: Osprey Publishing, 2005.

Martindale, Robert R. *The 13th Mission: The Saga of a POW at Camp Omori, Tokyo.* Austin, Tex.: Eakin Press, 1998.

McKie, Ronald. *Proud Echo: The Great Last Battle of HMAS Perth.* Sydney: Angus & Robertson, 1953 (published in the U.S. as *The Survivors*, Indianapolis, Ind.: Bobbs-Merrill).

Miller, Edward S. *War Plan Orange: The U.S. Strategy to Defeat Japan, 1897–1945.* Annapolis, Md.: Naval Institute Press, 1991.

Miller, John Grider. *The Battle to Save the Houston* (CL-81). Annapolis, Md.: Naval Institute Press, 1985.

Milner, Samuel. *The Undefeated.* Unpublished manuscript. CHC.

Minear, Richard H. *Victors' Justice: The Tokyo War Crimes Trial.* Princeton, N.J.: Princeton University Press, 1971.

Morison, Samuel Eliot. *History of United States Naval Operations in World War II*, Vol. 3: *The Rising Sun in the Pacific, 1931–April 1942.* Boston: Little, Brown & Co., 1948.

————. *History of United States Naval Operations in World War II*, Vol. 14: *Victory in the Pacific: 1945.* Boston: Little, Brown & Co., 1960.

Mullin, J. Daniel. *Another Six Hundred* (Destroyer Division 59 in the Asiatic theater, 1941–1942). Self-published, 1984. Collection of the USS *Houston* (CA-30) Survivors Association.

Mullins, Wayman C. (ed.). *1942: "Issue in Doubt"—Symposium on the War in the Pacific by the Admiral Nimitz Museum.* Austin, Tex.: Eakin Press, 1994.

Murray, Alan R. and Williamson Murray, *A War to Be Won: Fighting the Second World War.* Cambridge, Mass.: Belknap Press of Harvard University Press, 2000.

Murray, Sabina. *The Caprices* (short stories). Boston: Houghton Mifflin, 2002.

Nicholson, Arthur. *Hostages to Fortune: Winston Churchill and the Loss of the* Prince of Wales *and* Repulse. Phoenix Mill, U.K.: Sutton Publishing, 2005.

Ogburn, Charlton, Jr. *The Marauders.* Woodstock, N.Y.: Overlook Press, 1956.

Parkin, Ray. *Into the Smother*. Ringwood, Vict., Aus.: Penguin Books, 1963.

————. *Out of the Smoke: The Story of a Sail*. London: The Hogarth Press, 1960.

Payne, Alan. *HMAS Perth: The Story of a Six-Inch Cruiser, 1936–1942*. Garden Island, NSW, Aus.: The Naval Historical Society of Australia, 2000.

Perry, George Sessions, and Isabel Leighton. *Where Away: A Modern Odyssey*. New York: Whittlesley House/McGraw-Hill, 1944.

Persico, Joseph E. *Roosevelt's Secret War: FDR and World War II Espionage*. New York: Random House, 2001.

Piccigallo, Philip R. *The Japanese on Trial: Allied War Crimes Operations in the East, 1945–1951*. Austin, Tex.: University of Texas Press, 1979.

Pickett, Ernest, with K. P. Burke. *Proof Through the Night: A B-29 Pilot Captive in Japan*. Salem, Ore.: Opal Creek Press, 2001.

Potter, E. B. *Nimitz*. Annapolis, Md.: Naval Institute Press, 1976.

Prados, John. *Combined Fleet Decoded: The Secret History of American Intelligence and the Japanese Navy in World War II*. New York: Random House, 1995.

Pratt, Fletcher. *The Navy's War*. New York: Harper & Brothers, 1944.

Rawlings, Leo, with a supporting account by Bill Duncan. *And the Dawn Came up like Thunder*. London: Rawlings, Chapman Publications, 1972.

Rees, Laurence. *Horror in the East: Japan and the Atrocities of World War II*. Boston: Da Capo Press, 2001.

Reminick, Gerald. *Death's Railway: A Merchant Mariner on the River Kwai*. Palo Alto, Ca.: Glencannon Press, 2002.

Reynolds, E. Bruce. *Thailand's Secret War: The Free Thai, OSS, and SOE During World War II*. New York: Cambridge University Press, 2005.

Richardson, Adm. James O., as told to Vice Adm. George C. Dyer, USN (Ret.). *On the Treadmill to Pearl Harbor: The Memoirs of Admiral J. O. Richardson*. Washington, D.C.: U.S. Government Printing Office, 1973 (the manuscript was completed in 1958).

Rivett, Rohan. *Behind Bamboo: An Inside Story of the Japanese Prison Camps*. Sydney: Angus & Robertson, 1946.

Rowland, Robin. "Sugamo and the River Kwai." Paper presented to Encounters at Sugamo Prison, Tokyo, 1945–1952, The American Occupation of Japan and Memories of the Asia-Pacific War, Princeton University, May 9, 2003.

Schom, Alan. *The Eagle and the Rising Sun: The Japanese-American War, 1941–1943*. New York: W. W. Norton & Sons, 2004.

Schultz, Duane. *The Last Battle Station: The Saga of the USS* Houston. New York: St. Martin's Press, 1985.

Searle, Ronald. *To the Kwai and Back: War Drawings, 1939–1945*. New York: Atlantic Monthly Press, 1986.

Seiker, Fred. *Lest We Forget: Life as a Japanese POW*. Worcester, U.K.: Bevere Vivis Gallery Books, 1995.

Slone, Reuben. *The Light Behind the Cloud*. Waco, Tex.: Texian Press, 1992.

Smith, Nicol, and Blake Clark. *Into Siam, Underground Kingdom*. New York: Bobbs-Merrill Co., 1946.

Spector, Ronald H. *Eagle Against the Sun: The American War with Japan*. New York: Vintage Books, 1985.

————. *At War at Sea: Sailors and Naval Combat in the Twentieth Century*. New York: Viking, 2001.

Steijlen, Fridus (ed.). *Memories of "the East": Abstracts of the Dutch Interviews About the Netherlands East Indies, Indonesia and New Guinea (1930–1962) in the Oral History Collection*. Leiden, Neth.: KITLV Press, 2002.

Tamayama, Kazuo, and John Nunneley. *Tales by Japanese Soldiers (of the Burma Campaign, 1942–1945)*. London: Cassell, 2000.

Taylor, Jean Gelman. *Indonesia: Peoples and Histories*. New Haven, Conn.: Yale University Press, 2003.

Teel, Horace G. *Our Days Were Years: History of the "Lost Battalion," 2nd Battalion, 36th Division*. Quanah, Tex.: Nortex Press, 1978.

Thomas, David A. *The Battle of the Java Sea*. New York: Stein & Day, 1968.

Thompson, Kyle. *A Thousand Cups of Rice: Surviving the Death Railway*. Austin, Tex.: Eakin Press, 1994.

Toland, John. *The Rising Sun: The Decline and Fall of the Japanese Empire, 1936–45*. 2 vols. New York: Random House, 1970.

Tolley, Kemp. *The Yangtze Patrol: The U.S. Navy in China*. Annapolis, Md.: Naval Institute Press, 1971.

USS *Houston* and USS *Houston* (CA-30) Survivors Association. *Blue Bonnet* (newsletter), 1938–2006. CHC.

USS *Houston* (CA-30) Survivors Association. *The USS* Houston *(CA-30) in Poetry*, 1993.

Van der Vat, Dan. *The Pacific Campaign: The U.S.-Japanese Naval War, 1941–1945*. New York: Touchstone Books, 1991.

Van Oosten, F. C. *The Battle of the Java Sea*. Sea Battles in Close-Up Series. Annapolis, Md.: Naval Institute Press, 1976.

Velmans, Loet. *Long Way Back to the River Kwai: Memories of World War II*. New York: Arcade Publishing, 2003.

Webster, Donovan. *The Burma Road: The Epic Story of the China-Burma-India Theater in World War II*. New York: Farrar, Straus & Giroux, 2003.

Weissinger, William J., Jr. *Attention, Fool!* Austin, Tex.: Eakin Press, 1998.

White, W. L. *Queens Die Proudly*. New York: Harcourt, Brace & Co., 1943.

Whiting, Brendan. *Ship of Courage: The Epic Story of the HMAS Perth and Her Crew*. London: Allen & Unwin, 1992.

Winchester, Simon. *Krakatoa: The Day the World Exploded: August 27, 1883*. New York: HarperCollins, 2003.

Winslow, Walter G. *Ghost of the Java Coast*. Satellite Beach, Fla.: Coral Reef Publications, 1974.

————. *The Fleet the Gods Forgot: The U.S. Asiatic Fleet in World War II*. Annapolis, Md.: Naval Institute Press, 1982.

————. *The Ghost that Died at Sunda Strait*. Annapolis, Md.: Naval Institute Press, 1984.

Woody, Thomas B. *The Railroad to Nagasaki: An Account of Japanese POWs*. Self-published, 1992.

ARTICLES AND MONOGRAPHS

Andelman, David A. "Ex-Prisoners and Captors Join in a Walk Over Kwai Bridge," *New York Times*, October 26, 1976, p. 41.

Associated Press. "12 Allied Warships Lost in Java Battle—U.S. Cruiser *Houston*, Destroyer *Pope* Among Japanese Victims," *Los Angeles Examiner*, March 15, 1942, p. 1.

———. "Sunken Cruiser *Houston* Beat Off Jap Planes, Saved Convoy," *Boston Herald*, June 10, 1942. HRR.

———. "Tokyo Radio Tells of *Houston* Survivors," July 2, 1942. CHC.

———. "300 *Houston* Survivors Found in Jap Prison Camp in Thailand," dateline Washington, D.C., August 28, 1945. CHC.

———. "Houston Crew Accounted For," dateline Washington, D.C., August 29, 1945. CHC.

———. "Tragic War Mystery Clears—Lost Without a Trace in '42 Battle, 300 Houston Survivors Located," dateline Washington, D.C., August 29, 1945. CHC.

———. "110 More 'Lost Battalion' Members Safe in Calcutta," *Ft. Worth Star-Telegram*, September 8, 1945. Texas Military Forces Museum, Camp Mabry, Austin, Texas.

———. "Houston and Perth Sunk in Java Trap," *New York Times*, September 10, 1945, p. 1. HRR.

———. "Survivors Tell of Heroic Last Battle of Houston," September 12, 1945. HRR.

———. "Lost Battalion Salute Life-Saving Doctor," *Toledo Blade*, August 14, 1983. Texas Military Forces Museum, Camp Mabry, Austin, Texas.

———. "Bridge on the River Kwai Now Is Thailand Tourist Attraction," *San Diego Union*, August 11, 1985, p. A-32.

———. "Anger, Sorrow Still Run Deep Along River Kwai," dateline Kanchanaburi, Thailand, February 20, 1994.

Baldwin, Hanson W. "Saga of a Stout Ship—The *Houston*," *New York Times Magazine*, March 3, 1946, p. 5.

Bancroft, Arthur. "Prisoners of War: HMAS Perth Survivors" (monograph), Naval Historical Society of Australia, 1991.

Barrett, E. Miles, as told to Dorothy Rochon Powers. " 'My Greatest Adventure,' " *The Spokesman-Review*, October 3, 1951, p. 2. Collection of Michael Barrett.

Beaton, Terence R. "American POWs on the Railway." CHC.

———. "A Traveller's Guide to the Burma Railway," unpublished draft manuscript, 2003. CHC.

Beattie, Rod, and Neil MacPherson. "Death Railway Camps" (reference chart), revised September 29, 2005. www.mansell.com/pow_resources/camplists/death_rr/deathrailwaycamplist.html (last visited by the author on February 23, 2006).

Berney, Louis. "The Bridge on the River Khwae, 40 Years Later," *Washington Post*, February 3, 1985, p. E1.

Bernrieder, William A. "Port Houston's Latest Asset: The USS *Houston*," undated (circa 1927). CHC.

―――. "The United States Cruiser 'Houston,' the Pride of Our Navy and the City of Houston" (radio address), KPRC, October 11, 1930. William A. Bernrieder Papers, CHC.

Birkett, Gordon. "P40E/E-1 Operations in Australia, Part 5," unpublished. Courtesy of Gordon Birkett.

Boggett, David. "Notes on the Thai-Burma Railway, Part I: The Bridge on the River Kwai, the Movie," *Journal of Kyoto Seika University*, No. 19, 2000.

―――. "Notes on the Thai-Burma Railway, Part II: Asian Romusha, The Silenced Voices of History," *Journal of Kyoto Seika University*, No. 20, 2001.

―――. "Notes on the Thai-Burma Railway, Part IV: An Appalling Mass Crime," *Journal of Kyoto Seika University*, No. 22, 2002.

Boston Herald–New York Times Dispatch, "1000 Missing with *Houston* and *Perth* Prisoners of Japs," July 2, 1942. HRR.

Braswell, Janet. "Like the World Would End," *Hattiesburg American*, March 2, 1992, p. 1A.

Butler, Gary (ed.). "Lost Battalion Soldiers and USS *Houston* Crewmen Who Died while Prisoners of War," Lost Battalion Association, Texas Military Forces Museum, Austin, Tex. www.kwanah.com/txmilmus/lostbattalion/index.htm (last visited by the author on February 27, 2006).

Charles, H. Robert. "Saigon in World War II," *Leatherneck*, November 1989, p. 42.

Christian Science Monitor. "Civilian 'Tracks' *Houston* Men" (Fred G. Hodge), dateline September 14, 1944. HRR.

Clymer, A. Ben. "The Mechanical Analog Computers of Hannibal Ford and William Newell," *IEEE Annals of the History of Computing*, Institute of Electrical and Electronics Engineers, Vol. 15, No. 2, 1993, p. 19.

Conley, Jim. "Lost Battalion—Money, Equipment, Lives: Part of the Cost of Freedom," *Abilene Reporter-News*, August 13, 1982, p. 1. Texas Military Forces Museum, Camp Mabry, Austin, Texas.

Cooper, Carol. "The 'F' Force: The Endurance of 7,000 POWs in Thailand." www.cofepow.org.uk/pages/asia_thailand_f_force.htm (last viewed by the author on May 24, 2005).

Cotton, John. "Prisoner of War Camps in Japan—Zentsuji," *American National Red Cross Prisoners of War Bulletin*, Vol. 1, No. 2, July 1943. CHC.

Denning, Jill. "Veteran Recalls Imprisonment" (Frank B. Rhodes), *The Western Spirit* (Paola, Kan.), May 31, 1982, p. 1.

Duncan, I. L., J. H. Greenwood, T. L. B. Johnson, K. G. Mosher, and S. E. J. Robertson. "Morbidity in Ex-Prisoners of War," POW Association of Australia, June 1985. Papers of Charley L. Pryor, Jr.

"English Honor Tucson Officer" (Maj. Gen. Lowell W. Rooks), undated news article. HRR.

Falloon, Tom. "My Brush with History" (liberation of Omori camp, Tokyo), undated. CHC.

Faltot, David C. "Diving for the USS *Houston* in Sunda Strait," undated (circa 2004). Courtesy of David C. Faltot.

Fillmore, Clyde. Nine-part newspaper serialization (prepublication), edited by

George Works, of *Prisoner of War, Wichita Falls Times*, February 7–16, 1973. Texas Military Forces Museum, Camp Mabry, Austin, Texas.

Fulton, Robert B. II. "Fighting in the Java Sea," *Shipmate*, December 1998, p. 30.

Gang, Wu. "World War II Forced Labour Cases Voided in Japan," *China Daily*, May 25, 2004. www.chinadaily.com.cn/english/doc/2004-05/25/content_3334 15.htm (last viewed by the author on February 27, 2006).

Gray, Denis D. "Old Foes Will Meet Again on Bridge on the River Kwai," *Chicago Sun-Times*, October 25, 1976, p. 28.

Grundhoeffer, E. W. "Why There Should Be a USS *Houston*," U.S. Navy Recruiting Station, Houston, Tex., undated (circa 1927). CHC.

Hall, D. O. W. "Prisoners of Japan," Wellington, New Zealand: War History Branch, Department of Internal Affairs, 1949. www.nzetc.org/etexts/WH2-1 Epi/WH2-1Epi-fTit.jpg (last viewed by the author on February 27, 2006).

Hamlin, H. S., Jr. "The *Houston*'s Last Battles," *Shipmate*, May 1946, p. 9.

Harrell, John Allison, and John C. Reas. "USS *Houston* (CA-30) Roster of Enlisted Personnel and Locations and POWs," 1942–1945. USS *Houston* (CA-30) Survivors Association.

Hart, Thomas C. "What Our Navy Learned in the Pacific," *Saturday Evening Post*, October 3, 1942, p. 9. HRR.

Holton, Denny. "Cherokean Recalls 3 Years of Hell as POW" (Harry and O. C. McManus), *Cherokee Daily Times*, May 9, 1981, p. 1.

Houston Chronicle Magazine. "A Case of Unparalleled Patriotism," December 9, 1979. CHC.

Houston Press. "Roaring Welcome Given Cruiser" (CA-30 survivors visit USS *Houston*, CL-81), October 26, 1945, p. 1. CHC.

Japanese Monograph No. 164, "Railway Operations Record (1941–1945)," Japanese Department of the Army.

Japanese Monograph No. 101, "Naval Operations in the Invasion of Netherlands East Indies (December 1941–March 1942)," Japanese Department of the Navy.

Japanese Monograph No. 139, "Outline of South Seas Naval Force Operations and General Situation (December 1941–March 1942)," Japanese Department of the Navy.

Kehn, Don, Jr. "USS *Houston* (CA-30)/Naval Intelligence/Submarine Ops/Smith-Hutton," unpublished. Courtesy of Don Kehn Jr.

———. "American Heavy Cruiser USS *Houston* (CA-30) ('Northampton' Class)," unpublished, undated. Courtesy of Don Kehn Jr.

———. "History and Mystery (or, Seeing Is Misbelieving): A Reappraisal of the Sinking of USS *Edsall* (DD-219), 1 March 1942." Ca. 2002. Unpublished.

King, Cecil S., Jr. "Asiatic Fleet Odyssey," *Naval History*, Winter 1991, p. 74.

Levitt, H. A. "Ensign H. A. Levitt's List" (POW roster). USS *Houston* (CA-30) Survivors Association.

"List of Hellship Voyages," updated January 27, 2005. www.west-point.org/ family/japanese-pow/Ships.htm (last viewed by the author on February 27, 2006).

Loeb, Vernon. "Dreck Below the Bridge on the River Kwai," *Philadelphia Inquirer*, August 24, 1981, p. 1-A.

M'Mullen, Jim. "Battalion, Feared Lost in Java, Rough and Ready Lot," *Ft. Worth Star-Telegram*, June 10, 1942. Texas Military Forces Museum, Camp Mabry, Austin, Tex.

————. "West Texas Pays Tribute to 'Lost Battalion' on Day of Java's Fall to the Japs," *Ft. Worth Star-Telegram*, undated, ca. March 1943. Texas Military Forces Museum, Camp Mabry, Austin, Tex.

Mack, William P. "The Battle of the Java Sea," *Proceedings*, Vol. 69, No. 8, August 1943, p. 1052. HRR.

Martin, H. H. "Civil Responsibility of Japan for Maltreatment of Prisoners of War, Both Armed Forces and Civilians, During World War II," Washington, D.C., Claims Committee, Liberated Military Personnel (Japan), 1946. CHC.

Matsubara, Hiroshi. "Mitsui Case Breaks New Ground for Wartime Redress," *Japan Times*, April 27, 2002. www.japantimes.co.jp/cgi-bin/makeprfy.pl5?nn20020427a9.htm (last viewed by the author on June 7, 2005).

Miller, Melinda. "For Love of Fellow Man" (James E. "Red" Reynolds), *Houston Chronicle*, February 8, 1982, p. 4.

Mintzer, Jack Weiler. "The Long Journey Home: Fran Weiler's Ring Returns to Annapolis," *Shipmate*, September 2000, p. 10. Courtesy of Joe Kollmyer. www.usna.com/News_Pubs/Publications/Shipmate/2000/2000_09/journy.htm (last visited by the author on February 23, 2006).

Mobray, James A. "The Fabric of Air Warfare: Doctrine, Operational Experience, and Integration of Strategic and Tactical Air Power from World War I Through World War II," Maxwell AFB, Ala.: Air University Press, April 1991.

Morison, Samuel Eliot. "Notes on Writing Naval (not Navy) English," *The American Neptune*, Vol. IX, No. 1, January 1949, p. 5.

Morrow, Thomas J. "Ex-POW Wants to Relieve Hostages," *Escondido Times-Advocate*, January 20, 1980, p. A-1.

Moscow, Warren. "*Houston* Survivor Describes Battle," *New York Times*, undated. HRR.

Murray, Linda. "'It Was Easier to Die,'" *Hood County News* (Granbury, Texas), August 12, 1979.

————. "Eyewitness Account: The Bridge over the River Kwai," *Hood County News*, August 16, 1979, p. 4B.

————. "The Taste of Freedom: Some Will Never Know," *Hood County News*, August 19, 1979, p. 1B.

Nagatomo, Yoshitada. "Speech Delivered by Lieutenant Colonel Y. Nagatomo to Allied Prisoners of War at Thanbyuzayat, Burma," October 28, 1942. USS *Houston* (CA-30) Survivors Association.

Nally, Peter. "Diggers 'Fed Flesh of Chinese,'" *Gold Coast Bulletin* (Australia), February 10, 1989, p. 1. CHC.

Naval Historical Society of Australia. "HMAS *Perth*—Part II: Battle of Java Sea and Sunda Strait, 1942," Monograph No. 14, February 3, 1989.

————. "Prisoners of War: HMAS *Perth* Survivors," Monograph No. 132, including personal narrative by Arthur Bancroft, May 1991.

Naval War College. "Cruisers and Destroyers in the General Action," June 1937,

Section II, "Preliminary Survey of Employment of Cruisers and Destroyers in the General Action." www.gwpda.org/naval/usncdga2.htm (last visited by the author on February 27, 2006).

New York Times. "High Award Given *Houston*'s Captain," June 25, 1942. HRR.

———. "*Houston*'s Survivors Tell of Cruiser's Battle Against 16 Japanese Warships till She Sank," March 3, 1946. HRR.

Noble, J. Kendrick, Jr. "The Death of the *Houston*," *American Legion Magazine*, January 1951, p. 22. HRR.

Norbury, Kim. "Memoirs of Biscuits in Java, 50 Years On," *The Courier* (Ballarat, Australia), February 22, 1992, p. 3.

Norwood, I., and Emily L. Shek. "Prisoner of War Camps in Areas Other than the Four Principal Islands of Japan," Liaison and Research Branch, American Prisoner of War Information Bureau, July 31, 1946 (incorporated in Schwarz, "Burma-Thailand Death Railroad"). Papers of Charley L. Pryor, Jr.

Oakes, Porter. "Col. Tharp Hides Precious 131st Data," *Wichita Falls Times*, October 18, 1945. Texas Military Forces Museum, Camp Mabry, Austin, Tex.

Peters, C. Brooks. "Twelve Warships Lost by Allies in Java Sea, 5 of Them Cruisers; Japan Loses 7 Damaged or Sunk," *New York Times*, March 15, 1942, p. 1.

Pratt, Fletcher. "Americans in Battle—No. 1: Campaign in the Java Sea," *Harper's Magazine*, Vol. 185, No. 1110, November 1942, p. 562. HRR.

Ramsey, Sherry Sylvester. "Capt. Frederic Haynes Ramsey, USMC: A Profile of the Marine Commander on the USS *Houston* and a Review of How His Hometown Newspaper Reported the Sinking of His Ship," May 2004. Courtesy of Sherry Sylvester Ramsey and Col. Stephen F. Ramsey, USAF (Ret.).

Redding, Stan. "*Houston* Died in 'Fiercest' Naval Battle," *Houston Chronicle*, February 26, 1967, p. 23.

Reynolds, Gary K. "U.S. Prisoners of War and Civilian American Citizens Captured and Interned by Japan in World War II: The Issue of Compensation by Japan," Congressional Research Service, Library of Congress, updated July 27, 2001.

Riley, Frank. "A Poignant Walk Across Thailand's Storied Bridge on the River Kwai," *Los Angeles Times*, January 3, 1982, Part VIII, p. 1.

Robie, Marshall (ed.). "Program: Navy Week, Houston, Texas, October 26–November 3, 1945." Navy Mother's Club No. 2 of America.

Rooks, Albert H. "Sound Military Decision, Part I," Naval War College Staff Presentation, July 5–6, 1940. Cushing Library, Naval War College, Newport, R.I.

———. "Sound Military Decision, Part II," Naval War College Staff Presentation, July 25, 1940. Cushing Library, Naval War College, Newport, R.I.

———. "Sound Military Decision, Part III," Naval War College Staff Presentation, July 25, 26, 29, August 1, 3, 6, 1940. Cushing Library, Naval War College, Newport, R.I.

———. "Cruiser Warfare, 1914–1918, 1939–1940," Naval War College Staff Presentation, September 30, 1940. Cushing Library, Naval War College, Newport, R.I.

———. "Estimate of the Situation, Far East Area," November 18, 1941. NARA II.

Rose, Jim. "Diary of Death, Agony Written in POW Camp" (Frank Fujita), *Fort Worth Press*, August 16, 1968, p. 8. Texas Military Forces Museum, Camp Mabry, Austin, Tex.

Rowland, Robin. "Sugamo and the River Kwai," paper presented to Encounters at Sugamo Prison, 1945–52, Conference on the American Occupation of Japan and Memories of the Asia-Pacific War, Princeton University, May 9, 2003.

Rundle, Walter. "Survivors Describe Sinking of Cruiser *Houston* by Japs in Battle of the Java Sea," United Press dispatch, September 6, 1945.

San Francisco Maritime Park Association. "USS *Pampanito* (SS-383), The Third War Patrol, August 17–September 28, 1944." www.maritime.org/patrol3.htm (last viewed by the author on February 27, 2006).

Schneider, John F. "The History of KTAB and KSFO." www.bayarearadio.org/schneider/ksfo.shtml, Bay Area Radio Museum, San Francisco, 1997.

Schwarz, Otto C. "God's Hand Was on My Shoulder," *Faith at Work*, March 1962, p. 5. Collection of Otto Schwarz.

———. "Burma-Thailand Death Railroad," unpublished, June 1982. Collection of Charley L. Pryor Jr.

Seattle Post-Intelligencer. "Gallant Ship Goes Down With Guns Blazing: Sinking of the Houston," undated, ca. 1945. HRR.

Seattle Times. "Misdated Cable Gave Wife of Capt. Rooks False Hope," undated, ca. 1942. HRR.

———. "Medal of Honor Awarded to Captain Rooks," June 25, 1942. HRR.

Seiker, M. F. "The Thai-Burma Railway and Beyond, 1942–1945." CHC.

Shafter, Richard. "What's in a Name? The USS *Houston*," *Our Navy*, mid-July 1944, p. 24.

Sharp, John C. (ed.). "Japanese Documentary: Being a Collection of Papers from Japanese Sources Relating to Prisoner of War Camps in the Far East," translated and transcribed by James Whittaker at POW camps in Chungkai and Phet Buri, Thailand, 1945. USS *Houston* (CA-30) Survivors Association.

Sheeler, Jim. "The Enemy Was 'All Around Us,'" (Paul Papish), *Denver Post*, July 31, 2000, p. 1A. CHC.

Simmons, Walter. "How U.S. Cruiser *Houston* Fought 100 Ships Told," *Chicago Tribune*, April 22, 1945, p. 6. CHC.

Sissons, David. "Sources on Australian Investigations into Japanese War Crimes in the Pacific," *Journal of the Australian War Memorial*, Issue 30, April 1997. www.awm.gov.au/journal/j30/sissons.htm (last visited by the author on February 27, 2006).

Smith, George. "50th Anniversary of the Cruiser *Houston*'s Loss Approaches," *Ft. Worth Star-Telegram*, February 13, 1992, p. A22.

———. "Survivors Remember WWII Sea Battle, Capture by Japanese," *Ft. Worth Star-Telegram*, February 20, 1992, p. A18.

Smith, Virgil. "Where Is the Crew of the Ghost Cruiser *Houston*?" *The Oregonian*, undated, ca. 1944, p. 2. Collection of Lloyd and Dorothy Willey.

Stuart, Donald. "The Quiet Lion" (Sir Edward "Weary" Dunlop), *The West Australian*, January 22, 1977. CHC.

"The Story of HMAS *Perth*" (comic book), Navy Combat Series, No. 2, May 1955, Melbourne, Aus.: Gordon and Gotch. CHC.

Time. "World Battlefronts: Battle of the Pacific," January 26, 1942, p. 18.

———. "World Battlefronts: Battle of the Pacific," February 2, 1942, p. 23.

———. "World Battlefronts: Battle of Java," March 9, 1942, p. 16.

Timmons, B. N. "18 Texans of 131st Fly to Capital," *Ft. Worth Star-Telegram*, September 14, 1945, p. 1. Texas Military Forces Museum, Camp Mabry, Austin, Tex.

Tully, Anthony P. "Naval Alamo: The Heroic Last Months of the Asiatic Fleet: December 1941–March 1942." www.asiaticfleet.com/javaseaAug02.html (last visited by the author on February 23, 2006).

Tutt, Bob. "Good Ship *Houston* Went Down Fighting," *Houston Chronicle*, March 1, 1992.

———. "Despite the Years, Sailors Can't Forget USS *Houston*'s Last Fight," *Houston Chronicle*, March 1, 1992, p. 27A.

Ueno, Teruaki. "Japan PM Apologises over World War Two Dutch POWs," Reuters, May 2, 2005.

United Press. "Japanese Broadcast Hints Survivors from *Houston*," *Long Island Daily Press,* April 24, 1942. CHC.

———. "*Houston* Men Jap Captives?" dateline Sydney, Australia, July 1, 1942.

Waxman, Jerry. "USS *Houston*—A Story in Courage and Survival," *Katy Times*, February 24, 1999, p. 1.

Weintraub, Stanley. "The Kwai That Never Was," *Military History Quarterly,* Vol. 10, No. 4 (Summer 1998), p. 76.

Weissinger, William J., Jr. "A Final Roster of the Crew of USS *Houston* (CA-30)," July 1983. USS *Houston* (CA-30) Survivors Association.

Weller, George. "Writer Tells How Moon Betrayed Allies in Java Sea Battle," *Seattle Daily Times*, March 19, 1942, p. 1. HRR.

———. "Battle of Java: U.S. Sailors Tell of Action; Their Rescue Was a 'Miracle,'" Chicago Daily News Foreign Service, dateline March 27, 1942. HRR.

———. "Sailors Braved Fiery Death, Saved *Houston*, Her Gun Turret Ablaze," Chicago Daily News Foreign Service, dateline April 13, 1942. HRR.

———. "Luck to the Fighters," *Military Affairs*, Vol. VIII (Winter 1944), p. 259.

Whitehouse, Stuart. "Seattle Skipper Died on *Houston*," *Seattle Star,* undated. HRR.

"Wife Retains Hope *Houston* Captain Lives," undated, unattributed article. HRR.

Winslow, Cdr. Walter G. "The 'Galloping Ghost,'" *U.S. Naval Institute Proceedings*, Vol. 75, No. 552, February 1949, p. 155.

———. "Survivor Tells of Last Bloody Minutes of the USS *Houston*," *Houston Chronicle*, February 27, 1972, Section 4, p. 1.

Winston, George J., as told to Al Hirschberg. "We Built the Railway to Hell," *Argosy*, September 1959, p. 61. USS *Houston* (CA-30) Survivors Association.

Works, George. "Once POW, Always POW," *Wichita Falls Times*, February 11, 1973, p. 1. Texas Military Forces Museum, Camp Mabry, Austin, Tex.

INTERNET SITES

Cruiser Houston Collection, Special Collections and Archives, University of Houston Libraries. http://info.lib.uh.edu/sca/digital/cruiser/cruiserh.htm.

MacPherson, Neil. "Death Railway Movements." www.mansell.com/pow_resources/camplists/death_rr/movements_1.html (last visited by the author on February 22, 2006).

Mansell, Roger. Center for Research, Allied POWs under the Japanese. www.mansell.com/pow-index.html (last viewed by the author on February 27, 2006).

USS *Houston* (CA-30) Survivors Association. www.usshouston.org.

NOTES

Epigraph translation by Victor Davis Hanson of *Forsan et haec olim meminisse iuvabit*

Part 1: On Asia Station

CHAPTER 1 (pp. 7 to 13)

The account of the *Houston*'s ordeal on February 4 is built from interviews with survivors; Morison, *History of United States Naval Operations*, Vol. 3, 298; Prados, *Combined Fleet Decoded*, 266; Schultz, *The Last Battle Station*, 79–91; William J. Weissinger to Robert J. Cressman, Sept. 8, 1977; ONI, *The Java Sea Campaign, 1943*. **"He handled that ship . . ."**: H. Robert Charles, UNT interview, 21. **Captain Rooks as second coming of Mahan**: "Families Here Hold Hope for 22 Local Men," *Seattle Daily Times*, undated. **"The pilot found himself sitting on a picked chicken . . ."**: Hamlin, "The *Houston*'s Last Battles," 26. **"Mad as scalded dogs" and dud AA projectiles**: Otto Schwarz interview with the author; Winslow, *The Ghost That Died at Sunda Strait*, 90. **Damage to USS *Marblehead***: ONI, *Battle of the Java Sea*, 29–30. **Damage to *Houston*'s after turret**: Charles D. Smith narrative, Sept. 18, 1945, 2; Weissinger to Cressman, Sept. 8, 1977, 6; Weissinger to Otto Schwarz, Jan. 22, 1983; James Huffman interview with the author; Jack D. Smith, e-mail to the author, Sept. 2, 2003. **"I'm convinced they were never the same . . ."**: E. Miles Barrett, "My Greatest Adventure," 2. **"War came to us in a real way . . ."**: Charley L. Pryor Jr., UNT interview, Nov. 4, 1972, p. 73. **"I'm telling you, it was spooky"**: John E. Bartz, interview with the author.

CHAPTER 2 (pp. 14 to 19)

"The spit and polish of the U.S. Navy was ingrained in us": Donald Brain, UNT interview, 12. **FDR's 1938 cruise**: "Presidential Cruise, 1938," by Red Reynolds.

CHAPTER 3 (pp. 20 to 30)

Construction of the USS *Houston* (CA-30): Bernrieder, "Port Houston's Latest Asset: The USS *Houston*," 2, 5. "No detail, however small, was overlooked . . .": Bernrieder, KPRC radio address, Oct. 11, 1930. ***Houston*'s tenure as Asiatic Fleet flagship**: Kemp Tolley, foreword to Winslow, *The Fleet the Gods Forgot*, xi. "Seagoing fire departments": Tolley, *The Yangtze Patrol*, 170. "Like their officers, the men were regulars . . .": Thomas C. Hart, "Supplementary of Narrative," 19. **Nimitz on *Augusta***: Potter, *Nimitz*, 189–200. "We want the brawn of Montana . . .": Cdr. Francis H. Higginson, quoted in Spector, *At War at Sea*, 128. **John H. Wisecup's journey to the *Houston***: Wisecup, UNT interview, 6–9. **Background of James W. Huffman and Melfred L. Forsman** per their interviews with the author. **Shipboard culture of "officers' country"**: Spector, *At War at Sea*, 135–136. "Marines were never slow . . .": Tolley, *The Yangtze Patrol*, 170. Charley L. Pryor Jr. to his parents, July 1940, p. 2. "Everyone hates the Japs . . .": "The first sting of winter . . .": Tolley, 273. **Training of *Houston* personnel**: William J. Weissinger to Robert Cressman, Sept. 8, 1977, 3, 4. **Clymer, "a real tough old bird"**: Otto Schwarz, interview. "Other ships were struggling . . .": Robert B. Fulton, interviewed by Joe Kollmyer. **Prewar posture of U.S. Pacific Fleet**: Morison, *History of United States Naval Operations*, Vol. 3, 4–7, 33–43. "Japan was the only important nation . . .": Morison, *History of United States Naval Operations*, 5. **Japan's China policy**: Bix, *Hirohito*, 306–307. **Natural history of Indonesia**: Taylor, *Indonesia*, 1. **Prewar U.S. Army**: War Department, *United States Army in World War II*, 16. **U.S. attitudes toward Japan**: Bix, 334; Spector, 9; Morison, *History*, Vol. 3, 14. "About as hopeful as lighting a candle . . .": Tolley, *Yangtze Patrol*, 278–279. "He said the power of the Japanese was far greater . . .": Harold R. Rooks interview with the author. "It's a shame to wish away time at our age . . .": Albert H. Rooks to Edith Rooks, Aug. 29, 1941. "My opinion of the Jap situation keeps changing . . .": Rooks to Edith Rooks, Sept. 6, 1941. "Few Allied naval officers other than Captain Rooks . . .": Morison, 164. "Day after tomorrow it will be one month . . .": Rooks to Edith Rooks, Sept. 28, 1941. "The longer they keep from striking . . .": Rooks to Edith Rooks, Oct. 5, 1941. "They are really in what must be for them a very unsatisfactory position . . .": Rooks to Edith Rooks, Oct. 19, 1941. "The Jap situation is sizzling this week end . . .": Rooks to Edith Rooks, Oct. 18, 1941. "It is an interesting fact to me . . ." and "I have a feeling that fate is going to be kind to me . . .": Rooks to Edith Rooks, Oct. 19, 1941.

CHAPTER 4 (pp. 31 to 37)

***Houston* stripping down at Cavite**: William J. Weissinger Jr., interviewed by Samuel Milner, August 12, 1989, and Charley Pryor, UNT interview, Nov. 4,

1972, 53. *Houston's* movements as war loomed: Ship's log, Dec. 1941. **U.S. Navy strategy in the Far East**: Hart, "Supplementary of Narrative," 2–3, and Morison, *History of United States Naval Operations*, Vol. 3, 153–54. **"What did that thing say?"**: David C. Flynn, interview with the author. **"JAPAN STARTED HOSTILITIES. GOVERN YOURSELVES ACCORDINGLY."**: Thomas C. Hart, narrative, 36. **"A two-ocean war to wage with a less than one-ocean Navy . . ."**: Morison, *History of United States Naval Operations*, Vol. 3, 209. **Allied withdrawal from Philippines and setup of ABDA**: ONI, "The Java Sea Campaign," 6–14; Morison, Vol. 3, 281–82; Spector, *Eagle Against the Sun*, 123–125, 127–130; Schom, *The Eagle and the Rising Sun*, 252–59; and Leutze, *A Different Kind of Victory*, 262–263. **ABDA's internal conflicts**: Thomas C. Hart, "Supplementary of Narrative," 3–4; Hart, "Narrative of Events," 2; ONI, "The Java Sea Campaign," 14; Morison, *History of United States Naval Operations*, Vol. 3, 281–282; Spector, *Eagle Against the Sun*, 131. **"The Americans have held out on the Bataan Peninsula . . ."**: Wavell as quoted in Parkin, *Into the Smother*, 15. **Sketch of Admiral Helfrich**: Pratt, *The Navy's War*, 16.

CHAPTER 5 (pp. 38 to 44)

Houston convoy duty: Cdr. Arthur Maher, narrative, 3. **"It got to be so bad . . ."**: Winslow, *The Ghost That Died at Sunda Strait*, 58. **Life at Darwin**: Howard E. Brooks, interview with the author; Schultz, *The Last Battle Station*, 61–62. **"STURGEON NO LONGER VIRGIN"**: Morison, *History of United States Naval Operations*, Vol. 3, 283. **Battle of Balikpapan**: USS *Pope* (DD–225), "Night Destroyer Attack off Balikpapan, January 24, 1942, January 25, 1942," p. 1; ONI Combat Narrative, 18–21; Morison, Vol. 3, 285–290; Pratt, *The Navy's War*, 21. **Admiral Hart's "exaggerated ideas of Japanese efficiency"**: Leutze, *A Different Kind of Victory*, 273, quoting Wavell's letter to Churchill. **"A movement toward youth in all sea commands"**: Thomas C. Hart, "Supplementary of Narrative," 37. **"A worrier who never could sit back . . ."**: Hart's diary, quoted in Leutze, 321–323. **"I did not like to be commanding Admiral Helfrich on his own home ground"**: Hart, "Supplementary of Narrative," 37. **"I was scared of the old devil . . ."**: D. A. Harris, skipper of *Bulmer*, quoted in Leutze, 284. **Admiral King to Admiral Hart**: An **"Awkward situation"**: quoted in Leutze, 275. **"It's all on the laps of the gods"**: Hart, Feb. 5, 1942, diary entry, quoted in Leutze, 277. **"An island which was ours, but belongs to us no more . . ."**: Rooks, "Sound Military Decision," Part I, 60, 62.

CHAPTER 6 (pp. 45 to 49)

Repairs to *Houston*: Charles D. Smith, narrative Sept. 18, 1945, 2; Quentin C. Madson, "The Story of the USS *Houston*," 10. **"Oh, don't bother with me . . ."**: Howard E. Brooks, interview with the author. **"Suddenly, I had the weird impression . . ."**: Winslow, *The Ghost That Died at Sunda Strait*, 97. **"A weird silence enveloped the ship . . ."**: Winslow, 96. **"Well, the big news is that we have been in action . . ."**: Rooks to Edith Rooks, Feb. 9, 1942 (the letter is misdated Feb. 9, 1941). **"When it comes to judging the ability of men as cruiser**

captains. . . . Rooks still had perfect poise . . .": Thomas C. Hart to Edith Rooks, March 25, 1942. Rooks "didn't want our folks to accuse him of manslaughter . . .": George D. Stoddard, "The Sinking of the USS *Houston* and Life in Japanese Prison Camps," 2. "I think they looked at him as just another god": Gus Forsman, UNT interview, 16. "Admiration for the Captain bordered on worship": USS *Houston*, untitled report, Zentsuji Prison Camp, 1. "Everybody believed that the Good Lord . . .": Paul E. Papish, UNT interview, 10. "He always knew who he was . . .": Frank E. Gallagher, interview with the author. "After telling me that he would take his ship out again . . .": Hart, "Supplementary of Narrative," 19.

CHAPTER 7 (pp. 50 to 54)

"I am going out into the troubled zone this evening . . . May God protect and strengthen you": Rooks to Edith Rooks, Feb. 14, 1942. Admiral Hart's farewell: Leutze, *A Different Kind of War*, 277. "Well, boys, we all have a busy day tomorrow . . .": Ibid., 278. "Oh it was hard . . .": Hart diary, quoted in Leutze, 278. *Houston* convoy to Timor: ONI, "The Java Sea Campaign," 36; Winslow, *The Ghost That Died at Sunda Strait*, 100–101. "*I see the USS* Houston *is escorting four transports* . . .": John E. Bartz, interview with the author. Air attacks on *Houston*: USS *Houston*, "Action Report of the USS *Houston* (CA-30) in Defense of Convoy off Darwin, Australia, 16 February 1942." "She was a wonderful sight . . .": E. L. Cullis, "Vale *Houston*," *The Blue Bonnet*, newsletter of the USS *Houston* Survivors Association, Sept. 2001, 5. Rooks's seamanship under air attack: John D. Lamade, *USS Houston: December 8, 1941, to February 28, 1942*; Lloyd Willey, UNT interview, 22. "They dropped them so close to us . . .": Charley Pryor, UNT interview, 78. "I'd often wondered and worried . . .": Griff L. Douglas, UNT interview, 16–17. "You could just see them rocking up there": Lloyd V. Willey, UNT interview, 22. "All the sea boiled up and *Houston* was gone": E. L. Cullis, "Vale *Houston*," 5. "It was a proud moment": William J. Weissinger, interview with Samuel Milner, 4.

CHAPTER 8 (pp. 55 to 63)

The collapse of ABDA: ONI, *The Java Sea Campaign*, 44; British Admiralty, "The Battle of the Java Sea: 27th February 1942," 13; Prados, *Combined Fleet Decoded*, 257; Morison, *History of United States Naval Operations*, Vol. 3, 336. "I am afraid that the defense of the ABDA area has broken down": Prados, *Combined Fleet Decoded*, 257. The *Houston* at Tjilatjap: Winslow, *The Ghost That Died at Sunda Strait*, 108; Charles D. Smith, "USS *Houston* (CA-30) and Experiences in Jap Prison Camp," 4. "In a fatherly way, he draped his arm around my shoulder . . .": Winslow, 108. "Say, didn't I just hear a gate clang shut behind us?": Paul E. Papish, UNT interview, 29; see also Hamlin, "The *Houston*'s Last Battles," 10. "With all the confusion going on around us": Winslow, 109. "If this [naval force] is divided . . .": Wavell quoted in Payne, *HMAS Perth: The Story of the Six-Inch Cruiser*, 62. Background on the Seventeenth Pursuit Squadron: Craven and Cate, *The Army Air Forces in World War II: Plans & Early Operations, January*

1939 to August 1942, 383–87, 397–402; see also Edmonds, *They Fought with What They Had*, 288–290; U.S. Army Air Force, Historical Division, *Summary of Air Action in the Philippines and Netherlands East Indies*, 239–240; and Ingram, *A Worm's Eye View*, 13. "**It was the first time we'd ever fired at anchorage**": Charley L. Pryor, UNT interview, 82–83. "**At the end of three or four days of this**": Otto C. Schwarz, in "Death Becomes the Ghost," video. **Gathering of Combined Striking Force**: Hamlin, "The *Houston*'s Last Battles," 10; Mullin, *Another Six Hundred*, 205–206; Thomas, *The Battle of the Java Sea*, 156. "**There is a possibility in this action we may have some fighter protection**": Payne, *HMAS Perth*, 64. "You MUST CONTINUE ATTACKS TILL ENEMY IS DESTROYED": Helfrich to Doorman.

Part 2: A Bloodstained Sea

CHAPTER 9 (pp. 67 to 70)

The approach of the Japanese invasion force is based on Hara, *Japanese Destroyer Captain*, 72–76; Dull, *Battle History of the Imperial Japanese Navy*, 72; and Morison, *History of United States Naval Operations*, Vol. 3, 335. **Memories of the *Exeter***: Paul E. Papish, UNT interview, 36. "**A-Hunting We Will Go . . .**": Schultz, *The Last Battle Station*, 143. "**Even when we found that it was merely a bugle call . . .**": Hamlin, "The *Houston*'s Last Battles," 10. "NOTWITHSTANDING AIR ATTACK . . .": CZM (Helfrich) to E.C. (Doorman), INFO COMSOWESPAC (Glassford), Feb. 27, 1942. "WAS PROCEEDING EASTWARD . . .": Doorman to Helfrich, Feb. 27, 1942. "THIS DAY THE PERSONNEL REACHED THE LIMIT OF ENDURANCE . . .": quoted in Parkin, *Out of the Smoke*, 214. "**Throughout *Perth* there was general frustration . . .**": ibid., 215. "**The word spread like wildfire . . .**": Winslow, *The Ghost That Died at Sunda Strait*, 111.

CHAPTER 10 (pp. 71 to 81)

"AM PROCEEDING TO INTERCEPT . . .": USS *John D. Edwards*, Action Report, 2. **Rooks's "hurried but deadly serious" conference**: Winslow, *The Ghost That Died at Sunda Strait*, 112. Lamade would return stateside as an instructor at NAS Jacksonville. Later he went aboard the USS *Hancock* as Commander of Air Group Seven, striking at Japan. He named his fighter plane *T. Benny* in honor of the *Houston*'s senior aviator, Thomas B. Payne; Schultz, *The Last Battle Station*, 129. **Doorman's formation departing Surabaya**: Parkin, *Out of the Smoke*, 216; cf. Winslow, *The Ghost That Died*, 113, who wrote, "Such an unorthodox deployment of forces suggested that Doorman knew little about proven naval tactics, or chose to ignore them." Winslow did not account for the nagging mechanical problems of the destroyers. The British Admiralty's *Battle of the Java Sea* (Battle Summary No. 28) (fn. on 16) states the U.S. destroyer commander (Commander Binford) wanted the cruisers to scout for the destroyers in advance of any torpedo attack. "**A tactical instrument of collective genius . . .**": Hughes, *Fleet Tactics*, 74. **Communications within Doorman's squadron**: Morison, *History of United States Naval Operations*, Vol. 3, 342; but Winslow, at 113, says a Dutch liaison officer on the

Houston translated the orders, though he too mentions Lt. Otto Kolb on Doorman's staff on the *De Ruyter*, 124 fn., without explanation of his duties; see also Schultz, 143. **"Everyone knows that you cannot assemble eleven football players . . .":** Hamlin, "The *Houston*'s Last Battles," 10. **"ONE CRUISER, LARGE DESTROYERS, NUMBER UNKNOWN . . .":** Van Oosten, *Battle of the Java Sea*, 46; British Admiralty, *Battle Summary*, 77. **"TWO BATTLESHIPS, ONE CRUISER, SIX DE- STROYERS . . .":** British Admiralty, *Battle Summary*, 77; Winslow, *The Ghost That Died at Sunda Strait*, 113; Parkin, *Out of the Smoke*, 216–217. **Enemy bearings:** USS *John D. Ford* and USS *John D. Edwards* action reports. **"We realized help would come, but not today . . .":** Marvin Robinson, UNT interview, 15. HMS *Electra* **"twisting like a hare":** Cain, HMS *Electra*, 221–222. **The predicament about fleet air cover** was reflected by Admiral Helfrich, who stated: "All my previous re- quests for fighter protection had been refused. The lack of cooperation in this in- stance shows clearly that the fleet and the aircraft operating over the sea *must* be under the same command": British Admiralty, *Battle of the Java Sea*, 24, fn. 1. **Regarding air reconnaissance reports,** the British Admiralty further reports: "In order to minimize the delay attendant on the centralized system adopted by the [Dutch] Reconnaissance Group at Bandoeng, RADM Doorman urgently requested the Naval Seaplane Base at Moro-Krambagan, Surabaya to repeat to him immedi- ately all reports made by Reconnaissance Group flying boat pilots to their head- quarters at Bandoeng. However, since ABDAair and Recgroup (although they . . . [were] both at Bandoeng) [had] been separated, it frequently happened that recon- naissance signals only . . . [reached Doorman] after great delay": British Admiralty, 15. **Report of the U.S. air attack on troop transports:** Army Air Forces, "Summary of Air Action," 241–242. **"Our first shots were fired almost ahead . . .":** Hamlin, "The *Houston*'s Last Battles," 11. **"Jesus Christ, you just can't imagine . . .":** James W. Huffman, interview with the author. **"This is a thing that you couldn't do in peacetime . . .":** Hamlin, "USS *Houston* in Battle of Java Sea," 1. **"Near-miss underwater well aft":** Capt. Oliver Gordon in HMS *Exeter*, Dispatch on Battle of the Java Sea, para. 19. **"What possible bloody good can we do here?":** Captain Waller quoted in Parkin, *Out of the Smoke*, 218. **Regarding damage to Japanese ships during the engagement:** Judging claimed hits is difficult. However, most all Allied witnesses report seeing hits on a Japanese CA early in the engagement. Because no Japanese sources cite any dam- age, some historians have concluded that no Japanese ships were hit. See Prados, *Combined Fleet Decoded*, 261. However, numerous American and British observers reported hits on the enemy heavy. The abundance of simultaneous and specific Allied reports of damage to a Japanese heavy cruiser in this action cannot be negated by documentary silence on the other side. Capt. Oliver Gordon reported hitting a *Sendai*-class light cruiser after ten salvoes, forcing her to turn 180 degrees, and "she was last seen disappearing in a thick high column of smoke": *Exeter* dis- patch, para. 16. Prados, at p. 263, speculates that the smoke was of the Japanese ship's own making, concealing in by-the-book fashion the countermarch following a torpedo launch. **"I saw us hit this enemy cruiser one very good wallop in- deed . . .":** Hamlin, "USS *Houston* in Battle of the Java Sea," 1. N.B.: Hamlin also reported seeing a Japanese light cruiser "simply blow up and disappear in a tremendous column of smoke and spray and steam that must have gone up four or five hundred feet." However, all evidence indicates that the Japanese light cruisers in this battle survived. "**I whooped lustily and dashed for the voice tube . . .**": Hamlin, 2. **The Japanese cruiser was "put on fire early in the engagement . . .**": Maher, "Jap Prison Experiences," 6. "**The target was aflame both forward and amidships . . .**": USS *Houston*, Action Report. "**Clouds of black smoke poured out of her top . . .**": Parkin, *Out of the Smoke*, 224. *Exeter's* hits on the "**lower bridge structure**": *Exeter*, Dispatch, para. 18. "**The range was perfect**": Charles D. Smith, narrative, 7. **Premature explosions of Japanese torpedoes**: Hara, *Japanese Destroyer Captain*, 80.

CHAPTER 11 (pp. 82 to 87)

"**Salvo after salvo exploded into the sea around us . . .**": Winslow, *The Ghost That Died at Sunda Strait*, 116. "**Throughout this madness . . .**" and "**We were appalled . . .**": Winslow, 117. **Damage to *Houston's* communications apparatus:** Sholar quoted in Mullin, *Another Six Hundred*, 226; USS *John D. Edwards* action report. "**I'll never forget the *Perth* as she came by . . .**": Hamlin, "USS *Houston* in Battle of Java Sea," 2. "**The sea seemed alive with torpedoes . . .**": Winslow, 118. "**It was not going at sufficient speed to detonate**": Charles D. Smith, narrative, 6. "**There was only fifteen or twenty feet . . .**": Ibid. **Loss of the *Kortenaer*:** Her captain, Lt. Cdr. A. Kroese, and an officer from the *Witte de With*, Lt. Cdr. H. T. Koppen, believe *Kortenaer* was sunk by a submarine torpedo, but Japanese sources do not mention the presence of submarines in the Java Sea on February 27. See also British Admiralty, *Battle of the Java Sea*, 33; according to HIJMS *Haguro*, "Tabular Record of Movement," *Haguro* fired eight torpedoes at 1622 and hit *Kortenaer* at 1640. "**Passing close aboard . . .**" and "**No ship stopped to take on survivors . . .**": Winslow, 118; see also Quentin C. Madson, diary. "**The crystal ball was our only method . . .**": *John D. Edwards*, action report, para. 9. From his perch on the *Houston's* signal bridge, Walter Winslow, at p. 119, reported witnessing two startling events around this time. First, he saw the HMS *Jupiter*, returning from a torpedo run, breaking through the smoke screen near the *Houston* and launching a torpedo in the American cruiser's general direction. The missile traveled some five hundred yards before exploding, launching into the air two large tubular chunks of metal. An oil slick and a spread of flotsam rose from the deep. It was, Winslow surmised, a Japanese submarine, sunk right in their midst. The *John D. Edwards* action report, in paragraph 8, mentions "a torpedo apparently hit a submarine about 1,500 yards broad on our port bow, for a column of water and debris went up about 100 feet." Equally likely it was a Long Lance that passed near the *Jupiter* and self-destructed at the limit of its range. "**Enemy retreating west. Where is convoy?**": British Admiralty, *Battle of the Java Sea*, 41.

CHAPTER 12 (pp. 88 to 93)

Dutch report of the location of Japanese transports: ONI, *Java Sea Campaign*, 73. **Fetid conditions in *Houston's* turrets and magazines:** Otto C. Schwarz, interview with the author. "**As fast as we popped one group of lights . . .**": Winslow, *The Ghost That Died at Sunda Strait*, 123. "**Like a long string of**

Christmas lights": James Gee, UNT interview, 27. **Sinking of HMS *Jupiter***: British Admiralty, *Battle of the Java Sea*, 46, and ONI, *Combat Narrative*, 74. "**We stopped shooting star shells . . .**": Hamlin, "USS *Houston* in Battle of the Java Sea," 3–4. **Sinking of *Java***: Charley L. Pryor, UNT interview, 95; Parkin, *Out of the Smoke*, 239; Charles D. Smith, narrative, 7; and Weissinger, interview with Samuel Milner, 6. ***De Ruyter* "blew up with an appalling explosion . . .**": HMAS *Perth*, action report. "**It happened with the suddenness and complete-ness . . .**": Hamlin, "The *Houston's* Last Battles," 25. "**I thought it would fry us**": Parkin, 240. "**Captain Rooks frantically maneuvered . . .**": Winslow, 124–125. "**Counted nine separate and distinct explosions . . .**": Charles D. Smith, 7. "**The *Houston* and *Perth* raced on . . .**": Winslow, 125.

CHAPTER 13 (pp. 94 to 100)

"**Walking to the telephone building . . .**" and "**Java died that night . . .**": White, *Queens Die Proudly*, 223. "**They are done for**," and "**the last Japanese mistake of the battle**": Hara, *Japanese Destroyer Captain*, 85. "*HOUSTON AND PERTH* RETIRING TO BATAVIA . . .": *Houston* to COMSOWESPAC, Feb. 27, 1942. "**In the era before radar . . .**": Richardson, *On the Treadmill to Pearl Harbor*, 222–223. **The Japanese as "the world's most capable users of the torpedo"**: Rooks, "Estimate of the Situation, Far East Area," unpaginated. "**I don't think there was ever a minute . . .**": James Gee, UNT interview, 28. "**He was so very cheery . . .**": Glassford to Edith Rooks, May 21, 1942, 2. **Report that Sunda Strait was clear**: Hamlin, "USS *Houston* in Battle of Java Sea," 4. ***Houston* at Surabaya**: Dull, *Battle History of the Imperial Japanese Navy*, 71; Robert B. Fulton II, interview by Joe Kollmyer, 10; Lloyd V. Willey, UNT interview, 30. "OIL POSI-TION IS SERIOUS . . .": Helfrich, ABDAfloat message dated Feb. 21, 1942. ***Houston's* fuel situation**: According to Walter Winslow, "The *Houston*, it was de-termined, probably had enough remaining fuel to reach Australia," *The Ghost That Died at Sunda Strait*, 130. The *Houston's* Battle of Sunda Strait action report puts her bunkers at 350,000 gallons. However, the ship's assistant engineering officer, Robert B. Fulton, disputes that enough fuel was on hand for the ship to reach Australia. "**Concussion from the main batteries had played havoc . . .**": Winslow, 128–129. Other damage to *Houston*, action report, 7. "**He had been off-color for days**": McKie, *Proud Echo* (or *The Survivors*), 14. **Captain Waller's ser-vice in the Mediterranean**: Ibid., 18–19. **Regarding Admiral Doorman's employment of his light cruisers**: Admiral Helfrich later discussed why Doorman didn't separate his heavy and light cruisers, speculating that the poor sta-tus of communications made anything other than a simple single-column "follow me" approach unworkable; see British Admiralty, *Battle of the Java Sea*, Appendix P, 78. "**Everyone was lighthearted, and thinking that we had done our share . . .**": Lloyd V. Willey, interview with the author. "**Tom was hoisted on board . . .**": Winslow, 131.

CHAPTER 14 (pp. 101 to 103)

"**One was bad enough . . .**": McKie, *Proud Echo*, 5. **The cat "took off down that pier into Java . . .**": Reese, UNT interview, 20; cf. Lieutenant Hamlin's article

(p. 26), which states the *Houston* had no cat. "Like a cat, the *Houston* had expended eight of its nine lives . . .": Winslow, *Proceedings*, quoted in McKie, *Proud Echo*, 138. **Red Lead in "irons":** Hamlin, 26. **The animal seemed to know something:** Bee, *All Men Back*, 19. *Houston* **departing Batavia:** USS *Houston*, Zentsuji Report, 2. **"Many times before I had found solace in its beauty . . .":** Winslow, "The 'Galloping Ghost,'" 155. **"He felt that this moment at sundown was a dividing line . . .":** McKie, 12.

CHAPTER 15 (pp. 104 to 108)

Houston **approaching Bantam Bay:** USS *Houston*, action report, 1; Charles D. Smith, narrative, 9; Winslow, *The Ghost That Died at Sunda Strait*, 133; Bee, *All Men Back*, 20. **Background on Krakatoa:** Winchester, *Krakatoa*, 276–77. **"Ever since the night of the 23rd . . .":** Hamlin, "The *Houston*'s Last Battles," 26. **Piper "pacing the flag deck . . .":** McKie, *Proud Echo*, 17. **"They could hide a battleship out there . . .":** Charles, *Last Man Out*, 22. **"I looked in the same direction as the guns . . .":** Bee, 20. **"I found myself in my shoes before I was fully awake":** Winslow, 135. **"Our first salvos appeared to strike home . . .":** Bee, 20. **"We were desperately short of those eight-inch bricks":** Winslow, "The 'Galloping Ghost,'" 161. **"I figured we were in for trouble that night":** Stewart UNT interview, 16. **"ENEMY FORCES ENGAGED":** USS *Houston*, action report, 15.

CHAPTER 16 (pp. 109 to 121)

First minutes of Battle of Sunda Strait: Brooks, interview with the author, 26–27; "Batavia Battle," *Senshi Sosho*; Van Oosten, *Battle of the Java Sea*, maps at 56–57; Hara, *Japanese Destroyer Captain*, 86; Morison, *History of United States Naval Operations*, Vol. 3, 366. **"TWO MYSTERIOUS SHIPS ENTERING THE BAY":** Hara, 86; "Batavia Battle," *Senshi Sosho*, 483–487. **"There are four to starboard . . .":** Payne, *HMAS Perth*, 74. **"You could see the ships just all over . . ."** and **"We were firing at any target that [we] saw . . .":** Gee, UNT interview, 33–34. **"Momentarily, I caught a glimpse of tracers . . ."** and **"How reassuring it was to hear . . .":** Winslow, "The 'Galloping Ghost,'" 161. **"The largest landing yet attempted in the Southwest Pacific":** Morison, 365. **Dutch reconnaissance report:** Winslow, 131–132. **"The fight evolved into a melee . . .":** USS *Houston*, action report, 4. **Japanese attacks on *Houston* and *Perth*:** "Batavia Battle," *Senshi Sosho*; Tully, "Naval Alamo," www.asiaticfleet.com/javaseaAug02.html. **"The tactics were to expose the beam of one light . . .":** Parkin, *Out of the Smoke*, 251. **"It sounded like somebody throwing pebbles at the ship":** Schwarz, interview with the author. **"The whole ship was alive with orders . . .":** Parkin, 253. **"This kind of fighting demands the purest form of courage . . .":** sailor quoted in Spector, *At War at Sea*, 81. **"That is just what it sounded like . . .":** Brain, UNT interview, 37. **Damage to *Harukaze*:** Allyn D. Nevitt, "IJN *Harukaze*: Tabular Record of Movement," 1998 www.combinedfleet.com; also Rough Translation 1. *Houston*'s **hits on *Mikuma*:** "Report of Capt. Shakao Sakiyama of *Mikuma*," *Senshi Sosho*. **"We could see the whole outline of these Japanese destroyers . . .":** Howard Brooks, interview with the author. **"Oh Lord, sometimes you felt like you could reach out . . .":** John Bartz, interview with the author.

"The tin cans got so close to us . . .": John Wisecup, UNT interview, 18–19.
USS *Houston* engine room operations: Robert B. Fulton to the author, Oct. 26,
2004. "We were making full power . . .": Ibid. **First damage to the *Houston***:
Houston's Sunda Strait action report (p. 6) states that it was "presumably" a torpedo
to the port side; cf. George Detre, UNT interview, 30, who says it hit the starboard
side; Charles D. Smith says it was "a salvo of shells." A diagram sketched by divers
who visited the wreck and catalogued its wounds (collection of Don Kehn) shows
no damage consistent with a catastrophic torpedo hit on the port side. While there
is a relatively small gash at the waterline on the port side directly below the
number-two stack, the extent of the damage seems too limited to have been a torpedo hit and more in line with an armor-piercing shell. What damage may be in
evidence on the ship's starboard side lies buried in the silt of the Java Sea. "**When
the ship was underway my job was . . .**" and other quotes by Lieutenant
Fulton: Fulton to the author, Oct. 26, 2004, and Jan. 2, 2005. **Damage to boilers**: George Detre, UNT interview, 30–31.

CHAPTER 17 (pp. 122 to 127)

"**I wanted desperately to know . . .**": Winslow, *The Ghost That Died at Sunda
Strait*, 136. **Regarding the Navy's view of the utility of torpedoes on cruisers**:
in the view of the commander of the Scouting Force in 1933, Adm. Harris Laning,
"war games . . . since we have had light and heavy cruisers indicate that the offensive value of their torpedoes is practically nil," Friedman, *U.S. Cruisers*, 132.
Perth's **torpedo salvoes**: the ship's torpedo gunner reported hits on an aircraft carrier or tender, as well as two destroyers, though the claim seems optimistic. Parkin,
Out of the Smoke, 253. "**For God's sake shoot that bloody light out!**": McKie,
Proud Echo, 43. **Torpedo hit on *Perth***: this fish was reportedly from a spread of six
fired by the destroyer *Harakaze* at 11:56, per Payne, *HMAS Perth*, 75. "**Some vital
pulse had stopped**": Parkin, 254. "**What do we use after these?**": Ibid., 255.
"**Christ, that's torn it**" and "***Prepare* to abandon ship, sir?**": McKie, 43; Parkin,
at 254, recalled the conversation a bit differently. "**I don't want the Old Girl to
take anyone with her**": Parkin, 257. "**Across the sea and under the sky came
a great roar. From under X turret . . .**": Ibid., 260–261. "**Light, almost gay, in
that mad moment . . .**": McKie, 52–53. **Harper "was suddenly appalled . . .**":
Parkin, 262. Parkin noted that "after the fourth torpedo, the starboard list came off
her and she heeled slightly to port"; but W. A. Bee, in *All Men Back*, wrote that the
Perth was "listing heavily to port," 21; McKie quoted Lyons that it was "over on her
port side sliding down by the bows," *Proud Echo*, 46. "**Pieces could be seen flying
off as salvoes exploded . . .**": Parkin, 261. **Lt. Frank Gillan's escape from
*Perth***: McKie, 55–58. "**Her four propellers came clear of the sea . . .**": Parkin,
263. The *Perth* suffered 356 KIA, per Bee, *All Men Back,* 130. "**I'm the last man
out of that ship alive . . .**": McKie, 58.

CHAPTER 18 (pp. 128 to 131)

"**When Captain Rooks realized she was finished . . .**": Winslow, *The Ghost That
Died at Sunda Strait*, 137. "**We couldn't see . . .**" James Gee, UNT interview, 34.
Houston's **gunfire against transports**: USS *Houston*, action report, 6; see also

Imamura, quoted in Anthony Reid, *The Japanese Experience in Indonesia*, 33–34; Morison, *History of United States Naval Operations*, Vol. 3, 366. "Let the *Houston* have the credit": Toland, *Rising Sun*, Vol. 1, 353 fn. **Abandonment of *Houston*'s Central Station**: *Houston*, action report, 6; Clarence Schilperoort, interview with the author. "You didn't know where the hell you were . . .": David C. Flynn, interview with the author. "I thought I was looking at a moving picture": Schilperoort, interview with the author.

CHAPTER 19 (pp. 132 to 136)

Damage to *Houston* generally: USS *Houston*, Sunda Strait action report, 12. **Destruction of Turret Two**: USS *Houston*, action report; Charles D. Smith, "USS *Houston* (CA-30) and Experiences in Jap Prison Camp," 10; H. S. Hamlin, "Statement," 6. "Everything lit up . . ." and "I'm telling you what I did . . .": James Huffman, interview with the author, 5. **Casualties in Turret Two**: Smith, 11. "We knew the turret was on fire . . .": William J. Stewart, UNT interview, 19. "It was just like coming out of a blow torch . . .": Ibid., 20–21. **In the** ***Mikuma*, sailors boisterously celebrated** . . . : *Senshi Sosho*, Report of Capt. Sakiyama. "It's coming from all sides . . .": Paul E. Papish, UNT interview, 42. **Flooding of Turret One**: Hamlin, "Statement," 6–7. ***Houston* engaged by torpedo boats**: Winslow, *The Ghost That Died at Sunda Strait*, 140; Smith, "USS *Houston*," 11. "The ship seemed to be thrown sideways . . .": William J. Weissinger to Robert J. Cressman, Sept. 1977. **Roar of Japanese ships' firerooms**: Donald Brain, UNT interview, 38–39. "It was point-blank . . .": Frank King, UNT interview, 26. "It was invigorating to be in a battle like that . . .": Melfred L. Forsman, UNT interview, 32. "I thought I was going to get it . . .": Ibid. "You could hear them cooking": Winslow, 146. "My God, those magnesium flares just light a place up": Papish, 41.

CHAPTER 20 (pp. 137 to 145)

Movements of *Houston*: USS *Houston*, "Zentsuji Report," 3, and Battle of Sunda Strait action report, 7. "Because of the overwhelming volume of fire . . .": Sunda Strait Action Report, 8. "In a strong, resolute voice . . .": Winslow, *The Ghost That Died at Sunda Strait*, 140; per the *Houston*'s action report, the first abandon ship order went over the PA, and the second was blown by the bugler. Since Winslow personally recalls standing next to Captain Rooks when Rooks ordered the bugler to sound abandon ship, and since it seems Rooks was deceased when the second abandon ship order was passed, he must have used the bugler on the first abandon ship order too. "He never missed one beat on that bugle . . .": Lloyd Willey, UNT interview, 35. "If widely dispersed over the Far East . . .": Rooks, "Estimate of the Situation." **Wounding of Captain Rooks**: Charles D. Smith, "USS *Houston* (CA-30) and Experiences in Jap Prison Camp," 12; see also Winslow, 141. "He died within a minute": Charles D. Smith, "Casualty Affidavit No. 5"; see also Smith, "USS *Houston*," 12. "Rocking slowly back and forth, he held Captain Rooks . . .": Winslow, "The 'Galloping Ghost,'" 162. "We were really roaring along": Robert B. Fulton, interview with Joe Kollmyer. The *Houston*'s Sunda Strait action report, at p. 8, notes that the inert inboard screws were making about 210 rpm; the standard ratio for rpm to speed was 10 to 1. *Well, that's more like it*: Melfred L. Forsman, UNT interview, 34. **Captain Rooks's reported intention to ground the *Houston***: Quentin C. Madson, diary, 26; Weissinger to Robert J. Cressman, Sept. 8, 1977, p. 9; see also Weissinger, interview with Samuel Milner, 7; Seldon Reese, UNT interview, 25. **The report was disputed by**: Otto C. Schwarz, letter to the author, March 11, 2005, and Robert B. Fulton II, letter to the author, Jan. 2, 2005. **"We were really getting the devil knocked out of us . . ."**: James Gee, UNT interview, 35. **"No one in the magazine ever said . . ."**: James Gee, UNT interview, 35. **"I have never seen eight men face the absolute end so calmly"**: Marvin Robinson, quoted in Winslow, 158. **"Y'all come on out, and hurry!"**: Gee, Ibid. **"I told the boys, 'We've had it . . .'"**: Robinson, UNT interview, 20. **"We were going to go up . . ."**: Gee, 37. **"It looked like high noon on the boat deck . . ."**: Weissinger to Cressman, Sept. 8, 1977. **"When I got there it was just like the Fourth of July . . ."** and **"All of a sudden this guy jumped on top of me . . ."**: Otto C. Schwarz, interview with the author. **"Better go, Charlie. It's all over. Finished"** and other quotes between Charles and Standish: Charles, *Last Man Out*, 34. *Is this the way it is?*: Charles, UNT interview, 32–33. **"I nearly fell through a hole . . ."**: Hamlin, "Statement," 8. **"There were dead fish floating all around . . ."**: Seldon D. Reese, UNT interview, 27. **"I thought of her as she was when I joined her . . ."**: Hamlin, "The *Houston*'s Last Battles," 27. **"She was full of holes all through the side . . ."**: Hamlin, "Narrative," 8. **"She righted herself like a dog shaking water off its back . . ."**: Wisecup to Randall Sutherland, undated ca. February 1989, p. 4. **"Perhaps I only imagined it . . ."**: Winslow, *Proceedings*, 163. **Standish, "living up to Marine Corps legend . . ."**: John Wisecup to Randall Sutherland, undated, ca. Feb. 1989, 4. **"Not a word was uttered by anyone . . ."**: Wisecup to Sutherland, Feb. 10, 1989, 3. **"The Nation's safest insurance . . ."**: Bernrieder, address, 7.

Part 3: The Emperor's Guests

CHAPTER 21 (pp. 149 to 152)

The location of the *Houston*'s wreck: USS *Houston* (SSN-713), April 1993 track chart; see also navigation chart provided by Don Kehn Jr. **"I saw hundreds of unwounded men . . ."**: Harold S. Hamlin, "Statement," 8. **"There is an adage at war colleges . . ."**: Albert H. Rooks, "Estimate of the Situation," Section V, Paragraph (b). **"*EVERTSEN* REPORTS SEA BATTLE IN PROGRESS . . ."**: Rear Adm. William A. Glassford to *Houston*, sent 28/2328. Reaching Fremantle were the gunboats USS *Tulsa, Lanakai*, and *Isabel*, and the minesweepers *Whippoorwill* and *Lark*. See Morison, *History of United States Naval Operations*, Vol. 3, 379. **The best treatment of the loss of USS *Edsall* and the mystery of her crew's fate** is Don Kehn's article "History and Mystery . . ." and his work in progress, *Upon a Blue Sea of Blood*. **USS *Stewart*'s fate**: Morison, *History*, Vol. 3, 378. **"A magnificent display of very bad strategy"**: Admiral King as quoted in Morison, *History*, Vol. 3, 380. **"It drank the cup of defeat to the bitter dregs . . ."**: Ibid.

CHAPTER 22 (pp. 153 to 162)

"I took a deep drink of that sea water . . .": James Gee, UNT interview, 40. "You're just completely beyond exhaustion . . .": Charley L. Pryor, UNT interview, Nov. 4, 1972, 112. **Ens. John B. Nelson's boat**: Winslow, *The Ghost That Died at Sunda Strait*, 170–71 and Paul E. Papish, UNT interview, 49. "This jerk was picking up guys . . .": William M. Ingram, in Winslow, 149; see also Ingram, interviewed by Floyd Cox, 15. "We weren't ashore five minutes . . .": Ingram as quoted in Winslow, 149. "I could feel myself being carried out to sea . . .": Gee, UNT interview, 42. **Chaplain Rentz**: H. S. Hamlin, "The *Houston's* Last Battles," 27; Lloyd V. Willey, UNT interview, 40; Web site of the USS *Rentz* (-FFG-46), www.rentz.navy.mil/rentz_rentz.html. "You men are young, with your lives ahead of you": Hamlin, 27, and Walter L. Beeson, "Casualty Affidavit for Cdr. George S. Rentz." "The surface was dotted with all sorts of objects": William J. Weissinger to Robert J. Cressman, Sept. 26, 1977, 4. "Transports lined the beach as far as the eye could see . . .": John H. Wisecup to Randall Sutherland, Feb. 10, 1989, 4. "Strange guttural-snarling sounds . . ." and **Lt. Dalton's parley with the Japanese**: Weissinger, *Attention, Fool!* 10–12. "Nobody wanted us": Weissinger to Cressman, 5–6. **Ordeal of Frank Gillan's group of *Perth* survivors**: McKie, *Proud Echo*, 73–76, 88–91. "The deck looked like a used shoe store display": Wisecup to Randall Sutherland, Feb. 10, 1989, 1. **Ensign Smith and Red Huffman getting ashore**: Charles D. Smith, "USS *Houston* (CA-30) and Experiences in Jap Prison Camp." **Damage to Japanese landing force**: Weissinger to Cressman, Sept. 26, 1977, 4, and Winslow, 185.

CHAPTER 23 (pp. 163 to 170)

"Those Aussies—if you ever have to get captured . . .": Otto C. Schwarz, interview with the author; see also Pete Evans, UNT interview, 195. **Keith Gosden's capture**: McKie, *Proud Echo*, 54. *There's a plan for every man* . . .: Ibid., 101. **Toppers Island and Sangiang**: Parkin, *Out of the Smoke*, 1, 6, and McKie, 71–83. "They had both disappeared": William J. Weissinger to Robert J. Cressman, Sept. 26, 1977, 6. "If that's the sort they are . . .": McKie, 83. **John A. Thode**: McKie, 98–99. **On Princes Island**: Ibid., 102–103. **Capture by the Dutch**: Ibid., 106.

CHAPTER 24 (pp. 171 to 177)

"You are prisoners of war. Your lives will be spared": Charley L. Pryor, UNT interview, Nov. 4, 1972, 114; Otto C. Schwarz, "One Man's Story," 4–5. "All my life I was the kind of person . . .": Schwarz, videotaped interview, collection of Val Roberts-Poss. **Americans at Pandeglang**: William J. Weissinger to Robert J. Cressman, Sept. 26, 1977, 9. "You and the Japanese are brothers . . .": General Imamura, as quoted in Reid and Akira, *The Japanese Experience in Indonesia*, 35. **Sighting of Sergeant Standish ashore**: Griff L. Douglas, UNT interview, 40 (most survivors doubt he got off the ship). **Prisoners at Serang**: Bee, *All Men Back*, 130; Charles D. Smith, 14; Harold S. Hamlin, "Report of Service as Prisoner of War," 45; William J. Stewart, UNT interview, 36; Paul E. Papish, UNT interview, 60–61; and Rohan Rivett, *Behind Bamboo*, 89. "**They've now decided after several more counts . . .**": Ibid., 75. "**We thought we were dead pigeons . . .**": Edward Miles Barrett, diary entry for March 2, 1942. "**They just didn't want to believe we were off the** *Houston*": Pryor, UNT interview, Jan. 22, 1973, 10. "**For the first four or five days at Serang . . .**": Lanson H. Harris, interview with the author. "**We began to mellow out and to think**": Ibid. "**We were hungry to the point of it being actual torture . . .**": Pryor, UNT interview, Jan. 22, 1973, 16. "**After about two weeks, things began to get very uptight . . .**": Lanson H. Harris, speech to the Long Beach Yacht Club.

CHAPTER 25 (pp. 178 to 185)

"**From fragmentary reports received in the Navy Department . . .**": Navy Department, Communique No. 48. "**Nothing, however, has been heard from the HMAS** *Perth* **or the USS** *Houston* . . .": Navy Department, Communique No. 54. "**12 Allied Warships Lost in Java Battle . . .**": *Los Angeles Examiner*, March 15, 1942, 1. "**Kin of Missing Sad but Proud . . .**": *New York Herald Tribune*, dateline May 14, 1942. **Commander Maher, reported held in "the southern regions**": *Waltham News-Tribune*, "Some of Houston's Crew Saved, Japs Indicate." "**A new kind of war . . .**": Franklin D. Roosevelt, fireside chat, Feb. 23, 1942. "EVERYBODY WELL. LOVE, HAROLD ROOKS." Rooks to Edith Rooks, March 4, 1942. "**That means he and the ship are okay . . .**": "Misdated Cable Gave Wife of Capt. Rooks False Hope," unattributed, undated. "JUST HEARD THAT HOUSTON WAS SUNK . . .": Harold R. Rooks to Edith Rooks, March 14, 1942. "**Characteristic of you in having no hesitation . . .**": Hart to Edith Rooks, March 25, 1942, 1. "**I, myself, am by no means without hope . . .**": Ibid. "**It is with deep regret that I confirm the Navy Department's dispatch . . .**": Frank Knox to Edith Rooks, April 9, 1942. **Stivers "had word from a most responsible source**": J. W. Woodruff to Edith Rooks, April 22, 1942. **Rooks "a tower of strength in getting our scattered forces together . . .**": William A. Glassford to Edith Rooks, May 21, 1942, 1. "**There was a bell in the naval office . . .**": correspondence of William A. Bernrieder, CHC. "**There's never been anything like it, before or since**": "A Case of Unparalleled Patriotism," *The Houston Chronicle, Texas Magazine*, Dec. 9, 1979, 44. "**I'm ready to fight . . .**": Bob Tutt, "Reunion Set for Cruiser 'Volunteers,'" *Houston Chronicle*, May 11, 1992, 9A, 16A. "**On this Memorial Day, all America joins with you . . .**": *New York Times*, May 31, 1942, quoted in John Grider Miller, *The Battle to Save the Houston*, 6–7. "**An unparalleled gift of manpower**": Richard M. Morehead, "Texas Fills *Houston* Crew," undated United Press dispatch, dateline Houston, May 30, 1942.

CHAPTER 26 (pp. 186 to 190)

"**Officer? Any officer?**" **and Hamlin's parley with Japanese officer**: Paul E. Papish, UNT interview, 68–69. **Bicycle Camp "looked like the Hilton**": Lloyd V. Willey, UNT interview, 58–59. "**The whole camp froze . . .**": James Gee, UNT interview, 56. "**When a guy got out of line . . .**" **and "They were hard cases . . .**": John H. Wisecup, UNT interview, 39–40. "**They were looking for a soft billet . . .**": George Detre, UNT interview, 89. "**Some of them were so** short . . .": James Gee, UNT interview, 57. "**You did your damnedest to hold your feet . . .**": Seldon D. Reese, UNT interview, 58. "**After a while, hell, a bashing didn't . . .**": Wisecup, UNT interview, 41. "**The women and the kids had more intestinal fortitude . . .**": James Gee, UNT interview, 59. "**The Japanese soldier placed great emphasis on his masculinity . . .**": Charles, *Last Man Out*, 42. "**I'll always thank some good Christian missionary . . .**": Pryor, UNT interview, Jan. 22, 1973, 20. "**At nighttime you'd hear some noise . . .**": Ibid., 22. "**All these other Jap guards rushed out immediately . . .**": Willey, 63–64.

CHAPTER 27 (pp. 191 to 195)

Hill "**willed himself to die . . .**": Marvin Robinson, UNT interview, 130. Hill died at Serang on April 8, 1942. **Medical conditions in camp**: Raymond Day, "Saga of the *Houston*," 7–8, and Hamlin, statement, 2–3. "**This stuff is just like a knife in your guts**": John H. Wisecup, UNT interview, 43–44. "**Finally a British colonel interceded . . .**": Hamlin, "Statement," 2. "**He gave up a long time ago . . .**": John H. Wisecup, UNT interview, 31. "**Generally speaking, petty officers behaved splendidly . . .**": Hamlin, "Statement," 2. "**Organization was kept in every way . . .**": Ibid., 3. "**We were professional sailors . . .**": George Detre, UNT interview, 69. "**If you got your brass, you got a chance . . .**": Wisecup, UNT interview, 34. "**They would tell us about great naval battles . . .**": Charley L. Pryor, UNT interview, Jan. 22, 1973, 36. "**What's the matter, sailor?**": Paul E. Papish, UNT interview, 84.

CHAPTER 28 (pp. 196 to 202)

Arrival of the 131st: Donald Brain, UNT interview, 80, and Melfred L. Forsman, UNT interview, 78. **Lost Battalion battery associations**: Luther Prunty, UNT interview, 11. "**We felt very good because we felt that in numbers there was strength . . .**"": James Gee, UNT interview, 54. "**Whatever you needed, they seemed to come up with it**": Melfred L. Forsman, UNT interview, 79. "**How could there be so much water in the world?**": Jess Stanbrough, UNT interview, 38–39. **Lost Battalion's deployment on Java**: Ibid., 53–58, and Eddie Fung, UNT interview, 26. "**We were still in an *Alice in Wonderland* world . . .**": Stanbrough, UNT interview, 72. "**We would pass through a village . . .**": Thompson, *A Thousand Cups of Rice*, 37–38. "**There's only a few hundred of them over there . . .**": Ibid., 38–39. "**We entered right off the road, dressed in our fatigues . . .**": Stanbrough, quoted in Thompson, 40. "**The Australian Brigadier says . . .**" and "**At last we fully realized that the war had caught up with us**": Ibid., 40–41. "**We are forced to surrender . . .**": Ibid., 42. **Surrender of Lost Battalion**: Prunty, 38–39. "**We still had this eternal hope, prayer for the *Houston* . . .**": Wade H. Webb, UNT interview, 47–48. "**I guess that was the first time I'd seen a Jap . . .**": Roy M. Offerle, UNT interview, 36.

CHAPTER 29 (pp. 203 to 208)

Home life of *Houston* men: Otto C. Schwarz, interview with the author; H. Robert Charles, interview with the author and *Last Man Out*, 43–44. "**Hey, old**

Joe's really getting a pounding . . . !": Seldon D. Reese, UNT interview, 58. "He'd see a tin can—" and "They'd look at him and kind of shake their heads . . .": Charles, UNT interview, 81. "I don't know what there was in that man . . .": Charles, interview with the author. **Scavenging by work parties at Batavia**: Howard Brooks, interview with the author, 33; William M. Ingram, interview with Floyd Cox, 19; Charley L. Pryor, UNT interview, Jan. 22, 1973, 34; George Detre, UNT interview, 87; Raymond Day, "Saga of the *Houston*," 8a. "Hey, Jack, you've got a real treasure there . . ." and "You dumb bastard! Where's your truck?": Jack Feliz, UNT interview, 60–63. "This man stole many things": Lloyd V. Willey, UNT interview, 72. "He was the type of guy that could actually get you in trouble . . .": Marvin Robinson, UNT interview, 60.

CHAPTER 30 (pp. 209 to 216)

"Now when you get in a situation like that": Lanson H. Harris, speech, Long Beach Yacht Club. "If you had a chance to sabotage . . .": Paul E. Papish, UNT interview, 93. **Radios in camp**: John F. Schneider, "The History of KTAB/KSFO"; Horace Chumley, UNT interview, 38; Jess Stanbrough, UNT interview, 107; Thompson, *A Thousand Cups of Rice*, 50; Lloyd Willey, UNT interview, 74–75. "Oh, it looks to me at least six months . . .": Stanbrough, UNT interview, 111. "Hang in there . . ." and "Had anyone else tried to instigate such a thing . . .": Charles, *Last Man Out*, 44. "The Japanese knew he had it and laughed . . .": Seldon D. Reese, UNT interview, 63. "The guards poured out on the grounds to stop it then": Charles, *Last Man Out*, 44. "There were times you'd just say, 'Well . . .'": Papish, 104. "I never admitted that we were whipped": Melfred L. Forsman, UNT interview, 7. **Buying food**: Charley L. Pryor, UNT interview, Jan. 22, 1973, 33. **Pay rates**: Fujita, *Foo*, 106. **Controversy over funds**: Thompson, *A Thousand Cups of Rice*, 47–48. **Background on Lt. Roy E. Stensland**: La Forte and Marcello, *Building the Death Railway*, 30; Edmonds, *They Fought with What They Had*, 373–374, 385; Marvin Robinson, UNT interview, 93; Eldridge Rayburn, UNT interview, 85; P. J. Smallwood, UNT interview, 158; Daws, *Prisoners of the Japanese*, 224, 241. "Lieutenant Stensland, before you knew what was happening . . .": Lester C. Rasbury, quoted in La Forte, 61. "I thought he was a dead man . . .": Houston Tom Wright, UNT interview, 91–92.

CHAPTER 31 (pp. 217 to 223)

"This one day we were on a working party . . .": Lloyd V. Willey, UNT interview, 62. "I will obey all orders from the Japanese": Harold S. Hamlin, "Statement," 2. "At Serang were nearly all the survivors from the . . ." and "From first to last perhaps a hundred men . . .": Rivett, *Behind Bamboo*, 101–102. **Dispatch reporting U.S. prisoners at Batavia**: "*Houston* Men Jap Captives?" United Press, dateline Sydney, July 1, 1942. "I know many of the boys . . .": Mother of Crayton Gordon, quoted in Thompson, *A Thousand Cups of Rice*, 55. "I am proud of my two boys . . .": Ida Pearl Elliott Fujita, quoted in Fujita, *Foo*, 111–112. "As I marched my troops up and halted . . ." and "I was then taken . . .": Charles D. Smith, "USS *Houston* (CA-30) and Experiences," 16.

"If you do not sign the oath . . .": Hamlin, "Statement," 3. "You can always be sure that some Australians . . .": Jess Stanbrough, UNT interview, 129. "The three men were in obvious pain . . .": Hamlin, "Statement," 2. "There ain't a one of us who didn't think we were traitors . . .": John H. Wisecup, UNT interview, 51. "After the Fourth of July, all hell broke loose": Stanbrough, UNT interview, 120. "The Brown Bomber was our first infamous one": Stanbrough, 120. "He'd go pick out somebody . . .": Ibid., 131. Guard nicknames: Ilo B. Hard, UNT interview, 161, and Charley L. Pryor, UNT interview, Jan. 22, 1973, 42–43. "A soldier might tell you . . .": George Detre, UNT interview, 58.

CHAPTER 32 (pp. 224 to 227)

"The only man who could make five-gallon cans invisible . . .": Daws, *Prisoners of the Japanese*, 170. "Man, he had some gear . . .": John H. Wisecup, UNT interview, 54. "He became a sort of hero . . .": H. Robert Charles, UNT interview, 87. First group to leave Batavia: "Roster of Fitzsimmons Group," USS *Houston* Survivors Association. The Australian Army rank of brigadier was introduced in 1928 to replace the rank of colonel commandant, which had briefly replaced the rank of brigadier general in 1922. A brigadier is more a senior colonel rather than the lowest rank of general (much like a commodore is to an admiral in the navy). Hellship departures from Batavia: "List of Hellship Voyages." "The Japanese method of shipping troops . . .": C. D. Smith, "USS *Houston*," 17. "They just took a rifle butt and jammed it . . .": Julius B. Heinen, quoted in La Forte, *Building the Death Railway*, 80. "There had been cattle hauled in that ship . . .": H. Robert Charles, UNT interview, 86. "It was a night of darkness and heat . . ." and "like froth from a boiling saucepan": Parkin, *Into the Smother*, 6.

CHAPTER 33 (pp. 228 to 231)

"Once again, as in Batavia . . .": Rivett, *Behind Bamboo*, 131. "Oh my God, what in the world . . .": Charley L. Pryor, UNT interview, Jan. 22, 1973, 52. "Changi was a school for survivors": James Clavell, *The Guardian*, quoted in Reminick, *Death's Railway*, 77. "It was the strangest thing I've ever seen in my life . . .": Otto C. Schwarz, UNT interview, 81–82. "Why don't they make a run . . .": H. Robert Charles, UNT interview, 91. "Lay on one, Yank!": Pryor, 65–66. "Everybody just sat there spellbound . . .": Ibid., 92. "They'll be right at our sides": Schwarz, interview with the author, 11–12. "They had their own stuff cached away . . .": Charles, 93. "Those are the King's coconuts": Frank Fujita, UNT interview, 56; Pryor, 59–60. "You have got to take that man out . . .": Hamlin, quoted in Jack Bartz, interview with the author. "Well, my man! . . ." and "Pleased to meet you . . .": Rivett, *Behind Bamboo*, 134.

CHAPTER 34 (pp. 232 to 239)

"Hell, they are going to kill you . . .": Frank Fujita, UNT interview, 68. Fujita arrives in Japan: Fujita, *Foo*, 114, 123 fn. 4. "We carried on our own little war . . .": Fujita, UNT interview, 78. "He never even kicked": Ibid., 78. "They were anxious to find out almost anything . . .": Maher, "Jap Prison Experiences," 15. **Commander Maher in Japan**: Maher narrative, 13; see also Martindale, *The 13th Mission*, 109–10, 120. "**It was an honor, we understand . . .**": Raymond Day, "Saga of the *Houston*," 11. "**You're going to a health camp . . .**": Paul E. Papish, UNT interview, 124. "**Well, we ought to be out of the danger zone**" and "**Just incidentally, if . . .**": Julius B. Heinen Jr., UNT interview, 80. "**We heard this tremendous** *whomp* . . .": Charley L. Pryor, UNT interview, Jan. 22, 1973, 76–77. "**Just don't panic . . .**": Heinen, 81. "**What's the bid?**": Ibid., 82. **Damage to the** *Dai Moji Maru*: Raymond Day, "Saga of the *Houston*," 13–14; Charles D. Smith, "USS *Houston*," 18; Col. Tom Sledge, interview with the author and Roy Offerle, UNT interview, 85. "**Up above the water line . . .**": Pryor, UNT interview, Jan. 22, 1973, 79. "**I will give credit to the Japanese merchant captain . . .**": C. D. Smith, 18. **Rumors of a railway**: Pryor, 76; Donald Brain, UNT interview, 130.

CHAPTER 35 (pp. 240 to 245)

"**Hell, I know where we are . . .**": Donald Brain, UNT interview, 132–133. **The Battle for Burma and Japanese strategic plans**: Romanus and Riley, *Stilwell's Mission to China*, 100–101. "**We were still young and adventurous . . .**": James Gee, UNT interview, March 19, 1972, 4. **Colonel Nagatomo, "Very cocky, a king-of-the-walk type"**: H. Robert Charles, UNT interview, 98. **Welcoming speech**: Otto Schwarz and Howard Brooks, interviews with the author; Dan Buzzo, UNT interview, 131; and Gee, 13. "**It is a great pleasure to us to see you at this place . . .**": Nagatomo, "Speech Delivered at Thanbyuzayat," quoted in La Forte and Marcello, *Building the Death Railway*, 287–289. "**We will build the railroad if we have to build it over the white man's body . . .**": This last paragraph does not appear in the September 15, 1942, text of the speech found in the collection of Japanese POW documents edited by John C. Sharp. Nor is it included in Maj. W. E. Fisher's diary, which contains a transcript of Colonel Nagatomo's speech, nor in Rohan Rivett's *Behind Bamboo*. It is included in the text of the October 28, 1942, speech to the Fitzsimmons group, as published in La Forte and Marcello's *Building the Death Railway*, and also appears in Kyle Thompson's memoir, *A Thousand Cups of Rice*. Perhaps "We will build the railroad if we have to build it over the white man's body" may thus have been a special flourish for the Americans' benefit. "**Thanbyuzayat turned out to be the beginning of a real nightmare**": Gee, 18–19. "**I knew this guy meant business . . .**": Charles, UNT interview, 99.

Part 4: In the Jungle of the Kwai

CHAPTER 36 (pp. 249 to 252)

Japanese designs for the Burma-Thailand Railway: Davies, *The Man Behind the Bridge*, 91; the civilian consultant's name was Kuwabara. **For background on the Imperial Army's attitude toward prisoners**, see Herbert P. Bix's *Hirohito and the Making of Modern Japan*, 359–360. **Regarding Japan's treatment of its POWs**, see Bix, 207, where he discusses Emperor Hirohito's cover-up of the

Army's 1929 atrocities in Manchuria and the privy council's failure to ratify the full Geneva Prisoner of War Convention. "The groundwork for the future commission of war atrocities by the Japanese military was also being laid during this period," Bix writes. **Native Asian laborers on the railway**: see Boggett, "Notes on the Thai-Burma Railway," 42.

CHAPTER 37 (pp. 253 to 256)

My basic chronology of Branch Three's activities derives from the diary of Brig. Arthur L. Varley. **Establishment of Branch Five**: Harold S. Hamlin, "Statement," 4; Varley diary, 88. Maj. W. E. Fisher, the Australian doctor, observed the nomenclature "Thai POW Branch" for Burma railway construction units tended to keep the subsequent public focus on the Thailand end of the railway. In fact, in several respects the average prisoner's plight in Burma was worse. See Fisher, "Medical Experiences," 2. **Prisoners' duties on the railway**: See Charley L. Pryor, UNT interview, Jan. 22, 1973, 91–95; H. Robert Charles, UNT interview, 100–109; and the author's interviews with Howard Brooks and Otto C. Schwarz. **"You might spend a whole month making one fill . . ."**: Brooks, interview with the author. See also Lanson Harris, speech to Long Beach Yacht Club. **"There was a lot of rock . . ."**: Melfred L. Forsman, UNT interview, 144–145. **"We got beat up more for bending a shovel . . ."**: Brooks, interview with the author.

CHAPTER 38 (pp. 257 to 266)

Branch Three: Per Brigadier Varley's diary entry for March 28, 1943, Branch Three had 9,534 men, including 4,465 Australians, 481 British, 194 Americans, and 4,394 Dutch. **Background on Brigadier Varley**: Ramsey, "Courage Writ Large in a Steady Hand," *Sydney Morning Herald*, April 23, 2005. **"They all spoke cheerio and good luck messages . . ."**: Varley diary, June 6, 1942. **POW pay**: Varley diary, Feb. 19, 1943. **"Were there any good Japanese?"**: Fisher, "Medical Experiences," 47. **"If you poked your finger into your leg . . ."**: Otto C. Schwarz, interview with the author. **"You feel like your mind is a closed circuit . . ."**: Parkin, *Into the Smother*, 155. **"The J's require absolute proof . . ."**: Varley diary, entry for Nov. 11, 1942. **"A little quinine would have saved a lot of lives . . ."**: Schwarz, Ibid. **Henri Hekking's parley with Major Yamada**: Charles, *Last Man Out*, 78–79. **Rice "rotten and unusable . . ."**: Ibid., 114; see also Houston Tom Wright, UNT interview, 66. **"Melons were only hog feed . . ."**: William V. Bell to Mrs. Samuel H. Lumpkin, undated letter, circa June 1953. **"You don't worry about a day of reckoning . . ."**: Charles, *Last Man Out*, 114–115. **Dr. Hekking's jungle remedies**: Wright, 119–120, 150, 152; Charles, *Last Man Out*, 116. **"It was most distressing to him . . ."**: Ibid., 87. **Lumpkin's comment**: Per Ilo B. Hard, UNT interview, 170. **"He was the first man that I ever heard of . . ."**: Wright, 119–120.

CHAPTER 39 (pp. 267 to 269)

"The prisoners worked in a rather foolish fashion . . .": Charles D. Smith, "USS *Houston* (CA-30) and Experiences," 19. **Planes over Thanbyuzayat**: Varley, diary entry for March 1, 1943.

CHAPTER 40 (pp. 270 to 274)

"We'd get in there, and you'd hit one . . .": Charley L. Pryor, UNT interview, Jan. 22, 1973, 102. "An elephant's a smart bugger . . .": Ibid., 113. Spider rigs: Pryor, UNT#3, 41, and death of Japanese engineers: Luther Prunty, UNT interview, 114 and Donald Brain, UNT interview, 165. "It seemed impossible, but it worked . . .": Prunty, 115.

CHAPTER 41 (pp. 275 to 282)

"As we would go into a new working camp . . ." and "We kept our structure. We had our officers . . .": Otto C. Schwarz, interview with the author. "If a passing fly chose to step into your rice ration . . ." and "There were times when most of us felt . . .": Searle, *To the Kwai—and Back*, 122–123. "They would either die from the jolting about . . .": Varley, diary entry for April 10, 1943. "Major General Sasa has visited camp . . .": Varley, diary entry for April 14. Higuchi "knew nothing of medicine . . .": Fisher, "Medical Experiences," 52. Pryor as "nothing but the skin stretched over the bones": Charley L. Pryor, UNT interview, Jan. 22, 1973, 107–110. "It looked like an Army field hospital . . .": James Gee, UNT interview, March 19, 1972, 68–69. Red Cross inspection of Thanbyuzayat: Varley, diary entry for April 26, 28–30, 1943; Gee, 69; and Fisher, "Medical Experiences," 61. "Bless 'Em all": Otto C. Schwarz, interview with the author, and Rivett, *Behind Bamboo*, 192. Deaths at 80 Kilo Camp: of Lawrence F. Kondzela, March 13, 1943; James H. White, April 13, 1943; and Sgt. Joe Martin True Lusk, April 28, 1943. "I'm glad I'm sick because I'm not going to work . . .": Benjamin Dunn, UNT interview, 151–152. "Then he became depressed again": Fisher, 150. "He had tried to be tough with the guards at work . . .": Ibid. USMC Service Records for H. H. Dupler: NARA II. Dupler's burial: Varley, diary entry for May 15, 1943. "They were some of the biggest, strongest guys . . .": John H. Wisecup, UNT interview, 90–91.

CHAPTER 42 (pp. 283 to 290)

"It is as if the Wet were a baying animal . . .": Parkin, *Into the Smother*, 87. "The J. will carry out schedule and do not mind . . .": Varley, diary entry for May 18, 1943. "I don't remember any storms; I just remember rain . . .": Howard Brooks, interview with the author. "Within the first day and then with ever-mounting zeal . . .": Rivett, *Behind Bamboo*, 195. "It's awesome to hear a huge tree . . .": Ilo B. Hard, UNT interview, 163. "I remember on one occasion that a bridge had washed out . . .": Melfred L. Forsman, UNT interview, 170. "Finally they gave up on this truck thing . . .": Donald Brain, UNT interview, 181. "You would work whatever they decided you would work . . .": Otto C. Schwarz, interview with the author. "There seemed to be no bottom to the mud . . .": Charley L. Pryor, UNT interview, Feb. 20, 1973, 6. "That word 'Speedo' . . .": Howard Brooks, interviewed in video, "Secrets of the Dead." 80 Kilo established as a "hospital": Hamlin, "Statement," 5; Pryor, 7; and Smith, "USS *Houston* and Experiences," 20. "The least sick of the stretcher cases . . .": Smith, 20. "I looked in that hut, and I couldn't believe . . ." and "You know he's not going to live very long . . .": Dunn, 170; see also Luther Prunty, UNT interview, 141. **A jungle clearing, "the worst I have ever traveled on"**: Varley, diary entry for June 4, 1943. **"These poor devils do not appear to receive any treatment . . ."**: Ibid. **"My fears expressed so often during the past three months . . ."**: Varley diary, entry for June 4, 1943. **"It got cold about five o'clock each morning . . ."**: Clyde Fillmore, *Prisoner of War*, 78. **"Everybody died there. That was my station"**: Red Huffman, interview with the author.

CHAPTER 43 (pp. 291 to 295)

"Any way you could slow the Japanese down . . .": Melfred L. Forsman, UNT interview, 144. **"I know we Marines had a code among us . . ."**: H. Robert Charles, UNT interview, 107. **"The idea was that we'd crawl under there . . ."**: Ibid., 108. **"We agreed not to place the burden of secrecy on anyone . . ."**: Charles, *Last Man Out*, 135. **"I don't know how many it hurt or mangled . . ."**: Charles, UNT interview, 108; and *Last Man Out*, 134–136.

CHAPTER 44 (pp. 296 to 300)

Americans join H Force: Reminick, *Death's Railway*, 84; Crayton Gordon, UNT interview, 100. **"What we lost on that railroad . . ."**: John H. Wisecup, UNT interview, 63. **The embankment at Kinsayok**: Rod Beattie, quoted in "Secrets of the Dead: The Bridge on the River Kwai" (video). **"The road had petered out as the undergrowth changed . . ."**: Searle, *To the Kwai—and Back*, 105–106. **"This period of movement must mean something big . . ."**: Parkin, *Into the Smother*, 107. **"The head of the man holding the drill . . ."**: Parkin, 121, 123. **"Occasionally we caught glimpses . . ."**: Searle, 108. **"The daily blasting along this section is terrific . . ."**: Parkin, 167.

CHAPTER 45 (pp. 301 to 308)

"The radios were dismantled and smuggled . . .": Melfred L. Forsman, UNT interview, 166–167. **"I lived day by day . . ."**: Roy M. Offerle, UNT interview, 126. **"Jane, you've got a funny-looking thing here"**: Jane Harris, interview with the author. **"You come home from the station or airport . . ."**: quoted in Yellen, *Our Mother's War*, 13–14. **"Such a statement is either a deliberate evasion or . . ."**: Hodge, "Exchange of Information Sheet for Relatives of Personnel Attached to the U.S.S. *Houston*, Lost in Sundra Straits [sic], February 28, 1942," undated, revised to V-J Day, 1946. **"It is impossible to estimate the value of Mr. Hodge's work . . ."**: Smith, "Where Is the Crew of the Ghost Cruiser Houston?" *The Oregonian*. **Lieutenant Hodge's fate**: Statement of Leon W. Rogers, in dispatch from United States Naval Liaison Office, Calcutta, India, Enclosure a(2). **"One thing that has always discouraged me . . ."**: Edith Rooks to Hart, April 16, 1943, 8. **"Probably I should not have passed to you that rumor . . ."**: Hart to Edith Rooks, May 5, 1943. **"I must say more and more I feel the promise . . ."**: Edith Rooks to Hart, May 21, 1943, 2.

CHAPTER 46 (pp. 309 to 313)

Lieutenant Weiler's ring: Mintzer, "The Long Journey Home: Fran Weiler's Ring Returns to Annapolis," 10. **"There has got to be another way out . . ."**: Parkin,

Into the Smother, 101. **Flora and fauna of the railway**: Parkin, 72, 92–93, 111. "The thing eats faster than a cancer . . .": Charley L. Pryor, UNT interview, Feb. 1973, 3. "Had we known . . . that they'd wind up in a damn slop-hole grave . . .": Crayton Gordon, UNT interview, 141. "At first we made individual graves . . .": John Wisecup, UNT interview, 83. "I never will forget this . . ." and Wisecup's breakdown: Ibid., 84–85.

CHAPTER 47 (pp. 314 to 317)

"Nippon tearing Asia up into strips . . .": Dunlop, *War Diaries*, 221. **Jim Gee's hallucination**: Gee, UNT interview, March 19, 1972, 58. "This dream gave to me the strength . . .": Ibid. "Thank you for asking me to sponsor the USS *Rooks* . . .": Edith Rooks to Frank Knox, Dec. 7, 1943.

CHAPTER 48 (pp. 318 to 322)

Bombing of Thanbyuzayat: Varley, diary entry for June 12, 1943; Rivett, *Behind Bamboo*, 199–200. **Varley injured**: Varley, diary entry for June 15. **Life in the monsoon**: Benjamin Dunn, UNT interview, 143; Charles D. Smith, "Experiences," 20. "No medical officer or orderlies ever had to contend . . .": Lionel de Rosario, *Nippon Slaves*, www.ean.co.uk/Bygones/History/Article/WW2/ Death_Railway/html/songkurai.htm (last viewed by the author on March 10, 2005). "Nagatomo was astonished . . .": Varley, diary entry for July 1, 1943. **55 Kilo as "one of the worst, if not the worst camp . . .":** Fisher, "Medical Experiences," 8. **Aircraft of "a type not seen before"**: Varley, diary entry for July 9–12, 1943. "He was as regular as clockwork . . .": James Gee, UNT interview, March 19, 1972, 52. The Tenth Air Force's 80th Fighter Group flew P-38s over Burma starting in December 1942; www.talkingproud.us/HistoryBansheesE.html (March 16, 2005). "I guess they're going to wait for the rains . . .": Gee, UNT interview, 52.

CHAPTER 49 (pp. 323 to 330)

"*Fu*-ji-ta. Where is this *Fu*-ji-ta?": Frank Fujita Jr., UNT interview, 82; Fujita, *Foo*, 155–156. "They got mad as hell when I laughed . . .": Fujita, diary entry for June 6, 1943. "I figured my best bet is to keep my head . . .": Fujita, UNT interview, 84. "Look what we have here . . .": Fujita, UNT interview, 86; Fujita, diary, June 4, 1943. "I was bound and determined those sons of bitches . . .": Fujita, UNT interview, 90. **Japanese infantrymen, "small, illiterate, absurd . . ." and "They thanked us with bows . . .":** Fillmore, *Prisoner of War*, 85. **Prunty and Worthington "had a testament each"**: Luther Prunty, UNT interview, 129. **Charley Pryor at 80 Kilo Camp**: Pryor, UNT interview, Feb. 20, 1973, 16–18. "They'd tell you, 'I'm finished . . .'": John H. Wisecup, UNT interview, 81. "It was Wisecup, I guess, who would stand back there . . .": Paul E. Papish, UNT interview, 163. "Look, Charlie, your mind is like the muscle in your arm . . .": Jim Gee as quoted in Charles, *Last Man Out*, 132. "I don't have a friend": Dan Buzzo, UNT interview, 176. "Don't kid me. There are no eggs within a hundred miles": Ibid., 171–172. "Probably no single factor . . .":

Fisher, "Medical Experiences," 87. "A figure of six foot three inches emerges . . .": Parkin, *Into the Smother*, 105–106. "As small a thing as hiding, from yourself . . .": Marvin Robinson, UNT interview, 133. "It's people you've known, gone to school with . . .": Prunty, UNT interview, 135. Aborted escape by Forsman, Stensland, and Lattimore: Melfred L. Forsman, UNT interview, 189–191.

CHAPTER 50 (pp. 331 to 334)

Lumpkin "had the weight of the whole camp on his shoulders . . .": William V. Bell letter to Mrs. Samuel H. Lumpkin, 4. "It was hard to find anyone with such disregard for his self . . .": C. J. Vidler, letter "to whom it may concern," April 21, 1947. "Once the dysentery took a hold of him . . .": Roy Offerle, UNT interview, 135. "It was almost like a death blow to all of us . . .": Dan Buzzo, UNT interview, 175. "He didn't have it left in him . . .": Melfred L. Forsman, UNT interview, 186. "It was like a ghost town . . .": George Detre, UNT interview, 172. "You could smell that camp for miles": Eddie Fung, UNT interview, 124. "*Suffer* is a dangerous word here . . .": Parkin, *Into the Smother*, 93. "I find beauty in everything, even in death . . .": Frank Fujita, UNT interview, 53. "There is a lot to grumble about . . .": Ray Parkin, *Into the Smother*, 134. "It has become quite an institution . . ." and "*They'll be droppin' thousand-pounders when they come* . . .": Ibid., 215.

CHAPTER 51 (pp. 335 to 339)

Joining of the line at Three Pagodas Pass: Allen, "The 18th Division Royal Engineers," *Royal Engineers Journal*. 80 Kilo Camp abandoned: Smith, "USS *Houston* (CA-30) and Experiences," 21; Charley L. Pryor, UNT interview, Feb. 20, 1973, 16. Burials at 80 and 100 Kilo Camps: Smith, 21. "They had the bugle going all of the time . . .": Roy Offerle, UNT interview, 120. "It was more or less like a Toonerville trolley . . .": Melfred L. Forsman, quoted in La Forte and Marcello, *Building the Death Railway*, 256. "I think we all came to the conclusion . . .": James Gee, UNT interview, March 19, 1972, 79. "We were lucky": Ibid., 62–63. "In my opinion it is a virtue since ancient times . . ." and "We have exploited untrodden jungles . . .": Nagatomo quoted in Sharp, "Japanese Documentary," 22–23; see also Fisher, "Medical Experiences," 46. "Do you have anything to eat . . . ?" Houston Tom Wright, UNT interview, 165–166.

CHAPTER 52 (pp. 340 to 345)

Deaths in Branches Three and Five: Arthur L. Varley, diary entry for Jan. 11–19, 1944. Deaths in F and H Forces: Kinvig, *River Kwai Railway*, 198. Movements of A Force: Varley, diary entry for Nov. 7, 1943. The Japanese "seemed to indulge in a system of competitive bidding . . .": Harold S. Hamlin, "Report of Service as Prisoner of War," 5. "This camp was much better than anything we had seen . . .": Charles D. Smith, "USS *Houston* (CA-30) and Experiences," 21–22. "Like dining at the Savoy in Hollywood": Houston Tom Wright, UNT interview, 166. "He lost no telling how many dollars . . .":

Marvin Robinson, UNT interview, 138. "They'd chloroform the guy . . .": John H. Wisecup, UNT interview, 101. See also Wright, 170. **Construction of the bridge at Tamarkan ("the Bridge on the River Kwai")**: Davies, *The Man Behind the Bridge*, 100–103. "They were in a hurry to finish it . . .": Wisecup, UNT interview, 96. **Air attacks on the bridge**: U.S. Army Air Forces, Historical Office, *The Tenth Air Force: 1943*, 91.

CHAPTER 53 (pp. 346 to 351)

The Tenth Air Force: Army Air Forces Historical Office, *The Tenth Air Force: 1943*, 32–38. "A resourceful, able and wily enemy must be blasted from the jungles . . .": General Order No. 1, Headquarters, Eastern Air Command, Dec. 15, 1943, quoted in Ibid., 38. **January 1943 reconnaissance of railway**: Fritsche, "Liberators on the Kwai," 82. **Friendly casualties from air attacks**: Davies, *The Man Behind the Bridge*, 144; Kinvig, *River Kwai Railway*, 180–181. *Houston* **men lost on the** *Tamahoko Maru* were yeoman second class Robert P. Willerton and seaman first class Joseph J. Alleva, USS *Houston* Association crew roster; "List of Hellship Voyages," last updated January 27, 2005, www.west-point.org/family/japanese-pow/Ships.htm. **Lost Battalion hell ship KIA**: Fillmore, *Prisoner of War*, 151–153. **Submarine attack on** *Rakuyo Maru* **and** *Kachidoki Maru*: Kinvig, 188. **Death of Brigadier Varley**: Kelly, *Just Soldiers*, www.anzacday.org.au/history/ww2/anecdotes/survivors.html. "As men were received on board, we stripped them . . .": "USS *Pampanito* (SS-383): The Third War Patrol." "The first 'open source' information on conditions in the railway camps . . .": Kinvig, 188.

CHAPTER 54 (pp. 352 to 357)

"Look at the mighty Japanese air force . . .": Frank King, UNT interview, 138–139. **Failed air attacks on Burma bridges**: *The Tenth Air Force: 1943*, 105, 110–111. "When we protested the camp being located . . .": Fillmore, *Prisoner of War*, 94. "You cussed the planes and everyone in them . . .": Ibid., 101. "You want to cheer them for tearing up the bridge . . .": Roy Offerle, UNT interview, 141. "Prisoners will not laugh at Japanese guards . . .": Fillmore, 101. "That little P-51 came down with the B-24s . . .": Luther Prunty, UNT interview, 195. "My friends, American airmen . . .": Houston Tom Wright, UNT interview, 173. "I don't believe it . . .": James "Red" Huffman, interview with the author; see also Melfred L. Forsman, UNT interview, 204. "When the all-clear would go . . ." and "He was breathing under the ground . . .": Huffman, Ibid. **The AZON bomb**: Kinvig, 182. **Bombing of "Bridge 277" (the bridge at Tamarkan)**: Carl H. Frische, "Liberators on the Kwae," 88. "You could see they were worried . . .": John H. Wisecup, UNT interview, 115. "They had been very casual about guarding us . . .": Eddie Fung, UNT interview, 139–140. **Troops were advised to kill** "cautiously and circumspectly . . .": Brackman, *The Other Nuremberg*, 246. **Declaration regarding "liquidation" of prisoner populations**: Exhibit 2015, Tokyo War Crimes Trials, January 9, 1947, translated by Stephen H. Green, in Holmes, *Unjust Enrichment*, 123–124.

CHAPTER 55 (pp. 358 to 364)

Warship construction: Parshall, "Why Japan Really Lost the War." **"And you know, *whoosh!*"**: John H. Wisecup, UNT interview, 112–113. **Tonnage of bombs dropped on Japan, November 1944 to August 1945, and projections of September to December 1945**: Frank, *Downfall*, 306. **"Bombed Bullshit!"** Luther Prunty, UNT interview, 186. **"There wasn't an engine on that railroad . . ."**: Otto C. Schwarz, UNT interview, 143. **"You know, you Americans think you're smarter . . ."**: Schwarz, 135–136. **"Most of us stayed up to see the new year in . . ."**: Fujita, diary entry for Jan. 1, 1945. **"The Saturday morning raid was sure a rooter . . ."**: Ibid., entry for March 9, 1945; in that attack as many as 100,000 people died; see Frank, *Downfall*, 16–17. **U.S. prisoners at Ohasi**: Jess Stanbrough, UNT interview, 152–153; Arthur L. Maher, "Jap Prison Experiences," 24–25. **"It smelled like a fireplace burning pine wood . . ."**: Stanbrough, 155. **"We more or less accepted it philosophically"**: Maher, 25. **"I imagine they had an air gun up there . . ."**: Lloyd V. Willey, interview with the author. **Thai humanitarians**: Davies, *The Man Behind the Bridge*, 130–131; Kinvig, *River Kwai Railway*, 150–152. **Kempeitai activities**: Fisher, "Medical Experiences," 34; Willey interview with the author. **Siam becomes Thailand**: Nathaniel P. Davis, letter to Lawrence T. McCarthy, June 29, 1940. **Nighttime flights over Thailand**: Pryor, UNT interview, Feb. 20, 1973, 63, 72–73. **"I am your friend. I am with your friends . . ."**: Ibid., 77–78. **"If we run into Japanese, it will be bad for Japanese"**: Ibid., 78.

CHAPTER 56 (pp. 365 to 368)

OSS begins Thailand operation: "The Overseas Targets," 403; Smith, *Into Siam*, 17; Reynolds, "The Opening Wedge," 329, 339. Unbeknownst to the OSS, the codebreaking coup that produced the "Magic" intercepts of diplomatic signals gave Washington access to much of the information Donovan wanted out of Thailand. **"The opening wedge for postwar American economic . . ."**: Reynolds, 329. **Training of OSS field agents**: Smith, *Into Siam*, 48. **Training of Thai auxiliaries**: Ibid., 22, 25. **"They can throw their weight in wildcats"**: Ibid., 49. **The Thai agents killed by the Japanese** were Karawek Srivicharn or "Cary" and Sompongse Salyabongse or "Sal." Smith, *Into Siam*, 168–169, 302. **Pow reaches Bangkok**: Ibid., 180–183. **"A lamp had been lighted in the capital of Siam"**: Ibid., 183. **"Ruth"**: Reynolds, 330–331; "The Overseas Targets," 408. **"A double life is not an easy one,"** Smith, *Into Siam*, 233. **The OSS agents in Bangkok** were Maj. John Wester, a resident of Siam for eighteen years, and Dick Greenlee from Scarsdale, New York, who once worked as a tax lawyer in General Donovan's New York law firm. They flew by British seaplane to the waters off Thailand's southern coast and were spirited into Bangkok on a Thai Customs Department launch. See Reynolds, 336.

CHAPTER 57 (pp. 369 to 379)

Gus Forsman at Kanburi: Melfred L. Forsman, UNT interview, 202, 207–215. **"We learned, from these sources . . ."**: Fillmore, *Prisoner of War*, 106. **"Six years hell. We'll be lucky . . ."**: Forsman, 214. **Outram Road jail**: Daws, *Prisoners of the*

Japanese, 254–255; Lomax, *The Railway Man*, 158, 163–164. "A warder's boots would make a booming sound . . .": Lomax, 161–162. "This was a place in which the living . . .": Ibid., 164. Forsman at Outram Road: Forsman, 218–229. FDR's death: Larrabee, *Commander in Chief*, 647. Maj. Gen. Lowell Rooks in Germany: Ziemke, *The U.S. Army in the Occupation of Germany*, Chapter 15. POWs at Phet Buri (Cashew Mountain Camp) and Tayang airfield: Frank King, UNT interview, 147; Sharp, "Japanese Documentary," 27; Roy Offerle, UNT interview, 153; Luther Prunty, UNT interview, 200–201 (calling the camp White Pagoda Camp, west of Phet Buri, where an airstrip was being laid); James Huffman, interview with the author; Lanson H. Harris, speech, Long Beach Yacht Club; Lloyd V. Willey, UNT interview, 203–204. "Anything to get the hell out of camp . . ." and other quotes: Harris, speech. "You never tell anybody you're gonna escape . . .": Huffman, interview. "This is really stupid": Harris, speech. "You know, it's been three years . . .": Huffman, interview. Chinese dragon lore: Ingersoll, *Dragons and Dragon Lore*. "All of a sudden we looked up and here comes this clown . . .": Harris, speech. This was the second week of June 1945, per John C. Reas, letter to Pat Bozeman, April 26, 1988.

Part 5: Rendezvous with Freedom

CHAPTER 58 (pp. 383 to 390)

"About twenty minutes later, here come these Japs . . ." and other quotes from Lanson H. Harris: Harris, speech, Long Beach Yacht Club. "They would nearly kill you with the smoke . . ." and other quotes from James "Red" Huffman: Huffman, interview with the author. Major Bartlett "captured fifteen armed German soldiers . . .": Headquarters, ETO, U.S. Army, Certificate of Merit to Maj. Eben B. Bartlett Jr. Gallaher is referred to as "Virlen" and "Virlin" in other documents; re rank, Gallaher was promoted to sgt. on July 19; see OSS Records, Opero to Pattern, Aug. 17, 1945. Bartlett airdropped into Thailand: OSS, "Pattern Operational Report" (by Maj. Eben B. Bartlett Jr.), Sept. 28, 1945; Opero to Pattern, June 6, 1945; Pattern to Opero, June 11, 1945. Operation Salad (supply drops): OSS, "Report on Operation Salad," July 11, 1945; Smith, *Into Siam*, 203; Tenth Air Force, "Special Flight Intelligence Report," by Lt. Col. Robert A. Erdin, June 22, 1945. "THE WAY I FEEL ABOUT THIS BUSINESS . . .": Pattern to Opero, July 14, 1945. "IF JAPS COME IN HERE, SHALL WE FIGHT IT OUT . . .": Pattern to Opero, July 3, 1945. "PRESENT POLICY IS NOT TO HAVE ANY OF OUR GROUPS FIGHT . . .": Opero to Pattern, July 4, 1945. Reporting "lamentable": *War Report of the OSS*, 412. "Things are getting hot down there . . ." and conversations between Smith and Pow: Smith, *Into Siam*, 248. "Upon their arrival, a runner came . . .": OSS, "Pattern Operational Report." "I HAVE TWO PRISONERS OF WAR WITH ME . . .": OSS, Pattern to Opero, July 27, 1945. "He would get us apart," Red Huffman, interview with the author. "WHAT PARTICULAR INFORMATION DO YOU WANT . . . ?": OSS, Pattern to Opero, July 27, 1945. "Neither one of us would go": Huffman, interview with the author. "HAVE TOLD THEM THEY WOULD BE [EXFILTRATED] SOONEST . . .":

OSS, Pattern to Opero, July 28, 1945. **USS *Houston* KIA/MIA list (current to March 1, 1945):** OSS, Pattern to Opero, Aug. 7, 1945.

CHAPTER 59 (pp. 391 to 394)

"**All our men are bang-happy . . .**" and "**Another thing the fellows are anxious to get . . .**": Grassi quoted in Smith, *Into Siam*, 258–259. "**The only difficulty anticipated . . .**": Eben B. Bartlett Jr., untitled document, "From Pattern." "**Keep cautioning [your agents] against overt action . . .**": Smith, 284. "**Never forget Pearl Harbor**": USS *Indiana*, Ship's Log. **Bombardment of Kamaishi:** Cressman, *The Official Chronology of the U.S. Navy in World War II*. 334. Reportedly Admiral Halsey "firmly directed [the British task force] to attend to other targets, thus creating a distinct impression that the U.S. Navy regarded this operation as specific retaliation for Pearl Harbor." See Frank, *Downfall*, 158. "**Where were our planes . . . ?**": Jess Stanbrough, UNT interview, 161. "**There was a lot of people that had been captured . . .**": Ibid., 189–190. "**The prodigious land, sea and air forces of the United States . . .**": "Proclamation Calling for the Surrender of Japan," Potsdam, July 26, 1945. www.niraikanai.wwma.net/pages/archive/potsdam.html.

CHAPTER 60 (pp. 395 to 398)

Lloyd Willey at Tayang: Lloyd V. Willey, interview with the author. "**The Japs were very touchy . . .**": Ibid. A mood of "**impatience, frenzy and bewilderment**": Frank, *Downfall*, 290. **The P-51 pilot captured and tortured was Lt. Marcus McDilda:** Ibid. **Tensions between Japan and Soviet Union:** USSBS interrogation of Admiral Soemu Toyoda, 318–319. "**Since this is the shape of things . . .**": Frank, *Downfall*, 295–296, quoting a re-creation of the scene by Robert Butow, with modifications. "**The Imperial Army and Navy shall by no means return . . .**": Ibid., 326–327. "**The wishes of the imperial ancestors . . .**": Ibid., 318. **Imperial Palace coup:** Ibid., 317–321. "**A road to success will somehow be revealed . . .**": Ibid., 308–309. **Surrender negotiations:** Ibid., 300–301.

CHAPTER 61 (pp. 399 to 408)

"**Will they drop one on Saigon?**" Garth Slate, UNT interview, 214. "**Present plan tentatively approved . . .**": Opero (Col. Amos D. Moscrip) to Bartlett, Aug. 16, 1945. **OSS personnel supporting Major Bartlett:** OSS, Opero (Moscrip) to Pattern, Aug. 16, 1945; OSS Headquarters to Major Max Small, "Personnel on Operations," Sept. 5, 1945, 2. "**Cover is to be maintained . . .**": Opero (Goodell) to Pattern, Aug. 23, 1945. "**As soon as we found out in this camp . . .**": Charles D. Smith, "USS *Houston* (CA-30) and Experiences," 23. "**Hollywood couldn't have written . . .**": James Gee, UNT interview, March 19, 1972, 120. "**I gave them a short talk . . .**": OSS, "History, 'MAINLAND, PETBURI' Operation," Lt. Col. Amos D. Moscrip Jr., to Strategic Services Officer, IBT, Sept. 18, 1945. "**While the pictures may show the men to look fairly healthy . . .**": Moscrip, to Director, OSS Field Photographic Branch, "Operation Mainland," Sept. 16, 1945, 3. **Rescued Americans in Operation Mainland:**

OSS, "Operation Mainland, Chronology of Principal Events," 4, 9, 11. "**They cir-cled out and dived and wig-wagged**" and "*Cheer up, boys . . .*": Reynolds, diary, 234–235. "**Anyone having relatives on the crew of the *Houston* . . .**": Associated Press, "300 *Houston* Survivors Found in Jap Prison Camp in Thailand," dateline Washington, DC, Aug. 28, 1945. "**The appearance of the landing craft in the channel . . .**": Commander Task Group 30.6, "Action Report Covering Evacuation of Prisoners of War," III(1). "**With the end of the war, history started immediately to repeat . . .**": Ibid., VIII(1). "**The hand that fills in the blank pages in the book of war . . .**": Associated Press, "Tragic War Mystery Clears," dateline Washington, Aug. 29, 1945. **Commander Maher's visit with Captain Bahm**: Falloon, "My Brush with History." **Maher on the USS *Missouri***: Maher, USS *Houston* (CA-30) Survivors Association reunion speech, Aug. 12, 1983, Dallas; papers of Charley L. Pryor. "**In many ways these weeks have seemed the most difficult . . .**": Edward Miles Barrett, diary entry for Aug. 11, 1945. **Forsman's release**: Melfred L. Forsman, UNT interview, 234; Barrett, diary entry for Sept. 1, 1945. "**The war is over**" and "**That's impossible . . .**": Forsman, 236. "**The last time that I had seen that flag . . .**": Paul E. Papish, UNT interview, 171. "**They learned right quick . . .**": Garth Slate, UNT interview, 226–227. See also Wisecup, UNT interview, 120, and Dan Buzzo, UNT interview, 223.

CHAPTER 62 (pp. 409 to 418)

"**He had a piece of paper, like a government check . . .**": Lanson H. Harris, speech, Long Beach Yacht Club. "**I put two and two together with the telegram . . .**": Jane Harris, interview with the author. "**They treated us like real psycho cases . . .**": John H. Wisecup, UNT interview, 122. "**What are you going to do when you get out?**" Ibid., 125. "**Do you know where the *Houston* was sunk?**": James Huffman, interview with the author. "**That was bad for him . . .**": Jane Harris, interview with the author. "**They asked me questions like, 'Did you see this . . . ?'**": Lanson Harris, speech. "**You had a period of exuberance and then . . .**": Wisecup, UNT interview, 126. "**He told us the importance of exercise . . .**": James Gee, UNT interview, March 19, 1972, 56. "**I remembered the little amenities . . .**": Charles, *Last Man Out*, 178. "**We watched these pretty-looking girls . . .**" and "**Why didn't you let me know when I called you? . . .**": Jess Stanbrough, UNT interview, 208. "**With the thought of finding my step-father . . .**": Charles, 176. "**When I first came back . . .**" and "**I couldn't sleep . . .**": John Bartz, interview with the author. "**I was flying for five or six years . . .**": Lanson Harris, interview with the author. "**It came time when he was in twenty years . . .**": Jane Harris, interview. "**I was absolutely lost, like a fish out of water . . .**" and "**I spent the next three months . . .**": Otto C. Schwarz, UNT interview, 156–157. **The habits of a POW**: hot tea (Paul Papish, UNT interview, 149), burnt-rice coffee (Houston Tom Wright, UNT interview, 198), hard floors (Lloyd V. Willey interview), heads of lettuce (Donald Brain, UNT interview, 233). "**I resolved that although I might never be rich . . .**": Stanbrough, 213. Jess Stanbrough passed away in 1999. **Charles, "determined that the war would not be the biggest thing . . .**": Charles, *Last Man Out*, 189. **Encounter with**

Pack Rat McCone: Charles, interview with the author. "If I had my way about it, I'd find forty-nine other ex-POWs . . .": Morrow, "Ex-POW Wants to Relieve Hostages," *Escondido Times-Advocate*, A-1. "I don't know why, but all of a sudden . . .": Harris, speech. "I always had the philosophy . . .": Schwarz, 160.

CHAPTER 63 (pp. 419 to 431)

War Graves Commission activities: Lomax, *The Railway Man*, 230. Hirohito's culpability for war crimes: Bix, *Hirohito*, 360–367; Holmes, *Unjust Enrichment*, 128. "Murdering, maiming, and ill-treating prisoners of war . . .": Brackman, *The Other Nuremberg*, 84–85. "The law of war forbids . . .": Claims Committee, "Liberated Military Personnel (JAPAN), of Japan for Maltreatment of Prisoners of War," 2–3, quoting *Moore's Digest of International Law*, Vol. VII, 218. "In so far as the rules set forth in the convention . . .": U.S. For. Rel., 1918, Suppl. 2, 7, quoted in Claims Committee, "Civil Responsibility," 4. "Japan strictly observes the Geneva Convention . . .": International Military Tribunal for the Far East, War Crimes Trial transcript, 49713–49714. Tojo made similar assurances regarding civilian internees, 49715. "To observers in daily attendance at the tribunal . . .": Brackman, 254. Tojo ordered "all prisoners of war to engage in forced labor": Ibid., 263–264. "The Japanese idea about prisoners is very different . . .": Ibid., 267. Death Railway chain of responsibility: "General Outline of Construction Progress: Details of the Construction and State of Affairs in the Earlier State (from June 1942 to the middle of February 1943)" read into the trial record by prosecutor Sir Arthur Comyns Carr, Tokyo War Crimes Trials, Sept. 12, 1946, 5530–5536. "The confession of the Japanese Army with regard to the Burma-Siam railway": Tokyo War Crimes Tribunal, testimony of Sept. 13, 1946, 5570. "Well, he ain't going back to Korea . . .": Garth Slate, UNT interview, 229. "I had a debriefing by a lieutenant colonel . . .": There will be no citation here. The testimony of the brave individual making this confession may be found in the UNT oral history archive for those who must find it. Statistics of war crimes tribunals and convictions: NARA, Interagency Working Group, "Japanese Interim Report." "Those words hung him": Lloyd Willey, interview with the author. Nagatomo proceedings: Commonwealth of Australia, Department of the Army, Military Court. "Trial of Japanese War Criminals, including Lt. Col. Yoshitada Nagatomo and others," National Archives of Australia, http://naa.gov.au. Compensation to ex-prisoners, and limitations on legal redress: Reynolds, "U.S. Prisoners of War," 4–7. Multilateral Peace Treaty with Japan as "the cornerstone of U.S. security policy in the Pacific region": U.S. House of Representatives, Committee on the Judiciary, Hearing before the Subcommittee on Immigration, Border Security and Claims on the "Justice for United States Prisoners of War Act of 2001" (H.R. 1198), Statement of William H. Taft IV, Sept. 25, 2002. "A great nation does not repudiate its treaties,": Ibid. Mitsui Mining POW lawsuits: Wu Gang, "Forced Labour Case Voided in Japan," *China Daily*, May 24, 2004 (discussing the appeal of the Fukuoka District Court's verdict). The Fukuoka High Court overturned the award on appeal, holding the claim to be time-barred. www.chinadaily.com.cn/english/doc/2004–05/ 24/content_333378.htm (June 7, 2005). Apology of Prime Minister Junichiro

Koizumi: Ueno, Teruaki. "Japan PM Apologises over World War Two Dutch POWs," Reuters, May 2, 2005. **"If I had ever seen three or four of these guys . . .":** Charley L. Pryor, UNT interview, Nov. 4, 1972, 120–121. **"When you harbor something like that . . .":** Roy Offerle, UNT interview, 129. **"I wanted to volunteer to go to Japan . . .":** Melfred L. Forsman, interview with the author. **"When the roof fell in, a great funnel of smoke . . ."** Stephen Crane, "The Veteran," *McClure's Magazine*, June 1896, in *The Red Badge of Courage and Selected Short Fiction*, New York: Barnes & Noble Books, 2003, 179. **River Kwai tourist culture**: Loeb, "Dreck Below the Bridge on the River Kwai," *Philadelphia Inquirer*, 1-A, and Andelman, "Ex-Prisoners and Captors Join in a Walk over Kwai Bridge," *New York Times*, 66. **Perth survivors after the war**: McKie, *Proud Echo*, frontispiece. **"The fact is, the ones that obeyed the rules . . .":** Seldon D. Reese, UNT interview, 55. **"Well after almost 4 years our fate is to be decided . . .":** Fujita, diary entry for August 11, 1945.

MEN OF THE USS *HOUSTON* (CA-30) AND THE "LOST BATTALION"
(2ND BATTALION, 131ST FIELD ARTILLERY REGIMENT, 36TH INFANTRY DIVISION)
KILLED IN ACTION OR DIED IN CAPTIVITY, 1942–1945

Key

OFFICER'S RANKS
WO—Warrant officer
Ens.—Ensign
Lt. j.g.—Lieutenant (junior grade)
Lt.—Lieutenant
LCdr.—Lieutenant commander
Cdr.—Commander
Capt.—Captain

ENLISTED RATINGS
Numerals indicate a 1st, 2nd, or 3rd class rating. A "C" denotes a chief, e.g. CMM for Chief Machinist's Mate or ACM for Aviation Chief Metalsmith.

1stSgt.—First Sergeant (USMC or Army)
AM—Aviation Metalsmith
AMM—Aviation Machinist's Mate
AEM—Aviation Electrician's Mate
AerM—Aerographer's Mate
AOM—Aviation Ordnanceman
AR—Airship Rigger
ARM—Aviation Radioman
ART—Aviation Radio Technician
Bkr.—Baker
BM—Boatswain's Mate
Bug.—Bugler
Cpl.—Corporal (USMC or Army)
CK—Cook
CM—Carpenter's Mate
CCst.—Commissary Steward
Cox.—Coxswain
EM—Electrician's Mate
F—Fireman
FA—Fireman Apprentice
FC—Fire Controlman
GM—Gunner's Mate
HA—Hospital Apprentice
IC—Interior Communications Electrician
M—Metalsmith
Matt—Mess Attendant
ME—Metalsmith
ML—Molder
MM—Machinist's Mate
MoMM—Motor Machinist's Mate
MSgt.—Master Sergeant (USMC or Army)
Mus.—Musician
Pfc.—Private First Class (USMC or Army)
PhM—Pharmacist's Mate
PhoM—Photographer's Mate
PO—Petty officer
PR—Parachute Rigger
Ptr—Painter
Pvt.—Private (USMC or Army)
QM—Quartermaster
RM—Radioman
RT—Radio Technician
S—Seaman
SC—Ship's Cook
SF—Shipfitter
Sgt.—Sergeant (USMC or Army)
SK—Storekeeper
SM—Signalman
TM—Torpedoman's Mate
TSgt.—Technical Sergeant (USMC or Army)
WT—Water Tender
Y (or YN)—Yeoman

Last Name	First Name	Rank	Branch of Service	Date of Death	Place of Death	Cause of Death
Abate	Leo C.	F1c	USN	3/1/42	USS *Houston*	Enemy Action
Abrahamson	Chester E.	RM1c	USN	3/1/42	USS *Houston*	Enemy Action
Abrams	Russell E.	Y3c	USN	11/9/43	POW—80 Kilo Camp, Burma	Beriberi
Adams	Charles B.	Pvt.	USMC	3/1/42	USS *Houston*	Enemy Action
Adams	Richard L.	S2c	USN	3/1/42	USS *Houston*	Enemy Action
Adkins	Bruce	S2c	USN	2/4/42	USS *Houston*	Enemy Action
Ah	Fong	Matt1c	USN	3/1/42	USS *Houston*	Enemy Action
Airhart	Albert E.	S2c	USN	3/1/42	USS *Houston*	Enemy Action
Albers	Harold S.	AMM1c	USN	3/1/42	USS *Houston*	Enemy Action
Albin	Blumer T.	F2c	USN	3/1/42	USS *Houston*	Enemy Action
Albrecht	Edward A.	Pvt.	USMC	3/1/42	USS *Houston*	Enemy Action
Alderman	Harmon P.	CRM	USN	11/26/42	POW—Prison ship, South China Sea	Colitis
Alexander	J. G.	Sgt.	USA	9/26/43	POW—80 Kilo Camp, Burma	Tropical Ulcers
Alford	Charles W.	Bug1c	USN	3/1/42	USS *Houston*	Enemy Action
Allabaugh	Everett W.	S2c	USN	3/1/42	USS *Houston*	Enemy Action
Allen	Glen L.	S2c	USN	3/1/42	USS *Houston*	Enemy Action
Allen	Harold R.	S2c	USN	2/4/42	USS *Houston*	Enemy Action
Allen	Harper B.	S2c	USN	3/1/42	USS *Houston*	Enemy Action
Allen	Roy R.	S2c	USN	3/1/42	USS *Houston*	Enemy Action
Alleva	Joseph G.	S1c	USN	6/24/44	POW—Prison ship, South China Sea	Unknown
Allred	Max J.	SM2c	USN	3/1/42	USS *Houston*	Enemy Action
Almasie	John H.	S2c	USN	2/4/42	USS *Houston*	Enemy Action
Anderson	Carl B.	WT2c	USN	3/1/42	USS *Houston*	Enemy Action
Anderson	J. A.	Pfc.	USA	7/23/43	POW—100 Kilo Camp, Burma	Beriberi
Anderson	John W. Jr.	S2c	USN	3/1/42	USS *Houston*	Enemy Action
Anderson	Ralph H.	S2c	USN	3/1/42	USS *Houston*	Enemy Action
Andrews	David Z. Jr.	S1c	USN	3/1/42	USS *Houston*	Enemy Action
Anglin	Roy W.	SM2c	USN	3/1/42	USS *Houston*	Enemy Action
Anglini	Rudell H.	S1c	USN	3/1/42	USS *Houston*	Enemy Action
Anspaugh	George B.	S2c	USN	3/1/42	USS *Houston*	Enemy Action
Anthony	Arthur L.	S1c	USN	3/1/42	USS *Houston*	Enemy Action
Argo	Charlie D. Jr.	S2c	USN	3/1/42	USS *Houston*	Enemy Action
Armour	Floyd	S1c	USN	7/17/43	POW—100 Kilo Camp, Burma	Dysentery/Malaria
Arneson	Rayford	AMM3c	USN	3/1/42	USS *Houston*	Enemy Action
Ashmead	Morris L.	S1c	USN	3/1/42	USS *Houston*	Enemy Action
Ashton	Charles E.	MM1c	USN	3/1/42	USS *Houston*	Enemy Action
Ashton	James C.	F1c	USN	3/1/42	USS *Houston*	Enemy Action
Auston	Roy E.	S2c	USN	3/1/42	USS *Houston*	Enemy Action
Autio	Lauren E.	S2c	USN	3/1/42	USS *Houston*	Enemy Action
Awtrey	Palmer S.	S1c	USN	3/1/42	USS *Houston*	Enemy Action
Ayers	Ray C.	CQM	USN	3/1/42	USS *Houston*	Enemy Action

Last Name	First Name	Rank	Branch of Service	Date of Death	Place of Death	Cause of Death
Backer	Albert J.	S2c	USN	3/1/42	USS *Houston*	Enemy Action
Baerman	Donald G.	S1c	USN	9/27/43	POW—80 Kilo Camp, Burma	Dysentery
Bailey	Ira W.	Cox.	USN	2/4/42	USS *Houston*	Enemy Action
Bailey	James H.	RM3c	USN	3/1/42	USS *Houston*	Enemy Action
Bailey	Lester W.	S2c	USN	3/1/42	USS *Houston*	Enemy Action
Baize	Talbert W.	S1c	USN	3/1/42	USS *Houston*	Enemy Action
Baker	George D.	S2c	USN	3/1/42	USS *Houston*	Enemy Action
Baker	George W.	WT1c	USN	3/1/42	USS *Houston*	Enemy Action
Baker	Wayne S.	S1c	USN	3/1/42	USS *Houston*	Enemy Action
Barnes	Don H.		USA	2/3/42	B-17 bomber	Shot down
Barnett	Roger L.	F1c	USN	3/1/42	USS *Houston*	Enemy Action
Barney	Dwight M.	Sgt.	USMC	3/1/42	USS *Houston*	Enemy Action
Barr	George M.	GM1c	USN	3/1/42	USS *Houston*	Enemy Action
Barrett	Norvel S.	SF3c	USN	3/1/42	USS *Houston*	Enemy Action
Barrett	Raleigh	S1c	USN	3/1/42	USS *Houston*	Enemy Action
Barringer	Elra F.	FC2c	USN	3/1/42	USS *Houston*	Enemy Action
Barron	Floyd W.	Pvt.	USMC	3/1/42	USS *Houston*	Enemy Action
Bassett	Robert A.	MM1c	USN	3/1/42	USS *Houston*	Enemy Action
Batchelor	William C.	S1c	USN	10/1/43	POW—80 Kilo Camp, Burma	Tropical Ulcers
Baughn	Norvel W.	EM2c	USN	3/1/42	USS *Houston*	Enemy Action
Baxter	B. R.	Pfc.	USA	9/13/43	POW–80 Kilo Camp, Burma	Tropical Ulcers
Beatty	James R.	S2c	USN	2/4/42	USS *Houston*	Enemy Action
Beck	Oree C.	Pfc.	USMC	3/1/42	USS *Houston*	Enemy Action
Beckett	Robert A.	Pfc.	USMC	3/1/42	USS *Houston*	Enemy Action
Beinert	Joseph	BM	USN	2/4/42	USS *Houston*	Enemy Action
Bell	John R.	WT2c	USN	3/1/42	USS *Houston*	Enemy Action
Bender	George F.	S1c	USN	5/22/44	POW— Nakhon Pathom, Thailand	Chronic Dysentery
Benjamine	Leslie R.	QM3c	USN	3/1/42	USS *Houston*	Enemy Action
Benner	Calvin W.	EM1c	USN	6/27/43	POW—100 Kilo Camp, Burma	Thrombosis
Berhasek	Albert C. Jr.	Pvt.	USMC	3/1/42	USS *Houston*	Enemy Action
Bettinger	Phillip J.	QM2c	USN	3/1/42	USS *Houston*	Enemy Action
Biechlin	Louis E.	WO	USN	3/1/42	USS *Houston*	Enemy Action
Biechlin	Neal C.	Y2c	USN	3/1/42	USS *Houston*	Enemy Action
Bienert	J. B.	WO	USN	2/4/42	USS *Houston*	Enemy Action
Binder	William E. Jr.	S2c	USN	2/4/42	USS *Houston*	Enemy Action
Bingham	J. E.		USA	2/3/42	B-17 bomber	Shot down
Bingley	Harold L.	S1c	USN	3/1/42	USS *Houston*	Enemy Action
Bishop	Viva A.	Cpl.	USMC	3/1/42	USS *Houston*	Enemy Action
Black	Isaac A.	S1c	USN	3/1/42	USS *Houston*	Enemy Action
Black	Joseph G. Jr.	S1c	USN	3/1/42	USS *Houston*	Enemy Action
Blair	Kenneth S.	CSM (AA)	USN	3/23/44	POW— Tamarkan, Thailand	Beriberi

Last Name	First Name	Rank	Branch of Service	Date of Death	Place of Death	Cause of Death
Blake	Paul R.	GM3c	USN	3/1/42	USS *Houston*	Enemy Action
Bloch	Francis W.	S1c	USN	3/1/42	USS *Houston*	Enemy Action
Bock	Dudley C.	PH3c	USN	3/1/42	USS *Houston*	Enemy Action
Bonkoski	John A.	GM1c	USN	3/1/42	USS *Houston*	Enemy Action
Boone	Evans L.	S2c	USN	3/1/42	USS *Houston*	Enemy Action
Boorom	Richard W.	S1c	USN	3/1/42	USS *Houston*	Enemy Action
Booth	Charles W.	S1c	USN	3/1/42	USS *Houston*	Enemy Action
Boothe	Merton A.	MM2c	USN	3/1/42	USS *Houston*	Enemy Action
Boren	Lemuel M.	1st Lt.	USA	11/13/43	POW—80 Kilo Camp, Burma	Malaria
Botham	Willard R.	S1c	USN	2/4/42	USS *Houston*	Enemy Action
Bourgeois	Frederick J.	S2c	USN	3/1/42	USS *Houston*	Enemy Action
Bowen	G. M.	Sgt.	USA	12/11/43	POW—105 Kilo Camp, Burma	Pneumonia
Bowlby	Wilbur E.	S2c	USN	3/1/42	USS *Houston*	Enemy Action
Bowler	Morris R.	WT2c	USN	3/1/42	USS *Houston*	Enemy Action
Bowley	R. J.	Pvt.	USA	1/23/44	POW—Kanchanaburi, Thailand	Dysentery
Bowman	Byrl G.	S2c	USN	3/1/42	USS *Houston*	Enemy Action
Boyle	A. C.	Cpl.	USA	11/16/43	POW—80 Kilo Camp, Burma	Tropical Ulcers
Boynton	Dwight E.	S2c	USN	3/1/42	USS *Houston*	Enemy Action
Braathen	John W.	S2c	USN	3/1/42	USS *Houston*	Enemy Action
Bradley	Leonard E.	S2c	USN	3/1/42	USS *Houston*	Enemy Action
Brandt	Lester F.	Pfc.	USMC	3/1/42	USS *Houston*	Enemy Action
Branham	Lawrence R.	S2c	USN	8/17/43	POW—100 Kilo Camp, Burma	Tropical Ulcers
Brasfield	William L.	Pvt.	USMC	3/1/42	USS *Houston*	Enemy Action
Bray	C. B.	Sgt.	USA	9/8/43	POW—100 Kilo Camp, Burma	Dysentery/ Tropical Ulcers
Brill	Richard J.	GM3c	USN	3/1/42	USS *Houston*	Enemy Action
Brislin	Charles M. Jr.	RM2c	USN	3/1/42	USS *Houston*	Enemy Action
Brockman	Clarence A.	F2c	USN	3/1/42	USS *Houston*	Enemy Action
Brooks	Harold R.	S2c	USN	3/1/42	USS *Houston*	Enemy Action
Broom	D. C.	S2c	USN	3/1/42	USS *Houston*	Enemy Action
Brothers	Frank W.	S1c	USN	8/11/43	POW—114 Kilo Camp, Burma	Malaria
Brown	Allen R. Jr.	Y3c	USN	3/1/42	USS *Houston*	Enemy Action
Brown	Donald C.	S2c	USN	3/1/42	USS *Houston*	Enemy Action
Brown	Harold F.	BM1c	USN	3/1/42	USS *Houston*	Enemy Action
Brown	J. R.	Cpl.	USA	11/24/43	POW—100 Kilo Camp, Burma	Beriberi
Bruce	Herbert L.	S1c	USN	3MM/1/42	USS *Houston*	Enemy Action
Brust	James L.	Cox.	USN	3/1/42	USS *Houston*	Enemy Action
Bubnis	Joseph A.	S1c	USN	3/1/42	USS *Houston*	Enemy Action

Last Name	First Name	Rank	Branch of Service	Date of Death	Place of Death	Cause of Death
Buhlman	Clarence N.	S2c	USN	9/6/43	POW—80 Kilo Camp, Burma	Dysentery
Buice	William A.	F1c	USN	3/1/42	USS *Houston*	Enemy Action
Bujak	Stanley F.	S1c	USN	3/1/42	USS *Houston*	Enemy Action
Bulla	John Jr.	MM1c	USN	3/1/42	USS *Houston*	Enemy Action
Bunnell	Victor L.	TC1c	USN	3/1/42	USS *Houston*	Enemy Action
Buns	Arnold H.	S1c	USN	3/1/42	USS *Houston*	Enemy Action
Burns	Fred V.	MM1c	USN	3/1/42	USS *Houston*	Enemy Action
Burrell	Delbert F.	S2c	USN	3/1/42	USS *Houston*	Enemy Action
Burrell	Roy B. Jr.	S1c	USN	3/1/42	USS *Houston*	Enemy Action
Burton	Filmore E.	F1c	USN	3/1/42	USS *Houston*	Enemy Action
Bushell	Alfred	CMM	USN	3/1/42	USS *Houston*	Enemy Action
Bushnell	Edgar W.	CSK(AA)	USN	8/30/43	POW—100 Kilo Camp, Burma	Tropical Ulcers
Bussey	S. M.	Pvt.	USA	1/10/44	POW— Kanchanaburi, Thailand	Dysentery
Button	Charles J.	S1c	USN	3/1/42	USS *Houston*	Enemy Action
Byrd	J. R.	MM2c	USN	3/1/42	USS *Houston*	Enemy Action
Byrne	Dan J.	WT1c	USN	3/1/42	USS *Houston*	Enemy Action
Callahan	Melvin C.	S1c	USN	1/4/44	POW—133 Kilo Camp, Thailand	Tropical Ulcers/ Pneumonia
Caloway	Rhymond	S1c	USN	3/1/42	USS *Houston*	Enemy Action
Calvert	Arthur M.	S2c	USN	3/1/42	USS *Houston*	Enemy Action
Campbell	Creed B.	EM1c	USN	3/1/42	USS *Houston*	Enemy Action
Campbell	Rollin L.	S2c	USN	10/15/44	POW— Chungkai, Thailand	U.S. submarine
Campbell	Warren E.	S1c	USN	2/4/42	USS *Houston*	Enemy Action
Cantrell	James A.	S2c	USN	9/26/43	POW—80 Kilo Camp, Burma	Tropical Ulcers
Cantrill	Thomas S.	F1c	USN	3/1/42	USS *Houston*	Enemy Action
Caplicky	Joseph	F1c	USN	3/1/42	USS *Houston*	Enemy Action
Carlson	Clarence E.	F1c	USN	3/1/42	USS *Houston*	Enemy Action
Carlyle	Edward T.	S1c	USN	3/1/42	USS *Houston*	Enemy Action
Carney	George R.	Cox.	USN	3/1/42	USS *Houston*	Enemy Action
Carney	W. D.	Pvt.	USA	7/22/43	POW—100 Kilo Camp, Burma	Dysentery
Carsillo	Romeo L.	S1c	USN	3/1/42	USS *Houston*	Enemy Action
Carter	Frederick I. Jr.	QM3c	USN	9/16/43	POW—80 Kilo Camp, Burma	Tropical Ulcers
Carter	Gilbert G.	S1c	USN	3/1/42	USS *Houston*	Enemy Action
Caserio	Ebo R.	CMM	USN	3/1/42	USS *Houston*	Enemy Action
Casey	Leonard F.	MM2c	USN	3/1/42	USS *Houston*	Enemy Action
Cash	James L.	GM3c	USN	3/1/42	USS *Houston*	Enemy Action
Cassaday	William R.	Pvt.	USMC	3/1/42	USS *Houston*	Enemy Action
Caton	Laverne F.	SK3c	USN	3/1/42	USS *Houston*	Enemy Action

Last Name	First Name	Rank	Branch of Service	Date of Death	Place of Death	Cause of Death
Ceblak	Sylvester J.	RM3c	USN	3/1/42	USS *Houston*	Enemy Action
Chan	George	Matt1c	USN	3/1/42	USS *Houston*	Enemy Action
Chandler	Richard C.	S2c	USN	3/1/42	USS *Houston*	Enemy Action
Chandler	Thomas K.	S2c	USN	3/1/42	USS *Houston*	Enemy Action
Chang	SiAn	Matt1c	USN	3/1/42	USS *Houston*	Enemy Action
Chapman	George T.			4/28/44	POW—Nakhon Pathom, Thailand	
Chay	William	S1c	USN	3/1/42	USS *Houston*	Enemy Action
Cheadle	Clarence R.	FC3c	USN	3/1/42	USS *Houston*	Enemy Action
Cheng	Cheu S.	Matt1c	USN	3/1/42	USS *Houston*	Enemy Action
Cheng	Song S.	Matt1c	USN	3/1/42	USS *Houston*	Enemy Action
Cherry	Claude M. Jr.	F2c	USN	3/1/42	USS *Houston*	Enemy Action
Cherry	Travis J.	GM1c	USN	3/1/42	USS *Houston*	Enemy Action
Chie	Ke C.	Matt2c	USN	3/1/42	USS *Houston*	Enemy Action
Chien	Ling	Matt1c	USN	3/1/42	USS *Houston*	Enemy Action
Chih	Shou	Matt1c	USN	3/1/42	USS *Houston*	Enemy Action
Ching	Yu Chow	Matt1c	USN	3/1/42	USS *Houston*	Enemy Action
Chisholm	John K.	LCdr.	USN	3/1/42	USS *Houston*	Enemy Action
Chorman	Chester L.	S1c	USN	3/1/42	USS *Houston*	Enemy Action
Chow	Shing Foo	Matt1c	USN	3/1/42	USS *Houston*	Enemy Action
Christensen	Lester A.	S1c	USN	3/1/42	USS *Houston*	Enemy Action
Clark	William T.	MM2c	USN	3/1/42	USS *Houston*	Enemy Action
Clarkston	Leonard O.	S1c	USN	2/7/42	USS *Houston*	Enemy Action
Clingingsmith	Dale	S1c	USN	3/1/42	USS *Houston*	Enemy Action
Clymer	Shelton H.	BM1c	USN	3/1/42	USS *Houston*	Enemy Action
Coble	Joseph R.	S1c	USN	3/1/42	USS *Houston*	Enemy Action
Colbert	Patrick L.	MM2c	USN	3/1/42	USS *Houston*	Enemy Action
Colbert	Urban H.	Cox.	USN	3/1/42	USS *Houston*	Enemy Action
Collins	C. M.	Pfc.	USA	2/29/44	POW—Kanchanaburi, Thailand	Dysentery
Collins	Robert E.	S1c	USN	3/1/42	USS *Houston*	Enemy Action
Comer	Joseph G.	CEM	USN	3/1/42	USS *Houston*	Enemy Action
Connell	James H.	F1c	USN	3/1/42	USS *Houston*	Enemy Action
Conner	William A.	F1c	USN	3/1/42	USS *Houston*	Enemy Action
Cook	Joseph F.	F3c	USN	3/1/42	USS *Houston*	Enemy Action
Cooper	Dale R.	PO3c	USN	9/27/43	POW—100 Kilo Camp, Burma	Tropical Ulcers
Cooper	Lloyd F.	S2c	USN	3/1/42	USS *Houston*	Enemy Action
Copeland	James L.	GM3c	USN	3/1/42	USS *Houston*	Enemy Action
Corsberg	Howard C.	Pfc.	USMC	3/1/42	USS *Houston*	Enemy Action
Cox	C. A.	Cpl.	USA	10/4/43	POW—100 Kilo Camp, Burma	Dysentery
Cravens	J. R.	WO	USN	3/1/42	USS *Houston*	Enemy Action
Creed	Joe	EM2c	USN	3/1/42	USS *Houston*	Enemy Action
Crepps	Harry E. Jr.	S1c	USN	3/1/42	USS *Houston*	Enemy Action
Crippen	Marshall E.	Cox.	USN	3/1/42	USS *Houston*	Enemy Action
Cumming	George H. Jr.	ACMM	USN	3/1/42	USS *Houston*	Enemy Action
Curnite	Marion F.	MM3c	USN	3/1/42	USS *Houston*	Enemy Action
Czyzewski	Charles	PTR1c	USN	3/1/42	USS *Houston*	Enemy Action
Dagget	Marley W.	FC3c(M)	USN	3/1/42	USS *Houston*	Enemy Action

Last Name	First Name	Rank	Branch of Service	Date of Death	Place of Death	Cause of Death
Dale	Peter J.	RM1c	USN	3/1/42	USS *Houston*	Enemy Action
Daley	Robert M.	GM3c	USN	3/1/42	USS *Houston*	Enemy Action
Dalton	Charles E.	S1c	USN	3/1/42	USS *Houston*	Enemy Action
Daniels	Theodore D.	S2c	USN	2/5/42	USS *Houston*	Enemy Action
Darling	William E.	S1c	USN	3/1/42	USS *Houston*	Enemy Action
Darter	James R.	S2c	USN	3/1/42	USS *Houston*	Enemy Action
Davidson	Thomas A.	S1c	USN	3/1/42	USS *Houston*	Enemy Action
Davis	George E. Jr.	Lt.	USN	2/4/42	USS *Houston*	Enemy Action
Davis	Joseph S.	S1c	USN	3/1/42	USS *Houston*	Enemy Action
Davis	Stephen C.	S1c	USN	3/1/42	USS *Houston*	Enemy Action
Deats	L. F. Jr.	Cpl.	USA	9/10/43	POW—80 Kilo Camp, Burma	Tropical Ulcers
DeBord	Mark A.	Mus1c	USN	3/1/42	USS *Houston*	Enemy Action
Deck	**Leonard J.**	SC2c	USN			
DeFrantes	Emanuel E.	S1c	USN	3/1/42	USS *Houston*	Enemy Action
Delasio	F.	Pvt.	USA	12/23/43	POW—133 Kilo Camp, Burma	Pellegra
Dempsey	A. E.	Pfc.	USA	8/20/43	POW—100 Kilo Camp, Burma	Beriberi
Demoen	A. R.	CEM	USN	9/14/43	POW—80 Kilo Camp, Burma	Tropical Ulcers
DeShields	William M.	QM1c	USN	3/1/42	USS *Houston*	Enemy Action
Dethloff	Frank A.	WT2c	USN	3/1/42	USS *Houston*	Enemy Action
DeWald	William C.	AMM2c	USN	3/1/42	USS *Houston*	Enemy Action
Dexter	Robert E.	S1c	USN	3/1/42	USS *Houston*	Enemy Action
Dickens	W. H.	Pvt.	USA	1/1/44	POW—114 Kilo Camp, Burma	Pellegra
Dickerson	Lacy L. Jr.	S1c	USN	2/4/42	USS *Houston*	Enemy Action
Dickie	James C.	PTR2c	USN	3/1/42	USS *Houston*	Enemy Action
Dietrich	Normand W.	MM2c	USN	3/1/42	USS *Houston*	Enemy Action
Dietz	Edward J.	S1c	USN	3/1/42	USS *Houston*	Enemy Action
Dillon	Joseph E.	S1c	USN	3/1/42	USS *Houston*	Enemy Action
Dinan	Charles P.	F2c	USN	3/1/42	USS *Houston*	Enemy Action
Dittoe	Thomas P.	S2c	USN	3/1/42	USS *Houston*	Enemy Action
Dobkins	Mack	MM2c	USN	3/1/42	USS *Houston*	Enemy Action
Dodds	Lewis C.	S1c	USN	3/1/42	USS *Houston*	Enemy Action
Doiron	L. W.	Pfc.	USA	8/27/43	POW—100 Kilo Camp, Burma	Malaria
Dombrowski	Edwain S.	S1c	USN	3/1/42	USS *Houston*	Enemy Action
Dorrell	Tony R.	MM1c	USN	3/1/42	USS *Houston*	Enemy Action
Dotson	Robert	F1c	USN	3/1/42	USS *Houston*	Enemy Action
Doty	Carl	WT1c	USN	3/1/42	USS *Houston*	Enemy Action
Dowell	Thomas A.	Cox.	USN	3/1/42	USS *Houston*	Enemy Action
Dowling	William L.	S1c	USN	3/1/42	USS *Houston*	Enemy Action
Drago	Donald T.	S1c	USN	3/1/42	USS *Houston*	Enemy Action
Drake	J. P.	Pvt.	USA	8/1/43	POW—80 Kilo Camp	Dysentery

Last Name	First Name	Rank	Branch of Service	Date of Death	Place of Death	Cause of Death
Drake	Maryl L.	RM2c	USN	3/1/42	USS *Houston*	Enemy Action
Ducey	Ting	Matt1c	USN	3/1/42	USS *Houston*	Enemy Action
Dumas	Roy H.	S2c	USN	3/1/42	USS *Houston*	Enemy Action
Dupler	Harley H.	1stSgt.	USMC	5/14/43	POW— Thanbyuzayat, Burma	Dysentery
Durler	Ogden J.	CMM	USN	3/1/42	USS *Houston*	Enemy Action
Dutton	Archibald J.	CBM	USN	3/1/42	USS *Houston*	Enemy Action
Dykes	Birdine V.	FC3c	USN	3/1/42	USS *Houston*	Enemy Action
Dymanowski	Severyn F.	Mus1c	USN	3/1/42	USS *Houston*	Enemy Action
Eastwood	H. W.	Cpl.	USA	1/28/44	POW— Tamarkan, Thailand	Malnutrition
Ebaugh	Elmer M.	S2c	USN	3/1/42	USS *Houston*	Enemy Action
Ebaugh	Forest V.	S1C	USN	9/14/43	POW—100 Kilo Camp, Burma	Epilepsy
Edge	John W.	F1c	USN	3/1/42	USS *Houston*	Enemy Action
Edwards	Joe F.	TSgt.	USMC	3/1/42	USS *Houston*	Enemy Action
Egri	George J.	SC2c	USN	3/1/42	USS *Houston*	Enemy Action
Eiden	Herman G.	F1c	USN	3/1/42	USS *Houston*	Enemy Action
Ekberg	Oscar D.	MM1c	USN	3/1/42	USS *Houston*	Enemy Action
Eklund	R. L.	Pvt.	USA	1/3/44	POW—114 Kilo Camp, Burma	Pellegra
Elliott	Clarence F.	CFC	USN	3/1/42	USS *Houston*	Enemy Action
Elliott	Leslie L.	Cox.	USN	3/1/42	USS *Houston*	Enemy Action
Ellis	Frank D.	CWT	USN	2/24/44	POW—105 Kilo Camp, Burma	Amoebic Dysentery and Malaria
Elms	Lee G.	RM3c	USN	3/1/42	USS *Houston*	Enemy Action
Emmerth	William H.	Cox.	USN	3/1/42	USS *Houston*	Enemy Action
English	Henry A.	BM2c	USN	3/1/42	USS *Houston*	Enemy Action
Ermis	Robert L.	S2c	USN	3/1/42	USS *Houston*	Enemy Action
Eugates	John M.	S1c	USN	3/1/42	USS *Houston*	Enemy Action
Eustace	Milton J.	MM2c	USN	3/1/42	USS *Houston*	Enemy Action
Fanghor	Gene	GM2c	USN	12/19/42	POW—Ohasi, Japan	Diphtheria, pneumonia
Farnsworth	Franklin M.	AMM3c	USN	3/1/42	USS *Houston*	Enemy Action
Faulkner	H. L.	Cpl.	USA	9/8/43	POW—80 Kilo Camp, Burma	Tropical Ulcers
Faust	Ervin C.	S1c	USN	3/1/42	USS *Houston*	Enemy Action
Feely	James J.	S2c	USN	11/28/43	POW—80 Kilo Camp, Burma	Beriberi
Felice	Olind	WT1c	USN	3/1/42	USS *Houston*	Enemy Action
Felix	Irving A.	Y1c	USN	4/18/43	POW— Batavia, Java	Tuberculosis
Fiegel	Lawrence J.	S1c	USN	3/1/42	USS *Houston*	Enemy Action
Fincher	James G.	S1c	USN	3/1/42	USS *Houston*	Enemy Action
Florence	Robert C.	S1c	USN	3/1/42	USS *Houston*	Enemy Action

Last Name	First Name	Rank	Branch of Service	Date of Death	Place of Death	Cause of Death
Flowers	Homer L.	WT1c	USN	3/1/42	USS *Houston*	Enemy Action
Fontenot	Walter J.	F2c	USN	3/1/42	USS *Houston*	Enemy Action
Fook	Lau	Matt1c	USN	3/1/42	USS *Houston*	Enemy Action
Forgey	J. D.	Cpl.	USA	9/27/43	POW—100 Kilo Camp, Burma	Tropical Ulcers
Fornkahl	Raymond W.	S1c	USN	3/1/42	USS *Houston*	Enemy Action
Frantz	Harlan M.	SK3c	USN	3/1/42	USS *Houston*	Enemy Action
Freeman	Robert J.	S1c	USN	3/1/42	USS *Houston*	Enemy Action
Fritzsching	Richard L.	Pfc	USMC	3/1/42	USS *Houston*	Enemy Action
Froelich	Raymond W.	BM2c	USN	3/1/42	USS *Houston*	Enemy Action
Frost	Wilson L.	Cox.	USN	3/1/42	USS *Houston*	Enemy Action
Fussell	Donald E.	MM2c	USN	3/1/42	USS *Houston*	Enemy Action
Fussell	J. H.	F3c	USN	3/1/42	USS *Houston*	Enemy Action
Gagnon	Gilbert Jr.	S2c	USN	3/1/42	USS *Houston*	Enemy Action
Galusha	Eugene R.	HA1c	USN	3/1/42	USS *Houston*	Enemy Action
Gandy	Charley W.	S1c	USN	2/4/42	USS *Houston*	Enemy Action
Garrett	William E.	MM2c	USN	3/1/42	USS *Houston*	Enemy Action
Garwood	Edward D.	RM2c	USN	9/9/43	POW—80 Kilo Camp, Burma	Tropical Ulcers
Gary	James C. Jr.	CFC(AA)	USN	3/1/42	USS *Houston*	Enemy Action
Gentry	Stacy C. Jr.	S1c	USN	3/1/42	USS *Houston*	Enemy Action
George	Kelton B.	Cpl.	USMC	3/1/42	USS *Pecos*, sunk en route to Australia	Enemy Action
George	Marion E.	Pfc.	USMC	3/1/42	USS *Houston*	Enemy Action
Gerke	Arthur V. Jr.	HA2c	USN	3/1/42	USS *Houston*	Enemy Action
Gibbon	Leland A.	S1c	USN	3/1/42	USS *Houston*	Enemy Action
Gibson	James E.	S2c	USN	3/1/42	USS *Houston*	Enemy Action
Gillet	Frank A.	CWO	USN	3/1/42	USS *Houston*	Enemy Action
Gilliam	R. E.	Pvt.	USA	9/23/43	POW—100 Kilo Camp, Burma	Tropical Ulcers
Gillmore	Charles E.	S2c	USN	3/1/42	USS *Houston*	Enemy Action
Gingras	Richard H.	LCdr.	USN	3/1/42	USS *Houston*	Enemy Action
Giret	Andrew J.	FM1c(M)	USN	3/1/42	USS *Houston*	Enemy Action
Glatzert	P. A.		USA	6/24/44	POW—Prison ship, South China Sea	Unknown
Godfrey	Donald F.	S1c	USN	10/6/43	POW—100 Kilo Camp, Burma	Chronic Dysentery
Goodberlet	William F.	Pvt.	USMC	3/1/42	USS *Houston*	Enemy Action
Gorney	Roman T.	S1c	USN	2/4/42	USS *Houston*	Enemy Action
Graham	Joe B.	F2c	USN	3/1/42	USS *Houston*	Enemy Action
Graham	Joyner P.	BM2c	USN	2/4/42	USS *Houston*	Enemy Action
Graham	Richard G.	Y3c	USN	7/23/43	POW—80 Kilo Camp, Burma	Tropical Ulcers
Granger	Charles H.	F1c	USN	3/1/42	USS *Houston*	Enemy Action
Grasham	Stanley J.	S2c	USN	3/1/42	USS *Houston*	Enemy Action

Last Name	First Name	Rank	Branch of Service	Date of Death	Place of Death	Cause of Death
Gray	H.	Pfc.	USA	9/17/43	POW—80 Kilo Camp, Burma	Tropical Ulcers
Gray	James D.	Pvt.	USMC	3/1/42	USS *Houston*	Enemy Action
Green	Edward F.	Cox.	USN	2/4/42	USS *Houston*	Enemy Action
Griffin	C. R.		USA	10/44	Batavia, Java	Dysentery
Griffin	Everett F.	CPhM.	USN	3/1/42	USS *Houston*	Enemy Action
Grodzky	Henry S.	S1c	USN	3/1/42	USS *Houston*	Enemy Action
Guernsey	Charles E.	S1c	USN	3/1/42	USS *Houston*	Enemy Action
Guglietti	Albert D.	GM2c	USN	3/1/42	USS *Houston*	Enemy Action
Guthrie	W. L.	Pvt.	USA	9/10/43	POW—100 Kilo Camp, Burma	Tropical Ulcers
Guy	James A.	S2c	USN	9/12/43	POW—100 Kilo Camp, Burma	Beriberi
Guyer	Floyd G.	S1c	USN	3/1/42	USS *Houston*	Enemy Action
Gyugo	Paul Jr.	WT2c	USN	3/1/42	USS *Houston*	Enemy Action
Hall	Ervin L.	S1c	USN	10/2/43	POW—80 Kilo Camp, Burma	Tropical Ulcers
Hall	H. L.	Sgt.	USA	8/2/43	POW—100 Kilo Camp, Burma	Dysentery
Hall	Meredith C.	S1c	USN	3/1/42	USS *Houston*	Enemy Action
Hall	Raymond F.	HA2c	USN	3/1/42	USS *Houston*	Enemy Action
Hammer	H. B.		USA	6/24/44	POW—Prison ship, South China Sea	U.S. Submarine
Hampton	R. W.	1st Lt.	USA	7/31/43	POW—100 Kilo Camp, Burma	Dysentery
Hankinson	Delray M.	CCST	USN	2/4/42	USS *Houston*	Enemy Action
Hansen	Ralph R.	S1c	USN	8/22/43	POW—80 Kilo Camp, Burma	Dysentery
Hanson	Carlo H.	S1c	USN	2/4/42	USS *Houston*	Enemy Action
Hanson	Roger J.	S1c	USN	2/5/42	USS *Houston*	Enemy Action
Harder	Jack H.	WT1c	USN	3/1/42	USS *Houston*	Enemy Action
Hargrave	Dunice	Pvt.	USMC	3/1/42	USS *Houston*	Enemy Action
Harold	William R.	CM3c	USN	3/1/42	USS *Houston*	Enemy Action
Harper	David J.	Pvt.	USMC	3/1/42	USS *Houston*	Enemy Action
Harrell	Dero H.	Pfc.	USMC	3/1/42	USS *Houston*	Enemy Action
Harrington	Preston	QM3c	USN	3/1/42	USS *Houston*	Enemy Action
Harrison	J. W.		USA	6/24/44	POW—Prison ship, South China Sea	U.S. Submarine
Haskel	William D.	SC3c	USN	3/1/42	USS *Houston*	Enemy Action
Hatlen	Edwin A.	S1c	USN	12/21/43	POW—100 Kilo Camp, Burma	Beriberi
Hawkins	John B.	S2c	USN	3/1/42	USS *Houston*	Enemy Action

Last Name	First Name	Rank	Branch of Service	Date of Death	Place of Death	Cause of Death
Hayes	Gilbert W.	S1c	USN	3/1/42	USS *Houston*	Enemy Action
Hazen	Glenn E.	Pvt.	USMC	3/1/42	USS *Houston*	Enemy Action
Hebert	Melvin R.	S1c	USN	3/1/42	USS *Houston*	Enemy Action
Heleman	Donald N.	Sgt.	USA	8/45	Ohasi, Japan	
Hendricks	Robert H.	S1c	USN	12/30/43	POW— Kanchanaburi, Thailand	Dysentery
Henley	Doyle F.	SF3c	USN	3/1/42	USS *Houston*	Enemy Action
Hernandez	A.		USA	2/2/43	POW— Surabaya, Java	Tuberculosis
Herrera	L. M.		USA	9/44	POW— Nakhon Pathom, Thailand	Dysentery/ Beriberi
Hicks	J. W.		USA	8/25/43	POW—80 Kilo Camp, Burma	Tropical Ulcers
Hiddenga	Bouwe	CWT	USN	3/1/42	USS *Houston*	Enemy Action
Highfill	Denzil D.	Cox.	USN	3/1/42	USS *Houston*	Enemy Action
Hill	Clyde G.	MM2c	USN	3/1/42	USS *Houston*	Enemy Action
Hill	Donald W.	Pvt.	USMC	4/8/42	POW— Serang, Java	Jaundice/ Dysentery
Hinman	Earl E.	Cox.	USN	3/1/42	USS *Houston*	Enemy Action
Hirsch	Adolph A.	WT1c	USN	3/1/42	USS *Houston*	Enemy Action
Hirsch	Harry	F1c	USN	3/1/42	USS *Houston*	Enemy Action
Hirschberg	Louis	FM2c(M)	USN	11/26/43	POW—100 Kilo Camp, Burma	Tropical Ulcers
Hittle	Robert G.	SC3c	USN	8/17/43	POW—80 Kilo Camp, Burma	Tropical Ulcers
Ho	Chaun Hwa	Matt1c	USN	3/1/42	USS *Houston*	Enemy Action
Hoch	J. W.	Pvt.	USA	8/25/43	POW—80 Kilo Camp, Burma	Tropical Ulcers
Hodge	Ernest D.	Lt.	USN	3/1/42	USS *Houston*	Enemy Action
Hogan	James E.	WO	USN	3/1/42	USS *Houston*	Enemy Action
Hogue	John J.	WY2c	USN	3/1/42	USS *Houston*	Enemy Action
Hollingsworth	Leonard N.	WT2c	USN	3/1/42	USS *Houston*	Enemy Action
Hollowell	John A. Jr.	Cdr.	USN	3/1/42	USS *Houston*	Enemy Action
Holm	Herbert C.	FM2c	USN	3/1/42	USS *Houston*	Enemy Action
Holmes	Jason H. Jr.	WT2c	USN	3/1/42	USS *Houston*	Enemy Action
Holsinger	Frank O.	Cpl.	USMC	9/18/43	POW—80 Kilo Camp, Burma	Tropical Ulcers
Hoofer	Edwin F.	S1c	USN	3/1/42	USS *Houston*	Enemy Action
Hooper	Lloyd R.	AMM3c	USN	3/1/42	USS *Houston*	Enemy Action
Hostick	Ellis N.	GM3c	USN	3/1/42	USS *Houston*	Enemy Action
Houston	Dwight A.	GM2c	USN	3/1/42	USS *Houston*	Enemy Action
Hout	Melville A.	F1c	USN	3/1/42	USS *Houston*	Enemy Action
Howard	Fred M.	S1c	USN	3/1/42	USS *Houston*	Enemy Action
Hubbard	William R.	S1c	USN	3/1/42	USS *Houston*	Enemy Action
Hult	Sydney E.	S1c	USN	3/1/42	USS *Houston*	Enemy Action

Last Name	First Name	Rank	Branch of Service	Date of Death	Place of Death	Cause of Death
Humble	Ray K.	Pfc.	USMC	3/1/42	USS *Houston*	Enemy Action
Hunter	Lowell C.	CQM(AA)	USN	3/1/42	USS *Houston*	Enemy Action
Hurrell	Leslie T.	AMM2c	USN	3/1/42	USS *Houston*	Enemy Action
Husek	George E.	ME2c	USN	3/1/42	USS *Houston*	Enemy Action
Hutchinson	Bill M.	S2c	USN	7/5/43	POW—80 Kilo Camp, Burma	Dysentery
Hyser	Wayne H.	S1c	USN	3/1/42	USS *Houston*	Enemy Action
Isaacs	Edwin C.	S1c	USN	3/1/42	USS *Houston*	Enemy Action
Ivey	D. B.	Pvt.	USA	9/26/43	POW—80 Kilo Camp, Burma	Tropical Ulcers
Ivey	Jack	S2c	USN	3/1/42	USS *Houston*	Enemy Action
Iwanicki	John J.	S2c	USN	3/1/42	USS *Houston*	Enemy Action
Iwanicki	Stanley	S2c	USN	3/1/42	USS *Houston*	Enemy Action
Jackson	Edward	BKR1c	USN	3/1/42	USS *Houston*	Enemy Action
Jacobs	Paul Jr.	MM1c	USN	3/1/42	USS *Houston*	Enemy Action
James	Edward R.	EM2c	USN	7/21/43	POW—80 Kilo Camp, Burma	Dysentery
James	Harvey W. Jr.	S2c	USN	2/4/42	USS *Houston*	Enemy Action
Jaster	A. H.		USA	6/24/44	POW—Prison ship, South China Sea	U.S. Submarine
Jellison	Noeman B.	S1c	USN	3/1/42	USS *Houston*	Enemy Action
Johnk	Merle W.	MM1c	USN	3/1/42	USS *Houston*	Enemy Action
Johnson	Aaron L.	SF3c	USN	2/4/42	USS *Houston*	Enemy Action
Johnson	Douglas R.	S1c	USN	3/1/42	USS *Houston*	Enemy Action
Johnson	Edward I.	SK1c	USN	9/18/43	POW—100 Kilo Camp, Burma	Tropical Ulcers/ Dysentery
Johnson	Elmer E.	S1c	USN	3/1/42	USS *Houston*	Enemy Action
Johnson	Harold M.	S1c	USN	10/10/44	POW— Borneo, Dutch East Indies	Tuberculosis
Johnson	James C.	F2c	USN	3/1/42	USS *Houston*	Enemy Action
Johnson	Norman E.	S1c	USN	3/1/42	USS *Houston*	Enemy Action
Johnson	Robert R.	S2c	USN	3/1/42	USS *Houston*	Enemy Action
Johnson	William A.	S1c	USN	3/1/42	USS *Houston*	Enemy Action
Jones	Morris L.	S1c	USN	3/1/42	USS *Houston*	Enemy Action
Jones	S. A.	Pvt.	USA	9/11/43	POW—80 Kilo Camp, Burma	Tropical Ulcers
Jones	William S.	FC2c(M)	USN	3/1/42	USS *Houston*	Enemy Action
Jontz	Jay B.	Mus1c	USN	3/1/42	USS *Houston*	Enemy Action
Jowell	J. D.	Pvt.	USA	10/17/43	POW—80 Kilo Camp, Burma	Tropical Ulcers
Kadlec	Joseph	Pvt.	USMC	3/1/42	USS *Houston*	Enemy Action
Kaiser	Barnard R.	Y2c	USN	3/1/42	USS *Houston*	Enemy Action
Kalich	N. O. F.		USA	12/3/43	POW—Japan	Spinal Meningitis

Last Name	First Name	Rank	Branch of Service	Date of Death	Place of Death	Cause of Death
Kalous	E. B.	Pfc.	USA	9/16/43	POW—100 Kilo Camp, Burma	Tropical Ulcers
Kamler	Thomas J.	S1c	USN	3/1/42	USS *Houston*	Enemy Action
Kane	Charles J.	CSK	USN	3/1/42	USS *Houston*	Enemy Action
Karbowski	Adelbert L.	S2c	USN	3/1/42	USS *Houston*	Enemy Action
Kautter	Charles A.	EM2c	USN	3/1/42	USS *Houston*	Enemy Action
Keen	Owen J. Jr.	F2c	USN	3/1/42	USS *Houston*	Enemy Action
Keifer	Karl C.	Pvt.	USMC	3/1/42	USS *Houston*	Enemy Action
Keith	F. W.	Lt.CDR	USN	3/1/42	USS *Houston*	Enemy Action
Kelley	Floyd T.	PhM1c	USN	3/1/42	USS *Houston*	Enemy Action
Kelm	A. M.	Cpl.	USA	8/21/43	POW—100 Kilo Camp, Burma	Dysentery
Kendrick	**Arland W.**	**Pfc.**	**USMC**	**3/1/42**	**USS *Houston***	**Enemy Action**
Ketman	Robert E. Jr.	S1c	USN	9/5/43	POW—100 Kilo Camp, Burma	Bacillary Dysentery/ Tropical Ulcer
Keyno	John	Matt1c	USN	3/1/42	USS *Houston*	Enemy Action
Kielty	Martin T.	SC1c	USN	3/1/42	USS *Houston*	Enemy Action
Kiertianis	Stephen	MM1c	USN	3/1/42	USS *Houston*	Enemy Action
King	John W.	CMM	USN	3/1/42	USS *Houston*	Enemy Action
King	Virgil N.	S2c	USN	2/4/42	USS *Houston*	Enemy Action
Kirincich	Joseph N.	F3c	USN	3/1/42	USS *Houston*	Enemy Action
Kirkpatrick	William A.	SM3c	USN	3/1/42	USS *Houston*	Enemy Action
Kitchings	H. A.	Cpl.	USA	10/14/43	POW—100 Kilo Camp, Burma	Tropical Ulcers
Klymaszewski	Raymond L. R.	SC2c	USN	3/1/42	USS *Houston*	Enemy Action
Knoll	D. W.	Lt.	USN	3/1/42	USS *Houston*	Enemy Action
Knowlton	James T.	GM3c	USN	3/1/42	USS *Houston*	Enemy Action
Koelling	Vernon L.	Mus1c	USN	9/11/43	POW—80 Kilo Camp, Burma	Tropical Ulcers
Koepkey	Fred E.	MM2c	USN	3/1/42	USS *Houston*	Enemy Action
Kohn	Frank	S1c	USN	3/1/42	USS *Houston*	Enemy Action
Koller	John R.	Mus1c	USN	3/1/42	USS *Houston*	Enemy Action
Kollmyer	Kenneth L.	Lt. j.g.	USN	3/1/42	USS *Houston*	Enemy Action
Kondzela	Lawrence F.	S1c	USN	4/13/43	POW—80 Kilo Camp, Burma	Cerebral Malaria
Koo	Ah	OS3c	USN	3/1/42	USS *Houston*	Enemy Action
Koo	Yen F.	OS3c	USN	3/1/42	USS *Houston*	Enemy Action
Kormos	John	F3c	USN	3/1/42	USS *Houston*	Enemy Action
Koski	George P.	RM3c	USN	3/1/42	USS *Houston*	Enemy Action
Kulibert	Ira A.	S1c	USN	3/1/42	USS *Houston*	Enemy Action
Kunke	Czeslaus J.	GM2c	USN	8/23/43	POW—100 Kilo Camp, Burma	Tropical Ulcers
Kvach	Clarence D.	RM3c	USN	3/1/42	USS *Houston*	Enemy Action
Kyle	Grady H.	MM1c	USN	3/1/42	USS *Houston*	Enemy Action

Last Name	First Name	Rank	Branch of Service	Date of Death	Place of Death	Cause of Death
Lachman	Joseph F.	S2c	USN	3/1/42	USS *Houston*	Enemy Action
Lafferty	J. A.	WO	USN	3/1/42	USS *Houston*	Enemy Action
Laird	Jay R.	SM3c	USN	3/1/42	USS *Houston*	Enemy Action
Lalonde	Eldo F.	S1c	USN			
Lam	Ah S.	Matt1c	USN	3/1/42	USS *Houston*	Enemy Action
Lamm	Frederick W.	EM2c	USN	3/1/42	USS *Houston*	Enemy Action
Lanigan	Arthur W.	S1c	USN	3/1/42	USS *Houston*	Enemy Action
Lann	Carl J.	CRM	USN	3/1/42	USS *Houston*	Enemy Action
Lantz	William C.	S1c	USN	3/1/42	USS *Houston*	Enemy Action
Lattin	Claude W.	RM2c	USN	3/1/42	USS *Houston*	Enemy Action
Lawson	T. E.	Pvt.	USA	6/24/44	POW—Prison ship, South China Sea	
Layne	Guthrie F. Jr.	S1c	USN	3/1/42	USS *Houston*	Enemy Action
Ledbetter	Arthur V.	Pfc.	USMC	3/1/42	USS *Houston*	Enemy Action
Lee	Earl H.	S1c	USN	9/21/43	POW—100 Kilo Camp, Burma	Beriberi
Lee	Jack F.	FM1c	USMC	3/1/42	USS *Houston*	Enemy Action
Lee	Roy	S1c	USN	3/1/42	USS *Houston*	Enemy Action
Lee	Walter G.	AerM1c	USN	3/1/42	USS *Houston*	Enemy Action
Leo	Nicholas	CEM(AA)	USN	3/1/42	USS *Houston*	Enemy Action
Leung	**Mann Shing**	**Matt1c**	**USN**	**3/1/42**	**USS *Houston***	Enemy Action
Levchenko	Walter	S1c	USN	3/1/42	USS *Houston*	Enemy Action
Lewdansky	Joseph	WT2c	USN	3/1/42	USS *Houston*	Enemy Action
Lewis	Donald M.	S1c	USN	3/1/42	USS *Houston*	Enemy Action
Lewis	Jesse A.	Y2c	USN	3/1/42	USS *Houston*	Enemy Action
Liebla	Sylvan S.	EM1c	USN	3/1/42	USS *Houston*	Enemy Action
Lien	Zian Fah	Matt1c	USN	3/1/42	USS *Houston*	Enemy Action
Lindsley	Albert J.	S1c	USN	6/1/43	POW—100 Kilo Camp, Burma	Dysentery
Lindstaedter	Ben E.	S1c	USN	3/1/42	USS *Houston*	Enemy Action
Lindstrom	Jonas A.	S1c	USN	3/1/42	USS *Houston*	Enemy Action
Lochner	Francis J.	GM3c	USN	3/1/42	USS *Houston*	Enemy Action
Lofland	John A.	S2c	USN	3/1/42	USS *Houston*	Enemy Action
Looney	F. A.		USA	6/24/44	POW—Prison ship, South China Sea	U.S. Submarine
Lumpkin	Samuel H.	Capt.	USA	8/1/43	POW—100 Kilo Camp, Burma	Dysentery
Luna	E.	Pvt.	USA	9/22/43	POW—100 Kilo Camp, Burma	Beriberi
Luna	Jose	Mus1c	USN	3/1/42	USS *Houston*	Enemy Action
Lusk	Joe M. T.	Sgt.	USMC	4/28/43	POW—80 Kilo Camp, Burma	Malaria
Lutes	Eugene T.	S1c	USN	3/1/42	USS *Houston*	Enemy Action
Lynch	Charles L.	GM2c	USN	3/1/42	USS *Houston*	Enemy Action
Lyons	Harold V.	EM1c	USN	3/1/42	USS *Houston*	Enemy Action
MacDonald	Robert J.	S1c	USN	3/1/42	USS *Houston*	Enemy Action

Last Name	First Name	Rank	Branch of Service	Date of Death	Place of Death	Cause of Death
Macumber	Frank L.	CY	USN	3/1/42	USS *Houston*	Enemy Action
Mainey	L. H.	Ens.	USN	3/1/42	USS *Houston*	Enemy Action
Makris	Peter	F1c	USN	3/1/42	USS *Houston*	Enemy Action
Mallory	Fred F.	Ens.	USN	3/1/42	USS *Houston*	Enemy Action
Malone	Arbry K.	Pfc.	USMC	3/1/42	USS *Houston*	Enemy Action
Mamer	George F.	S1c	USN	3/1/42	USS *Houston*	Enemy Action
Manion	Tommy	S1c	USN	8/22/43	POW—100 Kilo Camp, Burma	Tropical Ulcers
Marsh	LeRoy W.	BM2c	USN	3/1/42	USS *Houston*	Enemy Action
Marsh	Walter L. Jr.	Pvt.	USMC	3/1/42	USS *Houston*	Enemy Action
Martin	Andrew M.	SK3c	USN	3/1/42	USS *Houston*	Enemy Action
Martin	James E.	Cox.	USN	3/1/42	USS *Houston*	Enemy Action
Martin	Pete	WT2c	USN	3/1/42	USS *Houston*	Enemy Action
Martin	Virgil	MM2c	USN	3/1/42	USS *Houston*	Enemy Action
Martinez	Alfred	S1c	USN	3/1/42	USS *Houston*	Enemy Action
Marton	Bela	BM2c	USN	3/1/42	USS *Houston*	Enemy Action
Marvel	Thomas H.	CMM	USN	3/1/42	USS *Houston*	Enemy Action
Massey	Allen O.	Cox.	USN	3/1/42	USS *Houston*	Enemy Action
Mathieu	James M.	S1c	USN	2/4/42	USS *Houston*	Enemy Action
Mattfeld	W. F.	Pvt.	USA	11/17/43	POW—114 Kilo Camp, Burma	Cardiac Arrest
Matthews	Forest C.	WT1c	USN	3/1/42	USS *Houston*	Enemy Action
May	Milton R.	FO3c	USN	3/1/42	USS *Houston*	Enemy Action
Mayo	Caswell A. III	Ens.	USN	3/1/42	USS *Houston*	Enemy Action
McCarty	Orville T.	CWT	USN	3/1/42	USS *Houston*	Enemy Action
McClaskey	James E.	S2c	USN	3/1/42	USS *Houston*	Enemy Action
McDonald	Paul M.	S1c	USN	3/1/42	USS *Houston*	Enemy Action
McFarlane	Thomas J.	PhM2c	USN	3/1/42	USS *Houston*	Enemy Action
McFee	Eugene A.	F1c	USN	3/1/42	USS *Houston*	Enemy Action
McGehee	Lesley V.	Em3c	USN	3/1/42	USS *Houston*	Enemy Action
McGrann	Robert P.	EM2c	USN	2/4/42	USS *Houston*	Enemy Action
McKenzie	Cletius J.	S2c	USN	3/1/42	USS *Houston*	Enemy Action
McMahan	R. W.		USA	6/24/44	POW—Prison ship, South China Sea	U.S. Submarine
McMullin	Mark D.	S1c	USN	3/1/42	USS *Houston*	Enemy Action
McNealy	Jack G.	MM1c	USN	3/1/42	USS *Houston*	Enemy Action
Meredith	Earl J.	AC	USMC	3/1/42	USS *Houston*	Enemy Action
Mesner	Lawrence R.	S1c	USN	3/1/42	USS *Houston*	Enemy Action
Metzger	Alvin W.	S2c	USN	3/1/42	USS *Houston*	Enemy Action
Mieth	William C.	F1c	USN	3/1/42	USS *Houston*	Enemy Action
Milgel	John L.	S2c	USN	3/1/42	USS *Houston*	Enemy Action
Miller	Carl W.	CGM(AA)	USN	3/1/42	USS *Houston*	Enemy Action
Miller	Franz L.	S1c	USN	2/4/42	USS *Houston*	Enemy Action
Miller	G. R.		USA	9/18/44	POW—Prison ship, South China Sea	U.S. Submarine
Miller	Homer E.	Pfc.	USMC	3/1/42	USS *Houston*	Enemy Action
Miller	James V.	Pfc.	USMC	3/1/42	USS *Houston*	Enemy Action
Miller	William D.	S2c	USN	3/1/42	USS *Houston*	Enemy Action
Mills	Frederick J.	S2c	USN	3/1/42	USS *Houston*	Enemy Action

Last Name	First Name	Rank	Branch of Service	Date of Death	Place of Death	Cause of Death
Mills	Sylvester	S1c	USN	3/1/42	USS *Houston*	Enemy Action
Moga	Rome J.	S1c	USN	3/1/42	USS *Houston*	Enemy Action
Montgomery	Edward J.	S1c	USN	3/1/42	USS *Houston*	Enemy Action
Moody	Leonard Jr.	S1c	USN	3/1/42	USS *Houston*	Enemy Action
Moon	Carl I.	S2c	USN	3/1/42	USS *Houston*	Enemy Action
Moore	G. E.		USA	10/43	POW— Kanchanaburi, Thailand	Dysentery
Moore	Howard L.	MM2c	USN	3/1/42	USS *Houston*	Enemy Action
Morris	James T.	S1c	USN	3/1/42	USS *Houston*	Enemy Action
Morrison	C. D.	Pfc.	USA	11/17/43	POW—80 Kilo Camp, Burma	Tropical Ulcers
Mount	Cecil V.	WT2c	USN	3/1/42	USS *Houston*	Enemy Action
Mullins	William D.	S1c	USN	3/1/42	USS *Houston*	Enemy Action
Murff	Andrew R.	WT2c	USN	3/1/42	USS *Houston*	Enemy Action
Musto	James W.	S2c	USN	6/21/43	POW—18 Kilo Camp, Burma	Dysentery
Myers	Sidney	Mus1c	USN	3/1/42	USS *Houston*	Enemy Action
Nebel	Alma R.	Cpl.	USMC	3/1/42	USS *Houston*	Enemy Action
Nelson	James D.	F2c	USN	3/1/42	USS *Houston*	Enemy Action
Nelson	John W.	RM2c	USN	3/1/42	USS *Houston*	Enemy Action
Nelson	Kenneth L.	S1c	USN	3/1/42	USS *Houston*	Enemy Action
Nethken	A. F.	Ens.	USN	3/1/42	USS *Houston*	Enemy Action
Newell	F. R.	Ens.	USN	3/1/42	USS *Houston*	Enemy Action
Newton	Willard A.	S1c	USN	3/1/42	USS *Houston*	Enemy Action
Newton	William D.	S1c	USN	3/1/42	USS *Houston*	Enemy Action
Nickelson	Raymond	MM2c	USN	3/1/42	USS *Houston*	Enemy Action
Nicoloa	Anthony	S1c	USN	3/1/42	USS *Houston*	Enemy Action
Nies	Dick K.	S1c	USN	2/4/42	USS *Houston*	Enemy Action
Niswonger	Duel L.	Cpl.	USMC	3/1/42	USS *Houston*	Enemy Action
Northcutt	James A.	S1c	USN	3/1/42	USS *Houston*	Enemy Action
Norvel	Richard	S2c	USN	3/1/42	USS *Houston*	Enemy Action
Novicki	Stanley E.	MM1c	USN	3/1/42	USS *Houston*	Enemy Action
Nowak	Edward B.	Mus1c	USN	3/1/42	USS *Houston*	Enemy Action
Nunnelley	Robert B.	MM1c	USN	3/1/42	USS *Houston*	Enemy Action
O'Hayre	Eddie P.	RM3c	USN	3/1/42	USS *Houston*	Enemy Action
O'Leary	Edward L.	S1c	USN	2/4/42	USS *Houston*	Enemy Action
Offerle	I. O.	Sgt.	USA	11/18/43	POW—80 Kilo Camp, Burma	Tropical Ulcers
Omoth	Robert E.	S1c	USN	8/16/43	POW—100 Kilo Camp, Burma	Cardiac Arrest
O'Neal	Joseph S.	CFS	USN	3/1/42	USS *Houston*	Enemy Action
Orcutt	Robert Y.	RM2c	USN	2/4/42	USS *Houston*	Enemy Action
Overturf	James G.	EM1c	USN	3/1/42	USS *Houston*	Enemy Action
Owen	Gerald N.	S2c	USN	3/1/42	USS *Houston*	Enemy Action
Owens	William L.	SM2c	USN	3/1/42	USS *Houston*	Enemy Action
Oxford	Ernest P.	WT2c	USN	3/1/42	USS *Houston*	Enemy Action
Panganiban	Edilberto	Mus1c	USN	3/1/42	USS *Houston*	Enemy Action

Last Name	First Name	Rank	Branch of Service	Date of Death	Place of Death	Cause of Death
Parish	Bartow H.	AMM2c	USN	8/16/43	POW—100 Kilo Camp, Burma	Beriberi
Parker	A. T.	Pvt.	USA	11/17/43	POW—80 Kilo Camp, Burma	Tropical Ulcers
Parsons	Charles E.	S1c	USN	3/1/42	USS *Houston*	Enemy Action
Pataye	John E.	S2c	USN	3/1/42	USS *Houston*	Enemy Action
Patten	Kenneth B.	S1c	USN	3/1/42	USS *Houston*	Enemy Action
Patty	John C. Jr.	Lt.	USN	3/1/42	USS *Houston*	Enemy Action
Pautsch	Phillip W.	WT2c	USN	3/1/42	USS *Houston*	Enemy Action
Pecena	Thomas F.	RM3c	USN	3/1/42	USS *Houston*	Enemy Action
Perkins	Jesse	BM2c	USN	3/1/42	USS *Houston*	Enemy Action
Perry	Earl	S2c	USN	3/1/42	USS *Houston*	Enemy Action
Peters	Charles A.	FC1c(M)	USN	3/1/42	USS *Houston*	Enemy Action
Peterson	Lennart O.	GM2c	USN	8/22/43	POW—80 Kilo Camp, Burma	Dysentery
Pfeil	S. A.	Pvt.	USA	8/11/43	POW—30 Kilo Camp, Burma	Dysentery
Phillips	David S.	S2c	USN	3/1/42	USS *Houston*	Enemy Action
Pierce	Arthur D.	MM1c	USN	3/1/42	USS *Houston*	Enemy Action
Pinkerman	William E.	CWT	USN	3/1/42	USS *Houston*	Enemy Action
Pistole	Frank L. H.	AMM3c	USN	12/26/43	POW—80 Kilo Camp, Burma	Beriberi/ Dysentery
Pittman	Clyde B.	RM2c	USN	3/1/42	USS *Houston*	Enemy Action
Pitts	G. E.	Pvt.	USA	1/14/44	POW—114 Kilo Camp, Burma	Pellegra
Plude	Leo	S2c	USN	3/1/42	USS *Houston*	Enemy Action
Polk	Farest G.	MM1c	USN	3/1/42	USS *Houston*	Enemy Action
Pool	Wilbur E.	CMM	USN	3/1/42	USS *Houston*	Enemy Action
Prattico	Louis	EM3c	USN	3/1/42	USS *Houston*	Enemy Action
Prentice	Jack H.	Cox.	USN	3/1/42	USS *Houston*	Enemy Action
Prescher	Harold H.	EM1c	USN	3/1/42	USS *Houston*	Enemy Action
Prince	Charles W.	S1c	USN	3/1/42	USS *Houston*	Enemy Action
Prouty	William D.	S1c	USN	3/1/42	USS *Houston*	Enemy Action
Pullen	Robert H.	S1c	USN	8/31/43	POW—100 Kilo Camp, Burma	Tropical Ulcers
Purcell	Mack C.	ME1c	USN	3/1/42	USS *Houston*	Enemy Action
Pye	Guy E.	GM2c	USN	8/12/43	POW—100 Kilo Camp, Burma	Tropical Ulcers
Quigley	Raymond A.	F1c	USN	3/1/42	USS *Houston*	Enemy Action
Racine	John "J"	GM2c	USN	3/1/42	USS *Houston*	Enemy Action
Rains	Joseph E.	S2c	USN	3/1/42	USS *Houston*	Enemy Action
Ramsey	Frederick H.	Capt.	USMC	3/1/42	USS *Houston*	Enemy Action
Raymann	James E.	F1c	USN	3/1/42	USS *Houston*	Enemy Action
Read	Herman R.	S1c	USN	3/1/42	USS *Houston*	Enemy Action

Last Name	First Name	Rank	Branch of Service	Date of Death	Place of Death	Cause of Death
Reburn	Paul A.	EM2c	USN	3/1/42	USS *Houston*	Enemy Action
Redwine	A. L.		USA	6/24/44	POW—Prison ship, South China Sea	U.S. Submarine
Reed	Clarence O.	RM2c	USN	8/23/43	POW—80 Kilo Camp, Burma	Dysentery
Reed	Norman	F1c	USN	3/1/42	USS *Houston*	Enemy Action
Reed	Reuben W.	Sgt.	USMC	3/1/42	USS *Houston*	Enemy Action
Rehfeld	Lester W.	S1c	USN	3/1/42	USS *Houston*	Enemy Action
Reider	John J.	MM2c	USN	3/1/42	USS *Houston*	Enemy Action
Reisinger	Robert R.	S1c	USN	3/1/42	USS *Houston*	Enemy Action
Rentz	George S.	Cdr.	USN	3/1/42	USS *Houston*	Enemy Action
Reves	Elbert L.	RM3c	USN	3/1/42	USS *Houston*	Enemy Action
Rhodes	B. E.		USA	3/2/42	Bandung, Java	Gunshot wound
Rhodes	William A.	TC1c	USN	3/1/42	USS *Houston*	Enemy Action
Rich	R. L.	Pfc.	USA	11/1/43	POW—80 Kilo Camp, Burma	Beriberi
Roach	George L.	S2c	USN	3/1/42	USS *Houston*	Enemy Action
Roach	Harold D.	BM2c	USN	3/1/42	USS *Houston*	Enemy Action
Robe	Walter	WT1c	USN	3/1/42	USS *Houston*	Enemy Action
Roberson	Norman L.	F2c	USN	3/1/42	USS *Houston*	Enemy Action
Roberts	David	Cdr.	USN	3/1/42	USS *Houston*	Enemy Action
Robertson	Robert N.	F1c	USN	3/1/42	USS *Houston*	Enemy Action
Robinson	John W. Jr.	F2c	USN	3/1/42	USS *Houston*	Enemy Action
Rocque	George T.	S1c	USN	3/1/42	USS *Houston*	Enemy Action
Rodgers	Louis	S2c	USN	3/1/42	USS *Houston*	Enemy Action
Rogers	Floyd	SK2c	USN	3/1/42	USS *Houston*	Enemy Action
Rogers	J. W.	Pvt.	USA	1/28/44	POW—Tamarkan, Thailand	Dysentery
Rohrbaugh	Mansfield J.	S1c	USN	3/1/42	USS *Houston*	Enemy Action
Roland	Junior W.	S2c	USN	3/1/42	USS *Houston*	Enemy Action
Rolf	Albert	SF3c	USN	3/1/42	USS *Houston*	Enemy Action
Rooks	Albert H.	Capt.	USN	3/1/42	USS *Houston*	Enemy Action
Rose	John J.	S1c	USN	2/4/42	USS *Houston*	Enemy Action
Ross	Russell R.	Lt.	USN	5/4/42	POW—Batavia, Java	Dysentery
Roszell	Lyle T.	S2c	USN	8/29/43	POW—Tarsoa, Thailand	Dysentery
Roth	John T.	MM2c	USN	8/5/43	POW—100 Kilo Camp, Burma	Dysentery
Rowan	Raymond H. Jr.	F1c	USN	3/1/42	USS *Houston*	Enemy Action
Ruddy	James R.	F1c	USN	3/1/42	USS *Houston*	Enemy Action
Ruscoe	Jackson	GM1c	USN	2/4/42	USS *Houston*	Enemy Action
Russell	C. E.	Pfc.	USA	9/7/43	POW—100 Kilo Camp, Burma	Sepsis, Amputation
Sadowski	Henry J.	EM2c	USN	3/1/42	USS *Houston*	Enemy Action

Last Name	First Name	Rank	Branch of Service	Date of Death	Place of Death	Cause of Death
Salazman	M. F.		USA	6/24/44	POW—Prison ship, South China Sea	U.S. Submarine
Sallis	James H.	SM1c	USN	3/1/42	USS *Houston*	Enemy Action
Sandercook	Theodore	BM1c	USN	3/1/42	USS *Houston*	Enemy Action
Sanders	Roy	CMM	USN	3/1/42	USS *Houston*	Enemy Action
Sass	Chester A.	FC3c	USN	3/1/42	USS *Houston*	Enemy Action
Saunders	Robert E.	GM3c	USN	3/1/42	USS *Houston*	Enemy Action
Sawer	Richard C.	S1c	USN	3/1/42	USS *Houston*	Enemy Action
Schandua	J. E.	Pfc.	USA	9/14/43	POW—100 Kilo Camp, Burma	Sepsis, Amputation
Schantz	Dale E.	EM3c	USN	3/1/42	USS *Houston*	Enemy Action
Schlosser	Charles M.	S1c	USN	3/1/42	USS *Houston*	Enemy Action
Schmitt	Milton W.	Pvt.	USMC	3/1/42	USS *Houston*	Enemy Action
Schnitzius	Woodrow B.	S2c	USN	3/1/42	USS *Houston*	Enemy Action
Schroder	John H. Jr.	MM1c	USN	3/1/42	USS *Houston*	Enemy Action
Schuelke	John H.	SC2c	USN	1/12/44	POW— Kanchanaburi, Thailand	Dysentery
Schuffenhauer	Louis O.	S1c	USN	3/1/42	USS *Houston*	Enemy Action
Schultz	L. D.		USA	6/24/44	POW—Prison ship	U.S. Submarine
Schultze	Francis B.	SF1c	USN	2/4/42	USS *Houston*	Enemy Action
Schwamle	Theodore	SF2c	USN	3/1/42	USS *Houston*	Enemy Action
Schwers	Julius F.	S1c	USN	3/1/42	USS *Houston*	Enemy Action
Scott	DeWitt T. Jr.	S1c	USN	3/1/42	USS *Houston*	Enemy Action
Seaton	Frederick L.	S1c	USN	3/1/42	USS *Houston*	Enemy Action
Seidel	Alfred G.	EM2c	USN	12/19/42	POW—Ohasi, Japan	Bronchitis
Sellers	Coleman IV	S2c	USN	3/1/42	USS *Houston*	Enemy Action
Sellers	Lewis E.	S2c	USN	3/1/42	USS *Houston*	Enemy Action
Sewell	D. H.	Cpl.	USA	9/27/43	POW—80 Kilo Camp, Burma	Tropical Ulcers
Shaver	H. D.	Pvt.	USA	9/6/43	POW—100 Kilo Camp, Burma	Dysentery
Shaw	E. E.	MSgt.	USA	8/25/43	POW—100 Kilo Camp, Burma	Tropical Ulcers
Shaw	Herbert D.	CM1c	USN	3/1/42	USS *Houston*	Enemy Action
Sheffield	LeRoy A.	MM2c	USN	3/1/42	USS *Houston*	Enemy Action
Shelton	Russell L.	S1c	USN	2/4/42	USS *Houston*	Enemy Action
Shemanski	Sylvester W.	S1	USN	3/1/42	USS *Houston*	Enemy Action
Shillings	George A.	S1c	USN	3/1/42	USS *Houston*	Enemy Action
Shipman	Ferlin F.	S1c	USN	2/4/42	USS *Houston*	Enemy Action
Shippy	Clair H.	S1c	USN	3/1/42	USS *Houston*	Enemy Action
Shireman	Raymond L.	MM1c	USN	3/1/42	USS *Houston*	Enemy Action
Short	Chester A.	WT2c	USN	3/1/42	USS *Houston*	Enemy Action
Shouse	Claude F.	Pvt.	USMC	3/1/42	USS *Houston*	Enemy Action
Shumaker	Clarence W.	S2c	USN	3/1/42	USS *Houston*	Enemy Action

Last Name	First Name	Rank	Branch of Service	Date of Death	Place of Death	Cause of Death
Siler	Joseph H.	S1c	USN	3/1/42	USS *Houston*	Enemy Action
Silva	E. J.	Pvt.	USA	8/3/43	POW—100 Kilo Camp Burma	Dysentery
Simpson	Ward H.	Pvt.	USA	1/30/44	POW— Kanchanaburi, Thailand	Tuberculosis
Sitton	Troy L.	F2c	USN	3/1/42	USS *Houston*	Enemy Action
Skidmore	Bruce D.	Lt.	USN	3/1/42	USS *Houston*	Enemy Action
Skinner	Alfred J.	BM2c	USN	3/1/42	USS *Houston*	Enemy Action
Skudlas	John J.	S1c	USN	3/1/42	USS *Houston*	Enemy Action
Slocum	Jim E.	Pfc.	USMC	3/1/42	USS *Houston*	Enemy Action
Smith	Andrew J.	MM1c	USN	3/1/42	USS *Houston*	Enemy Action
Smith	Carl F.	S1c	USN	3/1/42	USS *Houston*	Enemy Action
Smith	George	AMM2c	USN	3/1/42	USS *Houston*	Enemy Action
Smith	Gordon C.	FC2c	USN	2/4/42	USS *Houston*	Enemy Action
Smith	Horace P. Jr.	FC3c	USN	3/1/42	USS *Houston*	Enemy Action
Smith	Joseph R.	PhM1c	USN	3/1/42	USS *Houston*	Enemy Action
Smith	Loren R.	F2c	USN	3/1/42	USS *Houston*	Enemy Action
Smith	Sidney L.	LCdr.	USN	3/1/42	USS *Houston*	Enemy Action
Smith	Sammie D.	SK2c	USN	3/1/42	USS *Houston*	Enemy Action
Smith	Timothy B.	S2c	USN	3/1/42	USS *Houston*	Enemy Action
Smith	Walton Q.	MM2c	USN	3/1/42	USS *Houston*	Enemy Action
Smith	William S.	S1c	USN	3/1/42	USS *Houston*	Enemy Action
Snyder	Samuel E.	S1c	USN	3/1/42	USS *Houston*	Enemy Action
Soden	William J. Jr.	SC3c	USN	3/1/42	USS *Houston*	Enemy Action
Sokolowski	J. R.		USA	9/18/44	POW—Prison ship, South China Sea	U.S. Submarine
Sollberger	Roland A.	GM1c	USN	3/1/42	USS *Houston*	Enemy Action
Sorenson	Edwin N.	EM2c	USN	3/1/42	USS *Houston*	Enemy Action
Soule	Irvin G.	GM3c	USN	9/9/43	POW—80 Kilo Camp, Burma	Dysentery
Soy	Ah	OC3c	USN	3/1/42	USS *Houston*	Enemy Action
Sparkman	Leon S.	Sgt.	USA	6/24/44	POW—Prison ship, South China Sea	U.S. Submarine
Spencer	Charles L.	S1c	USN	3/1/42	USS *Houston*	Enemy Action
Spencer	Mason D.	S2c	USN	11/9/43	POW—80 Kilo Camp, Burma	Dysentery
Spillman	Andrew J.	GM3c	USN	3/1/42	USS *Houston*	Enemy Action
Spragle	Glenn W.	GM2c	USN	3/1/42	USS *Houston*	Enemy Action
Sprague	Robert M.	CMM	USN	3/1/42	USS *Houston*	Enemy Action
Sprayberry	James G.	SC2c	USN	3/1/42	USS *Houston*	Enemy Action
Stafford	William F.	S1c	USN	3/1/42	USS *Houston*	Enemy Action
Stahl	James C.	EM2c	USN	3/1/42	USS *Houston*	Enemy Action
Standish	Walter	MSgt.	USMC	3/1/42	USS *Houston*	Enemy Action
Stark	John N.	RM2c	USN	3/1/42	USS *Houston*	Enemy Action
Staver	L. P.		USA	5/23/45	POW— Singapore	Cancer

Last Name	First Name	Rank	Branch of Service	Date of Death	Place of Death	Cause of Death
Steele	Earl W.	S2c	USN	2/4/42	USS *Houston*	Enemy Action
Stevens	William W. Jr.	EM2c	USN	3/1/42	USS *Houston*	Enemy Action
Stevenson	Harold V.	S2c	USN	3/1/42	USS *Houston*	Enemy Action
Stewart	Glenn B.	QM1c	USN	3/1/42	USS *Houston*	Enemy Action
Stoker	Floyd E.	EM2c	USN	3/1/42	USS *Houston*	Enemy Action
Storie	Luther T.	CMM	USN	3/1/42	USS *Houston*	Enemy Action
Stout	G. W.	Pvt.	USA	10/31/43	POW—80 Kilo Camp, Burma	Tropical Ulcers
Stower	Donald G.	S1c	USN	3/1/42	USS *Houston*	Enemy Action
Street	Raymond A.	CY	USN	3/1/42	USS *Houston*	Enemy Action
Sturgill	Ollie J.	S1c	USN	3/1/42	USS *Houston*	Enemy Action
Swearingen	Lonnie D.	S2c	USN	3/1/42	USS *Houston*	Enemy Action
Szarke	Andrew S.	S2c	USN	3/1/42	USS *Houston*	Enemy Action
Szymala	Victor J.	MM2c	USN	3/1/42	USS *Houston*	Enemy Action
Tai	Chi Fah	OC2c	USN	3/1/42	USS *Houston*	Enemy Action
Tanberg	Albert N.	BK3c	USN	11/2/44	POW—Saigon, Indochina	Dysentery
Taraszkiewicz	Stanley	F2c	USN	3/1/42	USS *Houston*	Enemy Action
Tarrence	Earl L.	S2c	USN	2/4/42	USS *Houston*	Enemy Action
Taylor	Cecil L.	S1c	USN	3/1/42	USS *Houston*	Enemy Action
Tesar	Henry	GM3c	USN	2/4/42	USS *Houston*	Enemy Action
Thaxton	William L.	F1c	USN	3/1/42	USS *Houston*	Enemy Action
Thomas	B.		USA	10/27/43	POW— Kanchanaburi, Thailand	Beriberi
Thompson	Eldro W.	S2c	USN	3/1/42	USS *Houston*	Enemy Action
Tiemann	E. W.	Pvt.	USA	12/14/43	POW—100 Kilo Camp, Burma	Beriberi
Tisdale	William V.	S1c	USN	3/1/42	USS *Houston*	Enemy Action
Treanor	Halleran Jr.	WT1c	USN	3/1/42	USS *Houston*	Enemy Action
Tremonte	T. J.	Pvt.	USA	7/27/43	POW—80 Kilo Camp, Burma	Tropical Ulcers
Trim	Donald P.	Cox.	USN	12/11/43	POW—105 Kilo Camp, Burma	Tropical Ulcers
Truskoski	Thomas F.	S2c	USN	2/4/42	USS *Houston*	Enemy Action
Tsao	Ducey	OC2c	USN	3/1/42	USS *Houston*	Enemy Action
Tsiang	Packsen	Matt1c	USN	3/1/42	USS *Houston*	Enemy Action
Tsong	Ho Dee	Matt1c	USN	3/1/42	USS *Houston*	Enemy Action
Tucker	William E.	Mus1c	USN	8/9/43	POW—80 Kilo Camp, Burma	Tropical Ulcers
Tung	Ven Yung	Matt1c	USN	3/1/42	USS *Houston*	Enemy Action
Turman	Russell C.	Y3c	USN	3/1/42	USS *Houston*	Enemy Action
Tutas	James L.	S1c	USN	3/1/42	USS *Houston*	Enemy Action
Tye	Liu	OS2c	USN	3/1/42	USS *Houston*	Enemy Action
Tyre	Arlie W.	F2c	USN	3/1/42	USS *Houston*	Enemy Action
Uditsky	Samuel L.	WT1c	USN	3/1/42	USS *Houston*	Enemy Action
Ukena	Jewel Jr.	S1c	USN	3/1/42	USS *Houston*	Enemy Action

Last Name	First Name	Rank	Branch of Service	Date of Death	Place of Death	Cause of Death
Upperman	Max	Sgt.	USA	10/4/43	POW—100 Kilo Camp, Burma	Tropical Ulcers/ Beriberi
Ustaszewski	Sigmund H.	PhM2c	USN	3/1/42	USS *Houston*	Enemy Action
Valliere	Harry F.	SM3c	USN	3/1/42	USS *Houston*	Enemy Action
Van Slyke	Richard M.	F1c	USN	3/1/42	USS *Houston*	Enemy Action
Van Tilberg	Frank E.	S1c	USN	3/1/42	USS *Houston*	Enemy Action
Vancil	Kenneth A.	S2c	USN	3/1/42	USS *Houston*	Enemy Action
Vandenberg	Auverns E.	GM2c	USN	3/1/42	USS *Houston*	Enemy Action
Vanderauwera	Robert J.	FC3c	USN	3/1/42	USS *Houston*	Enemy Action
Vaughan	Houston A.	F.M.Sgt.	USMC	3/1/42	USS *Houston*	Enemy Action
Vaughn	James H. Jr.	F2c	USN	3/1/42	USS *Houston*	Enemy Action
Verley	Ralph A.	S1c	USN	3/1/42	USS *Houston*	Enemy Action
Verzwyvelt	James J.	EM3c	USN	3/1/42	USS *Houston*	Enemy Action
Villers	Donald D.	Mus2c	USN	3/1/42	USS *Houston*	Enemy Action
Villwock	Harvey H.	EM3c	USN	3/1/42	USS *Houston*	Enemy Action
Virchow	Harry H.	GM3c	USN	3/1/42	USS *Houston*	Enemy Action
Wai	Yau	Matt1c	USN	3/1/42	USS *Houston*	Enemy Action
Waite	Walter W.	Elec. (WO)	USN	3/1/42	USS *Houston*	Enemy Action
Walchuk	John	GM3c	USN	3/1/42	USS *Houston*	Enemy Action
Waldschmidt	Albert H. Jr.	MM1c	USN	3/1/42	USS *Houston*	Enemy Action
Wallace	John G.	Cox.	USN	3/1/42	USS *Houston*	Enemy Action
Wallen	Richard T.	Pvt.	USMC	3/1/42	USS *Houston*	Enemy Action
Walling	Nelson C.	F1c	USN	3/1/42	USS *Houston*	Enemy Action
Walts	Howard L.	S2c	USN	2/4/42	USS *Houston*	Enemy Action
Ward	Frank C.	EM2c	USN	9/21/43	POW—100 Kilo Camp, Burma	Tropical Ulcers
Ward	Willard G.	SF1c	USN	3/1/42	USS *Houston*	Enemy Action
Warner	John C.	Mus1c	USN	3/1/42	USS *Houston*	Enemy Action
Waters	N. H.	Cpl.	USA	9/2/43	POW—80 Kilo Camp, Burma	Tropical Ulcers
Watkins	Charles H.	MM2c	USN	3/1/42	USS *Houston*	Enemy Action
Watt	James E.	F1c	USN	3/1/42	USS *Houston*	Enemy Action
Weaver	Ben E.	GM1c	USN	3/1/42	USS *Houston*	Enemy Action
Weaver	Charles T.	EM2c	USN	3/1/42	USS *Houston*	Enemy Action
Weaver	David C.	CMM	USN	3/1/42	USS *Houston*	Enemy Action
Weber	Emery M.	S2c	USN	3/1/42	USS *Houston*	Enemy Action
Weiler	Francis B.	Lt. j.g.	USN	3/26/42	POW— Pandeglang, Java	Wounds
Weimer	Albert G.	SK2c	USN	3/1/42	USS *Houston*	Enemy Action
Wellbourn	Arthur F.	BM1c	USN	3/1/42	USS *Houston*	Enemy Action
Weller	Maurice E.	CCM	USN	3/1/42	USS *Houston*	Enemy Action
Wenholtz	Roy A.	MM2c	USN	3/1/42	USS *Houston*	Enemy Action
Werner	Paul W. Jr.	S1c	USN	3/1/42	USS *Houston*	Enemy Action
Westerfield	Dinavan H.	EM1c	USN	3/1/42	USS *Houston*	Enemy Action
Westerfelt	Robert	S1c	USN	3/1/42	USS *Houston*	Enemy Action
Weygant	Robert	S1c	USN	3/1/42	USS *Houston*	Enemy Action
Weyl	Joe W.	S2c	USN	3/1/42	USS *Houston*	Enemy Action

Last Name	First Name	Rank	Branch of Service	Date of Death	Place of Death	Cause of Death
Whatley	H. J.	Pvt.	USA	8/25/43	POW—100 Kilo Camp, Burma	Tropical Ulcers
Wheeler	Larkin H.	S1c	USN	3/1/42	USS *Houston*	Enemy Action
White	Charles E.	S1c	USN	3/1/42	USS *Houston*	Enemy Action
White	Glen D.	S2c	USN	3/1/42	USS *Houston*	Enemy Action
White	James H.	SF1c	USN	4/13/43	POW—80 Kilo Camp, Burma	Cerebral Malaria
White	Warren C.	MM2c	USN	3/1/42	USS *Houston*	Enemy Action
Whitehead	Wallace A.	SK2c	USN	3/1/42	USS *Houston*	Enemy Action
Whitney	Gaylord H.	CM2c	USN	3/1/42	USS *Houston*	Enemy Action
Widmeyer	Harry C.	S1c	USN	9/10/43	POW—80 Kilo Camp, Burma	Dysentery
Wienert	Ralph M.	CEM	USN	3/1/42	USS *Houston*	Enemy Action
Wilemon	Roy H.	S2c	USN	3/1/42	USS *Houston*	Enemy Action
Wiley	George M. Jr.	MM1c	USN	3/1/42	USS *Houston*	Enemy Action
Willenberg	Walter O.	S1c	USN	3/1/42	USS *Houston*	Enemy Action
Willerton	Robert P.	Y2c	USN	6/24/44	POW—Prison ship, South China Sea	Unknown
Williams	Alfred T.	CTC	USN	3/1/42	USS *Houston*	Enemy Action
Williams	Arlie	S1c	USN	3/1/42	USS *Houston*	Enemy Action
Williams	David M.	S1c	USN	6/1/44	POW— Chungkai, Thailand	Dysentery
Williams	Earnest D.	S2c	USN	3/1/42	USS *Houston*	Enemy Action
Williams	Joseph A.	CBM	USN	2/4/42	USS *Houston*	Enemy Action
Williamson	B. R.	Cpl.	USA	1/28/44	POW— Tamarkan, Thailand	Dysentery/ Malaria
Willis	Donnis W.	S1c	USN	6/10/43	POW—100 Kilo Camp, Burma	Dysentery
Wilson	Edwin P.	Pfc.	USA	6/13/43	POW— Thanbyuzayat, Burma	Bombing Attack
Wilson	James L.	S1c	USN	3/1/42	USS *Houston*	Enemy Action
Wilson	James R.	Pvt.	USMC	11/17/43	POW—114 Kilo Camp, Burma	Malaria
Wilson	Oscar W.	CRM	USN	3/1/42	USS *Houston*	Enemy Action
Wilson	Phillip E.	S1c	USN	3/1/42	USS *Houston*	Enemy Action
Wilson	Stewart S.	HA1c	USN	3/1/42	USS *Houston*	Enemy Action
Wilson	T. A.		USA	6/24/44	POW—Prison ship, South China Sea	U.S. Submarine
Wilson	Wayne L.	EM1c	USN	3/1/42	USS *Houston*	Enemy Action
Winters	Vic	SF1c	USN	2/4/42	USS *Houston*	Enemy Action
Wise	Glenn E.	FM2c	USN	2/4/42	USS *Houston*	Enemy Action

Last Name	First Name	Rank	Branch of Service	Date of Death	Place of Death	Cause of Death
Wise	Ray H. Jr.	S2c	USN	3/1/42	USS *Houston*	Enemy Action
Wismann	E.	Pvt.	USA	9/18/44	POW—Prison ship, South China Sea	U.S. Submarine
Wolf	Adrian W.	F1c	USN	3/1/42	USS *Houston*	Enemy Action
Wolf	Frank N.	QM2c	USN	3/1/42	USS *Houston*	Enemy Action
Wolfe	Glendon R.	S2c	USN	3/1/42	USS *Houston*	Enemy Action
Wolfe	Maurice A. Jr.	S2c	USN	2/4/42	USS *Houston*	Enemy Action
Woltz	D. G.	Pfc.	USA	10/6/43	POW—80 Kilo Camp, Burma	Dysentery
Wong	Far Ze	Matt1c	USN	3/1/42	USS *Houston*	Enemy Action
Wood	Sam W.	CWT	USN	3/1/42	USS *Houston*	Enemy Action
Woodruff	John F.	Lt. j.g.	USN	3/1/42	USS *Houston*	Enemy Action
Wooten	Melvin E.	S1c	USN	3/1/42	USS *Houston*	Enemy Action
Wynn	Marvin A.	S1c	USN	9/19/43	POW—80 Kilo Camp, Burma	Dysentery
Yannucci	Chester	Mus1c	USN	3/1/42	USS *Houston*	Enemy Action
Yates	Donald R.	F1c	USN	8/24/43	POW—80 Kilo Camp, Burma	Beriberi/ Pneumonia
Yell	A. B.	Cpl.	USA	9/18/43	POW—80 Kilo Camp, Burma	Dysentery
Young	Kenneth A.	S1c	USN	12/22/43	POW—105 Kilo Camp, Burma	Beriberi/ Malaria/ Dysentery
Zazzara	James J.	SK3c	USN	3/1/42	USS *Houston*	Enemy Action
Zeller	William L.	Cox.	USN	3/1/42	USS *Houston*	Enemy Action
Zimba	Louis John	GM1c	USN	2/4/42	USS *Houston*	Enemy Action
Zimmerman	Leonard	S2c	USN	3/1/42	USS *Houston*	Enemy Action

PHOTO CREDITS

Inset photograph of President Roosevelt at Charleston, South Carolina (Acme/UPI; Franklin D. Roosevelt Library)
Inset photograph of President Roosevelt reviewing the fleet at San Francisco (Wide World; Franklin D. Roosevelt Library)

Page Three
Inset photograph of the president's catch (Photo by R. B. Thompson, USN; Franklin D. Roosevelt Library)
Inset photograph of President Roosevelt and Adm. Claude Bloch (Associated Press/Acme/UPI; Franklin D. Roosevelt Library)

Page Four
Background photograph of Captain Rooks relieving Capt. Jesse. B. Oldendorf (Guthrie F. Layne, Jr., Collection, Cushing Memorial Library and Archives, Texas A&M University)
Inset photograph of Capt. Albert H. Rooks at age 45 (Courtesy of Harold R. Rooks)
Inset photograph of Thomas C. Hart (National Archives)
Inset photograph of Captain Rooks inspecting his crew (Cruiser Houston Collection, University of Houston Libraries)

Page Five
Photograph of *Houston* crewmen at play, 1931 (National Archives & Records Administration)
Photograph of *Houston* crewmen in China Station (Cruiser Houston Collection, University of Houston Libraries)

Page Six
Background photograph of the ship's company (Chief Storekeeper Carl Fox, USN; Cruiser Houston Collection, University of Houston Libraries)
Inset portrait of Cdr. Arthur L. Maher (Courtesy of Betty Maher)
Inset portrait of Cdr. George S. Rentz (Naval Historical Center)
Inset portrait of Lt. Harold S. Hamlin (U.S. Naval Academy)
Inset portrait of Lt. Robert B. Fulton (Courtesy of Rear Adm. Robert B. Fulton)

Page Seven
Inset portrait of Ens. Charles D. Smith (U.S. Naval Academy)
Inset portrait of Ens John B. Nelson (U.S. Naval Academy)
Inset portrait of Lt. Russel R. Ross (U.S. Naval Academy)
Inset portrait of Lt. j.g. Joseph Dalton (U.S. Naval Academy)

Page Eight
Background photograph of the *Houston*'s marine detachment (Cruiser Houston Collection, University of Houston Libraries)
Inset portrait of Sgt. Charley L. Pryor, Jr. (Courtesy of JoAnn Pryor Wychopen)
Inset portrait of Pfc. Jim Gee (Courtesy of Mrs. Shirley Gee)
Inset portrait of S1/c Melfred L. (Gus) Forsman (Courtesy of Dawn M. Lodge)
Inset portrait of S1/c John Bartz (Courtesy of John Bartz)
Inset portrait of Cox. James (Red) Huffman (Courtesy of James Huffman)

Page Nine
Inset photograph of Pfc. John Wisecup (Courtesy of James McDaniel)

Page Ten
Background photograph of the *Houston* passing through the Panama Canal (National Archives)
Inset photograph of an SOC floatplane (Cruiser Houston Collection, University of Houston Libraries)

Page Eleven
Inset photograph of AMM 3/c Lanson H. Harris (Courtesy of Jane & Lanson Harris)

Page Twelve
Background photograph of Turret One and Turret Two (Cruiser Houston Collection, University of Houston Libraries)
Inset photograph of the HMAS *Perth* (Cruiser Houston Collection, University of Houston Libraries)
Inset photograph of *Houston* five-inch gunners (Naval Historical Center)

Page Thirteen
Background photograph of the shore party heading for Tawi Tawi (Cruiser Houston Collection, University of Houston Libraries)
Inset photograph of Otto Schwarz (Collection of Otto Schwarz; Cruiser Houston Collection, University of Houston Libraries)
Inset photograph of the *Houston*'s baseball team (Cruiser Houston Collection, University of Houston Libraries)

Pages Fourteen and Fifteen
Japanese war art painting by Tokushiro Kobayakawa (1942) depicting Battle of Sunda Strait (Naval Historical Center)
Inset painting by Oliver Houston (1942) of sinking *Houston* (Naval Historical Center)

Page Sixteen
Photograph of Rear Adm. William A. Glassford at Memorial Day gathering (Cruiser Houston Collection, University of Houston Libraries)
Photograph of Thousand Volunteers enlistment ceremony (Cruiser Houston Collection, University of Houston Libraries)
Inset reproduction of President Roosevelt's Memorial Day message (Cruiser Houston Collection, University of Houston Libraries)
Inset photograph of Thousand Volunteers enlistment ceremony (Cruiser Houston Collection, University of Houston Libraries)

PHOTO AND ART INSERT II

Page One
Artist's rendering of life in Hintok Camp, Thailand (Sketches by John Wisecup, *After the Battle: Hintok!* By John Wisecup, Cruiser Houston Collection, University of Houston Libraries)
Inset layout of Bicycle Camp (Sketch by Raymond Day)

Page Two
Background photograph of the new *Houston* (Naval Historical Center)
Inset photograph of Lt. (jg) Harold R. Rooks (Courtesy of Harold R. Rooks)
Inset photograph of Lt. Col. Blucher S. Tharp (Texas Military Forces Museum)
Inset portrait of Sgt. Luther Prunty (Texas Military Forces Museum)
Inset portrait of Lt. James Lattimore (Texas Military Forces Museum)
Inset portrait of Capt. Winthrop H. Rogers (Texas Military Forces Museum)

Page Three
Inset photograph of Capt. Samuel L. Lumpkin (Texas Military Forces Museum)
Inset photograph of Tech. Sgt. Jess Stanbrough (Texas Military Forces Museum)
Inset portrait of Brig. Arthur L. Varley (Courtesy of Linda Douglas)
Inset portrait of Sgt. Frank Fujita (Texas Military Forces Museum)
Inset photograph of the new USS *Houston* at Newport News shipyard (National Archives)

Page Four
Photograph of USS *Pampanito* (National Archives)
Artist's rendering of the railway base camp at Thanbyuzayat, Burma (Sketch by Raymond Day; USS *Houston* Association)
Painting of atap hut interior (Cruiser Houston Collection, University of Houston Libraries)

Page Five
Photograph of 55 Kilo Camp (Cruiser Houston Collection, University of Houston Libraries)
Inset photograph of Pfc. Jim Gee (Courtesy of Shirley Gee)
Photograph of unidentified Burma prisoners (Cruiser Houston Collection, University of Houston Libraries)

Page Six
Background photograph of wooden railway trestle (Cruiser Houston Collection, University of Houston Libraries)
Inset photograph of cutting near Konyu (Cruiser Houston Collection, University of Houston Libraries)
Background photograph of finished railway (Cruiser Houston Collection, University of Houston Libraries)

Inset photograph of railway cutting (Cruiser Houston Collection, University of Houston Libraries)

Page Seven
Photograph of aerial view of wooden and concrete bridges under attack (Cruiser Houston Collection, University of Houston Libraries)
Inset photograph of a U.S. B-24 Liberator (Cruiser Houston Collection, University of Houston Libraries)
Inset photograph of collapsed concrete bridge at Tamarkan (Cruiser Houston Collection, University of Houston Libraries)
Photograph of the concrete bridge at Tamarkan (Cruiser Houston Collection, University of Houston Libraries)

Page Eight
Radio dispatch between OSS and Maj. Eben B. Bartlett (National Archives)
Inset photograph of Maj. Gen. William Donovan (OSS Records, NARA)

Page Nine
Radio dispatches between OSS and Maj. Eben B. Bartlett, Jr. (National Archives)
Inset photograph of Major Bartlett (OSS Records, NARA)

Page Ten
Background photograph of liberated railway POWs deplaning (Collection of Dorothy and Lloyd Willey)
Inset photograph of Major Bartlett with colleagues (OSS Records, NARA)

Page Eleven
Inset photograph of Col. John Coughlin and Lt. Gen. Raymond A. Wheeler (OSS Records, NARA)
Inset photograph of Epstein, Hamlin, and Maher (Cruiser Houston Collection, University of Houston Libraries)

Page Twelve
Background photograph of U.S. Air Transport Command C-47 landing at Rat Buri, Thailand (Cruiser Houston Collection, University of Houston Libraries)
Inset photograph of railway survivors (Cruiser Houston Collection, University of Houston Libraries)
Inset photograph of medical personnel (Cruiser Houston Collection, University of Houston Libraries)

Page Thirteen
Inset photograph of Lanson Harris (International Red Cross; collection of Jane and Lanson Harris)

Page Fourteen
Leaflet (Cruiser Houston Collection, University of Houston Libraries)

Page Fifteen
Background photograph of *Houston* survivors in Galveston (Marguerite Campbell, *Houston Post*)
Inset photograph of Albert H. Rooks, Jr. and Edith Rooks (National Archives)
Inset photograph of USS *Houston* survivors in Houston (Cruiser Houston Collection, University of Houston Libraries)

Page Sixteen
Photograph of *Houston* marine reunion (Cruiser Houston Collection, University of Houston Libraries)
Photograph of John H. Wisecup (Courtesy of James McDaniel)
Photograph of Frank Fujita (Don Kehn)
Photograph of James W. (Red) Huffman (James D. Hornfischer)
Photograph of Gus Forsman (Don Kehn)
Photograph of John Bartz (James D. Hornfischer)
Photograph of Edith Rooks (Cruiser Houston Collection, University of Houston Libraries)
Photograph of Jane and Lanson Harris (James D. Hornfischer)
Photograph of Wisecup in Thailand (Courtesy of James McDaniel)
Photograph of Otto Schwarz (Don Kehn)

INDEX